DAWN TO THE WEST

Japanese Literature of the Modern Era

POETRY, DRAMA, CRITICISM

A History of Japanese Literature, Volume 4
With a new preface by the author

DONALD KEENE

COLUMBIA UNIVERSITY PRESS   NEW YORK

Columbia University Press
Publishers Since 1893
New York   Chichester, West Sussex
Copyright © 1999 by Donald Keene
All rights reserved.

Library of Congress Cataloging-in-Publication Data
Keene, Donald.
Dawn to the West.
Includes bibliographies and indexes.
Contents: [1] Fiction— [2] Poetry, drama,
criticism.
I. Japanese literature—1868—   —History and
criticism. I. Title.
[PL726.55.K39 1987   895.6'09'004   87-17586
ISBN 0–231–11438–9 — 0–231–11439–7 (pbk.)

First published in hardcover by Holt, Rinehart and Winston
in 1984.

Printed in the United States of America
c 10 9 8 7 6 5 4 3 2 1
p 10 9 8 7 6 5 4 3 2 1

CONTENTS

PART FOUR: MODERN CRITICISM

PREFACE TO THE
COLUMBIA EDITION

IN JAPAN, AS IN many other countries, literature during the twentieth century has come to mean mainly the novel. This does not reflect any lack of good poets or playwrights. In Japan the twentieth century has been a period of unusual activity in poetry; innumerable poems have been composed both in traditional forms (like the tanka and haiku) and in modern forms influenced by European examples. The "haiku population" alone has been estimated at over a million people, and the "populations" of tanka and modern poets probably do not lag far behind. Of course, most of these millions of poets are amateurs whose books are published privately (if at all) in limited editions; but large numbers of amateur poets, most associated with a professional poet-teacher and a little magazine, support the poetic activity of the professionals.

A somewhat similar situation exists in the traditional theater. The Nō is maintained mainly by amateurs who study the singing and dancing of the roles, even if they have no hope of ever appearing in a public performance. They support the individual actors who teach them and subscribe to the magazine published by their particular school of Nō. A smaller number of people learn to recite the roles of a Bunraku play and form the "hard core" of audiences. However, when it comes to Kabuki and the various forms of modern theater, there is little support from disciples; the actors, like those elsewhere, depend for their income on the sale of tickets to spectators. The other face of this lack of support from amateur performers is that both Kabuki and the modern theater must attempt to attract audiences by presenting new or unusual works, but the repertories of the Nō and Bunraku theaters have changed extremely little during the past century or more.

A poet who has yet to establish a reputation will often publish at his own expense a slim volume of poems in an edition of 300 or 500 copies. The majority of these copies will be sent to critics who may be impressed enough to write a review or else a preface for the next collection of poems. Compared to the number of prizes offered by publishers to new novelists, there are relatively few shortcuts to popular success for poets, and this makes the dependence on the critics all the greater. A critic's recognition of genuine poetic talent will not only delight the poet but may also permit him to be one of the handful of contemporary poets who can live on royalties from books, readings, and editing the works of other poets.

Critics in Japan today read widely not only in the literature of their own country but also in works of contemporary criticism by Europeans and Americans. They may take advantage of new techniques to throw fresh light on works of classical Japanese literature, irritating traditional scholars. It commonly happens that a critic whose training has been in English or French literature will shift at some point to the study of Japanese literature. This is part of the familiar phenomenon of the "return to Japan" that affects many Japanese in their forties or fifties, whether or not they belong to literary circles. The most respected critics— like Kobayashi Hideo—are those who use examples drawn from Japanese literature to probe the question of what makes the Japanese so distinctive, so unlike Europeans, even after a century of study and love of European civilization. This kind of criticism is not fashionable in the West, but for Japanese, who hope that their traditional poetry and drama will not be overwhelmed by influence from abroad, it is heir to the criticism of such men as the eighteenth-century scholar Motoori Norinaga, the subject of Kobayashi's most impressive study.

The achievement of modern Japanese poetry, drama, and criticism is considerable, and deserves no less attention than has been accorded to the works of fiction that have been favored with Nobel Prizes.

DONALD KEENE
New York City
September 1998

PREFACE

THE SUBJECT OF THE two volumes of *Dawn to the West* is the literature written in Japan since the beginning of the new period inaugurated by the Meiji Restoration of 1868. During the fifteen or so years that I have been writing this book well-wishers have often asked me how far I had reached, the question arising from the natural assumption that I was writing in a chronological order. No doubt it would have been easier to discuss the literature written in any given year after completing my description of what had been written in the previous year, but this method seemed impractical. One cannot easily divide the activities of a writer into neat, twelve-month segments, certainly not if one wishes to give a coherent impression of him as an individual with an existence apart from the books he produced. I have chosen instead to cast my history into a pattern that is chronological only in general, following writers or movements from beginning to end, and not interrupting the narration to take stock afresh at the beginning of each year.

Certain writers obviously had to be given individual atten-

tion. Natsume Sōseki, Tanizaki Jun'ichirō, Akutagawa Ryūnosuke, and Kawabata Yasunari are so celebrated in Japan, and
have so often been translated into English, that they clearly deserved more extensive treatment than as figures in a movement,
even if I could find a movement to which these men belonged.
Other writers, including some I greatly admire, such as Arishima
Takeo, Shiga Naoya, and Dazai Osamu, were easier to treat as
central figures within a movement. The decision as to whether to
consider a particular writer independently or as a member of a
group was of necessity subjective and perhaps arbitrary, but the
author of a history of literature is bound to make decisions with
which not everyone will agree. Some writers, even men whose
books are still read, have been omitted altogether, whether
through inadvertence or because I decided they did not merit
attention. I apologize to readers for any inconvenience this may
cause, and hope that there are not too many such instances.

The Japanese literature written in the century or so since
1868 exceeds in volume all the Japanese literature that survives
from the preceding millennium. No one could read it all, and no
one wants to. Needless to say, I have read only a small fraction of
what has been published, but I have tried in every instance to read
every work I discuss, rather than rely on secondary accounts. I by
no means slight secondary sources. No one knows better than I
how much I am indebted to the work of Japanese and non-
Japanese scholars who have dealt with the literature of the period.
But when for reasons of time I had to choose between reading an
original work and an exegesis of the same work, I have chosen the
former.

During the period that I have been writing this history many
important works of scholarship have appeared, and I assume that
such works will continue to appear even while this book is published; but I have not been able to reconsider what I have written
on a man each time I hear a new book has appeared about him.
Once I have completed a chapter and moved on to the next one,
the temptation has been to think with relief that I have "disposed"
of it. Though I have later made many small revisions, it was simply not possible to keep rewriting. I have added to the bibliographies appended to each chapter the titles of recent books that
seem likely to be useful to readers wishing to pursue the subjects

further, even if I myself have been unable to incorporate their contents in my book. In the case of works of which complete translations have been published since I translated extracts for this book, I have adopted the titles used by the translators even when I have continued to use my own versions of quoted passages.

Modern Japanese literature is generally divided by Japanese scholars into three or four periods. Those who have adopted three divisions make them correspond to the reigns of the Emperors Meiji (1868–1912), Taishō (1912–1926), and Shōwa (since 1926); those who prefer four divide the Shōwa era into pre-1945 and post-1945 periods. I initially planned to disregard such divisions. Why, I thought, should I discuss Taishō literature as if it formed a distinct entity, when the Taishō period lasted less than fifteen years? But gradually I became aware that even if the division of literature according to the reigns of three emperors was illogical, it was difficult to ignore, just as it would be difficult for scholars of European literature to avoid such terms as "eighteenth-century literature." I have therefore used these conventional designations on occasion, reflecting not only the usage of Japanese critics but the feeling shared by many writers that they were different from those of the preceding reign.

In general, I have not discussed living authors, but a few took such prominent roles in movements of thirty or forty years ago that they could not be overlooked even though, happily, they are still publishing new books. Some writers who were initially excluded because they were living have since died, but it has not always been possible to find appropriate places for them when revising my manuscript.

The two volumes of *Dawn to the West* have been divided according to genre, fiction being placed in the first volume, other types of writing—poetry in various forms, drama, and literary criticism—in the second. Writers who wrote in a combination of genres have been considered in one place unless their contributions were of equal importance in different genres, in which case they may figure several times.

I have followed throughout the Japanese practice of referring to persons by their surnames followed by their personal names, rather than in the normal Western order; but there is unfortunately a problem involved in this usage. Many writers even of recent times are known by their literary names *(gō),* rather than by either their surnames or the names by which their mothers called them. I have referred to writers in the way followed by most Japanese today, rather than attempt to impose uniformity. Thus, Natsume Sōseki and Mori Ōgai are called Sōseki and Ōgai (Natsume and Mori alone would be unintelligible); but Akutagawa Ryūnosuke and Dazai Osamu, to give two instances, are called by their surnames. The use of literary names has all but died out among writers of prose, but is still normal among haiku poets especially.

Because I realize that some chapters may be read independently, I have not hesitated to repeat certain essential information, rather than oblige readers to search for earlier references. For the same reason, I have supplied bibliographies for each chapter. I hope that the index, which includes names of works, persons, and topics in the text, will otherwise help readers to find quickly subjects in which they are especially interested.

I have translated the titles of books and periodicals, subsequently referring to the former by the translations, but the latter by the original Japanese names. All Japanese terms used in the text are explained in the glossary. Japanese words are given in italics on first appearance, but later in roman type.

During the long years while I was engaged in writing *Dawn to the West* I was helped by many friends. Some obtained scarce works for me, others read the manuscript and made valuable comments, others typed it, and my editor, Karen Kennerly, asked innumerable searching questions about the substance and organization. To all of them I owe thanks. Special thanks are due to Takao Tokuoka who, while translating the book into Japanese, uncovered many mistakes, and to Barbara Ruch and Carol Gluck, whose enthusiasm for the book gave me the encouragement I needed when the task of completing it seemed Sisyphean.

DONALD KEENE
New York
May 1982

PART ONE

POETRY IN TRADITIONAL FORMS

INTRODUCTION

JAPANESE LITERATURE of the modern period began with the denial of the worth of traditional writings, especially those of the fifty or sixty years before the Meiji Restoration of 1868. It is true that not much literature of any kind—whether in keeping with or opposed to tradition—was published during the hectic days immediately after the Restoration, but the impetus for the creation of a new literature was provided by the steadily increasing flow of translations of European works in the 1880s and afterward.

In their enthusiasm for the possibilities of expression revealed by these translations, young Japanese poets openly declared that the time had come to jettison the old traditions. There were cries of protest from diehard practitioners of the familiar forms, but they had little success in holding back the tide of foreign influence.

It was not easy, however, even for young poets to abandon completely the old forms. The classical *waka* (which came to be known as *tanka*, or short poem, during the Meiji era) had been the most respected variety of Japanese literature for over a thousand years, and a knowledge of this poetry formed an important part of the literary background of all educated Japanese. The five lines of the tanka, which amounted to only thirty-one syllables, were certainly inadequate for expressing all that might be found in, say, "Intimations of Immortality" or "The Charge of the Light Brigade," both translated into Japanese in the 1880s; but everything that most Japanese wanted to convey in poetry could in fact be conveyed lyrically in the tanka or with the concentration of imagery typical of the even shorter haiku. Long familiarity with these poetic forms had not only bred in Japanese an intuitive awareness of what could be suitably expressed but seems to have inhibited them from wanting to express in poetry thoughts that might require longer verse forms. The poets of the past had tended to avoid experimentation because they did not wish to create an impression of novelty; they concentrated instead on perfecting the expression of familiar perceptions or emotions in the hopes of coming even slightly closer than their predecessors to the core of the thought conveyed.

Not all poets, even in the past, had been content with the tanka. Writing poetry in classical Chinese had been another possibility open to poets as far back as the eighth century. At times, especially during the medieval period, Chinese poems had formed an important part of the total poetic output, and even in the twentieth century some poets composed classical Chinese with skill. But at a time when modernization was adopted as an ideal and Japanese poets were excitedly discovering Wordsworth, Tennyson, and Verlaine, writing poetry in Chinese came to seem extremely old-fashioned, rather like the writing of Latin by contemporary Europeans.

Renga (linked verse), the characteristic poetic form of the fifteenth and sixteenth centuries, also survived into modern times, but almost entirely as the diversion of a few men who enjoyed thinking of themselves as *bunjin* (gentlemen of letters) of the past century.

The *haiku*, which had grown out of renga, continued to enjoy great popularity after the Meiji Restoration, though not one haiku poet of distinction was active. The haiku by this time had become a kind of national pastime, and even persons devoid of poetic talent felt little hesitation about dashing off seventeen syllables as a greeting to a host or as a memento of a pleasant gathering.

It would not have been surprising if the Meiji poets had totally abandoned the tanka and haiku as the mediums of their poetic compositions, much as the Meiji novelists turned their backs on the *gesaku* fiction of the early nineteenth century. In the 1890s Masaoka Shiki unleashed such devastating attacks on both tanka and haiku that self-respecting poets must surely have had doubts about continuing to employ these forms. However, Shiki himself led a reform movement that imparted new life to the tanka and haiku and personally contributed to both. Shiki, it may be noted, was responsible for the use of the word "haiku" to designate independent poems in seventeen syllables; earlier names, such as *haikai no renga*, had called attention to the antecedents of haiku in linked verse, a literary form that Shiki detested.

Thanks to the reforms effected by Shiki and his followers, even Japanese who were impatient with old usages discovered that a tanka or a haiku could be more effective in conveying certain perceptions, especially brief but memorable experiences, than any more modern form of poetry. A short poem is rather like a photograph: unlike an oil painting, which may demand days or months of concentrated effort, a photograph can be taken in less than a second, but it too reveals the artist's sensibility and his outlook on the world.

The tanka, whose early demise was at one time predicted by Shiki, enjoyed a new flowering in the twentieth century. The most popular of tanka poets, Ishikawa Takuboku, proved that specifically modern ideas could be conveyed even with a traditional form. His *shintaishi*, poems in the new style, were much inferior to his tanka. The brevity of the tanka—and even more so of the haiku—kept poetic conceptions from being diluted by additional stanzas of less vivid inspiration. Poet after poet demonstrated that the combination of traditional forms and new thoughts could yield superb results. Saitō Mokichi's tanka rank among the finest poetry of modern Japan, regardless of the form.

Haiku enjoyed a similar revival, though there was no haiku poet of the stature of Saitō Mokichi. Haiku poetry came under attack soon after the end of the Pacific War on the grounds that its standards were so obscure that a reader could not judge whether or not a particular haiku was good or bad unless he knew the name of the poet. Despite this and other attacks, haiku composition enjoyed unbroken popularity. The newspapers carried weekly tanka and haiku columns presided over by well-known poets who chose the best from the countless poems submitted by a nationwide readership. Most poets, no matter how obviously amateurish, and no matter how remote the place where they lived, belonged to an organization of tanka or haiku poets, which held regular meetings at which poems by members were discussed and published magazines featuring the members' compositions. There were literally hundreds of such magazines, an indication of the size of the tanka and haiku "population." It was, however, most unusual for any poet to attempt to compose in both forms.

Contrary to the predictions made during the Meiji era, the traditional poetry not only survived but flourished in the twentieth century, apparently because it perfectly suited the poetic impulses of the mass of Japanese as well as the handful of masters whose works were likely to withstand the test of time.

THE MODERN TANKA

THE EARLY PERIOD (1868–1893)

The new, enlightened reign of the Emperor Meiji opened inauspiciously, at least as far as poetry was concerned. Ōkuma Kotomichi and Tachibana Akemi, the two most accomplished waka poets of the late Tokugawa period, both died in 1868, the year of the Meiji Restoration. It is true that the first half of the nineteenth century was not a particularly brilliant period for waka poetry, but Kotomichi and Akemi were its most original spirits, men who might have written striking poetry that described Japan under the new regime, and their deaths left a void in the world of the waka. None of the other waka poets of the day had much to write about apart from the traditional bittersweet comments on the falling of the cherry blossoms or the reddening of the autumn leaves. Not that the waka was dead: innumerable waka poets, at the imperial court in Kyoto, in the shogun's capital at Edo, and in many small centers of waka composition, never doubted that the waka was the highest achievement of Japanese literature; they continued to produce vast quantities on traditional themes, oblivious to the rapid and sometimes violent changes that the country was experiencing. There were different schools of waka, each of which clung with pride to special traditions, but their differences are no longer of much interest. Some distinguished men, not generally recognized as poets, used the waka for other purposes—for example, to declare patriotic sentiments, bid farewell to the world, or record impressions of travels abroad—but these poems were soon forgotten.

Still, there were faint stirrings of a new spirit in the waka even at the very beginning of the Meiji era. A collection of waka published in 1868, *Fūka Shimbun* (News in Poetry), compiled by Inoue Fumio (1800–1871) and Ōkami Mimaki, bore a preface that insisted poetry must not confine itself to describing "flowers, birds, the wind, and the moon," but should exhort society, making clear what is true and false, promoting wisdom, and rebuking unworthy motives. The compilers included waka of their own composition on such contemporary events as the battles that had taken place earlier that year and the Imperial Court's decision to abolish the shogunate. The fact that barbarians had been permitted to visit the Imperial Palace was described in their poetry as an unmitigated disaster. But for all their patriotic indignation, the authors were thrown in jail for having published controversial views.[1]

For the most part, however, the waka of the new reign, at least for the first ten years, were almost indistinguishable from those of the past. In 1869 the Emperor Meiji commanded the court poet Sanjōnishi Suetomo to teach the art of poetry in the palace, and in 1874 the practice of holding poetry gatherings (*utagokai*) was inaugurated. The emperor was an enthusiastic waka poet; it is estimated that he wrote close to one hundred thousand waka in his lifetime, and his consort, the Empress Shōken, wrote about forty thousand.[2] Even at the end of the Meiji era the preferred school of waka remained that of the conservative Keien style originated by Kagawa Kageki a century earlier, though other poets had by this time blasted its old-fashioned notions of what made for beauty in poetry.

The influence of the new age showed itself only gradually in the tanka (as the waka came to be called), initially in comic or trivial details and only later in the basic conceptions of poetry.

Various collections of "one hundred poems by one hundred poets" were published, some funny, some didactic, and even one in roman letters, presumably to familiarize readers with the Western alphabet. Many tanka were composed on historical subjects. At first the poets confined themselves to Japanese history, but before long they encompassed the whole world. Even poems on Washington, Napoleon, or Peter the Great preserved the classical language and turns of phrase.[3] The Christian missionaries also used the tanka form to spread their teachings. One Christian collection, published in 1883, employed ancient pillow words at the head of poems that concluded with such untraditional expressions as *supirito santo*.[4]

In 1878 the first of the various collections proudly labeled *kaika* (enlightenment) appeared; the *Kaika Shindai Kashū* (Collection of Poems on New Themes of Enlightenment) included 472 tanka by 136 poets. The preface declared that ever since Japan came to enjoy relations with foreign countries the things the poet sees and hears—the traditional inspiration for poetry—have no longer been the same as in the past; poets must now write about trains, balloons, and other modern inventions, in keeping with the kaika spirit.[5] Not all of the poets represented in this collection expressed pleasure over the changes brought about by the Enlightenment. Suzuki Shigene (1814–1898), writing on the theme "Students of Foreign Learning," warned:

yoko ni hau	Even though you may learn
kani nasu moji wa	The crab-writing
manabu to mo	That crawls sidewards,
naoki mikuni no	Never forget
michi na wasure so [6]	The True Way of Japan.

Other poems in a lighter vein described newspapers, foreign umbrellas, ice sellers, thermometers, gas lamps, hospitals, the Yokosuka shipyards, and policemen. Certainly these topics were a far cry from those of the tenth-century *Kokinshū* or even from nineteenth-century imitations of the *Kokinshū*, and apart from their obviously "poetic" features, whether pillow words or archaic grammatical forms, there is nothing poetic about these tanka. The same held true of the collection *Kidai Hyakushu* (One Hundred Poems on Unusual Subjects) published in 1879. Though the subjects are unconventional, the language is stale, and the greatest effort is devoted to describing entirely modern inventions—the telegraph, the rickshaw, the bicycle, and so on—in old-fashioned language, from a generally reactionary point of view.[7]

It does not take extensive readings in these tanka to reach the premature conclusion that the form was incapable of adjusting to the new age. Perhaps if Ōkuma Kotomichi and Tachibana Akemi had still been alive a way might have been discovered out of the impasse, but neither poet's works were even known at the time. In 1882 three young men who had absorbed the new learning published *Shintaishi-shō* (Selection of Poems in the New Style), in which they rejected the tanka altogether, declaring it was inadequate to describe the modern world.[8]

The study of Western poetry and theories of poetry convinced other Japanese that the tanka could be no more than a plaything for dilettantes. The preface to Yuasa Hangetsu's *Jūni no Ishizuka* (The Twelve Stone Tablets, 1885) urged poets to abandon the tanka and create new poetic forms, rather than attempt to make improvements.[9] Mikami Sanji, writing in 1888, deplored the limitations of the tanka: in the attempt to express the traditional ideal of *mono no aware* it had sacrificed philosophical and esthetic depth. He proposed that formal restrictions on poetic expression be dropped, that the classical language be replaced in poetry by contemporary speech, that the subject matter be vastly expanded beyond what had hitherto been considered poetic, and that the Japanese write narrative and allegorical poetry and even poetic dramas. Suematsu Kenchō, another eager student of Western poetry, called for the revival of the *chōka* (long poem) of the *Man-yōshū* because it was the closest Japanese approximation to Western poetry.[10]

Many similar views were expressed in the literary journals of the 1880s and 1890s. Perhaps the most systematic plan to reform the tanka was offered by Hagino Yoshiyuki in 1887. His proposal was in four points: (1) instead of writing on prescribed topics the poet should describe real scenes and objects; (2) poetry should not be forced into alternating lines in five and seven syllables; (3) the tone of poetry should be made more masculine and conducive to a spirit of bravery; and (4) the language should be contemporary, not excluding words of Chinese or Western origins that already had been adopted into common speech.[11] The intimate connections between the tanka and the old aristocracy, the guardians of orthodoxy, were also decried by men involved in the new political currents. A democratic tanka that would describe life in Meiji Japan in modern language, filled with an optimistic, masculine spirit, became the professed aim of many opponents of the prevalent Keien school, though few succeeded in writing tanka that fulfilled these prescriptions.

The advocates of the Keien school by no means remained silent in face of such attacks. Ikebukuro Kiyokaze (1847–1900), who had received a Christian education, published articles denouncing poetry that used words of Chinese or Western origins, and insisted that a Japanese poem, by definition, must be composed in elegant language. He demonstrated his disapproval of the shintaishi (poems in the new style) by "translating" several into orthodox tanka and chōka. In 1890 he published an article stating that Japanese who had learned Western languages were generally ignorant of the true and unique Japanese style.

Continuing admiration for the poetry of Kagawa Kageki (1768–1843), the founder of the Keien school, was specifically reflected by the appearance of a biography of the poet in 1889; and in 1892 Ōnishi Hajime (1864–1900) published an article stating that Kageki's place in the history of the waka was similar to that of Wordsworth in English poetry of the nineteenth century. Ōnishi emphasized especially the naturalness of Kageki's poetry; Kageki, he insisted, had described real scenes and objects he had seen with his own eyes and had used contemporary language to express himself.[12] Ōnishi evidently hoped to win for Kageki the reputation of having been a pioneer. Indeed, Kageki's essays on poetics often strike us by the "modernity" of their approach, but despite what he wrote about poetry, he and his followers did not often describe real scenes; they clung to the standard poetic topics and, far from using contemporary language, hardly ventured beyond the vocabulary of the *Kokinshū*.

The opponents of the Keien school were divided into two main factions: those who despaired of the tanka altogether, believing with Toyama Chuzan that "thoughts which can fully be expressed in thirty-one or seventeen syllables are no more than wisps of incense or shooting stars"; [13] and those who believed that a study of the *Manyōshū* could enable Meiji poets to write in a manner appropriate to the new age.

OCHIAI NAOBUMI (1861–1903)

The first distinctively new poet of the Meiji period was Ochiai Naobumi, born a samurai of the Sendai clan. As a boy he studied *kokugaku* and Shinto, especially after being adopted by a Shinto scholar who was a follower of the zealot Hirata Atsutane. Later he went to Tokyo where, in 1889, he joined the S.S.S.(Shinsei Sha, or New Voices Society), a literary society headed by Mori Ōgai, and translated some of the European poetry included in the society's publication *Omokage* (Vestiges, 1889).[14] Soon afterward he became actively interested in the reform of the tanka and began to publish articles on the subject. In 1893 Ochiai, his brother Ayukai Kaien, Ōmachi Keigetsu, Yosano Tekkan, and others joined to form the Asaka Society, the name taken from the street in Tokyo where Ochiai lived. This society was intended to promote a new kind of tanka; Ochiai also formed a less successful society for writing shintaishi with Masaoka Shiki, Sasaki Nobutsuna, and others. The history of poetry (especially in the traditional forms) during the modern period could be written in terms of different societies and their members, beginning with Ochiai's; few poets chose to stand aloof because being a member of a society usually provided the possibility of being published in that society's magazine. The Asaka Society lasted only until 1895, when Tekkan and Kaien went to Korea, but despite its short life, it played an important role in the creation of the modern tanka.

Ochiai's efforts to improve the tanka were halfhearted, perhaps because his orthodox training in the Japanese classics prevented him from breaking completely with tradition. It was with difficulty that he managed to free himself from the influence of the Keien school, and only toward the end of his life did his tanka reveal any novelty, even of the least sensational kind. His chief importance was as the encourager of younger, more iconoclastic poets. Ochiai's poetic gifts were limited, but his works appeared at precisely the time when they could create the greatest effect. His first major poem, a tanka published in 1892, established his reputation with younger colleagues:

hiodoshi no	Dressed in armor
yoroi wo tsukete	Of crimson braid, buckling my
tachi hakite	Great sword at my side,
miba ya to zo omou	I think I shall go admire
yamazakurabana [15]	The mountain cherry blossoms.

This poem, though written on a familiar subject, the cherry blossoms, strikes a fresh note because of the conspicuously masculine tone, quite unlike the delicate tanka of the Keien school. Ochiai, a samurai educated in Shinto traditions, seemed to embody in this poem the familiar Japanese proverb "Among blossoms, the cherry blossoms; among men, the samurai." No doubt the mounting Japanese nationalism, which would soon find an outlet in the Sino-Japanese War of 1894–1895, also contributed to the extraordinary popularity of this tanka. The poet became known by the sobriquet of "Naobumi of the Crimson Braid." [16]

Another tanka, written in 1891 when Ochiai visited Hagidera, a temple in Tokyo famous for its *hagi* (bush clover), suggests the extent of his indebtedness to the old poetry, despite his professions of faith in the new:

Hagidera no	At Clover Temple
hagi omoshiroshi	How lovely are the clover!
tsuyu no mi no	Here I shall settle
okitsudokoro	A body fleeting as dew
koko to sadamen [17]	In its final resting place.

Although the first lines describe the poet's actual observation and the wish expressed in the last three lines was probably sincere, rather than a stock response to a set topic, the poem is crammed with the baggage of the old poetry: "dew," "clover," and "settle" were "related words" (*engo*) that had been used together innumerable times by poets of the past.[18] Ochiai was extremely fond of the hagi blossoms; he planted hagi in his garden in Tokyo and carefully transplanted it during his many moves, always referring to his house and himself as Hagi-no-ya. His preoccupation with hagi, reminiscent of many earlier poets' obsession with cherry blossoms, was so intense that one modern critic has accused Ochiai of monomania.[19] Of course, there is no objection to a poet's describing his love of the beauty of flowers in a poem, but

Ochiai, a professed member of the "new wave," was so tightly bound by the rhetoric of the past that we sense little of the man behind the conventional expression. Only later in life, especially during his final illness, did his poetry become more personal. His last tanka, written a week before his death, is genuinely affecting:

kogarashi yo	O winter wind,
nare ga yuku no	Tonight I shall sleep and dream
shizukesa no	Of the stillness
omokage yumemi	Of that landscape where you
iza kono yo nen [20]	reach
	Your final destination.

Ochiai Naobumi is remembered also for poems in other forms, including some *imayō* in four lines, each of seven plus five syllables; for the lyrics to long ballads, including one on Kusunoki Masashige that remains a popular favorite; and for shintaishi whose lines were generally cast in patterns of seven and five syllables.[21] His views on the art of poetry were influential, though they differed little from those of many other poets of his day. On one occasion, addressing a society of "old-style" poets, he proclaimed himself a man of the "new style" and offered this criticism:

> If we examine the poems of the "old school" as to their materials, expression, diction, and thought, we shall find that they are all imitated from the poets of former times, and there is nothing novel or interesting about them. For example, what birds do they mention in their poems? In spring do they not confine themselves to the skylark, the song thrush, and the pheasant? For summer is not the cuckoo the only bird? And in autumn they mention the snipe and quail, in winter the plover. The birds included in the successive waka anthologies are indeed fortunate, for they can be sure everybody will write poetry about them, but birds like the canary, the peacock or the parrot, no matter how beautiful their voices or their feathers may be, are ignored by the old-style poets.[22]

Similar criticism of approved and nonapproved birds and flowers had been made by Tachibana Akemi years before, without noticeable effect; but Ochiai influenced many younger men because the time was ripe for reform of the tanka. His society, the

Asaka Sha, was the incubator for a new generation of tanka poets. Yosano Tekkan (1873–1935) and Kaneko Kun'en (1876–1951) were specially favored disciples. The two men later parted company, but both remembered Ochiai Naobumi with gratitude and affection. Kaneko Kun'en recalled in 1936: "The first time I met my teacher he told me that a poem without individuality was no poem at all. He ended by remarking, 'Ochiai's poems must be Ochiai's, and in the same way Kaneko's poems must be Kaneko's.' His resonant voice still echoes in my ears. I would be hard put to express how much these words encouraged me." [23]

TEKKAN, AKIKO, AND THE *MYŌJŌ* POETS

Ochiai's chief successor was Yosano Tekkan (also known as Yosano Hiroshi [24]), who has often been credited with creating the modern tanka. Tekkan was born in Kyoto, the son of a Buddhist priest who had achieved some distinction as a waka poet. Although Tekkan's formal education did not extend even to middle school, he was carefully instructed in the composition of poetry by his father, and he studied the Japanese and Chinese classics by himself. Even as a child he associated with his father's disciples, including Amada Guan (1854–1904), a poet of considerable influence. At the age of sixteen Tekkan, unable to gain admission to middle school, complied with his father's wishes and took orders as a Buddhist priest, though this vocation had no appeal for him. In 1892, at nineteen, he ran away from Kyoto to Tokyo, and in the following year became a pupil of Ochiai Naobumi. Tekkan was prominent in the founding of the Asaka Society and, on Ochiai's recommendation, was put in charge of the Arts and Letters column of the newspaper *Niroku Shimpō* in 1894. In this newspaper he published serially his attack on the traditional tanka poets called *Bōkoku no Ne* (Sounds Ruinous to the Country, 1894–1895), which bore the subtitle "Abuse Directed at the Unmanly Waka of Today." This work severely criticized the adherents of the Keien and similar schools, declaring that their poetry was weak and vulgar, effeminate, and minor. Tekkan advocated a masculine poetry in the traditions of the *Manyōshū*. With this publication he took his place at the head of the movement of new poets, displacing the milder Ochiai.

Tekkan's manifesto began to appear at an opportune moment, just before the outbreak of the Sino-Japanese War, in July of 1894. This war was to arouse many poets to write in precisely the virile manner Tekkan advocated. Tekkan himself composed tanka to encourage the Japanese troops, to denigrate the Chinese, or to celebrate victories. In April 1895 he went to Korea to teach Japanese at a school in Seoul. His stay was relatively short, but it inspired him to write a number of tanka, especially during the summer of 1895, when he lay in a Seoul hospital suffering from typhoid fever. Ten tanka begin with the lines *Kara ni shite/ ikade ka shinan* (How can I die in Korea?), including:

Kara ni shite,	Here in Korea,
ikade ka shinan.	How can I possibly die?
ware shinaba,	If I should die,
onoko no uta zo,	The poetry of real men
mata sutarenan [25]	Would again be abandoned.

The prefatory note to another poem written about this time explains how a school had been founded by the Japanese in Seoul where he taught some seven hundred pupils the Japanese classics and the composition of Japanese poetry. Tekkan wrote when the school was opened:

Kara yama ni,	In Korean mountains
sakura wo uete,	I plant a cherry tree,
Karabito ni,	And I shall teach Koreans
Yamato onoko no,	To sing the songs
uta utawasen. [26]	Of the men of Yamato.

That autumn, after leaving the hospital, Tekkan wrote a famous tanka expressing his indignation over Queen Min's oppression of the pro-Japanese party in Korea:

Kara yama ni	In Korean mountains
aki kaze tatsu ya,	The autumn wind has risen;
tachi nadete,	As I stroke my sword
ware omou koto,	I am by no means wanting
naki ni shi mo arazu. [27]	In righteous indignation.

Tekkan's early tanka perfectly embodied the ideals set forth in *Sounds Ruinous to the Country*. Rejecting the elegant, effeminate tanka being composed at the time, he turned to the simple, martial tone found in the *Manyōshū*. He even went so far as to deny the validity of love poetry, on the grounds that it tended to be too effeminate. Tekkan deplored the belief of some critics of literature that morality and literature were quite separate; he characterized such men as "destroyers of the country."

Tekkan asked in his essay, with seeming seriousness, why, at a time when some people favored ending prostitution and others a prohibition on the consumption of liquor, nobody had as yet advocated banning the modern tanka. Indulgence in sex and liquor harms the body and the effects are immediately apparent, but dilettantism corrodes the spirit and the effects are more insidious. The danger to one's health lies not in liquor and sex themselves but in overindulgence; but the danger in the tanka lay in men's corrupting its functions and spreading the poison. Modern tanka poets blindly follow those of the past, and it has been many years since poets listened directly to the music of the cosmos. The most conspicuous proof of the blindness of contemporary poets is their worship of Kagawa Kageki and their calling him "the saint of the waka." Each successive wave of imitation only lowers the standards; poets today are incapable even of attaining Kageki's level, let alone that of the poets of the distant past.[28]

Tekkan concluded *Sounds Ruinous to the Country* by declaring that although it has always been his practice to refer to his seniors with deference, he can no longer be reticent, for when it comes to discussing poetry there are no seniors or juniors. "The poison of imitation has already infected the elders, and their poison is in turn about to infect the next generation." He asserted that he had written his essay in the hopes that poets infected by this malady would examine themselves and discover whether or not it is true that "revolution is a stage in progress."[29]

Tekkan's essay by no means silenced the opposition.[30] Moreover, it was not long before Tekkan himself changed: as the result of falling desperately in love with his future wife, he abruptly abandoned his opposition to love poetry. Nevertheless, his manifesto had a salutary effect, and it established Tekkan as the chief spokesman of the younger poets. He followed his essay with the poetry collection *Tōzai Namboku* (The Four Directions, 1896). The book came well recommended, with prefaces by Ochiai Naobumi, Mori Ōgai, Masaoka Shiki, Saitō Ryokuu, and others. The poet's own preface recalled his early career. Even in his youth, he claimed, he had already written some seven thousand tanka, of which he could now remember barely a fiftieth. In compiling this collection he had rejected all these examples of juvenilia.[31] He declared, "My poems, whether tanka or shintaishi, have not been composed in adulation of anyone, nor have I licked at anyone's leavings; I think I may fairly say that my poems are *my* poems." [32]

The Four Directions contains 279 tanka, forty-five shintaishi, and a few renga sequences. Some poems are prefaced with explanations describing the circumstances of composition. One bears the preface, "On Hearing that the Chicago Exposition Has Opened":

Shikago e wa	To Chicago
mazu okuramaku	I would like to send
omou ka na	First of all:
Fuji no shirayuki	The white snows of Fuji,
mi Yoshino no hana [33]	The cherry blossoms of Yoshino.

This is not only an inept poem, but egregiously unoriginal. The reader is likely to wonder why Tekkan could think of sending to Chicago in 1893 nothing less predictable than the most hackneyed of all symbols of Japan. Despite Tekkan's insistence on "manliness" (*masuraoburi*) in poetry, most poems in the collection that do not specifically describe Tekkan polishing his sword or listening to tigers roar are conventionally pretty rather than intense. He objected to the tanka in the court anthologies compiled after the *Manyōshū*, but he sometimes borrowed shamelessly even from such poetry:

yo no naka ni	I wish that somewhere
aki yori hoka no	In the world there were a town
sato mo ga na	Where fall never came;
omou koto naku	I would gaze up at the moon,
tsuki nagamen [34]	Not thinking of a thing.

It does not take much of a literary detective to discover that Tekkan derived his poem from this one of Princess Shikishi in the *Shin Kokinshū*:

nagame wabinu	Weary of brooding,
aki yori hoka no	I wish I had a house where
yado mo ga na	Autumn never came;
no ni mo yama ni mo	But would the moon be as bright
tsuki ya sumuran [35]	On the fields and mountains?

Not only is Tekkan's tanka derivative, but it dilutes the effects of Princess Shikishi's superb poem. If Tekkan had intended his poem as a parody we might enjoy his virtuosity, but clearly such was not his intent. His early tanka, despite his claims to originality, tend to follow closely the old themes, and the caesura usually occurs after the third verse, in the *Shin Kokinshū* manner. Tekkan used the artificial vocabulary of the old waka, avoiding modern language even when he described contemporary events, and usually concluded his poem with *ran*, *keri*, *kana*, and the other "poetic" particles, or else with nouns. Only in his specifically "masculine" poems did he adopt the style and diction of the *Manyōshū*; this "return" to earlier Japanese poetry produced, paradoxically, more modern poems than his *Shin Kokinshū* style.

In February 1899 Tekkan organized the Shinshi Sha (New Poetry Society), and in April 1900 the society published the first issue of its organ, the magazine *Myōjō* (Morning Star). Tekkan's collection *Tekkanshi* (1901) showed a marked improvement in his poetic techniques, and revealed how greatly his attitude had changed on the seemliness of love poetry:

koi to na to	Love or reputation—
izure omoki wo	Which is the more important?
mayoisomenu	I have begun to waver.
wa ga toshi koko ni	My age at this point in time
nijūhachi no aki [36]	Is twenty-eight autumns.

The difference in his viewpoint can be traced to his meeting Hō (also pronounced Ōtori) Akiko in August 1900 while on a visit to Osaka. They fell in love, and in the following year Akiko left home for Tokyo. Her poetry, first published in the collection *Midaregami* (Tangled Hair, 1901), is intensely romantic, and she seems to have infected the stern Tekkan with her ardor. Their magazine *Myōjō* would be known above all for its emphasis on romantic passion, not for the masculine strength Tekkan had so often announced as his ideal. Tekkan married Akiko in the summer of 1901, soon after the publication of *Tekkanshi*.[37] His next collection, *Murasaki* (Purple, 1901), belongs to a quite different world from its predecessors, as the title suggests. The opening poem sets the tone:

> *ware otoko no ko*
> *iki no ko na no ko*
> *tsurugi no ko*
> *shi no ko koi no ko*
> *aa modae no ko* [38]

> I am a male child,
> A child of temper, a child of pride,
> A child of the sword,
> A child of poetry, a child of love,
> And ah! a child of anguish.

The effect of this poem cannot be conveyed in translation; it depends on the repetition of the word *ko* (child), the boldness of the meter, and the freedom of the diction (*iki* and *shi*, words of Chinese origin, had normally not been allowed in the tanka). The poem has an immediacy and impetuosity quite unlike the self-conscious heroics of Tekkan's early works. Tekkan was influenced not only by Akiko but by Yamakawa Tomiko (1879–1909), another woman poet with whom he became friendly in 1900. In this tanka he still asserts, in his masuraoburi manner, that he is a male, proud, and armed with a sword, but the last two lines indicate the contradictory part of his nature that makes him a poet, a man of sensitivity and love.

In the sixth issue of *Myōjō* the "rules" of the Shinshi Sha were first announced: (1) We believe it is an innate faculty to enjoy the beauty of poetry. Our poetry is therefore our pleasure. We consider it shameful to compose poetry for the sake of an empty name. (2) We love the poetry of our predecessors, but we cannot stoop to spade the fields that they have already cultivated. (3) We shall show our poetry to one another. Our poems do not imitate those of our predecessors. They are our poems, or rather, they are poems each one of us has invented for himself. (4) We call our poems "national poems" (*kokushi*); they are new poems of the nation, national poems of the Meiji era, national poems that stem from the lineage of the *Manyōshū* and the *Kokinshū*.[39]

Tekkan, perceiving that his manly ideals—as expressed, for example, by his advocacy of a Japanese invasion of Korea—were giving way before the conflicting demands of his destiny as a poet, wrote this verse, included in *Purple*:

so ya risō	That way my ideals,
ko ya ummei no	This way my destiny—
wakareji ni	At the crossroads
shiroki sumire wo	A white violet;
aware to naku mi [40]	Moved, I stand weeping.

Tekkan, despite himself, realized that his lot would be cast with poetry; the white violet that moved him to tears was probably intended as a symbol for feminine beauty.

Tekkan's biggest collection, *Aigikoe* (Love Poems, 1910), was a selection of one thousand poems composed during the previous eight years. Mori Ōgai's preface states: "Who first created and nurtured what we now call the 'new wave' of the tanka? No one save Yosano can reply, 'I did.' " [41] This judgment is fair; although Tekkan's poetry before long lost much of its appeal, his insistence that the tanka must be individual and personal inspired younger poets to write in this form. However, instead of calling his poems either waka or tanka he preferred *kokushi* (national poetry) or *tanshi* (short poetry), in order to place the tanka squarely in the realm of modern poetry and wrest control from amateurs who composed tanka as a mere diversion.

Tekkan continued to write poetry, both tanka and shintaishi, for the rest of his life, but his important work ended in 1910 with the publication of *Love Poems*.

Yosano Akiko (1876–1942), born in the commercial city of Sakai, received an excellent education, particularly in the Japanese classics. She read *The Tale of Genji* several times while still at school, and knew most of the poems in the standard court anthologies by heart.[42] Her earliest preserved tanka, dating from 1896, are completely conventional, on such assigned topics as "deer on a mountain peak," but she fell under the spell of the shintaishi poets, especially Shimazaki Tōson and Susukida Kyūkin. Through their poetry she directly absorbed the Japanese Romanticism of the *Bungakkai* group, and indirectly the European Romanticism that had inspired them. She began to compose shintaishi, and this form of poetry, more suitable to her outbursts of passion and her narrative intent than the tanka, might well have become her normal medium of expression had she not happened to read in 1897 a tanka by Tekkan that powerfully impressed her. She was moved to write in the same vein, and her tanka were soon strikingly more individual than those she composed a few years earlier.

Akiko's meeting with Tekkan in 1900 determined her career as a poet. She began to contribute to *Myōjō* from the second issue, and achieved instant fame with the publication of *Midaregami* (Tangled Hair) in 1901. It has often been assumed that these poems, brimming with romantic ardor, reflect her own turbulent love life, but this is unlikely; she was so strictly raised by a puritanical father that the passionate affairs she described probably existed only in her imagination.[43] Only after she met Tekkan were her emotions quickened by an actual object of love. At first she never met him unchaperoned. As it happened, the chaperon, Yamakawa Tomiko, was also romantically interested in Tekkan, and Tekkan for his part was still in love with his wife. Tomiko was forced by her parents to marry another man and Tekkan's marriage soon afterward broke up in a divorce, leaving the field open for Akiko, whose poems became more overt in their expressions of love. But even these love poems could not have prepared readers for the intensity of *Tangled Hair*. The first poem of the collection announced the arrival of an important poet:

yo no chō ni	A star once whispered
sasameki tsukishi	The full extent of her love
hoshi no ima wo	In the curtains of night;
gekai no hito no	Now, a creature of the world below,
bin no hotsure yo [44]	Sleepless, my locks are twisted.

Like many of the tanka in *Tangled Hair* this one is hard to understand because of the irregular syntax and the private meanings of certain words. A few months after the publication of *Tangled Hair* Tekkan explained this poem: "The words of joy exchanged within the curtains of night in heaven are sweet and satisfying as honey, but I, a star-child fallen to the world below, am wasted now by the unattainability of love; behold how my lusterless sidelocks are twisted!" [45] Another commentator suggested that Akiko, likening herself to a star enjoying the celestial delights of love, looked down on the world of mortals and saw what anguish love brought them. Still another commentator interpreted the poem as meaning that in heaven, on the night of the seventh day of the seventh moon, two stars meet happily, but down below in this world the poet, beset by the torments of love, has disheveled her hair by tossing and turning in bed.[46]

Probably Tekkan's explanation was closest to Akiko's intent, if only because he knew her best when she wrote this tanka, but the fact that it can be interpreted so variously suggests the obscurity of her elliptic style. Akiko did not learn this obscurity from Tekkan, whose poems are usually straightforward; her initial inspiration had come from the shintaishi, and the obscurity of her tanka may have resulted from attempting to cram into thirty-one syllables a complexity of thought more easily expressed in a longer verse form. Her difficulty in accommodating her thoughts to the tanka is indicated by another poem in *Tangled Hair*:

uta ni kike na	Ask my poetry—
tare no nohana ni	Who denies the crimson among
akaki inamu	The flowers of the field?
omomuki aru ka na	That is where the meaning lies—
haru tsumi motsu ko	The girl guilty with the spring.

Not only are some lines irregular in length, but the use of words is peculiar: "crimson" (like purple, red, or pink) was used by the *Myōjō* poets to symbolize love, and such words as "spring," "guilt," and "child" were loaded with special meanings. The sense of the poem would seem to be that the poet, though considered guilty by stern moralists, tells the truth when she writes about love; she can no more deny love than reject red flowers, the most beautiful in the field; only through poetry can this love be conveyed.[47]

Again and again in the collection, as the title foreshadows, hair is used as the symbol of youthful beauty and love:

sono ko hatachi	The girl is twenty;
kushi ni nagaruru	Oh, the beauty of black hair
kurokami no	Flowing through her comb
ogori no haru no	In the pride of her spring!
utsukushiki ka na.[48]	

This assertion of pride in her beauty flew in the face of the feudal morality, which insisted that women be modest, but it was typical of Akiko's self-assurance. Often she pitted herself against convention or exulted in her uncontrollable passions. *Tangled Hair*, not surprisingly, was an immediate sensation and sold an unprecedented number of copies for a book of poetry. Akiko had established herself as a leading tanka poet. She also wrote shin-taishi throughout her career; the most famous of these, addressed to her brother with the Japanese army at Port Arthur, urged him not to die for his country. This earned her such bitter reproaches for her lack of patriotic spirit that she felt obliged to explain that women have always disliked war. The poem, typical of Akiko's outspoken views and perhaps reflecting her merchant-class background, was certainly not typical of the *Myōjō* school, headed by Tiger Tekkan.

Although Yosano Akiko continued to produce important volumes of poetry in the 1920s and 1930s, her greatest popularity ended with the demise of *Myōjō*. Her defiant poems were no longer so startling to a new generation of readers, and Akiko looked less convincing at fifty in the role of the emancipated woman than at twenty. The mainstream of the modern tanka was to head in a different direction from hers. In later years Akiko detested even to hear *Tangled Hair* mentioned, no doubt because it irritated her to think that her first collection was fated to be the one for which she would be remembered. Though her later poetry was technically and artistically superior, flaming youth rather than the ripeness of age was what the public asked of Akiko, and they found it in *Tangled Hair*. Like Théophile Gautier, always remembered in terms of the red vest he wore to the opening of *Hernani*, even when he was an old man, Akiko captured so vividly the headstrong emotions of a sensual girl that readers never permitted her to grow up.

The chief achievement of the *Myōjō* poets was to win for the tanka a place in the new literature denied it by enthusiasts for Western forms of expression.[49] These poets were characterized by their insistence on the importance of the individual, their love of beauty, the admiration they expressed for art, their nostalgia for distant times and places, their craving for a kind of supra-realism and, above all, their awareness of belonging to a group sharing an unorthodox, revolutionary spirit.[50] Even at the height of its popularity, however, the *Myōjō* poetry stood apart from contemporary Japanese literature, prevailingly naturalistic during the decade after the Russo-Japanese War. The New Poetry Society was held together by the Yosanos, but not all members reacted with enthusiasm to them or to the principles of the society. Some poets drifted away from the tanka to modern poetry (like Takamura Kōtarō); others, like Kubota Utsubo (1877–1967) and Mizuno Yōshū (1883–1947), after sharing the Shinshi Sha ideals for a time broke away to form their own schools; and still others, like Kitahara Hakushū and Yoshii Isamu, though fundamentally in agreement with the principles of the Shinshi Sha, became increasingly disenchanted with the Yosanos. By the time *Myōjō* ceased publication with its hundredth issue in 1908 it had fulfilled its mission in the world of the tanka.

KITAHARA HAKUSHŪ (1885–1942)

The successor to *Myōjō* was *Subaru* (Pleiades), published from 1909 to 1913, initially under the editorship of Ishikawa Takuboku. *Subaru* printed not only tanka but poetry in other forms, plays, and even novels, including Mori Ōgai's sensational *Vita Sexualis*, the publication of which led the authorities to ban the sale of the magazine. But *Subaru* was characterized above all by the hedonistic, sensual tanka of Kitahara Hakushū and Yoshii Isamu (1886–1960). The latter continued to write in much the same vein for the rest of his long career, though he shifted his activities from Tokyo to Kyoto, gaining fame as the poet of the Gion geisha district. Hakushū, a much more considerable figure, developed into a major poet, in both the tanka and the shintaishi, and was known also for his folk and children's songs.

Hakushū was born into a wealthy Kyushu family. He went to Tokyo to study English, but left Waseda before graduation to devote himself entirely to poetry. He joined the Shinshi Sha in 1906 and published in *Myōjō*, associating especially with Yoshii Isamu and Ishikawa Takuboku. In 1908 he began to attend the poetry sessions held at Mori Ogai's house, where he met Itō Sachio, Saitō Mokichi, and other members of the *Araragi* group. In the same year he joined various artists and poets in founding the Pan no Kai (Devotees of Pan), a group of admirers of foreign literature and art who met periodically to drink and discuss their mutual interests. In January 1908 Hakushū left the Shinshi Sha, one of the crises that led to *Myōjō* ceasing publication the following November. Soon after *Subaru* first appeared in January 1909, Hakushū joined its staff. In March he published *Jashūmon*, a collection of shintaishi.

In 1913 Hakushū's first collection of tanka, *Kiri no Hana* (Paulownia Blossoms), appeared. Sometimes these tanka closely parallel his shintaishi in expression, and an awareness of French symbolism pervades both forms. He composed the following tanka at one of the regular sessions at Mori Ōgai's house:

haru no tori	Birds of spring,
na naki so naki so	Don't sing, please don't sing!
aka-aka to	A blaze of red
to no mo no kusa ni	In the grass outside my window,
hi no iru yūbe [51]	The sun sets this evening.

This impromptu composition was placed by Hakushū at the head of *Paulownia Blossoms*, an indication of its importance for him. The poet, though normally fond of birds singing, finds they disrupt his mood of melancholy as he watches the sun sink in the grassy fields outside his window, and bids them be silent.[52] The meaning of the poem is enhanced by its musical qualities, especially the repetition of *naki so naki so* in the second line and *aka-aka* in the third, followed by the four *o* sounds in the fourth. Hakushū composed a shintaishi on the same subject, using similar language. He defined at length why he chose on occasion to compose tanka, despite its musty heritage and its constricting length:

The tanka is a small, green, ancient precious stone. It is an extract distilled from the sentiments of the long-ago Age of Pathos. It is old, but hard to discard. That perfected, beautiful form has been given an incomparable, sad luster by the many different memories of Orientals going back two thousand years. Over its surface moves an iridescent light and a modest fragrance like almond water, or else the rhythm of a simple *lied* played on a one-stringed koto or on an old Japanese flute. Does it not make one nostalgic? Just as the young Rossetti expressed the joys of *The House of Life* through the old form of the sonnet, I too, after having allowed my entire senses to vibrate in some extravagant and untrammeled new symphonic work, see no reason why I should not happily pluck a lonely, one-stringed old koto with new, sad fingertips. Does not even the vulgar man of the city at moments in his busy round of bank affairs at times cast a casual but delicate glance at a bowl of cineraria? I should like in such a manner to become intimate with the scent of the tanka.

*

That small, green, old, precious stone often lies on my palm damp with fresh perspiration filled with the lingering scent of spices, and I touch it with fingertips stained with whiskey or yellow sponge cake. Depending on the time, the place and the variations in my moods, it may reflect the faint fragrance of paulownia flowers, or shine with the pale green of grass and young leaves, or even be spotted with a drop of red blood from the scratch of an imperceptible thorn.

Of course I love the gentle touch of this old, precious stone. I would also like to impart to it a special, deep luster with the fresh and delicate perspiration of my modern sensibilities and the intense breath of restless youth. But I know the deep pathos that emanates from its perfected form. To tell the truth, I am convinced that nothing is so sad as a completed object, and nothing is so lonely in all the world as a waitress past forty who has failed as a wife but into whose eyes occasionally comes a delicate look, like that of a young geisha. The hearts of young people yearn after more complicated, unlimited, incomplete music. They go to Manet, Degas, Gauguin, Andreyev; they are attracted by the feeling and form of Strauss, Baudelaire, Rodenbach. When I am fatigued by the pleasure of their strong colors, the old color of that little emerald at times transmits softly through my fingers the sad overtones of my soul. It is like the taste of a glass of old champagne when one is suffering some temporary illness.

The old, small emerald should be hidden in a crystal box behind the bottles of some titillating Western liquor and of hashish. The old one-stringed instrument should be stood in the pale green shade beside a French piano and looked at quietly. That is how I think of tanka.

And I truly love it.

*

If my modern poems are strong-colored oil paintings of the Impressionist school, my tanka must be the moisture of turpentine oil faintly stirring on the underside. This lonely dampness is the green of the small precious stone in my heart, and it is the elegant sobbing of a one-stringed koto.[53]

The preciosity and complexity of the expression exactly corresponded to the heady exoticism of the tanka in *Paulownia Blossoms*:

hiyashinsu	Hyacinths,
usu murasaki ni	Pale lavender.
sakinikeri	Opened their blossoms
hajimete kokoro	The day my heart
furuisomeshi hi [54]	First began to tremble.

Mention of the hyacinth, a foreign flower, was typical of Hakushū's exoticism; other tanka in the collection mention the amaryllis blooming as the poet kissed a girl, a spring night in Paris, Rimbaud wandering the streets, an evening when Hakushū heard a clarinet play. A most affecting example combines a fin-de-siècle unhealthiness with the sound of a foreign musical instrument (even though it is the harmonica!) to create an "oriental" scene:

yameru ko wa	The sickly child
hamonika wo fuki	Played his harmonica
yo ni irinu	Until it grew dark:
morokoshibatake no	Over the fields of Chinese corn
ki naru tsuki no de [55]	The yellow moonrise.

A note of romantic love often accompanies the exoticism:

fukura naru	My senses are stirred
boa no nioi wo	By the fluffy fragrance of
atarashimu	A feather boa:
jūichigatsu no	A secret meeting with her
asa no aibiki [56]	One morning in November.

Sometimes the meaning is not even hinted at, though the reader can sense the poet's emotion:

te ni toreba	Taken in my hand
kiri no hansha no	The newspaper was pale green
usuaoki	In light reflected
shimbunshi koso	From the paulownia leaves;
nakamahoshikere [57]	It made me want to cry.

Hakushū does not say why he felt like crying. Perhaps the contrast between the sordid content of the newspaper in his hand and the faint presence of nature in the green light filtered through the leaves brought on tears too deep for words. The poet's sensitivity transcends the ordinary principles of cause and effect.

Hakushū's tanka sometimes resemble those of the *Shin Kokinshū* in structure, thought, and diction, though not in imagery; unlike many tanka poets active around 1910, he was not affected by the *Manyōshū*.[58] His romanticism had little in common with the "manliness" of the heroic past.

Hakushū led a private life in keeping with the fin-de-siècle mood of his poetry. His romantic exaltation suffered a setback in 1912 when, after having become deeply involved with a married woman, Hakushū and the woman were sued by her injured husband for adultery. The two were thrown into jail for some days while awaiting trial, but were finally acquitted. The shock of arrest was, however, so great that Hakushū was no longer capable of "singing like a little bird in the clear spring sky." [59] His reputation, which had been enhanced by each successive collection of poetry, was now damaged, at least in the eyes of the vulgar public, and he fled to a fishing village where he and his newly won wife

attempted to begin a new life. The simple life helped to heal the
wounds he had suffered, but his next volume of tanka, *Kirara Shū*
(Mica Collection, 1915), was in a quite different mood from
Paulownia Blossoms. He wrote of the change: "I destroyed the
tone of *Paulownia Blossoms*. *Mica Collection* was crude, but the
fresh green of turnip leaves and the silver glint of a globefish had
brought me vitality and health. The pale violet of paulownia flowers and the milky yellow of sponge cake had already become a
dream of some distant season beyond the sea." [60]

Mica Collection contains some sensual poems, but they lack
the nervous tension and the feverishness so abundant in *Paulownia Blossoms*; often they describe the joy and satisfaction of being
in love with a woman who was no longer a secret paramour but
the wife who shared his happiness.[61] Hakushū turned to Buddhism, reading Japanese literary works that had been written under Buddhist influence and composing poetry in the same vein.
His third tanka collection, *Suzume no Tamago* (Sparrow Eggs,
1921), reveals his mood of religious awareness most clearly. During the period when he compiled this collection Hakushū was
troubled by fresh marital difficulties and lived in poverty, but the
poetry is filled with a kind of resignation:

susukino ni	The smoke rising
shiroku kabosoku	Whitely and thinly over
tatsu kemuri	The *susuki* fields
aware naredomo	Stirs me with sorrow, but
kesu yoshi mo nashi [62]	I know no way to quench it.

Hakushū does not explain why the thin column of smoke rising
over the endless plumes of susuki grass distressed him so greatly;
perhaps it symbolized his own thoughts.

Most of the tanka Hakushū published during the rest of his
career were marked by a similar quiet acceptance and by his quest
of a "new *yūgen*." The gradual approach of blindness lent somber
overtones to the poems of his last years. These tanka are affecting
in their understatement, but have none of the brilliance of imagery associated with Hakushū's name. A tanka, published in the
collection *Kurohi* (Black Cypress, 1937), is especially moving:

teru tsuki no	I can verify
hie sadaka naru	The coldness of the shining moon
akarido ni	From the glass door;
me wa korashitsutsu	As I stare, straining my eyes,
shiite yuku nari [63]	Each moment I grow blinder.

In 1949 a collection of some twelve hundred tanka and chōka on travel written between 1923 and 1926 was posthumously published, with the title *Unasaka* (Sea Borders). These tanka are occasionally experimental, using the vernacular, breaking the conventional metrics, or dividing into three or four lines:

shiruku hatto no	The governor, in a silk hat,
chiji san ga dete miteru	Comes out and has a look
tento no soto no	At the distant Alps
tōi Arupusu [64]	Outside the tent.

Not only is the language highly colloquial but the scene described is comically modern: the governor of some rural prefecture, dressed up to inaugurate a country fair, steps out of a tent in his top hat and notices the grandeur of distant scenery. In other poems of *Sea Borders* Hakushū expressed sympathy with the farmers in a village that had been condemned to make way for a dam. Such poems constitute only a minor element in Hakushū's oeuvre, though they figured prominently among the works of poets of the Naturalist school.

THE NATURALIST POETS

The poets classed as members of the Naturalist school differed so markedly among themselves that it is often hard to detect their common features. Most were first stimulated into writing tanka by their reading of the *Myōjō* poets, but before long came to express strong opposition to the involved expression and insistence on superhuman passions; they preferred to direct their attention instead (in the manner of the Naturalist novelists) to ordinary yet poignant incidents and perceptions drawn from daily life.

Kubota Utsubo (1877–1967), the senior Naturalist poet, continued to the end of his long lifetime to publish tanka of distinction, as well as poems in other forms (including the chōka) and many studies of classical Japanese literature. Unlike the *Myōjō* poets, he attained his greatest distinction as a poet relatively late in life. His closest approach to the thematic material of the Naturalist school is found in a poem like the following one, published in 1915:

sono te mote	He learned the sadness
meshi kuu koto no	Of eating food earned with his
kanashisa wo	hands,
shirinitarikeru	The young factory worker.
shōnen shokkō [65]	

The subject matter of this tanka is suitable for a Naturalist poem, but its effect depends above all on the exact choice of words. For example, the drawn-out syllables *shirinitarikeru*, which can be translated into English as "found out" or "discovered," contain something like a sigh of grief, and this protracted, pure Japanese word is followed by the clipped syllables of *shōnen shokkō*, bringing in a contrasting note of harsh reality. Kubota Utsubo's poetry often has a perfection of diction that defies translation, though his themes and imagery are less compelling than those of other members of the Naturalist school.

Wakayama Bokusui (1885–1928) published his first collection, *Umi no Koe* (Voices of the Sea), in 1908, while a student at Waseda University. The poems are filled with romantic expressions of grief and longing that hardly differ from those written by members of the *Myōjō* group, but—perhaps owing to his country background—they also possess a vitality and a feeling for nature that set his work apart from the more conceptual imagination of, say, Yosano Akiko. A poem from *Voices of the Sea* suggests his special kind of melancholy:

shiratori wa	The white seagull—
kanashikarazu ya	Is it not saddening
soro no ao	It should hover, undyed

umi no ao ni mo	By the blue of the sky
somazu tadayou [66]	Or the blue of the sea?

The meaning of the second line has been much debated; some commentators insist that the question is addressed to the seagull ("Are you not sad you should hover?"), others that Bokusui empathizes with the seagull or that he himself is the seagull, and still others that the poem is an example of Romantic symbolism.[67] Most likely, the second line is addressed to a third person, asking if he does not share the poet's sadness at the sight. The background of the tanka is the poet's unhappy love affair, though this is not expressed. The seagull is not a symbol for the poet; rather, the poet, gazing at the seagull so unaffected by its surroundings, senses in it something peculiarly congruent to his own loneliness.

iku yama kawa	How many mountains
koesariyukaba	And rivers must I cross before
sabishisa no	I reach that country
hatenan kuni zo	Where my loneliness will end?
kyō mo tabi yuku [68]	Today too I shall journey.

This tanka was written while Bokusui was traveling in Okayama. The physical hardships he experienced when making his way over rough terrain impart strength to the romantic conception of a far-off land without loneliness. Bokusui seems to have been influenced by a poem by the German lyricist Carl Busse (1872–1918), which speaks of a place "beyond the mountains" where happiness may be found. Busse's poem had been published in a Japanese translation by Ueda Bin in 1905, and no doubt its combination of romanticism and poetic realism helped Bokusui to crystalize his experience.[69]

Bokusui established his reputation with the collection *Betsuri* (Separation, 1910). It included some one thousand tanka written between 1906 and 1908, while he was still a student. His next collection, *Rojō* (On the Road, 1911), further enhanced his reputation, though the manner is sometimes surprisingly conceptual:

unazoko ni	They say there lives
me no naki uo no	At the bottom of the sea
sumu to iu	A fish without eyes;

| *me no naki uo no* | How I envy |
| *koishikarikeri* [70] | That fish without eyes! |

Maeda Yūgure wrote about this poem: "The eyeless fish at the bottom of the sea presumably symbolizes the author's desolation and depression. His attempt to identify his mental state with a blind fish in the depths of the sea suggests a kind of passionate longing." [71] Another poem in the collection, composed by the ruins of the Castle of Komori, is celebrated:

katawara ni	This is what they said,
akikusa no hana	The flowers of autumn grasses
kataruraku	Blooming at my side:
horobishi mono wa	How we yearn for the things
natsukashi ka na [72]	That have perished forever!

These early poems are still Bokusui's most popular works; like other tanka poets who won fame with outpourings from the heart, he could not arouse the same enthusiasm for later poems describing periods of disillusion or of resignation. His collections *Shi ka Geijutsu ka* (Death or Art?, 1912) and *Minakami* (Headwaters, 1913) reveal a marked change in his outlook. These tanka, often dismissed today as "dark and decadent," sometimes break the rules of metrics or employ colloquial language. Perhaps such changes can be attributed to the influence of Ishikawa Takuboku, with whom Bokusui had become friendly,[73] but these poems are bitter and weary in a manner foreign to Takuboku:

haha wo omoeba	When I remember my mother
wa ga ie wa tama no	My house is cold as jewels;
gotoku tsumetashi	When I remember my father
chichi wo omoeba	It is warm as mountains.
yama no gotoku	
atatakashi [74]	

The sentiment is startling and perhaps unprecedented. Certainly Japanese did not often think of their mothers in terms of coldness, nor, for that matter, were mountains a normal simile for warmth. The lines, moreover, are so irregular that it may not even make sense to divide them into the conventional five lines of a tanka.

The irregularity conveys the impression of emotions too powerful for Bokusui to force into conventional language or metrics.

Even when the form more closely approximates that of a usual tanka, it is often totally uncharacteristic of tanka expression:

chichi to haha	The sight of my father and
kuchi wo tsugumite	mother,
mukaiaeru	As they faced each other
sugata wa ishi no	Their lips clamped shut,
gotoku sabishiku [75]	Was lonely as stones.

The emotions that gave rise to these tanka are conveyed with unusual impact. The tanka had traditionally been sung in plangent tones, not flung at the world, nor gasped out in anguish. Bokusui's Naturalism—the unvarnished depiction of scenes from his daily experience—threatened to explode the form.

Bokusui apparently decided after publishing *Headwaters* that he had gone too far in his experimentation with the tanka; at any rate, his later collections use conventional vocabulary and form. A sequence on the *yamazakura*, a variety of cherry blossoms that flowers when the leaves are on the tree, was especially praised. Bokusui also wrote many tanka on travel and drink, usually in the understated manner adopted by many Japanese poets in their late years. Most critics approved of this change, pleased that Bokusui had shaken off his "decadence." But his best work—certainly the poems with the most marked individuality—are in the earlier collections. The lyricism of *Separation* and the harshness of *Death or Art?* and *Headwaters* are equally moving: these collections contain some of the finest Japanese short poems of the twentieth century.

Maeda Yūgure (1883–1951), for a time one of the most outspoken opponents of the Shinshi Sha, was first inspired to write poetry by reading *Myōjō*, and for years, even while he fulminated against the romantic excesses of the *Myōjō* poets, his own tanka contained much that reminds us of Yosano Akiko.[76] As a youth he was so high-strung he had to leave middle school without graduating. In later years he sometimes insisted on the ordinariness of his life, but however humdrum his daily routine may have been, it is not hard to detect a nervous sensitivity in his most typical poems.

Yūgure sent his first compositions in prose and poetry to various magazines. Most were rejected without a word of encouragement, but Onoe Saishū (1876–1957), a distinguished tanka poet who ran the poetry column of the periodical *Shinsei* (New Voices), urged him to continue his efforts. Yūgure went to Tokyo and became Saishū's pupil. In 1905, when Saishū founded the Shazensō Sha (Plantain Society), Yūgure, Bokusui, and various others became members. The poets of this society, opposing the *Myōjō* school, insisted on clarity and simplicity of expression, and on using materials drawn from ordinary experiences.

Yūgure's first collection, *Shūkaku* (Harvest), published in 1910, was a worthy companion to Bokusui's *Separation* of the same year, and people soon were referring to them as the twin stars of the Naturalist tanka. A sample poem from *Harvest* describes Yūgure's lonely life at the time:

fuyu fukaki	From the night streets
yoru no machi yori	Dark with the winter's depth,
kaerikite	I return to my room;
chiisaki hibachi no	All alone, I blow the embers
hi wo hitori fuku [77]	Of my little charcoal stove.

He later wrote of such poetry: "I want above all to write poetry using my own life as its basis. I will be quite satisfied if the extremely common life of an entirely ordinary man can be glimpsed, even a little, through my poetry." [78] Bokusui criticized *Harvest* for not having penetrated deeply enough into the harsh ugliness of real life. It cannot be denied that Yūgure's expression tended to be tepid, certainly when compared with Bokusui, but he was uncompromising in his Naturalism:

hokori uku	Above the big desk
kōseishitsu no	In the proofreaders' room
ōtsukue	Where the dust hovers,
mono uki kao no	Three or four weary faces
mitsu yotsu narabu [79]	Lined up side by side.

Although Yūgure was an extremely prolific poet—over forty thousand tanka are preserved—his publications were comparatively few. His style began to shift from Naturalism to a distinctly more modern style in his collection *Ikuru Hi ni* (On a Day of Life, 1914), but in 1919 he went to live in a remote mountainous district and composed no poetry for four years. In 1923 he began to write again, describing nature as he had seen it in the wilderness. In the following year he, Kitahara Hakushū, Kinoshita Toshiharu (1886–1925), Koizumi Chikashi (1886–1927), Toki Zemmaro (1885–1980), and others formed a group to publish the magazine *Nikkō* (Sunlight), and devoted it to Modernism.

In 1929, as the direct result of his first ride in an airplane, Yūgure started to write tanka in the colloquial; the experience was so new and so overwhelming that he felt he could not capture it in more conventional language:

> *shizen ga zunzun karada no naka*
> *wo tsūka suru—yama, yama, yama.*

> Nature passes swish-swish through
> my body—mountains, mountains, mountains.

> *niji, niji, ganzen sū mētoru no kyori*
> *no sematte, mado garasu wo*
> *sure sure tobu niji!* [80]

> Rainbows, rainbows.
> Pressing to within a couple of yards of my eyes,
> grazing the window glass,
> leap the rainbows!

For the next fifteen years Yūgure wrote tanka in irregular forms, disregarding the old traditions of versifying and diction, and calling his poems "tanka" because of their internal rhythm, not because they satisfied any formal requirements. The content of the poetry ventured far beyond the realm of Naturalism:

> *doa hissori akete,*
> *hadaka rōsuku*
> *shirojiro tomoshite kuru hakuchi no shōjo*

> Stealthily opening the door,
> a naked candle whitely lit,
> in comes a crazy girl.

watakushi wa tachimachi fubuki to nari,
seppen to nari, hyōhyō to shite
hyutte no mado akari ni muragaru [81]

Suddenly I turn into a snowstorm,
into snowflakes, and buoyantly swarm
around the light from the hut window.

Yūgure's poems gradually took on a political coloring as the world situation grew tense in the late 1930s. He wrote tanka on such subjects as the signing of the Soviet-German Non-Aggression Treaty, the Nomonhan Incident in Manchuria, and the conclusion of the Tripartite Pact by Japan, Germany, and Italy. Though not even the most ardent nationalist could have objected to Yūgure's views, he seems to have become apprehensive about the propriety of writing irregular, specifically modern poetry at a time when "pure" Japanese values were being exalted; and from 1942 he returned to the regular tanka form and classical language. Even after the end of the war Yūgure retained the classical diction, but the lines become irregular once again, as in the following example:

aru hi oitaru monogoi	One day an old beggar came.
kitareri	His face was dirty,
kao yogoretaredo	But his smile was gentle.
odayaka ni waraeri [82]	

Toki Zemmaro (also known as Aika), the fourth of the major Naturalist poets, was born in Tokyo, and this distinction sets off his poetry from that of Bokusui, Utsubo, and Yūgure, all of whom turned to nature for inspiration and comfort. Zemmaro first began to study tanka while at middle school, and became the pupil of Kaneko Kun'en, who was, as we have seen, the pupil of Ochiai Naobumi. Kun'en, a minor tanka poet, never fulfilled his early promise. He flirted with almost every school of tanka, at one time experimenting with "free" tanka of irregular lengths, in the manner of Maeda Yūgure; but it is hard to detect any individuality. Kun'en has been styled a "city poet," [83] and a kind of urbane detachment, distinguishing him from the more intense country poets, was his most conspicuous quality. Perhaps this "city" nature attracted Toki Zemmaro to a poet with whom he shared little else.

At Waseda University, where he associated with Wakayama Bokusui and other tanka poets, Zemmaro read widely in European literature. After graduation he became a journalist, working from 1918 to 1940 for the *Asahi Shimbun*. Zemmaro first attracted attention with the collection *Nakiwarai* (Smiling Through the Tears, 1910), which consisted of 143 tanka written entirely in roman letters, printed in stanzas of three lines each. Nothing could have been more antithetical to the atmosphere engendered by the traditional anthologies of tanka than these pages of businesslike roman letters; undoubtedly Zemmaro was trying by this dramatic expedient to free the tanka of its old associations. Ishikawa Takuboku, reviewing *Smiling Through the Tears*, stated that the strongest impression left by the book was that Zemmaro was less like a tanka poet than any other tanka poet of the day.[84] It is true that he still used the classical language, but the material was drawn, in the Naturalist manner, from commonplace events. Nevertheless, a suggestion of romantic love clings to these poems, as if in unconscious admission of the poet's youth:

Tsuma to futari,
Toaru Kashiya wo mini iritsu,
Usukuragari no Haru no awaresa.[85]

My wife and I, the two of us,
Went to look at a certain house for rent.
Ah, the sadness of spring in semidarkness!

The poet and his wife, searching for a place to live, enter a house for rent, and are repelled by the contrast between its gloomy mustiness and the spring day outside. The thought is not profound, and the words have little melodic beauty, but the poet is obviously saying something of importance to him, not merely conjuring up pretty images. The division into lines of six, twelve, and fourteen syllables was not intended to establish any new metrical scheme, but to emphasize the meaning. No matter how he divided the tanka, however, Zemmaro usually kept close to the traditional total number of syllables. The three-line form, invented by Zemmaro, was soon afterward adopted by Ishikawa Takuboku, who used it in his two collections of tanka.

Zemmaro's next volume, *Tasogare* (Twilight, 1912), was dedicated to Takuboku, a mark of his friendship. The two met first in January 1911. Takuboku recorded in his diary that Zemmaro suddenly telephoned him one day. "It's funny that the first meeting of two men who write the same kind of poetry should be over the telephone when we couldn't see each other." [86] The two poets shared many views and even planned to publish a magazine together, but these plans never materialized, perhaps because their political convictions differed too markedly for them to cooperate; by this time Takuboku was a revolutionary, in favor of practical action, but Zemmaro wanted to work only within the framework of literature. [87] The opening poem of *Twilight* was:

te no shiroki rōdōsha koso kanashikere.
kokkin no sho wo,
namida shite yomeri

The grief of the worker with white hands!
He has read, in tears,
A book banned by the state.

"The worker with white hands" probably refers to Zemmaro himself, a member of the intelligentsia, and the prohibited book no doubt contains socialist thought; but his helplessness to correct the ills of society reduces him to tears. In 1910, following the trial and execution of Kōtoku Shūsui on the charge of having plotted to assassinate the emperor Meiji, the government imposed censorship on all books and magazines, and totally banned those that advocated socialism. Perhaps the prohibited book mentioned in this tanka is Kropotkin's *La conquête du pain*, translated by Kōtoku Shūsui in 1909.

A poem on a similar theme seems to refer to Takuboku, whose interest in the Kōtoku case had converted him to socialism:

wa ga tomo no, shindai no   From the suitcase
shita no,   Under my friend's bed

> kaban yori I borrowed a forbidden book.
> kokkin no sho wo karite
> yuku ka na [88]

But Zemmaro's socialism was mild, and vitiated by rising social position and a happy family life:

> kakumei wo tomo to kataritsu
> tsuma to ko ni miyage wo kaite
> uchi ni kaerinu

> I talked about the Revolution with my friend,
> Bought a present for my wife and kid,
> Then went back home.

He was grateful to Takuboku for his guidance, and his collection *Zatsuon no Naka* (Amidst the Din, 1916) opens with a sequence dedicated to Takuboku's memory:

> hito no yo no   He who taught me
> fuhei wo ware ni   To feel dissatisfaction
> oshietsuru   With the world of men
> kare ima arazu   Is no longer here;
> hitori wa ga kanashi [89] How sad to be alone!

Zemmaro did not abandon his social concerns in the 1930s; when the pressure of the militarists to conform became stronger, he turned from poetry to scholarly research, rather than write propaganda.

Toki Zemmaro possessed fewer innate gifts than the other leaders of the Naturalist tanka movement, and he suffers especially when compared with Takuboku, but his voice is distinct, and his various experiments over the years suggest how Takuboku might have developed as a poet if he had lived fifty years longer.

ISHIKAWA TAKUBOKU (1886–1912) [90]

Takuboku is undoubtedly the most popular and beloved tanka poet of modern times, not only because of the great individuality of his poetry but because his life captured the imagination of the Japanese. He was born in a remote village of northern Japan, and his education went no further than middle school, but the diffusion of education during the Meiji era was such that Takuboku was at little disadvantage when compared to his associates who had attended school in the big cities. His father was a Buddhist priest. By dispensation of the government, priests had been permitted to marry in the Meiji era, but for the first six years of his life Takuboku was officially registered as a bastard, which was considered less of a stigma than being a priest's son. He left school at sixteen apparently bored and exasperated by old-fashioned teachers, but he had received an excellent education both in traditional Japanese learning and in English. He began to write tanka while a student. In 1902, after making his decision not to return to school for further education, he went to Tokyo to reconnoiter the literary scene. He met the Yosanos, the reigning monarchs of the tanka, and was inspired to throw himself into tanka composition. He wanted to remain in Tokyo, and considered making his living as a translator of Ibsen, but ill health forced him to return home. Nevertheless, he was able that year to publish some tanka in *Myōjō*, his first, precocious literary recognition.

More of his tanka appeared in *Myōjō* the following year, and he also published in a local newspaper a series of articles on the thought of Richard Wagner. His tanka and shintaishi began to be accepted by other literary magazines and to attract the attention of the leading poets. In 1905 he published in a small edition his first collection of shintaishi, *Akogare* (Yearning), with a preface by the distinguished translator Ueda Bin and an afterword by Yosano Tekkan. The poems were unabashedly imitative of the Romantic manner of such established men as Kambara Ariake and Susukida Kyūkin, but they were by no means without talent. Takuboku, encouraged by the reception of his book, published a literary magazine of his own, but only one issue appeared.

In 1907 Takuboku traveled to Hokkaidō in search of employment. He worked for various newspapers before returning in 1908 to Tokyo, leaving his mother, wife, and child behind in Hokkaidō. He resumed his contacts with the Yosanos and their group, and wrote tanka with great enthusiasm. He also published serially in a newspaper his novel *Chōei* (Shadow of a Bird).

Takuboku seems to have impressed everyone as a genius. Although he constantly complained of his poverty, he was an incurable spendthrift, recklessly throwing away whatever money came into his hands. His diary in roman letters (*Rōmaji Nikki*) kept in 1909 vividly describes his life at the time, especially his frustrations at not being able to write successful fiction, his chief ambition. He worked for several years as a proofreader for the *Asahi Shimbun*, but his diary reveals how often he failed to show up for work, taking off the day in the hopes that he would be able to write a story. Usually he would spend such days fruitlessly, making one or more false starts at a story that ceased to interest him after the first page. But when *Subaru*, the successor to *Myōjō*, began publication in 1909 Takuboku was chosen as the editor and publisher, a position he kept for about two years.

Takuboku's fame is based mainly on two collections of tanka, *Ichiaku no Suna* (A Handful of Sand, 1910) and the posthumous *Kanashiki Gangu* (Sad Toys, 1912). He also wrote shintaishi, but they have not enjoyed the popularity of his tanka; they express strong convictions, both emotional and political, but betray an insufficient mastery of his materials.[91] Takuboku himself recognized that the tanka was ideally suited as a medium for his characteristic sudden and intense flashes of emotion. In a "dialogue" written in 1910 Takuboku and an imaginary friend discuss the future of the tanka. The friend cites the theory of Onoe Saishū that the tanka is doomed, but Takuboku answers cynically that the tanka will survive as long as archaisms persist in poetic expression and the language of Japanese poetry is not made uniformly colloquial. He goes on to point out how the old insistence on alternating lines in five and seven syllables is breaking down. He himself intends to write poetry in language as close to contemporary speech as possible, and if these tanka do not fit into thirty-one syllables he will add as many more syllables as he thinks necessary. "If even then a man can't write tanka it's not because the words or the form is old, but because his head is old!" he comments. The tanka will henceforth be divided into whatever patterns of line the poet deems appropriate to the internal necessity of the particular poem. He concludes:

> People say that the tanka form is inconvenient because it's so short. I think it's shortness is precisely what makes it convenient. Don't you agree? We are constantly being subjected to so many sensa-

tions, coming both from inside and outside ourselves, that we forget them soon after they occur, or even if we remember them for a little while, we end up by never once in our whole lifetimes ever expressing them because there is not enough content to these sensations to sustain the thought. Most people look down on such sensations; even if they don't, they let them escape with almost no show of interest. But anybody who loves life cannot despise such moments. . . . Although a sensation may last only a second, it is a second that will never return again. I refuse to let such moments slip by. The most convenient way to express these experiences is through the tanka which, being short, does not require much trouble or time. It's really convenient. One of the few blessings we Japanese enjoy is having this poetic form called the tanka.[92]

Takuboku valued the tanka because it enabled him to capture momentary experiences while still white-hot, without feeling any necessity of inflating their importance so as to make them worthy of a longer poetic form. In his essay *Kuu beki Shi* (Poems to Eat, 1909) he wryly describes how he composed shintaishi when he first began, at the age of sixteen. He felt obliged to make everything he saw "poetic":

Say I saw a tree about six feet high standing in an empty lot with the sun shining on it. If I were in any way moved by it, I'd end up by turning the empty lot into a vast wilderness, the tree into a mighty tree, the sun into either the rising sun or the setting sun and, if that weren't bad enough, I turned myself into some poet or wanderer contemplating the scene. If I didn't make myself into a sorrowful young man, the feeling would have been all wrong for the kind of poems I was writing those days and I couldn't be satisfied with it myself.[93]

Takuboku hated especially the atmosphere of "romantic agony" surrounding poets. He remembered with distaste an experience in Hokkaido: "The courteous old politician who took me to the newspaper in Kushiro introduced me to somebody with the words, 'He's a shintaishi poet.' I have never felt so brutally humiliated by anyone's goodwill as I did at that moment." [94]

Takuboku's tanka do not proclaim his romantic ardor in the manner of the *Myōjō* poets, though for a time they influenced him; nor did he seek to identify himself with nature (for a poet reared in the country he was remarkably uninterested in plants or scenery); nor, obviously, was he attempting to evoke memories of the *Manyōshū* or some other ancient collection; his tanka were, in his words, his "sad toys." Takuboku revised many of his tanka when they were republished, but he excelled at impromptu composition, and he seems to have considered spontaneity the essential element of a tanka; even if a tanka were expanded to forty-one or fifty-one syllables, the form would not perish as long as it remained wedded to the evocation of a particular moment of perception.[95]

Takuboku's tanka share little with the traditional tanka in diction, mood, or subject. When they succeed it is not because of their evocative charm but because they hit us with both fists. They are sometimes explosively harsh, sometimes perilously close to being sentimental, but each poem, whether good or bad, is indivisibly connected with Takuboku's personality. Appreciation of his poetry is often associated with admiration for him as a man, whether as a rebel against the old poetic conventions or as a revolutionary imbued with socialist thought. Takuboku's tanka are almost always about himself or people he knew, only rarely on imagined scenes. He used the classical language throughout, despite his advocacy of the colloquial, but so freely that only the verb endings reveal that the language is classical. Certainly the tone is colloquial, and the poems make no concession to elegance of effect. Even if they have few overtones of the kind thrown off by the traditional tanka, they often have symbolic content. The opening two tanka of the collection *A Handful of Sand* suggest the tone of the entire work:

> *tōkai no kojima no iso no shirasuna ni*
> *ware nakinurete*
> *kani to tawamuru*

On the white sand of the shore of a small island in the Eastern Sea,
My face wet with tears,
I play with a crab.

hō ni tsutau
namida nogawazu
ichiaku no suna wo shimeshishi hito wo wasurezu

I won't forget the man—
Not bothering to wipe away the tears
That rolled down his cheeks,
He showed me a handful of sand.

The imagery of the first tanka evokes the loneliness and futility of Takuboku's life: the small island in the Eastern Sea is Japan itself, the white sand the blank emptiness of his life, the crab his minor daily preoccupations.[96] In the second poem the symbolic intent is obvious; the handful of sand is all the man has to show for his life. Other poems in the same sequence are more optimistic:

dai to iu ji wo hyaku amari
suna ni kaki
shinu koto wo yamete kaerikitareri

I wrote the character Great
More than a hundred times in the sand,
Forgot about dying and went away.

From 1908 to 1910 Takuboku lived alone in Tokyo. He promised his family in Hokkaidō he would send for them as soon as he had the money, but in his improvidence made no serious attempt to improve his finances. He was desperately eager to establish himself as a novelist, but his genius was best suited to the short compass of a tanka; his novel is badly constructed and surprisingly conventional, and his short stories, though better, are interesting mainly as records of what Takuboku was thinking at a particular time. The finest of his prose is in the diaries and letters.

Even before Takuboku first went to Tokyo he had read a considerable amount of European literature, mainly in English. In his diaries he quoted from a wide variety of works, from "Dover Beach" to short stories by Gorki. In his last years he became interested in socialist thought, and copied out extensive passages from Kropotkin's *Memoirs of a Revolutionist*.[97] Direct influence from these readings is found in his shintaishi, notably *Hateshi naki giron no ato* (After Endless Arguments, 1911), but his tanka contain few overt references to his revolutionary beliefs, perhaps because of the limitations of the form.

Kubota Utsubo, in a eulogy published in 1915, three years after Takuboku's early death, stated that Takuboku had set in place a great new foundation for the poetic movement; he had transcended personal emotions and experiences to deal with the relations between the poet and society.[98] Some tanka of this description are indeed found in *Sad Toys*, but surely Takuboku will be remembered most for highly personal, completely unconventional thoughts that have little to do with the poet's relations with other men:

tehajime ni	said the
mazu Fuji-san wo	first thing
kuzusan to	I'd do
ware ii kimi wa hareyaka	is smash Mt. Fuji—
ni emu [99]	you laugh
yogoretaru tabi haku toki	give me
no	the creeps
kimi waruki omoi ni	some memories
nitaru	like putting on
omoide mo ari [100]	dirty socks

Takuboku in such poems and in his diaries reveals himself as perhaps the first Japanese writer who would have been totally intelligible to his contemporaries in the West. He is full of quirks, but ruthlessly honest with himself. His explanation of why he chose to keep his diary in roman letters is typical: "Why did I decide to keep this diary in Romaji? Why? I love my wife, and it's precisely because I love her that I don't want her to read this diary. No, that's a lie! It's true that I love her, and it's true that I don't want her to read this, but the two facts are not necessarily related." [101]

For all his modernity, however, Takuboku had no literary posterity, unless we choose to consider as such the unrelated "proletarian tanka" movement of the 1920s and early 1930s. The mainstream of the modern tanka would be formed by a group of poets whose poetry had quite different sources of inspiration from

Takuboku's; for them the portrayal of nature (*shasei*), rather than the assertion of the poet's feelings and beliefs, was the only true purpose of the tanka. If Takuboku laid foundations for a new poetic art, it was for the shintaishi, and not the tanka, though his tanka were his finest achievement.

MASAOKA SHIKI (1867-1902)

About the same time that Yosano Tekkan was first proclaiming the importance of freedom and individuality in the tanka, another kind of reform was being carried out by a poet of totally different principles, Masaoka Shiki. Shiki's influence was important even during his short lifetime, and after his death his disciples and their disciples would assume positions of commanding importance in the world of the tanka. Only during the last four years of his life did Shiki give himself seriously either to the composition of tanka or to tanka criticism. His earlier writings had been devoted mainly to creating the modern haiku, and his career as a whole is most easily discussed in terms of his work in the haiku,[102] but his contributions to the modern tanka were no less important.

Shiki learned to compose tanka as part of his early education, and some dismally inept examples from this period have been preserved. As a young man he showed no particular interest in writing tanka, and seems to have been convinced that the *Kokinshū* represented the apogee of the art. A chance meeting in 1893 with Ayukai Kaien, the younger brother of Ochiai Naobumi, first made him realize that a reform of the tanka, similar to the kind he was then carrying out in the haiku, was long overdue.[103] His preferences in tanka quickly shifted from the *Kokinshū* to poetry in the style of the *Manyōshū*, and under the influence of Amada Guan and other spiritual descendants of the *kokugaku* scholars he decided that the tanka had been emasculated by the *Kokinshū* poets and their imitators.

Shiki expressed his new convictions in a series of ten short essays entitled *Utayomi nu atauru Sho* (Letters to the Tanka Poets, 1898). The first essay, predictably, lamented the present state of the tanka; Shiki declared, "Honestly speaking, it has not flourished since the *Manyōshū* and Sanetomo." Shiki praised the thirteenth-century Minamoto Sanetomo's originality, profundity, and poetic skill, and deplored the inferior reputation he had been assigned, despite his unique ability to evoke the masculine strength of the *Manyōshū*.

Shiki's second letter began: "Tsurayuki is a bad poet and the *Kokinshū* is a stupid collection." He admitted that he himself had worshiped the *Kokinshū* even a few years before, supposing that the tanka's sole function was to be elegant and that the *Kokinshū* was the essence of elegance. Now, having shaken off this misconception, he was annoyed with himself, like a lover who is disillusioned to discover he has been infatuated with an unworthy woman. Shiki made light of the characteristic ingenuity of *Kokinshū* poetry; the collection now seemed to him to consist exclusively of bad puns and toying with words. The *Shin Kokinshū*, he grudgingly admitted, was somewhat superior, but the number of truly excellent poems could be counted on one's fingers. Shiki next turned his attention to Kagawa Kageki, a blind admirer of the *Kokinshū* and especially of Tsurayuki's poetry. Despite his lamentable failings, Kageki had written some good poems, better at any rate than Tsurayuki's, no doubt because he lived in more enlightened times. Unfortunately, Kageki's good and bad poems were inextricably mixed, and his followers had tended to imitate the bad ones.

Shiki's third letter attacked the tanka poets for their ignorance of other kinds of poetry; they knew nothing about haiku—though the form is closely related to the tanka—much less about Chinese poetry, and they were unaware whether or not such a thing as poetry even exists in the West. If, however, they were asked if novels and plays merited being called literature, they would probably stare in amazement, for they were not only certain that the tanka is the highest form of literature, but considered it the only form.

Other points brought up in subsequent letters included the conflicting claims of strength against melody, ingenuity against objective description, sincerity against artificiality. Shiki's preferences are always predictable, but he made one concession to conventional poetic ideals: obviously, he said, there must be some emotional basis even to the seemingly objective description of such a sight as a willow at the end of a bridge; unless the poet thought the sight was beautiful, he would never have been moved to write the poem. However, he continued, good tanka and haiku were more likely to be written objectively than subjectively, and that was why he recommended objectivity.

Shiki answered the arguments of historical relativists who claimed that even though the *Kokinshū* might seem stale or trivial to modern readers it probably had a quite different meaning in its own time; he agreed, but declared that his intention was not to describe poetry in historical perspective but to judge it in terms of absolute literary values. To nationalists who complained that his criticism of the tanka would threaten what they termed "the bastion of Japanese literature" he replied that, in its present state, the tanka was so frail that one shot from a cannon would crumble it. Japan could not rely on bows and arrows to defend itself in the Meiji era but must protect itself with warships and cannons, even though these were purchased from abroad at high price; similarly, the tanka could survive only if it incorporated modern methods, even if they, too, had to be imported.[104]

Shiki next presented his famous concept of *shasei*, "copying life," as a technique of modern poetry. He apparently borrowed this ideal from his friend, the Western-style painter Nakamura Fusetsu (1866–1943). Shiki was at pains, however, to make it clear that he did not propose using realism to the exclusion of the imagination; realistic techniques in poetry could be applied even to subjects that went beyond normal realistic expression.

In his seventh letter Shiki discussed specifically how to reform the tanka. He started with the objection raised by some critics that the tanka was worn out and so thoroughly rotten that reform was impossible. Shiki replied that although the spirit of the tanka had declined, the form still merited preservation. He guaranteed that he could transfuse a new spirit into the tanka and make it sound again. The first failing was the poetic diction, the limited vocabulary of the tenth-century collection, the *Kokinshū*. Some people, he said, opposed his suggestion that foreign words and literary conceptions should be employed in the tanka, accusing him of attempting to destroy Japanese literature; but their attitude was basically mistaken. Shiki believed that any poem composed by a Japanese, even if in Chinese, Sanskrit, or some European language, formed a part of Japanese literature, just as victories won at sea by Japanese sailors on ships purchased in England and using German guns were indubitably Japanese victories. He concluded: "Any word used literarily is a part of the Japanese poetic vocabulary."

The eighth and ninth letters were devoted to poems Shiki admired by Sanetomo and various *Shin Kokinshū* poets. In the tenth and final letter Shiki listed some of the failings of the contemporary tanka, including the use of engo (related words) and fancy, "poetic" names for ordinary things. He wrote, underlining the words, "It is my basic principle to express as clearly as possible the poetic quality I myself feel to be beautiful." [105] For this reason, he said, he did not hesitate to use common words when they seemed appropriate. His concluding paragraph, however, comes as a surprise:

> There are some people who suppose that when I advise poets to "write about new things" I refer to such so-called artifacts of civilization as trains and railways, but this is a serious misapprehension. Most of the "artifacts of civilization" are unpoetic and difficult to include in poetry. If one wishes nevertheless to write about them, one has no choice but to mention something poetic as well. If no such combination is made, and the poem simply states that "wind blows over the rails" it is extremely bleak. The poem will be more attractive if the poet at least combines this statement with some other object such as violets blossoming beside the rails, or poppies scattering after the train has passed, or susuki plumes nodding.[106]

Shiki's insistence that every tanka must contain some element of beauty remained at the heart of his poetry and that of his school. The techniques he favored may have been realistic, but his attention was always focused on sights that poets had traditionally considered beautiful. Even when he used foreign words or modern Japanese terms that to a traditionalist would have seemed vulgar, the thought is seldom startling.

Shiki's tanka, written to exemplify his theories, are essentially in the traditional manner. The greatest departures are in vocabulary. In March 1899 Shiki founded the Negishi Tanka Society to encourage composition in the manner he advocated, and eventually attracted a group of poets who became his disciples. These men, for the most part country-bred and rather older than the members of rival poetic groups, were headed by Itō Sachio (1864–1913) and Nagatsuka Takashi (1879–1915). The members, despite their proclaimed intent of reforming the tanka, were conservative, untouched by the new thought and culture introduced from the West. Far from considering the tanka as merely a "short poem" in the manner of the Shinshi Sha, they turned to the past, especially to the *Manyōshū*, for inspiration; the *Myōjō* poets accordingly derided them as men who wished to stroll down the Ginza wearing ancient robes and court caps.[107]

Shiki's reputation as a haiku poet and critic had already been established, but he was a novice at composing tanka, and his readings in the tanka of the past were extremely limited. Despite his lavish praise for the *Manyōshū* in his letters to the tanka poets, he scarcely knew anything about the anthology except what he read in the works of commentators; it was only in 1900 that he first became directly acquainted with the original works and adopted their style in his own poems.[108] The poets who gathered around Shiki were attracted to him as a man, rather than as a fount of learning about the tanka. Compared to the other tanka groups of the day the Negishi Tanka Society was not only traditional and old-fashioned, but also tended to be nationalistic; it was progressive only with respect to the reform of the tanka.[109]

Shiki, stimulated by his disciples, between 1897 and 1900 wrote most of the tanka included in the posthumous collection *Takenosato Uta* (Poems from the Bamboo Village, 1904). This volume consists of 544 tanka, fifteen chōka, and twelve *sedōka* selected from among the more than two thousand poems in various forms (apart from haiku) composed between 1882 and Shiki's death in 1902. The prolonged illness of his last years did not prevent Shiki from engaging actively in the meetings of his poetry society or from rediscovering such forgotten tanka poets as Tachibana Akemi and Hiraga Motoyoshi. His illness occasioned some of his most moving tanka, though it became harder and harder to find "poetic" elements to include in descriptions of his sickroom. One tanka, written in 1898, bears the headnote "On first getting up and leaning on a stick":

yotose nete	Four years spent in bed—
hitotabi tateba	I got up for the first time
ki mo kusa mo	To find the trees and plants,
mina me no shita ni	All of them, before my eyes,
hana sakinikeri [110]	Had burst into flower.

In his last years Shiki could not even leave his bed. His world was limited to his room and a corner of the garden visible from his pillow. "Nature," his chosen subject, tended to be the flowers brought by visitors. Often he wrote sequences of related tanka, like one with the prefatory note:

> After finishing dinner I was lying on my back looking to the left when I noticed that the wisteria arranged on my desk had responded to the water in the vase and were now at their peak. I murmured to myself, "How charming, how lovely!" and vague nostalgic recollections of the Heian romances flitted through my head. I felt strangely moved to write some tanka. Considering how neglectful I have lately been of the art of poetry, I took up my brush with some uncertainty.

Shiki wrote ten tanka, beginning with:

kame ni sasu	The wisteria cluster
fuji no hanabusa	Thrust into the vase
mijikakereba	Is so short
tatami no ue ni	It does not reach
todokazarikeri [111]	As far as the tatami.

This tanka probably cannot be successfully translated. It certainly is not impressive in English, despite its high reputation in Japan. The surface meaning of the poem seems to be merely that the cluster of wisteria on Shiki's desk does not hang down far enough to reach the floor. The most high-flown panegyrics were lavished on this poem by Shiki's followers, who believed it contained a profound perception of truth: "The poet, for whom it had become completely impossible to come into direct contact with the majesty of the mountain peaks or the surging motion of the sea, turned to the spray of flowers in a vase at his bedside and expressed his solitary thought in this poem." [112] If, however, the poem also had a subjective meaning related to Shiki's life as an invalid, and it was not simply an objective description of the wisteria cluster, another, even more affecting meaning emerges: Shiki, lying immobile, sees wisteria blossoms that seem to stretch toward his pallet on the tatami; but their beauty does not reach him. Many critics, though they praise the poem, deny that anything more was intended than a realistic description. Surely, however, the sixth poem of the sequence implies more:

kame ni sasu	The wisteria cluster
fuji no hanabusa	Thrust into the vase
hana tarete	Lets its blossoms hang
yamai no toko ni	Close to my sickbed
haru kuren to su	Spring approaches an end.

Perhaps the wisteria poems did not mean very much to Shiki in any case. If we can believe his journal, they were jotted down without corrections; their importance may owe more to the value attached to poetry composed under such tragic circumstances regardless of intrinsic beauty.

Shiki's main contributions to the modern tanka were his critical essays and the instructions he gave his disciples. He was tempermentally suited more to the haiku or the poem in Chinese than the tanka, and could not himself create the kind of poetry his intelligence discerned.

SACHIO AND TAKASHI

In 1903, the year after Shiki's death, the magazine *Ashibi* was founded as the organ of the Negishi Tanka Society with the avowed purpose of continuing his traditions in the tanka. The magazine continued to appear irregularly until 1908 with Itō Sachio as its guiding spirit. At first only a handful of poets were involved with the publication, but gradually new men like Saitō Mokichi, Shimagi Akahiko, and Nakamura Kenkichi (1889–1934) were attracted. Sachio was forced by personal reasons to give up *Ashibi*, and another poet, Mitsui Kōshi (1883–1953), edited the successor magazine, *Akane*, for six issues in 1908–1909. A quarrel between Sachio and Kōshi prompted the former to found *Araragi* in 1908. After a slow start it established itself as the most important tanka magazine, and maintained this position under Shimagi Akahiko (from 1913 to 1926) and Saitō Mokichi (from 1926 to 1953). Masaoka Shiki's school, a relatively small circle during his lifetime, became after 1910 the dominant force in modern tanka.

The chief principle of this school was shasei, the ideal of objectivity laid down by Shiki, but the meaning of the term varied from poet to poet. Nagatsuka Takashi (1879–1915) took Shiki most literally and wrote completely objective descriptions of nature in a *Manyōshū* style. In 1910 he also published the long novel *Tsuchi* (Earth), written in shasei prose, about the hardships of a farmer's life he had personally experienced as a young man; this work differs from later "proletarian" writings on the peasantry in that Takashi put forth no thesis, but seems to have had no other object than to present an accurate description of his subject, in keeping with the shasei ideals.

Itō Sachio (1864–1913), Shiki's senior tanka disciple, came to entertain quite different interpretations of shasei. His first exchange of views with Shiki occurred in 1899, when the two men clashed on whether or not the form of a poem dictated its content. Shiki thought not; at one point he declared, "I see no objection to saying that a tanka is a long haiku, a haiku a short tanka. The only difference between the two is in the form." [113] Sachio, on the other hand, was convinced that the tanka was better suited to treating time than space, but that the haiku treated space better. He believed that the two genres of poetry should be kept absolutely distinct, though Shiki had been pleased to discover themes shared by Buson, the haiku poet he most admired, and the tanka poet Tachibana Akemi.

In 1900, despite their quarrel, Shiki published three poems by Sachio in his tanka column in the newspaper *Nippon Shimbun*, and Sachio went to pay his respects. His former antagonism instantly melted away, and he came to revere Shiki. In 1906 he published an essay called "The Shiki I Worship" in which he wrote, "The Shiki I saw was perfect and immaculate, a brilliant, glittering Shiki." [114] Sachio, an unusually stubborn and opinionated man, was constantly quarreling with other poets, but his loyalty to Shiki was intense. Yet there were unspoken differences in their views. For example, Sachio placed much greater emphasis than Shiki on the music (*shirabe*) of the tanka, advocating the use of the characteristic *Manyōshū* "music," syntax, and vocabulary even when describing contemporary events. His preference for a more subjective style of tanka than Shiki's shasei envisaged was revealed in 1905 in his exchange of views with Nagatsuka Takashi, who consciously sought his materials in external objects rather than in emotions with himself, and who characterized the process of writing tanka as "coming into direct contact with nature and depicting it from life." This was close to Shiki's own conception of shasei, but Sachio insisted that it was impossible to achieve objectivity within the tanka form because, unlike a haiku, a tanka did not exist as an independent unit but as part of a "belt" joined by the subjective personality of the poet. Sachio's criticisms of Takashi in the end carried him even to attacking his adored Shiki, despite his professions of unvarying loyalty: at one point he declared that Shiki's poetry and criticism "viewed from a contemporary standpoint are obviously extremely elementary." [115] Sachio's interpretation of shasei was colored by his temperament, and eventually he came to consider that the tanka was not so much an objective description of nature as a "cry," the direct expression of a "vibration of the emotions." [116] In practice, however, Sachio's expression of his emotions was often indirect, as in a famous tanka composed in 1909:

hito no sumu	Leaving behind me
kunibe wo idete	The world where other men live,
shiranami ga	I reached the border
daichi futawakeshi	Where the white waves divided
hate ni kinikeri [117]	The earth into land and sea.

Sachio was known also for his advocacy of the *rensaku*, or tanka sequence. This represented his solution of how to surmount the limitations imposed on poetic expression by the thirty-one syllables of the tanka and convey the "belt" of thoughts arising from the poet's continuity of personality. A series of connected poems could produce the impression of a single, long poem, even though each poem was able to stand completely on its own. Sachio devised rules for the rensaku, rather in the manner that the old renga and haiku poets had laid down "codes" for their arts. He stated that (1) there can be purely objective but not purely subjective rensaku; (2) rensaku must deal with the present, and if some poems in a sequence describe nostalgic recollections or imaginings of the future, they should be linked with the present; and (3) rensaku must be carefully organized and not merely present in sequitur.[118] Rensaku became the normal form of expression of many tanka poets, who might group under a single title thirty or forty tanka, each intended to add one telling stroke to the picture being composed.

SHIMAGI AKAHIKO (1876–1926)

Araragi, the journal founded by Itō Sachio, continued throughout his period of editorship to consider as its two guiding principles shasei (however defined) and worship of the *Manyōshū* as the source of Japanese poetry. The same principles were maintained by his successor, Shimagi Akahiko. Akahiko's reputation is based mainly on the poetry of his later years, filled with a calm sense of resignation, but his style changed several times before he settled on what would be his characteristic vein. He began to write tanka in 1893, at first in the style of the kokugaku scholars. Nothing in this poetry reveals its time; its tedious perfection transcends the centuries. In June 1895 Akahiko published a long shintaishi called "The Song of the Men of a Maritime Nation," in a mood of appropriate exhilaration over the victory in the Sino-Japanese War. The poem has a *Manyōshū* flavor, evidence that his tastes had turned in that direction, perhaps moved by the new nationalism of the age. Akahiko wrote mainly shintaishi and even an occasional chōka during the 1890s, but in 1900 he submitted fourteen tanka to the *Nippon Shimbun*. Shiki selected only one for his column, but he became more favorably disposed toward Akahiko later that year when Akahiko published an article strongly attacking Yosano Tekkan's deficient scholarship, his excessive fondness for novelty, and his total inability to capture poetic beauty; this criticism, at a time when the *Myōjō* poets ruled the roost, marked Akahiko as a potential adherent of Shiki's still small and weak following.

In 1903 Akahiko began to publish a tanka journal called *Himuro* in his native prefecture of Nagano. Although it had only a small circulation and the contributors were for the most part unknown, Akahiko was so confident that it indicated the future path of the tanka that he sent a copy to Itō Sachio for his criticism. Six months later Sachio's own journal, *Ashibi*, started to appear. Akahiko felt no sense of rivalry; he contributed to *Ashibi* and joyfully welcomed Sachio the next year to Lake Suwa. He evidently felt that he and Sachio were exploring parallel paths, and he was impressed also by the poetry of Nagatsuka Takashi. Akahiko gave up his job as an elementary school teacher in Nagano and tried chicken breeding for a year in 1907, but when this failed he returned to teaching, and in 1909 was appointed as an elementary school principal. In that year he discontinued publication of *Himuro*, stating that its mission had been assumed by *Araragi*.

Akahiko's poetry by this time was highly competent, even judged by Tokyo standards. In 1905 he published a collection of shintaishi jointly with Ōta Mizuho (1876–1955), but his most impressive poetry remained his tanka, which became more conspicuously imbued with the spirit of shasei. A few years later he declared that his tanka were born of the powerful emotions stirred within him by the majesty of nature and the noble nature of man. Clearly, however, he was more interested in nature than in man; comparatively few of his tanka deal with human problems.[119]

Akahiko's first important collection of tanka, *Bareisho no Hana* (Potato Flowers, 1913), was also a joint venture, this time with Nakamura Kenkichi, a disciple of Sachio and a central figure in the *Araragi* group. The tone of the collection was set by Akahiko's poem:

mori fukaku
tori nakiyamite
tasogaruru
ko no ma no mizu no
hono akari ka mo [120]

Deep in the forest
The birds cease their singing;
Ah, the glimmering light
Of water glimpsed through the trees
As day draws to a close!

Many of Akahiko's poems describe quiet scenes of dawn, dusk, or night. His feelings sometimes are intense, but more often are meditative, a mood that would be associated with him. A poem from a rensaku written in 1912 about a lonely railway station in the mountains evoked perfectly the atmosphere:

tamatama ni	Once in a while
kisha todomareba	A train stops here, and then
fuyu sabi no	You hear in this station
yama no umaya ni	In the lonely, winter mountains
hito no oto su mo [121]	The sound of people's footsteps.

Akahiko published this collection under the name Kubota Kakibito. Kubota was his real surname, and Kakibito was derived from *Kaki*nomoto no *Hito*maro. He did not adopt the name Shimagi Akahiko until 1913. In that year he visited a show of the late French Impressionists in Tokyo, and was particularly impressed by the work of Gauguin. He took the name Shimagi (Island Tree) Akahiko (Red Man) under the influence of Gauguin's Tahitian scenes and colors.[122] In the same year he visited the southerly island of Hachijō-jima, hoping to find on Japanese soil landscapes reminiscent of Gauguin. The island was a paradise for Akahiko, perhaps because he had a passionate affair with a local woman. His outlook on literature abruptly changed, and he now found his earlier poetry excessively dry and bland. He wrote in a letter, "Has not the time come for me to dye my poems directly with the black blood and the red blood flowing through my veins?" [123] He declared that the Japanese were basically sensual, citing the poetry of the *Manyōshū* and even of the *Kojiki*, and attributed to Confucian and Buddhist influences the curbing of the original Japanese élan. This influence had given rise to some poetic masterpieces, such as Bashō's haiku with their understatement and suggestion; but the Japanese of the Meiji era, thanks to Western influence, had entered a new age of sensuality. The tanka he wrote at this time display an intensity that embarrassed the orthodox *Araragi* poets, who found them "discordant."

sugu soko ni	Right over there,
awa wara no hatake,	A field of millet and straw,
shirakaba no saketaru	The split trunk of a birch tree,
miki,	An animal woman
kemono no onna [124]	

These two years were exceptional in Akahiko's orderly life. He tended to be contemplative rather than passionate, and was even criticized for his overintellectuality. His view of shasei was that it involved intent observation of an object by the poet; this would result in an interplay between the poet's mind and the object, which in turn produced a direct expression of feeling. He considered this kind of expression was characteristic of the "oriental" poet's quiet manner, and that the concentrated, simple form of the tanka was ideally suited to such expression. A quiet tone pervades his later collections, which include *Hio* (Whitebait, 1920), *Taikyo Shū* (Great Void Collection, 1924), and the posthumous *Shiin Shū* (Persimmon Shadow Collection, 1925). Unlike the tanka of his two passionate years, the later ones are regular:

yūyakezora	The sky at sunset
kogekiwamareru	Blazing to incandescence,
shita ni shite	And underneath it
kōran to suru	The stillness of the lake
mizuumi no shizukesa [125]	As its waters turn to ice.

mizuumi no	Out on the lake
kōri wa tokete	The ice has melted,
nao samushi	But still it is cold.
mikazuki no kage	The crescent moon's reflection
nami ni utsurou	Glitters on the waves.

A tanka written during his final illness has been especially praised:

Shinanoji wa	When will it turn spring
itsu haru ni naran	Along the Shinano Road?
yūzuku hi	After the evening sun
irite shimaraku	Has set for a while there lingers
ki naru sora no iro [126]	A yellow color in the sky.

The lingering yellow light makes the patient eager for the spring, which comes late to the wintry province of Shinano. The metrics of this tanka are somewhat irregular, perhaps because Akahiko had no time to correct it before he died.

Akahiko was known also for his children's songs and for his commentaries to the *Manyōshū*. His preference in *Manyōshū* poetry was for the early songs, rather than for the masterpieces of Hitomaro (though he borrowed Hitomaro's name), much less the more intellectual Okura. Perhaps his years as a school teacher and principal led him to prefer the simplicity of the early poetry. From 1914, when he became the editor of *Araragi*, he was chiefly responsible for making the school the strongest force in the tanka, and his own objective, simple style in the later collections influenced even other schools. He achieved in the end detachment and tranquillity, distilling from his experiences a remoteness that may have been his ultimate triumph over the emotional intensity he had briefly but unforgettably revealed.

SAITŌ MOKICHI (1882–1953)

Akahiko's successor was Saitō Mokichi, probably the most important tanka poet of the twentieth century. He was adopted as a boy by a wealthy doctor with the understanding that he himself would follow his adopted father's profession. In 1905 he accordingly entered the medical school of Tokyo University. Soon afterward he happened to read a collection of tanka by Masaoka Shiki that so impressed him that he became a pupil of Itō Sachio the following year. He began to contribute poetry to *Ashibi*, and his tanka appeared in the first issue of *Araragi* in 1908. After his graduation in 1910 he worked in various Tokyo hospitals, specializing in mental illnesses. His experiences with deranged persons provided him with unique materials for his poetry.

Mokichi's first collection, *Shakkō* (Red Light, 1913), created a great impression not only on tanka poets but on the literary world in general. The attention this collection attracted was extended to all the *Araragi* poets, though they previously had been rather isolated. *Red Light* contains 834 tanka written between 1905 and 1913.[127] Although the style recalls the *Manyōshū*, its themes, far from being archaistic, reveal a distinctly modern sensibility. The tanka are clustered in rensaku, arranged under such topics as "Fireflies and Dragon Flies" or "My Mother Is Dying." The sequence of fifty-nine poems on his mother's death (his real and not his adopted mother) determined the reputation of the entire collection. These poems, divided into four sections, described the poet's hurried journey back to his native province, his vigil by his mother's sickbed, the funeral and cremation, and his recuperation afterward. Although the diction employed was that of a thousand years earlier—many tanka end in such *Manyōshū* forms as *ka mo* and there are even *makurakotoba*—the effect is entirely modern. The most vivid sections of the rensaku describe his anxious hours by his mother's side just before her death:

shi ni chikaki	I lie beside my mother
haha ni soine no	Who is close to death—
shinshin to	Piercing cries
tōda no kawazu	Of frogs in distant fields
ten ni kikoyuru [128]	Echo from heaven.

The cries of the frogs not only recall boyhood days but they suggest voices from heaven summoning his mother's soul.

> *kuwa no ka no*
> *aoku tadayou*
> *asaake ni*
> *taegatakereba*
> *haha yobinikeri*

> At daybreak
> When the smell of mulberry leaves
> Greenly hovers,
> It was so unendurable
> I called to my mother.

The chilly air of early morning brings a raw smell of mulberry leaves, used for feeding silkworms; unable to bear the remembrances they evoke, the poet cries out, "Mother!"

nodo akaki	Two red-throated
tsubakurame futatsu	Swallows perch on a crossbeam:
hari ni ite	My mother who nurtured me
tarachine no haha wa	Is dying.
shinitamau nari	

The poet, fearful that any moment may be his mother's last, happens to glance up and see two swallows on a crossbeam overhead, and the redness of their throats seems somehow ominous. Mokichi here joined two seemingly unrelated statements, but each imposes its authority and persuades the reader there is an underlying connection. One critic suggested that mention of the swallows had a Buddhist significance, alluding to the birds and beasts that gathered to watch over the Buddha's death.[129] Mokichi does not make it clear why he mentions the red throats of the swallows, but we can be sure that the perception was close to the center of his agony. Perhaps he meant to intensify the contrast between the early spring swallows building their nest on the crossbeam with the death of his mother. The use of *tarachine no*, a makurakotoba of uncertain meaning, which modified "mother," and the archaic diction also lent a dimension in time to the poet's experience, Mokichi joining the endless procession of poets who have watched their mothers die amid the indifference of nature.

Another rensaku in *Shakkō* describes a love affair that occurred in the year of his mother's death. Mokichi made superb use in these poems of such reduplicated Japanese words as *hatsuhatsu*, *horohoro*, *honobono*, and *shinshin*, and of the typical verb endings and particles of the *Manyōshū*. Sometimes the beauty of his words carried its own conviction, though the meaning was not immediately apparent:

ki no moto ni	When, under the tree,
ume hameba sushi	I bite into a plum, how sour!
osana tsuma	The time has passed
hito ni sanizurau	When my childlike bride
toki tachinikeri [130]	Used to blush before people.

No relationship is stated between the two halves of the poem, and probably the poet would have been hard pressed to spell it out. Nagatsuka Takashi gave as his opinion: "When the poet composed this poem he probably, for reasons he could not explain, felt compelled to express his thought this way. An underlying strength binds the two unrelated statements together indissolubly." Some poems were so ambiguous that Mokichi felt obliged to state his own interpretation, in response to those of other critics:

aka nasu no	Beyond the spot
kusarete itaru	Where red tomatoes were rotting

tokoro yori	I walked,
ikuhodo mo naki	Not very far.
ayumi narikeri [131]	

Nagatsuka Takashi explained the technique employed was similar to that of a haiku: the poet, thinking vaguely about something else as he walks along, suddenly realizes that he passed some rotting tomatoes a little while before, and the experience is encapsulated in this form. Mokichi, replying to criticism that the poem was ambiguous or even a hoax played on the public, defended it against "commonsense logicality." He declared that the poem meant exactly what it said: somebody had thrown away the overripe tomatoes; the poet noticed them as he passed; a few steps later an image grazed his mind. It does not make any difference what this image, plumbed from his subconscious, might have been, but the ending in *-keri* indicates that the poet felt an emotional response to the image, as so frequently in the poetry of a thousand years earlier. This, Mokichi said, was what he meant by shasei.

Mokichi's definitions and explanations of shasei went far beyond Shiki's simple insistence on the importance of "depicting life." Sometimes he explained the concept in terms of the aesthetics of Far Eastern painting, but his most famous definition, published in 1919, was, "Shasei means depicting life by empathizing with real objects." [132] Elsewhere he wrote, "For us shasei is not a means, a technique or a process, it is the totality." He apparently meant that shasei, contrary to Shiki's belief, was not merely a way of imparting actuality to a tanka by basing it on some observed aspect of nature, as contrasted to the conventional imagery of the old-fashioned tanka, but the whole of the poem; the poet, penetrating the aspect of nature before him, reaches to its fundamental nature and identifies himself with it.[133] For Mokichi shasei meant something quite different from an objective depiction of life. He believed that the tanka was by nature lyrical, and that it should express the poet's feelings; it might happen, then, that the poet would not need to depend on external objects to express his inner feelings. However, if the poet turned to external objects, he must penetrate their essence, not merely decorate his own feelings by mentioning flowers and birds. This identification with the external object closely resembles the theory of *Einfühlung* (empathy) in the works of Theodor Lipps (1851–1914), and no doubt there was influence from the German aestheticians; but whatever the source, Mokichi's interpretation of shasei gave his works their uniqueness, and accounts for the extraordinary reputation he acquired. Even men who bitterly opposed Mokichi's nationalistic political views were moved to express admiration for his poetry.[134]

Mokichi's popularity stemmed not only from his extraordinary combinations of perceptions but from his superb choice of language. He wrote, "The nature of the tanka is for it to be sung, rather than spoken." [135] Or again, "The tanka is definitely not simply concerned with the meaning of the words or the symbolic intent of the words; the musical effect produced by the sequence of sounds is most important." The sounds were the outpouring of internal emotion; empathy was the act of penetration into the nature of the external object.[136]

Mokichi's qualifications as a poet were established with his first collection. He continued to write prolifically: not only did he publish seventeen volumes of tanka, but works in many other forms, and his *Complete Works* appeared in fifty-six volumes. Yet all of his efforts as poet or scholar had to be fitted into a busy medical career, which sometimes (as when he went to Nagasaki in 1916 or to Europe in 1921) separated him from other poets of his school. Altogether he wrote some sixteen thousand tanka. His most productive period was in the early 1930s, but his best poetry is contained in *Red Light*, his second collection *Aratama* (The New Year, 1921), and the late *Shiroki Yama* (White Mountains, 1949). *The New Year* opens with the rensaku "The Black Cricket," including:

furisosugu	Into light
ama tsu hikari ni	Pouring down from the sky
me no mienu	I drove
kuroki itodo wo	A blind, black cricket.
oitsumenikeri [137]	

The poem states merely that the author has driven into the sunlight a cricket that was hiding in a dark corner, but one cannot escape the implication that the poet's own mental state is being described.

Another rensaku in the collection, "Road without a Fork," opens:

aka-aka to	In glaring sunlight
ippon no michi	A road without a fork
tōritari	Lies straight before me.
tamakiharu wa ga	This, I know, will be my life,
inochi narikeri [138]	As long as I live.

Probably Mokichi actually saw a straight road before him in blazing early autumn light, and it made him realize that this was the road he must walk. The poem was written shortly after Itō Sachio's death had deprived him of guidance in his poetry. There are allusions to Saigyō and Bashō, and *tamakiharu* was a makurakotoba used to characterize a whole life. Mokichi saw the life ahead of him as one of unswerving devotion to poetry, like Saigyō or Bashō in the past.

In the 1930s Mokichi began to write patriotic poetry, and during the war years *Araragi* became an instrument of the war effort. Years before (in November 1923) he had been in Munich at the time of Hitler's *putsch* and wrote:

kōshin no	I can hear the marchers' singing—
utagoe kikoyu	I wonder if
Hitler no	Hitler's speech
enzetsu sude ni	Has already ended.
hatetaru koro ka [139]	

Mokichi expressed admiration for Hitler as late as the end of World War II. In April 1945 he was evacuated to the country, and his hospital in Tokyo burned to the ground in an air raid the next month. Mokichi, stunned by the defeat of Japan, began to wonder in self-examination if he himself did not bear a share of the responsibility for having pushed Japan into the war. Late in 1946 he wrote:

kuragari no	I too am one
naka ni ochiiru	Who has lived in a century

tsumi fukaki	Full of guilt
seiki ni itaru	That drops into darkness.
ware mo hitori zo [140]	

The tanka in *White Mountains*, written in the grief and resignation of old age, are among his most unaffected and moving.

It is easy to understand why Takuboku, who wrote simply and forcefully about modern life, should have enjoyed such popularity, but Mokichi's popularity is puzzling. His poems are difficult and their expression is indirect. It is true that many people, knowing of his reputation as a great poet, praised his works without understanding them, but his importance is beyond question. He proved that the tanka, even if written in an archaic style, could still move the Japanese more than any modern poetic form. He explained this in terms of the inheritance from the past, the poetry that is in the blood of the Japanese. It is curious, however, in view of the complexity of his thought and his particular admiration for Hitomaro, that Mokichi never wrote chōka, which are not only equally Japanese but the glory of the *Manyōshū*. He apparently felt that he lacked the breadth of Hitomaro; but even if he could not compose a single, sustained poem, he achieved similar effects with his rensaku.

A non-Japanese may experience trouble in appreciating Saitō Mokichi's work. Some tanka, it is true, are impressive even in translation, thanks to the effectiveness of their imagery, but much of the magic of his poetry depends on its particular music, and translation often reduces a melody to a few bluntly expressed images. There is no problem, however, in understanding his enormous prestige, if only in terms of what *Araragi* meant to the Japanese literary world during the period when he was the editor. Many poets have written tanka since Mokichi's death in 1953, some with notable skill and intelligence, but perhaps he will be remembered as the last truly great poet of this quintessentially Japanese poetic form.

THE OTHER POETS

Almost all the tanka poets discussed above were born between 1876 and 1886, but their life-spans, ranging from Takuboku's twenty-six years to Kubota Utsubo's ninety, differed so markedly that it is hard to remember that these men were all very nearly contemporaries. Most of these poets were associated with a group, a journal, and an identifying label, but there were other poets, who are known for their distinctive styles and their reluctance to conform to the dictates of any school.

Kinoshita Toshiharu (more often known as Rigen, 1886–1925) studied initially under Sasaki Nobutsuna (1872–1963), a conservative tanka poet and scholar of Japanese literature. Later he was influenced by Kitahara Hakushū, Kubota Utsubo, and the *Araragi* poets; but gradually he evolved his own style, characterized by an unaffected use of the colloquial and by irregularities in the metrics that were occasioned not by any desire to express scorn for traditional poetics but by the internal needs of the poem. His effortless compositions became popular among general readers, who no doubt found them easier to absorb than Saitō Mokichi's tanka; they have an unmistakable freshness both in the perceptions and in the language, as the following example may suggest:

machi wo yuki	I was walking through the street;
kodomo no soba wo	Just as I passed by some children
tōru toki	I caught the fragrance
mikan no ka seri	Of tangerines—
fuyu mata kuru [141]	Winter is coming again.

Rigen appended this explanation: "Winter is already hurrying its advance riders into the autumn by the time the candy shops begin to display green tangerines. What is so sharply scented, so sour, so freshly fragrant as green tangerines? And the first to make an assault on these green tangerines are the children playing in the streets. They are the most sensitive to the fragrance and color of the green fruit." The tanka poet Kawata Jun (1882–1966) pointed out that, despite the seeming ordinariness of the scene, this was the first poem ever to have been composed on the scent of tangerines.[142]

The irregularity of Rigen's tanka often took the form of lines in eight syllables that are divided into two hemistiches of four syllables each. The following example is from *Ichiro* (One Road, 1924), the collection that enjoyed the highest reputation:

ushiguruma	The ox-cart grinds along
nosshiri omomi	At such a heavy, plodding pace
kishimi yuku ni	That pebbles in the road
tsuburete merikomu	Crushed by the sinking wheels
dōro no jari oto [143]	Groan under the weight.

There is an extra syllable in the third, fourth, and fifth lines, and the effect in the fourth and fifth lines especially is to emphasize the heaviness of the ox-cart. The colloquial word *nosshiri* and the Chinese-derived word *dōro* also give freshness to the poem. It should be noted that the first version of this tanka was metrically regular, but Rigen when making his revision deliberately violated metrics to convey a desired effect.

Kinoshita Rigen's poetry is said to have been colored by his early associations with the *Shirakaba* group. Like most of the others in this group, he came from an aristocratic family; his could boast the sixteenth-century poet Kinoshita Chōshōshi as a collateral ancestor. The humanitarian views of the *Shirakaba* writers are not immediately apparent in Rigen's most famous verses, but his aristocratic background is perhaps suggested by the refined, understated quality.

Two other poets of the same generation have left a more lasting impression on later readers, Aizu Yaichi (1881–1956) and Origuchi Shinobu (usually known by his Buddhist name Shaku Chōkū, 1887–1953). Aizu wrote his tanka entirely in *kana*, separating the words as in English, but his subject matter was largely derived from his appreciation of the Buddhist art in Nara. He made his first visit to Nara in 1908, but did not publish his first collection of tanka, *Nankyō Shinshō* (New Songs of the Southern Capital), until 1924. Although this collection is highly praised today, the sales at the time were disappointing, and Aizu had to publish (in 1934) his next collection at his own expense.[144] Aizu was known above all as a calligrapher, both of Chinese characters and of Japanese kana, and a full appreciation of his tanka is possible only when one examines them in Aizu's distinctive calligraphy. Despite his present popularity, he seems to rank no higher than as a minor poet.

Shaku Chōkū is a much more considerable figure. His tanka are also somewhat unconventional in visual terms because phrases are divided by spacing and there is even internal punctuation, thus violating the old conception of the tanka as a single thread of beaten gold. His first collection, *Umi Yama no Aida* (Between the Sea and the Mountains, 1925), already displays his characteristic style, as in this tanka:

> *hito mo uma mo*
> *michi yukitsukare shininikeri*
> *tabine kasanaru hodo no*
> *kasokeki* [145]

> Men and horses too
> Have died exhausted on the road.
> After so many nights on this journey
> I have found a quietness of heart.

In the preface to this poem Chōkū described the gravemounds of horses, and even stone monuments of the horse-headed Kannon, that tell of the many horses who have died on the road. At almost every pass in the mountains too there is the grave of some man who has died on the road, perhaps of a pilgrim making his weary way from shrine to shrine, hiding from his family the terrible marks of some disease for which he seeks a miraculous cure. The traveler is moved by these sights, but it is a quiet emotion, for he too has known the hardships of many nights on the way.

Chōkū's tanka are often difficult, not only because of the complexity of the thought, but because he used archaic words, gleaned from his studies of the *Kojiki*, *Manyōshū*, and other early writings. (Under his lay name, Origuchi Shinobu, he published many volumes describing his discoveries in ancient literature and in folklore.) Sometimes a seemingly modern word is given a gloss to indicate it must be read in a forgotten pronunciation, or an entirely modern sentiment is clothed in archaic language. Such tendencies not only reveal his predilection for the old writings but for masuraoburi, the "manly way" associated with the *Manyōshū* by poets of the *Araragi* school. Chōkū joined the school in 1909 and for twelve years was active as a proponent of masuraoburi as the ideal of tanka; but in 1918 Saitō Mokichi severely criticized Chōkū for his eccentricities, such as the use of punctuation.[146]

Chōkū at first put up with this criticism, but in 1921 broke with the *Araragi* poets, though he continued to emphasize masuraoburi.

Chōkū's admiration for the manly virtues exalted by the *Manyōshū* poets was put to the test in the 1930s when Japan became steadily more deeply involved in war. The following tanka, published in 1937, indicates the ambivalence of his feelings:

ikite ware kaerazaran to,	After sending off
utaitsutsu,	Soldiers who were singing,
hei wo okurite	"We don't expect to return alive,"
ie ni iritari [147]	I went back into my house.

Perhaps, as commentators have opined, this poem expressed Chōkū's indignation over the February 26, 1936, army coup and the outbreak in the following year of the China Incident; but there may be more personal overtones, specifically his fears for Fujii Harumi (1907–1944), the young scholar he eventually adopted as his son.

Such emotions did not, however, prevent Chōkū from expressing the most fervent commitment to the war, which began in December 1941. His tanka on such subjects as the Imperial Rescript declaring war on America and England and on the fall of Singapore are filled with intense emotion, as he urges the Japanese forces to strike the enemy or proclaims the joy of the entire people at serving under the emperor. He was by no means alone in this enthusiasm for the war. Saitō Mokichi, the doyen of tanka poets, set the tone of the public poems, which have been termed "poems in uniform." [148] Even a poet like Toki Zemmaro, who had frequently aroused controversy in the past with his outspokenly antiwar tanka, executed a rapid volte-face, and was soon writing no less patriotically than the most earnest advocates of masuraoburi.[149] Chōkū's poems in uniform include the following, published in 1942 in his collection *Tenchi ni noberu* (Declaration to Heaven and Earth):

himugashi no	Now is the moment
tōki shisō ni	When we must decisively strike

modoku mono	Whatever opposes
ima shi	The profound philosophy
danjite utarazaru	Of the Orient.
bekarazu	

yorokobite	Joyously
ima wa tatakau	We now are fighting.
taetaeshi anadori no	How truly long a time
ge ni hisashikarishi ka [150]	We endured their contempt!

In the first verse Chōkū expresses his belief in the traditional Japanese (or oriental) ways of thought, and his conviction that the time had come for the Japanese to expel, as foreign bodies in their system, the contrary kinds of thought that had been taken in from the West; many tanka poets treated similar themes. He expresses in the second verse the commonly held belief that the racial prejudice directed against the Japanese and other Asian people had been too long endured; the moment had come when endurance was no longer possible. These statements of belief seem sincere, but they do not arise naturally from the negative views on war that Chōkū had not long before been expressing. The declaration of war seems to have swept away Chōkū's doubts, and made of him as enthusiastic an advocate of total, unsparing warfare as any rank propagandist; but even in his most jingoistic verses he usually maintained a certain nobility of tone.[151]

With virtually no exceptions the tanka poets, as the transmitters of ancient Japanese literary tradition, expressed themselves in the most positive and even bloodthirsty terms when declaring their hatred of all who opposed the will of the emperor.[152] Slogans were twisted into tanka, and the most banal conceptions were dignified by archaic, "poetic" language, as in this example by Chōkū:

ippeisotsu	One soldier
kimi wo zo tanomu.	Places his trust in our Master.
ippeisotsu no ue mo,	And above this one soldier,
wa ga ōkimi wa	Our great Lord
shiroshitamaeri [153]	Has deigned to rule.

The shock of the death of his adopted son on Iwo Jima inspired Chōkū to write in quite a different tone:

omou ko wa tsui ni kaerazu.
kaeraji to iishi kotoba no
amari masashiki [154]

My beloved son has finally not returned.
His words, saying he probably would not return,
Have proved all too true.

Although Chōkū, like innumerable other tanka poets, composed poetry expressing profoundest grief on learning of Japan's defeat, it did not take long for a sharp reaction against the war to find voice in their poetry. For some tanka poets the end of the war brought liberation, for others it was a test, and for still others it brought a deep sense of loss, but in every case it conspicuously stimulated creative activity.[155] Saitō Mokichi, who had been the most outspoken of the public poets, began to write totally private poetry, revelatory of his attempts to find solace for his fallen ideals in the natural beauty of the scenery in the countryside where he was living. The defeat proved to him, in the words of Tu Fu, that "the country has fallen, but its rivers and mountains remain," and he was able to find comfort in the abiding beauty of the land, the renewed harvests. But for Chōkū the defeat brought a double loss: first, it was the negation of the traditions of Japan, the land of the gods, to which he had so long given himself; second, it meant the death of his beloved disciple and son.

Perhaps Chōkū's finest poetry is in the collection *Yamato Oguna* (Men of Yamato), published posthumously in 1955. The poignant grief he felt over Harumi's death is disclosed in a rensaku of unusual emotional warmth, as in this example:

tatakai ni hateshi wa ga   The time has surely come
 ko wo   For me to say at last
kaese to zo   "Give me back the son
iubeki toki to   Who perished in the war!"
nariyashinuran [156]

THE POSTWAR POETS

One of the first tanka poets to emerge after the war, Satō Satarō (1909–1987), had joined *Araragi* at the age of seventeen, and always considered himself to be a faithful disciple of Saitō Mokichi. He gained his first recognition in 1940 with his collection of tanka, *Hodō* (Pavement), in which he described ordinary scenes from the daily life of the middle class, but with a sharpness of perception and a care with words that distinguished him. However, it was only after the war, when he gave up his job with the Iwanami Publishing Company to devote himself entirely to poetry, that he obtained wider fame. At the beginning of 1947 he wrote, "When the war came to its sad conclusion, I vowed to make a fresh start, rousing myself to fresh determination. Sensing a vague new direction in how I wanted to compose poetry, I made great efforts to pursue it, but 1946 ended without my having been able to implement my determination or to escape in any way from the old state of things. Now, as the year is about to begin, I have resolved to try to create new circumstances both in my life and in my composition of poetry." [157]

The task of tanka poets who wished to maintain something of the traditional tone and content in their works was complicated by the publication in 1946 of the article "Daini Geijutsu" (Second-Class Art) by Kuwabara Takeo. Although Kuwabara's attacks were leveled specifically at the haiku, much of what he wrote was directly applicable to modern tanka as well, and some poets were so discouraged by the harshness of his evaluations of the role that the traditional poetry played in modern society that they abandoned tanka. Satō Satarō, however, chose to interpret Kuwabara's remarks as defining the possibilities of the tanka in terms of its depth, rather than in terms of its inability to communicate the wide range of thought possible in a modern poem or in a short story.[158] His collection *Kichō* (Ebbtide, 1952) was a reaffirmation of his belief in the tanka. It is faithful to the traditional form, and the manner is that of the shasei advocated by Mokichi and his school; his poems are distinguished not by novelty but by the impression they give of inner depths behind the plain surface, as in this tanka of 1959:

shirafuji no　　　　　　　The sound of bees
hana ni muragaru　　　　Clustering in the blossoms

hachi no oto	Of white wisteria:
ayumisakarite	Now they have walked away
sono oto wa nashi [159]	And their sound is heard no more.

Japanese commentators have noted that it is characteristic of Satō Satarō's tanka to attempt to hear sounds that lie at the depths of other sounds; here, he is not listening to the sounds of the bees but to the soundless sound that grows louder in the emptiness after the bees have departed.

Other postwar poets were more outspoken in their replies to Kuwabara's charge that the traditional Japanese poetry was no more than a "second-class art." For example, Tsuchiya Bummei (1890–1990), whose tanka had been known even before the war for their variety of subjects drawn from the daily lives of ordinary people, listed the objections raised to the tanka—that it was old-fashioned, that there was no distinction between writers and the audience, that it was incapable of expressing modern life—and replied point-by-point: "I admit that the tanka is simple, but far from expecting that a form of literature which is so extremely close to the lives of people will disappear, I believe that it will continue to exist within the social structure, no matter what kind of structure that may be. Moreover, I believe that it is this poetry with simple roots, this tanka which will fill in the gaps and the estrangement between commercial literature and life." [160] Tsuchiya was convinced that the tanka was ideally suited to become the literature of the working classes because it had no need of heroes or geniuses, and in the tanka column he edited in *Araragi* he included tanka by people in all walks of life, to demonstrate its vitality and its peculiar closeness to the average Japanese.

Opposition to the theory of "second-class art" was voiced in a different way by Kimata Osamu (1906–1983). In the magazine *Yakumo*, which he helped to found in 1946, he made this statement of its principles: "We will attempt to break through the feudalism of tanka circles and, working against a background of the postwar rise of democratic literature, effectuate a revolution in tanka literature." [161] The magazine dealt severely with tanka poets who had been wartime collaborators, and proclaimed the conviction of the editors that the tanka must be a responsible medium for the expression of the poet's deepest concerns; it should not be the elegant amusement of ladies and gentlemen.

Although Kimata had begun his career as a disciple of Kitahara Hakushū, and in his early tanka had successfully captured the quality of yūgen so prized by Hakushū at this time, he gradually drifted away from this kind of poetry as he became more involved with society. A poem written in February 1946 evokes the hardships of the immediate postwar days:

mujin zu no	I am so clumsy
nayami no naka ni	Even at squirming my way
agaku sae	through
kyō no tsutanaki	The innumerable
ware ga ikizama [162]	Troubles plaguing us today—
	What a way for me to live!

Kimata's best poems, however, are not necessarily those that reflect most closely his concerns with postwar Japan; a lingering affection for Hakushū continued to color his tanka long after he asserted the close connection between the poet and his society, and it is for these poems that he is most likely to be remembered.

The most engaged of the postwar tanka poets was undoubtedly Kondō Yoshimi (b. 1913). Although his point of departure was initially the *Araragi* school, he gradually became convinced that individual happiness or salvation was not possible unless the poet chose to participate in politics. He became aware too that no power existed without evil; however beautiful the ideals of a revolution, when it is accomplished it is inevitably the substitution of one form of evil for another.[163] His poems surprise us by their individuality and refusal to go along with the prevailing sentiments. In 1945, when most tanka poets were expressing their grief over the defeat, Kondō wrote these poems:

itsu no ma ni	Before I knew it,
yo no shōsen ni	At night on the subway line
hararetaru	Young men were stripping
gun no gariban wo	The mimeographed notices
seinen ga hagu	The army had pasted there.

yo wo ageshi	I kept it intact
shisō no naka ni	When the whole world was
mamorikite	seething
ima koso sensō wo	With "philosophy"—
nikumu kokoro yo [164]	Now I'll give them a taste
	Of my hatred for the war!

Kondō's involvement with the contemporary scene did not end with the immediate postwar period. There are tanka on the Korean war, on the demonstrations against the Security Treaty in 1960, on the Vietnam war. These poems are not only expressions of the strong emotions aroused by political events, identifying the poet with the many members of society who have been similarly aroused, but they serve indirectly to defend the validity of the tanka as a means of communicating to the people, in a form they most readily understand, thoughts that can comfort or inspire. Not all of Kondō's tanka are on political matters—a particularly affecting series is devoted to his love for his wife—and his finest collection was perhaps his first, *Sōshunka* (Poems of Early Spring, 1948), though it was the most lyrical and least openly political of his works. Kondō, nevertheless, was a committed poet, perhaps the poet who most effectively demonstrated that the tanka need not be a second-class art, even in our time.

The postwar period witnessed also a revival of the tanka written by women, notably Ubukata Tatsue (b. 1905), Gotō Miyoko (1898–1978) and Saitō Fumi (b. 1909). The women poets had been active during the war, especially Saitō Fumi, the daughter of a general with conspicuous right-wing tendencies; and after the war they felt a need to express something more than the delicacy and sensitivity traditionally associated with the feminine tradition. In 1951 Shaku Chōkū published an important article entitled "Nyonin no uta wo heisoku shita mono" (What Has Obstructed Poems Written by Women), an attack on the *Araragi* group for having promoted masuraoburi and shasei to the exclusion of the feminine virtues in Japanese poetry. This essay seems to have given women poets courage to write in the mood of vertigo (*gyakujō*), which had been the hallmark of Japanese women writers for centuries; a notable example of this development is *Senkō* (Pale Red, 1950), the collection that brought Ubukata Tatsue acclaim. Gotō Miyoko's poems were about maternal love, certainly an unexceptionable theme, but there is something distinctly modern in her unsparing avowals of the possessiveness this involves.

Some of its prewar associations continued to cling to the tanka even after the many changes effected by the postwar poets. The right wing in its sporadic displays of nostalgia for the Japanese past sometimes commemorated its violence in the traditional form: before Mishima Yukio and his followers invaded the headquarters of the Japanese Defense Force in November 1970 they each prepared a valedictory tanka in the customarily elliptic manner and old-fashioned diction.

However, there have also been avant-garde tanka poets who have done much to restore its contemporary validity in the eyes of the literary world. Tsukamoto Kunio (b. 1922) and Okai Takashi (b. 1928) are both difficult poets, depending on free associations and on overtones provided by the Chinese characters they use as well as the sounds. Tsukamoto especially has given the tanka a complexity unimaginable even to as subtle a poet as Saitō Mokichi; his expression is sometimes almost perversely obscure because of private references to Christianity or to poets and musicians of the West. No single poem can suggest his range, but the effect can be intuited perhaps through the following examples:

panya kamado ni	By the bakery oven
bara-iro no shita	Rose-colored tongues
tsumikasane	Pile one on another;
keburi tatsu	The smoke is rising on
Rōtoreamon kinichi [165]	Lautréamont's anniversary.

Kokutō ga	Cocteau is dead;
shini shirogane no	The silver hair rustles;
kami soyogi	The snow that falls on
sakareshi sake no	Salmon flesh split apart.
niku ni furu yuki [166]	

Vachikan ni	Even though there is a God
kami wa aru tomo	In the Vatican,
haha ga tatsu	The crimson dahlia
daria no ne no	My mother cuts
Shamu sōseiji [167]	Has Siamese-twin roots.

Despite the obscurity of these tanka, and despite the consternation they aroused among more conventional tanka poets, Tsukamoto, in Mishima Yukio's words, "revived the dignity of a verse form close to extinction." [168]

Okai's tanka are more easily understood, though in their way no less defiant of tradition than Tsukamoto's, as the following will suggest:

"Non!" naze?	*"Non!"* why not?
"Nazette . . ." kasaneoku	"Why not . . ." snow lying
tebukuro no	On gloves folded
yuki tokenagara	One on the other, melting
umi nasu taku wa [169]	Creates a sea on the table.

In this tanka by Okai the language is colloquial, though Tsukamoto used the classical grammatical forms in even his most modern poems. The classical language has the virtue not only of greater concision, a matter of importance to poets writing in short forms, but of greater precision. Okai, however, expressed his discontent that not greater attention had been paid to bridging the gap between modern content and the traditional vocabulary and constructions used in the tanka.

> Our efforts to enrich the poetic vocabulary by choosing words from contemporary Japanese is necessary, I believe, in order that the modern tanka be truly modern tanka. But I am convinced, on the other hand, that the belief the Japanese we normally speak and use to express ourselves can serve *just as it is* as the language of the tanka is a misapprehension, which poses the greatest threat to the vitality of the tanka. Poets of the popular "mass" variety cheerfully adopt the clarity and directness of daily speech, but words of this kind, when used in a poem, show a surprising tendency to lose their strength, perhaps because these words have been bred and nurtured by prose.[170]

Okai went on to discuss the legitimate uses even of archaisms in the vocabulary and constructions; the additional expressive powers that they impart to the tanka poet are not easily surrendered.

The tanka seems likely to survive as almost every traditional

Japanese art has survived. For some it will be no more than the avocation of amateurs, but other poets will no doubt continue to find it a peculiarly congenial medium to express even their most deeply felt and untraditional thoughts.

NOTES

1. Koizumi Tōzō (ed.), *Gendai Tanka Taikei*, I, pp. 4–6, 429. Ōkami Mimaki, an obscure figure, was also known as Kusano Mimaki.
2. Kimata Osamu, *Kindai Tanka no Shiteki Tenkai*, p. 4.
3. Koizumi, *Gendai Tanka Taikei*, I, p. 385.
4. *Ibid.*, p. 101. The collection *Seika* (pp. 97–105) was compiled by Catholic missionaries.
5. *Ibid.*, p. 118. The collection was compiled by Ōkubo Tadayasu (1830–1886), but the preface was by Hoshino Chiyuki.
6. *Ibid.*, p. 125.
7. *Ibid.*, p. 387. Among the examples of "pure Japanese" words invented by tanka poets were *sujikanemichi* for *tetsudō* (railway) and *abumikuruma* for *jitensha* (bicycle).
8. *Nihon Gendaishi Taikei*, I, p. 25.
9. *Ibid.*, p. 116.
10. Koizumi, *Gendai Tanka Taikei*, I, pp. 388–89. Suematsu Kenchō (1885–1920) published this article in 1884. Suematsu is also remembered for his partial translation of *The Tale of Genji*, published after he had studied in England from 1878 to 1886.
11. *Ibid.*, p. 395.
12. *Ibid.*, p. 396.
13. *Nihon Gendaishi Taikei*, I, p. 25.
14. Ochiai translated the long poem by J. V. von Scheffel, *Der Trompeter von Säkkingen* (1854), for the most part into stanzas of four lines, each consisting of twelve syllables with a caesura after the seventh, in the manner of *imayō* poetry. The second and fourth lines rhyme, as in the original. Ochiai changed the bugler of the original into a flautist because he feared Japanese would be unable to imagine a girl being attracted to a man because of his bugling! For text, see *ibid.*, pp. 241–48.
15. Koizumi, *Gendai Tanka Taikei*, II, p. 3.
16. Kimata Osamu, *Kindai Tanka no Kanshō to Hihyō* (henceforth abbreviated as *KTKH*), p. 34.
17. *Ibid.*, p. 37.
18. *Ibid.*
19. Nakashio Kiyoomi, "Ochiai Naobumi," p. 87.
20. Kimata, *KTKH*, p. 45. See also *Gendai Tanka Zenshū*, I, p. 306.
21. Nakashio, "Ochiai Naobumi," pp. 78, 81.
22. Koizumi Tōzō, *Meiji Karon Shiryō Shūsei*, p. 687.

23. Shimma Shin'ichi, *Kindai Tankashi Ron*, p. 8.

24. He used the name Tekkan from 1890 to 1905, the most productive years of his career.

25. *Gendai Tanka Zenshū*, I, p. 13.

26. *Ibid.*

27. Kimata, *KTKH*, p. 53.

28. Koizumi, *Meiji*, pp. 560–61.

29. *Ibid.*, p. 568.

30. Takasaki Masakaze, one of his principal targets of attack in this essay, as late as 1912 wrote a defense of love poetry in precisely the manner of the preface to the *Kokinshū*. See *ibid.*, pp. 547–55.

31. This statement throws doubt on the authenticity of the juvenile tanka published for the first time in 1933. See Kimata, *KTKH*, p. 48.

32. Koizumi, *Gendai Tanka Taikei*, II, p. 33.

33. *Ibid.*, p. 42.

34. *Ibid.*, p. 37.

35. See Iwatsu Motoo, *Tanka Koten to Kindai*, pp. 210–11, and Kōhashi Kenji, *Yosano Tekkan*, p. 13.

36. Kimata, *KTKH*, p. 56.

37. For an account of the complications stemming from this marriage, see Yosano Akiko, *Tangled Hair*, trans. Goldstein and Shinoda, pp. 9–16.

38. Kimata, *KTKH*, p. 57.

39. *Myōjō*, No. 6, September 1900, p. 68. In subsequent issues the second "rule" began: "We love the poetry of our predecessors, both of the East and of the West."

40. Kimata, *KTKH*, p. 60. Also, *Gendai Tanka Zenshū*, I, p. 67.

41. Koizumi, *Gendai Tanka Taikei*, II, p. 81.

42. Yosano Akiko later made a modern-language translation of *The Tale of Genji* and of other works of classical literature.

43. Satake Kazuhiko, *Zenshaku Midaregami Kenkyū*, p. 13. *Midaregami* was published under the author's maiden name, Hō (or Ōtori) Akiko.

44. *Ibid.*, pp. 1–4.

45. Kimata, *KTKH*, p. 144.

46. *Ibid.*, p. 145. The meeting of the two stars once a year, often alluded to in Chinese poetry, was celebrated in Japan as the Tanabata Festival.

47. Satake, *Zenshaku*, pp. 4–5.

48. *Ibid.*, p. 9. For a different translation, see Hiroaki Sato and Burton Watson, *From the Country of Eight Islands*, p. 431.

49. Koizumi Tōzō, *Kindai Tanka Shi*, p. 385. *Bungakkai*, the predecessor to *Myōjō* in publishing Romanticist works, did not carry tanka.

50. *Ibid.*, p. 386.

51. Kimata, *KTKH*, p. 213. Also, *Kitahara Hakushū*, p. 288.

52. There was some controversy as to whether the bird is in a cage inside the house, Wakayama Bokusui's opinion, or outside in the fields, as Kimata Osamu believed. See Kimata, *KTKH*, p. 214.

53. *Kitahara Hakushū, Miki Rofū, Hinatsu Kōnosuke*, pp. 204–06. The essay was written on May 27, 1910.

54. Ōishi Issaku, *Kindai Shūka Kanshō*, pp. 129–30. Also, *Kitahara Hakushū*, p. 288.

55. Yoshida Seiichi et al., *Gendai Tanka Hyōshaku*, pp. 169–70. Also, *Kitahara Hakushū*, p. 290.

56. Kimata, *KTKH*, pp. 216–17. Also, *Kitahara Hakushū*, p. 301.

57. Kimata, *KTKH*, p. 217. Also, *Kitahara Hakushū*, p. 291.

58. The relations between Hakushū and the *Araragi* poets, particularly Saitō Mokichi, were complicated. The *Araragi* poet Koizumi Chikashi (1886–1927) criticized Hakushū for not attempting to penetrate to the essence of the objects he described in his poetry, in the shasei manner, but Saitō Mokichi was clearly influenced by Hakushū. See Kimata, *KTKH*, pp. 214–15, and Kubota Masafumi, *Gendai Tanka no Sekai*, pp. 61–62.

59. Kimata Osamu, "Kitahara Hakushū," p. 423.

60. *Kitahara Hakushū, Miki Rofū*, p. 228.

61. See Yoshida, p. 175.

62. Kimata, *KTKH*, p. 228. Also, *Kitahara Hakushū*, p. 321.

63. Kimata, *KTKH*, p. 239. Also, *Kitahara Hakushū*, p. 389.

64. Kubota, pp. 64–65.

65. Kimata, *KTKH*, p. 494.

66. *Yosano Tekkan, Yosano Akiko, Wakayama Bokusui, Yoshii Isamu* (henceforth abbreviated *YYWY*), p. 203. Also, *Wakayama Bokusui Zenshū*, I, p. 41. See also Sato and Watson, p. 447.

67. Yoshida, *Gendai Tanka*, p. 151.

68. *YYWY*, p. 209.

69. Yoshida, *Gendai Tanka*, p. 154.

70. *YYWY*, p. 223. See also *Wakayama Bokusui Zenshū*, I, p. 249.

71. Ōishi, *Kindai Shūka*, p. 103.

72. *YYWY*, p. 226. Also, *Wakayama Bokusui Zenshū*, I, p. 163.

73. Bokusui composed in memory of Takuboku the undistinguished tanka: "A cherry tree blossomed at the bottom of the early summer cloudiness—and you have died, utterly exhausted!" Bokusui was present at Takuboku's deathbed. For the tanka, see *YYWY*, p. 235.

74. *Ibid.*, p. 38.

75. *Ibid.*, p. 242.

76. Maeda Tōru, "Maeda Yūgure," p. 319.

77. Kimata, *KTKH*, p. 470.

78. *Ibid.*, p. 471.

79. *Ibid.*

80. *Wakayama Bokusui, Kubota Utsubo, Toki Zemmaro, Maeda Yūgure*, p. 318.

81. *Ibid.*, p. 328.

82. *Ibid.*, p. 354.

83. Kubota, *Gendai Tanka no Sekai*, p. 39.

84. *Takuboku Zenshū*, IV, p. 253.

85. Kimata, *KTKH*, p. 516. The romanization here is Toki Zemmaro's; in selections from later collections the romanization is mine.

86. Quoted in Kimata, *KTKH*, p. 524.

87. *Ibid.*, p. 525.

88. This and the following poem are given in *Wakayama Bokusui, Kubota Utsubo*, p. 203.

89. *Ibid.*, p. 221.

90. The exact date of Takuboku's birth has been much debated, but the date given in the official records, Feb. 20, 1886, is probably right. See Iwaki Yukinori, "Takuboku Shusshō Nengappi ni kansuru Mondai."

91. Yoshimoto Takaaki, "Takuboku Shi ni tsuite," p. 222.

92. "Ichi Rikoshugisha to yūjin to no taiwa," in *Takuboku Zenshū*, IV, p. 284.

93. Takuboku, *Poems to Eat*, trans. Carl Sesar, pp. 15–16.

94. *Takuboku Zenshū*, IV, p. 209.

95. *Ibid.*, IV, p. 294.

96. *Ishikawa Takuboku Shū*, p. 57. The appeal of this poem is not in possible symbolic overtones but in the sentimental, although still valid, picture of a lonely child on a beach.

97. *Takuboku Zenshū*, IV, pp. 351–58.

98. Kubota Utsubo, "Takuboku no Uta," p. 63.

99. Takuboku, *Poems to Eat*, p. 146.

100. *Ibid.*, p. 77.

101. Donald Keene, *Landscapes and Portraits*, p. 167.

102. For a discussion of Shiki and the haiku, see pp. 92–106.

103. Robert H. Brower, "Masaoka Shiki and Tanka Reform," p. 387.

104. *Shiki Zenshū*, VII, p. 37; also, *Ishikawa Takuboku, Masaoka Shiki, Takahama Kyoshi*, pp. 295–301.

105. Brower, p. 395.

106. *Shiki Zenshū*, VII, p. 50; also, *Ishikawa Takuboku*, p. 311.

107. Shimma Shin-ichi, *Kindai Kadan Shi*, p. 59.

108. Koizumi Tōzō, *Kindai Tanka Shi*, p. 507.

109. *Ibid.*, p. 516.

110. *Shiki Zenshū*, VII, p. 238; also, *Ishikawa Takuboku*, p. 230.

111. *Shiki Zenshū*, VI, pp. 408–09; also, Ishikawa Takuboku, p. 255. See Janine Beichman, *Masaoka Shiki*, pp. 117–21, for a translation of and commentary on the ten tanka.

112. Saitō Mokichi, quoted by Brower, "Masaoka Shiki," p. 408.

113. Kitazumi Toshio, *Shaseiha Kajin no Kenkyū*, p. 32. Shiki later revised his opinion.

114. *Ibid.*, p. 64.

115. *Ibid.*, p. 74.

116. Kimata, *KTKH*, p. 10.

117. *Ibid.*, p. 274.

118. Kimata Osamu, *Kindai Tanka no Shiteki Tendai*, pp. 51–52.

119. Kitazumi, *Shaseiha Kajin*, pp. 213–14.

120. *Ibid.*, p. 220.

121. Yoshida, *Gendai Tanka*, p. 202.

122. Kitazumi, *Shaseiha Kajin*, p. 229.

123. *Ibid.*, p. 230.

124. Kubota, *Gendai Tanka no Sekai*, p. 119.

125. Yoshida, *Gendai Tanka*, p. 205.

126. *Ibid.*, p. 221.
127. The tanka of this collection were originally arranged in reverse chronological order, but in the 1921 revision Mokichi rearranged them in chronological order.
128. This and the following two tanka are in *Saitō Mokichi*, p. 73. For a complete translation of "Shinitamau Haha," see Amy Vladeck Heinrich, *Fragments of Rainbows*, pp. 158–66.
129. Kimata, *KTKH*, pp. 307–08.
130. The tanka and the following comment are from Kimata, *KTKH*, pp. 302–03.
131. *Ibid.*, pp. 304–05.
132. Mokichi explained *jissō kannyū* in terms of the German words *Anschauung* and *Hineinschauen*. See Kitazumi, p. 306.
133. Mokichi's identification of shasei with the principles of Chinese painting was apparently mistaken; the term as used by Chinese artists meant the depiction of birds and flowers in a realistic manner, without making the attempt to penetrate their essences. Another style of painting, called *sha'i*, attached greater importance to capturing the spirit of the object portrayed. Shiki was therefore correct in taking shasei to be a means of achieving fidelity to the object depicted. See Kitazumi, pp. 283–90.
134. The left-wing poet and critic Nakano Shigeharu was a devoted admirer of Mokichi's tanka, as he revealed in *Saitō Mokichi Nōto*.
135. Kitazumi, *Shaseiha Kajin*, p. 306.
136. *Ibid.*, p. 329.
137. *Saitō Mokichi*, p. 83.
138. The words *aka-aka to* recall Bashō's celebrated haiku: *Aka-aka to/ hi wa tsurenaku mo/ aki no kaze*. *Inochi narikeri* is a line of a celebrated waka by Saigyō: *Toshi takete/ mata koyubeshi to/ omoiki ya/ inochi narikeri/ Saya no Nakayama*. Text in *Saitō Mokichi*, p. 87.
139. Kimata, *KTKH*, p. 320.
140. *Ibid.*, p. 329.
141. Yoshida, p. 276.
142. Kawata Jun, *Kinoshita Toshiharu*, p. 50.
143. Yoshida, *Gendai Tanka*, p. 280.
144. Ueda Shigeo, *Aizu Yaichi*, p. 200.
145. Yoshida, *Gendai Tanka*, p. 308.
146. Details of Mokichi's charges are given in Iwata Tadashi, *Shaku Chōkū*, p. 42. The original article appeared in *Araragi* for May 1918.
147. Yoshida, *Gendai Tanka*, pp. 316–17. The poem was first printed in a magazine in 1937 but not included in a collection by Chōkū until *Tōyamahiko* (Distant Echoes, 1948).
148. See Ueda Miyoji, "Kaisetsu," to Ōoka Makoto, Tsukamoto Kunio and Nakai Hideo (ed.), *Gendai Tanka Taikei*, I, p. 333.
149. Iwata, *Shaku Chōkū*, p. 168.
150. *Ibid.*, p. 169.
151. *Ibid.*, p. 171.
152. Keene, *Landscapes and Portraits*, pp. 304–06.

153. Iwata, *Shaku Chōkū*, p. 169.
154. *Ibid.*, p. 204.
155. Ueda Miyoji, "Kaisetsu," p. 331.
156. Yoshida, *Gendai Tanka*, p. 319.
157. Ōoka Makoto et al., *Gendai Tanka Taikei*, VI, p. 330.
158. *Ibid.*, p. 332.
159. Yoshida, *Gendai Tanka*, p. 327.
160. Ueda Miyoji, *Sengo Tanka Shi*, pp. 31–32.
161. *Ibid.*, p. 47.
162. Yoshida, *Gendai Tanka*, p. 340.
163. Ōoka Makoto et al., *Gendai Tanka Taikei*, VI, p. 342.
164. Ueda Miyoji, *Gendai Kajin Ron*, p. 59.
165. Ōoka Makoto et al., *Gendai Tanka Taikei*, VII, p. 47.
166. *Ibid.*, p. 48.
167. *Ibid.*
168. Yukio Mishima and Geoffrey Bownas (ed.), *New Writing in Japan*, p. 24.
169. Ōoka Makoto et al., *Gendai Tanka Taikei*, VII, p. 146.
170. *Ibid.*, p. 173.

BIBLIOGRAPHY

Note: All Japanese books, except as otherwise noted, were published in Tokyo.

Beichman, Janine. *Masaoka Shiki*. Boston: Twayne, 1982.
Brower, Robert H. "Masaoka Shiki and Tanka Reform," in Donald H. Shively (ed.), *Tradition and Modernization in Japanese Culture*. Princeton, N.J.; Princeton University Press, 1971.
Gendai Tanka Zenshū, 15 vols. Chikuma Shobō, 1980–81.
Haga Tōru. *Midaregami no Keifu*. Bijutsu Kōron Sha, 1981.
Heinrich, Amy Vladeck. *Fragments of Rainbows*. Columbia University Press, 1983.
———. "My Mother Is Dying: Saitō Mokichi's 'Shinitamau Haha,' " in *Monumenta Nipponica*, XXXIII, No. 4, 1978.
Ishikawa Takuboku, in Nihon Bungaku Kenkyū Shiryō Sōsho series. Yūseidō, 1970.
Ishikawa Takuboku, Masaoka Shiki, Takahama Kyoshi, in Nihon no Bungaku series. Chūō Kōron Sha, 1974.
Ishikawa Takuboku Shū, in Nihon Kindai Bungaku Taikei series. Kadokawa Shoten, 1969.
Ishikawa, Takuboku. *A Handful of Sand*, trans. Shio Sakanishi. Boston: Marshall Jones, 1934.
———. *Poems to Eat*, trans. Carl Sesar. Kodansha International, 1966.
———. *The Romaji Diary*, trans. Donald Keene, in *Modern Japanese Literature*. New York: Grove Press, 1956.
Itō, Sachio. *Songs of a Cowherd*, trans. Shio Sakanishi. Boston: Marshall Jones, 1936.

Iwaki Yukinori. *Takuboku Hyōden.* Gakutōsha, 1976.

———. "Takuboku Shusshō Nengappi ni kansuru Mondai," in *Ishikawa Takuboku.*

Iwata Tadashi. *Shaku Chōkū.* Kinokuniya Shoten, 1972.

Iwatsu Motoo. *Tanka Koten to Kindai.* Waseda Daigaku Shuppanbu, 1959.

Kajiki Gō. *Saitō Mokichi.* Kinokuniya Shoten, 1970.

Kawata Jun. *Kinoshita Toshiharu.* Ondori Sha, 1957.

Keene, Donald. *Landscapes and Portraits.* Tokyo: Kodansha International, 1971.

Kimata Osamu. *Kindai Tanka no Kanshō to Hihyō.* Meiji Shoin, 1964.

———. *Kindai Tanka no Shiteki Tenkai.* Meiji Shoin, 1965.

———. *Shōwa Tanka Shi,* 4 vols., in Kōdansha Gakujutsu Bunko series. Kōdansha, 1978.

Kitahara Hakushū, in Nihon no Shiika series, Vol. IX. Chūō Kōron Sha, 1968.

Kitahara Hakushū, Miki Rofū, Hinatsu Kōnosuke, in Nihon Gendai Bungaku Zenshū series, Vol. XXXVIII. Kōdansha, 1963.

Kitazumi Toshio. *Shaseiha Kajin no Kenkyū.* Hōbunkan, 1955.

Kōhashi Kenji. *Yosano Tekkan.* Shinshōdō, 1943.

Koizumi Tōzō. *Kindai Tanka Shi.* Hakuyōsha, 1955.

———. *Meiji Karon Shiryō Shūsei.* Kyoto: Ritsumeikan Shuppanbu, 1940.

———(ed.). *Gendai Tanka Taikei,* 10 vols. Kawade Shobō, 1953.

Kubota Masafumi. *Gendai Tanka no Sekai.* Shinchōsha, 1972.

Kubota Utsubo. "Takuboku no Uta," in *Ishikawa Takuboku.*

———. *Yosano Akiko.* Ondori Sha, 1950.

Maeda Tōru. "Maeda Yūgure," in *Meiji no Kajin.*

Masaoka, Shiki. "A Drop of Ink," trans. Janine Beichman-Yamamoto, in *Monumenta Nipponica,* XXX, No. 3, 1975.

———. *Peonies Kana,* trans. Harold J. Isaacson. Tokyo: Weatherhill, 1972.

———. "The Verse Record of My Peonies," trans. Earl Miner, in *Japanese Poetic Diaries.* Berkeley: University of California Press, 1969.

Meiji no Kajin, edited by Meiji Jingū. Tanka Kenkyūsha, 1969.

Mishima, Yukio, and Geoffrey Bownas. *New Writing in Japan.* Harmondsworth, England: Penguin Books, 1972.

Myōjō. Facsimile edition. Kyoto: Rinsen Shoten, 1964.

Nakano Shigeharu. *Saitō Mokichi Nōto.* Chikuma Shobō, 1942.

Nakano Yoshikazu. *Shin Tanka no Rekishi.* Shōrinsha, 1967.

Nakashio Kiyoomi. "Ochiai Naobumi," in Waka Bungaku Kai (ed.), *Kindai no Kajin.* Ōfūsha, 1969.

Nihon Gendaishi Taikei, 10 vols. Kawade Shobō, 1954–55.

Nihon no Shiika series, 31 vols. Chūō Kōron Sha, 1967–69.

Nishimoto Akio. *Kitahara Hakushū no Kenkyū.* Shinseisha, 1965.

Ōishi Issaku. *Kindai Shūka Kanshō.* Ōfūsha, 1969.

Ōoka Makoto, Tsukamoto Kunio, and Nakai Hideo (eds.). *Gendai Tanka Taikei,* 12 vols. Kadokawa Shoten, 1972.

Saitō Mokichi, in Nihon no Shiika series, Vol. VIII. Chūō Kōron Sha, 1968.

Saitō Mokichi, in Nihon Shijin Zenshū series, Vol. X. Shinchōsha, 1967.

Satake Kazuhiko. *Zenshaku Midaregami Kenkyū.* Yūhōdō, 1957.

Sato, Hiroaki, and Burton Watson (eds.). *From the Country of Eight Islands.* Garden City, N.Y.: Doubleday, 1981.

Shaku Chōkū, Aizu Yaichi, Kubota Utsubo, Toki Zemmaro, in Nihon no Shiika series, Vol. XI, Chūō Kōron Sha, 1969.

Shiki Zenshū, 25 vols. Kōdansha, 1975–76.

Shimma Shin'ichi. *Kindai Kadan Shi.* Hanawa Shobō, 1968.

———. *Kindai Tankashi Ron.* Yūseidō, 1969.

Takata Namikichi. *Shimagi Akahiko no Kenkyū.* Iwanami Shoten, 1941.

Takuboku Zenshū, 8 vols. Chikuma Shobō, 1967–68.

Takuboku. *Poems to Eat,* trans. Carl Sesar. Tokyo: Kodansha International, 1966.

Ueda Miyoji. "Kaisetsu," in Ōoka Makoto et al., *Gendai Tanka Taikei,* I.

———. *Sengo Tanka Shi.* San'ichi Shobō, 1974.

Ueda Shigeo. *Aizu Yaichi.* Bungei Shunjū, 1969.

Wakayama Bokusui, Kubota Utsubo, Toki Zemmaro, Maeda Yūgure, in Nihon Shijin Zenshū series. Shinchōsha, 1968.

Yamamoto Kenkichi. *Shaku Chōkū.* Kadokawa Shoten, 1972.

Yosano, Akiko. *Tangled Hair,* trans. Sanford Goldstein and Seishi Shinoda. Lafayette, Ind.: Purdue University Press, 1971.

Yosano Tekkan, Yosano Akiko, Wakayama Bokusui, Yoshii Isamu, in Nihon no Shiika series, Vol. IV. Chūō Kōron Sha, 1969.

Yoshida Seiichi, Motobayashi Katsuo, and Iwaki Yukinori. *Gendai Tanka Hyōshaku.* Gakutōsha, 1966.

Yoshimoto Takaaki. "Takuboku Shi ni tsuite," in *Ishikawa Takuboku.*

THE MODERN HAIKU

HAIKU POETRY AT THE time of the Meiji Restoration was even more desperately in need of a revival than the tanka. Not a single poet of distinction was writing; indeed, it had been almost one hundred years since anyone had composed haiku of unmistakable literary worth. This does not mean that haiku was a dying art. Far from it: there were many schools and innumerable practitioners. Most poets followed the style of the "three masters of the Tempō era" (Hōrō, Sōkyū, and Baishitsu), delighting in the ingenuity associated with those poets. Superficial wit was the hallmark of men like Hozumi Eiki (1823–1904), who was admired for such verses as:

> *hototogisu*　　　　　The nightingales—
> *koi ni nenu yo no*　　When I was young it was love
> *wakakarishi* [1]　　　That kept me awake.

The point of this haiku is precisely the opposite of what a modern reader might suppose: the poet is congratulating himself on his present refined tastes that induce him to stay up late at night to hear the nightingales, contrasting this happy state with the folly of his youth, when love kept him from sleeping. Little emotion can be detected behind this or other poems by Eiki and his school. The cleverness of the conception intrigued rich gentlemen looking for some pastime to fill their idle hours, and the patronage of such men was earnestly sought by haiku masters, whose main source of income was the fees obtained for correcting haiku composed by their pupils. Soon after the Restoration, while conditions were still unsettled and unfavorable to leisurely pursuits, one haiku master hit on the idea of installing a large box outside his house into which busy pupils could deposit haiku along with a flat correction fee of eight *mon* each.[2]

The various haiku schools emphasized petty differences as crucial indications of superiority, and great attention was paid to lineage. Some masters acquired such titles as the sixth Kikaku, the fifth Sampū, and so on, though no one dared call himself the second Bashō. When one man succeeded to the "title" of the eighth Kikaku in 1887, it cost him three hundred yen, an enormous sum at the time.[3] Ceremonies were frequently held in honor of Bashō, less out of piety than out of the desire to reaffirm the special connections of a particular school with the great Master.

Regular monthly meetings of each haiku school were held at which the haiku of members were judged. These were known as *tsukinami* ("monthly"). The term at first merely designated the regular nature of the gatherings, but tsukinami came to be used by Masaoka Shiki as a term of abuse, in denigration of the stale verses composed at such sessions.

The turbulent events of the Meiji Restoration did little to ruffle the composure of haiku poets. The battle at Ueno between the government forces and the adherents of the shogunate, the first disturbance of the peace of Edo for three hundred years, inspired this haiku by Torigoe Tōsai (1803–1890):

mimi tojite	I will shut my ears
hana wo kokoro ni	And, thinking only of blossoms,
hirune kana [4]	Enjoy my nap.

Perhaps the poet intended to express defiance at the external events that impinged on his tranquil observation of nature, but the false front of an estheticism that transcended vulgar realities is not appealing. A haiku by Hozumi Eiki, written about the same time, bears the title "On Fleeing the Battlefield at Ueno":

chi wo nagasu	Rain washes away
ame ya orifushi	The blood: just at that moment
hototogisu [5]	A nightingale sings.

The *hototogisu* (rendered here as "nightingale") was described in legends as having coughed blood; that no doubt was why Eiki mentioned the bird in his sanguinary poem.

On the whole, however, the haiku poetry composed immediately after the Restoration was serenely indifferent to the many changes. The first event to arouse a marked reaction was the decree at the end of 1872 proclaiming the adoption of the solar calendar beginning on January 1, 1873. Of all varieties of Japanese poetry the haiku was most closely associated with the seasons; a haiku without a seasonal word was contemptuously dismissed as being "miscellaneous." The seasonal words used by Bashō had been constantly expanded by later poets, and in 1803 the novelist Bakin classified some 2,600 of them.[6] However, the adoption of the solar calendar upset all the old associations: New Year no longer occurred at the beginning of spring but in the dead of winter, and the Tanabata Festival brought no first breath of autumn wind when it was celebrated in the middle of July. In 1874 a progressive haiku master compiled a new list of seasonal words, shifting their calendar associations by one month; for example, spring now began in February, rather than at New Year. New seasonal words were coined to evoke the realities of life in modern Japan, such as the first day of school, January 18.

The haiku poets of the day, occupied with such petty matters, were not aware that their art had become stagnant and even meaningless. They rejoiced in the undiminished number of pupils and in the respect that they still commanded, despite the change of regime. Their good opinion of themselves was confirmed in 1873 when the Ministry of Religious Instruction (*Kyōbushō*) appointed four haiku masters as special instructors, charged with identifying haiku poetry with the policies of the Meiji government.[7] Bashō was established as a legitimate object of divine worship in 1879, and elaborate commentaries on his haiku demonstrated that he had preached filial piety and the other Confucian virtues.[8] The government obviously wished to assert traditional Japanese values at a time when a flood of Western ideas had swept over the country, threatening the old morality. Haiku poets were urged especially to embody in their works "respect for the gods and love of country," to clarify "the principles of Heaven and the Way of man," and to inculcate "obedience to the will of the Court under the emperor."[9] They responded that this was indeed their deepest desire, and asserted that one could count on the fingers of both hands the number of men who had displayed as profound devotion to the gods, the emperor, and the country as Bashō in his haiku on the ancient pond. This may be why the government in 1885 recognized the "Old Pond Church" (Furuike Kyōkai) as a religious body, affiliated with the Bashō sect of Shintō.[10]

Despite the official protection, the haiku came under sharp attack from the advocates of modern poetry (shintaishi), who expressed their doubts that short poems could adequately treat the complexities of modern life. For such reformers as Tsubouchi Shōyō the haiku was merely the pastime of dilettantes who praised flowers and the moon because they had nothing to say about the serious matters of life. Such criticism, inspired by Western theories of literature, would not have troubled haiku poets of the past because it never occurred to them that the haiku was supposed to fulfill the lofty purposes of "literature." The first to assign the haiku this function, hitherto restricted to the Chinese classics and the waka in the imperial anthologies, was one Mori Sankei who declared in 1890, "Haikai is a form of literature and of art. It must therefore manifest a noble spirit and lofty thought."[11] But the same writer recognized that few contemporary haiku poets were capable of living up to this prescription. Only if poets abandoned the practice of composing on prescribed topics that often bore no relation to their own emotions would the haiku be able to hold its own against the new shintaishi and revive the glory of native poetic traditions.[12]

Suzuki Shōkō was perhaps the first critic to compare the distinctive features of the shintaishi and haiku. The shintaishi, being of Western origins, shared the qualities of Western poetry, which seeks to exhaust every emotion, leaving nothing to the imagination. Moreover, he continued, "We Japanese seem to love nature more than artifice. The Europeans and Americans desire perfection, but we Japanese seem to prefer things that have not yet attained this state. The Europeans and Americans love bustle, but we Japanese prefer quiet." [13] He was convinced that the shintaishi could not long prosper because it was basically alien to Japanese tastes. This affirmation of the superiority of a native literary form to one derived from Europe was in keeping with the "Japanism" that became increasingly evident after 1890. Although the future prosperity of the shintaishi showed that Suzuki Shōkō's prognostication of doom was mistaken, it is noteworthy that a reaction in favor of the haiku had taken place, even though there were no outstanding poets who could by their work demonstrate that the haiku was still a viable literary form.

MASAOKA SHIKI (1867-1902)

The tentative cries for reform of the haiku made by such men as Suzuki Shōkō called attention to the problems involved, but these efforts paled to insignificance beside the achievement of Masaoka Shiki who almost singlehandedly restored the haiku to an important place in Japanese poetry after first subjecting it to devastating attacks. Katō Shūson (b. 1905) declared that there had been two great "waves" in the history of haiku, represented by Bashō and Shiki, and that no modern practitioners could ignore either man.[14]

Shiki's first important statement of his view on haiku was presented in a series of articles published in 1892 under the title *Dassai Shooku Haiwa* (Talks on Haiku from the Otter's Study).[15] He opened with a brief recapitulation of the history of haikai poetry. This section contains few surprises, but his account picks up interest when he reaches his predictions of the future of haiku. He began, characteristically in a man of the modern age, with a reference to a new science, mathematics: "Present-day scholars who have studied mathematics say that the number of possible waka, haiku and similar forms of Japanese poetry is unquestionably limited, as one can easily calculate from the number of permutations possible with a mere twenty or thirty syllables. In other words, the waka (generally called the tanka) and the haiku must sooner or later reach their limits. We have already reached the point where it is quite impossible to compose a wholly original poem." Shiki deplored the ignorance of those who supposed (out of ignorance of science) that it would always be possible to compose new tanka and haiku. "In fact, both the tanka and the haiku are already fast approaching their death throes." The innumerable thousands upon thousands of tanka and haiku composed since ancient times all seem different on first glance, but under careful examination it becomes apparent how many are alike. Pupils plagiarize their teachers, and men of later generations plagiarize their predecessors. A man who can convert the stone of old poems into the jade of new ones is acclaimed as a master poet, even though he never presents an original idea.

> It is true that the individual poets bear the guilt for the mediocrity of the poetry composed in later times, but the narrowness of the range of the tanka or haiku must also be a factor. People ask how much longer the life of the tanka and haiku has to run. I reply that although no one can predict, of course, when it will become impossible to compose any more poems in these forms, the haiku is already more or less exhausted. Even if one grants that it still maintains a spark of life, surely its end must come during the Meiji era. The tanka has more syllables than the haiku and therefore, speaking in mathematical terms, the possible number of permutations greatly exceeds that of the haiku; but in practice only elegant words can be used in the tanka, and their number is so extremely limited that the range is even narrower than for the haiku. That is why I believe that the tanka was more or less exhausted even before the Meiji era began.[16]

Shiki's simplistic calculation of the potential number of tanka and haiku in terms of permutations of the seventeen or thirty-one syllables was not really essential to his judgment that the tanka was already exhausted and the haiku would certainly be dead before long. This statement was far more sweeping than any previous attack on traditional Japanese poetry. Shiki did not merely point out the inadequacies of traditional poetry to express the life of the new age, but insisted that it could no longer fulfill any literary function. He recognized that "contemporary affairs and things are totally unlike those of the past." Not only had swords given way to guns, but the peculiar features of Japanese society were fast vanishing. Formerly people rode or walked according to their station in life, but now commoners rode in the same vehicles as noblemen. The waka, Shiki asserted, was totally unable to respond to this changed situation because of its rigorous insistence on purity of diction, and the haiku, though it did not absolutely reject new words, certainly did not welcome them.[17]

Shiki followed this challenging section of *Talks on Haiku* with a rather bland discussion of Bashō's disciples and of the birds and plants most commonly mentioned in Japanese poetry. Only when he turned his attention to a book on haikai poetry by a contemporary poet did he let loose with his familiar sarcasm in an attack on the author's opinions on the grammar of the haiku. "The author urges poets to adopt the ancient grammar in writing haiku today, but I would like to ask him one question: When he speaks of ancient grammar, to which age does he refer? Remote antiquity? The Nara period? The Heian period? Or perhaps the Muromachi period? Whatever age he may have in mind, why must we cling to the grammar of the past? Is grammar incapable of changing with the times?"[18] Shiki was especially distressed by the examples of modern haiku given by the author: "My first reaction to this book was one of weariness and boredom, but the extreme ineptness and superficiality of the haiku given as examples finally made me want to vomit."[19] Such intemperance must have startled readers, but there can be no doubting the genuineness of Shiki's disgust.

On the whole Shiki was pessimistic about the future of the haiku, but his very expressions of despair suggested that he did not in fact consider the haiku beyond redemption. At first he confined his attacks to the tsukinami poets of recent times, but in a series of articles published in 1893 in the newspaper *Nippon* (which he joined in 1892 after failing his examinations at Tokyo University) he chose a new subject, the hitherto sacred poetry of Bashō himself. By Japanese reckoning 1893 marked the two-hundredth anniversary of the death of Bashō. Irritation over the excessive adulation offered the Master at innumerable celebrations may have inspired Shiki to produce in *Bashō Zatsudan* (Chats on Bashō) what was probably the harshest criticism ever directed at the Saint of Haiku. Shiki explained the worship of Bashō in terms of the popular appeal of his poetry, which had endeared him to the public at large, but questioned whether such adulation was a true indication of its literary worth. From these doubts he passed to an examination of what he labeled Bashō's "bad poems," declaring his intention of analyzing Bashō as a literary figure rather than as the object of cult worship. Even though he attacked specific haiku, he paid Bashō the indirect tribute of referring to his works as literature (*bungaku*), using a term that was normally reserved for compositions in Chinese and similarly elevated forms of writing.

Shiki opened his discussion of the "bad poems" with a bombshell: "I would like to state at the outset my judgment that the majority of Bashō's haiku are bad or even doggerel, and not more than a tenth can be called first-rate. Even barely passable verses are as rare as morning stars." [20] He listed eleven haiku by Bashō that were generally acclaimed as masterpieces and analyzed each. Only the first, the celebrated haiku on the frog jumping into the pond, elicited his praise; he called it "the most necessary verse in the history of haiku," a poem that exists on a plane of its own, without reference to the conventional considerations of good or bad. Apart from its historical significance as the work that heralded Bashō's characteristic style, it was highly exceptional in its unadorned expression, which defied the common preference for ingenuity and decoration.

Shiki's praise of the frog poem bore no resemblance to the normal inarticulate cries of wonder on the part of Bashō's devotees who, if asked the meaning of the poem, would answer that it was a mystery, incommunicable in speech. His opinions had the precision associated with Western-oriented scholars: Bashō, he explained, was able, thanks to the use of suggestion, to convey the silence of the ancient pond, remote from the city and the clamor of men's voices, without once mentioning it.[21] Shiki believed that the poem, like the Zen adept's calling a willow green and a flower red, described as exactly as possible an actual experience. The poem, he was sure, had flashed into Bashō's head in the form of the second and third lines: "A frog jumps in/ The sound of the water." There was no statement of subjective impressions, no prolongation of the experience either spatially or temporally. Bashō later added the first line, "The ancient pond," merely in order to establish the setting.

Shiki's treatment of the other ten haiku by Bashō was much harsher. He declared that the famous poem on the mallow-flower by the road (*Michinobe no . . .*) was popular only because of the didactic interpretation as a warning against standing out from the crowd. He rejected the praise of other commentators for the melody of the poem and their claims that no other plant could be substituted for the mallow-flower, even giving two modified versions of the haiku, which he considered superior to Bashō's original. He concluded, "In short, this verse as literature ranks at the very bottom." [22] Other famous poems by Bashō were denounced as plagiarism or close adaptations of earlier haiku, and Shiki was especially irritated by any display of ingenuity. His final judgment was that Bashō's poetry, all in all, was no more than a junk heap of bad and good works indiscriminately thrown together.

Shiki, however, denied that he thought Bashō's poetry was worthless; on the contrary, his good haiku possessed the qualities most lacking in Japanese literature: masculinity and grandeur. Poetry embodying these qualities is found in the *Manyōshū* and even earlier works, but with the exception of Minamoto Sanetomo, no poet of later times possessed them. The haiku of the Teitoku and Danrin schools had reeked so much of stale vulgarities as to be unworthy of the name of literature; Bashō's poetry was the first in centuries to display virility and amplitude.[23]

Shiki's praise of Bashō, no less than his criticism, revealed that he had already formed his ideals of poetry. His later advocacy of the waka of Sanetomo, Hiraga Motoyoshi, and other "masculine" poets exactly corresponded to what he praised in Bashō. Conversely, his dislike of the feminine qualities in Japanese literature reflected his samurai background and his basically unromantic nature. On occasion, it is true, he admired poetry in a romantic vein, but his greatest enthusiasm was reserved for the *Manyōshū* and for poets working in the *Manyōshū* traditions.

By this time Shiki was thoroughly contemptuous of the "three masters of the Tempō era" and poets of their line, whom he characterized as frogs in a well, unable to discern the great sea. As yet he had not discovered Buson, and his praise for Bashō, though grudging, represented the limit of his admiration for haiku. Even so, when it came to Bashō's linked verse (*haikai no renga*) he declared categorically, "The hokku is literature. *Haikai no renga* is not literature. That is why I have not discussed it." [24] He believed that linked verse depended on nonliterary elements, especially shifts in subject, for its effects, and that poets had not conceived of it in terms of a literary whole. Finally, Shiki, discussing Chinese influences on Bashō, contended that he was the first Japanese writer to have completely absorbed such influences.[25]

This essay on Bashō exudes the brashness of youth, and no one could assent to all of Shiki's judgments, but even his mistakes effectively awakened people from complacent admiration for the Master. Bashō could no longer be taken for granted as the incarnation of the spirit of the haiku; his defenders would have to prove his excellence.

Shiki's writings between 1894 and 1896 revealed a steadily deepening admiration for Buson. A little earlier (in 1893) he had merely mentioned Buson among the poets of the late eighteenth-century, and apparently considered Ōshima Ryōta to be the most provocative poet of that period,[26] but he soon changed his mind and declared that Buson was the most distinguished of the "five great poets" of the era. He now wrote slightingly of Ryōta's vulgarity and coarse tone.[27] So pronounced an about-face indicated that Shiki was still not settled in his critical views, despite the confidence of his tone, but he was learning his trade rapidly; after praising Buson in 1894 as the greatest haiku poet after Bashō, he never afterward wavered in this opinion. Other essays of the period praised Buson for his pictorial qualities, his nostalgia for the past, and his ability to recount a story in a bare seventeen syllables. The climax of his writings on Buson came in the long essay "Haijin Buson" (Buson the Haiku Poet, 1896). It opened with a reiteration of Shiki's doubts concerning the divinity of Bashō, the Saint of Haiku. He complained that Buson was neglected: "The haiku of Buson are the equal of Bashō's and in some respects superior. He has failed to win the fame due him mainly because his poetry is not for the masses, and because the haiku poets after Buson were ignorant and lacking in discrimination." [28]

In the section on the "positive beauty" he found in Buson's haiku, Shiki declared, "In general, oriental art and literature tend toward negative beauty, occidental art and literature toward positive beauty." However, in both Orient and Occident negative beauty was typical of the past and only later gave way to positive beauty. Bashō's art, he insisted, was essentially negative, though he wrote some haiku of grandeur and sublimity. Most of Bashō's successors considered negative beauty to be the only kind, and rejected sensual charm, vivacity or originality as aberrations of expression, much as devotees of oriental art decried Western art as vulgar. Buson, by contrast, was a poet of positive beauty, and summer, the most "positive" of the four seasons, was the time of year he loved best. Bashō rarely wrote about peonies, a voluptuous summer flower, but Buson composed no fewer than twenty haiku on the subject, including several masterpieces. "Young leaves," another "positive" summer subject, appeared in Bashō's haiku merely as seasonal appurtenances, but Buson wrote ten haiku about them, capturing their particular brilliance.[29]

Shiki next discussed Buson's pictorial qualities. Shiki's interest in this subject was aroused by his meeting in 1894 with the Western-style painter Nakamura Fusetsu (1866–1943), from whom he learned about the principle of shasei (copying life). At first Shiki showed not the least appreciation of Western paintings, but under Fusetsu's guidance he learned to distinguish the qualities of Japanese and Western art. After six months of conversations with Fusetsu he came to believe that haiku poetry and painting were in essence identical arts.[30] The aspect of Fusetsu's theory of art that most powerfully impressed Shiki was the central importance he gave to shasei in reproducing sights and experiences. Shiki first attempted to incorporate shasei in his haiku when he went on an excursion in August 1894 with Fusetsu and the haiku poet Naitō Meisetsu (1847–1926). He composed various poems, including

> *hatsuaki no*
> *ishidan takashi*
> *sugi kodachi*

> The stone flight of steps
> Looms high in early autumn
> Amidst the cedars.

Fusetsu commented that such a poem would be easy to convert into a painting.[31]

Shiki later recalled that his reading of *The Essence of the Novel* by Tsubouchi Shōyō had opened his eyes to realism (*shajitsu*) in art and to copying nature (*mosha*). Futabatei Shimei's *The Drifting Cloud* had also taught him "what realism was." [32] By

1897 his criticism of haiku came to be expressed largely in terms of effectiveness in producing clear, pictorial impressions. He admired especially the style of Kawahigashi Hekigotō (1873–1937), declaring that each haiku by Hekigotō was "exactly like a small painting in the shasei style." [33]

Shiki was aware of the danger of apparent artlessness inherent in the shasei style, but even the most realistic work involved selection, and selection itself was an art. Another danger, that a work of art might give pleasure solely because it exactly resembled the object portrayed, was less acute in the case of shasei poetry than of shasei painting, but verisimilitude was not to be scorned. An accurate depiction of flowers in the shasei style should arouse an even stronger reaction than the flowers themselves, because the artist has arranged them and eliminated extraneous surroundings. It is true that the poetic overtones tend to disappear when clarity of expression is the chief objective, but the overtones are no more essential to a haiku than the impressions directly produced; both partake of beauty, and it is impossible to say which is more important.[34]

Shiki believed that haiku poetry was closest of all literary forms to paintings. In other forms of poetry the emphasis is on time, rather than on space, but the haiku is too brief to go beyond the present moment, and must therefore evoke space instead.

Shiki's interpretation of the meaning of shasei changed over the years, especially after he had come to appreciate the Chinese ideal of *heitan* (plainness and blandness), but he continued to relate poetry to painting. In 1892 Shiki had advocated the "positive beauty" of Western art, but he admitted in *Wa ga Haiku* (My Haiku, 1896) that he had changed his mind: "A man who formerly loved the extremely unusual and the grandiose has come to love plainness and blandness instead. This surely must indicate that he has reached a state at which his emotions have developed sufficiently for him to make more subtle distinctions." [35] Shiki's interest in heitan beauty may have been stimulated by changes in the prevalent style of oil painting. In 1893 Kuroda Seiki (1866–1924), an outstanding painter in the Western style, returned from Paris and introduced to the Japanese a new style, the *plein air* manner of Raphaël Collin (1850–1916), a minor French artist under whom many Japanese painters studied. At first Shiki was critical, finding the style too artless to depict the magnificent, the bold, or the profoundly tranquil,[36] but by 1899 he was comparing the new Meiji haiku to *plein air* paintings.[37] A haiku written in this style might seem bland and unprovocative, but the apparent blandness was merely the surface under which lay hidden deep flavors that could be appreciated only after careful savoring. By 1902 he stated, "Shasei is heitan." [38] In his last years Shiki, confined to his sickbed, had little direct contact with nature, and perhaps that was why he came to think of shasei not as a means of depicting nature in the raw but as the heitan surface beneath which the poet's deepest emotions could be glimpsed.[39]

Shiki's activities as a critic earned for him the reputation of having been the founder of modern haiku. He occupied a similar position with respect to the modern tanka too, though this form was not so close to him as the haiku; his first and last poetic impulses were expressed in the haiku. He was by nature an unusually practical and intellectual poet, despite his repeated insistence on simplicity and his rejection of "intellectualization." His training in the Confucian classics as a young man probably accounted for this strong element of rationalism, which went better with the haiku than the more lyric tanka. He was at times able to approach the "positive beauty" he admired in Buson, but rarely the loftier realm of Bashō's poetry.

Shiki's first haiku of distinction was composed in 1890, the year after he coughed blood and took the name "Shiki." [40] During the course of his short life he composed over eighteen thousand haiku, as well as many tanka and other varieties of poetry.[41] The early haiku are occasionally of interest, whether because of a perception of nature or a glimpse of his personal life, but only after his meeting with Nakamura Fusetsu in 1894 and his adoption of shasei as his guiding principle did his haiku acquire maturity. In the summer of 1894, in between jobs, he spent his days wandering in the suburbs, notebook in hand, composing haiku in the shasei manner. According to his own account, it was then that he first came to make the shasei techniques a natural part of his expression, as in:

> *hikuku tobu*
> *aze no inago ya*
> *hi no yowari* [42]

See how low it flies,
That locust on the paddy walk—
The sunshine weakens.

It is autumn. The rice has been harvested, and the locust, deprived of a place of concealment in the paddy field, rests on the raised path. At Shiki's approach it flies up, but so weakly it does not rise very high. The sunshine has also lost its summer intensity. Shiki's close observation of the locust is saved from triviality (always a danger in shasei haiku) by his perception that not only the locust but the sun itself has weakened.

In 1895 Shiki volunteered as a war correspondent. He should have realized that his delicate health would be unequal to the strain, but he persuaded himself that life would not be worth living unless he could see service at the front in China. His stay there (mainly at Chin-chou) lasted little more than a month, but the poetry he composed was important to the development of his shasei style; he described unfamiliar scenes with accuracy and evocativeness:

nagaki hi ya	The long days—
roba wo oiyuku	The shadow of a lash
muchi no kage [43]	Chases a donkey.

Shiki captured the spaciousness of the Chinese landscape with the long shadows of a spring day stretching into the distance. Other haiku composed in China were more closely associated with the warfare; one described the sickening sight of corpses strewn around a gun emplacement, another the fewness of the swallows after a battle had ended.[44] Shiki also wrote some tanka and poems in Chinese on the same experiences, evidence of how deeply they had affected him. None of these poems ranks among Shiki's major poems, but travel abroad extended the range of his shasei expression.

On the ship returning to Japan, Shiki had a violent bout of coughing blood apparently brought on by seeing a shark. When the ship reached port six days later Shiki was carried ashore and taken to a hospital in Kobe in a critical state. His family rushed to his bedside from Tokyo, to be present at his last moments, but he miraculously recovered. By autumn he was traveling again, to his old home in Matsuyama and to Nara, where he composed a famous verse:

kaki kueba	As I eat a persimmon
kane ga naru nari	I hear the temple bell toll:
Hōryūji [45]	Hōryūji.

No connection is stated between the persimmon and the sound of the temple bell, though commentators have unconvincingly equated the coldness of the persimmon and the sound; but the atmosphere of the quiet village by the ancient temple is effectively conveyed. The poem bears the headnote "Resting at a teashop at the Hōryūji," but the poem was originally composed at the Tōdaiji; Shiki changed the name of the temple, finding that the atmosphere of the Hōryūji more exactly corresponded to what he had in mind when he composed the haiku than the somewhat noisier surroundings of the Tōdaiji. Such a change suggests how much more than bare observation was involved in creating a successful haiku in the shasei style.

After returning to Tokyo in October 1895, Shiki again took up his life as a poet and critic. In December he formally asked his disciple Takahama Kyoshi (1874–1959) to become his successor. A few months earlier, while lying in the hospital and near death, he had made the same proposal without eliciting a response, but this time Kyoshi unambiguously refused.[46] Shiki was bitterly disappointed, afraid that he would die without leaving a literary posterity. He nevertheless continued until the time of his death in 1902 to lead an exceedingly busy life. Even when confined to his sickbed he received a steady stream of visitors and kept up literary activities that might have exhausted someone in perfect health. He published two extensive diaries and wrote a third for his private reference; these are our best sources of information on the thoughts and emotions of a man who rarely expressed himself overtly in his poetry.

As the diaries reveal, Shiki was definitely a man of the new era. He was interested in all the latest importations and did not hesitate to mention them in his poetry:

akikaze ni	Spilling over
koborete akashi	In the spring breeze, how red—
hamigakiko	My tooth powder!

Kyoshi wrote of this poem, "At the time what interested us most was that Shiki had been able to compose a haiku on anything so commonplace as tooth powder. It provided us with a strong stimulus at a time when shasei was still in its infancy." [47]

More and more frequently Shiki's haiku alluded to his illness, as in this verse written late in 1896:

Snow When I Was Sick

ikutabi mo	Again and again
yuki no fukasa wo	I asked the others how much
tazunekeri	Snow had fallen.

Behind the apparently straightforward statement lies the unspoken anguish of the man who cannot leave his sickbed even to step into the garden and measure the snowfall for himself. Yamamoto Kenkichi wrote of this haiku: "In such sickbed compositions Shiki was already exploring a unique poetic domain which was not that of either Bashō or Buson. . . . His style, intentionally borrowed from Buson's ever since discovering Buson's haiku in 1893, came in this year to possess at last individuality of expression." [48]

When Shiki became immobile toward the end of 1896 his tiny garden became virtually his only source of poetic inspiration. The love he expressed for the flowers he could glimpse from his bed was quite extraordinary; his life seemed to have become one with the plants. "The objects he saw were so restricted in numbers that his eyes truly began to see. Shiki's shasei reached its heights at this point." [49] Other men in Shiki's predicament might have yielded to self-pity, but his samurai training made him shun overt expressions of weakness in his poetry.[50]

Even Shiki's impromptu poems were often tinged with deep pathos because of the implicit circumstances of his illness. Some of them, written in the impersonal shasei style, were for long overlooked because their implications were not detected. The following haiku, ignored by most professional haiku critics for years, is now often acclaimed as his masterpiece:

keitō no	Cockscomb—
jūshigo hon mo	I'm sure there are at least
arinu beshi	Fourteen or fifteen stalks.

This verse unfortunately loses everything in translation, but even the original excited derisive remarks from various poets who, questioning the absoluteness of its terms, made such substitutions as "seven or eight stalks" or "withered chrysanthemums" for "cockscomb." [51] One critic defied anyone to define the differences between seven or eight stalks and fourteen or fifteen stalks; but, as Yamamoto Kenkichi pointed out, the sound of the words is important, and anyone who argues exclusively on the basis of meaning does not understand the nature of poetry. The slight differences in shading (rather than of meaning) given the haiku by the grammatical particles and verb endings also communicate overtones to a sensitive Japanese reader that cannot be analyzed in translation. Yamamoto wrote:

> Every masterpiece is a flower on a precipice, to be picked only with spiritual danger. The risk is life itself. It is too much to hope every poetry-lover will unfailingly grasp all subtleties of the creative act, but no artistic masterpiece exists without the danger of its being misunderstood. It is a tremendous assertion for the poet to have said, "There must be fourteen or fifteen stalks of cockscomb." After we read this poem we cannot imagine the possibility there could have been more or fewer cockscomb than fourteen or fifteen.[52]

The first discoverer of this poem was Nagatsuka Takashi, a disciple of Shiki's in tanka rather than haiku, who was struck by the profound impression it conveyed of Shiki's emotions as he gazed from his bed at the cockscomb in his garden.[53] Shiki, watching the proudly erect plants, wishes he could be like them, though he knows that his bedridden life is fast ebbing away. Probably Shiki composed the haiku easily, even artlessly, as he looked at the garden, unaware that he had created a masterpiece of haiku; but the depth of his feelings and his skill at shasei composition revealed themselves in a work that was uniquely his own.

Shiki's last three haiku, written the day before his death on September 19, 1902, have been acclaimed by other critics as his finest poems. Unfortunately again, they lose much in translation. The first and perhaps most effective was:

hechima saite	The sponge-gourd has flowered!
tan no tsumarishi	Look at the Buddha
hotoke kana [54]	Choked with phlegm.

Sap from the sponge-gourd (*hechima*) was used as a medicine to stop coughs or break up phlegm, but his family had been too busy ministering to the other symptoms of Shiki's final illness to remember to collect the sap on the night of the fifteenth, as prescribed. Now the vine is in flower. Shiki, sensing that nothing can cure him or even alleviate his pain, sees himself objectively (and even with a touch of haikai humor) as a Buddha-to-be choking on his phlegm.

Shiki is today remembered above all as a critic, a pioneer in the revival of both haiku and tanka who wrote at a time when it seemed most unlikely traditional poetry could survive in the complex new world of Meiji Japan. His harsh criticism of linked verse all but killed this art, and if he had continued to attack haiku and tanka he might well have obtained the same results. It is true that his sharp criticism of Bashō did little to diminish the Master's reputation, but that may have been because Shiki's criticism of Bashō was always tempered with expressions of admiration. He borrowed much from Buson, but remained a totally different poet, never taking on Buson's romanticism or his absorption with the Heian past. His best haiku are given their particular coloration by his samurai stoicism and his suffering. Few are truly memorable, but he stands nevertheless at the head of the twentieth-century revival of the haiku.

Among Shiki's friends two deserve special mention as haiku poets, Naitō Meisetsu and Natsume Sōseki. Meisetsu, an official of the Matsumae clan, worked at the Ministry of Education in Tokyo after the dissolution of the clans and also served as the director of the residence of the former clan. In 1887, while Shiki was living at this residence, he and Meisetsu became acquainted. Shiki influenced Meisetsu, twenty years his senior, into taking up haiku in 1892. Meisetsu was temperamentally a bunjin of the old style, genially dabbling in poetry without deeply committing himself.[55] Sōseki and Shiki met in 1888 when they became classmates in Tokyo. Shiki at first guided Sōseki in Chinese poetry, but he later transmitted to Sōseki his interest in haiku. Sōseki's early haiku were often comic, but his best haiku were composed during a short period in 1910 when he was so seriously afflicted by a stomach complaint that he believed death was near; the presence of death gave his poetry a new intensity. Perhaps Sōseki's most affecting haiku, at least in translation, bears the title, "Hearing in London the News of Shiki's Death":

kiri ki naru	See how it hovers
ichi ni ugoku ya	In these streets of yellow fog,
kagebōshi [56]	A human shadow.

A figure seen wandering in the fog suggests to the poet his dead friend making his way to the Yellow Springs of the afterworld.

SHIKI'S SENIOR DISCIPLES, HEKIGOTŌ AND KYOSHI

After Shiki's death two disciples, Kawahigashi Hekigotō (1873–1937) and Takahama Kyoshi (1874–1959), contended for leadership in the world of haiku. Both men, like Shiki, came from samurai families in Matsuyama. Hekigotō was the first to meet Shiki. As a boy he had not been much interested in haiku, but in 1888 his brother wrote him from Tokyo urging him to meet Shiki, who knew all about the fascinating new sport called baseball. He had given Shiki a bat and ball to take to the boy when he returned to Matsuyama.[57] Shiki was delighted to explain baseball to Hekigotō, and also took the occasion to initiate him into haiku. Some verses written by Hekigotō in 1890 bear Shiki's corrections.

In 1891 Hekigotō left middle school in Matsuyama to pursue his studies in Tokyo. He spent several months preparing for high school entrance examinations, but failed. Just about this time a letter arrived from his classmate and close friend, Takahama Kyoshi, asking for an introduction to Shiki. That summer Shiki and Hekigotō both returned to Matsuyama, and with Kyoshi threw themselves into haiku composition with such energy as to establish Matsuyama as the center of the new haiku. Hekigotō's compositions improved rapidly, and he even became known as a boy prodigy. At the time Shiki still hoped to write novels, but a story he published in 1892 was so severely criticized by Kōda Rohan that he abandoned his hopes. His disciples Hekigotō and Kyoshi in later years would surpass Shiki as writers of fiction, but their lasting reputations were also to be in haiku.

In 1893 Hekigotō and Kyoshi entered the Third High School in Kyoto. Soon afterward Hekigotō published an article in a school magazine predicting the imminent demise of the haiku, basing his arguments on the same theory of permutation that Shiki had used the year before. At the time his ambition was to become a great man of letters, and haiku seemed to be no more than a diversion; it did not occur to him, in view of his precocious and effortless success, that it required intensive study to become a master.[58] Shiki at first singled out Hekigotō's haiku for special praise, but when the young man refused to study haiku seriously, Shiki criticized him sharply: "He has not shown the slightest improvement since the spring of 1894. A precocious prodigy has turned into a mediocrity." [59]

Despite the harshness of these remarks, Shiki was still amicably disposed toward Hekigotō, though his samurai patience was tried by reports that reached him that Hekigotō and Kyoshi, then sharing a room, were indulging in liquor and prostitutes. When Shiki left for China in 1895 he placed Hekigotō in charge of the selection of poems for the haiku column of the *Nippon Shimbun*, a signal honor for a young man just turned twenty-one.

A split developed in 1897 between Hekigotō and Kyoshi, who had been the closest of friends. Hekigotō had spent a month in the hospital with smallpox, and when he was released he learned that the young lady of the lodging house, previously his sweetheart, had shifted her affections to Kyoshi, who married the girl in June. The shock induced Hekigotō to work more seriously at his haiku. In October 1897 he became the haiku critic for the newly founded magazine *Hototogisu*.[60]

In 1899 Shiki, reviewing haiku activity during the previous year, traced with satisfaction the spread of the Nippon-style, as his school was known (from the *Nippon Shimbun*). He praised

Hekigotō's masterly, firm brush strokes and Kyoshi's lofty vitality. He professed that he could not predict which would emerge as the winner if the two men were to engage in a test of skills.[61]

That year, 1899, represented the apogee of Shiki's work as a haiku poet and critic. Soon afterward he shifted his attention to the tanka and then his rapidly worsening illness kept him from much activity in haiku. Relations between his two chief disciples continued to deteriorate. In 1902 Hekigotō anonymously published an article in *Hototogisu* stating that "Kyoshi is 47 percent haiku poet and 53 percent businessman. He has thrown himself into his business and his haiku have become inept."[62] Kyoshi retorted angrily, and Shiki, fearing a further rift between his disciples, declared that he himself had written the anonymous article. But the damage was done. Immediately after Shiki's death an announcement in the *Nippon* reported that Hekigotō would henceforth edit the haiku column. Kyoshi for his part became the editor of *Hototogisu*, and the other poets of the new haiku divided their allegiances between two publications, which had formerly both served as forums for Shiki's theories. The lines were drawn fairly clearly between Hekigotō's advocacy of shasei, contemporaneity, and progress in the haiku, and Kyoshi's conservatism and emphasis on tradition.

Hekigotō followed Shiki's theories quite literally, always insisting on the supreme importance of shasei. "Depict the details," he urged his pupils. But he was more impatient than Shiki with the formal requirements of haiku, and his modernity often took the form of deliberately breaking the rules. This haiku, written at a hot-spring resort in 1903, was typical:

onsen no yado ni	At the hot-spring inn
uma no ko kaeri	A baby colt was hatched out:
hae no koe [63]	The buzzing of flies.

The awkward combination of the baby colt (an endearing creature) and the irritating flies was undoubtedly intended to create an impression of novelty, and Hekigotō had probably observed just such a scene. The haiku proved only that *any* real scene exactly described does not necessarily make a good poem. The irregular length of the first line, the compulsion to avoid any suggestion of staleness, implicit in saying that a colt was "hatched," and the crude attempt to "capture" reality display the worst failings in Hekigotō's later poetry.[64]

Kyoshi, on the other hand, showed signs of losing interest in haiku, and *Hototogisu* rapidly changed into a general literary magazine. In 1905 Sōseki chose to serialize *Wagahai wa Neko de aru* (I Am a Cat) in its pages. *Hototogisu* came to stand for artistic writing, at a time when Naturalism was rising to the height of its popularity, rather than for Shiki's shasei. Kyoshi did not abandon the haiku, but he now seemed "lazy and careless" to some critics, as if his heart were not really in haiku.[65] In 1907 he published his most famous story, "Fūryū Sempō," in *Hototogisu* and continued to write other prose works for the rest of his life; his most impressive work in prose was *Kaki Futatsu* (Two Persimmons), an autobiographical account of his relations with Shiki, published in 1915.

In the meantime Hekigotō had become universally acknowledged as the leading figure in the world of haiku. In 1906 he published the collection *Zoku Shunkashūtō*, a selection of 4,000 examples from among the 1,150,000 haiku he had read between 1902 and 1906 as the haiku critic of *Nippon*. He constantly urged newness in the haiku, insisting that its special characteristic was its ability to treat materials that would be out of place in any other form of poetry. Haiku could effectively depict even the "vulgar" things of the world, whether the humble appurtenances of the traditional Japanese life or the unfamiliar new importations. Some poets, influenced by such remarks, actually visited poverty-stricken villages to observe conditions there, instead of celebrating rustic beauty in the traditional manner. Hekigotō, convinced that his new style was meant for all of Japan and not only for the professional poets in Tokyo, traveled throughout the country (from Hokkaido to Okinawa) in 1907–1911, carrying the new haiku to local poets. These journeys enhanced his national fame. Ōsuga Otsuji (1881–1920), later acclaimed as the outstanding haiku theorist of the day, declared that "Hekigotō is like a god in his choice of haiku." His poems, collected in *Sanzenri* (Three Thousand Miles, 1910), an account of his travels, were reported by Otsuji to have astonished the whole country by their brilliance and clarity.[66]

Although Otsuji wrote with the deference of a disciple, he had already passed Hekigotō in his understanding of the new haiku. In an article published in 1908 he stressed the importance of indirection in haiku expression. Shiki had insisted on shasei, the direct depiction of nature, by way of reaction to the stale conceits and repetitions of conventional phraseology of the tsu-kinami poets, but his attacks had proved so successful that it was now time for another aspect of haiku—suggestion—to be given greater attention. An exclusive reliance on shasei was likely in the end to make readers feel dissatisfied with the shortness of the haiku form, since a description of nature could obviously be expanded to much greater lengths than seventeen syllables; but if the poet employs indirection even a haiku can contain the whole universe.[67]

Otsuji's views on haikai, at first expressed in letters to Hekigotō, were centered around the belief that a "new tendency" in recent haiku favored the use of indirect expression. No longer would it suffice for a haiku merely to record impressions in the shasei manner; by evoking the associations of the season and the other phenomena described it could express thoughts far more complicated than those of direct observation. These views, presented in organized form in 1908, indicate that Otsuji was aware of symbolism, then enjoying great popularity with the shintaishi poets; indeed, he used the word "symbol" (*shōchō*) when discussing the seasonal themes of haiku: "The impressions aroused by the seasonal themes are a kind of symbol. However, we reject conventional symbols. . . . Our symbols arise intuitively, from our experiments; they are not clear-cut conceptions or signs. . . . Seasonal themes alone do not serve as symbols, but when, because of the arrangement of a poem, their special characteristics emerge, they may be said to have been used symbolically." [68] Otsuji's use of the word "symbol," it must be said, was extremely vague; at times he seems to have meant little more than that the haiku should suggest more than it stated. This, of course, had always been true of haiku in the past. Thanks to his use of symbolism, Hekigotō's poetry grew conspicuously more obscure.

Initially Otsuji and Hekigotō saw eye to eye on the "new tendency." Otsuji cited this verse by Hekigotō (written in 1906) as particularly fine:

omowazu mo
hiyoko umarenu
fuyu sōbi

Quite to my surprise
Some little chicks have been born:
Winter roses

There is no obvious connection between freshly hatched chicks and the winter roses, but the effect of both images is similar: the poet is surprised that in the winter he should see roses or hear the peeping of chicks. Otsuji considered this a splendid example of suggestion because the poet had not made the trite comment, "How unusually warm it is for winter!" [69] Hekigotō had come to believe that the haiku had gone beyond Shiki's bare descriptions of external objects to more introspective observations, but before long he adopted even more radical views: in 1909 he published articles expressing his conviction that taste in the haiku must henceforth conform to the Naturalism prevailing in other branches of literature, emphasizing a closeness to daily life, regionalism, and concern with social problems.[70] His first break with Otsuji was as the result of his advocacy in 1910 of the principle of "no-centeredness" (muchūshin-ron), by which he meant that natural phenomena should be described exactly as they are without imposing any human standards. This view was praised by Naturalist writers, but not by Otsuji, who insisted that the fusion of nature and man was essential to the haiku.

Kyoshi, who had stopped composing poetry in 1909, returned to the world of haiku in 1912, once again running a column in *Hototogisu*. His conservative tastes were more congenial to amateur poets than Hekigotō's progressive opinions, as we can infer from the sudden shift of contributors back to *Hototogisu*. Unlike Hekigotō, whose haiku were becoming more and more baffling, Kyoshi insisted on simplicity, and his patient guidance of beginners brought him new disciples. A poll taken in 1911 showed Hekigotō ranked second only to Meisetsu in popularity, but from then on his fortunes rapidly waned. Unabashed by these signs of disenchantment, Hekigotō went on to advocate even more unorthodox views. By 1915 he had come to oppose a fixed form for the haiku and was willing to allow the colloquial in place of the classical language. He still favored the use of seasonal words, but the unconventional content of his haiku exposed him to an attack by Otsuji for his "imitation of Western diabolism." [71] Hekigotō's free haiku no longer had the familiar haiku shape, but tended to run on to prosaic lengths. He himself preferred to call them "short poems" (*tanshi*). This poem, written in 1918, was typical of his new manner:

> *ringo wo tsumami*
> *iitsukushitemo*
> *kurikaesaneba naranu*

> I pick up an apple;
> I've said everything that was to be said,
> But still must repeat.

The meaning seems to be that the speaker, having attempted in vain to persuade another person of something, picks up an apple, perhaps aimlessly, only to try once again to convince his intractable opponent.[72] The poem has twenty-four syllables and is close to the colloquial in phrasing; the mention of the apple, the only "seasonal word," is misleading, for the poem was written in January, not in summer, the season associated with apples. Though rather effective as a short poem, this is hardly a haiku, and there is no trace of shasei. Konishi Jin'ichi wrote of such poems, "When one reaches this point, haikai and haiku disappear, both in name and in reality. . . . Hekigotō, having valiantly forged ahead on his own road, had come finally to destroy the road before him." [73]

The collection of essays *Shinkō Haiku e no Michi* (The Way to the Newly Risen Haiku, 1929) was Hekigotō's most complete statement of his views. He declared that the "short poem" was based on momentary stimuli and impressions aroused by the poet's surroundings, and that the expression of his feelings had to be fresh, based on a sensitivity that was not hamstrung by tradition or conventionality. He rejected the fixed form of the haiku as a childish example of blind adherence to convention, and dismissed as mere externals any distinctions between literary and colloquial language.[74] His persistent opposition to convention made him a controversial figure, but although he continued in middle age to travel around the country propagating his views among poets, he no longer attracted much attention. In 1933, at a celebration in honor of his sixty-first birthday, he announced his retirement from haiku. Many men had considered themselves to be disciples of Hekigotō, but few followed him to his ultimate conclusions. Konishi commented, "The path he took led in the end to failure, but I would like to think of it as a brilliant failure." [75]

In 1928, the year before Hekigotō set forth his views on the new haiku, his long-time rival Takahama Kyoshi issued the even more famous declaration that haiku was essentially the art of "singing about flowers and birds." Nothing could better illustrate the divergence in the paths of the erstwhile friends and fellow disciples of Shiki. Kyoshi's adherence to the shasei principle had from the first been ambivalent; unlike Shiki, who believed in describing only what was before his eyes, Kyoshi insisted that the literary associations of an object formed an essential part of its nature. Shiki reportedly told him, "If you examine a moonflower closely your previous mental images will completely disappear, leaving only a new, shasei appreciation in your mind." Kyoshi replied, "If you sweep away all the mental images related to the moonflower, you are destroying the many different kinds of poetic associations with which the poets of the past endowed this flower. . . . It would be the same thing as blotting out one's mental images of the famous sites and monuments of the past." [76] If the literary associations were stripped from, say, the spring rain, it would be depressing rather than poetic. Only by admiring the spring rain across the poetic associations built up over the centuries could one appreciate its charm. Kyoshi suggested also that the sights before the poet's eyes—the objects of shasei—were of interest mainly as stimulants for emotions already present within him; but Hekigotō continued to insist that the poet's business was to filter sights and sounds through the selective mechanism of his "ideals." Perhaps it was mainly by way of opposition to Hekigotō that Kyoshi had come to insist on the necessity of subjective elements in haiku and of a sense of time in the form of past associations. [77]

Kyoshi was initially the underdog in his rivalry with Hekigotō, though he had begun brilliantly and had made the stronger impression on Shiki. Many critics consider Kyoshi's finest haiku to have been one he wrote in 1900 at twenty-six:

tōyama ni	In the distant hills
hi no ataritaru	A patch where sunlight touches
kareno kana	The withered meadows.

Yamamoto Kenkichi wrote of this poem, "It is an astonishing verse that defies paraphrase. The language is quite ordinary, with nothing that calls attention to itself, but the reader senses something of incalculable importance in this commonplace landscape. The combination of 'withered meadows' and 'distant hills' is not especially memorable in itself; the critical factor is the words 'a patch where sunlight touches' linking the nouns. This line, though not in the least extraordinary in itself, makes both 'distant hills' and 'withered meadows' come alive." [78] The reader should sense something mysterious and indefinable in the single patch of brightness in the bleak wintry landscape, perhaps even a promise of salvation.

A few years after this auspicious beginning, Kyoshi withdrew from haiku composition. No doubt his decision was at least partly occasioned by irritation over Hekigotō's great popularity. Only when Hekigotō's "new tendency" poetry began to arouse unfavorable reactions did Kyoshi return to haiku; the financial difficulties of *Hototogisu* in the 1910s may also have inspired this decision, though his writings suggest Kyoshi felt an internal compulsion. His new haiku, in marked contrast to Hekigotō's complexities, were simple and conservative:

Kamakura wo	Cold of winter,
odorokashitaru	Still lingering, has astonished
yokan ari	All Kamakura.

This haiku, composed in 1914, is simplicity itself, at least on the surface, but as Yamamoto pointed out, if "Tokyo" or "Shizuoka" were substituted for "Kamakura" there would be no poem.[79] Only an expert, a man who has himself written haiku, can fully appreciate the skill of this and many similar poems by Kyoshi. An outsider might find this haiku no more than a simple statement of fact arranged in seventeen syllables, but if he remembers that Kamakura was known for its mild climate, he may sense the particular significance of mentioning Kamakura in a poem about "lingering cold." Even admitting the exceptional professional competence of this haiku, it is not exciting, nor is there any suggestion of modern concerns. Kyoshi claimed that by stating that the lingering coldness of early spring had surprised Kamakura, instead of the people of Kamakura, he had made the verse haikai.[80] No doubt, considering that Kyoshi was then living in Kamakura, some personal meaning was also involved. But after Hekigotō's experimentations with the new haiku, this poem seems extremely tame.

Kyoshi differed with Hekigotō and other Modernists in his insistence on the necessity of including a seasonal word and of observing strictly the division of the seventeen syllables into lines of five, seven, and five syllables. In 1912, just before his active return to the world of haiku, he wrote in *Hototogisu*: "The haiku, as I understand it, is a kind of classical literary art. To call it such is not to denigrate it as being stale; a classical literary art is a special one composed under certain long-established rules. The poet who stands within the discipline is free to work as unconstrainedly as he pleases. What are the conventions of haiku? The main ones are the interest in seasonal topics, the limitation to seventeen syllables, and the poetic tone." [81] Kyoshi considered his conservativism to be an affirmation of proud convictions, as a haiku written in 1913 suggests:

harukaze ya	In the spring wind,
tōshi idakite	Nursing my fighting spirit,
oka ni tatsu [82]	I stand on a hill.

Mention of the "spring wind" clearly identifies the season, and perhaps spring was also the most appropriate season for a poet to assert his readiness to fight for his ideals; but the object of Kyoshi's struggles was a return to the past, not a bold step forward. Konishi wrote, "Kyoshi returned the conception of 'haiku' established by Shiki to the sense of 'haikai' that had existed before Shiki's revolution. Or, to put it in stronger terms, he took a poetic form that Shiki had struggled to make into a first-class art and established it once again as second class." [83]

This judgment is severe, but it is confirmed by Kyoshi's limitation of the range of haiku expression to conventionally admired sights of nature. A celebrated haiku composed in 1906 demonstrated Kyoshi's great skill, but probably also his limitations:

kiri hitoha	A paulownia leaf
hi atarinagara	Caught all the while in sunlight
ochinikeri [84]	Flutters to the ground.

The fall of a single paulownia leaf was a hackneyed poetic image used as a harbinger of the coming of autumn, the seasonal indication here. Kyoshi accepted the conventions in mentioning the fall of the leaf, but gave the haiku life by describing how the leaf was caught in sunlight all the way down from the tree to the ground. Kyoshi himself believed that this poem expressed in microcosmic form the wonder of heaven and earth; but it takes an exceptionally sensitive reader to discover such dimensions.

Shiki chose Kyoshi, rather than Hekigotō, as his successor, apparently because he felt that Kyoshi had the orderly intelligence needed to carry out his revolution in the haiku. He also admired the simplicity and blandness (*heii tampaku*) of Kyoshi's expression.[85] Kyoshi's haiku are by no means devoid of passion or imagination, but their "blandness," like the blandness of the poetry he selected for *Hototogisu*, characterized his work. He spoke often of shasei, but its importance was never so great as to break the rules of haiku in an attempt to achieve greater verisimilitude. He insisted that poets must experience nature before describing it; he once remarked that it was possible to visualize fallen leaves in a wood, but unless a poet actually saw them, he might not imagine their silence. The basic feature of his shasei was the intent examination of a sight of nature, followed by a clear expression of the feelings the sight evoked in the poet. A shasei verse ideally mingled objectivity and subjectivity. Kyoshi and his disciples frequently went on excursions, the purpose of which was "To come in contact with nature and to catch something of the new life of nature." But the sites chosen for these excursions were generally in the neighborhood of Tokyo, and the nature caught by the poets tended to be of the garden variety, rather than the untamed nature of the distant mountains.[86]

Kyoshi was celebrated for his advocacy of "flowers and birds" as the subject matter best suited to haiku. "Flowers and birds" paintings constituted an important branch of Chinese art.[87] Emperor Hui-tsung (ruled 1101–1125), a major bird-and-flower painter, had a passion for "literal renderings of the real appearances of things; he reprimanded his painters for the most trivial lapses from accuracy." [88] The emperor insisted that painters depict objects true to form and color, but the results were not photographic fidelity to nature but (in Cahill's words) "a crystalline clarity, a sense of perfection ideally achieved. These pellucid vi-

sions are derived closely from nature, but set forth with such absolute assurance as to create their own, separate reality." [89] This, no
doubt, was the importance of shasei to Kyoshi. He was indebted
also to Bashō, especially to the famous description at the opening
of *Oi no Kobumi* (Manuscript in My Knapsack) where Bashō insisted that everything the poet sees must be "flowers," and that the
poet must make friends with the four seasons. Kyoshi was convinced that a haiku that ignored the seasons or dwelt on human
affairs to the exclusion of nature could not properly be called a
haiku. He believed that it was a mistake for haiku poets to try to
keep abreast of modern developments and reflect them in their
poetry; like the Nō (an art of which he was especially fond), haiku
had been perfected in the past, and attempts to absorb modern
influences could only result in its destruction.[90]

Kyoshi's conservatism alienated some poets, but he attracted
enormous numbers of others to the *Hototogisu* school and built
up an organization that extended to every part of the country,
enabling the haiku to survive the changes in Japanese life and
literature during the first half of the twentieth century. Indeed, the
history of *Hototogisu* during this period is more or less the history
of the haiku itself.[91] But at a time when the other literary arts
were seeking to come to grips with modern problems, *Hototogisu*
remained aloof. This was not necessarily a mistake; the haiku
Kyoshi wrote during the war years 1941–1945, for example, maintained a detachment that contrasted favorably with the near hysteria exhibited in other literary forms. Yet even this virtue suggests
a basic weakness in his style of haiku: it could not normally be
used to express man's deepest concerns but only momentary perceptions. Flowers and birds add joy to life, and the changing of
the seasons is eternally worth celebrating, but surely Bashō attempted something more profound in his haiku.

A quiet tone of "oriental" appreciation of the small beauties
of life fills Kyoshi's poetry. This is particularly apparent in his
poems set in nontraditional places. When he visited Europe in
1936 he described in haiku the sights of the journey, sometimes
ineptly ("Belgium/ a country without mountains/ tulips!"), sometimes in a manner hardly to be distinguished from a haiku about
Japan ("There stands an old castle/ and amidst the young green
leaves/lingering snow").[92] The journey convinced Kyoshi that the
Japanese should be proud of the haiku because there was nothing

like it elsewhere. His experiences while traveling across an unfamiliar continent did not alter in any way his outlook on the works of man; and despite his proud claims for the haiku, he had in effect reduced its importance by restricting its compass.

Kyoshi made of haiku a national avocation. He encouraged poets even of minor talent, provided he could detect something fresh in the poems they submitted to *Hototogisu*. Haiku became the literary art of the common man; social class, education, political views, and other elements in the makeup of individual poets were obliterated by the consuming attention paid to flowers and birds. When Kuwabara Takeo published his essay "Daini Geijutsu" (Second-Class Art) in 1946, attacking modern haiku as a pastime rather than as a serious literary form, some haiku masters wrote strong retorts, but Kyoshi accepted the judgment with the ironic remark that he was pleased that haiku had at last been promoted to being second class! He was satisfied with the approval of persons who, having themselves composed haiku, could appreciate the beauty and exactness of his poems. In his late years especially Kyoshi was idolized, surrounded by admirers who fought for the least memento of a man who had become a legend in his own day.

POETS OF FREE RHYTHM

Hekigotō's experiments with haiku in irregular forms gave rise to a school of nontraditional poets, many of whom left their mentor behind. Ogiwara Seisensui (1884–1976), the chief figure of this new movement, had become interested in haiku while still a high school student, but at Tokyo University dropped it in favor of German literature, only once again to be stimulated into composing haiku by Hekigotō's example.

In 1911 Seisensui founded the magazine *Sōun* (Layers of Cloud) as an organ of Hekigotō's New Tendency School, but it was not long before he was questioning Hekigotō's theories, especially with respect to the importance of the seasonal words. As early as 1912 he declared that seasonal words were "useless" and "inartistic," no more than a form of dilettantism, and urged that the haiku should move instead in the direction of light and strength."[93] The use of seasonal words was officially ended by *Sōun* in 1914. In the meantime Hekigotō had severed his connections with the magazine, taking his followers with him. Seisensui, having made this decisive step, moved to open criticism of the New Tendency poetry, asserting that it lacked a "soul." He stated in the introduction to *Shizen no Tobira* (The Portals of Nature, 1914):

> The haiku is a poem of impressions. However, there is no point merely in expressing impressionistically whatever impressions have met one's eyes. No matter how small the impression may be, it should evoke great nature itself and one's whole being. When the poet believes he has penetrated the surface and outlines of nature and discovered something inside, or when he thinks he has grasped something deep within himself, not in the manner of the events described in a diary, his feelings may be described as a response that can be felt flashing like lightning. If the poet makes a grandiose statement of this response, it will be a failure; he will in fact lose the experience. Only by expressing it suggestively, in short words, will it be possible to communicate the feeling.
>
> The haiku tends to originate in impressions and move toward symbols. The haiku is a poem of symbols.[94]

Seisensui, despite his iconoclasm with respect to the fixed form of the haiku or the necessity of including seasonal words, was convinced that it was the only poetic form capable of catching in a pure and intense state momentary, transcendentally important perceptions. This was perhaps the most persuasive argument that could be offered for continuing to employ a form perfected by the masters of the past in a world totally unlike the present, and for devoting one's energies to utterances so brief that they are likely to seem trivial to outsiders. Seisensui believed that a haiku must be all dynamite. Naturally this could be true only of a very short poem, but the exact length was unimportant: if the poet's emotions could be conveyed adequately in fifteen syllables, why add a useless two extra syllables merely in order to make the poem scan? Or if they could not be compressed into seventeen syllables, what did it matter if there were a few extra? The internal rhythm of the poem, dictated by the nature of the experience that inspired it, was what mattered. Seisensui's poetry was irregular, and sometimes even defied division into three lines, as in this example:

sora wo	*ayumu*	It walks	the heavens
rōrō to	*tsuki hitori*	Radiantly	the moon, alone.

The choice of words was of crucial importance: the onomatopoetic *rōrō* has the meaning of "brightly" but suggests by its sound the fullness of the moon; and the final word, *hitori*, at once personifies the moon as being alone and implies that the poet is also alone.[95] Some poems by Seisensui depend so heavily on their sounds as to be almost incommunicable in translation, but Seisensui insisted that, unlike Hekigōtō, his haiku did not deliberately break the rules of prosody; they observed natural rules, in accordance with their inherent movement.[96] He gave as an example of the free rhythm of his haiku:

chikara ippai ni naku ko to
naku tori to no asa

Morning with a baby crying with all its might
And a crowing rooster.

Other haiku by Seisensui display a startling use of metaphor:

tsuma no tsuioku no	I suck at
suppai mikan wo	The sour tangerine of
suute iru [97]	Memories of my wife.

The repetition of the sounds *tsu* and *su* and the use of the colloquial also help to give this haiku its distinctive music.

Seisensui was not only a poet but a distinguished scholar of poetry and published many books of haiku criticism. He nevertheless remained an outsider, unaffected by the mainstream of developments in the modern haiku, and unable to persuade many others of the validity of his free rhythms. All the same, he attracted a number of disciples, two of whom gained fame almost as much for their unusual lives as for their poetry, Ozaki Hōsai (1885–1926) and Taneda Santōka (1882–1940).

Ozaki Hōsai's early life followed the typical pattern of success for Japanese men of politics and industry: he graduated from the First High School in Tokyo and then from the Law Department of Tokyo Imperial University. He accepted a position with a prominent insurance company and rapidly moved up in the firm; but suddenly, for reasons never clarified, he resigned his post. He resumed his career, however, taking an important post in 1923 with a company in Korea, only to give up his job without explanation in the same year. He returned to Japan with his wife, then left her. From this time until his death he lived at various Buddhist temples, usually working in some menial capacity. While at a small temple within the compound of the Chion-in in Kyoto he met Seisensui. He had been interested in haiku since high school, and had contributed to *Sōun* since 1916, but only now did he begin to compose haiku in his distinctive manner. After a drunken bout that disgraced him at the Chion-in, he went to the Suma Temple near Kobe, where he wrote many of his best-known haiku, including:

ichinichi	All day long
mono iwazu	I don't say a word:
chō no kage sasu [98]	A butterfly casts its shadow.

This verse evokes the loneliness of Hōsai's life and the momentary consolation he feels when a butterfly casts its shadow on the *shōji*, or the floor of his tiny room. Another poem refers to his life in wryer tones:

tsukemono oke ni
shio fure to
haha wa unda ka [99]

"Shake some salt
In the pickle tub!"
Is that why my mother bore me?

He watches himself performing the humble, even demeaning task of salting the vegetables in a pickle tub, part of his work at the temple, and wonders if that was what he was born for. But there is no note of self-pity, no suggestion of resentment over his fall in social status; one even senses something humorous in his questioning whether his mother's labors in bringing him into the world and her efforts to send him through the university and make him a splendid member of society had as their aim such lowly employment. These poems lack anything resembling regularity of meter, and seasonal words appear only accidentally. Sometimes his indifference to the formal requirements of the haiku is even more striking:

seki wo shite mo	Even though I cough
hitori [100]	I am alone.

This poem, written at a little temple on the island of Shōdo, alludes to his illness and the self-imposed solitude of his last years. The brevity of the poem was in keeping with the trend in *Sōun* at this time, which reached its limits in a famous example by Ōhashi Raboku (1890–1933):

hi e yamu [101]	I am sick with the sun.

Perhaps most typical of Hōsai's years spent in great poverty as a mendicant priest is a haiku written while on Shōdo:

ashi no ura araeba
shiroku naru [102]

When I wash the soles of my feet
They become white.

This seemingly bald statement had a special meaning for Hōsai, which he described in a letter: "The parts of our bodies we use most cruelly are the soles of our feet. . . . They silently comply with this cruel usage. Are they not to be pitied? . . . When I wash them, they turn white, and seem to look me in the face and say, in their lonely way, 'Thank you.'" His Buddhist piety found expression in another well-known verse:

iremono ga nai	Nothing to put it in—
ryōte de ukeru [103]	I'll take it in my hands.

Perhaps the poem refers to the coarse food he received when he begged, perhaps to the enlightenment he gained by abandoning everything. Hōsai died unattended except for an old fisher couple who watched over his last moments.

Hōsai's poems, written in the colloquial and observing none of the traditional features of the haiku, have nevertheless acquired a following; one admirer declared that Hōsai, together with Bashō, Buson, and Issa, was one of the rare poets whose haiku once read are never forgotten.[104]

Taneda Santōka's last years resembled Hōsai's, though his earlier life, shadowed by a tragic childhood, had been quite different. He began to compose haiku as a boy, and pursued this avocation through the various hardships that dogged him. About 1915 he became interested in the *Sōun* style of haiku. In the following year the family business went bankrupt and Santōka moved to Kumamoto, where he started a secondhand bookshop. He made so little money he could not support a family, and he was forced in 1920 by his father-in-law to give up his wife. Santōka, becoming interested in Zen philosophy, went in 1924 to live in a temple, where he took the tonsure soon afterward. From 1927 he began his wanderings all over Japan, which continued until shortly before his death. He led the life of a mendicant priest, traveling with a bamboo hat and staff in the traditional manner. The main influence on his poetry was that of Bashō, but he was much moved by the life and death of Hōsai, whose house and grave on Shōdo Island were the object of one pilgrimage.

Santōka never stayed long anywhere, but he managed to publish seven collections of haiku and various works in prose. His haiku, in the colloquial, were irregular in form and usually lacked seasonal references. This haiku reflected the hardships of his travels:

teppatsu no naka e	Into my iron begging-bowl
arare [105]	A shower of hail.

Santōka provided a description of the circumstances of the poem, a lonely winter's journey. As he went his way, begging from passersby, hail suddenly began to fall, striking every part of him, body and soul. His bamboo hat and priestly robe rattled with the hail, and the iron begging-bowl gave off metallic sounds. He attempted to capture the experience in a poem, trying first, "Today I was beaten by the hail," but rejecting this as sentimental. He finally settled on the present version, feeling it was incomplete but being unable to change a word. This seemingly artless statement was his way of describing a painful experience, even to the word *teppatsu*, which not only means a begging-bowl but suggests the sound of the hail.[106]

Hōsai and Santōka, though memorable figures, exerted little influence on the development of the modern haiku. Nakatsuka Ippekirō (1879–1946), another poet of free rhythms, was more closely associated with the world of haiku, especially through his magazine *Kaikō* (Sea Crimson), which began publication in 1915. He was a disciple of Hekigotō, but quickly surpassed his teacher in Modernism, experimenting with colloquial free verse as early as 1912. He may even have anticipated Seisensui in this respect; one critic has claimed that the modern haiku began with Ippekirō.[107] He also experimented with extremely brief poems, such as this example of 1932:

> *kusa aoao*   The grass is green, green!
> *ushi sari*[108]   The cattle have gone.

The popularity of such forms, which first appeared in *Sōun*, spread to *Kaikō*. When people criticized his free verse as not being haiku, he replied that it did not make the least difference to him what they were called. His poetry was too far in advance of its time to create much impact on circles dominated by conservative poets, but won admirers among much later men.[109]

THE *HOTOTOGISU* POETS

During the 1920s and 1930s the predominant style of haiku was definitely not that of the Modernists but of Takahama Kyoshi and his disciples associated with *Hototogisu*. The members of the *Hototogisu* school were extremely varied, even though all of them normally cast their poems into patterns of five, seven, and five syllables. Most agreed with Kyoshi's conservative views on the methods of the haiku, but unmistakably different personalities were revealed in their poetry. Many felt compelled to break away eventually and to found sub-schools, each with its own haiku magazine.

MURAKAMI KIJŌ (1865–1938)

Murakami Kijō, the oldest of Kyoshi's disciples, was born in the Edo residence of the Tottori clan, the eldest son of a samurai. He had ambitions of becoming a military man, like many others of his generation, but an ear injury when he was eighteen compelled him to give up this career. He next took up the law, but again his near deafness cut short his career as a judicial officer, and at thirty he could find no better employment than as a court scribe in the provincial town of Takasaki. His life continued to be darkened by deafness and a poverty aggravated by having a family of ten children. His interest in haiku was first aroused by Shiki's writings and he wrote him for guidance. Kijō later contributed not only haiku but *shaseibun* (sketches from life in prose) to *Hototogisu*. Almost entirely self-taught in haiku, he first received recognition in 1913 when a haiku gathering in Takasaki was presided over by Takahama Kyoshi and Naitō Meisetsu. The following poem by Kijō was chosen by Kyoshi as the best of all submitted:

hyakushō ni	A skylark soars,
hibari agatte	And for the farmers
yo aketari [110]	The day has dawned.

Kyoshi, impressed by the poem, urged the people of Takasaki not to forget they had the haiku poet Kijō among them. When he learned of Kijō's poverty and deafness, Kyoshi did what he could to assist him; but the greatest joy for Kijō was this first public praise, which gave him the confidence to launch into his most important period of poetic composition, between 1914 and 1920. In later years (especially after 1925), when his poverty was relieved and he had obtained recognition, Kijō's compositions became conventional and repetitious.[111]

Kijō's haiku, though composed in the traditional form and employing classical diction, had little to do with the flowers and birds associated with the *Hototogisu* school. One famous haiku described a blind dog bumping into things as it wanders in the early spring cold; the poem is affecting in itself, but becomes doubly interesting when we realize that here, as so often in Kijō's works, mention of this pathetic animal was obliquely intended as a reference to himself. Yamamoto Kenkichi wrote of Kijō's poetry, "Self-pity was always involved in his love for living creatures." [112]

The haiku that established Kijō's position as a poet was the first one in which he openly alluded to his deafness:

jirōshu no
you hodo mo naku
samenikeri [113]

Before I·could get drunk
On that saké that cures deafness
I was sober again.

This haiku, published in *Hototogisu* in 1914, may have discharged Kijō's feelings of inferiority because of his deafness: the saké he mentioned (a seasonal word for spring because it was sold at the spring festival of certain shrines) was drunk by people hard of hearing, but Kijō could afford so little it had no effect.

A poem published in *Hototogisu* in 1915 attracted the attention of Ōsuga Otsuji:

fuyu hachi no	The bee in winter
shinidokoro naku	Walks around, nowhere for him
arukikeri [114]	To lay down and die.

Otsuji was so impressed that he compared Kijō to Issa, to the former's advantage. Kyoshi, going even further, said, "When people speak of Issa in the past and Kijō in the present, this is insulting to Kijō." [115] Both poets shared a sympathy for the helpless little creatures of nature, but Kijō evinced none of Issa's resistance to the forces bearing down on the weak and defenseless; he is resigned, ready to accept fate. In the end, Yamamoto Kenkichi found this acceptance of fate (and, by implication, of his own position in life) limited his poetic horizon, and his poetry rarely rises to great heights.[116] Only on occasion did he depict more than a small corner of nature, but his personal integrity and samurai fortitude in the face of adversity saved his poetry from being wholly negative. Something of his strength is suggested by this poem:

gantan ya	It's New Year's morning!
fudoshi tatande	A neatly folded loincloth
makuragami [117]	Above my pillow.

Kijō intended on New Year's Day to wear fresh, clean clothes, even to his underwear; mention of this article (and placing it above his pillow) suggests the inborn dignity of the man.

Although Kijō's reputation was never again as high as during the period when he was first discovered, it has not dimmed altogether, thanks to the accents of the common people he brought to the modern haiku.

IIDA DAKOTSU (1885–1962)

Dakotsu was also known as a country poet, though his background and literary manner differed totally from Kijō's. As a child he displayed precocious gifts for haiku composition, and after he entered Waseda University in 1905 he became completely absorbed in literature, associating with such classmates as the poets Wakayama Bokusui and Toki Zemmaro and reading especially in the new Naturalism. He met Kyoshi that year and first began to publish in *Hototogisu*. His work attracted favorable attention, and from 1908 until 1912 he also published in the haiku column of the *Kokumin Shimbun* edited by Kyoshi and later by Matsune Tōyōjō (1878–1964). His poems were regularly selected among the best three of each issue of the newspaper.

In 1909 he was ordered by his family to leave Tokyo and return home. He sold all his books and broke his ties with the world of learning; henceforth he would lead the life of a country gentleman. Nevertheless, he continued to contribute to *Kokumin Shimbun* and, after Kyoshi had returned to active haiku composition and made *Hototogisu* a haiku journal again, Dakotsu quickly established himself as a central *Hototogisu* poet. Although his early works reveal influence from the New Tendency poets, his mature career was to be as an orthodox poet who invariably observed the use of seasonal words, the prescribed seventeen syllables, and classical grammar. Konishi described Dakotsu as a poet who transcended all notions of newness or oldness, a true exemplar of Bashō's *fueki* (unchangingness), whose haiku were unconcerned with passing fashions.[118] His qualities as a poet are suggested by an early haiku:

imo no tsuyu	Dew on the taro leaf:
renzan kage wo	The chains of hills and
tadashū su	mountains
	Correctly range their forms.

Dakotsu noticed close by him large drops of dew on a taro leaf; in the distance, mountain peaks stood imposingly in the clear autumn light with an air of formal decorum.[119] The loftiness of the tone has impressed every commentator, and the juxtaposition of the dew on the leaf and the mountains against the sky is the mark of a master. Yamamoto Kenkichi wrote of this poem that its nobility and orthodoxy of tone made it worthy to open some great linked verse sequence; only Dakotsu among modern haiku poets achieved this loftiness.[120] There is little apparent modernity in either the language or the imagery, though the personification of the mountains "correcting" their posture was probably new.

A haiku composed in 1915 was traditional in diction and in its use of a seasonal word, but the conception was more modern:

oba yuite	A light stab of pain
karuki itami ya	When my aunt passed away—
waka kaede [121]	The young maples.

Grief over the death of his aunt moves the poet, but the grief is "light," for she is old and death has come as naturally as young leaves to the maple. The thought behind the poem is not in the least startling, but no poet had spoken with such serenity about an event that normally excited conventional if not deeply felt grief.

A poem written in 1926 had the title "Going by Boat Along the Fuji River":

gokukan no	Walls of stone
chiri mo todomezu	Do not hold back even the dust
iwabusuma [122]	Of the dead of winter.

The severity of the landscape—great cliffs, like the sliding doors of a room, standing over the river in bitter-cold wind, catching not even dust—has a grandeur no other modern haiku poet could match. The nobility of Dakotsu's poetry presents special problems in translation because it is conveyed by an uncanny use of words, rather than by striking images or unusual sentiments.

Dakotsu was associated with the periodical *Ummo* (Mica) from 1915 until his death. Although the organ of what was technically a separate school, it clearly belonged to the *Hototogisu* traditions.

HARA SEKITEI (1886–1951)

Takahama Kyoshi in *Susumubeki haiku no michi* (The Path on Which Haiku Must Advance, 1918) stated that the best of the "new poets" were Kijō, Dakotsu, and Hara Sekitei. Kijō stood in a class by himself, but Dakotsu and Sekitei shared a specifically modern intelligence that undoubtedly owed much to the Naturalist movement. Dakotsu was more intellectual, Sekitei more physical and intuitive. Nakamura Kusatao wrote that Dakotsu seemed to want to keep a firm grip on something within himself that might unify his life, but Sekitei seemed to be aspiring to elevate the uncertainties and agitation within him into a vital luminosity.[123] Sekitei's rather unbalanced nature verged on eccentricity even in his most tranquil periods, and by the end of his life took the form of a debilitating nervous condition that left him helpless.

Sekitei was the son of a doctor in Shimane Prefecture and expected to follow his father's profession. However, his interests, even while he was a medical student, were confined mainly to poetry, and he failed out of school. As early as 1908 he had founded a haiku club and contributed to the regional haiku competitions of *Hototogisu*. This may have been what emboldened him to visit Kyoshi in 1912 and ask his assistance in obtaining a job. Kyoshi strongly urged him to go back home, and Sekitei obeyed. Just at this time a brother, working as a doctor in the remote recesses of the Yoshino mountains, asked Sekitei to help him. His stay in Yoshino was brief, less than two years, but almost all the poems for which he is now remembered were composed during that period. He made his debut in *Hototogisu* in 1912 with this haiku:

chōjō ya	The crest of the hill—
koto ni nogiku no	The camomiles especially
fukareori	Are blown by the wind.

This poem hardly seems exceptional, but it created a sensation when first published. Yamamoto Kenkichi, analyzing what was new in it, suggested that it was the poem's unpretentiousness; the effect of the whole is as free and light as the flowers in the wind Sekitei pictured. The use of the particle *ya* in the first verse, the agreeably amateurish use of *koto ni* in the second verse, and the almost prosaic ending in *ori* all contributed to the mood.[124] Nakamura Kusatao read more into the haiku. The poet, arriving at the top of the hill after a long climb, feels the sensation of relief he evokes by the particle *ya*. The use of *koto ni* (especially) indicates that the camomiles were not the only flowers blown by the wind but the ones the poet happened to notice. The prosaic *ori* at the end suggests a complete yielding of the flowers to the wind. Kusatao thought the haiku was surprisingly like Bashō's famous, "Going a mountain road/ something attracted me/ violet blossoms," but he interpreted Bashō's poem as the expression of a man who has turned his back on the world but cannot forbear moments of longing for it, whereas Sekitei's was permeated by a more instinctive, physical sense.

Such analysis of what appears (certainly in translation) to be a mere observation suggests the problems of anyone outside the tradition attempting to analyze the haiku. No amateur, not even a cultivated Japanese, would be likely to sense the naïve freshness of *koto ni* or the less than normally portentous use of *ya*, yet such considerations are very much to the point when discussing haiku of the *Hototogisu* school, conservative in form and diction, and revealing freshness mainly in such touches.

Another haiku of his Yoshino period shows Sekitei at his best:

kaei basa to	Blossom shadows blur—
fumu beku arinu	I might have stepped on them!
soba no tsuki	Moon of the mountain path.

This haiku was acclaimed by Nakamura Kusatao as the finest Sekitei ever composed.[125] He interpreted the poem in these terms: a path winds round the mountain. At this season of year every peak and valley at Yoshino is swathed in cherry blossoms. The poet is walking on the path rather late at night. The blossoms filling the valleys seem to shine a snowy white, and overhead there are also blossoms. On the path, as the poet ascends, the shadow of the blossoms is sharply etched. The mountain is windless and silent, and he is about to tread boldly over the motionless shadows. He feels almost as if he is to stride over blossoming trees and the prospect stirs feelings of divinity within him; but the omnipresent shadows of the cherry blossoms also inspire something akin to dread, so great that the poet hesitates to disturb their world. For a time he stands there hesitantly, gazing at the shadows of the flowers exactly as if they grew on the path.[126] To suggest this much in the seventeen syllables of a haiku is a prodigious accomplishment, but of course the range and depth of what is suggested inevitably depend largely on the reader; no one without Kusatao's great familiarity with haiku could have derived such intense pleasure and beauty from this poem.

The haiku is complicated further by the words *basa to*, normally used of dancers moving, or shadows blurring with movement, but probably here employed mainly for their onomatopoetic value, suggesting the abruptness of the poet's entry onto the scene. The use of the sound of *b* in the key words *basa*, *fumubeku*, and *soba* also imparted a particular stability to the poem.[127] A haiku with such complexities could give fresh life even to that most hackneyed of subjects, the cherry blossoms at Yoshino.

Another, simpler poem written in 1913 seems to have been of special importance to Sekitei:

sabishisa ni	In his loneliness
mata dora utsu ya	Once again he strikes the gong—
kabiya mori [128]	The deer-fire watchman.

A watchman deep in the mountains burns fires all night long in order to scare off wild boars and deer who might otherwise ravage the crops. Sometimes he also beats a gong for the same purpose. In this haiku the watchman has just struck the gong only to strike it again, perhaps seeking in his solitude to reassure himself of his own existence and to dissipate his feelings of loneliness.

The importance of this poem is indicated by Sekitei's decision, when he founded a magazine of his own in 1921, to give it the name *Kabiya* (deer-fire). His health began to deteriorate in 1923, and although he continued to compose haiku and select poetry for *Kabiya* until 1940, he was an invalid most of the time. His most important collection, *Kaei* (Blossom Shadows, 1937), took its name from the opening line of his finest poem.

MAEDA FURA (1889–1954)

Maeda Fura was ranked by Takahama Kyoshi alongside Hara Sekitei as a poet who had brought distinction to *Hototogisu* after his own return to the world of haiku in 1914. He contrasted the "prodigal and uninhibited" talents of Sekitei (which he likened to the spring or summer) and with the "concision and vigor" of Fura's poetry (which reminded him of autumn or winter).[129] This contrast was supported by the favorite haunts of the two men: Sekitei lived in the mountains of Yoshino, known for a thousand years for their brilliant displays of cherry blossoms and maple leaves; Fura preferred the forbidding, powerful mountains of central Japan, or else the dark landscapes of the Japan Sea coast. Fura, sensitive to such differences, once commented that he found it absolutely intolerable for a haiku "nurtured by the snows of the Japan Sea coast to be placed on the same sheet of paper with a haiku that conveys the brightness of the Pacific Coast side of Japan." [130]

Fura's life was one of travel, sometimes on journeys as far away as Korea or Taiwan, but more often on the branch lines of the railways crisscrossing the "rear side" of Japan, on lonely trains passing through the scenic grandeur of remote regions. He spent a long time in central Japan, absorbing the "music" of each of the famous mountains, and many of his most successful works evoke the particular qualities of Komagatake, Asamayama, Mizugakiyama, and other peaks. Fura's haiku lack the charm of Sekitei's.

He is the least known of the "four great disciples" of Kyoshi who flourished in the 1910s, partly because of the austerity of his sometimes sublime poetry, partly because he spent much of his life on the Japan Sea coast and the journal he edited, *Kobushi* (Magnolia), published in Toyama, attracted little attention elsewhere. His unwillingness to compromise with popular tastes cost him fame in his day, but he is now considered by such critics as Yamamoto Kenkichi to rank alongside Iida Dakotsu in the lofty tone of his haiku. The grandeur of nature is powerfully conveyed in many poems, including

oku Shirane	The depths of Shirane—
ka no yo no yuki wo	The snow sparkles with a light
kagayakasu [131]	From another world.

Mention of *ka no yo* (the other world; that is, the world of the dead or the blessed) gives a conceptual note to the poem that goes beyond observation; but although it is subjective in its appreciation, the haiku conveys exactly the essential beauty of snow in the deep mountains.[132]

Fura's most distinctive quality, however, was probably his concern for human affairs, which set him apart from many poets of the day who were so absorbed in shasei descriptions of scenery as to exclude human considerations.

hito korosu	Perhaps—I don't know—
ware ka mo shirazu	I may have killed somebody!
tobu hotaru [133]	Flitting fireflies.

This verse is unusual because haiku rarely express doubts, and it is given its particular tone by the strange state induced in the poet by the ghostly sight of fireflies. Perhaps he has been moved to thoughts of *hitodama*, the spirits of the dead which hover as will-o'-the-wisp lights. A more genial vein is evident in

mushi naku ya	How the insects cry!
ware to yu wo nomu	On the wall my shadow is
kagebōshi [134]	Drinking tea with me.

This evocation of a lonely autumn evening is given its humor by the shadow mimicking the poet. There may also be overtones of

Li Po's famous poem on drinking wine with his shadow as his companion.

Finally, a haiku that combines Fura's interest in human affairs and remote landscapes:

fuyu umi ya	The sea in winter—
hito iwa ni ite	A man sitting on a rock
Uo wo matsu [135]	Waits for a fish.

SUGITA HISAJO (1890–1946)

Another poet of the *Hototogisu* school during the early 1920s who merits special attention is Sugita Hisajo. In the long history of haiku there have been few women poets of distinction. Bashō's disciple Hata Sonome (1664–1726) enjoyed celebrity in her day, and Kaga no Chiyojo (1703–1775) wrote a few haiku that everybody knows, but not many other women poets come to mind. In the 1910s, however, several women began to write for *Hototogisu*. Hisajo was the most conspicuous and the best poet. She had a good education, and for a time was interested in writing fiction or tanka, but under Kyoshi's influence she became a contributor to *Hototogisu* in 1916, and gave up other literary activity. Soon she was a rival of Kijō, Dakotsu, and Sekitei in the monthly competition as to whose poem would head the issue.

Considerable surprise was expressed over the appearance of an important woman poet. The haiku, unlike the tanka, did not consist of lyrical perceptions or revelations but had to include an intellectual apprehension of the world. Male poets were reluctant to credit women with this degree of objectivity. The sensitivity that was expected of Japanese women in their writings was considered to be unsuited to haiku. Sonome's poems had been praised not for their feminine delicacy but for their "masculine, free and easy" manner.[136] Meiji women haiku poets, perhaps by way of overcompensation, tended to exclude subjective elements from their haiku, to the point that their compositions were often bare, prosaic examples of shasei that lacked the internal strength to raise observation to a higher plane.[137]

However, Hisajo managed, thanks to her forceful personality, to establish herself as a poet with a distinct voice, though in so doing she made many enemies. She married a painter, a suitably romantic profession for a lady poet's husband, but he took a job teaching school in Kyushu. She recalled with indignation that she "gave up diamonds, gave up a carriage, all to marry an artist, and then he didn't paint one picture! Instead, he stooped to becoming a country school teacher!" [138] Hisajo's mention of diamonds brings to mind the scene in Ozaki Kōyō's *The Demon Gold* in which a beautiful young woman of good family is seduced by the diamond flashed at her by a banker, but this, alas, was not to be Hisajo's life. She complained:

tabi tsugu ya	I darn my husband's socks—
Nora to mo narazu	I became not Nora
kyōshi-zuma [139]	But a teacher's wife!

She would have liked to become an emancipated woman like Nora in *A Doll's House*, but instead she mends her husband's *tabi*, not even comforted by diamonds.

Hisajo's haiku often borrow vocabulary or images from *The Tale of Genji*, which she devotedly read. In one essay she compared various contemporary haiku poetesses to characters in this novel, declining to compare herself to any one figure because she was convinced that she combined the best features of all! Needless to say, Hisajo did not settle down gracefully to being a country teacher's wife, but was constantly involved in love affairs. The note of romantic love she brought to the haiku recalls Yosano Akiko of *Tangled Hair*; as Konishi pointed out, the modern haiku tended always to be thirty years behind the tanka.[140]

Hisajo's waywardness, her conceit, and her absolute refusal to conform resulted in her expulsion from *Hototogisu* in 1936. She was not permitted to visit Kyoshi, and was kept at a distance even by friends and relatives, leading in her last years to an extreme nervous breakdown. Her haiku were not collected until 1950, after her death. She does not rank nearly so high in reputation as Kyoshi's four "great" disciples, but as the first notable woman haiku poet in centuries she lent a distinctive note to the art.

HINO SŌJŌ (1901–1956)

Sōjō was another exceptionally interesting minor poet whose haiku (at times similar to Hisajo's in expression and ardor) reveal a modern consciousness at work. Much of his life as a poet was spent in the effort to achieve reforms in the haiku, though he aimed at nothing so dramatic as the destruction of form already effected by the New Tendency poets. His work is interesting for the early period, when strong erotic overtones—whether the result of his study of Buson, his experiences with Kyoto prostitutes, or merely his imagination—gave his haiku a distinctive coloring, and for his very late works when, bedridden, he attained a simplicity of expression that most closely approached the traditional functions of this art.

It was about 1920, when *Hototogisu* was in the doldrums, that the haiku of Sōjō, then a student at the Third High School in Kyoto, began to attract attention by their freshness and freedom from convention. Of course there had been youthful haiku poets before, but the haiku (in contrast to the tanka or shintaishi) was still considered to be the poetry of old men, the tiny vehicle into which a lifetime of experience and understanding of nature was poured in crystalline drops. Sōjō's haiku, however, frankly mentioned such experiences as sending for a prostitute one spring evening:

haru no hi ya	Lamplight in the spring—
onna wa motanu	A woman's throat hasn't got
nodobotoke [141]	An Adam's apple.

The sensual beauty of the woman's neck certainly contrasted vividly with the flat examples of shasei more typical of *Hototogisu* at the time.

It is not always clear from Sōjō's poetry whether or not he is describing his own experiences; he himself admitted that his haiku contained fictional elements, but this divergence from the resolutely serious efforts of the orthodox *Hototogisu* poets gave his work a special allure. His most celebrated composition was the sequence (*rensaku*) called *Miyako Hotel* (1934), describing the wedding night of a couple at the lavish hotel in Kyoto. The haiku evoking the bride's embarrassment on the morning after was typical:

uraraka na	In the radiance
asa no tōsuto	Of morning the breakfast toast
hazukashiku	Is somehow shaming.

The series evoked violently opposed reactions: Murō Saisei acclaimed it as opening a new path in the art of haiku by proving that haiku was not merely the diversion of old men: but Kubota Mantarō, an amateur haiku poet of distinction, denounced it as being no better than the sentimentalism of a popular song. The eminent haiku poets Mizuhara Shūōshi and Nakamura Kusatao, though otherwise of quite different outlooks, were equally repelled by Sōjō's sensationalism.[142]

Sōjō's haiku began to appear regularly in *Hototogisu* in 1920, the year he also founded the magazine *Kyōganoko*, which became the bastion of the *Hototogisu* school in the Kansai region. He produced his first collection in 1927, and in 1929 became a member of the board of *Hototogisu*. However, in 1935 he began to publish another magazine, *Kikan* (Flagship), which carried experiments in rensaku and seasonless haiku; this so shocked the orthodox *Hototogisu* poets that he was expelled from their number in the following year. *Kikan* came under fire from the authorities in 1940, as part of the campaign to suppress unorthodoxy of any kind as being potentially subversive, and Sōjō withdrew from the world of haiku. When he resumed composition after the end of the war in 1945, it was to write some quietly resigned poetry reflective of his ill health and long period of adversity. The main thrust of all his poetry was directed at the concerns of human existence, rather than at the nature detachedly observed by Kyoshi and his school. Although this inevitably put him in conflict with the orthodox *Hototogisu* poets, it gave his haiku a special appeal for many readers.

THE REVOLT AGAINST *HOTOTOGISU*

As far back as the seventeenth century there were bitter disputes over the proper way to write haiku. Disciples of the same master often quarreled over which one most faithfully transmitted his teachings. In some cases a strong if unfocused dislike of the prevailing school of haiku might breed rebellion within the ranks and—much more rarely—a man with poetic convictions of his own might decide that the time had come to found a school that would openly defy the mainstream. It would have been strange if something similar had not happened in the 1920s, when Takahama

Kyoshi and the *Hototogisu* poets dominated the world of haiku poetry. Some mavericks, beginning with Kawahigashi Hekigotō, had already displayed their independence of *Hototogisu*, but their influence was too limited to speak of their having established rival schools. This distinction belonged to Mizuhara Shūōshi (1892–1981).

Shūōshi was born in Tokyo, the son of a doctor, and himself planned at an early age to follow his father's profession. He was a brilliant student, but his father, in order to prevent the boy from dissipating his talents, forbade him to read novels. The boy, however, secretly read such works as the novels of Izumi Kyōka and Tsubouchi's translations of Shakespeare, and while at high school was so attracted by the tanka of Wakayama Bokusui, Kubota Utsubo, and others that he determined that even after he had become a doctor he would write tanka. Despite his growing interest in other literary forms, he remained indifferent to the haiku. Years later he recalled, "I was convinced that haiku were all outdated evocations of the joys of tranquillity, and doubted that anything of much interest was to be found even in some new style emanating from that source." [143]

In 1914 he entered the medical school of Tokyo University. Before his final examinations in 1918, bored with his medical texts, he happened to read the recently published work by Takahama Kyoshi, *The Path on Which Haiku Must Advance*, a book that changed his views on haiku completely. He was attracted by the work of the *Hototogisu* poets discussed by Kyoshi, notably Murakami Kijō, Maeda Fura, Iida Dakotsu, and Watanabe Suiha (1882–1946), but above all Shūōshi was excited by the brilliance of Hara Sekitei. He began to subscribe to *Hototogisu*, but seems not to have considered composing haiku himself.

In 1919, after graduation from medical school, Shūōshi entered the serology laboratory at the university. An assistant urged him to join a haiku club whose members were all graduates of the Tokyo University Medical School. The leader of the group was a disciple of Matsune Tōyōjō, and the club was affiliated with Tōyōjō's *Shibukaki* group. Shūōshi would have preferred to study the *Hototogisu* style, but he was persuaded to attend the meetings. As his interest in haiku composition deepened he could not help comparing unfavorably the *Shibukaki* poets to those of *Hototogisu*: "I felt that the breath of air direct from nature, which emanated from the pure shasei of the *Hototogisu* poems, was more beautiful. Sekitei had especially keen eyes, and his haiku, searching out the profound beauties of nature, seemed to describe and display them with unconstrained expression before the reader." [144] The petty attacks on Kyoshi constantly made by the *Shibukaki* poets irritated Shūōshi, and he realized also that the *Hototogisu* principle of shasei was far more to his taste than the conceptual techniques of Tōyōjō.

Shūōshi's break with Tōyōjō and *Shibukaki* took place in October 1920. At a meeting of the poetry club, Tōyōjō proposed an experiment: he would write on a piece of paper a topic for each man present. This topic would not be a seasonal subject, but something in the nature of a Zen riddle: for example, "One bird sings and the mountain grows ever darker. Then the bird stops singing. Why is this?" Tōyōjō would go into the next room and wait for each man to complete his haiku on the assigned topic. If he approved of the haiku, he would give the man another topic; if not, the man would have to rewrite. Shūōshi, disgusted by this childish procedure, announced his resignation from the club the next day.[145]

He decided to join *Hototogisu* instead. At the time the prestige of this magazine was enormous. The competition to have poems accepted was so severe that if a man had even one haiku accepted in a whole year he was considered to be a poet of some importance. Shūōshi nevertheless felt confident he would eventually be recognized. To prepare himself, he spent every free day in the outskirts of Tokyo, making notes in his poetry diary. His insistence on contact with nature originated at this time. He began submitting haiku to *Hototogisu* late in 1920.

In April 1921, to Shūōshi's boundless delight, four haiku were selected for the famous *zatsuei* (miscellaneous composition) column of *Hototogisu*. In May he first attended one of the regular monthly meetings and met Kyoshi. These meetings were not always well attended by the best-known poets of the *Hototogisu* school, mainly because each had a haiku magazine of his own that he was anxious to promote. Perhaps also the established poets had lost patience with the unwritten rules governing the selection of poetry for *Hototogisu* and with the lack of criticism on the judgments passed by Kyoshi and his colleagues. The poet who enjoyed the reputation of being the most successful was a nonentity,

Nishiyama Hakuun (1877–1943), whose haiku were praised for their flawless incarnation of Kyoshi's principle of "objective description of nature" (*kyakkan shasei*).[146] Shūōshi's enthusiasm was by now so intense that he never missed any meetings, though he privately regretted the rigidity of approach.

In April 1922 Shūōshi was introduced in Kyoto to Yamaguchi Seishi (b. 1901), who was about to go to Tokyo and enter the Law Department of Tokyo University. Shūōshi felt immediate friendship for the young man, already a talented haiku poet, and when he reactivated the dormant Tokyo University Haiku Society later that month he invited Seishi to be a member, along with Nakada Mizuho (1893–1975), Tomiyasu Fūsei (1885–1979), and Yamaguchi Seison (b. 1892), all young poets who would distinguish themselves within the *Hototogisu* ranks. When word reached Kyoto of this reorganized society, Hino Sōjō acclaimed the "Newly Arisen Haiku" (*Shinkō Haiku*) of these Tokyo intellectuals. This term would later be used specifically of the haiku composed by Shūōshi and his associates during the period 1931 to 1940.[147]

One more event of literary importance occurred in April 1922: a Buddhist priest founded a periodical called *Hamayumi*, and invited Shūōshi to join the board. After some show of reluctance occasioned by the old-fashioned name of the periodical, meaning the exorcising bow used by a diviner, Shūōshi accepted, and before long *Hamayumi* became the organ of the Tokyo University Haiku Society. Its connections with *Hototogisu* were emphasized by the appointment of Kyoshi's nephew as judge of the zatsuei. Shūōshi's association with the *Hamayumi* group was important in his development as a poet because the atmosphere of its meetings was conducive to study and mutual criticism, unlike the benevolent despotism that prevailed under Kyoshi. Shūōshi continued also to publish in *Hototogisu*, and from 1923 his haiku were regularly selected.

In 1923 Shūōshi's associate at the serology laboratory, Takano Sujū (1893–1976), who had hitherto been scornful of Shūōshi's devotion to haiku, suddenly asked for instruction, and before long became passionately interested in composing haiku. From this casual beginning Sujū developed into an important poet, and eventually became Shūōshi's chief antagonist in the struggle over shasei.

In December 1924 seven poems by Shūōshi were chosen to head the zatsuei column of *Hototogisu*, incontestable proof of his high reputation within the school. These haiku were all in the objective mood favored by Kyoshi, describing with no trace of subjectivity appropriately poetic scenes. Now that he had proved his mastery of the style of "objective description of nature," Shūōshi attempted to promote new developments in the haiku. His earlier interest in the tanka had convinced him of the importance of melody in poetry,[148] and he decided that melody was no less important to the haiku than to the tanka.

The importance of the sound of a poem to the total effect it produces is so obvious as hardly to need stating, but the emphasis of the haiku poets had always been elsewhere. The music of poetry was often enough discussed by tanka poets, and it may be that the haiku poets, in order to dissociate their art from this overly familiar concept, deliberately omitted the sound from their theorizing about haiku, concentrating instead on techniques, content, and form. But, of course, the haiku poets (subconsciously at least) had always chosen words with overtones both of meaning and of sound that corresponded most closely to their intent. Shūōshi's contribution was to make this process conscious.

The form and melody of the haiku became inseparably entwined in Shūōshi's mind:

> In the most frequently employed form of haiku the five syllables of the first line conclude with the particle *ya*, and the five syllables of the third line with a noun. Once a poet falls into the habit of this stereotyped expression, his conceptions lose their vitality. Even though various other forms are possible in haiku, the majority of poets follow the stereotype. I have endeavored first of all to do away with the stereotype, and next to include as much modulation as is possible within the prescribed seventeen syllables and to free the melody.[149]

Shūōshi's companion and confidant at this time was Yamaguchi Seishi. The two men differed in their habits (Seishi could rarely be persuaded to accompany Shūōshi on his poetry-making excursions into the countryside), but both were intensely serious about the composition of haiku. Shūōshi often visited Katsushika, on the outskirts of Tokyo, and tried to combine in his haiku the present drab appearance of the place with the poetic associations of the past, imparting a new complexity to his haiku. He and Seishi sometimes used the vocabulary of the *Manyōshū*, arousing the derision of many critics, even those (as Shūōshi wryly commented) who had never so much as held a copy of the *Manyōshū* in their hands.[150]

Kyoshi showed himself surprisingly tolerant of such experiments, insisting that the two poets had not abandoned the principle of objectivity, even though subjective impulses could be detected beneath the surface.[151] Shūōshi and Seishi were not even reprimanded for having eliminated the traditional *kireji* ("cutting words") such as *ya*, *kana*, and *keri*, or for having added extra syllables when necessary, but there was no discussion or criticism of what they had attempted. Shūōshi steadily rose within the *Hototogisu* organization until he was appointed an editor in 1928. In the same year, however, he began to take a more active role in the publication of *Hamayumi*, renamed *Ashibi* at his request; perhaps he sensed that he would soon need another forum for his poetry and criticism.

In 1929 Kyoshi's celebrated declaration that haiku was about flowers and birds appeared in *Hototogisu*. Shūōshi was dissatisfied with the declaration itself, but especially with the chorus of approbation not only from the *Hototogisu* poets but from the satellite haiku magazines, which welcomed this principle with all but religious fervor.[152]

Shūōshi published his first major collection of haiku, *Katsushika*, in 1929. Contrary to the normal practice of *Hototogisu* poets, he did not ask Kyoshi for a preface, but wrote his own, which included this definition of the two different ways of considering nature: "One is to make it one's practice to be completely faithful to nature, making one's own mind a blank; the other is to retain an attachment to one's own thoughts while respecting nature." Obviously Shūōshi considered himself to belong to the second category.[153] Shortly after publication of *Katsushika* Shūōshi ran into Kyoshi, who remarked that he had read one section, wondering all the while, "Is this all there is to it?"[154] Naturally, this reaction came as a great disappointment; many critics have since acclaimed *Katsushika*, together with Seishi's collection *Tōkō*

(Frozen Harbor, 1932), as one of two works that brought about the modernization of the haiku.[155]

Beginning in January 1931 a dialogue between Nakada Mizuho and a disciple was serialized in *Hototogisu*, reprinted from the obscure Niigata haiku magazine where it had appeared over a year earlier. The third installment, dealing with Shūōshi and Sujū, consisted of a bitter attack on Shūōshi for failing to maintain orthodox *Hototogisu* objectivity and shasei. It was certainly most peculiar that an article from a provincial magazine should have been reprinted so conspicuously in *Hototogisu*, and Shūōshi was furious. Obviously someone was behind this affront—presumably Kyoshi himself—and Shūōshi felt he had no choice but to leave *Hototogisu*. His opportunity came in July 1931 at a haiku-making excursion. He informed Kyoshi that he had lost all interest in poetry. Kyoshi did not seem surprised; he realized that Shūōshi was breaking his long connections with *Hototogisu*.[156]

In October 1931 Shūōshi published in *Ashibi* his most famous essay, "Shizen no Makoto to Bungeijō no Makoto" (Nature's Truth and Literary Truth). "Nature's truth" was what the *Hototogisu* poets (most recently, Sujū) had aimed at; "literary truth" (which Shūōshi ranked much higher) did not stop at the accurate depiction of nature but displayed the poet's individuality. "Nature's truth" was the ore from which the poet refined "literary truth." Shūōshi singled out for special attack Sujū's haiku, which he castigated for their lack of modernity.[157]

The historical importance of Shūōshi's article far outweighed its intrinsic merits as criticism. Its message was simple and not unexpected (in view of his previous work), but it presented a challenge to *Hototogisu*, hitherto sacrosanct, signifying that a new movement in haiku had begun. Young poets gathered around Shūōshi; the average age of the *Ashibi* group at this time was only thirty, ranging downward from Shūōshi himself, who was forty, to Ishida Hakyō, nineteen. The meetings of these poets were marked by lively discussions, quite unlike the authoritarian decorum of *Hototogisu* sessions. The sales of *Ashibi* doubled, but there was virtually no response in *Hototogisu* to the challenge; Kyoshi's policy seems to have been one of ignoring the upstarts.

One new feature of *Ashibi* from 1932 was the popularity of the rensaku, groups of haiku on one general theme. A dispute arose between Shūōshi and his close friend Seishi as to the proper organization of a rensaku: Shūōshi considered the rensaku to form an organic whole, and even stated that seasonal words could be omitted from individual members of a sequence because the season was adequately conveyed by the whole; but Seishi believed that the rensaku must be an arrangement of existing haiku to form a new whole, rather than an independent form.[158] For a time Shūōshi was so enthusiastic about rensaku (presumably because it provided a means of transcending the limited expressive possibilities of a single haiku) that he virtually gave up other types of composition; but by 1937 he turned from rensaku because he had reached the conclusion that it endangered the independence of the individual haiku.

Ashibi continued to attract new poets, partly because of Shūōshi's democratic handling of haiku gatherings, partly because his emphasis on modern life (scenes of the city and suburbs, and references to other arts such as painting, sculpture, and films) was more exciting than Kyoshi's birds and flowers. Yamaguchi Seishi, who had remained with *Hototogisu* despite the unconventionality of his themes, which had aroused controversy among the *Hototogisu* poets, finally decided in 1935 to join *Ashibi*, precisely at a time when more radical poets like Takaya Sōshū (b. 1910) left *Ashibi* because they were disappointed by Shūōshi's conservatism on such subjects as the necessity of having seasonal words in each haiku. Shūōshi devoted ten issues of *Ashibi* in 1936 to a sustained attack on "seasonless" (*muki*) haiku, reflecting the importance he attached to this matter. Younger poets, especially in Kyoto, chafed at such traditional restrictions; the ill-fated "proletarian haiku" movement of the 1930s was an expression of impatience with all established forms, advocating instead the importance of content.[159] *Ashibi* came increasingly to seem like a middle ground between the unbending conservatism of *Hototogisu* and the controversial experiments of the radical poets. It attained its greatest prominence in 1937 when it published not only Shūōshi and Seishi but a half-dozen other outstanding poets, and the magazine itself was a bulky 140 pages.[160]

Shūōshi continued to develop his art, but his most celebrated haiku were those in his first collection, *Katsushika*. Three poems will suggest the prevailing tone and the exquisite sensibility:

haru oshimu	The holy statue
onsugata koso	Yearning for departed springs
tokoshinae [161]	Is eternity.
ashibi saku	I touched the door
kondō no to ni	Of the Golden Hall where
wa ga furenu [162]	Andromedas bloom.
kitsutsuki ya	The woodpeckers
ochiba wo isogu	Hurry the falling leaves
maki no kigi [163]	Among meadow trees.

The background for the first poem was supplied by Shūōshi, who recalled that at the time of composition (1927) he felt a desire to add something distinctive to the usual descriptions of nature. He was uninterested in the alternative of portraying daily life, in the manner of the realistic haiku poets. He happened to read a book about the old temples of Nara, and this induced him to visit the sites. He was impressed by the great statue known as the Kudara Kannon, especially by its smile, a wistful recollection of the past. The language of this haiku is archaic, but the melody is flawless, and it differed markedly in conception from the *Hototogisu* poetry.

The second haiku, also about Nara, is one of several mentioning *ashibi* (the andromeda), the flower that gave its name to Shūōshi's magazine. The statement that he touched the door of the old temple suggests his nostalgia for the past, which is given additional poignance by the flowers that bloom, unaffected by the passage of time.

The third haiku is even more striking. Yamamoto Kenkichi wrote, "His poems escape the traditional mood of the haiku and open the way to a unique, radiant domain filled with the qualities of Western painting. It is worthy of note that his landscapes, permeated by fresh sensations, provided the direction for his subsequent modernization of the haiku." [164]

The beauty of Shūōshi's haiku was praised by Konishi as being "not of this world." Unfortunately, it is almost impossible to suggest in translation the surprising effect of an altered particle or the personal meaning for the poet of what appears to be objective description. It is true that some haiku, like the following one written in 1938, have a surface beauty communicable even in translation, but the implications for a Japanese sensitive to haiku surely go beyond anything a Western reader would imagine:

Ruri numa ni	The cascade tumbles
taki ochikitari	Into the Emerald Pool
ruri to naru [165]	And turns emerald.

"The Emerald Pool" was a proper noun, but Shūōshi used it for its meaning as well. He sensed eternal mystery in the quiet emerald pool before him, endlessly drinking in the white of the fall and turning it green. "We too are made to feel apprehensive lest we be sucked into the pond and turned emerald," commented Yamamoto Kenkichi.

Shūōshi's intensity of expression gave his haiku their great fame. An archetype of beauty governed his depiction of nature and choice of subjects. This was his reaction to the "objective," even mindless, manner of the shasei poets when they portrayed sights, but it easily lent itself to abuse in lesser hands, for his conceptualization was not too far removed from the attitudes of the tsukinami poets before Shiki's revolution. Again, Shūōshi's lyricism is often lovely, but tanka melodies in the haiku could be deadly if used ineptly. It was Konishi's opinion that "A follower who lacked Shūōshi's natural gifts and his pellucidly clear mind and who imitated only his external forms could not resist the tendency to form a third tsukinami school on the heels of the second, that of *Hototogisu*. This perhaps was the basic limitation of Shūōshi's haiku." [166]

YAMAGUCHI SEISHI (1901–1994)

Seishi was born in Kyoto but at the age of eleven was taken by his father to distant Karafuto (Sakhalin) where his father edited a newspaper. He returned to Kyoto in 1917, but his stay in Karafuto would be recalled in many haiku. In 1920, while at the Third High School in Kyoto, he joined the haiku club and received instruction from Hino Sōjō, among others. Two years later he entered the law department of Tokyo University, where he became a founding member of the Tokyo University Haiku Society under the circumstances already described. Even while still an undergraduate his talents were recognized, and his poems appeared frequently in *Hototogisu*. At this early stage in his career the influence of Shūōshi was especially important. The two men studied the *Manyōshū* together and planned the changes in haiku style associated with Shūōshi's name.

Seishi first met Takahama Kyoshi in 1922 at a gathering in Kyoto. Along with many others he submitted haiku for the master's judgment, and was overjoyed when his received the highest praise. The kind and protective look Kyoshi bestowed on the young man "nailed" him to haiku for life.[167] Two years later, while studying for examinations, Seishi contracted through overwork and neglect a series of ailments culminating in pleurisy. He never again fully recovered his health, though he was active not only as a poet but as a company executive.

Many poems in Seishi's first collection, *Tōkō* (1932), allude to his youth. "Korsakov," written in 1926, described an old Russian settlement in Karafuto:

tōkō ya	The frozen harbor—
kyūro no machi wa	Nothing to look at now but
ari to no mi [168]	The old Russian town.

Almost all of his Karafuto poems are set in winter, when the harbors are frozen and ships cannot enter port. A certain bleakness of aspect, monochromatic and without much human involvement, marked much of Seishi's poetry. His scenes tended to be large, like the frozen wastelands of Karafuto, rather than carefully observed details of nature in the shasei manner. Unlike Shūōshi, he felt little attraction toward the Japan of the past; he wrote rarely even about Kyoto, where he was born and lived much of his life.[169] His interest in the harsh Karafuto landscapes or in the specifically modern scenes of other parts of Japan gave his poetry an unconventionality that excited young poets of the day. The following haiku was written in 1927 when Seishi visited northern Kyushu on company business:

shichigatsu no	The green July peaks
aomine mijikaku	Seem close enough to touch—
yōkōro [170]	A blast furnace.

Seishi is not contrasting the beauty of nature and the ugliness of man's works, but juxtaposing the strength (and even beauty) of the blast furnace with the grandeur of the mountains. A haiku of 1933 provided a similar juxtaposition:

natsukusa ni	The steam engine's wheels
kikansha no sharin	Grind to a halt as they reach
kite tomaru [171]	The summer grasses.

This poem, composed in Osaka Station, evokes the power not only of a great steam engine, but of vigorous young summer grass by a siding. Seishi captures perfectly a momentary observation, in the shasei tradition, but his subject matter is specifically modern. Seishi is known as the most material of poets, and he rigorously excluded any touch of personal emotion. When he dealt with nature (as opposed to factories and trains), he did not take it as axiomatic that nature must be admired:

karikari to	With a dry crackling
tōrō hachi no	The praying mantis devours
kao wo hamu [172]	The face of the bee.

This extremely harsh verse treats nature with a deliberate lack of sentimentality.

Seishi was famous for the unconventional subjects he introduced into his haiku, including dance halls, skating rinks, rugby whistles, typists in an office, stockholders at a board meeting, and May Day parades. Kyoshi once remarked that Seishi's choice of subjects and defiance of tradition made it likely he would eventually abandon haiku, much as Shimazaki Tōson turned to the novel once he could no longer confine himself to thoughts expressed gracefully in poetry, but Seishi remained faithful to the haiku. His refusal to become involved with his subjects, even when he described highly controversial issues or when (as in 1944) he wrote poetry amid a national disaster, was perhaps what enabled him to confine his expression to the seventeen syllables of the haiku.

Seishi did not immediately join Shūōshi's revolt against *Hototogisu*, though his estrangement from the *Hototogisu* regulars was apparent. He published the collection *Kōki* (Yellow Flag) in 1935 without asking Kyoshi's prior approval, and later that year accepted a formal invitation to join *Ashibi*, breaking his ties with *Hototogisu.* Obviously he did not feel totally at home among the *Ashibi* poets either, if only because he felt less passionately than Shūōshi the absolute necessity of including seasonal references in every haiku. On the other hand, he was much closer to the *Ashibi* poets than to those of *Kyōdai Haiku* (Kyoto University Haiku), who not only espoused seasonless haiku but made it the vehicle of social criticism, directed especially against the hostilities in China. In 1937, the year of the second China Incident, Seishi published perhaps his most famous haiku:

natsu no kawa	River in summer:
akaki tessa no	The end of a red iron chain
hashi hitaru	Soaks in the water.

The poet Saitō Sanki (1900–1962) stated that this poem was his choice as the best of the more than five thousand haiku by Seishi.[173] Another poet, Hirahata Seitō (b. 1905), a longtime associate of Seishi's, declared, "As was true of Bashō's verse, 'The departing spring/Birds weep and in the eyes/Of fish, the tears,' there is such an inexplicable richness of content that the full meaning could not be revealed even in a novel the length of *A Dark Night's Passing.* What other literary art could possibly convey adequately the meaning of Seishi's short poem in seventeen syllables about the river in summer?" [174] Such extreme praise is likely to baffle a non-Japanese reader, even after he studies the more coherent explanation by Yamamoto Kenkichi:

> The scene is one commonly observed at the mouths of rivers in port towns and such places. "Red iron chain" might be interpreted as meaning an iron chain that has been painted red, but I prefer to take the red as being rust on the chain. There is something truly ominous in the mention of the end of the chain soaking in the water, but if one pursues the thought, there is also something indefinably attractive about the scene. The place is on the outskirts of a city, a river or canal near the sea. Factory buildings can be seen nearby, and the tide is probably high. The poem suggests an abun-

dance of water. Needless to say, the water is turbid and has a rancid odor; and the end of the long chain hangs, heavier than stone, in the water. The poetic sensitivity of the writer who could capture this forsaken, ominous scene was indeed acute.[175]

There can be no doubt that the haiku is effective, though Kaneko Tōta (b. 1919) complained of its lack of a critical spirit.[176] A Western reader is nevertheless likely to have difficulty in understanding why such a scene, however effectively captured, should be acclaimed as the masterpiece of a lifetime. If not even a long novel could fully express all that is contained in the seventeen syllables, clearly mysteries impenetrable to ordinary criticism are involved. Yet surely the poem is not an example of the emperor's new clothes. Konishi Jin'ichi, who shared the general admiration of this haiku, though he did not consider it to be Seishi's best poem, began his discussion of Seishi by expressing confidence that he alone could be assigned a place in the history of haiku that will be written hundreds of years in the future.[177]

Seishi published only one book of criticism (in 1938), and even though he often explained the backgrounds of his haiku, rarely attempted to indicate what ultimate statements he had in mind. He thought of his haiku as poems (*shi*) that observed certain special requirements, such as mention of the seasons, but he was a modern man, desirous above all of communicating with other modern men. Even when he used the vocabulary and syntax of the *Manyōshū*, it was not with any archaistic or pious intent, but because he found the *Manyōshū* vocabulary fresher, less trammeled by overuse, than the conventional haiku language. Seishi's use of the old language was poles apart from the conservative usage of Kyoshi or the heavy-handed archaisms of the tanka poets; he was using it as the most basic expression, tracing poetry back to its sources.

After a long period of illness when he composed little poetry, Seishi began to write again in a prodigious burst of energy late in 1944, during the depths of the war. His collection *Gekirō* (Raging Waves, 1944) consists mainly of haiku composed between July and October of that year. Little overt reference is made to the war, though it deeply affected Seishi. A haiku suggested indirectly his feelings of emptiness:

umi ni dete	Moving out to sea
kogarashi kaeru	The winter storm has nowhere
tokoro nashi [178]	For it to return.

The storm wind, blowing meaninglessly out to sea, may have symbolized the poet himself once his poems had been composed.

During the war, fearful that his poetry might be lost, Seishi
entrusted his manuscripts to a disciple, Hashimoto Takako (1899–
1963), a poet of considerable distinction in her own right, who was
even called the "female Seishi." Takako left the *Hototogisu* group
with Seishi, and when Seishi founded the haiku magazine *Tenrō*
(Dog Star) in 1948, breaking his long association with Shūōshi,
she again followed him, helping to make this magazine the outstanding forum of the postwar haiku.

Seishi continued to compose poetry of great individuality,
but his style and vocabulary shifted from time to time. A haiku
written in 1947 attracted more than usual attention:

banryoku ya	Among all things green
wa ga te ni kugi no	My palms are unmarked even
ato mo nashi [179]	By traces of nails.

The reference to the New Testament (the story of Doubting
Thomas in John 20) has been interpreted as meaning that Seishi,
standing amid the eternal vitality of nature ("all things green"),
sees that his palms are not torn by the wounds of Jesus' suffering;
he is just an ordinary human being with no special claim to glory.
Of course Seishi was acquainted with the passage in the New
Testament, but this haiku is apparently not a disclosure of Christian piety. The modern haiku, however lofty its tone, rarely
touched on religion.

KAWABATA BŌSHA (1897–1941) AND LATER *HOTOTOGISU* POETRY

The modern haiku poet whose works were most clearly
marked by religiosity was Kawabata Bōsha. This coloration of his
poetry was apparently not only the result of constant illness but of

the kind of puritanism aroused in him by childhood experiences. His parents ran a geisha house in Tokyo, and the boy, believing this profession to be sinful and sympathizing with the often overworked geishas, turned to Buddhist meditation as an escape from the circumstances surrounding him.[180] In 1923, after the Great Earthquake destroyed his house in Tokyo, he went to live at the Tōfuku-ji in Kyoto, where he studied Zen Buddhism for four years. At first he planned to become a painter, no doubt under the influence of his half-brother, the distinguished artist Kawabata Ryūshi (1885–1966), but he gave up this plan soon after the death of his teacher, Kishida Ryūsei (1891–1929), apparently convinced that his health would not permit this career. The last twenty years of his life were spent in perpetual bouts of illness; the last ten recall Masaoka Shiki's in the intensity of his suffering.

Bōsha began contributing to *Hototogisu* about 1915 and continued his associations with this magazine until his death, unaffected by the newly arisen haiku movement. Indeed, Takahama Kyoshi found in Bōsha a perfect exemplar of his art of "flowers and birds." Bōsha's poetry avoids mention of social change; it was not that he lacked social awareness (he was interested in the Tolstoian endeavors of the *Shirakaba* school of novelists), but he did not think the haiku was a proper medium for such concerns. An early haiku hints at his rejection of worldly involvement:

yomise haya	Night stalls—already
tsuyu no saikoku	Dew lies on *Success Stories*
risshihen	*Of the Western Lands.*

The scene described is of the wares of a secondhand bookseller spread out on the ground at some night market. Among the books is the Meiji period translation of *Self-Help* by Samuel Smiles, a book that had once fired the imaginations of ambitious young Japanese. Now it lies neglected, its paper covers wetted by the night dew. The word "already" (*haya*) evokes the poet's surprise that it is so late dew has already formed; but it also conveys his realization that the ideals of the past have already been discarded.[181]

Bōsha wrote an exceptional number of poems about the dew. His first collection, *Kawabata Bōsha Kushū* (1934), opened with twenty-six haiku on the dew. No doubt he associated his own life, in the traditional manner, with the ephemeral dew, but he insisted paradoxically on its strength, as if to proclaim his intensity of purpose, despite his frailty:

kongō no	A single dewdrop
tsuyu hitotsubu	A diamond of hardness
ishi no ue [182]	Lies on the stone.

Obviously, this was not the standard way to refer to the dew, but Bōsha sensed a strength and absoluteness even in the quickly vanished dew; indeed, a dew of diamond hardness was the symbol of his entire work.[183] People at the time sometimes spoke of Bōsha's "Pure Land," a realm of lasting dewlike beauty.

Another haiku in the same sequence seems to refer more overtly to his condition:

shiratsuyu ni	On the white dewdrops
aun no asahi	Shines the alpha and omega
sashinikeri [184]	Of morning sunlight.

A-un, the first and last letters of the Sanskrit alphabet, were used also to describe the first and last breaths a man took in his life. Bōsha's life was as perishable as the dew, he realized, but this dew could hold for a moment the brilliance of the sun and the beginning and end of life itself.

Bōsha's allegiance to the *Hototogisu* school was so unswerving that one critic called him a "martyr" to the cause of "flowers and birds." [185] His most extensive piece of literary criticism, on Kyoshi's haiku, served only to demonstrate his lack of any firm critical basis for his instinctive preference for "flowers and birds" as the themes of poetry. His haiku were exquisitely fashioned, brilliantly effective in their use of onomatopoeia, and filled with a richness of metaphors unmatched in other modern haiku, but the range was limited. Many poems employed Buddhist imagery, but toward the end of his life the imagery was sometimes Christian, as in this haiku of 1939:

hana anzu	Apricot blossoms—
jutai kokuchi no	A buzzing of wings proclaims
haoto bibi [186]	The Annunciation.

The Japanese words for annunciation (*jutai kokuchi*) literally mean "notification of conception." The surface meaning is that an insect buzzing (*bibi*) among the apricot blossoms informs us of the conception of the flowers; but there are the half-spoken overtones of the "buzzing" of the angel's wings as the angel told Mary she was to give birth. The poem has been compared to Fra Angelico's *Annunciation*, and Bōsha's identification of this Christian scene with the humble sight of a bee fertilizing a flower was typical of his attempts to discover religious truth in even the simplest natural phenomena. Yamamoto Kenkichi admired Bōsha's pantheism, comparing him in this respect to the great Japanese poets—Hitomaro, Saigyō, and Bashō—and crediting Bōsha with a unique ability to see the invisible.[187]

Bōsha's last poem overtly referred to his illness:

ishimakura	A pillow of stone—
shite ware semi ka	Have I become a locust?
naki shigure [188]	This dinning of tears.

In his agony Bōsha finds his pillow as hard as stone, and the ringing in his ears sounds as sharp as the din of locusts. The cries of locusts, as we know from Bashō's celebrated haiku, can pierce even rocks, even the stone of Bōsha's hard pillow.

Bōsha's name was often linked with that of his friend Matsumoto Takashi (1906–1956). The son of a famous Nō actor, Takashi would have followed this career himself had he not developed lung trouble as a boy. For the rest of his life he was afflicted with various nervous ailments. He gave up Nō and began to compose *Hototogisu*-style haiku instead, studying with Kyoshi himself from the time he was fifteen. Takashi's poetry, crowned by his collection *Sekkon* (Soul of Stone, 1953), resembles Bōsha's in his appreciation of flowers and his use of metaphors, but there is a note of sensuousness not present in Bōsha:

yūjoya no	Nightfall in autumn
tsukawanu heya no	In the room at the brothel
aki no kure [189]	Nobody uses.

The circumstances are clearly quite different from those in a poem by Bōsha, but the lonely atmosphere is similar. More important, perhaps, is the fact that these two poets had chosen to associate themselves with the *Hototogisu* principle of celebrating "flowers and birds," at a time when Shūōshi's more dynamic school had won many young poets.

One other poet whose life was cut short by illness deserves mention, Hasegawa Sosei (1907–1946). During most of his career he belonged to the *Hototogisu* group, though for a time he wrote for the quite differently oriented *Kyōdai Haiku*.[190] His poems in *Hototogisu* were marked by a lyricism reminiscent of the tanka, but he gained his greatest fame from the haiku written in 1938–1939 while serving as an artillery officer in China. These poems, collected in *Hōsha* (Gun Carriage, 1939), were in no way critical of the war, but make their points simply, thanks to Sosei's mastery of language. He was taken ill in China and was an invalid for the rest of his life. The poems of his last years, describing the gradual worsening of his condition, are among his most affecting, sometimes realistic, sometimes lyrical, usually tinged with "oriental resignation."

THE POETS OF HUMANITY

NAKAMURA KUSATAO (1901–1983) [191]

Kusatao, though born in Amoy, China, where his father was the Japanese consul, was educated mainly in Matsuyama. Quite naturally he became interested in haiku of the *Hototogisu* school, so long associated with that city. In 1925 he went to Tokyo University to study German literature. His first real awakening to poetry occurred in 1927 when, after his father's death, he suffered a nervous breakdown and, to soothe his turbulent emotions, read tanka by Saitō Mokichi. These tanka made Kusatao realize for the first time that a poet need not compose for other people's benefit; it sufficed if he wrote for his own satisfaction. In later years Kusatao would return to this discovery and apply it to his own poetry.

He met Kyoshi in 1929 and, returning to Tokyo University after an absence, joined the Tokyo University Haiku Society. In 1931, still at the university, he transferred to the Japanese Literature Department, graduating at last in 1933. In the meantime he had become friendly with Matsumoto Takashi and Kawabata

Bōsha. He attended a meeting of the *Hototogisu* group at which he denounced the melodious rhythms of Shūōshi's haiku, then at the height of their popularity. Kusatao's first published collection, *Chōshi* (Eldest Son, 1936), included poems submitted to *Hototogisu* between 1929 and 1936. This collection, so called not only because he was in fact an eldest son but because he believed himself to be bound by the traditional obligations of one, was filled with a fresh lyricism that pleased even those who would later object to the obscurities and irregularities of his work, but Kusatao's special poetic qualities are unmistakable:

furu yuki ya	The falling snow—
Meiji wa tōku	How far away Meiji
narinikeri [192]	Has receded!

This haiku, according to Kusatao's own explanation, was composed as he walked through the section of Tokyo where he had attended elementary school twenty years earlier. On this cold day, when the streets were deserted, it seemed as though time itself had been frozen. It began to snow. Suddenly four or five pupils rushed out of the school in black uniforms with gold buttons. The sight made the poet aware of the passage of time; in his day, the Meiji era, the pupils all wore kimonos.[193] At least this was how Kusatao explained the haiku, but Konishi Jin'ichi, who admired the poem, insisted that if this was indeed the meaning, the haiku was a failure: the atmosphere of the poem suggests some old quarter of Tokyo, not the fashionable suburb where Kusatao attended school.[194] No wonder Kusatao was so reluctant to explain his poems.

The ambiguity of many haiku gave Kusatao the reputation of being a "difficult" poet. He explained: "The principal cause of the obscurity of my haiku is that my character is insignificant, my techniques immature, and my expression inadequate." [195] After this modest disclaimer, he went on to suggest why his poems were appreciated only by a few people and misunderstood by most: it was because "when I compose poetry I compose only for myself." He wrote haiku out of internal necessity, not to please other people, and he therefore often ran counter to their tastes. He also acknowledged that his poetry in recent years (by which he meant

1935–1939) was difficult because it expressed not only sensations or perceptions of beauty but "truth" and "ideas." [196]

Unlike Shūōshi and Seishi, Kusatao remained faithful to the *Hototogisu* school until the war years when, fearful that his own unfounded reputation of being a "dangerous thinker" might affect Kyoshi, he prudently refrained from contributing any poetry to *Hototogisu*.[197] The poems in his early collections were selected by Kyoshi, who frequently expressed his admiration, but a world separated Kusatao from the "flowers and birds" of Kyoshi, and his extremely personal tone contrasted with the blandness of the standard shasei techniques. He most closely resembled Kawabata Bōsha in his tone and in his ability to make symbols of his perceptions and experiences. A Western sensibility, the product of his reading and his knowledge of Western art, is also apparent in his haiku:

gekkō no	On the moonlit wall
kabe ni kisha kuru	A flash of sudden light
hikari kana [198]	As a train approaches.

This poem of 1933 suggests the approach of the train not in terms of its roar but of the poet's perception of the change in light as the engine's searchlights, from the distance at first, touch the surface of the moonlit wall. The train, an ugly product of modern civilization, is perceived in the manner of an impressionist painting.

Kusatao was an enormously prolific poet, and subjects of every variety, from transparently clear descriptions of sights of nature to intensely compressed stories, were somehow fitted into the haiku form. His poems on insects and animals were especially remarkable for their clarity of observation. This example was written just after the end of the war in 1945:

tōrō wa	The praying mantis
basha ni nigerareshi	Looks like a buggy driver
gyosha no sama [199]	Whose horse and buggy ran away.

The exactness of this observation is compelling, but Kusatao was even more celebrated for the humanism of his poetry. In contrast to such contemporaries as Shūōshi or Seishi, who rigorously excluded from their aesthetic or intellectual perceptions anything smelling of human affairs, Kusatao again and again struck home with haiku of powerful humanity, as in this 1939 verse:

banryoku no	Amidst all things
naka ya ako no ha	Verdant, my baby
haesomuru	Has begun to teethe.

Kusatao led a conspicuously happy family life; one critic even compared him to Jesus Christ at the head of a "holy family"! [200] His joy over his infant is perfectly expressed in this example of "montage" juxtaposition of the world of nature and the teething baby. The word *banryoku*, first used by Kusatao but later adopted by many poets, was derived from a line by the Sung poet Wang An-shih in describing a pomegranate; perhaps there was some implied comparison between the baby's teeth and pomegranate seeds.[201] Knowledge of this allusion is by no means essential to appreciation of the haiku, but it suggests the great care Kusatao gave to even seemingly uncomplex poems. The stiffness of the Sino-Japanese word *banryoku* may have been intended to convey the vigorous growth of the plants, whereas the repeated *a* sounds in *naka ya ago no ha hae* more likely were used for the baby's softness. This haiku has been acclaimed as one of Kusatao's masterpieces.

Kusatao's haiku often have somber overtones, as in this one composed in 1937:

shoku no hi wo	I used a candle flame
tabakobi to shitsu	To light my cigarette:
Chiehofu ki	Chekhov's anniversary.

The atmosphere evoked by the poem does not seem to be that of Kusatao's house but of some gloomy room in northern Europe. Virtually no seasonal element is present, though a diligent student might know that Chekhov died on July 15. The atmosphere, as Konishi Jin'ichi remarked, is novelistic rather than typical of the haiku; in fact, many young men of the day who had intended to write novels turned to haiku under Kusatao's influence, finding them less trouble to compose.[202]

During the war years, a fellow poet denounced to the police as subversive some haiku by Kusatao on the death of Kawabata Bōsha in 1941. Kusatao, forced to compromise if he wished to be published at all, consoled himself with the thought that even his faint gestures of resistance might be of value. A haiku composed in 1944 when thirty of his pupils were conscripted for military service has been interpreted by some commentators as an expression of his resistance:

yūki koso	The courage to go on—
chi no shio nare ya	*That* is the salt of the earth:
ume mashiro [203]	Pure white plum blossoms.

The mention of plum blossoms in the last line was included not merely to indicate the season; they were a familiar symbol of purity and bravery (because they bloom in the depths of winter), and they "echo" the color of the salt. But did Kusatao seek to inspire the boys to go and die for their country, or was he urging them to resist the temptation to follow the suicidal impulses of their fellows? This ambiguity is typical of the haiku, and either interpretation is possible. The quotation from the New Testament recalls Bōsha's, though Kusatao, an admirer of Nietzsche, was not often inspired by the Bible. Another biblical example is postwar, from 1946:

sora wa taisho no	The sky is the blue
aosa tsuma yori	Of the Beginning; from my wife
ringo uku [204]	I accept an apple.

Despite the overtones of Adam and Eve, the scene described was real, the cramped quarters where Kusatao and his family lived just after the war. The life was hard but, he tells us, the sky shone with the blue of peace, and when he accepted an apple from his wife it was a gesture of renewal.

Kusatao's really obscure poems are difficult even for Japanese critics to untangle, and would be almost meaningless in translation. The popularity of his haiku, despite such difficulties, was related to his personality as a poet, which survived even in poems that defied parsing. Some poems, expressive of his political convictions, were less ambiguous, but have lost much of their impact because they dealt with ephemeral problems.[205] It is unlikely he will be remembered for such poems. He will probably be read instead for the sidelights on the warm, humanistic convictions he more lastingly expressed in his unquestionably superior works.

KATŌ SHŪSON (1905–1993)

Shūson as a young man was attracted to the modern tanka, especially those by Ishikawa Takuboku, which he knew by heart, and began composing tanka (without any formal guidance) while still in middle school. The long illness of his father, imposing a great strain on the family finances, forced Shūson to give up plans to attend high school. After his father's death in 1925 he went to Tokyo and obtained a teacher's certificate. In 1929 he obtained his first post, at a middle school in Kasukabe, a small town in Saitama Prefecture. Two years later fellow teachers at the school induced him to take up haiku, and although his inclinations were still directed toward the more lyrical tanka, he agreed. In order not to be humiliated by the others, he diligently studied the haiku of Murakami Kijō, the poet they most admired.

The accidental discovery that Mizuhara Shūōshi (in his capacity as a physician) was regularly visiting a hospital in Kasukabe involved Shūson deeply in haiku. He would wait at the hospital gate for Shūōshi and the two men would walk together along the nearby rivers and canals, discussing haiku. Shūson was profoundly moved by Shūōshi's collection *Katsushika*, realizing for the first time the nature of the world treated by the haiku. His early poetry was written under its spell, describing scenes around Kasukabe in Shūōshi's elegiac manner. Shūson later expressed embarrassment over his "escape" into nature and away from the difficulties of his own life. He wrote about two haiku composed in 1931, "Nowadays when I stumble on these poems I feel as if I were looking at soulless dolls. But at the time devoting myself entirely to such subjects was one way of forgetting the contradictions inside me." [206]

Shūson, like Kusatao, would be known as a poet of social consciousness, and his early works were thus atypical. But even his early haiku sometimes suggested an involvement with people alien to Shūōshi, as in this example of 1931:

wata no mi wo	As she goes on picking
tsumiite utau	The cotton bolls she never
koto mo nashi [207]	Breaks into song.

A girl picking cotton is an attractive, even romantic sight that recalls Bashō's haiku on the Oku rice-planters whose song was "the beginning of poetry"; but the hard-working, mechanical labor of cotton-picking provided no occasions for song.

In his poems composed between 1935 and 1937 Shūson demonstrated even more conspicuously his sympathy with the lives of the farmers, which he learned about from their children, his pupils. Four haiku on "the hardships of farming" described treading the barley plants (*mugifumi*). In the spring his pupils were obliged to stay away from school in order that they might patiently, mechanically tread the barley shoots to strengthen them. Shūson, watching them, felt as if they were silently treading on their own roots, stamping into the earth their hopes in a dull realization of their bondage to the soil. Shūson recalled: "After I had made the rounds of my students' houses with such thoughts in my mind, I came gradually to understand my own haiku. I realized I was naturally headed in the direction of demanding from life the right to live. This was something like a firming of my haiku, like the children's treading on the barley shoots." [208]

In 1937, with Shūōshi's encouragement, Shūson moved with his family to Tokyo, to become a student once again, this time in the Japanese Literature Department of Tokyo Bunrika University. His life in Tokyo extended the range of Shūson's subjects to include urban scenes; instead of describing the birds singing along the rivers or the falling leaves in the forests, he wrote about the city streets and especially about the human conditions he observed. From July 1937, when a clash at the Marco Polo Bridge in Peking initiated the second China Incident, until the end of the war in 1945, Shūson's poems were dotted with references to friends or students going off to the front, to his own pacifist sentiments or (at the end) to his resigned acceptance of his role in a life-or-death struggle. A poem composed in 1939 suggested his choked emotions:

hikigaeru	The squatting toad:
dare ka mono ie	Say something, somebody,
koe kagiri [209]	As loud as you can!

The toad was used as the symbol of the patient, heavy attitude of the Japanese people as the war situation grew steadily more oppressive.[210] At a time when no one dared voice overt opposition to the policies of the militarists, Shūson despondently begged someone to speak. The obscurity of this verse, which juxtaposes without explanation a toad and a plea for speech, helped give Shūson the reputation for difficulty he shared with Kusatao. This was not the only cause of his obscurity, but his desire to speak, in riddles if necessary, undoubtedly contributed to the ambiguity. Another haiku written about the same time more openly touched on the war, though the poet's feelings were still hidden:

tsui ni senshi	One ant struggled
ippiki no ari	And struggled, but in the end
yukedo yukedo [211]	Died in battle.

The incident described—the speaker apparently has squashed with his finger an ant crawling on the floor, only for it to drag itself forward on its remaining legs until it finally dies—might have been merely a genre scene if written in more peaceful times, but the reference to the fighting in China was unmistakable. Only the indirection of this haiku enabled Shūson to escape being censored or even imprisoned, but by the same token the obscurity lessened the impact: the poet's sentiments were intelligible only to those who to some extent already shared them.

Shūson spoke with the utmost contempt of haiku poets who described scenes of fighting in China on the basis of newsreels and the like. He contended that no one who had not actually experienced warfare could write about it; the most a poet could do was to reflect the changes within himself the war had brought about. Shūson remained as always preoccupied with the "human" question of how he should live, and tended to look on society as a projection of his own deepest reflections. Perhaps that is why his resistance to the war, once Japan had become totally involved in 1941, was less pronounced than that of men whose principles were more abstract.[212]

Shūson published in 1939 a collection of haiku called *Kanrai* (Winter Lightning). In the preface he declared, "In the haiku I place greatest importance on human life. I search for haiku that have for their foundations the truth about life. . . . I aspire to truth before beauty. I would like to seize the truth of things with startling strength." [213] Such statements are not in themselves remarkable, but the relative lack of interest Shūson manifested in nature, the traditional subject matter of the haiku, and his insistence on truth rather than beauty, would set off this collection (and the subsequently founded magazine *Kanrai*) from Shūōshi's style of poetry.[214] Shūson did not deny the importance of the seasonal elements in haiku, but sought them in depth, rather than in mechanical formulae. His insistence on humanism attracted an exceptional number of the younger poets, including such men as Kaneko Tōta and Sawaki Kin'ichi, who emerged as leaders of the postwar haiku.

Shūson's haiku written at the outbreak of the Greater East Asia War adumbrated the effect of the declaration of war on every household in the country:

jūnigatsu	The eighth of December—
yōka no shimo no	On how many million roofs
yane ikuman [215]	The frost this morning.

"Frost" was unexceptionable as a seasonal word for December, but here it lent a tension, and even a note of apprehension, to the scene.

Most of Shūson's wartime poems were personal and did not deal directly with military developments, but he composed haiku on such subjects as the death of Admiral Yamamoto, and the final charge of the garrison on Attu.[216] When, after the battles at Midway and Guadalcanal in 1942, Japanese reverses threw into doubt the awaited victory, Shūson identified himself with his country in a way impossible for him when Japan had been victorious in China and Southeast Asia. He turned for comfort to the Japanese past, especially the poetry of Bashō. When accused after the war ended by Nakamura Kusatao of having cooperated with the militarists, he did not deny this charge; defeat in war seemed to threaten the very existence of Japan, and Shūson became a quite ordinary Japanese, eager to do his utmost to save his country. No longer the critic of policies that now seemed irreversible, he declared in 1944, "I believe that the time has come when the haiku no longer sings of war, but the war itself gives birth to haiku." The distance between haiku and the war had been all but obliterated, he declared, describing how, with the steadily deteriorating situation in the South Pacific, it had become improper for haiku poets to choose the war as only one of many possible subjects; there could now be no such separation between the poet and the war. The destiny of the country involved the life of each Japanese, and it was the poet's task to go on living and writing, staring death in the face. In that way he might produce haiku of the intensity of Bashō's when he set out on a journey, convinced that death awaited him.[217]

In 1944 Shūson was sent by the Japanese Army Information Section to Mongolia. The ostensible purpose of this and similar journeys sponsored by the army was to familiarize writers with the other peoples of Japan's new empire. Shūson, the first haiku poet sent on such a mission, traveled from July to October through much of China and Mongolia and wrote some nine hundred haiku, which were not published, however, until 1948. He returned to Japan just before the first of the B-29 air raids on Tokyo. From this time until the end of the war Shūson's poetry was concerned almost exclusively with the destruction. Perhaps the most moving of his haiku bore the prefatory note: "On May 23rd there was a large-scale air attack late at night. Carrying my sick brother on my back, I went wandering through the flames all night long in search of Michiko and Akio." [218]

hi no oku ni	In the depths of fire
botan kuzururu	I saw how a peony
sama wo mitsu [219]	Crumbles to pieces.

Shūson's poems describing his war experiences were collected in *Hi no Kioku* (Memories of the Fire, 1948). Half the poems had to be omitted, for fear of annoying the American Occupation authorities, and the whole collection was not published for some years.[220]

Shūson's last collection, *Sammyaku* (Mountain Ranges), published in 1955, displayed his ripest skill as a poet.[221] The haiku are quiet, often about nature, whether observed in the mountains or his own garden while he recuperated from a protracted illness. Shūson often described himself as an ordinary (*heibon*) man. His poems, when not touched by war or similar external circumstances, tended to be quiet, and the influence of Bashō was especially congenial, even in modern contexts:

manhōru no	From the bottom
soko yori koe su	Of a manhole, a voice sounds—
aki no kure [222]	Nightfall in autumn.

The equivalence of the senses between the voice emanating from the depths of the earth and the loneliness of an autumn dusk suggests the world of Bashō's late poetry, and demonstrates Shūson's success in evoking that world.

ISHIDA HAKYŌ (1913–1969)

Hakyō's name was often linked with Kusatao's and Shūson's both because he treated "human" subjects and because his haiku were more than usually difficult. Some of his most affecting poems were, like Shūson's, written at the end of the war and during the bleak days immediately afterward, but although the men shared much, their outlooks on poetry came to differ markedly.

Hakyō was born in Matsuyama, like so many other famous haiku poets. In 1928, while at middle school, he began to write haiku, and before long he and his friends had formed a haiku club. In 1930 he was introduced to Igasaki Kokyō (1896–1935), a disciple of Shūōshi's, and under his tutelage began to submit haiku to *Ashibi*. Hakyō was exceedingly prolific, dashing off close to two thousand haiku each month, and submitting only a small fraction to *Ashibi*. Early in 1932 one of his haiku was chosen to head an issue of *Ashibi*, and on the strength of this success, Kokyō urged him to go to Tokyo, where he entered the Literature Department of Meiji University. Shūōshi took him under his protection, and two years later appointed Hakyō an editor of *Ashibi*. In 1933 Hakyō published his first well-known haiku:

basu wo machi
ōji no haru wo
utagawazu [223]

I wait for a bus,
Not doubting that spring has come
To the avenue.

The poem suggests the excitement of the country-bred Hakyō in the big city. Even as he waits for a bus on some busy street, he is sure that spring has come, observing the difference in the light, the clothes of the passersby, and other untraditional sights of spring. Many early poems are in this vein, but before long Hakyō turned to more "human" themes, sometimes in the vein of autobiography. In 1937 he became an editor of the newly founded journal *Tsuru* (The Crane), and, although he retained his connections with *Ashibi*, published many important poems there.

In the spring of 1937 Hakyō was joined in the *Ashibi* editorial office by Katō Shūson, and for the next three years the two men worked together. The mutual influences of these poets were probably stronger than either received from elsewhere, When they first met, Shūson was known mainly for his haiku describing rustic scenes, and Hakyō for his city poems; but before long they came to be moved by the same urge to seek out humanity in their poetry.[224] The obscurity of expression they shared with Kusatao was the result of a common desire to impart weight and density to their haiku. Hakyō at this time read widely in European fiction of the nineteenth century. Though this influence is not immediately apparent, storytelling elements dominate such haiku as the following example of 1939:

onna ku to   "A woman has come!"
obi makiizuru   I go out, tying my sash—
sarusuberi [225]   Crepe myrtle blossoms.

The scene is a bachelor apartment. Mention of the crepe myrtle tells us it is summer, and the young man is probably lounging around in his underwear. At word that he has a lady visitor he hastily puts on his kimono and is tying the sash even as he hurries out to meet her. It does not matter whether the woman is a total stranger or his mistress; the effect is to convey the atmosphere of a bachelor's life in rather humble quarters. Yokomitsu Riichi predicted (inaccurately) that Hakyō would certainly write novels, but Hakyō replied, "Haiku are my 'I novels.' " [226]

Hakyō's poetic interests took a different turn during the early war years when he "rediscovered" Genroku haiku, especially Bashō's collection *Sarumino*. He began to express the conviction that haiku must be poetic, distinctly unlike prose, and he felt increasingly dissatisfied with the *Ashibi* school,[227] because it scorned the conventional *kireji* and sometimes, in the desire to be strong and modern, risked being prosaic or even banal. He asserted that he had had his fill of haiku in which everything was spelled out, and announced that haiku was *not* literature. His denial of Shiki's cherished principle was a reassertion of the special domain of the haiku, unlike that of any other form of literature, rather than a denial of the haiku's worth. Although the subject matter and the prevailing thought of his poems at this time were certainly not in the vein of *Sarumino*, the expression would not have startled Bashō. In September 1943, when Hakyō was conscripted, he composed this haiku:

karigane ya	The migrant geese—
nokoru mono mina	Everything remaining here
utsukushiki [228]	Is beautiful.

This haiku evokes the poet's emotions as he sets out for service at the front in China. It is the season when migrant geese pass overhead. Hakyō, noting that nothing has changed since he received his conscription papers, finds all the familiar sights he is about to leave beautiful. The first line concludes, like those of so many traditional haiku (but few written by poets of the *Ashibi* school), with *ya*, an example of Hakyō's use of the traditional *kireji*, in his *Sarumino* manner.

Hakyō was assigned to a carrier-pigeon unit in North China. This assignment was indeed a curious accident: Hakyō's love of birds and small animals, revealed in many haiku, was so pronounced that many critics likened him to Issa.[229] A few months later, however, he contracted pleurisy and was sent back to Japan for discharge. For the rest of his life he was to be afflicted by long bouts of illness. A haiku written while he lay ill in China suggests how deeply the spirit of the Genroku haiku permeated him even in moments of greatest distress:

nemu no tsuki	Moonlight spilling
koborete mune no	Through the acacia blossoms
hienikeri [230]	Sends chills to my chest.

The verb ending *keri* of the last line would certainly have been considered archaic by the *Ashibi* poets, but effectively conveyed the shock of the juxtaposition of the moon and his illness.

Hakyō's poems written at the end of the war and during the hard years afterward perfectly captured his impressions and emotions. The poems are particularly affecting in their evocations of the wretched lives led in the burned-out ruins of Tokyo. In March 1946 Hakyō put up a shack for himself and his family where they lived in poverty. A poem written in that year was explained in these terms by Hakyō: "A bombed-out site. The scene is a shack someone has thrown up. There are no proper walls or ceiling. The only touch of decoration bespeaking the presence of a woman is a water plantain stuck in an empty can at one corner."

rokugatsu no	It's June
onna suwareru	And a woman is sitting
aramushiro [231]	On a coarse straw mat.

The haiku effectively contrasts the beauty of the woman with the meanness of the surroundings.

Hakyō underwent two major operations in 1948, but wrote many memorable poems about this time. His collection *Sha-kumyō* (Clinging to Life, 1950) was acclaimed as a monument of the modern haiku.[232] One poem in this collection attracted particular attention:

yuki wa shizuka ni	The snow is quiet,
yutaka ni hayashi	Abundant, precipitous:
kabane shitsu	The mortuary.

Hakyō supplied an explanation for this haiku. There had been a brief but intense fall of snow. He wrote in his work notebook:

Yuki wa shizuka ni yutaka ni hageshi ("It is snowing quietly, abundantly, fiercely"), but changed the middle syllable of the last word to *hayashi* (swift). "It was snowing so hard I wrote down *hageshi* (intense) without thinking, but having once said that, there was nothing left to say." He felt that the word *hageshi* was "crude, explanatory, and incoherent." The "montage" use of "mortuary" also troubled Hakyō. Wouldn't garage, kitchen shed or pharmaceutical storeroom have done just as well? He chose the mortuary, a building at some distance from the hospital, because it seemed more appropriate to a haiku, and because this little building could easily be blotted out by a sudden, heavy snow. Yamamoto Kenkichi, not knowing the actual circumstances of the composition of this haiku, interpreted it quite differently: he believed that the emphasis was on the lonely, bleak chamber where a body is reposing before being cremated the next day. The snow falling outside intensifies the stillness within the room and establishes a contrast between the grief of the mourners and insentient nature.[233] Yamamoto obviously discovered more in the poem than Hakyō had consciously included, but this does not mean he was mistaken. The ambiguity of the haiku, the result of its brevity, omission of necessary grammatical particles and avoidance of "explanation," inevitably gives rise to varying interpretations. Indeed, this was precisely what appealed to Hakyō; if he had wished to make a clear statement with no danger of being misunderstood, he would never have written haiku.

POSTWAR HAIKU

The purpose and functions of the modern haiku were called into question almost as soon as the war ended. In the November 1946 issue of the magazine *Sekai*, Kuwabara Takeo of Kyoto University published the article "Daini Geijutsu" (Second-Class Art), a discussion of the modern haiku. The immediate stimulus for the article may have been provided by the extraordinary display of interest in the haiku during the preceding year, when at least twenty-five haiku magazines were either revived or newly founded. Adopting the technique of I. A. Richards in *Practical Criticism*, he asked various intellectuals to evaluate fifteen haiku, ten by recognized masters such as Nakamura Kusatao, Iida Dakotsu, and Takahama Kyoshi, and five by completely unknown amateurs, not revealing the poets' names. The responses were chaotic, a proof to Kuwabara that no objective standards of excellence existed. He complained that some of the haiku by modern writers were so obscure that nobody would make the effort to understand them unless they knew in advance the poems were by masters. It is not necessary to "translate" into contemporary French a poem by Baudelaire or Verlaine, but without a translation or paraphrase few readers, even among persons of great literary sensitivity, could grasp the meaning of many modern haiku. Some haiku poets (like Shūōshi) have stated that unless a man has composed haiku himself he cannot hope to understand them; but if this is true, it is a most damning judgment of the haiku. Would the same be said of a novel, a film, or a work of sculpture? Other men have claimed that it was not possible to judge a haiku poet's worth by one poem, and it might therefore happen that a rank amateur's composition would seem superior to a lesser verse by a master, but would it ever happen that even a single short story by a great writer would be thought inferior to one by a rank amateur? [234]

Kuwabara also derided the factionalism in the modern haiku and the fundamental lack of concern with serious issues.[235] Earlier in 1946 he had written about the modern Japanese novel, "The haiku spirit has lingered on among novelists since the Meiji era, and thereby inhibited the development of the modern novel. I believe it would be wise therefore to forget haiku for the time being, in the interests both of future literature and of the lives of our people." [236] He recognized that attempts had been made to revivify the haiku, but concluded that it could never be the vehicle for the complexities of modern life.

The outcry from offended haiku poets was deafening. Needless to say, the masters were indignant and offered many rebuttals that pointed out the flaws in Kuwabara's methodology; but some younger poets were so shocked that they considered giving up haiku altogether, and no one could deny that the first serious discussion of the haiku since the defeat had been provoked. Replies to Kuwabara's charges were made both by the conservative poets and by such independently minded men as Yamaguchi Seishi and Nakamura Kusatao. Regardless of the point of view, the arguments advanced against Kuwabara's essay generally turned on his lack of qualifications to judge haiku, an art with its own special rules that could not be fully comprehended by every amateur connoisseur of literature. These poets insisted, moreover, that they were trying to the best of their abilities to incorporate modern thought into their poetry; if Kuwabara failed to detect this intent, it was no doubt because of the elliptical expression characteristic of haiku. But Katō Shūson wrote, "It is no longer possible to go on composing haiku without being aware that the haiku's survival is uncertain." [237]

The definitions of the purpose of haiku made during the following decade no longer devolved on such familiar issues as the necessity of maintaining the seventeen syllables and the seasonal words of the haiku, but on such subjects as "the quest of the oriental concept of nothingness" and "the impossibility of pure cognition through the emotions." The social content of the haiku, also mentioned by Kuwabara, became of special concern in 1953 when the importance of socialist ideology to the haiku was proclaimed.[238] In the development of the haiku during the period since 1925 two works were of special significance: Kyoshi's famous proclamation that the haiku must be devoted to flowers and birds and Kuwabara's attack on the modern haiku as a second-class art. Though totally dissimilar in content, both set off fruitful discussions on the meaning of the survival of the haiku in the twentieth century.

The immediate postwar years were marked by the return to haiku of various poets who had been badly treated or even imprisoned by the militarists. The most interesting of them was Saitō Sanki (1900–1962), whose sophisticated poetry was not directly connected to any tradition of modern haiku.[239] This distinctiveness may have been the result of his residence abroad from 1925 to 1929, when he practiced as a dentist in Singapore. Unlike many Japanese abroad, Sanki enjoyed the life there and made friends from different countries. Indeed, he might never have returned to Japan had not two disasters struck: the activities of the Japanese army in China precipitated an anti-Japanese boycott that affected his practice, and he himself had a serious case of typhoid fever. He returned to Japan in despair, with no prospects of suitable employment. He felt like a stranger in his own country, but quite by chance he was encouraged to take up haiku, and he threw himself into poetry to forget his troubles. He was thirty at the time, unusually late for a haiku poet to take up his career, and his poems naturally lacked the youthful ardor associated with beginners, but he brought to the haiku a special freshness, above all in the language. An early haiku is revelatory:

kan'ya ake	A cold night's dawning:
akai zōka ga	That red paper flower
mata mo aru	Is still there today.

The language of this haiku was characterized by Yamamoto Kenkichi as being close to "broken Japanese."[240] The first line contains the ponderous Sino-Japanese expression *kan'ya* (cold night); the second is colloquial; and the third opens with *mata mo*, a typical *Manyōshū* phrase, only to conclude with a colloquial verb. Sanki obviously paid no attention to these anachronisms, or perhaps he was attempting to shock. The traditionalists, needless to say, found the poem jarring and unfinished, but younger poets welcomed the dryly unsentimental language and the rigorous avoidance of the "fragrances" of the old haiku diction. This poem evokes the author's feelings as he opens his eyes to see once again a paper flower, no doubt the beautifying touch contributed by his wife or girl friend to his room, dusty and cheerless on a cold morning.

Sanki had joined the *Kyōdai Haiku* poets in 1934, sharing in their unconventionality, if not their advanced political views. His remarkable aptitude won him the reputation of being a "wizard of haiku," and he enjoyed great popularity. He was arrested in 1940 along with other *Kyōdai Haiku* poets and detained for over two months before being released with a suspended indictment. He gave up haiku until after the war, when he took up again his sardonic, often erotic compositions. A haiku written in 1947 captured the rare feelings of common humanity shared by people undergoing the same hardships:

uete mina	Starving, how friendly
shitashi ya nowaki	Everyone is! The autumn wind
tōku yori [241]	Comes from the distance.

The following haiku, written about Hiroshima in 1947, was provided with this background by Sanki: "Night streets that still shriek. The traveler's mouth is clamped shut. He opens it only to eat a smooth boiled egg, just wide enough to admit the egg."

Hiroshima ya	At Hiroshima
tamago kuu toki	When I eat a boiled egg
kuchi hiraku	I open my mouth.

Sanki's note confirms the surrealistic quality of the poem. One commentator likened the face of the traveler, stunned into horrified silence by what he has seen of the devastation of the atomic bomb, to the featureless shell of an egg, as if all individual traits had dissolved.[242]

Although Sanki was closely associated with poets who insisted on the importance of social consciousness, he himself apparently had no hopes for a liberation by revolution; instead, he waited with eagerness for the one day when the world would collapse of itself. His nihilism did not prevent him from feeling the warm solidarity with the people he expressed in this haiku of 1952:

kuraku atsuku	In the dark and heat
daigunshū to	I wait for the fireworks
hanabi matsu	Along with the crowd.

Sanki explained this poem (in which he took special pride): "One would have supposed that people would have had as much of noise and light as they could possibly stand during the air raids and fires, but the teeming multitude, desiring nothing better than to see the brilliance of fireworks, stands dark and hot with expectation. This seems to me to be something like a symbol of modern society."[243]

Sanki's unconventional subject matter and treatment exerted a marked influence on the haiku composed by many other men during the postwar years. Tomizawa Kakio (1902–1962), an old friend of Sanki's, was even bolder in his rejection of traditional elements in the haiku like the seasonal words and in his vocabulary was almost identical with that of the *gendaishi* (contemporary poetry). His poems exclude flowers and birds, except ironically, and the atmosphere is prevailingly dark and cold, as in this poem written in 1949:

> *gunkan ga shizunda umi no*
> *oitaru kamome* [244]

> An aged seagull
> Over waters where a warship foundered.

Kakio's aim of establishing haiku as a poetic art without either secret traditions or inherent limitations of subject matter was otherwise expressed in his founding in 1948 of a short-lived magazine that printed indiscriminately tanka, haiku, and modern poetry, a revolutionary innovation to most poets, who considered the three forms not only totally distinct but mutually exclusive.[245]

During the immediate postwar years there was great activity in haiku circles, despite the disillusionment induced by Kuwabara's famous article. In 1947 the New Haiku Poets' Association (*Shin Haikujin Remmei*) was founded. Its members included almost all the most distinguished haiku poets and critics, but there was no unity of opinions among them. The younger poets wanted to break away from all the haiku conventions; not only did they do away with the seasonal words and the fixed form in seventeen syllables, as many other haiku poets before them, but they introduced hitherto forbidden subject matter, in the attempt to expand the range of expression. Haiku on aspects of nature unaffected by the seasons, on parts of human anatomy, and on social issues of a totally "unpoetic" nature reflected their impatience with the traditional flowers and birds and even with beauty itself.[246] Their references to demonstrations, labor disputes, and the like gave their haiku topicality, but ran the risk of becoming ephemeral, rather in the manner of the Danrin school's references to contemporary gossip. A competition for haiku on May Day 1948 produced such anonymous winners as:

> *mēdē no*   When one links arms
> *ude kumeba ame*   On May Day, even the rain
> *atatakashi* [247]   Is warming.

Obviously the sentiments expressed are sincere, but the poem lacks any specifically haiku quality. The outbreak of the Korean War in 1950 stirred many haiku poets into expressing their reactions, sometimes as baldly as in the May Day poem, sometimes with the skill of Nakamura Kusatao, who at this time stood at the forefront of the committed haiku poets:

chōchō no	A butterfly
ōkō kōrudo	Traverses the sky
uōa no naka [248]	Amidst the Cold War.

Such haiku were possible because the authors were free of the fear of political censorship or of being ostracized by fellow poets.

Political developments were naturally not the only new subjects of haiku poetry. Every object that met the poet's eye, whether a postage stamp or a wheelchair, had become a legitimate subject of haiku, and words of foreign origin dotted the new poems, flaunting their Modernism. But if the vice of the traditional haiku had been blandness and conventionality, the new ones tended to be prosaic or obscure. The novelty of the most avant-garde or even revolutionary haiku was also often vitiated by the conservatism of its diction. Most haiku, regardless of content, were still composed in the classical language,[249] and to a surprising extent the seventeen syllables were maintained. The relative concision of the classical language suited the brief haiku form better than the colloquial, and the form itself had to be preserved in some manner if a haiku were not to degenerate into a mere short statement.

Kaneko Tōta, who emerged as the most articulate of the younger poets, took particular pride in this haiku:

dore mo kuchi	How lovely their mouths,
utsukushi banka no	All of them: a late summer
jazu ichidan	Jazz combo.

The haiku contains the seasonal word *banka* (late summer), but Tōta insisted that he included it not out of any obligation to the old rules, but because it exactly fitted the poem he wanted to write about a jazz combo. He was struck by the redness of the lips of the young musicians in the bright sunshine, and mentioning the late summer gave definition to the scene; however, he assured readers, if he had thought of an even more suitable expression, he would certainly have used it, regardless of whether it contained a seasonal association or not.[250]

Tōta explained how he, a professional haiku poet, set about composing a poem. He gave the seven stages of a single haiku that resulted in this final version:

tsuyoshi seinen
hikata ni tamanegi
kusaru hi mo

How strong they are, the young men,
Even on a day when onions
Rot on the dry beach.

He explained the circumstances of the poem: one summer day he noticed some onions lying on the beach, perhaps fallen into the sea when a ship was being unloaded. He also noticed some young men capering around on the beach. His first attempt at depicting this scene was:

tamanegi korobu	On the dry beach
hikata ni tsudou	Where onions roll around
seinenra [251]	Gather the young men.

He was pleased to have noticed the onions, rather than some more conventional object on a beach (such as shells or baby crabs); mention of onions would be unusual enough to make the reader pause. But this first effort was little more than a bare description of what the poet had observed. Such a description might have suited a *Hototogisu* poet, but Tōta felt the need for greater tension and subjectivity. In the effort to achieve these qualities, he inevitably moved toward greater obscurity of expression, omitting certain information necessary for easy understanding. The final version is unquestionably a superior poem and would be immediately recognizable as such by any person seriously interested in haiku, but its appeal to a wider public was limited by the modern techniques the poet employed. This was true not only of Kaneko

Tōta, but of most poets of his generation. An anonymous article published in February 1957 declared that the modern haiku had become a literature without readers. "In brief, one can say with respect to haiku that the reader is the writer himself." [252] The article estimated that as many as a million amateur poets, belonging to haiku organizations each headed by some well-known poet, supported the publication of many magazines chiefly for the pleasure of seeing their own poems in print.

Needless to say, even if the haiku of these amateurs are by no means masterpieces, they do no harm, and composing a poem in seventeen syllables can be not only a pleasant creative activity but positively therapeutic. The question remains, however, how much more can the contemporary haiku be than a diversion? Is it possible to write poetry with a specifically modern intelligence about matters of deep concern to modern men and still satisfy some definition of the haiku? Clearly some poets succeeded in this endeavor, but their poems ran the danger of becoming unintelligible, if only because of the compression involved in fitting complex thoughts into so short a form. If a poet is content with the applause of the discriminating few, he can write poems of the utmost difficulty, but if he believes in the social message of his haiku, he will normally wish to communicate with a wider public.

The importance of the social significance of haiku was first brought to public attention in 1953 by Nakamura Kusatao when he published the collection *Ginga Izen* (The Milky Way as Before). In the afterword he declared that his poems represented a "violent confluence" of elements of a conceptual and social nature with purely poetic elements, and he stressed the compulsion he felt as a member of society to treat directly phenomena of historical importance he had witnessed with his own eyes.[253] In the following year Sawaki Kin'ichi (b. 1919), the leading spirit of the magazine *Kaze* (The Wind), stated that he meant by haiku of social significance poems of progressive tendencies, especially those inspired by the ideology of socialism. Kaneko Tōta about the same time affirmed that the poet had to consider himself as existing within a social context and that he must display his awareness of the attitudes of those who sought to solve social problems.[254] Their ideological approach to the haiku was strongly opposed by Yamamoto Kenkichi, and sharp exchanges of opinion were published by both sides. The results were inconclusive, and

Kaneko's interests eventually turned from ideological to more strictly literary concerns. But Sawaki continued to stand at the forefront in composing haiku of social significance. A series of haiku describing the salt fields of the Noto Peninsula he visited in 1955 included this example:

enden ni	In the salt fields
hyakunichi sujime	One hundred days of raking
tsuketōshi [255]	Lines in the sand.

The picture here is of a primitive and infinitely laborious process. Buckets of sea water are repeatedly dumped, all day long, into sand plots exposed to the hot summer sun. The water evaporates, leaving the salt. The sun is hot enough to make this crude method of salt extraction possible only for about one hundred days in the year. The raking of the sand, generally left to the women, was (like the rest of the process) back-breaking labor. Sawaki's poem, effectively depicting the scene, earned the praise of such men as Mizuhara Shūōshi and Yamaguchi Seishi for its rare success in incorporating into the poem itself theories of social consciousness often advocated by critics of haiku.[256]

It is unlikely that the haiku can ever be the most effective form a writer can use to convey his indignation over, say, a political system that tolerates the terrible working conditions in the salt fields. An indictment in some other form—whether of journalism, fiction, or modern poetry—would certainly be more likely to produce a strong effect, but if the haiku is the manner of expression most congenial to a particular poet, he must somehow combine the message of his criticism with distinctively poetic elements, whether the haiku form (meticulously observed by Sawaki in this poem), a traditional vocabulary, or perceptions of beauty that link the new poem with haiku history.

Experiments in the 1950s and 1960s attempted directly or indirectly to determine the limits of haiku expression. For the poets of the *Seigen* group like Itami Mikihiko (b. 1920), the determination to wrest the haiku from the domination of aged masters led to an insistence on modern language and imagery, but within the traditional haiku form. Other men wrote haiku of hermetic obscurity. In 1946 Yamamoto Kenkichi had stated that the haiku was "not an art of sentiments but of cognition," and that it was "a means of arriving at ideas through a form of its own in seventeen syllables." [257] He gave as the three distinctive features of haiku: its humor, its function as a greeting, and its impromptu quality. None of these features in fact marked the postwar haiku, which was usually solemn, introspective, and carefully wrought. The doom of the haiku, announced by Kuwabara in 1946, did not take place, but its survival as a serious medium of poetry was something of a mystery. The death of Takahama Kyoshi in 1959 left a void not only within the *Hototogisu* establishment but in the world of haiku as a whole, regardless of school. It is difficult to say of a poetic art that is supported by a million or more devotees that it may be dying, but there are few signs of the kind of revival that might restore the haiku to its traditional place of importance in Japanese literature.

NOTES

1. Katō Shūson, "Meiji Haiku Shi," I, p. 5.
2. Katsumine Shimpū, *Meiji Haikai Shiwa*, p. 14.
3. Katō, "Meiji Haiku," p. 7.
4. *Ibid.*, p. 12.
5. Katsumine, *Meiji Haikai*, p. 8.
6. This was Bakin's compilation *Haikai Saijiki*. See Katō, "Meiji Haiku," p. 21.
7. Matsui Toshihiko, *Kindai Hairon Shi*, p. 30.
8. *Ibid.*, pp. 34–36.
9. *Ibid.*, p. 31.
10. *Ibid.*, pp. 32, 37.
11. Quoted in *ibid.*, p. 46.
12. Quoted in *ibid.*, p. 47.
13. *Ibid.*, p. 50.
14. Katō, "Meiji Haiku," p. 1.
15. *Dassai*, one of Shiki's literary styles, referred to *dassaigyo*, the alleged habit of the otter of catching a great many fish and spreading them out before eating; by extension, it meant a scholar who gathers many reference books around him.
16. *Shiki Zenshū*, IV, p. 166.
17. *Ibid.*, pp. 166–67.
18. *Ibid.*, p. 204.
19. *Ibid.*, p. 206.
20. *Ibid.*, p. 230.
21. *Ibid.*, p. 234.
22. *Ibid.*, p. 238.

23. He gave as examples of Bashō's grandeur such verses as *Natsukusa ya, Samidare wo atsumete, Araumi ya,* and *Tsuka mo ugoke,* all from *Oku no Hosomichi.*

24. *Shiki Zenshū,* IV, p. 258.

25. *Ibid.,* pp. 266–67.

26. *Ibid.,* p. 295. This quotation is from *Saitan Kanwa* (1893).

27. *Ibid.,* pp. 363, 368. Quotations from *Haikai Taiyō* (1895).

28. *Ibid.,* IV, p. 625.

29. *Ibid.,* pp. 626–29.

30. Entry for June 26, 1901, in *Bokujū Itteki.* See *Shiki Zenshū,* XI, p. 219.

31. Matsui, *Kindai Hairon,* p. 75. For the full account of this occasion, see *Shiki Zenshū,* XIII, pp. 595–97. Shiki proposed to Fusetsu that they wage a competition between painting and haiku, but when he saw Fusetsu's sketches he declared that the haiku had lost the competition. One sketch is reproduced on p. 597.

32. *Ibid.,* p. 76.

33. *Ibid.,* p. 84.

34. *Shiki Zenshū,* IV, pp. 505–06. From *Meiji Nijūkunen no Haikukai* (1897).

35. *Ibid.,* pp. 482–83. Shiki says in the same essay (p. 483) that at one time he worshiped the West but now, by way of reaction, he has come to look down on the West and he worships only Japanese things.

36. Matsui, *Kindai Hairon,* p. 110, quoting an article written in 1895.

37. *Shiki Zenshū,* V, p. 169. Quotation from *Haiku Shimpa no Keikō* (1899).

38. Matsui, *Kindai Hairon,* p. 112. Quotation from *Byōshō Rokushaku,* entry for June 26, 1902. (*Shiki Zenshū,* V, p. 290.)

39. Matsui, *Kindai Hairon,* p. 114.

40. Donald Keene, *Landscapes and Portraits,* p. 159. The bird known as *hototogisu* in Japanese or *shiki* in Sino-Japanese was reputed to cough blood.

41. Katō, "Meiji Haiku," p. 51.

42. Matsui Toshihiko, *Masaoka Shiki,* p. 120. See also *Shiki Zenshū,* II, p. 108.

43. Matsui, *Masaoka Shiki,* p. 127. See also *Shiki Zenshū,* II, p. 174.

44. See Keene, *Landscapes,* p. 264, and Katō, "Meiji Haiku," pp. 63–64.

45. Ōno Rinka, *Kindai Haiku no Kanshō to Hihyō,* p. 15. See also *Shiki Zenshū,* II, p. 325.

46. Kyoshi wrote the long autobiographical novel *Kaki Futatsu,* which describes his dread of being dominated by Shiki and his decision to make his way independently. Text in *Ishikawa Takuboku, Masaoka Shiki, Takahama Kyoshi.*

47. Matsui, *Masaoka Shiki,* p. 139. This haiku was composed in 1896. See also *Shiki Zenshū,* II, p. 414.

48. Yamamoto Kenkichi, *Gendai Haiku,* p. 15. See also *Shiki Zenshū,* II, p. 610.

49. Yamamoto, *Gendai Haiku,* p. 19.

50. He reserved his complaints for the secret diary *Gyōga Manroku,* which he never intended to publish.

51. Quoted by Yamamoto, *Gendai Haiku,* pp. 26–27. For a further discussion of this haiku, see Janine Beichman, *Masaoka Shiki,* pp. 64–67.

52. Yamamoto, *Gendai Haiku,* p. 26.

53. Ōno, *Kindai Haiku,* p. 22.

54. *Ibid.*, p. 23. See also *Shiki Zenshū*, III, p. 473.

55. Takeda Ōtō, *Naitō Meisetsu Kenkyū*, pp. 1–2.

56. Ōno, *Kindai Haiku*, p. 33. For a more extensive selection of Sōseki's haiku, see Makoto Ueda, *Modern Japanese Haiku*, pp. 38–47.

57. Abe Kimio, *Kawahigashi Hekigotō*, p. 13.

58. *Ibid.*, p. 18.

59. *Ibid.*, p. 22.

60. The magazine was originally founded in Matsuyama in 1897 as the organ of Shiki's Nihon school of haiku, but soon ran into financial difficulties. Takahama Kyoshi was able to borrow money to keep the magazine going, then moved it to Tokyo, where the first issue appeared in October 1898. See Kiyozaki Toshirō, *Takahama Kyoshi*, pp. 31–32.

61. *Shiki Zenshū*, V, p. 154.

62. Kiyozaki, *Takahama Kyoshi*, p. 36.

63. Abe, *Kawahigashi Hekigotō*, p. 159.

64. Kyoshi charged that the second and third lines of the poem did not go together, and suggested several more plausible variants, but Hekigotō replied that he had not even thought of harmonizing his images; he had merely reported what he had actually seen. (Matsui, *Kindai Hairon*, p. 136.) This was the first open break between the two men.

65. Ōsuga Otsuji, quoted in Ōta Kōson, "Meiji Haiku Shi," II, p. 90.

66. Abe, *Kawahigashi Hekigotō*, p. 47.

67. Ōta, "Meiji Haiku," pp. 106–07. See also Murayama Kokyō, *Ōsuga Otsuji Hairon Shū*, p. 22.

68. Matsui, *Kindai Hairon*, p. 178. Murayama, *Ōsuga Otsuji*, pp. 21–22.

69. Murayama, *Ōsuga Otsuji*, pp. 20–21; Matsui, *Kindai Hairon Shi*, p. 177.

70. Abe, *Kawahigashi Hekigotō*, p. 60.

71. *Ibid.*, p. 80. See Murayama, *Ōsuga Otsuji*, pp. 94–99, for Otsuji's devastating appraisal of Hekigotō's poetry.

72. See Abe, *Kawahigashi Hekigotō*, p. 202; also, Yamashita Kazumi et al., *Kindai Haiku Shū*, p. 138.

73. Konishi Jin'ichi, *Haiku*, p. 196.

74. Abe, *Kawahigashi Hekigotō*, pp. 100–101.

75. Konishi, *Haiku*, p. 196.

76. Matsui, *Kindai Hairon*, p. 132.

77. *Ibid.*, pp. 133–35.

78. Yamamoto, *Gendai Haiku*, p. 44.

79. This discussion may recall the passage in *Kyoraishō*, which describes why a poem by Bashō about the departing spring could refer only to Ōmi.

80. Kiyozaki, *Takahama Kyoshi*, p. 182.

81. *Ibid.*, p. 66.

82. *Ibid.*, p. 179.

83. Konishi, *Haiku*, p. 198.

84. Kiyozaki, *Takahama Kyoshi*, p. 177.

85. *Ibid.*, p. 30.

86. *Ibid.*, p. 103.

87. James Cahill, *Chinese Painting*, pp. 67ff.

88. *Ibid.*, pp. 73–74.
89. *Ibid.*, p. 74.
90. Kiyozaki, *Takahama Kyoshi*, pp. 106–07.
91. *Haikai Daijiten*, p. 163.
92. Kiyozaki, *Takahama Kyoshi*, p. 122.
93. Ōno Rinka, "Ogiwara Seisensui," p. 79.
94. Akiyama Shūkōryō, "Ogiwara Seisensui," pp. 199–200.
95. Ōno, "Ogiwara," p. 81. See also Yamashita, pp. 177 and 441, for a somewhat different interpretation.
96. Yamashita, *Kindai Haiku Shū*, p. 41.
97. *Ibid.*, p. 183.
98. Akiyama Shūkōryō, "Ozaki Hōsai," p. 220.
99. *Ibid.*, p. 221.
100. *Ibid.*
101. Konishi, *Haiku*, p. 202.
102. Akiyama, "Ozaki," p. 226. See also Yamashita, *Kindai Haiku Shū*, pp. 193, 443.
103. Akiyama, "Ozaki," p. 225.
104. *Ibid.*, p. 219.
105. Ōno Rinka, "Taneda Santōka," p. 90. For translations of poetry by Santōka, as well as detailed biographical information, see James Abrams, "Hail in the Begging Bowl."
106. Ōno, "Taneda," p. 91.
107. Izawa Motoyoshi, "Nakatsuka Ippekirō," p. 194.
108. Ōno, *Kindai Haiku*, p. 86.
109. For extensive translations of haiku by Ippekirō, see Soichi Furuta, *Cape Jasmine and Pomegranates*.
110. Matsumoto Asahi, "Murakami Kijō," p. 31.
111. Nakamura Kusatao, "Murakami Kijō," pp. 126–27.
112. Yamamoto, *Gendai Haiku*, p. 70.
113. Matsumoto, "Murakami Kijō," p. 34.
114. *Ibid.*, p. 37.
115. Quoted in Yamamoto, *Gendai Haiku*, p. 68.
116. *Ibid.*, p. 70.
117. Matsumoto, "Murakami Kijō," p. 39.
118. Konishi, *Haiku*, p. 208.
119. Dakotsu is quoted in Ōno, *Kindai Haiku*, p. 164; see also Yamashita, p. 445.
120. Yamamoto, *Gendai Haiku*, p. 79.
121. *Ibid.*, p. 81.
122. *Ibid.*, pp. 81–82.
123. Nakamura Kusatao, "Hara Sekitei," p. 138.
124. Yamamoto, *Gendai Haiku*, pp. 92–93.
125. Nakamura, "Hara," p. 139.
126. *Ibid.*, pp. 139–40.
127. Yamamoto, *Gendai Haiku*, p. 93.
128. Ōno, *Kindai Haiku*, p. 199.

129. Quoted from *Susumubeki Haiku no Michi* in *ibid.*, p. 182.
130. *Ibid.*, p. 182.
131. Yamamoto, *Gendai Haiku*, p. 106.
132. Ishida Hakyō, "Maeda Fura," p. 161.
133. Yamashita, *Kindai Haiku Shū*, p. 229.
134. *Ibid.*, p. 232.
135. *Ibid.*, p. 234.
136. *Haikai Daijiten*, p. 424.
137. Yamamoto, *Gendai Haiku*, p. 141.
138. Quoted in *ibid.*, p. 140.
139. *Ibid.*, p. 140.
140. Konishi, *Haiku*, p. 217.
141. Katsura Nobuko, "Hino Sōjō," p. 229.
142. *Ibid.*, p. 231; Azumi Atsushi, "Hino Sōjō," p. 245.
143. Mizuhara Shūōshi, *Takahama Kyoshi*, p. 6.
144. *Ibid.*, p. 10.
145. *Ibid.*, pp. 16–17.
146. *Ibid.*, p. 28.
147. Kōhashi Kenji, "Gaisetsu Shinkō Haiku Shi," p. 8.
148. Mizuhara, *Takahama Kyoshi*, p. 98.
149. *Ibid.*, p. 99.
150. *Ibid.*, p. 101.
151. Ishida Hakyō and Fujita Shōshi, *Mizuhara Shūōshi*, p. 48.
152. Mizuhara, *Takahama Kyoshi*, p. 184.
153. Ishida and Fujita, *Mizuhara Shūōshi*, p. 64.
154. Mizuhara, *Takahama Kyoshi*, p. 214.
155. Ishida and Fujita, *Mizuhara Shūōshi*, p. 65.
156. Mizuhara, *Takahama Kyoshi*, pp. 255–57.
157. Ishida and Fujita, *Mizuhara Shūōshi*, pp. 72–73.
158. *Ibid.*, pp. 87–99.
159. *Haikai Daijiten*, p. 692; Konishi, pp. 204–05.
160. Ishida and Fujita, *Mizuhara Shūōshi*, p. 102.
161. Yamamoto, *Gendai Haiku*, pp. 148–49.
162. Yamashita, *Kindai Haiku Shū*, p. 327.
163. Yamamoto, *Gendai Haiku*, pp. 155–56.
164. *Ibid.*
165. *Ibid.*, p. 156.
166. Konishi, *Haiku*, p. 220.
167. Ōno, *Kindai Haiku*, p. 255.
168. *Ibid.*, p. 256.
169. *Ibid.*
170. Yamashita, *Kindai Haiku Shū*, p. 351. See also p. 464 for Seishi's own explanation of this poem.
171. Ōno, *Kindai Haiku*, p. 260.
172. *Ibid.*, p. 259.
173. Quoted in *ibid.*, p. 263.
174. Hirahata Seitō, *Yamaguchi Seishi*, pp. 58–59.

175. Yamamoto, *Gendai Haiku*, p. 168.
176. Hirahata, *Yamaguchi Seishi*, p. 58.
177. Konishi, *Haiku*, p. 220.
178. Ōno, *Kindai Haiku*, p. 270.
179. Yamamoto, *Gendai Haiku*, p. 177.
180. Kōsai Teruo, "Kawabata Bōsha," p. 447.
181. Ōno, *Kindai Haiku*, p. 323.
182. *Ibid.*, p. 322.
183. Konishi, *Haiku*, p. 211.
184. Ōno, *Kindai Haiku*, pp. 332–33.
185. Ishihara Yatsuka, "Kawabata Bōsha," p. 202.
186. Ōno, *Kindai Haiku*, pp. 332–33.
187. Yamamoto, *Gendai Haiku*, p. 232.
188. *Ibid.*, pp. 242–43.
189. *Ibid.*, pp. 251–52.
190. *Kyōdai Haiku* was founded in 1933 as a forum for present and former Kyoto University haiku poets. At first it followed *Hototogisu* traditions, but gradually criticism of "flowers and birds" was expressed. In 1935 the magazine changed character: the contributors were not restricted to people connected with Kyoto University and the poetry showed social consciousness, especially antiwar sentiments. It was suppressed in 1940 by the police for violating the Peace Preservation Law.
191. The name is pronounced *Kusadao* by at least half the authorities, including *Daijimmei Jiten*. I have followed *Nihon Kindai Bungaku Daijiten*. The poet's own preference was not clear.
192. Ōno, *Kindai Haiku*, p. 256.
193. Nakamura Kusatao, "Jiku Jikai," pp. 80–81.
194. Konishi, *Haiku*, p. 232.
195. Nakamura, "Jiku," p. 74.
196. *Ibid.*, pp. 74–79.
197. Hirahata Seitō, in *Nihon Shijin Zenshū*, XXXI, p. 251.
198. Kōsai Teruo, *Nakamura Kusatao*, p. 135.
199. *Ibid.*, p. 176.
200. Hirahata, *Nihon*, p. 253.
201. Kōsai, *Nakamura*, p. 162.
202. Konishi, *Haiku*, p. 235.
203. Kōsai, *Nakamura*, p. 173.
204. *Ibid.*, p. 179.
205. For example, the haiku "At the bases/even the goldfish sing/smoke of DDT," composed in 1955. See Kōsai, *Nakamura*, p. 215.
206. Quoted by Tagawa Hiroshi, *Katō Shūson*, p. 38.
207. *Ibid.*, p. 215.
208. Quoted by *ibid.*, p. 48.
209. Ōno, *Kindai Haiku*, p. 406.
210. The toad should not suggest anything repulsive. I have added the word "squatting" in the translation because "toad" alone seemed inadequate as a translation of the polysyllabic *hikigaeru*.

211. Tagawa, *Katō Shūson*, p. 236.
212. *Ibid.*, p. 79.
213. *Ibid.*, p. 89.
214. Shūson resigned from the *Ashibi* group in 1942.
215. Tagawa, *Katō Shūson*, p. 250.
216. See examples in *ibid.*, p. 110.
217. Katō Shūson, "Haiku, Sensō," pp. 20–22.
218. Michiko was the name of a daughter, Akio of a son.
219. Tagawa, *Katō Shūson*, p. 268.
220. *Ibid.*, pp. 140–41.
221. He continued to write prolifically in later years, but these haiku were not collected.
222. Yamamoto, *Gendai Haiku*, p. 382.
223. Ōno, *Kindai Haiku*, p. 381.
224. Ishizuka Tomoji, "Ishida Hakyō," p. 485.
225. Ōno, *Kindai Haiku*, p. 384.
226. Yamamoto, *Gendai Haiku*, p. 328.
227. Hakyō resigned from *Ashibi* in 1942 at the same time as Katō Shūson.
228. Ōno, *Kindai Haiku*, p. 387.
229. Yamamoto, *Gendai Haiku*, p. 331.
230. *Ibid.*, p. 335.
231. Ōno, *Kindai Haiku*, p. 391.
232. Konishi, p. 249.
233. Yamamoto, *Gendai Haiku*, p. 352.
234. Kuwabara Takeo, "Daini Geijutsu," p. 57.
235. See Matsui Toshihiko, *Shōwa Haiku no Kenkyū*, p. 300, for excerpts from writings by Kuwabara published earlier in 1946 illustrative of his thesis that the Japanese turned to Western literature because it discussed seriously how men should live.
236. Quoted in Matsui, *Shōwa*, p. 300.
237. *Ibid.*, pp. 303–07.
238. *Ibid.*, p. 308.
239. There is a provocative account of Saitō Sanki in Matsuda Osamu, *Yami no Yūtopia*, pp. 240–99.
240. Yamamoto, *Gendai Haiku*, pp. 394–96.
241. Takaha Shugyō, "Saitō Sanki," p. 209.
242. *Ibid.*, p. 213.
243. Quoted in *ibid.*, p. 220.
244. Takayanagi Shigenobu, "Tomizawa Kakio," p. 247.
245. *Ibid.*, p. 246.
246. Kaneko Tōta, *Haiku*, pp. 73ff.
247. Kusumoto Kenkichi, *Sengo no Haiku*, p. 55. This haiku is attributed to the New Haiku Poets' Association. It was composed at a time when group compositions were thought to be superior to poems by individuals.
248. *Ibid.*, p. 64.
249. A discussion of haiku written in the colloquial is given in *ibid.*, pp. 82–84.
250. Kaneko, *Haiku*, pp. 68–71.

251. *Ibid.*, p. 113.
252. "Dokusha wo motanai Bungaku," p. 141.
253. Kusumoto, *Sengo no Haiku*, pp. 93–94.
254. *Ibid.*, p. 103.
255. Akimoto Fujio, "Sawaki Kin'ichi," p. 493.
256. Kusumoto, *Sengo no Haiku*, pp. 280–81.
257. Matsui, *Kindai Hairon*, p. 556.

BIBLIOGRAPHY

Note: All Japanese books, except as otherwise noted, were published in Tokyo.

Abe Kimio. *Kawahigashi Hekigotō.* Ōfūsha, 1964.
Abrams, James. "Hail in the Begging Bowl: The Odyssey and Poetry of Santōka," in *Monumenta Nipponica*, XXXII, No. 3, Autumn 1977.
Akimoto Fujio. "Saitō Sanki," in *Haiku Kōza*, VIII.
———. "Sawaki Kin'ichi," in *Haiku Kōza*, VI.
Akiyama Shūkōryō. "Ogiwara Seisensui," in *Haiku Kōza*, VIII.
———. "Ozaki Hōsai," in *Haiku Kōza*, VIII.
Azumi Atsushi. "Hino Sōjō," in *Haiku Kōza*, VI.
Beichman, Janine. *Masaoka Shiki.* Boston: Twayne, 1982.
Cahill, James. *Chinese Painting.* Geneva: Skira, 1960.
"Dokusha wo motanai Bungaku," in *Bungakkai*, February 1957.
Furuta, Soichi. *Cape Jasmine and Pomegranates: The Free-Meter Haiku of Ippekirō.* New York: Grossman Publishers, 1974.
Haikai Daijiten. Meiji Shoin, 1957.
Haiku Kōza, 9 vols. Meiji Shoin, 1970.
Hirahata Seitō. *Yamaguchi Seishi.* Ōfūsha, 1963.
——— (ed.). *Nihon Shijin Zenshū*, 34 vols. Shinchōsha, 1966–69.
Ishida Hakyō. "Katō Shūson," in *Haiku Kōza*, VI.
———. "Maeda Fura," in *Haiku Kōza*, VI.
——— and Fujita Shōshi. *Mizuhara Shūōshi.* Ōfūsha, 1963.
Ishihara Yatsuka. "Iida Dakotsu," in *Haiku Kōza*, VIII.
———. "Kawabata Bōsha, Hito to Sakuhin," in *Nihon Shijin Zenshū*, XXXI.
Ishikawa Takuboku, Masaoka Shiki, Takahama Kyoshi, in Nihon no Bungaku series. Chūō Kōron Sha, 1967.
Ishizuka Tomoji. "Ishida Hakyō," in *Haiku Kōza*, VIII.
Izawa Motoyoshi. "Nakatsuka Ippekirō," in *Haiku Koza*, VIII.
Kanda Hideo and Kusumoto Kenkichi. *Kindai Haiku.* Yūseidō, 1965.
Kaneko Tōta. *Haiku.* Hokuyōsha, 1972.
Katō Shūson. "Haiku, Sensō," in *Haiku Kenkyū*, April 1944.
———. "Meiji Haiku Shi," in *Haiku Kōza*, VII.
Katsumine Shimpū. *Meiji Haikai Shiwa.* Taiseidō, 1934.
Katsura Nobuko. "Hino Sōjō," in Sawaki Kin'ichi, *Kindai Haijin.*
Keene, Donald. *Landscapes and Portraits.* Tokyo: Kodansha International, 1971.

Kiyozaki Toshirō. *Takahama Kyoshi.* Ōfūsha, 1966.
Kōhashi Kenji. "Gaisetsu Shinkō Haiku Shi, I," in *Haiku,* November 1956.
Konishi Jin'ichi. *Haiku.* Kenkyūsha, 1952.
Kōsai Teruo. "Kawabata Bōsha," in *Haiku Kōza,* VIII.
———. *Nakamura Kusatao.* Ōfūsha, 1969.
Kusumoto Kenkichi. *Sengo no Haiku,* in Kyōyō Bunko series. Shakai Shisō Sha, 1966.
Kuwabara Takeo. "Daini Geijutsu," in *Sekai,* November 1946. Also in Muramatsu Takeshi (ed.), *Shōwa Hihyō Taikei,* III. Banchō Shobō, 1974.
Kyōgoku Tosō. "Hara Sekitei," in *Haiku Kōza,* VI.
Matsuda Osamu. *Yami no Yūtopia.* Shinchōsha, 1975.
Matsui Toshihiko. *Kindai Hairon Shi.* Ōfūsha, 1965.
———. *Masaoka Shiki.* Ōfūsha, 1967.
———. *Shōwa Haiku no Kenkyū.* Ōfūsha, 1970.
Matsumoto Asahi. "Murakami Kijō," in Sawaki Kin'ichi, *Kindai Haijin.*
Minato Yōichirō. "Gaisetsu Shinkō Haiku Shi, II," in *Haiku,* November 1956.
Mizuhara Shūōshi. *Mizuhara Shūōshi Kushū.* Bokuyōsha, 1972.
———. *Takahama Kyoshi.* Bungei Shunjū Shinsha, 1952.
Murasawa Kafū. *Ishida Hakyō no Haiku.* Gakubunsha, 1966.
Murayama Kokyō (ed.). *Ōsuga Otsuji Hairon Shū,* in Kōdansha Gakujutsu Bunko, 1978.
Nakamura Kusatao. "Hara Sekitei," in *Haiku Kōza,* VI.
———. "Jiku Jikai," in *Haiku Kenkyū,* March 1939.
———. "Murakami Kijō," in *Haiku Kōza,* VI.
Nakanishi Hodo. "Maeda Fura," in Sawaki Kin'ichi, *Kindai Haijin.*
Nihon Shijin Zenshū, 34 vols. Shinchōsha, 1966-69.
Ōno Rinka. *Kindai Haiku no Kanshō to Hihyō.* Meiji Shoin, 1967.
———. "Ogiwara Seisensui," in *Haiku Kōza,* VI.
———. "Taneda Santōka," in *Haiku Kōza,* VI.
Ōta Kōson. "Meiji Haiku Shi, II," in *Haiku Kōza,* VII.
Saitō Kiyoe. "Taneda Santōka," in *Haiku Kōza,* VIII.
Sawaki Kin'ichi. *Kindai Haijin.* Ōfūsha, 1973.
Shiki Zenshū, 25 vols. Kōdansha, 1975-78.
Tagawa Hiroshi. *Katō Shūson.* Ōfūsha, 1966.
Takaha Shugyō. "Saitō Sanki," in Sawaki Kin'ichi, *Kindai Haijin.*
Takayanagi Shigenobu. "Tomizawa Kakio," in Sawaki Kin'ichi, *Kindai Haijin.*
Takeda Ōtō. *Naitō Meisetsu Kenkyū.* Kōransha, 1934.
Ueda, Makoto. *Modern Japanese Haiku: An Anthology.* Tokyo: University of Tokyo Press, 1976.
Yamamoto Kenkichi. *Gendai Haiku,* in Kadokawa Bunko series. Rev. ed., 1971.
Yamashita Kazumi et al. *Kindai Haiku Shū,* in Nihon Kindai Bungaku Taikei series. Kadokawa Shoten, 1974.

PART TWO

POETRY IN NEW FORMS

INTRODUCTION

THE TERM "MODERN POETRY" could properly be used to describe all poetry, both traditional and nontraditional, composed in Japan ever since the beginning of the Meiji era; but it refers here specifically to the shintaishi (poetry of the new style), originally written under the direct influence of translations of European poetry. The most obvious difference between "poetry of the new style" and traditional Japanese poetry was its length. Poets who had been accustomed to concentrate their expression into the thirty-one syllables of a tanka or the seventeen syllables of a haiku were enabled, like their counterparts in the West, to give free rein to their inspiration in poems that were unrestricted in their length. Of course, there had been long poems even in Japan. The most impressive poetry in the eighth-century collection *Manyōshū* is in the form of chōka (long poems), which range up to 150 lines or so. But the chōka was abandoned by subsequent poets, and only in the eighteenth century, after a millennium of neglect, was it revived, though even then without much success. The shintaishi poets were aware of the chōka tradition and often suggested its influence in their translations from European languages. Another tradition, still very much alive at the time of the Meiji Restoration, was that of writing *kanshi*, poems in Chinese. Although the kanshi were often no more than distant echoes of the themes of the major Chinese poets, and their content was severely limited by preconceptions as to what might legitimately be described in poetry, the connections between the kanshi and the shintaishi were felt by young intellectuals even as they were turning from Chinese to Western civilization.

It is important to bear in mind that these elements in the existing poetic traditions facilitated the acceptance of the new poetry imported from the West, but this does not diminish the importance of translations of European poetry in the creation of the shintaishi. Translations provided direct inspiration for many poems, especially those written in the early or middle Meiji period. The poems translated were unsystematically chosen. Not surprisingly, some poems that were popular in the 1880s but have since been forgotten were among those translated. For the most part, however, the selection was of poetry much beloved in the English-speaking world: "The stag at eve had drunk its fill . . . ," "Tell me not, in mournful numbers . . . ," "Cannon to the right of them . . . ," etc.

The Japanese of the 1880s were not satisfied, however, merely with translating, but attempted to write their own long poems in the new manner. In the distant past, when poetry in Chinese was first introduced to Japan, the Japanese, carefully following the metrical and rhyme schemes devised in China, had expressed in Chinese not so much what they wanted to say as what they could say in a foreign language. The shintaishi, though derived from foreign examples, were composed in Japanese, and the poets even felt a sense of liberation as they described whatever had stirred their spirits as men of the new Meiji era, daringly breaking the rules of the old prosody. In their excitement over writing poetry that was freed of the former restrictions, many Japanese did not realize that even in the case of shintaishi certain subjects were best left to prose, and some wrote unintentionally comic verse that suggested misplaced earnestness. Again and again the new poets insisted that they, unlike their ancestors, had such complex thoughts that it was impossible to squeeze them into the tiny compass of a tanka or haiku. This claim was later contested by poets who continued to write in the traditional forms, but the state of the tanka and haiku in the early Meiji era lent conviction to accusations that they had outlived their usefulness.

Despite the youthful abandon of the early translations and original examples of shintaishi, the poets revealed an unexpected conservatism with respect to poetic diction and meter. Each line of a poem usually consisted of a combination of units of seven and five syllables, in the traditional manner, and the vocabulary was drawn almost entirely from classical Japanese literature, with a minimum admixture of the new words that were daily being invented to cope with the unprecedented flood of new things and ideas. Only as the translations became numerous and fidelity to the originals became a matter of pride did the forms and language reflect the break with tradition.

In the 1880s the Japanese were profoundly moved by Gray's "Elegy Written in a Country Church-Yard." Twenty years later they were reading translations of French Symbolist poetry. With bewildering speed the Japanese had caught up with current European literature. Symbolist poetry proved especially attractive to Japanese poets, presumably because it was closer in its effects to traditional Japanese poetic expression than the narrative or philosophical poetry that the first translators had tackled.

Modern poetry was less adventurous than fiction in its language even after it had left behind the archaisms of the traditional poetry. A novel written in classical language was an oddity in the twentieth century, but the poets were reluctant to abandon a medium of expression that was at once more concise and more evocative than the colloquial. Some poets experimented with the colloquial only to turn back to the classical language. Only after 1945 did the use of the colloquial become general.

For most Japanese critics, as well as for the public, literature in the twentieth century has meant, above all, the novel. Poetry, despite its long traditions, has had to take second place, not because it was inferior—modern Japanese poetry is in fact of exceptional quality—but because its place was harder to maintain in a world of publishing that catered increasingly to the preferences of a mass market. It may be, however, that future historians of Japanese literature will remember the twentieth century for its poetry as much as for any other variety of literature.

THE MEIJI PERIOD (1868–1912)

THE BEGINNINGS: THE AGE OF TRANSLATIONS

The creation of the shintaishi can be traced to the publication in 1882 of the volume *Shintaishi Shō* (Selection of Poetry in the New Style), compiled by Toyama Masakazu (Chuzan), Yatabe Ryōkichi (Shōkon), and Inoue Tetsujirō (Sonken).* The collection consisted of nineteen poems, fourteen translated from English (including Longfellow's English version of a poem by Charles d'Orléans), and five original Japanese poems by the compilers. "Elegy Written in a Country Church-Yard," "The Psalm of Life," soliloquies from *Hamlet*, *Henry IV*, and *Henry VIII*, and a variety of other poems were included, in one case in alternative translations by two different men. The translators were all well acquainted with English: Toyama Masakazu (1848–1900) had studied in London before going on to the University of Michigan, where he

---

* Poets of the Meiji period and some of the Taishō period are referred to by their literary names (*gō*) rather than their surnames, in keeping with Japanese custom.

194

studied science and philosophy; Yatabe Ryōkichi (1851–1899) graduated in botany at Cornell in 1876; and Inoue Tetsujirō (1855–1944) had studied philosophy in Berlin. None of these men possessed much poetic talent, but this did not inhibit them in either their translations or their original poems. The three were junior professors at Tokyo University when they happened to discover a mutual interest in translating European poetry. Inoue's prefatory note to his translation of Longfellow's "The Psalm of Life" related the background:

> I had long wished to compose poetry in a new style but, being well aware of the difficulty of such a project, I decided to prepare myself by studying Japanese and Chinese poetry and prose of both ancient and modern times. Later, as I gradually approached the point of trying to write poetry in a new style, Shōkon showed me one day his translation of a passage from *Hamlet*. The language included colloquialisms, but it was actually more artistic than the recondite old waka and kanshi. I expressed my admiration and printed the translation in the sixth issue of a literary journal.[1] Next, Chuzan produced a translation of the same speech from *Hamlet* and also a translation of Cardinal Wolsey.[2] I realized then that, regardless of whether one is talking about the past or present, it is safe to say that the popularity of a new style of poetry is a matter of chance, and not necessarily the result of the perfection achieved after a hundred polishings. Perhaps, I thought, what Shōkon and Chuzan had written were the first poems of a new style. I myself translated "The Psalm of Life" by Longfellow, so as not to leave to my friends the sole credit for having created this new style of poetry. My translation was in general similar to those by my friends, but whereas they did not employ rhyme, I tried using it as an experiment.

Inoue followed this account with some general observations on poetry including:

> Waka written in the Meiji era must be waka of the Meiji era. They should not be old waka. Kanshi written by Japanese should be Japanese poems and not Chinese poems. This is why we decided to compose poetry in a new style. The rules for rhyming, the level of the vocabulary and the rest must be evolved gradually; they cannot be laid down at a single time.[3]

Inoue's prescription that poetry must be of its own time and place would be obeyed by the poets of the shintaishi, no matter how deeply they might be indebted to foreign influences. Inspiration was borrowed from abroad, but the language of the poems was easily intelligible Japanese, and the people and scenes described were contemporary Japanese. The kanshi composed in the past often imitated Chinese models so closely as to be almost indistinguishable from poetry written by Chinese, but it was obviously not possible for a Japanese to write poetry in his own language yet pretend to be a European; imitation of European models did not make the poets Europeans but modern Japanese.

The shintaishi poets learned, moreover, through their readings in foreign languages, that the European poets used everyday language, rather than a special poetic diction preserved from antiquity. The poets of the waka were still obliged to observe the tenth-century diction of the *Kokinshū*, and the kanshi poets continued to embellish their poems with obscure allusions to the Chinese poetry of a millennium earlier, but the shintaishi poets reveled in the freedom to use the language of modern Japan. Yatabe Ryōkichi in the preface to his translation of Gray's "Elegy" insisted on this point: there was far greater variety in European poems than in Japanese, but they were always written in the language of everyday life.

> They never borrow words from foreign countries, nor do they pad their language with archaic words used a thousand years before. The result is that anyone, even a small child, can understand poetry, providing he knows the language of the country. . . . My colleague Chuzan and I, after consultation together, chose some Western poems and translated them as an experiment, using the language of daily speech.[4]

Yatabe further stated, in the preface to his original poem "Sentiments on Visiting the Great Buddha at Kamakura":

> In general, the peoples of the entire globe, and not only the Western countries, use the language of ordinary speech when they compose poetry. That is why they are all able to express easily and directly what they feel in their hearts. The same was true of Japan in remote

antiquity, but poets of recent times use Chinese vocabulary when they compose kanshi and archaisms when they compose waka. They avoid the language of daily life as vulgar. How could this but be a misconception? [5]

The use of modern language and the direct and unaffected expression of the poet's feelings were not the only lessons the translators learned from the West. The subject matter of the poems in *Selection of Poetry in the New Style* included many areas of human experience that had never been treated in Japanese poetry. "The Charge of the Light Brigade," translated by Toyama, inspired his own poem "Battōtai" (The Drawn-Sword Unit) which, he claimed, was the first war poem ever composed in Japan.[6] The translations of Shakespeare suggested the possibilities of the new kind of dramatic poetry that Tsubouchi Shōyō would write, combining foreign and Japanese traditions. Each of the fourteen translated poems in the book provided its own particular stimulation to the Japanese.

In their enthusiasm over the horizons that seemed to be opening before them, some Japanese poets concluded that *any* subject could be legitimately treated in verse. Toyama, for example, wrote the extremely long poem *On the Principles of Sociology*, which included this explanation of the theory of evolution: [7]

The characteristics the parents possess
Are transmitted by heredity to the children;
The fit go on flourishing,
The unfit perish.
In the present world, all that exists—
Bellflowers, pampas grass, the wild valerian,
Plum blossoms and cherry blossoms, clover and peonies,
And, associated with peonies, the Chinese lion-dog,
And butterflies that alight on the rapeflower leaves,
Song thrushes that warble among the trees,
Robins that hunt for food by the gate,
Cuckoos that tell their name amidst the clouds,
Plovers that call their friends and kin,
Deer who, longing for their dear ones, cry
In the deep mountains, trampling the maple leaves,

Sheep and oxen who, not knowing the reason,
Plod ahead, driven by the sound of a horn,
And monkeys too, close to the sheep—
How stupid they are!—and even man,
Called the soul of all creation,
His present body and his abilities too—
If traced back to their source have all
Little by little, with each generation,
Improved, and are the result
Of a steady accumulation.
With an acuteness of vision
Unmatched throughout history,
The ones who determined this was so
Were Aristotle, Newton and one
Neither better nor worse than they in ability,
Mr. Darwin, whose discovery it was,
And, no inferior to him, Spencer,
Who developed the same principles.[8]

The theories of Darwin and Herbert Spencer, even when cast into regularly alternating phrases in seven and five syllables, do not make poetic reading. This is a bad poem, not only because the principles of sociology are better expressed in prose, but because the conventional prettiness of detail—especially the mentions of flowers and animals often described in the waka—contrasts so peculiarly with the theme. Yatabe's poem on his visit to the Great Buddha at Kamakura reflected in a different way the theory of evolution: contrasting the function of the Great Buddha in former times, when it served as an object of worship, to its present status as a tourist attraction, he attributed the change to the workings of the principle of evolution. These poems are read today only as survivals of the stone age of modern Japanese poetry, but the mistakes of the young translators, as well as their small poetic triumphs, would be of immense value to later poets.

The *Selection of Poetry in the New Style* was described by the poet Hinatsu Kōnosuke as being "no more than an accidental accumulation of incompetent pieces absolutely undeserving of being discussed in terms of the artistic value of the contents."[9] The only translation for which he had even a grudging word of praise was Yatabe's version of Gray's "Elegy," which, for all its clumsy expression, revealed a modicum of feeling. Toyama's translation of a poem by Charles Kingsley was rated as "worse in its faltering tone than the composition of a junior high school student." [10] The attempts at rhyme, to which the Japanese language is unsuited, also evoked Hinatsu's derision. It is hard not to agree. Consider the attempt at rhyme in this original poem by Yatabe:

haru wa monogoto yorokobashi
fuku kaze totemo atatakashi
niwa no sakura ya momo no hana
yo ni utsukushiku miyuru kana
nobe no hibari wa ito takaku
kumoi haruka ni maite naku [11]

In spring everything is full of charm,
The blowing wind is really warm.
Cherry and peach, blossoming bright,
Make an unusually pretty sight.
The lark of the moors, very high,
Sings as it soars far in the sky.

The compilers had apprehensions about the reception this poetry would be accorded. Yatabe wrote in his preface to the collection: "Even if our poems win no favor among people today, it may be that future generations of modern Japanese poets will attain the heights of Homer or Shakespeare. Some great poet, impressed by the new style of this collection, may display more skill and write poetry that will move men's hearts and make the very gods and demons weep."[12]

The collection certainly did inspire ridicule, and the gods and demons were probably less moved than by the *Kokinshū*, whose preface claimed this power for poetry. But, despite its clumsiness, the power of genuine emotions was sensed by the reading public. *Selection of Poetry in the New Style* sold so well that it was reprinted in 1884 from woodblocks (the 1882 edition had been printed from movable type) in order to facilitate running off additional copies.

The success of *Selection of Poetry in the New Style* occasioned the publication between 1882 and 1895 of five collections with the overall title of *Shintai Shiika* (Verses in the New Style). These volumes contain chiefly original poetry on subjects drawn from Japanese history as well as modern events. Komuro Kutsuzan (1858–1908) contributed an "Ode to Liberty" that has been acclaimed as an "unknown 'Marseillaise' of Japan." It opens:

> In Heaven I will be a free ghost,
> On Earth I will be a free man.
> O Liberty, Ah Liberty, Liberty O
> The ties that bind us together
> Were pledged by Heaven, Earth and Nature
> To last a thousand, nay, eight thousand generations,
> As long as the world will last;
> How can these bonds vainly be broken?
> And yet, there are in this world
> Clouds that hide the moon, winds that scatter the blossoms;
> Man is not the master of his fate.
> It is a long tale to tell, but many years ago
> There was a country called Rome where,
> So that they might give the people Liberty
> And establish a republican government,
> Many men endured bitter hardships. . . .

The poem concludes:

> From ancient times, for Liberty's sake,
> Many men have parted company
> Or have been torn apart by death.
> How can it be, though our lands differ,
> That we men of the Orient
> Should not be one with them at heart?
> Liberty for man
> Is the natural Way of Heaven and Earth.
> My friends, bestir yourselves! Strive!
> Let it not be said that we are a servile people.
> I have finished my story.
> The time is spring, and to a dreaming nation
> A bell, rousing us from slumber,
> Has sounded, clearer than ever before.[13]

This poem is no more impressive in language or imagery than the examples in *Selection of Poetry in the New Style*, but we cannot doubt that Komuro Kutsuzan was expressing his deepest concerns. His failure stemmed from a basic lack of poetic talent and from his use of outdated imagery—clouds that hide the moon and the like—that went with the traditional meter of lines in seven plus five syllables. Yet there is something touching about Komuro Kutsuzan's dream of liberty, and it was entirely proper for him to have attempted to describe his vision in a shintaishi.

Political beliefs inspired many other shintaishi, but the subject matter of early Meiji poetry was by no means restricted to sociological or political themes. The first volume of shintaishi published by a single poet, *Jūni no Ishizuka* (The Twelve Stone Tablets) by Yuasa Hangetsu (1858-1943), was inspired by Christian theology. This long poem (in 700 verses), originally delivered by the author at the time of his graduation from Dōshisha University in 1885, dazzled his audience by its flow of language. Hangetsu retained the imagery of the old Japanese poetry and chose a style reminiscent of the chōka, imparting to the untraditional subject matter a dignity missing from other shintaishi on unfamiliar themes.

Even more successful shintaishi were found in the translations by Mori Ōgai and his associates of the S.S.S. (Shin Seisha), which appeared in the collection *Omokage* (Vestiges, 1889). These translations, however, did not please the original translators of *Selection of Poetry in the New Style*, who considered that the smoothly worded, archaistic translations in *Vestiges* had betrayed their original purpose in introducing Western poetry to Japan: instead of expanding the range of Japanese poetry, the translators of *Vestiges* had chosen only foreign poetry that could be easily rendered into the Japanese language. The best-known poem in *Vestiges*, the translation of Ophelia's song "How should I your true love know?" from *Hamlet*, was not only rendered into alternating phrases in seven and five syllables but maintained a traditional purity of diction.[14] There was little to suggest that a new age had begun for Japanese poetry, but the *Vestiges* translations, unlike those in the pedestrian *Selection of Poetry in the New Style*, succeeded as poetry and can still be read with pleasure.

One of the rare shintaishi poets of interest before Shimazaki Tōson burst on the literary scene was Miyazaki Koshoshi (1864-

1922), whose collected poems, though full of echoes of Wordsworth, Longfellow, and Felicia Hemans, were given an individual quality by the poet's genuine feeling for the countryside scenes he described. Koshoshi, convinced that the pastoral life was infinitely preferable to the meaningless bustle of the city, wrote with cynicism about the Rokumeikan, the emblem of the Enlightenment, where Japanese sweating in their foreign finery politely chatted as they danced; and he contrasted these slavish imitators of the West with honest farmers toiling in the fields. Koshoshi is hardly a major poet, but his praise for the bucolic life (seemingly influenced as much by Wordsworth as by his own tastes) and his effortless use of traditional meters in describing entirely untraditional scenes, influenced the lyric poets of the next generation, notably Shimazaki Tōson.[15]

The Sino-Japanese War of 1894–1895 inspired poets to compose many tanka and haiku, but heroic deeds were obviously better commemorated in a shintaishi (or a kanshi) than in a mere thirty-one or seventeen syllables. Toyama Chuzan, one of the original *Selection* "poets," composed various poems on subjects such as the gallant bugler who kept his bugle pressed to his lips even after receiving a fatal wound.[16] His most famous war poem, "Ryojun no Hirō Kani Taii" (Captain Kani, the Hero of Port Arthur), begins:

> *Kaibyaku irai imada katsute, kyō no gotoku kokkō no kagayakeru*
> * wa nashi.*
> *Kaibyaku irai, imada katsute kyō no gotoku, wa ga hōjin no meiyo no*
> * kōdai naru wa nashi.*
> *Ryōun nari kōfuku nari, kono jiki no sōgū seru no Nihonjin wa. . . .*[17]

Never, since the country was founded, has our national glory shone
  so brightly as it does today;
Never, since the country was founded, has the fame of our
  countrymen been so lofty and grand as today.
How fortunate, how happy we are to be Japanese, alive in such
  glorious times!

Toyama, despite the all too apparent failings of his poem, was attempting something far more ambitious than the S.S.S. poets with their elegantly rendered translations: not only is his vocabulary totally unlike the traditional Japanese poetic diction (many words are of Chinese origin), but he totally disregards metrics and the conventional embellishments of the waka. The poem is blatantly patriotic (as were many other Meiji poems), and its expression hardly differs from the speeches delivered by Toyama at various gatherings; but it was nevertheless seriously considered by critics of the day, who praised or condemned the bold innovations. The most frequent complaint was that the reader could not distinguish this poem from prose; poetry, it was declared, had to obey metric rules of some kind or else it stopped being poetry. Toyama, undaunted by such criticism, asserted that, as one of the originators of the shintaishi in the 1880s, he had the privilege of creating a new style of poetry in the 1890s, and he predicted that future poets would follow him. To this the critic of *Waseda Bungaku* replied: "If what he writes is to be called 'poetry,' virtually all the orators of the past must have been poets. It would seem that he intends to abolish the distinction between prose and metrical expression." [18]

The critic Takayama Chogyū, entering the discussion at this point, announced that poetry was distinguished from prose by its contents, rather than by any external form. He quoted Coleridge's statement: "Poetry is not the proper antithesis to prose, but to science. Poetry is opposed to science, and prose to metre." [19] In 1898 Chogyū published an essay on Walt Whitman recalling that "while we Japanese were reviling the shintaishi of Dr. Toyama, the Americans were enthusiastically reading Whitman." [20]

Another member of the original *Selection* group, Inoue Tetsujirō, published in 1896 the long poem *Hinuyama no Uta* (Song of Mount Hinu), as a challenge to the poetic circles of the day. He declared that he had deliberately mixed elegant and plebeian speech, words of Chinese and Japanese origins, and that he had borrowed the general format of his poem from the *Divine Comedy*. He wished to prove that it was not only possible to write poetry in the same language used in newspaper articles and other contemporary prose, but that this language was more suitable to describing the concerns of modern men than the pseudo-*Man'yōshū* diction adopted by many poets.[21] *Hinuyama no Uta* was unsuccessful, but it helped, both directly and indirectly, to stimulate the vogue for narrative poetry in the following decade.

The debate on the appropriate language for poetry did not at once result in poetry being composed in the colloquial, in the manner that prose by this time had come to be written in, the *gembun itchi* style. This was partly because the poetry composed in the new style by Toyama and Inoue was not only inept but halfhearted in its modernization, inexplicably resorting to archaic forms of vocabulary whenever the poets felt a need for elevated expression.[22] The modern-language movement led by Toyama and Inoue failed, less because of its own inadequacy than because of the appearance in August 1897 of Shimazaki Tōson's collection *Wakana Shū* (Seedlings); the extraordinary success of this volume, written almost entirely in the traditional "elegant language" and phrased in alternating passages in seven and five syllables (though arranged in longer lines), inevitably inhibited serious discussion of more modern poetic language and forms. Tōson believed poetry had to be written in a special, elevated language, in accordance with recognized Japanese metrics. When, eventually, he came to prefer the language of everyday life, he turned from poetry to prose.[23]

SHIMAZAKI TŌSON (1872–1943)

Tōson may fairly be called the creator of modern Japanese poetry. Earlier examples of shintaishi are quoted in textbooks, but his poetry was the first of lasting merit, which succeeded both in terms of modern content and pleasing poetic expression.

Tōson was born in the Valley of Kiso in central Japan, but moved to Tokyo when he was nine. His father, an opponent of foreign thought and culture, saw to it that Tōson received a firm grounding in the Chinese classics, but after graduating from elementary school Tōson decided to learn English like the other boys; soon he was so infatuated with these studies that even the smell of the paper in the English textbooks intoxicated him.[24] In 1887 he entered Meiji Gakuin, a school founded by missionaries ten years before, and in the following year he was baptized. Even though Tōson ceased to be a practicing Christian a few years later, the influence of the Bible is especially apparent in his poetry and other early writings.

Tōson had originally entered Meiji Gakuin mainly in order

to perfect his English for commercial purposes, but by his third year he was completely absorbed in literature. He neglected his classroom studies, but privately read both the classics of Western literature (including Dante and Shakespeare) and writings of the Tokugawa period, particularly the novels of Saikaku and the plays of Chikamatsu, which were just being rediscovered. Soon after graduation he began to publish translations in *Jogaku Zasshi*; in 1892 his translation in four installments of Shakespeare's *Venus and Adonis* appeared. The strong attraction this romantic early work of Shakespeare's held for Tōson may perhaps be explained in terms of his youth. With each succeeding installment of his translation, which was called *Natsukusa* (Summer Grass), he moved further and further away from the original, adopting a style close to that of Jōruri in recounting the tale of the unhappy Adonis. This translation in turn influenced Tōson's original poem "Yosaku no Uma" (Yosaku's Horse), a poem in eighty lines published in 1895; the vocabulary, syntax, and structure show marked indebtedness to *Venus and Adonis*, but the subject matter (suggested by Chikamatsu's play *Yosaku from Tamba*) and the pessimistic tone reflect his own interests and mood at the time. Tōson, later recalling this period, said that he was convinced at the time he could not live much beyond twenty-five.[25] His depression was occasioned by family problems, an unhappy love affair, and the conflict he felt between his ideals and reality.

Tōson's reputation was established with the publication of "Akikaze no Uta" (Song of the Autumn Wind) in the November 1896 issue of *Bungakkai*. The poem was probably inspired by Shelley's "Ode to the West Wind," and the few direct parallels in expression have often been analyzed by Japanese scholars; but the two poems are entirely dissimilar in nature. Unlike Shelley, who addresses the wind directly ("Thou from whose unseen presence . . ."), Tōson is calm and detached. His poem by no means matches Shelley's in scale, richness of imagination, or intensity, but it is nevertheless of great importance to modern Japanese literature, both historically and intrinsically. It was the first shintaishi to reveal a mastery of the form, and its expression (if not its content) has been treasured by generations of readers. Each line is in twelve syllables with a caesura after the seventh. It opens quietly:

Shizuka ni kitaru aki	Softly blowing, the autumn wind
kaze no	Has risen from the western sea;
Nishi no umi yori	You can even see the course
fukiokori	they fly
Maitachisawagu	The dancing, blustering white
shirakumo no	clouds.
Tobite yukue mo miyuru	
ka na	

Obviously an entirely different mood has been established from Shelley's "O wild West Wind, thou breath of Autumn's being." The serenity of these opening lines has often suggested to Japanese critics the contrast between "oriental" calm and the turbulence of the "occidental" spirit, and they sometimes confess they are stirred more deeply by the poet's identification with the wind and by his unspoken overtones than by Shelley's powerful but alien personification. The first two lines of Tōson's poem, according to one critic,[26] "effortlessly evoke in our minds an extremely natural, lyrical quality. . . . They present us with an overall view of the autumn wind. The next two lines, one feels, convey with great fidelity an autumn sky filled with scudding, refreshing white clouds." Another critic wrote, "The deep, submerged note of pathos in Tōson's poem is normally not to be found in Western poetry; instead one senses the violent efforts of the poet who rages or shouts with the autumn wind." [27]

The non-Japanese reader, comparing the poems by Shelley and Tōson, is likely to prefer Shelley's. Nothing in Tōson's poem matches the brilliance of Shelley's comparison of the leaves caught in the wind to "ghosts from an enchanter fleeing"; and his urgency and personal conviction make Tōson's expression seem bland. But "blandness" (*tan*) was a quality highly praised by critics of Chinese poetry, and Tōson's dispassionate descriptions (and the melodies of his words) no doubt still appeal to many Japanese readers more than the unfamiliar rhetoric of the English poet. Japanese commentators frequently stress the implied meanings behind Tōson's words, but the examples they cite are unimpressive; one commentator pointed out that the line "You can even see the course they fly" subtly hints that the autumn sky, against which the white clouds stand out, is no doubt blue,[28] but this is hardly a memorable use of suggestion.

Other overtones, such as those found in the second stanza, are untranslatable:

*Yūkage takaku aki wa ki
    no
Kiri no kozue no koto no
    ne
Sono otonai wo kiku toki
    wa
Kaze no kitaru to
    shirarekeri*

The evening light slants high;
Autumn is in the yellow-topped
    kiri.
When you hear its sounding harp
You know the wind has come to
    call.

Here the poet makes effective use of alliteration and sound repetition (*ki no kiri no kozue no koto no*), and the syntax is so involved as to be intelligible only by intuition. Moreover, the poetic associations of the *kiri* (paulownia) would be apparent only to a Japanese: the koto is made of kiri wood and, traditionally, the fall of a single kiri leaf was taken as the first hint of the coming of autumn. Such overtones, plus the beauty of the sounds and the freshness of the syntax, make this stanza appealing to Japanese readers, though the meaning is surely less exciting than that of a stanza by Shelley.

The best stanza of the poem is untraditional in expression and may well be indebted to Shelley:

*Michi wo tsutauru Baramon no
Nishi ni higashi ni chiru gotoku
Fukitadayowasu akikaze ni
Hirugaeriyuku ko no ha ka na*

Scattering East and scattering West,
Like the Brahman priests who spread the Way,
See the leaves flutter in the autumn wind
That blows and tosses them!

The simile of leaves in the wind being likened to Brahman priests traveling east and west from India to transmit their teachings is without precedent in Japan. Perhaps, as numerous commentators have claimed, it was occasioned by Shelley's mention of an "enchanter." [29] The simile no doubt was also intended to suggest the ochre, or yellow, robes of the Buddhist priests of Southeast Asia, the color of autumn leaves, and perhaps also the fluttering of these garments as the priests walked.[30]

The "Song of the Autumn Wind" could not have been written without Western influence. The form is at sharp variance with Japanese traditions, and the poem possesses a depth and intensity that clearly distinguishes it from any waka on the subject of the autumn wind.[31] Not only does Tōson fail to mention the natural objects normally associated with the autumn wind in the waka—dew, hagi flowers, the moon, and so on—but he added totally unconventional imagery of the kind discussed above. Tōson, when compared with Shelley, seems conspicuously "oriental," but when compared with Saigyō, whose waka he loved, Tōson's "occidental" character is no less apparent.

A month after "Song of the Autumn Wind" appeared, Tōson published six poems under the general title *Usugōri* (Thin Ice), a reference perhaps to the approach of winter in Sendai, the city in the north of Japan where he composed most of this poetry. Later, when the poems were included in his collection *Seedlings* he changed their title to *Rokunin no Otome* (Six Maidens). Each of the six women portrayed represents a different social class or condition: Oyō is a court lady, in service at the palace; Okinu a blind girl; Osayo a musician who has devoted her life to her art; Okume a girl of headstrong passions ready to swim a swollen river to join her lover; Otsuta a woman of wit and intelligence; and Okiku a maiden who warns other women not to fall in love. The six poems differ in their total length and in the shape of their individual stanzas, but they are uniformly in alternating phrases of seven and five syllables, and the language is "pure" classical Japanese.

The poems are not only pleasing as melody but distinctively Japanese in their expression. Many commentators have noted the wisdom of Tōson's decision to place his *Six Maidens* at the head of the collection *Seedlings*, thereby establishing the romantic tone that henceforth would be associated with all of Tōson's poetry. The most effective poem of the sequence is the third, about Osayo, the girl who remains unmarried so that she may pursue her career as a musician. The poem begins:

> *Ushio samishiki araiso no*
> *Iwa kage ware wa umarekeri*

Ashita yūbe no shirogoma to
Furusato tōki mono omoi

Okashiki mono ni kurueri to
Ware wo iurashi yo no hito no

Ge ni kuruwashi no mi naru beki
Kono toshi made no otome to wa

I was born in the shadow of a cliff
On a rough shore with lonely tides.

My todays and yesterdays have swiftly passed
And my thoughts return to that distant home.

I gather that people are whispering
I must be strange or even deranged.

Truly I must seem a madwoman,
To have reached this age and still be unwed!

In the Meiji era any woman still unmarried at twenty-five was considered to be an old maid. Osayo hints at her loneliness even as she describes the joy of playing her flute.

The description of Osayo's birth on a lonely shore may have been inspired by the prose-poem "Le Centaure" by Maurice de Guérin,[32] and the tedious enumeration of the seven emotions Osayo summons up with her flute may have been intended to evoke the Seven Muses, but the interest of this and the other poems in *Six Maidens* does not lie in discovering how ingeniously Tōson incorporated Western materials into his poems; rather, it is in Tōson's insistence on romantic love. He conveyed the intensity of the emotions of his six contrasting women, and fully sympathized with them. Yoshida Seiichi commented, "The significance of Tōson's poetry in the history of Japanese literature and thought was that it represented a liberation of the emotions, especially the romantic emotions, from feudalistic dictates. He wrote with passion, above all when he wrote from a woman's viewpoint, of the moving beauty of love, hitherto considered a sin." [33]

Tōson was perhaps the purest lyrical poet of modern Japan, but the romantic expression of his poetry did not necessarily reflect his own experiences. His only love affairs prior to composing

Seedlings had been unsuccessful, and the women described in his poems seem to have been inspired mainly by his readings. Nevertheless, his declarations ring true. His best love poem, "Hatsukoi" (First Love), begins:

Mada agesomeshi maegami no
Ringo no moto ni mieshi toki
Mae ni sashitaru hanagushi no
Hana aru kimi to omoikeri

Yasashiku shiroki te wo nobete
Ringo wo ware ni ataeshi wa
Usukurenai no aki no mi ni
Hito koisomeshi hajime nari

When I saw you under the apple tree
Your front hair swept back for the first time,
I thought, seeing the flower-comb in front,
That you were a flower too.

Stretching out your gentle, white hand,
You gave me an apple.
I felt a first stirring of love
In the pale crimson of that autumn fruit.

The poem convincingly evokes the atmosphere of first love, in Japan or anywhere else. The language is marvelously fluent Japanese, though the imagery, beginning with the mention of the apple orchard, is certainly not traditional. The scene Tōson depicted was probably imaginary, and may even have been inspired by the story of Adam and Eve, but diligent research has revealed that when Tōson was nine or ten the lady in the house next door used to pick apples and throw them to him.[34] The lines "Stretching out your gentle, white hand,/You gave me an apple" are particularly effective because they picture, in a manner unknown to earlier Japanese poets, the offering that symbolizes the confession of first love. The girl's youthful beauty is indicated, in Japanese fashion, by mention of how her hair was arranged for the first time in the style of a girl of sixteen; in the Meiji era the style of a woman's hair, which signified her age and marital status, was a crucial element in any description. The young man responds to her beauty by becoming (in the third stanza) drunk with the wine of love, a Western image. The resolution is the indirectly phrased revelation that the young man visited the girl so often a path was worn through the orchard.

The poem is less about the poet's love of a particular woman than about love itself. The emphasis on the "firstness" of this love is given not only by the title but by the use of different words related to "beginning," as well as by mention that the girl's hair had just been combed in an adult style and that the apple was turning red. This poem has enjoyed special popularity with young readers, and Tōson has often been called the foremost writer of love poetry of the Meiji era.

Other poems in *Seedlings* revealed the influence of Japanese love poetry, especially the kind found in the Jōruri of Chikamatsu. The poem "Yotsu no Sode" (Four Sleeves) is based on the story of the love of Onatsu and Seijūrō, described in Chikamatsu's *Gojūnenki Uta Nembutsu* (A Song of Prayer for the Fiftieth Anniversary). Tōson does not dwell on the tragic consequences of their love but on its blazing intensity:

> *Otoko no kuroki me no iro no*
> *Onatsu no mune ni utsuru toki*
> *Otoko no akaki kuchibiru no*
> *Onatsu no kuchi ni moyuru toki* [35]

> When the look in the man's black eyes
> Falls on Onatsu's breast,
> When the man's red lips
> Burn on Onatsu's mouth. . . .

"Kasa no uchi" (Inside the Umbrella), in the same collection, refers to the love of Umegawa and Chūbei in Chikamatsu's *The Courier for Hell*.

Another element in Tōson's lyricism seems to have been derived from the Japanese translations of Christian hymns written in alternating lines of eight and six syllables. "Nigemizu" (Mirage Waters) begins:

> *Yūgure shizuka ni*   In the still of evening,
> *Yume min to te*   Thinking I will dream,

| *Yo no wazurai yori* | From the troubles of the world |
| *Shibashi nogaru* | I hide myself a while. |

These lines echo almost word for word a hymn:

Yūgure shizuka ni	In the still of evening,
Inori sen to te	Thinking I will pray,
Yo no wazurai yori	From the troubles of the world
Shibashi nogaru	I hide myself a while.

But Tōson's poem is about love, not religious devotion, and its theme is the poet's conviction that the griefs and joys of love are in essence the same.[36]

Edwin McClellan has aptly said of the poetry in *Seedlings:* "These poems may strike the modern Western reader as being at best rather unoriginal. But what may seem to us today undistinguished lyrical verse—and here we are speaking merely of the content, not the language—can very easily have seemed novel and exciting to the Japanese public of 1897."[37] The influences on Tōson from Wordsworth, Shelley, or the Bible made his poetry seem fresh to Japanese readers, but he carefully refrained from startling them with unfamiliar language or overly Western imagery. The poems were easily absorbed, and for at least fifty years afterward young Japanese regularly memorized the most famous ones.

The defects of Tōson's collection did not pass unobserved even in his day. His deliberate vagueness, though sometimes praised for its richness of suggestion, was more often condemned as mere "mystification,"[38] and the style characteristic of his obscurer poems was given the appellation *mōrō-tai*, "style of dimness." One critic declared: "Poetic expression is of necessity vague . . . but vagueness in thought is not to be tolerated. This is where Tōson's vagueness reveals itself. His style is not necessarily obscure, but the thought at times is truly mystifying. For this reason the poems to which he apparently devoted his most careful attention are for the most part vague and failures." The same reviewer also criticized Tōson for his diffuseness and for his proclivity for using such loaded expressions of grief as "Ahh!" or "How sad I am!" which are not only unattractive in themselves but weaken the effect of the entire poem.[39]

Other critics were more friendly. Kambara Ariake contrasted Tōson's naturalness of language (probably the result of the influence of Wordsworth's views of poetic diction) with the archaizing of academic poets of the day: "Mr. Shimazaki's language by no means consists of a fastidious selection of rare words; on the contrary, an examination of his words one by one will reveal their astonishing plainness. This choice of words has the effect of creating a beautiful, unfamiliar music. The patterns of melody stir in the sky of the mind the faint glimmers of heat waves shimmering over spring fields." [40]

Tōson published three other collections: *Hitoha Fune* (A Leaflike Boat, 1898), which consisted mainly of prose sketches; the eighteen poems of *Natsukusa* (Summer Grass, 1898); and *Rakubai Shū* (Fallen Plum Blossoms, 1901). The five poems in *A Leaflike Boat* included one of his most impressive works, "Washi no Uta" (The Eagle's Song). *Summer Grass* shows a marked decrease in his lyricism and expressions of a romantic nature; its philosophic tone may owe something to *Faust*. The final collection represented a further step away from the lyricism that had brought him fame only three years before. The poems in *Fallen Plum Blossoms* were written mainly while Tōson was teaching at a school in Komoro in the mountains of Nagano Prefecture. The most poignant section is a sequence treating his love for a woman who may have been the model for Osayo in *Six Maidens*. The best-known poems, however, are in a melancholy vein typified by "Chikuma-gawa Ryojō no Uta" (Song of the Weary Traveler by the Chikuma River).[41] It begins:

Komoro naru kojō no hotori
Kumo shiroku yūshi kanashimu

By the old castle in Komoro
In white clouds the wanderer grieves.

These lines suggest immediately the influence of Byron—the lonely Childe Harold wandering through various landscapes—but there is also a hint of the Chinese traveler-poet Tu Fu, perhaps as rendered by Bashō in *The Narrow Road of Oku*: "The country has fallen but its mountains and rivers remain; when spring comes to the castle the grass turns green again." The note of acceptance, so foreign to the turbulent romanticism of Tōson's early poetry, finds its strongest expression in the stanza:

Aa kojō nani wo ka katari
Kishi no nami nani wo ka kotau
Inishiyo wo shizuka ni omoe
Momotose mo kinō no gotoshi

Ah, what does the old castle tell,
What do the waves against the banks reply?
Think calmly of the world gone by;
A hundred years are as yesterday.[42]

After publishing this highly successful collection Tōson bade farewell permanently to the world of poetry. In the preface to his *Collected Poems*, published in 1904, he recalled movingly the beginnings of the shintaishi movement, concluding: "Ah, poetry for me was a whip with which to scourge myself. My youthful breast spilled over and became four volumes, rootless grasses without flower or fragrance. As a memento of my youth, I have raked together these grasses of verse filled with memories, and I offer them to whoever would be my friend." [43] In his preface to a collection of poems by Yamamura Bochō published in 1913 he also recalled: "I loved poetry as I might love a woman, and I parted from poetry as from a woman I loved." [44]

Tōson's decision to abandon poetry was irrevocable, whatever lingering attachment remained. His gradual evolution as a poet from the lyricism of *Seedlings* to the philosophic poetry of *Fallen Plum Blossoms* seems to have prepared him for the sober autobiographical writings that henceforth would be associated with his name. He also set a pattern for many other twentieth-century Japanese poets, whose activity as poets abruptly concluded when they reached thirty or forty and the last vestiges of youthful lyricism in them had disappeared. Tōson probably felt he had nothing more to say in the poetic forms he had explored and perfected. As early as 1900 he had begun writing poetical sketches in prose, his *Chikuma-gawa no Suketchi* (Sketches of the Chikuma River). In 1902 he published a first, unsuccessful story, and two years later began writing his important novel *Hakai* (The Broken Commandment).*

DOI BANSUI (1871-1952) [45]

Bansui has frequently been paired with Tōson as one of the "twin stars" of Japanese poetry in the 1890s. Unlike the poverty-ridden Tōson, however, Bansui grew up in affluence, the son of a Sendai pawnbroker with literary inclinations. He began his study of English in his native city, and in 1894 entered the English Department of Tokyo University. He later became an editor of the literary magazine *Teikoku Bungaku*, to which he contributed some of his best-known poems. In 1889 he graduated, and two years later published his first collection, *Tenchi Ujō* (Heaven and Earth Have Feelings).

Even before this publication Bansui was well known, thanks to the efforts of his friend Takayama Chogyū, who, in an essay published in 1897, had compared his poetry to that of Shimazaki Tōson and of the now forgotten poet Takeshima Hagoromo (1873-1967):

> I admire Tōson's melodies, but not his diction or thought. His language is weak and his thought vague. I admire Hagoromo's diction, but not his thought or melody. His thought is shallow and his melody monotonous. . . . Bansui is no match for Tōson in melody and he is, I suppose, inferior to Hagoromo in diction. But he far surpasses both men in the loftiness of his thought and the purity of his feelings.[46]

When *Heaven and Earth Have Feelings* appeared, Chogyū published anonymously a highly laudatory review, acclaiming Bansui for having brought "fresh light and life" to the "infantile poetry world." He regretted that Bansui's poetry was as yet imperfectly understood, and felt compelled therefore to explain its virtues. First of all, he states, the extreme seriousness of the poetry is

---

* His career as a novelist is treated elsewhere.

noteworthy. In order to lift the tone of his poetry and avoid any impression of monotony created by regular patterns of lines in alternating groups of seven and five syllables, Bansui frequently adopted the tone of the kanshi. Moreover, as a worshiper of Victor Hugo and an avid reader of the Bible, Virgil, and Dante, he wrote poetry rich in religious and transcendental emotions. "His poems are not idle songs but have the ring of prayer." The most conspicuous feature of his poems is their reflectiveness. "Most of the poems are lyrical, not impromptu lyrics in the manner of Goethe, Heine, or Shelley, but meditative lyrics like those of Schiller and Swinburne." [47]

Much was made of Bansui's learning. Not only was he a graduate of Tokyo Imperial University, but he was fluent in English, German, French, and Italian, and even in Greek and Latin. The most obvious influences on his poetry, however, came from Chinese literature and history, which Bansui studied in his youth. His long poem *Hoshi otsu Shūfū Gojōgen* (A Star Falls: Autumn Wind over Wu-chang-yüan) is an account of the death of the great Chinese general Chu-ko Liang. Though Western influence is apparent, especially in the use of a recurrent refrain, the whole is a tissue of allusions to Chinese history, carefully worked into alternating phrases in seven and five syllables. The lean severity of this poem earned for Bansui the reputation of being a masculine poet, unlike the more sensitive, "feminine" Tōson, and the heroic tone and lofty ideals made such poetry suitable for adaptation as school songs. Although Bansui also wrote a fair number of love poems, these lyrical works were all failures. He is remembered for long poems that skillfully employ the rich vocabulary of Chinese (unlike Tōson, who generally confined himself to "pure" Japanese) and for a few short poems like "Kojō no Tsuki" (Moon over the Old Castle, 1898) and "Yū no Hoshi" (Evening Star, 1898) with its famous verse:

Aa Karudea ni makibito no
Nare wo mishi yori shisennen
Hikari wa towa ni wakō shite
Yo wa kaku made ni oishi ka na [48]

Ah, four thousand years have passed
Since a shepherd in Chaldea saw you.

Your light is eternally young,
But how old the world has grown!

The contrast between eternal nature and the transience of man is hardly startling, but not only is it gracefully expressed, it brings biblical history into the Japanese ken, as Bansui otherwise did for Chinese history. Another popular poem, "Hoshi to Hana" (Stars and Flowers), reveals a different aspect of Bansui, the sensitive, even sentimental side he kept hidden under his austere, contemplative mask:

Onaji 'shizen' no on-haha no
Mi-te ni sodachishi ane to imo
Mi-sora no hana wo hoshi to ii
Wa ga yo no hoshi wo hana to iu.[49]

Older and younger sister, reared
By the hands of the same mother, Nature,
We call the flowers in the sky stars,
The stars in our world, flowers.

Ueda Bin, the distinguished translator, singled out this poem for special condemnation, pointing out the artificiality of referring to stars as the "flowers of the sky." He rhetorically declared, "Such desperate attempts to imitate some French poet make no sense even to those of us familiar with the original poems. Why should anyone have supposed they were worthy of attention in our day?" [50]

Bansui in fact commanded the attention of the young intellectuals of the day, who were intoxicated especially by the grandiloquent manner of his historical poems, if not by the more intimate "Stars and Flowers." In his use of a nontraditional vocabulary, borrowed largely from Chinese classics, and his choice of themes not previously treated in Japanese poetry, though common in Chinese or Western literature, Bansui fulfilled the dreams of the *Selection of Poetry in the New Style* poets better than Tōson or any other poet of the time, but he had no direct literary posterity. His influence no doubt was unconsciously absorbed by the students who sang his poems, but the course of Japanese modern poetry was to lie in a different direction. Bansui continued to produce volumes of poetry after *Heaven and Earth Have Feelings*, but as one critic opined, "It would be no exaggeration to say that Bansui's importance as a poet ended with *Heaven and Earth Have Feelings*."[51] His last major work was the complete translation of the *Odyssey*, published in 1943.

SUSUKIDA KYŪKIN (1877-1945)

The two best-known poets of the age after Tōson and Bansui were Susukida Kyūkin and Kambara Ariake. Their names are often linked, but they shared little as poets, and they must be considered separately. Ariake stood at the forefront of the Symbolist movement, which exercised great influence over all twentieth-century Japanese poetry, but Kyūkin's modernity consisted mainly in inventing new forms for Japanese poetry, rather than in content or style. The forms he adopted from the West, including the sonnet, ode, and narrative poem, did not thrive in Japan, though there were occasional practitioners. Even though Kyūkin's influence on later poetry was limited, he clearly belongs to a later stage in the development of the shintaishi than Tōson. He wrote not only lyrics but poetry in which the intellect as well as the heart was involved and he experimented with meter in a way foreign to earlier poets. He borrowed from the West to enrich his understanding of Japan.

If he had continued to write poetry through his maturity he might well have developed into a more commanding figure, but short of adopting Symbolism, the course of future Japanese poetry, neither he nor any other Japanese poet could remain in the mainstream. With Kyūkin the influence of nineteenth-century European poetry reached fruition. He realized better than any other poet the Meiji ideal of "combining the best of East and West" but chose not to take the next step of entering the twentieth century.

Kyūkin was born to a wealthy and cultivated family near the city of Kurashiki in Okayama Prefecture. His marks at school were outstanding, but he left middle school without graduating, apparently because of his aversion to gymnastics. Although he was later recognized as an exceptionally learned poet, he was largely self-taught; perhaps it was the compulsion of the autodidact to display his knowledge that inspired Kyūkin's conspicuous use of arcane language and literary references.

Kyūkin's poetry first appeared in 1897 in the magazine *Shinchō Gekkan*. The poetry editor, Gotō Chūgai (1866–1938), impressed by the work of an unknown youth, selected thirteen shintaishi for publication. The grateful Kyūkin continued to publish his work in the same magazine until Chūgai moved to a more important one as its poetry editor. The rival literary journal *Teikoku Bungaku* at once attacked Chūgai for his espousal of the poetry of an utter unknown, but he did not waver in his support. In 1899 Kyūkin's first collection, *Boteki Shū* (A Flute at Dusk), appeared in Osaka. To the publisher's intense surprise, the book sold five thousand copies in the first two months, at a time when even popular novels usually sold a bare two thousand copies. Even the *Teikoku Bungaku* critic was so impressed by the sales that he admitted that Kyūkin ranked next after Tōson and Bansui. Yosano Tekkan, recently returned from Korea, wrote a poem expressing his admiration, and Kyūkin, overjoyed by this recognition from an important literary figure, wrote his thanks in seventeen stanzas, including:

> *Wazurai ōki yo wo sakete*
> *Ima shi no ryō ni yomigaeru*
> *Metorazu, yukazu tendō no*
> *Kiyoki zo hō to omou mono.*[52]

> Shunning a world full of misfortune,
> I return to life now in poetry's domain;
> Taking no bride, going to no other's house,
> I will maintain an angelic purity.

These sentiments no doubt appealed to Tekkan, who (before he met Akiko) had similarly rejected the pleasures of love in favor of the Spartan severity of the poet's calling. Kyūkin, despite the tenderness of his pen name ("weeping violets"), maintained until he was in his thirties his resolve not to be bound by marital ties.

Japanese critics have sometimes linked this decision to the marked lack of ardor in Kyūkin's poetry. His intellectuality, which certainly contrasted with Tōson's effusive cries of love, kept his poetry from ever enjoying much popularity among the young and impressionable; but it also saved Kyūkin from falling into the banality and sentimentality of which Tōson was sometimes guilty. Only in his last collection of poetry, *Ochiba* (Fallen Leaves), published two years after Kyūkin's late (by Meiji standards) marriage in 1906, did he suddenly burst forth into poems on love. It has been conjectured that Kyūkin, having long denied himself the joys of marriage, now first realized how much he had missed, and wrote of love with a poignance born of this awareness.[53] If we accept this hypothesis, however, we must sadly note that after publishing *Fallen Leaves*, Kyūkin wrote no more poetry, suggesting that happiness in marriage did not inspire him for long.

Kyūkin's poetry at almost every turn reveals influence from the nineteenth-century English poets, especially Keats and Browning. He made no secret of his borrowings, including on occasion an epigraph quoting Keats, or imitating the recurrent refrain from some well-known European ballad. Obviously he felt extremely dissatisfied with the kind of shintaishi written by Tōson and Bansui, and turned to the West for an escape from the mellifluous mediocrity of the typical Japanese poem of the 1890s. First of all, he borrowed European forms, notably the sonnet (which he called *zekku* after the short Chinese verse-form). The nineteen sonnets in his first collection consist of fourteen lines each of fourteen syllables, marked by a caesura after the eighth syllable.

Sometimes also Kyūkin turned to the West for thematic materials or merely for a point of departure. His sonnet "Kōrogi" (The Cricket) was not only based on Keats' sonnet "On the Grasshopper and the Cricket" (1816), but bears the epigraph from Keats: "The poetry of earth is never dead. . . ."[54] Nevertheless, the atmosphere in Kyūkin's poem is distinctly Japanese:

> The serving maid is asleep, the kitchen cold;
> At midnight when mice are snug in their nests,
> By the dying warmth of the hearth, without a friend,
> Its song untutored, a cricket shrills . . . .[55]

Kyūkin's indebtedness to Keats was demonstrated by his borrowing of both sonnet and ode forms from Keats and in the adoption in his own poems of the major themes of the "Ode to the Night-ingale" and the "Ode on a Grecian Urn." Kyūkin's "Kokyō no Fu" (Ode on an Ancient Mirror) drew inspiration from both of Keats's great odes, though its subject matter, the images reflected in the mirror a court lady used long ago, betrayed no foreignness. The court lady, unhappy in love, cut her hair and became a Bud-dhist nun, throwing away her mirror, the symbol of worldly van-ity. Kyūkin's language was perfectly appropriate to the Heian scene he described, a discreet combination of archaisms used to suggest the distant world of the court lady, and a more modern language for the poet who conjures up the past. It is quite possible to read this poem without once thinking of Keats, though the overtones have a familiar ring. In some of Kyūkin's poems the inspiration is more obvious. "Boshun no Fu" (Ode on Late Spring) contains these lines:

Tsumetaki muro ni kamosarete
Wakamurasaki no iro fukaku, awa saku sake no sakazuki wo
Wa ga kuchibiru ni fukumase yo

Let my lips imbibe
A cup of wine, a dark young purple, with winking bubbles,
Brewed in some cool cellar . . . .

The resemblances to Keats are inescapable: [56]

Oh, for a draught of vintage that hath been,
Cool'd a long age in the deep-delved earth.
. . . .
O for a beaker full of the warm South,
Full of the true, the blushful Hippocrene,
With beaded bubbles winking at the brim,
And purple-stained mouth.

Direct borrowings of this kind were, however, rare. Kyūkin nor-mally assimilated whatever he borrowed, and cast his thoughts or images into moving and effective Japanese.

In his third collection, *Nijūgo Gen* (A Lute of Twenty-five Strings, 1905), Kyūkin, ever in search of new forms, turned to narrative poetry. The 699 lines of *Amahasezukai* (The Courier of Heaven), although not remarkably long by European standards, represented a milestone in the development of extended poetic composition in Japanese. The subject matter of the poem, various legends concerning Izanagi and Izanami, the first man and woman, was naturally based on Shinto materials, but it also included Buddhist elements and even traces of Keats's "Hyperion." Kyūkin's long poems were only intermittently effective, perhaps because the monotonously regular rhythms of his Japanese prosody could not sustain so long a work. The same factors that had inhibited the writing of chōka during the thousand years after the *Manyōshū* still seemed to impose limits on the length of Japanese poems.

The best-known work in *A Lute of Twenty-five Strings* is "Kōsonjuka ni tachite" (Standing under the Gingko Tree), a poem in one hundred lines, each of twelve syllables regularly divided after the seventh syllable. The poem opens with a description of the sun shining on the Piazza di Spagna in Rome and the famous steps swarming with beggars. This passage, inspired by Mori Ōgai's translation of Hans Christian Andersen's *Improvisatoren*, is followed (without break or explanation) by a description of the sun shining over a bleak fishing village in the north, and then of its shining on a landscape in Kyūkin's native Okayama. The effect is impressionistic; Kyūkin presumably intended to capture, by contrast with other scenes, the distinctive qualities of the surroundings in Okayama where a great gingko tree stands. The tree is likened to a warrior sending arrows of leaves into the advancing autumn wind; and the loss of leaves after each charge in turn reminds the poet of Ishtar's descent into the underworld, where she leaves a garment at each of seven gates. The effect produced by these sudden shifts of scene and by the rich vocabulary is not one of unity but of a beauty that imposes its own logic. The reader is left at the end with an imprecise but unforgettable impression of the ancient tree.

Kyūkin's most important collection, *Hakuyōkyū* (The Constellation Aries, 1906), has been acclaimed as one of two masterpieces of Meiji poetry.[57] It is famous for two long poems, both directly inspired by Western examples but nevertheless faithful to the Japanese landscapes depicted. *Aa, Yamato ni shi aramashikaba*

(Oh, to Be in Yamato) opens with lines that seem to parody Robert Browning, but quickly becomes a quite different work:

Oh, to be in Yamato
Now that November's there!
I would follow a path through the wood
Where the gods descend, sunlight through the unleaved tops,
My hair drenched in the early morning dew,
To Ikaruga. On a day when tall grasses
In the fields of Heguri wave like a golden sea,
And the tops of dusty windows whiten in the pale sunlight
I would stare in wonder at the gold lettering of a precious ancient
   book,
At a Korean lute, a sacred wine vessel, frescoes on a wall,
Pausing in the shadows of a column;
In a temple of beauty graced with eternal flowers, deep in the
   sanctuary,
Where burning incense befuddles the senses like a vat
Of wine many times distilled—
I would grow drunk on that perfume!

The first section of the poem, given above, describes Yamato in early morning. Kyūkin's long poems are often divided into sections according to the time of day or season of the year; in this poem the characteristic sights of morning are followed by those of noon and dusk, each so described to suggest the dusty grandeur of the ancient capital—an effect heightened by the use of many archaic words drawn from the *Manyōshū* and other old texts. Despite the obvious borrowing from Browning in the opening lines, the poem cannot be dismissed as mere imitation. Kyūkin, resorting to the familiar device of Japanese poetry, made an "allusive variation" on Browning's statement of his desire to be in another country because it was uniquely beautiful at a particular time of year; but his poem, unlike Browning's, is devoted to recollections of the distant past, rather than a nostalgic re-creation of remembered sights.

In *Bōkyō no Uta* (Song of Homeward Thoughts), the other important poem of *The Constellation Aries*, Kyūkin borrowed from Goethe the refrain at the end of each stanza: *Kanata e, kimi to iza kaeramashi* ("There would I return with you!"). The source was Mignon's song "Kennst du das Land?" in *Wilhelm Meister*:

> *Dahin! Dahin*
> *Möchte ich mit dir, o mein Geliebter, ziehn.*

The scenes evoked in Kyūkin's poem are not of a distant land where orange trees bloom but of the Kyoto the poet knew when he lived there, depicted in each of the four seasons. In contrast to his poem about Yamato, he does not look back to the ancient glories of Kyoto, but restricts himself to the modern city. Even so, his longing for the past is unmistakable. The third stanza, describing autumn outside Kyoto, is perhaps the best:

> The old city: over a path through fields where yellow alder leaves
> flutter
> A winnower-girl, softly singing, homeward leads her light-brown
> ox;
> The sun darts a last glance at the pagoda spire,
> Then, as dusk falls, slowly shuts his eyes; deciduous trees, thinned
> now,
> Are like old mourner-women, shawls wearily pulled over their
> heads,
> Standing in grief; the evening moon, glimmering through the trees,
> Casts a dreamy sidelong glance; the bluish echoes of a temple bell
> Recall to the traveler on his pilgrim's round his home.
> —There, there, I would return with you!

These lines are untraditional in their metaphors and personification and in their effective combination of archaisms with ancient-sounding neologisms. The meter, less experimental than in some poems by Kyūkin, consists of lines of twenty-four syllables, each divisible into phrases of seven, five, seven, and five syllables.[58]

Kyūkin's concern with form, language, and tradition (and his conspicuous intellectuality) have given him the name of a "Parnassian." Certain poems in fact indicate he was influenced by Leconte de Lisle, read in Ueda Bin's translations. The Parnassian qualities that brought Kyūkin's poetry acclaim and respect in its day have ever since prevented it from maintaining a wide following. The archaic language provides special pleasure to readers thoroughly familiar with the *Manyōshū*, *The Tale of Genji*, and the medieval war tales, but such knowledge can no longer be assumed. The major poems, when reprinted in recent years, have had to be provided with vocabularies of obscure words and sometimes with complete translations into modern Japanese before readers could surmount their difficulties. Even with such aids their Parnassian remoteness denies them the popularity still enjoyed, say, by Tōson's lyricism. Kyūkin was dissatisfied with the standard poetic diction, established by the *Kokinshū*, but instead of adopting the more obvious expedient of enriching this vocabulary with that of contemporary speech, he resuscitated even more archaic language. As a result he puzzled even his admirers and denied himself the possibility of successors.

In 1906, when Kyūkin published *The Constellation Aries*, he was the leading figure in the world of Japanese poetry, and he has retained a distinguished place in its history, but the accidental circumstance that he ceased to compose poetry just as Symbolism was emerging as the dominant trend means that he stands isolated, the author of four or five anthology pieces rather than a founder of modern poetry.

UEDA BIN (1874–1916)

Before the Japanese poets could enter the twentieth century they had to learn what the creators of modern European poetry had written. More than anyone else, it was Ueda Bin who taught them. Bin's fame is due almost entirely to his translations, though he also published original works of poetry and prose. He came from a distinguished family of scholars. Both his father and grandfather had traveled to Europe, and as a child he played with Western toys. He attended an English school in Tokyo and at eighteen began to publish translations of Shelley and Byron that attracted favorable attention. In 1894 he entered the English Department of Tokyo Imperial University, where he became friendly with members of the *Bungakkai* group. He was also a founder of *Teikoku Bungaku* and contributed an article on Belgian literature to the first issue. In 1896, the year that Lafcadio Hearn accepted a post at the university as a teacher of English literature, Bin became his student. At the time the subjects he studied were all

taught by non-Japanese; Hearn and Raphael von Koeber (1848–
1923), the German-Russian philosopher, were of particular importance in Bin's development. After graduation in 1897 he continued his studies under Hearn and von Koeber. An essay on
William Collins, written in English, won him praise from Hearn
as "a student in ten thousand." [59]

Bin had also studied French in high school. In 1896 he published an article on the death of Paul Verlaine, introducing his
work to Japan. Two years later he published an article in *Teikoku
Bungaku* on "New Voices in French Poetry," introducing both the
Parnassians and Symbolists, the earliest systematic presentation of
poetry that would have enormous importance in Japan.[60]

In 1899 Bin published his first book, *Yaso* (Jesus), largely
under the influence of Renan's *Vie de Jésus*. In the same year he
also published in English *The Victorian Lyre*, a collection of Victorian poetry for school use that included FitzGerald's *Rubaiyat*,
some Rossetti and Swinburne, and even some Kipling. During
this period Bin by no means neglected his readings in Japanese
literature. He shared in the revival of interest in the classics of the
1890s that was occasioned in part by way of reaction to the craze
for Western literature, and received instruction from Ochiai Naobumi in the *Manyōshū* and *Shin Kokinshū*. His virtuoso talent for
writing archaic Japanese, as much as his ability to read foreign
languages, lay behind the success of his later translations.

Even after he began to win a name as a translator of English
and French, Bin continued his studies of European languages,
adding Italian and German. His translations published during
1902–1903 included his famous versions of "Über den Bergen" of
Carl Busse and the "Song" from *Pippa Passes* of Browning, both
of which became anthology pieces.

The year 1905 was probably the most memorable of Bin's
life. In the June issue of *Myōjō* he published a study of Mallarmé's Symbolism and translations of Verhaeren, Régnier, Verlaine, and Rodenbach. In October his collection of translations of
poetry, mainly by French (and Belgian) Symbolists, appeared under the title *Kaichōon* (Sound of the Tide); it was dedicated to
Mori Ōgai. The translations were acclaimed as masterpieces, and
their reputation has not diminished. Although the process of making these highly polished translations was slow and difficult,

the final versions seem effortless re-creations in Japanese of the theme and moods (if not the words) of the translated texts. A particularly celebrated example is his version of Verlaine's "Chanson d'automne":

Les sanglots longs	Aki no hi no
Des violons	Vioron no
De l'automne	Tameiki no
Blessent mon coeur	Mi ni shimite
D'une langueur	Hitaburu ni
Monotone.	Urakanashi.

Bin's translation is far from literal. He altered *blessent mon coeur* to the more familiar Japanese expression *mi ni shimite* (pierces my body), and only suggested *d'une langueur monotone.* But how much superior his Japanese version is to the English one!

The wailing note
That long doth float
From Autumn's bow,
Doth wound my heart
With no quick smart,
But dull and slow.[61]

A comparison of Bin's translation with later Japanese versions of the same poem also reveals his ability to capture the spirit and melody of the original, even at the cost of some of the language.

Sound of the Tide consisted of fifty-seven poems by twenty-nine poets. Fourteen of the poets were French. Bin's translations revealed to Japanese for the first time the distinctive nature of French poetry, especially of the nineteenth century. The translations of English and German poetry, no less carefully executed, had less impact if only because these literatures were already fairly well known. Among the French poets Bin (as he mentioned in the preface) felt the greatest affinity with the Parnassians, especially Leconte de Lisle and José Maria de Heredia. His translations of these poets, employing more flexible patterns of meter than elsewhere in the collection, are his finest work but, as Bin was aware, the day of the Parnassians had passed. The poetry of the Symbolists had greater appeal for the readers. Bin's preface stated that

> the use of symbols in poetry is by no means a modern invention; no doubt it is as old as the hills. However, the conscious use of symbols as the central feature of poetic composition probably first began some twenty years ago in the new French poetry. . . . The function of symbols is to help create in the reader a mental state similar to that in the poet's mind. Symbols do not necessarily communicate the same meanings to everyone. The reader who quietly savors symbolist poetry is enabled by it to enjoy an indescribable pleasure, in accordance with his own sensibilities, which the poetry has not specifically indicated. As a result, the interpretation of a given poem will vary according to the period. The essential thing is that a similar mental state be evoked.[62]

Bin's theories of Symbolism, first enunciated in this preface, were based largely on those of E. Vigié-Lecoq in *La poésie contemporaine, 1884–1896*, and he illustrated them with references to the same poem by Verhaeren that Vigié-Lecoq had used.[63]

The reception given *Sound of the Tide* was extraordinary. According to Yosano Tekkan, it provided the "same nourishment to Meiji and Taishō poetry that Po Chü-i's *Works* had afforded Heian literature." [64] Probably no other work of modern poetry, with the possible exception of Tōson's poems, has enjoyed such popularity, but its chief importance was as an inspiration to the next generation of poets. A distinguished critic has attacked *Sound of the Tide* for having created a "buffer zone" between European and Japanese poetry by creating poems intended to be "poetic" rather than faithful to the sense or construction of the originals.[65] But, leaving aside the question of what the course of Japanese poetry might have been if Bin's translations had been more faithful to the originals and less easily digestible by Japanese readers, one can only marvel that he succeeded better than any English translator in rendering Mallarmé, Verhaeren, and Régnier into an idiom entirely congenial to his countrymen. The same critic (Shinoda Hajime) has also stated, "Anyone who denies Mallarmé is a part of Japanese poetic tradition is a chauvinist who does not appreciate the work of the modern Japanese poets." [66] Although more accurate translations of Mallarmé than Ueda Bin's were later rendered, none surpassed his in their influence, which is apparent in the work of the first Japanese Symbolist poets, Kambara Ariake, Kitahara Hakushū, and Miki Rofū.

KAMBARA ARIAKE (1876–1947)

Kambara Ariake in later years traced his awakening as a poet to an experience of 1895 when, as a young man of nineteen, he was traveling to Kyushu. As he gazed over the Inland Sea from his boat he noticed a flutter of white wings and a seagull disappear into the evening darkness. The sight stirred him strangely. "It was the guidance of the seagull that day that eventually made me a poet," he later recalled.[67] The poem that flashed into his mind after watching the seagull was not preserved in its original state, but a revised version, written about 1900, was included in his first collection under the title "Umashi Obama" (Lovely Shore). This poem may have represented Ariake's awakening as a poet, but he had loved poetry even as a child, when he and his sister memorized poems from *Selection of Poetry in the New Style*, especially "Elegy Written in a Country Church-Yard" and "The Charge of the Light Brigade." [68] He was fascinated by the magic of Western Romanticism when he read the poems translated in *Vestiges*; and as a boy of fifteen he read Kitamura Tōkoku's *Song of Paradise* with profound admiration. Later he entered an English-language academy where he attended lectures on Shakespeare and Byron. On his journey to Kyushu he carried with him a copy of *Childe Harold's Pilgrimage*. These and other foreign influences were of paramount importance to his development as a poet, but he was also deeply interested in the oldest Japanese literature, especially the *Kojiki* and *Izumo Fudoki*, and he later employed their archaic vocabulary even in poems expressing a modern sensibility.

After Ariake's return from Kyushu he wrote a story that won first prize in a competition judged by Ozaki Kōyō.[69] He wrote a few other short stories before he turned definitely to poetry, and Kōyō helped to get them published. Ariake continued to read the works of the English Romantic poets with enthusiasm, but he was most deeply affected by the poetry of Dante Gabriel Rossetti, whom he learned about from the notes of a friend who had attended Hearn's lectures on English poetry at Tokyo University in 1899. His passion for Rossetti's poetry, which moved him to translate "The Blessed Damozel" as early as 1900, remained with him throughout his life as a poet; and it grew more profound with the years, even after his readings had ranged far beyond Rossetti in complexity and subtlety. Not even Susukida Kyūkin's admiration for Keats matched Ariake's unconditional worship of Rossetti. This devotion enabled him to absorb the techniques of modern Western poetry more completely than any previous Japanese. He was styled "the Japanese Rossetti."

Ariake's first collection, *Kusa Wakaba* (Grass and Young Leaves, 1902), compared with his later poetry is relatively simple, melodic, and regular. Some poems might even be mistaken for works by Tōson, whose final collection *Fallen Plum Blossoms* was published just a year before *Grass and Young Leaves*. Unquestionably Ariake was under Tōson's influence; an admiring letter from Tōson, describing his impression of *Grass and Young Leaves*, indicates how congenial he in turn found Ariake's poetry.[70] But even in this early work there are poems much more advanced than anything by Tōson. The most famous, "Kaki no Kara" (The Oyster's Shell), is an allegory that depicts the oyster (the individual) as being unhappily imprisoned in its shell (society), unable to appreciate the beauty and grandeur of the surrounding world, and powerless to achieve its ideals. The final stanza expresses the hope that one day a great storm will ravage the sea and break open the shell, freeing the oyster from its prison.[71]

The influence of Rossetti is not apparent in "The Oyster's Shell" or elsewhere in the collection; however, the brief preface, written in Heian-style prose, opens with the statement: "Within the gentle heart Love shelters him, as birds within the green shade of the grove," an unacknowledged quotation of two lines from the thirteenth-century poet Guido Guinizelli, as rendered by Rossetti in *The Early Italian Poets*.[72] Ariake had by this time completed his first successful "sonnets" in the Rossettian manner; but he withheld these poems for future publication, perhaps feeling they did not go well with his earlier poetry.

His second collection, *Dokugen Aika* (Elegies on a Single String, 1903), included translations of both Rossetti and Keats, but the most distinctive works were the original sonnets and ballads composed under the influence of Rossetti. In the sonnets written by Kyūkin the meter tended to break down monotonously into short units of fixed length.[73] Ariake adopted a long line of seventeen syllables that permitted him to maintain an impression of variety. In later years he stated that he had borrowed his unconventional rhythms from the Japanese translations of Christian hymns.[74] His familiarity with hymns did not represent the limit of his interest in Christianity; like many other young intellectuals of the 1890s he was attracted by Christian idealism, and a distinctly religious note—whether in the form of prayers or references to spiritual life—is found in many works.

Kambara Ariake never explicitly stated his reasons for writing sonnets. The very fact that so many poets of the West had chosen this form was probably a justification in itself; like them, he may have found it congenial to express his thoughts within a fixed form of relatively brief compass that imposed a discipline welcome to a poet of his essentially conceptual (rather than lyrical) bent, but Ariake's sonnets were unlike European sonnets in that he did not intentionally use rhyme. The early sonnets were sometimes successful, but his best works in this form appeared in his fourth collection, *Ariake Shū* (1908), in which he lifted the Japanese sonnet to its highest level of attainment.

The other influence from Rossetti in *Elegies on a Single String* is the prominence of the literary ballad with a recurrent refrain. The materials for Ariake's ballads were derived from such disparate sources as the legends in the various *fudoki*, Swinburne's *Itylus*, and a collection of South Sea myths and songs compiled by an English missionary.[75] Ariake stated that his aim was not merely to retell in elegant language various old legends but to trace the psychological development involved. "Rossetti's ballads excel in precisely this quality," he declared.[76]

Ariake's ballads are by no means easy to comprehend: the language is archaic; the references to the *Kojiki* and other ancient texts are left unexplained; and the syntax is unusually complicated. *Elegies on a Single String* was nevertheless well received; the review by Tsunajima Ryōsen (1873-1907) in *Myōjō* was all but ecstatic in its praise of the freshness, audacity, charm, and nobility of Ariake's poems.[77]

Ariake's third collection, *Shunchō Shū* (Birds of Spring,

1905), represented a marked advance in his poetic techniques. The long preface includes such statements as:

> If anything in the crystallization of one's sensations concerning nature and human existence differs from that of the past, it surely requires new forms for its expression. At the approach of summer people prepare to discard their spring clothes, but those with old habits long planted in their minds hate making the effort to consider anything new.

The great efforts of modern poets to break the dead weight of tradition sometimes has led to excesses, it is true, but this was inevitable considering the magnitude of the task of loosening the bonds of the old poetic diction and making Japanese a medium capable of expressing the subtleties of modern thought. "For this reason I have been resigned all along to the criticism that my poems are obscure." Ariake insisted especially on the importance of vivid expression of the sensory impressions. Without this vitality, literature tends to consist of patchwork imitations.

The next important statement in his preface concerned synesthesia, the mingling of the senses so often preached by the Symbolist poets:

> The senses—sight, hearing and so on—have become confused and mingled in the mental impressions of modern man; that is why there are such things as the "sound of silver light" or the "color of a sonority." These refer to the mind's eye or the mind's ear, but it is possible also to detect with our sense of smell the fragrance of a soul. Only a man ignorant of the intensity of the senses would say of the sense of smell that it is vulgar.

Ariake gave instances of synesthesia in classical Japanese literature, mentioning Sei Shōnagon and Bashō in particular, and said of the latter that he was the most Symbolist writer in all of Japanese literature. He cited examples of Bashō's use of synesthesia, such as the famous haiku that describes the voices of seagulls as being "faintly white," and denounced the attempts of the commentators to find philosophic or didactic meanings in such poems. These views on synesthesia probably were derived from articles published by Ueda Bin and Mori Ōgai in 1900 and 1901.

In the last section of the preface Ariake briefly discussed the prose-poem, first being attempted in Japan at this time. He scornfully dismissed most as no more than prosy examples of "fine writing," and suggested that the closest the Japanese had ever come to approximating this art perfected by Baudelaire and Mallarmé was in the *haibun* written by Bashō's disciple Sodō.[78]

The preface is obscurely worded and contains puzzling references, but the main points are clear enough: Kambara Ariake was groping toward the standpoint of the Symbolists. His distinctively Symbolist style is first noticeable shortly after 1904, when Ueda Bin published in *Myōjō* a translation of Verhaeren's "Parable" under the title "Symbolist Poem." Bin's next presentation of Symbolism was in June 1905, when he published translations of seven poems under the general title "Symbolist Poems." In the meantime Ariake, relying mainly on his ingenuity, wrote the series of poems in the Symbolist manner included in *Birds of Spring*, published in July 1905. This collection is headed by one of Ariake's important poems, which opens:

FALLEN EARS FROM THE SUN

Fallen ears from the sun, drops from the moon—
Who has tasted the leavings,
Who has garnered the overflow?
Is this how the world passes by?
Alas, who will answer, unhesitant,
When asked, "Have you trodden the steps of the sun
To the shrine of the moon, the depth of the scent?" [79]

"Fallen ears from the sun" and "drops from the moon" are both used as symbols for instants of time, day and night. The poet asks rhetorically who has savored each moment to the utmost, who has penetrated the mystery of time ("the shrine of the moon") to its essence ("the depth of the scent").[80] The theme of the complete poem—the rapid passage of time and the importance of seizing each moment—of this poem of twenty-eight lines was by no means unusual even within Japanese traditions, but the imagery and metaphors were modern. The poem is not Symbolist—surely only one meaning is intended—but the complexity and obscurity of expression invited comparison with the Symbolists. Many critics complained that they could not understand the meaning, and Ariake, who spent the last half of his life revising his early poetry, felt obliged to simplify some of the lines.[81] As usual in such cases, Ariake's simplifications tended to weaken the poems by making their expression—their chief distinction—prosy or even banal; but in the original versions the language, though obscure and ambiguous, is movingly evocative, thanks to the effective imagery.

"Asa nari" (It Is Morning) in the same collection would seem (once the reader had penetrated the surface complexities of vocabulary and syntax) to be a realistic description of daybreak over the polluted waters of a river flowing through Tokyo. It begins:

> It is morning. Before long the turbid river,
> Giving off a tepid smell, seems to wash away
> The foetal membrane of night. Along the white walls
> —The row of warehouses of a riverside market—
> It is morning; the river haze hangs humidly.[82]

As this line-by-line translation indicates, the word order is strained: for example, although the haze presumably hangs over the white walls, the two are separated by statements that dangle syntactically in midair. The most striking image is of the darkness of night being washed away by the light coming down the river. The use of the words "foetal membrane of night" (*yoru no e*) not only suggests the birth of a day but the tepid odor of afterbirth clinging to the river.

The poem, eight stanzas of five lines each, describes refuse floating in the river; a dirty bridge over which geishas, worn out by their night's exertions, wearily cross at daybreak; seagulls searching for food; the colors of the river at dawn; and the activity starting up in the market as it grows light. The final stanza returns to the expression of the first, with an unexpected twist at the end:

> It is morning. Shapes take on their colors again,
> And now sunlight shines along the turbid river.
> It is morning, and the white walls
> Of the row of market warehouses along the river
> Are already glistening.—Is this, I wonder, my mind? [83]

The abrupt question at the end, introducing for the first time a subjective note into what has seemed an entirely objective description of the scene, indicates that the poet's mind, at first obscured like the warehouse walls by darkness and haze, has suddenly cleared; his depression has lifted with the coming of day. The last line has caused some critics to opine that the entire poem should be read symbolically, but probably only the final perception—the equation between the suddenly illumined walls and the poet's state of mind—has symbolic overtones; the remainder of the poem is what it seems to be, the description of an actual scene.

The scene itself is so unusual as to require some comment. It has hitherto not been considered a function of poetry to describe warehouses, floating debris in a foul-smelling river, or bedraggled prostitutes crossing a creaking bridge. Not until 1907, when Kawaji Ryūkō created a sensation with his "Hakidame" (Rubbish Heap), did the Naturalist poets begin to treat such subjects. Ariake anticipated this enlargement of the realm of poetry.

"It Is Morning" was highly praised by Ueda Bin, always Ariake's most perceptive critic, as the best poem in the collection: "It is true that it takes some effort to appreciate this poem, and it may be that my interpretation of the meaning is not the same as the author's. But presumably it does not matter, since the author is a Symbolist poet, if readers do not interpret the meaning exactly as the poet intended." [84]

Kambara Ariake's last collection, *Ariake Shū* (1908), is by general consent his finest achievement, and it is often ranked alongside Susukida Kyūkin's *The Constellation Aries* as marking the summit of modern (*kindai*) poetry. Despite the renown it enjoyed in later years, it was not greeted with any special enthusiasm when it appeared, perhaps because Ueda Bin was abroad at the time. Moreover, a group of younger writers, dissatisfied with Ariake's remoteness of style, had founded the Waseda Poetry Society in the previous year with the announced intention of extending to poetry the attitudes of the Naturalist movement.[85]

The sonnet at the head of the collection, "Chie no Sōja wa Ware wo mite" (A Learned Physiognomist, Looking at My Face), heralded a new development in Ariake's poetry:

A learned physiognomist, looking at my face, told me today:
"Your features are clouded with signs of misfortune.

If you supinely let your thoughts stray to love, clouds and squalls
Will darken your sky; flee the danger before it strikes."

He told me to flee from you and your loveliness,
From the wavy folds of your black hair, softer even
Than green pastures, than undulant grassy fields.
—But what will be the judgment you pass?

I shut my eyes and see myself in the twilight,
Trudging with lowered head to the ends of an endless desert—
You might suppose I was a starving beast on the loose.

That figure, that drab and weary figure—
The man who can flee from you and embark on an arid journey!—
If not—a whirlpool of fragrance, a storm wind of color.[86]

The poem depicts the conflict between the poet's desires and his intellect, which, in the guise of a fortune-teller, predicts disasters if he allows himself to be trapped in sensual pleasure. The resolution is the poet's decision to yield to the fragrance and color of passion, rather than condemn himself to the bleak monotony of a life without pleasure. The poem is striking because it is so conceptual, rather than being given to easy expression of the emotions. Hagiwara Sakutarō wrote of this sonnet that "like purple smoke rising from an incense burner in a monastery, it is at once extremely sensual and meditative." [87]

Kambara's most celebrated work is the sonnet, in the same collection, called "Matsurika" (Jasmine):

Gracefully you roll up the gauzy curtains
Of my clouded, weary heart, choked with grief, and brilliantly
One day your face is revealed in the languid, seductive
Brightness of poppies blooming in fields of enticement.

Even as, allured by whisperings that melt my soul,
I embrace you again, I feel I shall weep.
The most secret of sorrows, the trap of dreams—in your arms
My aching arms were imprisoned.

Again, one evening, I could not see you, but there came
The indefinable soft rustling of your spun-silk garment—
That was all I heard, and my heart at that moment was riven.

In a room at night fragrant with the scent of jasmine
Your smile, mingled in that odor, sought my wound,
Sank into it, perfumed it, elegantly, again and again.[88]

The women described in the poem is no doubt a phantom evoked in the successive stanzas by the senses of sight, touch, hearing, and smell. This mingling of the senses, together with the deliberate obscurity of expression, mark this as a Symbolist poem. It reveals not only the influence of Mallarmé but the fin-de-siècle weariness, or even decadence, that fills many of Ariake's works. Various Japanese commentators have stated that in this sonnet Kambara Ariake demonstrated that he had fully absorbed Western influence and was capable of creating independently Symbolist poetry of his own.[89] Indeed, the poem has been acclaimed as the masterpiece of Japanese Symbolism, but Shinoda Hajime has expressed reservations:

> What captivates us is not the poem itself so much as its "poetic" aspects. For example, the images revolving around the jasmine and those concerning love are intertwined in this poem with consummate skill and describe a complex and many-leveled interior landscape; but if we recall the poetic world of Mallarmé, what a despair-making difference there is! In Mallarmé's poetry psychological and logical images join together dazzlingly; or, as they come apart, mental visions of multifold meanings appear and disappear one after another; but in the end it is the power of the words themselves that awesomely reveals before our eyes the presence of the poem. In contrast, the words of "Jasmine" are exceedingly feeble and empty. Rather than speak of a world of multilevel meanings, we might more properly say that two varieties of images surrounding the jasmine and love explain each other, and that both are superficial. This style of poetry might more properly be called allegoric rather than symbolic.[90]

Shinoda's strictures suggest the difficulty of evaluating absolutely not only Ariake's poetry but any Japanese poetry written in a European manner. Kambara Ariake earns our respect for having assimilated the styles of two nineteenth-century masters, Rossetti and Mallarmé, and he richly deserves his place in literary history; but is his poetry more than a provincial version of the English or French original genius? Unquestionably he attempted to impart a distinctively Japanese flavor to his poems, using an archaic vocabulary and allusions to Japanese literary traditions, and exploiting the auditory possibilities of the Japanese language; but the content of "Jasmine" and the manner of presenting the poetic thought were foreign to Japanese tradition and seem contrived. Japanese poetry abounds in expressions of love, especially rejected or recollected love, but the poets never spoke of choking and groaning or of a woman's smile sinking into the "wound" of the poet's spiritual anguish. Ariake's archaisms—real or invented— enhanced the beauty of the poem especially for readers unable to accept modern Japanese speech as a medium for poetry. This beauty, however, tended to remain pleasing sounds, rather than suggestion at the profoundest level, as might be said of Mallarmé's poetry. Only with the development of a distinctive poetic language in the 1920s would it be possible to write poetry that was at once new and wholly Japanese.

Ariake, at any rate in his Symbolist vein, is a difficult poet. Usually his poetry is printed in Japan without commentary, or with notes only on the least perplexing points, such as the botanical nomenclature for the flowers mentioned. In the few cases where more extensive commentaries exist, comparison immediately reveals what sharp differences there are in interpretation. It is a measure of Ariake's success as a poet that readers (presumably less competent at interpreting the poems than specialists) can take pleasure in his works even without fully grasping the meaning. No doubt his poems will be read even if their meanings become utterly obscure, if only for their "poetic" effects.

Ariake's influence on later poets was considerable, though indirect. Shinoda commented, "Modern Japanese poetry, ever since the founding of the 'Japanese Symbolist School,' has always aimed at a Symbolist 'climate.' It is impossible to discuss modern Japanese poetry without taking this 'climate' into account." [91]

Kambara Ariake's significant work as a poet ended with *Ariake Shū*. In 1922 he published *Ariake Shishū* (Collected Poems of Ariake), including some new works along with favorites from his earlier collections, but none of the new poems was of great value. His flame as a poet was burned out. Like Shimazaki Tōson,

Susukida Kyūkin, and many other modern Japanese poets, his inspiration came early but also departed early. His last thirty years were spent as a poet of the past.

KITAHARA HAKUSHŪ (1885–1942)

Susukida Kyūkin and Kambara Ariake stopped writing poetry about the same time. Although they were born within a year of each other and their careers as poets spanned the same period, Kambara Ariake seems to belong to a later generation, one that also includes Kitahara Hakushū and Miki Rofū, though the latter two men went on developing as poets long after Kambara Ariake fell silent. Hakushū was not only an exceptionally gifted poet, but also an exceptionally popular one. In contrast to the poetry of Susukida Kyūkin and Kambara Ariake, whose obscure and archaic language made appreciation largely cerebral, Hakushū's poems gave the pleasure of music. Though sometimes complex and sometimes (especially in his early period) expressed in exotic language, these poems still speak to the heart.

Hakushū was born in Yanagawa in Kyushu. As a child his delicate health and high-strung disposition often kept him from school, and he passed his time reading and writing poetry. A tanka he sent to the magazine *Bunko* (Library) in Tokyo was accepted for publication in 1902, and the next issue of the magazine carried twelve of his poems at the head of the tanka section. Hakushū continued to compose tanka until an annoying incident made him give up tanka altogether: a poem he wrote in which he described Kaguyama as a "female" mountain, was sharply attacked by a tanka critic who insisted in a long article that the mountain was actually male. Such pedantic criticism so irritated Hakushū that he abandoned the tanka in favor of modern poetry.* His father, eager to have Hakushū succeed him in the family brewery, strongly disapproved of his writing poetry; but in

---

* The term *shintaishi* stopped being used at this time except as a designation for early Meiji period examples. The new word, *gendaishi*, literally "contemporary poem," was used of poetry in untraditional forms. The term will be translated as "modern poetry."

1904, with the connivance of his mother and brother, Hakushū ran away from home. He went to Tokyo, where he registered at the English Preparatory School of Waseda University.

Hakushū's modern poetry began to appear in *Bunko* regularly. The April 1904 issue, for example, was given over entirely to a long poem of his, altogether some four hundred lines. This early poetry was marked by a stringing together of beautiful phrases, which earned Hakushū the nickname of "the Izumi Kyōka of poetry." [92] In 1906, responding to an invitation from Yosano Tekkan, he joined the Shinshisha, and soon was publishing his poetry in *Myōjō*. Through the Shinshisha he came to know not only the Yosanos but Yoshii Isamu, Kinoshita Mokutarō, Ishikawa Takuboku, and other young poets. He took up tanka composition again in 1907 when he participated in a contest sponsored by *Myōjō*; a critic declared that his tanka exhibited much the same features as his modern poetry—a delight in exaggeration and illusions, and a penchant for subjects that were voluptuous, strange, tragic, novel, and coarse, and for such words as blood, silver, iron, death, red, crimson, black hair, and fragrance.[93]

In July 1907 Hakushū and some Shinshisha friends traveled to Kyushu. This journey stirred in Hakushū and Kinoshita Mokutarō (1885–1945) an interest in the period of the "southern barbarians," when Portuguese and Spaniards created a Christian culture in parts of Kyushu, especially Nagasaki and Amakusa. An exoticism, directed toward his own country's past, was to color many of Hakushū's early works. The journey was otherwise of importance in that, not long after their return, Hakushū, Kinoshita, Yoshii, and others left the Shinshisha, apparently dissatisfied with Yosano Tekkan's high-handed manner of treating them and their genius. In January 1908, the same month in which he resigned from the Shinshisha, Hakushū published his first important poem, entitled (significantly) "Muhon" (Rebellion) in the magazine *Shinshichō* (New Thought Tides). Other magazines immediately showed interest in the young poet, and the most important journal of the day, *Chūō Kōron*, offered him space in its poetry column. The important poems in Hakushū's first collection, *Jashūmon* (The Heretics, 1909), first appeared in this magazine.

One other event of 1908 was of special importance to Hakushū: he and a group of poets and artists, headed by Kinoshita Mokutarō and Ishii Hakutei, founded the Pan no Kai (Devotees of Pan) to promote aestheticism and "art for art's sake." The name was derived, of course, from that of the frolicsome Greek demigod, but the word *pan* also had overtones of an "all-embracing" society of artists. Perhaps too, judging from the Western restaurants where the Devotees regularly assembled, it also referred to the society's preference for bread (*pan*) rather than rice! The group as a whole was opposed to the Naturalism that had so dominated Japanese fiction since Shimazaki Tōson's *The Broken Commandment* (1906) and Tayama Katai's "The Quilt" (1907). The Devotees of Pan practiced a cult of beauty that embraced both the exoticism of the West together with a nostalgia for the Japanese past, especially the late, overripe Edo period. A short poem by Hakushū expressed the combination. It is called "Kin to Ao to no" (Gold and Blue, 1910).

> A *nocturne* in gold and blue,
> A duet of spring and summer,
> In young Tokyo the songs of Edo,
> Shadows and light in my heart.[94]

At the height of its glory, in 1909 and 1910, the Devotees of Pan attracted most of the best young writers, with the exception of those directly involved with the Naturalism advocated by *Waseda Bungaku*. The meetings were attended by such men as Takamura Kōtarō, Tanizaki Jun'ichirō, Osanai Kaoru, Nagai Kafū, and Watsuji Tetsurō—all destined to become leading figures in the literary world.

In 1909 the first issue of the magazine *Subaru* (Pleiades) appeared. Its staff consisted of a core of former Shinshisha poets including Hakushū, Ishikawa Takuboku, Kinoshita Mokutarō, and Yoshii Isamu, with Mori Ōgai acting as general adviser. *Subaru* quickly established itself as the leading literary magazine, occupying a position similar to that enjoyed by *Myōjō* a decade earlier. It continued to appear until 1913, but its period of greatest importance was 1909–1911, the same as for the Devotees of Pan. Insofar as *Subaru* had an editorial policy, it stood for aestheticism. Its manner was urbane and its contents suggested the editors' leanings toward exoticism.

Hakushū shared and helped to shape the tastes revealed in *Subaru*. His maiden volume, *The Heretics*, had a most distinctive appearance: the cover was half in a brilliant red cloth imprinted with a design from the Namban (Southern Barbarian) Temple, and half in a batik cloth with designs of animals and plants. The contents reveal everywhere the same combination of a love of color and exoticism. Most of the 120 poems had been written just the year before publication, in 1908, when Hakushū was at the height of his infatuation with fin-de-siècle decadence.

Hakushū paradoxically dedicated the book to his father, who had so sternly opposed his becoming a poet. There is also a prefatory inscription, obviously inspired by the words over the gates of hell in Dante's *Inferno*: "He who passes here enters the multitude of sufferings of *melodia*; he who passes here enters the bitter anaesthetic of the nerves." Hakushū followed these gnomic remarks with a preface stating his intent:

> The vital element in poetry is suggestion, not any mere explanation of phenomena. Is it not the main purpose of our symbols to seek out the faint sobbing of the spirit amid the infinite vibrations of artistic effects we cannot describe adequately in writing or in speech, and to exult in the pathos of self-contemplation as we yearn for the pleasures of faint and faraway music? That is why we revere mysteries, delight in dreams and fantasies, long for the crimson of putrefied decadence. Ah, we believers in the modern heresies cannot forget, even on our couch of dreams, the grief of marble sobbing in the pale moonlight, the eyes of the Sphinx tormented by the thick, crimson-tinctured fogs of Egypt; or *romantisch* music laughing in the sunset, and the doleful shrieks of the mind before and after the crucifixion of an infant; or the ceaseless spasms of decomposing yellow wax; the smell when the third string of a violin is rubbed, the acute nerves of whiskey choking inside clouded glass, the heavy scent of the sighs of poisonous grasses the color of the human brain; and the sorrow of song thrushes wearily singing in the paralysis of the senses. But above all, most precious is the touch of crimson velvet as it escapes into the sound of a faint horn.[95]

The sentiments expressed in the preface reek of the mannered decadence of an Oscar Wilde, and the mingling of the senses brings to mind the Symbolists. Hakushū's Symbolism was quite different in nature from Kambara Ariake's intellectual preoccupations: it was an indulgence of the senses, hedonistic and sometimes not fully controlled. The exotic language and the kaleidoscopic display of images make the poems in *The Heretics* bewildering on first reading; the poet Murō Saisei recalled that when he first read the collection at the age of twenty-one he had no idea what the poems were about.[96] But even the uninitiated cannot fail to be moved by the beauty of language and the melodies. Many poems were later set to music.

Hakushū's modern poetry was generally written in combinations of units in the standard five and seven syllables, though often he varied this pattern. The language included colloquialisms, dialectal expressions from Yanagawa, and obscure seventeenth-century terms of Portuguese or Dutch origin; but Hakushū rarely employed the archaisms so dear to Susukida Kyūkin and Kambara Ariake. He used his marvelous command of language mainly to create moods, rather than present ideas. The moods he evoked were varied, but nostalgia, whether for his own boyhood or for the survivals of the Edo past—the Christian mementos and the white-walled storehouses—frequently figures in these poems. Joined to this nostalgia is a seemingly contradictory delight in such specimens of contemporary exotica as whiskey, feather boas, and fountains. The flowers in his poems tend to be foreign—acacia, water hyacinths, and heliotropes, but never cherry blossoms. He wrote a series of poems on foreign animals, including the elephant, the leopard, and the camel. But above all there hangs over Hakushū's early poetry an odor of decadence—the frenzied weeping of violins, the shrieks of unborn infants, the blood-red light of the sunset, the sighs of pale yellow fountains, the dripping of chloroform. The opening poem, "Jashūmon Hikyoku" (Secret Song of the Heretics), displays his love of exoticism and decadence to the full. It begins:

> I believe in the heretical teachings of a degenerate age, the
>   witchcraft of the Christian God,
> The captains of the black ships, the marvellous land of the Red
>   Hairs,
> The scarlet glass, the sharp-scented carnation,
> The striped calico of the Southern Barbarians, the arak, the *vinho
>   tinto* . . . .

Later on he states:

> I have heard their cosmetics are squeezed from the flowers of
>   poisonous herbs,
> And the images of Mary are painted with oil from rotted stones.

The last of the five stanzas declares:

> Oh, vouchsafe unto us, sainted padres of delusion,
> Though our hundred years be shortened to an instant, though we
>   die on the bloody cross,
> It will not matter; we beg the Secret, that strange dream of crimson:
> Jesus, we pray this day, bodies and souls caught in the incense of
>   yearning.[97]

The poem is dotted with foreign words like *kirishitan, kapitan, biidoro, anjabeiiru (anjebier)*, and *araki*. It expresses an infatuation with exotic objects and beliefs so profound that the speaker professes his willingness to renounce his allotted span of life for the sake of one intense moment of voluptuous revelation. The profusion of foreign words, most transcribed in perversely bizarre Chinese characters, creates the impression of a marvelously strange world, imagined in terms of odors, colors, and sounds entirely unlike those of traditional Japan. It probably makes little difference what specifically Hakushū may have meant by the last stanza. Elsewhere in the book he wrote:

> My symbolist poems are mainly expressions of emotional pleasures
> and sensory impressions. . . . It is a mistake therefore for anyone
> who plans to read my poetry to search for intellectual clarity or for
> a conceptual framework free of fantasy. In short, my most recent
> tendency is to feel the rhythm of the faint vibrations of internal life,
> and to devote myself exclusively to creating musical symbols that
> will reproduce this rhythm in the same tuning.[98]

Other poems in *The Heretics* are closer to Kambara Ariake's variety of Symbolism, but the best works are marked by Hakushū's distinct poetic personality. "Muhon" (Rebellion) is unique in its scale and symbolic power. The four stanzas depict the mounting waves of pent-up feeling beating against the narrator, his feelings being symbolized by the sounds of a violin, at first mournful, next anguished, then insane, and finally "blind."

The cover of Hakushū's second collection, *Omoide* (Memories, 1911), was adorned with a picture of the playing-card Queen of Diamonds, and the title page was in roman letters; but despite these obvious exoticisms, the book is filled with nostalgic evocations of Hakushū's boyhood. An extremely long preface explained the background and importance to the poet of these memories. The book, he declared, should be read as a history of his feelings or even as the account of his sexual desire. He described Yanagawa, a deserted town where the crumbling walls of the storehouses built in feudal times awakened nostalgic recollections of the past. He told of the scenery, the changes brought by the seasons, his own boyhood. As the eldest son he was known as *tonkajon* in the local dialect, a name he liked to use in the form Tonka John. He remembered that when he was a child he was so frail he was known as *biidoro bin*, or glass bottle. Some of these recollections appeared in the poetry of *Memories*; the first poem, "Joshi" (Prelude), related impressionistically his childhood experiences in terms of the sights, smells, and sounds of Yanagawa. The most famous poem in the collection is "Itoguruma" (Spinning Wheel):

> Spinning wheel, spinning wheel, slow and deeply spun by hand,
> Evenings when the spinning wheel gently turns are melancholy.
> In the room with a wooden floor where two gourds, gold and red,
>   have rolled,
> In the room with the wooden floor marked "Public Clinic,"
> The old woman left in charge sits alone, forlorn.
> She is deaf and blind, but now it is May,
> And the dust of faintly fragrant bits of down stirs memories.
> The single white bone standing in the glass cupboard is strange;
> How moving the moonlight shining slantwise along the canal!
> Spinning wheel, spinning wheel, slow and silent hand-spun silk,
> Evenings when those remembrances softly turn are melancholy.

This poem is not characteristic of a period when Hakushū more commonly flaunted his high-strung sensibilities, but it beautifully captures with a sense of melancholic nostalgia his boyhood recollections. In the bare, bleak room of the town clinic the only sound is that of the spinning wheel. In the growing darkness the boy makes out the form of the old deaf-and-blind woman at the wheel, and the solitary white bone in a specimen case. The sound and sight are reinforced by the smell of the down, giving the memories a synesthetic complexity. Hakushū even supplied a customary exotic touch in naming the gourd *bōbura*, from the Portuguese *abobora*.

Memories was honored by a publication party, the first in modern Japan. Ueda Bin, the guest of honor, delivered a speech praising the book. He concluded by declaring that he "worshiped" Kitahara Hakushū, the poet from Yanagawa. Hakushū, needless to say, was moved to tears of joy. Bin apparently admired especially the short songs in the collection, some in the old *imayō* form of four lines, each consisting of seven plus five syllables:

> *Aoi sofuto ni furu yuki wa*
> *Sugishi sono te ka, sasayaki ka*
> *Sake ka, hakka ka, itsu no ma ni*
> *Kiyuru namida ka, natsukashi ya* [99]

> The snow falling on my blue felt hat—
> Her remembered hand? Her whispering?
> Saké? Peppermint? Tears that dissolve
> Before you know it? I feel nostalgic!

Another poem relates the incident when, as a small boy, Hakushū offered his girl friend a butterfly, only to have it rejected: "I smeared the fearful powder, blue and gold, upon your lips because you would not weep." [100] A fight with his younger brother is recalled poignantly in "Zabon no Kage" (Under the Pomelo), and other childhood events figure prominently. These poems, if not remarkable, are irresistibly appealing. It is easy to imagine why, when a poll was conducted in 1911 to determine the most popular poet in Japan, Hakushū won. *Memories* especially, with its theme of nostalgia for lost childhood and the vanishing remains of the past, appealed to contemporary Japanese readers, who could easily share Hakushū's emotions.

Hakushū was at the height of his fame when, as previously

described, [101] he was suddenly arrested in July 1912 on the charge of having seduced his neighbor's wife. He and the lady were subsequently acquitted, but Hakushū withdrew from Tokyo and the world of poetry. In 1913 he published his first collection of tanka, *Kiri no Hana* (Paulownia Blossoms), and *Tōkyō Keibutsu Shi oyobi sono ta* (Scenes of Tokyo and Other Poems), his third collection of modern poetry. *Scenes of Tokyo* resembled *The Heretics* in content, contrasting with both *Memories* and *Paulownia Blossoms*. Fascination with the West and an exoticism directed toward the vestiges of Edo culture (the twin tastes of the Devotees of Pan) are prominent. Many poems describe Tokyo during the rainy season, when everything seems to rot. The tone is one of world-weariness as the poet describes his mixed attraction and loathing for the city. "Kambō" (Vista) evokes with vignettes the sordid, polluted Tokyo seen (as through a telescope) on a hot July day from the dome of the St. Nicolai Russian Orthodox Church; at the conclusion Tokyo is described as looking like a vast graveyard, and the cathedral bell seems to be tolling for the whole city, not only for the person for whom funeral rites are being conducted. Hakushū's method is impressionistic, using unconnected scenes to convey the deadly torpor of a summer afternoon in the sprawling city.[102]

Hakushū, a most prolific poet, continued to publish one or more volumes, both modern poetry and tanka, during the next few years, despite his complicated marital life. In 1919 he also published his first collection of the children's songs for which he would become renowned, and the first of his works of autobiographical fiction. His next important collection of modern poetry was *Suiboku Shū* (Ink Drawings, 1923). The title itself suggested the great change in Hakushū's outlook; in place of the red-and-gold coloring of his earlier poetry, he was now using Chinese ink to achieve the astringent beauty of a monochrome, and the overtones were not those of French Symbolism but of *yūgen*. A sequence of twenty-two poems, the longest only four lines and the short ones a bare two lines, were composed under the title *Gekkō Biin* (Faint Overtones of Moonlight). These poems are dotted with words like *honoka*, *kasuka*, and other expressions suggesting barely perceptible sights in the moonlight. The first poem describes a cluster of *asuwahinoki*, an evergreen whose name means literally "tomorrow I shall be a cypress":

Tsuki no yo no	On a moonlit night
Asuwahinoki no	The *asuwahinoki*'s
Nan to naki	Indefinable
Haru no kasukesa	Springtime obscurity.

Yoshida Seiichi wrote of this poem:

Merely by saying "On a moonlit night/The *asuwahinoki*'s," he captured in a truly impressionistic manner the dark, quietly clustering trees, the whole scene bathed in moonlight, and the hazy shadows lying on the ground. These shadows are motionless if one thinks they are, or barely moving if one thinks so, and in their faint presence one senses the dim, smoky stillness of an absolutely calm spring night. This is not reasoned but intuited.[103]

The qualities praised suggest the domain of the tanka rather than of the modern poem. Hakushū denied that these short songs were in any traditional form, but he was undeniably moving during this period in the direction of Japanese overtones, the recognition of barely perceptible shifts of light or color. Hakushū himself referred to this style as the "new yūgen." The second song of the sequence illustrates the combination of traditional sensitivity and modern Impressionism:

Tsuki no yo no	On a moonlit night
Tabako no kemuri	The smoke of a cigarette:
Nioi no mi	Only its fragrance
Murasaki naru.	Is violet in color.

The best-known poem in *Scenes of Tokyo* is "Karamatsu" (Chinese Pines). The success of this poem depends largely on the sounds, words of pure Japanese origins written in regular lines of five plus seven syllables. Hakushū brilliantly exploited the special music of the Japanese language:

Karamatsu no hayashi wo sugite
Karamatsu wo shimijimi to miki.
Karamatsu wa sabishikarikeri.
Tabi yuku wa sabishikarikeri.

Passing the forest of Chinese pines
I looked profoundly at the Chinese pines.
How lonely were the Chinese pines!
How lonely it was to travel!

The repetitions of the word *karamatsu*, each time followed by a different particle, and the long-drawn-out syllables of *sabishi-karikeri* contribute a peculiar sadness to the words, almost apart from their meaning. The recognition of the identity of the loneliness of the pines and the poet's own loneliness is expanded in later stanzas as the poet wanders in the woods, but in the end, like Saigyō asking the cuckoo to make him lonely, he rises above the grief of loneliness to its joy:

Yo no naka yo, aware narikeri.
Tsune nakedo ureshikarikeri.
Yamagawa ni yamagawa no oto,
Karamatsu ni karamatsu no kaze.

The world—how lonely it is!
How inconstant, and yet how joyous!
In the mountain streams, the sound of the mountain streams
In the Chinese pines, the wind of the Chinese pines.

The sentiments expressed by Hakushū seem so close to the poetry of the past that we may be deluded into supposing that he had forfeited his identity as a modern poet; but clearly he was aware that he was performing a traditional act, that he was experiencing traditional sentiments. His acceptance of the sound of the mountain stream as no more, no less than the sound of a mountain stream suggests that he no longer thought of nature as a symbol of anything except itself. Nevertheless, Hakushū remained an observer. The language, natural in Saigyō, represented for Hakushū a deliberate choice of a distant idiom, not very different from his earlier savoring of the exoticism of Portuguese and Dutch words. The poem is highly conscious of its effects and succeeds because of Hakushū's poetical genius, not because he had miraculously turned himself into a Japanese of the past.

Kaihyō to Kumo (Sea Leopards and Clouds, 1929), Hakushū's last important collection of modern poetry, carried his discovery of Japan even further back than Saigyō, to the *Kojiki* and *Nihon Shoki*, the sources of Japanese literature. The opening poem, "Minakami" (The Source), evokes the world of the Shinto gods through descriptions of primeval nature—water, sunlight, mountains, and rocks. A series of poems describing the whiteness of egrets, peonies, and vegetables, and even the nature of whiteness itself, is associated with the purity of Shinto, carrying Hakushū's aesthetics to its furthest limits.[104]

Sea Leopards and Clouds also contains experimental poetry in a totally dissimilar vein. One poem, "Kōtetsu Fūkei" (Landscape in Steel), insists on the presence of the divine even in the most modern, inhuman objects:

> *Kami wa aru, kaiki na kikan ni aru.*
> *Kami wa aru, mootaa to kaiten suru.*
> *Kami wa aru, tanku to hashiru.*
> *Kami wa aru, hōdan to sakuretsu suru.*[105]

The gods are present, they are in the weird steam engine.
The gods are present, they turn with the motor.
The gods are present, they run with the tank.
The gods are present, they explode with the shell.

Other poems are even more experimental. "Gogatsu no Yoru no Sora" (Night Sky in May) uses English "readings" for the Chinese characters:

hoshi da, a	It's a star, ah!
guriin	Green
guriin	Green
guriin	Green
guriin [106]	Green

Such poems were undoubtedly influenced by the Expressionism and Futurism introduced to Japan in the 1920s. Hakushū experimented with these new techniques even as he returned in other poems to the most ancient Japanese materials.

Some critics believe that Hakushū's best poetry was written toward the close of his career, when he was growing blind. These poems were mainly tanka, rather than modern poetry. Yoshida Issui, the distinguished poet, characterized Hakushū's poetry in these terms: "If the tanka was Hakushū's blood, his artery, his modern poems were the configurations of his sensory perceptions." [107]

Hakushū had many followers, in both the tanka and the modern poem. The two outstanding modern poets of the next generation, Hagiwara Sakutarō and Murō Saisei, were both in his direct line. Among his contemporaries he was closest to Kinoshita Mokutarō (1885-1945), whose short poetic career lasted only from 1908 to 1912. Kinoshita, an ardent member of the Devotees of Pan, tried to achieve in his poems a blend of the West and old Japan "like an Edo woodblock print copied in oils." [108] His best poems celebrate the city of Tokyo around 1910, rather in the manner of Hakushū's *Scenes of Tokyo*. "Serii-shu" (Sherry Wine), dedicated to the proprietor of a bar, describes the pleasures of a winter evening spent sitting near a stove, flushed with wine. From the distance the poet hears the voice of a lady *gidayū* singer, a perfect combination of West and East. Kinoshita's poems, less complex than Hakushū's, vividly capture that period when the "best of East and West" was not only an ideal but the reality of the young hedonists of Tokyo.

MIKI ROFŪ (1889-1964)

Hakushū's name is also linked with Miki Rofū's, less because of their resemblances than their dissimilarities. Rofū was also precociously successful: he published his first collection in 1905, when only sixteen, and established his reputation four years later with the collection *Haien* (The Overgrown Garden, 1909). Unlike Hakushū, however, he was subdued, meditative, and rather commonsensical, and he lacked Hakushū's urbanity. His poetry was praised for its unaffected lyricism; indeed, the poems he wrote with the least effort and the least consciousness of his mission as a poet were his best. "Furusato" (Old Home), his most popular poem—the one engraved in stone in his native town—was composed in 1907, when he was eighteen. It describes how a girl weeps to hear the sound of a flute on a moonlit night and concludes with the question:

To tose henu	Ten years have passed:
Onaji kokoro ni	Do you still weep
Kimi naku ya	With the same feelings,
Haha to narite mo [109]	Now that you are a mother?

The expression is extremely plain, but there is something touching in the perception of how time dulls the senses. This was the vein in which Rofū excelled, and his most popular poems, set to music, preserved his simple lyricism. However, Rofū considered his Symbolist poems to be his most important work. He was influenced by translations of French poetry, not only those of Ueda Bin but those of Nagai Kafū, which were later collected in *Sango Shū* (Corals, 1913). Rofū proudly styled himself a Symbolist, but insisted that his poetry was nonetheless within the Japanese tradition:

> It is an undeniable fact that Symbolist poetry was transmitted to Japan thanks to the influence of the French Symbolist poets, but its spirit . . . has existed from ancient times in Japan. I do not mean anything as vague as saying Symbolism is as old as the hills; I mean that the Japanese literary spirit has revealed itself in the form of splendid Symbolist writings. If we consider the poetic style Bashō developed in the haiku, we shall see that, despite the difference in name, it was this same spirit that permeated Bashō's mind at that time. The yūgen style is what we today call the Symbolist style. The special feature of this style is that it avoids explanations and prizes suggestion instead. It does not divide phenomena into minute categories but looks at them as a whole and simplifies them, attempting insofar as possible to transcend reality.[110]

Elsewhere Rofū claimed that the Japanese variety of Symbolism not only antedated that of Verlaine and Mallarmé, but went further than they did toward their ideals. "I am happy that I am in the spirit of this tradition," he declared. He soon passed beyond praising the Symbolism of the tanka and haiku and declared that Nō, Japanese painting and pottery, and, indeed, all the Japanese arts were Symbolist. He even stated his conviction that Confucius was a Symbolist.[111]

The readiness with which the Japanese poets took to Symbolism can be explained in terms of their participation in a world movement in poetry; but Rofū was no doubt correct in saying that Japanese tradition made Symbolism especially congenial. Obscurity was never considered a fault in a Japanese poem, and the indirection of the haiku masters at times surpassed that of any Symbolist. But although this may explain why the Japanese poets found Symbolism to their taste, it does not account for the particular variety of ambiguity practiced by Miki Rofū and his fellows, which had little to do with Japanese tradition.

Rofū's most important collection, *Shiroki Te no Karyūdo* (The Hunter with White Hands, 1913), earned him a place alongside Hakushū in the usual histories of Japanese literature. The poems are not only complex but reveal greater depth than Hakushū's, as well as considerable direct borrowing from the French Symbolists. His chosen time of day was dusk, unlike Hakushū, who preferred the brightness of noon. A good example of Rofū's Symbolist style is "Yuki no Ue no Kane" (Bell over the Snow):

In my heart at twilight a snow of memories
Gently falls and accumulates,
Monotonous, without charm.

Buried sorrows sleep below.
My voice is pent up, covered over;
I lean my breast against a burning tombstone.

And yet the beauty of the sound of an echoing bell
—The coolness of tears that have dried—
Serenely, serenely swelling out.

My heart dreams on,
About to embark on an endless journey.
Ah, a wind from the distant valley
Slackly, faintly rouses my breast.

A silver sunset of sadness
Smiles deep within me.
Delicate green grass in the snow—
Ah, green grass, like you my longing gropes forth
Far, far away. With hands that are delicate too.[112]

The precise meaning of the poem would be impossible to state. No doubt the poem is recalling an unhappy love affair when suddenly a fresh stirring of hope passes over him, and from within his memories a hand stretches out toward happiness. The mood is nostalgic, but not in Hakushū's manner; rather, Rofū is groping for memories that elude him and is taking comfort from imprecise flickerings of hope.

Rofū was a more serious but less talented poet than Hakushū. The contrast between the two men is suggested by the different effects of a visit to the Trappist monastery in Hokkaidō. Rofū, profoundly impressed, became a Catholic and lived several years in the monastery. Hakushū wrote a poem about the monastery cows whose mooing seems to say, "Our udders are full. Holy Mary." Rofū's seriousness unfortunately did not often result in notable poetry. The last thirty years of his life, when he was intermittently afflicted by mental illness, produced almost no work of significance.

THE TAISHŌ PERIOD (1912–1926)

JAPANESE SCHOLARS customarily divide modern poetry into works composed during the reigns of the three emperors—Meiji, Taishō, and Shōwa. In general, one may say that during the Taishō era the apprenticeship of Japanese poets to the European masters—whether Shelley, Keats, or Mallarmé—was succeeded by the mature and independent achievements of first-rate poets.

In retrospect the years 1909 to 1918, the end of the Meiji era and first seven years of the Taishō era, may seem the most brilliant period of modern Japanese poetry.[113] Not only did it see the mature achievements of such "Meiji" poets as Kitahara Hakushū and Ishikawa Takuboku, but it marked the impressive beginnings of the careers of the leading "Taishō" poets. The number of poets at this time is also surprising; Fukunaga Takehiko said of this period, "It was an age when it was not very difficult to become a poet, provided one had some talent." [114]

The Taishō era was notable also for the extraordinary variety of publications on the theory of poetry, occasioned by the importations of the views of such European schools as Futurism, Expressionism, Constructivism, Imagism, and Surrealism, as well as by reconsiderations of native Japanese traditions. The early Taishō poets were often reacting against the profusion of neologisms and obscurities in the works of Susukida Kyūkin, Kambara Ariake, or Kitahara Hakushū. Murō Saisei stated in 1949, "The poems of my predecessors, from whom I was trying to learn how to write poetry, were all so incomprehensible that my own poor poems never became difficult." [115] New experiments in free verse that broke all the rules of traditional Japanese composition also provoked much debate on the function of metrics. Hagiwara Sakutarō, writing much later, declared:

> The true, artistic free verse is based on the spirit of regular meter; it is created by making and breaking metered verse. The man who starts off writing Chinese characters abbreviated in whatever manner his own whims dictate, without a proper foundation in the "bones" of orthodox penmanship, will never succeed in writing characters correctly. Poets who have not been trained from childhood in the orthodox poetics certainly will not be able to compose even free verse.[116]

It is striking how many poets of the Taishō era composed in the classical diction, even after they had established reputations with their colloquial verse, as if to reassert their associations with Japanese poetic tradition.

Foreign theories of meter and rhythm appealed to many Japanese poets, often as an alternative to their own traditions. The first issue of the journal *Mirai* (The Future), the organ of the Miraisha headed by Miki Rofū, carried in 1914 an article on rhythm in poetry based especially on Vance Thompson's *French Portraits;* [117] this work supplied the first theoretical basis for free verse in the concept that each poet has his *rythme personnel*, which he must discover for himself. However, as increasingly eccentric "personal rhythms" made their way into print, a natural reaction occurred. The poet Fukushi Kōjirō (1889–1946), dissatisfied with free verse, was pleased to discover that French poetry, like Japanese traditional poetry, was written in syllabics. He explained his basic position: "I am convinced that the rhythm of the Japanese language is derived from syllabics, without any relation to accent;

and that, moreover, this is true not only of the fixed poetic forms that have existed in Japan since antiquity—the tanka, popular song, haiku, and chōka—but also of the free verse which has become the banner of the new Japanese poetry." [118] By implication, Fukushi rejected rhythm—personal or otherwise—as an element in Japanese poetry, except insofar as it conformed to traditional patterns of syllabics. A foreign theory of poetry, that of syllabics, was thus borrowed to bolster ancient Japanese poetical practice.

On the whole, however, the period was marked by experimentation rather than by the reassertion of tradition. Most of the new European movements enjoyed only brief periods of popularity before being succeeded by even fresher developments. The longest-lived was Futurism. In 1920 David Davidovich Burliuk (1882–1962), known as the father of Futurism in Russia, became a refugee in Japan. He created a powerful impression with an exhibition of five hundred examples of Russian Futuristic painting, and for a time Futurism, whether in art or poetry, came to embrace such new fashions as Dada and Cubism. The movement, a violent reaction against the previous generation, reached its height in 1922–1925 in Japan. The most conspicuous figure was Hagiwara Kyōjirō (1899–1938), whose collection *Shikei Senkoku* (Verdict of Death, 1925) is considered a landmark in the development of a distinctly modern poetry; one critic stated that this volume "ended the 'modern poem' and established the direction of the 'contemporary poem.' " [119] The title itself was ostentatiously "unpoetic," and the aim of the collection has been defined as a "passionate attempt to achieve a subjective unity between the world-view of revolutionary poetry and the methods of the poetic revolution." [120] Hagiwara Kyōjirō's poetry often attempts by visual means—characters printed in different faces of type or in different sizes from the rest of the text—to impose directly an awareness of the poet's turbulent emotions. Onomatopoeia is a feature of almost every poem, and some poems even display meaningless combinations of letters or dots and triangles in place of words. (The name of the Dadaist periodical that appeared in 1924–1925 was typical: GE. . .GIMGAM. . .PRRR. . .GIMGEM.) But Hagiwara Kyōjirō's anarchistic, revolutionary message was sometimes expressed less eccentrically, though not less forcefully, as in "Ai wa shūryō sareta" (Love Is Completed):

> Countless fingernail scratches on my mother's breast, some oozing
>   blood!
> Or else red welts of blows!
> Scars from a stoning! Bite marks!
> Ah, all those painful red scars
> Are scars necessary for the survival of your dear children!
>
> We have not forgotten your breasts, but there's nothing to suck
>   now.
> Ravaged and abandoned like an empty house—
> Ah, love has already been completed!
> And yet now, once again, I kick my mother's breast!
> For the sake of my sweethearts of the new century!
> For the sake of all that is youthful in the new world!
> Ah, to destroy in one clean sweep
> The old traces of our father—that is our principle! [121]

The revolt against the past, even the beloved past, culminates in a rejection of the mother's love and the father's authority. It is more clearly stated here than in the inarticulate exclamations, meaningless fragments of conversation, and repetitions of words or noises in Hagiwara Kyōjirō's other poems, but the latter are more typical. The destruction of the old forms of expression, a principle borrowed from the Italian Futurists, naturally led to an impatience with all conventional speech.

Other poets of the time (like Senge Motoharu, 1888–1944) expressed their dissatisfaction with society by adopting the "humanism" preached by the *Shirakaba* (White Birch) group, or by becoming Christians like Yagi Jūkichi (1898–1927), though this happened less frequently than in the Meiji era, or by favoring political changes, like the poets of the Minshū-ha (People's School). Still other poets withdrew so completely from society into their private worlds as to become hermetic. Hinatsu Kōnosuke (1890–1970) is so extreme an example of this tendency that he has been called "the eccentric among eccentrics." [122] His poetry is complex, formalistic, and forbidding to the outsider. At a time when most poets were writing free verse in the colloquial, he resolutely clung to the classical language; and at a time when some poets were using kana almost exclusively, Hinatsu filled his poems with Chinese characters—sometimes giving them private or extremely obscure readings or using them as hieroglyphs that indicate meanings by their shapes. But under the camouflage of exotic characters and diction, the thought is often simple to the point of banality; perhaps Hinatsu chose such materials merely in order to demonstrate he could create a poem even out of trivialities.[123] Probably also, as a result of his long study of foreign literatures, Hinatsu felt obliged to determine what was quintessentially Japanese—for example, the visual aspect of a poem—instead of concerning himself with fashioning distinctive sounds and rhythms in the manner of the major poets of his time.

Two poets of the Taishō era who enjoyed great popularity in their own time (for quite different reasons) now seem of mainly historical importance. The two men, Satō Haruo (1892–1964) and Horiguchi Daigaku (1892–1981), born in the same year and lifetime friends, composed in entirely dissimilar styles. Satō, remembered also as a novelist, wrote affecting poems rather in the manner of Shimazaki Tōson, using a vocabulary and meter that were thus doubly archaic. One poem, similar in style to Satō's evocations of his beloved Wakayama countryside, but totally unalike in content, stands out: "Gusha no Shi" (Death of a Fool, 1911), which describes the hanging of Ōishi Seinosuke, who was found guilty of participating in Kōtoku Shunsui's alleged plot to assassinate Emperor Meiji. On the surface the poem deplores the folly of the would-be culprit, but it is possible to interpret the poem as an expression of the poet's grief.[124] This poem is certainly not typical of those that won Satō a great following, like "Suihen Getsuya no Uta" (Song on a Moonlit Night by the Water, 1921), which begins:

Setsunaki koi wo suru yue ni
Tsukikage samuku mi ni zo shimu.
Mono no aware wo shiru yue ni
Mizu no hikari zo nagekaruru.[125]

Because I am desperately in love
The moonbeams stab me coldly.
Because I know the pity of things
I am grieved by the light in the water.

Not only is the diction completely conventional (with even a *mono no aware* thrown in), but the lines are metrically exactly like Shimazaki Tōson's, the usual seven plus five syllables. Yet this poem was not merely an exercise: Satō was describing his passionate love for Tanizaki Jun'ichirō's wife, the most sensational event in the literary world of the 1920s. Even in a poem written under such circumstances, let alone those on less turbulent subjects, Satō is pleasingly old-fashioned. For this reason his poetry continued to appeal to readers left behind by more complex developments.

Horiguchi Daigaku, though an amusing, urbane poet in his own right, is remembered chiefly for his translations of modern French poetry. His collection *Gekka no Ichigun* (A Moonlit Gathering, 1925) exercised an enormous influence over later Japanese poetry, surpassing even that of *Sound of the Tide*. The son of a diplomat, Horiguchi learned French, the language of diplomacy in countries where his father was stationed, and his knowledge of the language was exceptional. His tastes were first formed by the poetry of Remy de Gourmont, and later by Henri de Régnier, Jules Laforgue, and Albert Samain, finally moving on to Francis Jammes, Guillaume Apollinaire, Jean Cocteau, and Max Jacob. He translated works by all these poets and many more *(A Moonlit Gathering* contains 340 poems by 66 poets). Most of his versions were in the colloquial, and the freshness of his language explained much of the influence of the collection on subsequent Japanese poetry. One scholar put it: "Unlike Ueda Bin, who attempted to 'Japanize' the original poems by employing poetic conceptions already existing in Japanese literature, Horiguchi made the Japanese language fit the images in the original poems. For that reason, he produced simple and witty lines of poetry, employing the language of everyday speech, a language which had never before been considered poetic." [126]

The travails of the Meiji poets were brought to fruition in the Taishō era.

HAGIWARA SAKUTARŌ (1886–1942)

Hagiwara is by common consent the chief figure of modern Japanese poetry. He is not an easy poet, and the exact interpretations of many works elude the exegesis of even his most devoted admirers, but his work both commands the respect of other poets and critics and is popular with the general public. The novelist and poet Fukunaga Takehiko gave a representative evaluation: "Hagiwara Sakutarō is the outstanding writer of Japanese modern poetry; it is a recognized fact that his works constitute the most beautiful crystallizations of the Japanese language." [127]

Hagiwara was born in Maebashi, an unremarkable city famous chiefly for its gusty winds. He is known as a poet of nostalgia, and a number of moving poems are recollections of Maebashi; but these are essentially references to his own past, rather than affectionate descriptions of buildings or landscapes. Although imposing mountains are visible from Maebashi, and the nearby countryside was still beautiful in Hagiwara's youth, he frequently expressed his lack of interest in the country and his love of the crowds and excitement of a big city. Eventually he moved to Tokyo, but his early collections were composed in Maebashi, where he lived in comfortable circumstances as the chief literary light of a provincial town.

Hagiwara first began to submit his poetry to *Myōjō*, *Bunko*, and other Tokyo magazines while he was still in middle school. Poetry absorbed him so completely that he neglected his studies; he did not graduate from middle school until he was twenty and kept up his spasmodic attempts to finish high school until he was twenty-five; he was apparently under no pressure from his family to earn a living. Hagiwara also studied the mandolin and the guitar, even intending at one time to become a professional musician. So far little suggested he would develop into the great Japanese poet of the twentieth century.

In 1913 Hagiwara published some tanka in the magazine *Zamboa* (Pomelo), then being edited by Kitahara Hakushū. An infatuation with Hakushū's poetry colored his early work, and this association with *Zamboa* marked the beginning of his serious work as a poet. Twenty-seven was unusually late for a start; most Meiji poets produced all of their important work before they were thirty. But Hagiwara seems to have been in no hurry to impress the literary world. In 1914, having reconciled himself to living in Maebashi, he built a study in the corner of his parents' garden, furnished entirely in Western style. There he drank black tea, still an exotic beverage in Maebashi, played the mandolin, and read European literature. He began to attend Christian churches and

visit the houses of foreign missionaries, enjoying this approximation of life abroad. It was about this time that he wrote the poem
Ryojō (Going Away). It begins:

> I think I would like to go to France,
> But France is so very far away;
> At least I will try to take a trip of my own choosing,
> Wearing a new suit of clothes.[128]

In June 1914 he and the two poets Murō Saisei and Yamamura Bochō formed the Ningyo Shisha (Mermaid Poetry
Society), which had as its avowed purpose the study of poetry,
religion, and music. Hagiwara's interest in Christianity lingered
on a few years longer. One night in April 1916 he experienced a
kind of religious ecstasy, the source no doubt of the distinctly
religious tone in part of his first collection, *Tsuki ni hoeru* (Howling at the Moon), published in February 1917. Words like *tsumi*
(sin), *inoru* (to pray) and *zange* (confession) dot the first half of
the collection, as in the well-known poem "Tenjō Ishi" (A Hanging in Heaven, 1914):

> *Tōyo ni hikaru matsu no ha ni,*
> *Zange no namida shitatarite,*
> *Tōyo no sora ni shimo shiroki,*
> *Tenjō no matsu ni kubi wo kake.*
> *Tenjō no matsu wo kouru yori,*
> *Inoreru sama ni tsurusarenu.*[129]

> Onto pine-needles glittering in the distant night
> Drip the tears of his confession;
> White in the sky of the distant night
> The pine of heaven where he hangs.
> For having loved the pine of heaven
> He has been strung up in a posture of prayer.

This difficult poem has been analyzed in these terms: "What is
meant by the 'pine of heaven' where a man is hung? Obviously it
does not refer to a tree. The 'pine of heaven' stands for the sacred,
for God, for purity, and so on. It is a place of confession, designated in visionary terms. When the poet speaks of being 'strung

up in the posture of prayer,' this metaphor expresses the intensity of his confession; while in this posture his confession is completed by death." [130] Hagiwara wrote on a picture of the Crucifixion he owned at the time the words "A Hanging in Heaven."

The poem is certainly not typical of Hagiwara's early poetry as a whole, but it displays one important characteristic: apart from its religiosity, it is striking because of the obscurity of expression, which arouses not a sense of bewilderment or irritation but of mystery and depth, similar to the effect of yūgen in the classical tradition. Although Hagiwara is celebrated as the first master of the free-verse, colloquial poem, this work (like many others in *Howling at the Moon*) was in the classical language and in regular meter, each line consisting of seven plus five syllables.

A few months later Hagiwara wrote the short poem "Kaeru no Shi" (Death of a Frog, 1914), also included in *Howling at the Moon*:

Kaeru ga korosareta,
Kodomo ga maruku natte te wo ageta,
Minna issho ni,
Kawayurashii,
Chidarake no te wo ageta,
Tsuki ga deta,
Oka no ue ni hito ga tatte iru.
Bōshi no shita ni kao ga aru.[131]

A frog was killed.
The children, forming a circle, raised their hands;
All together
They raised their adorable,
Blood-smeared hands.
The moon came out.
Someone is standing on the hill.
Under his hat is a face.

This poem is in the colloquial, and the meter is free, confirming Hagiwara's self-assertive claim: "Before this collection not a single poem had been written in colloquial language of this style, and before this collection the animation in the world of poetry one senses today did not exist. All the new styles of poetry sprang from this source. All the rhythms of the lyric poetry of our time were engendered here. In other words, because of this collection a new epoch was created." [132]

The fact that the language of this poem is simple—common words drawn from daily speech—does not mean that the meaning is obvious. The last line startles not by unusual imagery but by the flat statement of a seemingly irrelevant fact: of course there was a face under the man's hat, but why mention it? Is this the face of an adult watching the children at their cruel sport? Or of the poet himself, as a child detachedly observing his companions? The ambiguity compounds the basic unreality: Did the children really lift their blood-smeared little hands in the moonlight? The poem is an enigma that somehow strikes the heart, fulfilling the definition of poetic expression Hagiwara gave in the preface to the collection:

> The object of poetic expression is not merely to evoke an atmosphere for its own sake. Nor is it to describe illusions for their sake. Nor, for that matter, is it to propagandize or make deductions about any particular variety of thought. The true function of poetry is, rather, to scrutinize the essential nature of the emotions vibrating in a man's heart and to disclose these emotions to the full through poetic expression. Poetry is a capturing of the nerves of the emotions. It is a living, functioning psychology. [133]

Later in the preface he wrote:

> What I hope for from readers of my poetry is that they will perceive through their senses not the ideas expressed on the surface nor the "circumstances," but the feelings that are the internal core itself. I have expressed my "grief," "joy," "loneliness," "fear," and other complicated and particular emotions difficult to express in words or sentences through the rhythm of my poetry. But rhythm is not an explanation; it is a communion of mind with mind. Only with the man who can without words sense that rhythm can I converse, taking his hand in mine. [134]

Despite the difficulties involved in interpreting Hagiwara's poems, the reader never receives an impression of willful obscurity. His disciple Miyoshi Tatsuji, contrasting Hagiwara's ambiguities with those of Kitahara Hakushū, claimed that Hagiwara rejected the "mystification" of the late Symbolist poets, and treated by preference events and emotions associated with ordinary life. Miyoshi went so far as to suggest that Hagiwara, despite his reiterated dislike of the Naturalists, was actually influenced by their manner of expression; [135] certainly some of his most affecting poems are direct to the point of Naturalism. "Yogisha" (Night Train, 1913), Hagiwara's first important poem, describes the break of day in the oppressive atmosphere of a night train, where the poet and another man's wife share passion and despair.[136] But the more typical poems in *Howling at the Moon* go beyond direct personal experience to the realm of the vision, as in "Take" (Bamboo, 1915):

> On the shining ground bamboo grows,
> Green bamboo grows;
> Below the surface bamboo roots grow.
>
> Roots gradually tapering,
> From the root ends fine hair grows,
> Faintly smoldering fine hair grows.
> It faintly trembles.
>
> On the hard ground bamboo grows,
> On the ground, sharply, bamboo grows,
> Precipitously bamboo grows;
> The frozen knots piercingly cold,
> Under the blue sky bamboo grows,
> Bamboo, bamboo, bamboo grows.[137]

The rhythm of the poem creates its atmosphere; obviously Hagiwara did not intend it as a realistic description of growing bamboo. The season is early spring, when the bamboo breaks the hard ground; but the poet's thoughts turn to the invisible roots extending fine hairs into the darkness of the soil. It has been suggested that these images are related to the poet's psychological state. A few years earlier he had written of "always stretching his hands toward the light" but of "falling instead, increasingly, into a dark abyss." [138] The morbid sensitivity of his poetry is suggested by the fine hairs extending into subterranean depths. The poem not only expresses Hagiwara's feeling for bamboo but his own psychology.

Hagiwara's first poem in the colloquial, "Satsujin Jiken" (A Case of Murder, 1914), was of crucial importance in his development as a poet. Kawaji Ryūkō (1888-1959) had published some graphically realistic poems in the colloquial a few years earlier, and Kitahara Hakushū had also experimented with the colloquial, but Hagiwara was essentially correct when he boasted of being the first to employ this medium successfully. "A Case of Murder" opens with these lines:

> *Tōi sora de pisutoru ga naru.*
> *Mata pisutoru ga naru.*
> *Aa watakushi no tantei wa hari no ishō wo kite,*
> *Koibito no mado kara shinobikomu,*
> *Yuka wa shōgyoku,*
> *Yubi to yubi no aida kara,*
> *Massao no chi ga nagarete iru,*
> *Kanashii onna no shitai no ue de,*
> *Tsumetai kirigirisu ga naite iru.*[139]

> In the distant sky a pistol resounds.
> Again the pistol resounds.
> And my detective, in his clothes of glass,
> Slips in through the lady's window.
> The floor is of crystal.
> From between her fingers
> Deathly pale blood flows,
> And on the unhappy woman's corpse
> A chilly grasshopper sings.

The colloquial is used to superb effect, its casual tone making the unbelievable "facts" related seem all the more extraordinary. The cold, glassy surface of the poem and the atmosphere of fantasy share much with other poems in the collection, but it also has the faintly humorous overtones of a silent film.

When *Howling at the Moon* was first published it fell under the ban of the censors because it contained two poems adjudged to be harmful to public morals. These poems, "Airen" (Love) and "Koi wo koi suru Hito" (A Man Who Loves Love), are without question sensual, but hardly a danger to morals. "Love" concludes:

> Ah, I hug your breasts tightly to me;
> And you press with all your strength against my body.
> In this manner, in the middle of this deserted field,
> Let us play as snakes play.
> I will treat you with piercing tenderness, in my fashion,
> And smear your beautiful skin with juice from green leaves of
>   grass.[140]

In some poems Hagiwara experimented with the musical values of the colloquial and of onomatopoeia. In "Kaeru yo" (You, Frog!) he twice gives the line:

> *Gyo, gyo, gyo, gyo, to naku kaeru.*[141]

> "Gyo, gyo, gyo, gyo," cries the frog.

These sounds, to at least one Japanese commentator, conveyed an impression of "blank loneliness." [142] Other examples of Hagiwara's use of onomatopoeia included dogs barking in the distance (*no-oaaru, to-oaaru, yawaa*),[143] and roosters crowing *to-otekuu, to-orumou, to-orumou*.[144] Hagiwara explained the latter:

> I have represented cockcrows heard in the distance from my bed at daybreak with the sounds *too-ru-mor, too-te-kur,* and have employed these sounds as the principal idea-words of the poem. Properly speaking, the crying of animals, the noise of turning machinery and the like are purely auditory; unlike words, they have no meaning of their own to put forth; they can therefore be interpreted as expressing anything one pleases, according to the subjective feelings of the listener. As a consequence, such sounds make excellent materials that provide a maximum freedom of use in the expression of poems centered around musical effects.[145]

Years later (in 1933) Hagiwara recalled:

> Among the poems I wrote years ago there is one called "Niwatori" (Rooster). To tell the truth, this was an adaptation of Poe, and my

representation of the rooster's crowing as *totekuu, mouruto* and so on was an attempt to produce a poetic effect similar on the whole to Poe's "Raven" by means of similar techniques of expression.

He analyzed "The Raven" in these terms:

> The expressive effect of Poe's unrhymed (*sic*) poem "The Raven" results from the repeated echoes of the gloomy, eerie sounds of such words as *nevermore* and *Leonore*, which sound like the wind blowing from some lonely, distant graveyard. Poe intentionally repeated these words, and made the feelings produced by their periodic repetition serve as the motifs of the entire poem. If these sounds were removed from "The Raven," nothing would remain; the poem would be no more than a meaningless arrangement of letters. Could any translator, no matter how gifted, transfer this effect to Japanese? This example makes it evident how impossible it is to translate poetry.[146]

Hagiwara's fascination with Poe and his use of sound suggests his connection with Baudelaire, another great admirer of Poe.

Whether or not dogs barking in the distance actually sounded like *no-aaru, to-oaaru, yawaa* to Hagiwara, he used the transcription to superb effect in a poem suggesting a child's terror at hearing strange noises at night; *no-oaaru to-oaaru, yawaa* evoke the mystery of the dark far better than a mere *woof-woof.* Onomatopoeia is also at the heart of the short poem "Neko" (Cats):

Makkuroke no neko ga nihiki,
Nayamashii yoru no yane no ue de,
Pin to tateta shippo no saki kara,
Ito no yō na mikazuki ga kasunde iru.
"Owaa, komban wa"
"Owaa, komban wa"
"Owaaa, koko no ie no shujin wa byōki desu"[147]

Two jet-black cats
On a melancholy night roof:
From the tips of their taut tails
A threadlike crescent moon hangs hazily.
"Owaa, good evening."

"*Owaa*, good evening."
"*Owaaa*, the master of this house is sick."

Hagiwara's interest in sound was not restricted to animal noises. Many poems deliberately employ repetitions of words and phrases in the interests of rhythm. "Shun'ya" (Spring Night, 1915) opens:

Asari no yō na mono,	Something like a mussel,
Hamaguri no yō na mono,	Something like a clam,
Mijinko no yō na	Something like a water-flea ....
mono	

Later in the poem these lines occur:

Soyo soyo to shiomizu nagare,
Ikimono no ue ni mizu nagare ....[148]

Soyo-soyo the salt water flows,
Over living creatures the water flows ....

Such uses of sound create a peculiarly dreamlike atmosphere, evocative of a spring night. The words go beyond their conventional meanings to approach the realm of pure sound.

The insistence on sound, as opposed to verbal meaning, should not, of course, suggest that Hagiwara intended his poetry to be read as pure melody, nor that the poet is absent from his creations. The portrait of the poet dimly visible behind the early poems is of an acutely sensitive man with a masochistic sense of guilt. Although Hagiwara lost his interest in Christianity, he retained an awareness of original sin that continued to torment him.[149] His long poem *Sabishii Jinkaku* (A Lonely Character, 1917), written while under the influence of Dostoevski, has been interpreted as a release from his guilt and inferiority complexes.[150] Dostoevski certainly figured prominently in his thoughts. In the preface to *Howling at the Moon* he wrote:

People, individually, are always, eternally, perpetually in terrible solitude. . . . Our faces, our skins are all different, one from the other, but as a matter of fact each human being shares traits with all the others. When this commonality is discovered among fellow human beings, "morality" and "love" among humankind are born. When this commonality is discovered between human beings and plants, "morality" and "love" in nature are born. And then we are never lonely again.[151]

This was the "salvation through love" Hagiwara found through Dostoevski. He also explained his opposition to the "sensual mysticism of the school of Mallarmé and to the Symbolist poetry of that school" as a result of his contact with "the philosophy of Dostoevski." [152]

Hagiwara's second collection, *Aoneko* (The Blue Cat, 1923), was greeted with even greater enthusiasm than *Howling at the Moon*. In 1934, when he published the "definitive edition" of *The Blue Cat*, he explained in the preface the circumstances of composition and the meaning of the title:

> Mr. Hinatsu Kōnosuke, in the second volume of his *History of Poetry in the Meiji and Taishō Eras*, has stated that my *Blue Cat* is merely an extension of *Howling at the Moon* and contains no changes or development, but as far as I am concerned, this collection was a *poésie* that sprang from totally different and separate origins. My maiden collection *Howling at the Moon* had a purely imagistic vision for its poetic domain, and its basic quality was a physiological terror, but *The Blue Cat* is quite different; the basic nature of its *poésie* arises entirely from pathos. There are no tears or pathos in *Howling at the Moon*. . . .
>
> There is no collection of my poetry I think of with such nostalgia and sadness as *The Blue Cat*. The images and the vision in its poems are magic-lantern pictures reflected on a retina of tears; though I wipe them away, these representations of grief keep returning again and again, like mist on a windowpane on a rainy day. *The Blue Cat* is not an Imagist collection. Together with my recently published *The Iceland*, it is for me a collection that sings of pure feelings. . . .
>
> I have frequently been asked about the meaning of the title of the book, *The Blue Cat*. I intended by the word "blue" the English word: that is, I used it to embrace the meanings of "hopeless," "melancholy," and so on. . . . The meaning of the title is, in other words, "a melancholy-looking cat." Another meaning, also found in

the title-poem "The Blue Cat," was the result of imagining that the bluish-white sparks from electric lines reflected on the sky over a big city were a huge blue cat. This meaning conveyed the intense yearning I felt for the city while writing these poems in the country. In addition, I was infatuated with Schopenhauer when I compiled the collection, and a world-weary, passive ennui based on his philosophy of the negation of the will, together with the Hinayana Buddhistic pessimism of bliss through annihilation, inevitably lurked beneath the sentiments in the poems.[153]

Fukunaga Takehiko characterized the differences between *Howling at the Moon* and *The Blue Cat* in other terms: "In *Howling at the Moon* he believed in what he could see with his eyes. The sick man's world really existed. But here he believed in what he could not see, and attempted to see conceptual objects beyond his life, to fix his fugitive emotions." [154]

The Blue Cat is marked by the frequent use of the word *yūutsu* (melancholy or depression), and the collection has been termed "a confession of failure in life." [155] The title poem is especially important. The first half describes his longing for the metropolis, its excitement, tall buildings, and beautiful women; the second half, in a more characteristic vein, suggests more elusively the nature of his fascination with Tokyo:

> Ah, the only thing that can sleep at night in this huge city
> Is the shadow of one blue cat,
> The shadow of a cat that tells the sad history of mankind,
> The blue shadow of the happiness we are ever seeking.
> That must be why, in quest of such a shadow,
> I have longed for Tokyo even on days of sleet;
> But huddled with cold against a back-street wall,
> This beggar who resembles a man—what is *he* dreaming of? [156]

The last lines indicate the poet's awareness of the misery crouching in the streets of the city he longs for so passionately; but because the beggar is treated with irony rather than compassion, Hagiwara's lack of concern with social issues shocked the critics; even his disciple Miyoshi Tatsuji compared these lines to Bashō's equally "unfeeling" verse on seeing an abandoned child at Fuji River.[157] Hagiwara was interested only in his inner feelings; the beggar was not so much a fellow human being in distress as a projection of his own uncertainties.

The Blue Cat contains poems that represent Hagiwara's most successful experiments with the modern Japanese language. "Kuroi Fūkin" (Black Harmonium, 1918) opens:

> *Orugan wo o-hiki nasai   onna no hito yo* [158]

> Play the organ, please, good woman!

Not only is there alliteration on words beginning with *o*, but this vowel occurs seven times out of the sixteen in the line. Of the twenty-eight lines in the entire poem, eleven begin with *o* and nine with *a*, the vowel with which *o* is associated in the quoted line. Apart from these effects of repetition, the distinctively colloquial rhythms produce effects that would have been impossible in classical Japanese. Hagiwara's use of alliteration and related consonants suggests at least indirect influence from the French Symbolists like Gustave Kahn, who in 1885 wrote, "Free verse, instead of being, as in old verse, lines of prose cut up into regular rimes, must be held together by the alliterations of vowels and related consonants." [159]

When the "definitive edition" of *The Blue Cat* was published, Hagiwara added various poems composed after the original compilation in 1923. "Neko no Shigai" (The Corpse of a Cat) was among these additional poems. It has been described as being "the apogee of the love poetry composed after the early works in *The Blue Cat*." [160] It concludes:

> We have no past, no future,
> And have faded away from the things of reality.
> Ula!
> Here, in this weird landscape
> Bury the corpse of the drowned cat! [161]

In his notes to the poem Hagiwara wrote:

> This Ula is not a real woman, but a ghost-woman dressed in vaporous garments who breathes amid the images of a love poem. She is a lovable, melancholy woman smeared with the fresh blood of pas-

sion. This nostalgically remembered woman always reminds me of music. It is a music connected sadly and inconsolably to the past, present, and future, that breathes painfully in a calendar of eternal time.

That is why the central theme of the poem is concentrated on the sound *Ula*. If the reader can sense the musicality of Ula by pronouncing the name, he can probably grasp quite clearly the main thought of the poem; if he fails to sense it, he probably will be unable to understand the meaning of the poem as a whole. To put it in different terms: *Ula* serves the same function with respect to the formal structure of the composition as *Nevermore* or *Leonore* to Poe's "Raven." [162]

Hagiwara elsewhere compared the world evoked by this poem, which reflects his own life at the time of composition, to "The Fall of the House of Usher":

My family life in every way resembled "The Fall of the House of Usher." There was no past, no future, and the portentous, accursed, empty present—a present appropriate to the House of Usher—had faded away from the "things of reality." This ominous, squalid situation was symbolized by the muddy corpse of the cat. Ula! Don't touch it! I was always, instinctively afraid. I shuddered, weeping in my dreams.[163]

The poem has also been interpreted as Hagiwara's farewell to the poetic world he created in *The Blue Cat*: this is the corpse he intends to bury.[164]

In 1925 Hagiwara moved definitively to Tokyo. In the same year he published the collection *Junjō Shōkyoku Shū* (Short Songs of Pure Feelings). The first half of this book consists of early poems antedating even *Howling at the Moon*, the second half of ten poems composed in 1924 describing scenes at Maebashi. The early poems include such famous works as "Night Train," the later ones some of Hagiwara's masterpieces. Although, as we have seen, Hagiwara had a special place in his heart for *The Blue Cat*, there is something morbid about these poems, and the reader may turn with relief to the "pure feelings" of the later collection. A period of ten years separates the composition of the first and second halves of the book, but Hagiwara himself felt that unity was provided by their both being in the same style, poems written in plangent literary language.

Hagiwara did not state his reasons for returning to the classical language after ten years of brilliant colloquial poems. Undoubtedly the choice was dictated by the materials he used, remembered scenes more easily described in the classical language, with its own distant associations, than the aggressively contemporary modern language. When he published his last collection of poetry, *Hyōtō* (the cover bears the English title *The Iceland*), in 1934 he stated that his use of the literary language was a "retreat" after years spent opposing it and perfecting free verse in the colloquial. "But," he went on, "when I wrote the poems in *The Iceland*, the literary language was for me an absolutely necessary poetic diction. In other words, it was impossible to express the emotions in that collection in any other language but the literary one." [165] No doubt much the same reasons impelled Hagiwara to choose the literary language for his "poems of pure feeling." A well-known work in this series was the short "Koide Shindō" (New Koide Road, 1925):

> The new road opened here
> Goes no doubt straight to the city.
> I stand at a crossway of this new road,
> Uncertain of the lonely horizon around me.
> Dark, melancholy day.
> The sun is low over the roofs of the row of houses.
> The trees in the wood have been sparsely felled.
> How, how to change my thoughts?
> On this road I rebel against and will not travel
> The new trees have all been felled.

Compared to the poems in *The Blue Cat*, the meaning is clarity itself, though commentators have emphasized the obscurities.[166] But even if fine points can be debated, there is no mistaking the poet's sense of desolation over the road that now rips through the forest he had loved.

Other poems in the sequence are dominated by the same mood, and sometimes the same turns of phrase recur. The finest poem, "Ōwatari-bashi" (Ōwatari Bridge), was praised by Miyoshi

Tatsuji in these terms: "It is not only the jewel among Hagiwara Sakutarō's poems, but a masterpiece that occupies a prominent place among the countless poems written since shintaishi became free verse." [167]

> The long bridge they've erected here
> No doubt goes from lonely Sōsha Village straight to Maebashi
>   town.
> Crossing the bridge I sense desolation pass through me.
> Carts go by loaded with goods, men leading the horses.
> And restless, nagging bicycles.
> When I cross this long bridge
> Twilight hunger stabs me.
>
> Ahh—to be in your native place and not go home! [168]
> I've suffered to the full griefs that sting like salt.
> I grow old in solitude.
> How to describe the fierce anger today over bitter memories?
> I will tear up my miserable writings
> And throw every scrap into the onrushing Tone River.
> I am famished as a wolf.
> Again and again I clutch at the railing, grind my teeth,
> But it does no good: something like tears spills out,
> Flows down my cheeks, unstanched.
> Ahh—how contemptible I have been all along!
> Past me go carts loaded with goods, men leading the horses.
> This day, when everything is cold, the sky darkens over the plain.

The self-hatred and nihilism that mark this poem reached even greater extremes of expression in Hagiwara's last collection of poetry, *The Iceland,* which consisted of poems composed between 1916 and 1933. These poems are not only in the classical language.but have (for Hagiwara) an exceptionally high proportion of words of Chinese origin. Hagiwara characterized the poetry in *The Iceland* as "screams" (*zekkyō*) of anger, hatred, loneliness, denial, doubt, and all the other strong emotions he felt.[169] Words of Chinese origin, with their sharper contours, were better suited to such expression than the softer Japanese words. The poems are otherwise marked by the strong influence of

Nietzsche.[170] The best-known work in the collection, "Hyōhaku-sha no Uta" (The Wanderer's Song), especially reveals the influence of *Also Sprach Zarathustra*. The poet sees himself as a lonely wanderer:

> You, wanderer!
> You come from the past and go by the future,
> Pursuing your eternal nostalgia.

The poem concludes:

> Ah, man of loneliness,
> You climb the slope of the sad sunset
> And wander over the precipice of will-lessness,
> But you will not find a home anywhere.
> Your home surely does not exist! [171]

The value of this poem and, indeed, of the entire collection *The Iceland* has been much debated by Japanese poets and scholars. Hagiwara's outstanding disciple, Miyoshi Tatsuji, labeled the collection the work of a jejune and decadent period in Hagiwara's life. He found that it consisted of "odd repetitions and distasteful retrogressions" and that, for a collection by Hagiwara, the workmanship was extremely poor.[172] His strictures were echoed by Naka Tarō, who believed that Hagiwara, having realized that the springs of his creative imagination had dried up, was forced to describe a commonplace world of which he himself probably felt ashamed.[173] But *The Iceland* has also had its defenders, some because they welcomed the light it sheds on a particularly unhappy period of Hagiwara's life, others because they are convinced that this collection was the crowning masterpiece of his career.[174]

The poems in *The Iceland* are almost without exception gloomy in tone, with frequent repetitions of such words as *sabishiki* (lonely), *yūshū* (melancholy), *kyomu* (nothingness), *kodoku* (solitude), and *uree* (grief). It is easy to imagine why certain critics have read these poems mainly as autobiographical documents describing Hagiwara's lonely life after separating from his wife. But they are certainly more than items of historical interest; the poems have a lean, stark beauty that is not the product of an exhausted mind but of a ripe and austere one.

During the years between the publication of *The Iceland* in 1934 and his death in 1942 Hagiwara composed almost no poetry. He wrote numerous works of poetical criticism including a famous essay on Buson, aphorisms, and brief studies of the nature of Japanese culture. The great esteem he enjoyed during his lifetime has never wavered since.

MURŌ SAISEI (1889-1962)

Murō Saisei, a close friend of Hagiwara's, was an important poet in his own right. His life began unhappily: he was the illegitimate child of an elderly ex-samurai and a household maid. Saisei's father, embarrassed by this late addition to his family, left the infant at a nearby temple, where Saisei was raised by the priest and his common-law wife. The boy left elementary school without graduating, much to the approval of his foster-mother, who at once sent him to work as a page at a local law court. Saisei early showed literary aspirations, and began to write haiku while only fourteen. In 1906 a piece he submitted to a Tokyo literary magazine was accepted, and a poem written the next year was singled out for special praise by the editor of *Shinsei* (New Voices). Saisei thereupon decided he would become a poet, and for the next few years was active in poetry circles in his native Kanazawa. He wrote not only modern poetry but haiku and tanka, and read the poetry of Kitahara Hakushū with special enthusiasm. In 1909 he gave up his job at the court and became a reporter for various local newspapers. He went the next year to Tokyo, where he called on Hakushū, who encouraged him to write for his magazine, *Zamboa*. Hagiwara Sakutarō, then unknown, was so impressed by some poems Saisei published in the March 1913 issue of *Zamboa* that he invited him to Maebashi, the beginning of their long and fruitful friendship.[175] In 1916 sixty poems by Saisei were published in the magazine *Kanjō* (Emotions), which was founded that year by Hagiwara, Saisei, and Yamamura Bochō.

Saisei published his first volume of poetry in 1918 at his own expense, with money he raised after the death of his foster father by selling the temple furnishings. The collection, called *Ai no Shi Shū* (Love Poems), consisted of poetry in the colloquial, much of it more devoted to social concerns than the title would suggest. Saisei was at pains to insist, at various stages of his career, that his poetry was free of ideas: "The most sensible decision I ever made was to refuse to touch anything except lyrical subjects in my poetry. No doubt it was because I happened to be lucky enough never to be able to formulate any ideas that I was not intimidated by anything so difficult as 'thought.' " [176] But in his first collection some poems touch dangerously on the realm of ideas, as this one, merely called "Unfinished Poem":

> A red, red sunset—
> Below, streets and houses packed together.
> Looking at them wearies me.
> What reflections do they give?
> Voices of street hawkers at the twilight hour
> Spread from them to my heart,
> The voices of many kinds of lives,
> Mingled with the sad scent of a late autumn shower.
> I listen, my face pressed against the window.[177]

Saisei's next collection, *Jojō Shōkyoku Shū* (Short Lyrics), was in a more characteristic vein, and includes some of the finest lyrics composed in modern Japan. It was acclaimed after publication in September 1918. Hagiwara wrote, "This slim volume of poems is the only collection of beautiful lyrics to have appeared in Japan since Kitahara Hakushū's *Memories*. I doubt that it will be easy in the future, for that matter, to find a better example of this kind of art." [178]

These early lyrics by Saisei were marked by a freshness of expression that seemed to bring new life to the classical language. It is difficult at times to communicate the quality of the poems because the particular words used and their sounds are of even greater importance than the meaning, as in the following example, called "Snakes":

> *Hebi wo nagamuru kokoro hebi ni naru*
> *Gin'iro no surodoki hebi ni naru*

Dokudami no hana aojiroku
Kusaretaru fukii no nioi hebi ni naru
Kimi wo omoeba kimi ga yubi
Surusurusuru to hebi ni naru [179]

The mind that contemplates snakes becomes a snake.
It becomes a silver, sharp-edged snake.
It becomes a snake, pallid as nightshade blossoms,
Reeking of polluted artesian wells.
When I think of you, your fingers
Turn, slithering, into snakes.

The repetitions of the words *hebi ni naru* (turn into snakes) is given special force in the last line by the onomatopoetic adverb *surusurusuru*, which suggests the slithering motion of the snakes and the rapidity of the transformation.

A more conventional kind of lyricism is found in the same collection in poems like "Semigoro" (The Time of Cicadas):

Izuko to shi naku
Shii to semi no nakikeri
Haya semigoro to narishi ka
Semi no ko wo toraen to shite
Atsuki natsu no sunachi wo fumishi ko wa
Kyō izuko ni ari ya

Natsu no aware ni
Inochi mijikaku
Miyako no machi no tōku yori
Sora to yane no anata yori
Shii to semi no nakikeri [180]

Somewhere or other
Sheee—the cicadas are singing.
Is it already the season for cicadas?
A boy runs over the hot summer sand
Hoping to catch some cicadas—
Where has he gone today?

In the sadness of summer,
How short its life is!
From the distant city streets,

Beyond the sky and the roofs,
Sheee—the cicadas are singing.

The sound of the cicadas singing, a prolonged *sheee*, produces a melancholy effect at the beginning and end of the poem.
The poet, living in the crowded city, hears from somewhere the
familiar insect cries, and recalls himself as a boy, running not over
city pavement but over the sand in open sunlight. The sound of
the cicadas presumably comes from some nearby tree, but to the
poet it seems to come from an infinite distance of time, rather
than space. As the poet Ōoka Makoto pointed out, Saisei's most
typical poems are those in which a man, now living in the city,
recalls the countryside of his boyhood.[181]

The poems in Saisei's later collections are more direct, some
so direct that they are hardly distinguishable from prose, and
much of the magic has been lost. Even within the same collection
he sometimes used the colloquial, sometimes the classical language; the latter's elegiac quality lends additional pathos to his
words. The first of the following poems is in the colloquial, the
second in the classical. Both appeared in *Tsuru* (Cranes, 1928):

TOMORROW

"Tomorrow we'll play again!
Come play tomorrow, and don't forget the time!"
The children, now that it was getting dark, parted.
I went to where they had been playing and had a look.
There was nothing suggesting the scent of fresh grass.
It didn't seem like a place one could have any fun.
In fact, there was even a cold wind blowing.
All the same, they're going to play again tomorrow!
This is where they promised to meet, then separated.[182]

The poem evokes the private world of children who enjoy playing
even in an empty lot that seems to an adult to be devoid of attraction; but he has lost their secret. Another poem from *Cranes*,
"Setsunaki Omoi zo shiru" (I Have Known Heartbreaking
Thoughts) is more intense:

I love taut-stretched ice;
I love tense and searing thoughts.

I have seen ice flash like rainbows;
I love those flowers that are not flowers.
I share the feelings of whatever lies deep inside the ice,
And feel the passion within that swordlike thing.
I have always lived inside a cramped existence,
Groaned inside the desolation of human life.
That is why I love taut-stretched ice,
And love such tense and searing thoughts.[183]

Saisei exercised great influence over many young poets, including Nakano Shigeharu, Miyoshi Tatsuji, and Hori Tatsuo, but lacked the depth of intellect of Hagiwara that might have permitted him to keep growing as a poet. His lyricism eventually lost its freshness, and he was obliged to turn to writing prose for an income. His stories were successful almost from the beginning, and "Ani Imōto" (Brother and Sister, 1934) [184] created a sensation when first published, with its brutally realistic description of the relationships in a laboring-class family. Saisei's more poetic fiction was typified by the "I novel" *Anzukko* (1957), which brought him new fame. It may be as a writer of fiction, rather than as a poet, that he will ultimately be remembered, but his early collections of lyrics are remarkably beautiful and deserve their high reputation.

YAMAMURA BOCHŌ (1884–1924)

One other early associate of Hagiwara's deserves special mention as a poet, Yamamura Bochō, who joined with Hagiwara and Saisei in publishing two short-lived poetry magazines. While in Maebashi he became a Christian under the influence of a female missionary who taught him English. The townspeople taunted Bochō for being the "kept man" of the foreign "heretic," but he persisted in his faith, later attending a theological school and eventually becoming a minister. Once Bochō took up his clerical duties, however, he began to rebel at the formalism of the church and turned increasingly to poetry as an outlet for his confused but intense feelings. His first major collection, *Seisanryō Hari* (Sacred Prisms, 1915), contained poetry as arcane and baffling as any of the period. "Geigo" (Incoherent Muttering), for example, consists of thirteen lines, each composed of two nouns, the first the designation of a variety of crime, the second some object associated in the poet's mind with that crime. It begins:

settō kingyo	theft goldfish
gōtō rappa	burglary bugle
kyōkatsu kokyū	blackmail fiddle
tobaku neko [185]	gambling cat

The associations vary from the easily understood link between theft and "gold" fish, to the similarity between the gloomy atmosphere surrounding blackmail and the plaintive sounds of the *kokyū*, or Chinese fiddle, to the furtive secrecy of gambling and the movements of a cat.

A more famous (and even more perplexing) poem in the same collection is called "Dansu" (Dance). To suggest the wild movements and voluptuousness of the dancers, he used words more for their sounds than their meanings:

> *arashi*
> *arashi*
> *shidareyanagi ni hikari are*
> *akambo no*
> *heso no me*
> *suigin hisuteria . . . .*[186]

> hurricane
> hurricane
> let there be light in the weeping willow
> sprouts from the navel
> of an infant
> mercury hysteria . . . .

Hinatsu Kōnosuke denounced such poetry as a mere "showing off of eccentricity to impress amateurs" and called Bochō a "hack poet." [187] But Hagiwara provided lengthy explanations for each line, relating the words by the texture of the sound to the movements of a dance. Hagiwara eulogized Bochō as a pioneer, recalling the violent opposition that poems like "Incoherent Muttering" aroused when first published:

Unusual lines like "burglary bugle" were an out-and-out rebellion against the accepted views of the poetry circles of the time. It would be impossible today even to imagine the hostility and hatred such lines aroused among poets. When one realizes that Yamamura Bochō was persecuted by the members of the poetry circles because of these lines, it is like seeing a nightmare out of the last century, so greatly have poetry circles changed since then.[188]

Hagiwara distinguished three periods in Bochō's poetry: first, the extreme obscurity and "Cubism" of the poetry in *Sacred Prisms*; second, the poetry of such collections as *Kaze wa kusaki ni Sasayaida* (The Wind Whispered in the Grass and Trees, 1918), characterized by a warm humanism influenced by the Tolstoyism of the *Shirakaba* school and the poetry of Whitman; and finally, the poetry of *Kumo* (Clouds, 1921), which achieved an "oriental" detachment and simplicity.[189] Certainly it is a far cry from "Dance," or from the even more extraordinary "Fūkei" (Landscape, 1915), a poem in twenty-seven lines of which twenty-four are identical—"A field full of rape blossoms"—to the sober poems of his second period treating the life of old fishermen or the coming of spring, or to the absolute bareness of his last collection. It is almost unbelievable that the same poet, in the space of six years, could write such strikingly different styles of poetry, but Hagiwara detected a basic consistency in the man and his outlook under the outward changes. A childlike wonder at the world took totally dissimilar forms of expression in the obscure early poems and in the unaffected descriptions of nature in his last collection, but itself remained unchanged. Perhaps that is why Yamamura Bochō, like a surprising number of other twentieth-century Japanese poets, was a successful writer of children's songs and stories.

MIYAZAWA KENJI (1896–1933)

Miyazawa stands apart from other important poets of his time both because of his physical remoteness from the poetry-making circles and because of his spiritual remoteness from the kinds of anguish that tormented Hagiwara and the other central figures of the time. Though one can trace the influence of Kitahara Hakushū, Hagiwara Sakutarō, and other modern poets, whom he read assiduously, on his works, his life among farmers, more than any literary influences, colors his poetry.

Miyazawa was born the son of a well-to-do pawnshop-owner in the northerly prefecture of Iwate, but (apparently out of sympathy for the hard-pressed farmers who patronized his father's shop) Miyazawa himself turned against commerce altogether. His parents were devout believers in Jōdo Buddhism, but after a reading of the Lotus Sutra in 1915, which made him tremble with joy, he became converted to Nichiren Buddhism. It has been said that he lived his entire life in accordance with the spirit of this sutra, which he kept by him always.[190] His writings, mainly poetry and children's stories, contain an unusual number of words of Buddhist significance, and even though specifically Buddhist teachings do not often surface in his works, they were never far from his mind. Miyazawa's deathbed request, made to his father, was that he print an edition of one thousand copies of the Lotus Sutra in Japanese translation and distribute them to friends with a note saying: "The purpose of the work of my entire lifetime was to deliver this sacred book into your hands, and to enable you to enter the Highest Path by bringing you into contact with the Buddha's teachings." [191] Such piety, contrasted to the indifference to Buddhism on the part of most modern Japanese poets, helps to explain the life Miyazawa led.

Miyazawa began writing poetry as a schoolboy, composing over a thousand tanka. Although these poems were crude in execution, they already prefigure the fantasy and intensity of emotion that would later be revealed in his mature work. His earliest modern poetry was written under the influence of Ishikawa Takuboku and Kitahara Hakushū; with the exception of some poems written in the classical language toward the end of his life, when he lay on a sickbed, his modern poems were all in the colloquial, sometimes even in dialect. He wrote by preference in irregular, sprawling forms, but occasionally composed a tanka even as late as 1921.

In 1918 Miyazawa graduated from the Higher Agricultural School in Morioka in the north of Japan and was appointed a special research assistant in geology, soil science, and fertilizers. Later that year his younger sister Toshi, who was studying at a university in Tokyo, fell ill, and Miyazawa and his mother went to Tokyo to look after her. He remained there until his sister had recovered early in the next year. In 1919 his sister compiled a collection of 662 of his tanka for publication. Miyazawa himself edited a volume of extracts from the writings of Nichiren, and in the following year joined a Nichiren Buddhist society. That winter he went through the streets of the city shouting the invocation of Nichiren Buddhists: *Namu Myōhō Renge Kyō* ("Hail the Lotus Sutra of the Wonderful Law").

While at home in January 1921 he made several unsuccessful attempts to convert his family to Nichiren Buddhism. He was much discouraged, but one day a miracle occurred: some volumes of the writings of Nichiren fell off a shelf and struck him. Taking this as a divine revelation, he instantly determined he would go to Tokyo and take a more active part in proselytization. Forty minutes after making this decision, Miyazawa was on the train, carrying with him only the Lotus Sutra, an umbrella, and travel money.[192]

As soon as Miyazawa arrived in Tokyo he went to the Kokuchūkai (Pillar of the Nation Society), where he offered his services in whatever way might be helpful in spreading Nichiren's teachings. At first his offer was politely rejected, but eventually he engaged in street propagation of the faith. During his stay in Tokyo he also wrote an enormous number of pages of children's stories—supposedly three thousand pages a month—and sold one story at the end of the year for five yen, the only money he received during his lifetime for his writings. In September 1921 he returned home because of his sister Toshi's renewed illness, and became a teacher at the Agricultural School in the town of Hanamaki in Iwate Prefecture.

Miyazawa began composing the poems that were eventually included in his first collection, *Haru to Shura* (Spring and the Demon), in 1922. About this time, his interest was also aroused in Western music, and he began to collect records, especially of Bach and Beethoven. His love of music undoubtedly affected the poetry he wrote during this period. In November 1922 his sister Toshi died, a traumatic shock from which Miyazawa never recovered. On the day of her death he composed three poems that stand near the head of his entire body of poetry. The incredible speed was typical of Miyazawa: some months earlier, he wrote three long poems, including one over nine hundred lines in length, in three days. When caught in a frenzy of poetic composition he wrote almost automatically, with no preconceived plan of how long his poem would be, and seemingly without thought of future revisions.

The first of Miyazawa's three poems on the death of Toshi (or Toshiko, as he also calls her), called "Eiketsu no Asa" (The Morning of Eternal Parting), is the longest and most affecting:

Before this day is over,
My sister, you will go far from here.
It's sleeting, and strangely bright outside.
    (Please bring me some sleet.)
The sleet falls unbrokenly
From clouds the gloomier for being tinged with red.
    (Please bring me some sleet.)
Thinking I would fetch some snow for you to eat
In these two chipped china bowls
With designs of water-shields in blue,
I leaped out into this dark sleet,
Like a bent rifle-bullet.
    (Please bring me some sleet.)
From lead-colored clouds
The streaming sleet sinks.
Ah, Toshiko,
Now, when you are about to die
You have asked me
For a bowl of refreshing snow
With which to brighten the rest of my life.
Thank you, my brave sister.
I'll be glad to go, right away.
    (Please bring me some sleet.)
That terrible, terrible fever on you, at breaks in your gasps
You have asked me
For a last bowl of snow from the sky,
The world they call the Milky Way, the Sun, the atmosphere . . .
. . . On two slabs of granite
Forlornly the sleet accumulates.
I stand on them unsteadily.
I will accept the last food
For my beloved sister

From glistening pine branches
Laden with transparent, icy drops
That preserve, pure white, a two-phased system of snow and water.
You will also be saying goodbye
To these bowls with the blue pattern you remember
From the time we were growing up together.
    (I'm going all by myself.)
That's right, you will be leaving us today.
Ah, my brave sister,
Inside the dim screens and mosquito netting
Of that sick room with shut doors,
You burn gently, palely.
No matter where I choose to gather snow,
It is too white, everywhere.
This beautiful snow has come
From that frightening, turbulent sky.
    (If I'm born again as a human being,
      Next time I don't want to suffer this way
        Only because of myself.)
I pray now from the heart
To the snow in these two bowls you will eat
That it will turn somehow into manna from heaven
And bring holy nourishment soon
To you and to all others.
I pray, and will give in return my entire happiness.

The lines have no metrical pattern, but Miyazawa seems to
have learned from Hagiwara Sakutarō that intensity of feeling can
maintain an unmistakable level of poetry, even without recognizable poetic devices. The sentences in parentheses are uttered by
Toshiko in dialect so unlike standard Japanese that Miyazawa
gave translations at the end of the poem; they supply a kind of
musical refrain, the more effective because nearly unintelligible.
Most of the poem is absolutely direct in expression, but the reader
is likely to be startled by the words "two-phased system" (*nisōkei*),
which no doubt reflect unconsciously Miyazawa's scientific training. The poem does not suggest it has been extensively revised; its
effect comes instead from the impression of words torn from the
heart, presented without artifice. The subject matter makes this

manner of composition feasible, but it can readily be imagined what difficulties would be involved in maintaining the poetic intensity when describing an event of less compelling emotional quality.

The third of the poems on Toshi's death, *Musei Dōkoku* (Voiceless Lamentation), is equally effective. Miyazawa's descriptions of her beauty, even in her terrible sickness, are interrupted by Toshi's pathetic exclamations (given in dialect) which express her fear that she must look and smell unpleasant. In this poem Miyazawa referred to himself as "walking the *shura*'s way." *Shura* (from the Sanskrit *asura*) designated the realm of envious, eternally fighting demons, of the Six Ways of the world after death. He called himself a shura because of his constant struggle against the pride, envy, and lust he felt within him. *Spring and the Demon*, the title of his first collection, symbolized by "spring" the forces of nature, the source of good for Miyazawa, and by "demon" (or *shura*), the forces of evil. Miyazawa was so determined to overcome the evil forces he sensed in himself that he sometimes wandered all night in the woods in order to subdue the waves of sexual desire; a close friend wrote that Miyazawa died a virgin.[193]

Miyazawa's life was consecrated to the welfare of the farmers of the desperately poor northeast region. He resigned his post as a teacher in 1926 in order to become a farmer himself. He instructed the other farmers not only in superior methods of cultivation, but in music, poetry, and whatever else might enrich their bleak lives. In August 1926 he formed the Rasuchijin Society for this purpose. When someone asked what "Rasuchijin" meant, Miyazawa replied that it had no special meaning, but *chi* (earth) and *jin* (man) were probably in his mind. The society lasted two years. Miyazawa gave it his full energies, yet managed to find time also to compose many poems. The poems are long and tend to ramble. One friendly critic said of Miyazawa's longest poem, *Koiwai Nōjō* (Koiwai Farm), that it would have been better if it were only one-half, or even one-third, as long.[194] But Miyazawa's excellences as a poet revealed themselves only when the impetuous flights of his imagination were given free rein. The poems of this period often describe the hardships of tilling the poor soil, or even contain advice on fertilizers and irrigation. This may not sound like promising material for poetry, but Miyazawa managed to breathe intensity into his descriptions by evoking the terrible presence of famine, as in the poem "Opus 1063":

Ours are simple fences in the Ainu style.
We plotted and replotted mulberry trees
In our inch of garden,
But even so, couldn't make a living.
In April
The water in the paddy-fields was black,
Tiny eddies of dark air
Fell like pellets from the sky
And birds
Flew by with raucous cries.
These fields full of horned stones
Where horsetails and wormwood have sprouted
Are cultivated by women
Dropping their litters
Patching together the ragged clothes of the older children,
Cooking and doing the village chores,
Shouldering the family discontents and desires,
With a handful of coarse food
And six hours sleep the year round.
And here
If you plant two bushels of buckwheat you get back four.
Are these people, I wonder,
So much unlike
The many revolutionaries tied up in prisons,
The artists starved by their luck,
Those heroes of our time? [195]

The farmers did not all respond favorably to Miyazawa's self-sacrificing devotion to their welfare. Some sneered at him as a young man from the city merely playing at being a farmer; others, disappointed when his fertilizers did not produce the hoped-for results, only manifested their anger.[196] Miyazawa did not idealize the farmers. In one especially powerful poem, "Sono Chichi to au" (Meeting His Father), a farmer tells Miyazawa bluntly that all his efforts have done nobody any good.[197]

In the summer of 1928 Miyazawa fell ill, and by the end of

the year his illness had worsened into acute pneumonia. He had become a confirmed vegetarian, and it was extremely difficult to persuade him to eat more nourishing food. Once, when he was tricked into eating carp liver, he wept to discover it.[198] During his illness he began writing poetry in the classical language. Gradually he recovered, and in 1931 he took a job as the consultant for a rock-crushing company. He traveled about advising on improvements in the manufacture of calcium carbonate. In September, while visiting Tokyo, he was again stricken with pneumonia, and he was sent back to Hanamaki in a grave condition. On November 3, 1931, he wrote in his notebook what has become his most popular poem:

> *Ame ni makezu*
> *Kaze ni mo makezu*
> *Yuki ni mo natsu no atsusa ni mo makenu*
> *Jōbu na karada wo mochi*
> *Yoku wa naku*
> *Keshite ikarazu*
> *Itsumo shizuka ni waratte iru . . . .*[199]

> Undaunted by the rain,
> Undaunted by the wind,
> Undaunted by the snow or the summer heat,
> With a strong body
> And no desires,
> Never losing my temper,
> I will always keep smiling . . . .

This poem is much less Kiplingesque in the original than it may seem in translation. All the same, it is by no means one of Miyazawa's best poems, and it is ironic that this should be the one poem for which he is universally known, a poem inscribed for inspirational purposes on plaques and souvenir towels, and memorized by would-be emulators of his steadfast purpose. The poem is affecting, it is true, but less because of its contents than because of the background. One cannot help but be struck by the picture of Miyazawa writing this poem of resolution and self-encouragement even as he lay at the point of death.[200]

Miyazawa's health improved somewhat in 1932, but he remained a convalescent. He continued to write poetry, to study (mainly mathematics and calligraphy), and to advise farmers about their crops. In the autumn of 1933 his health seemed sufficiently improved for him to stand in his doorway to watch the procession of a local Shinto shrine pass by. Some farmers, seeing Miyazawa, supposed he must have entirely recovered, and engaged him for about an hour in conversation about fertilizers. Exhausted by this protracted discussion, he died the next day, after writing his final request to his father for the edition of the Lotus Sutra.

Miyazawa's children's stories, especially "Kaze no Matasaburō" (Matasaburō Rides the Wind) and "Ginga Tetsudō no Yoru" (Nights on the Railroad to the Milky Way, *c.* 1921) enjoy great popularity, but he is important above all as a poet. His poems at their best are fiercely involved, less with his personal griefs or sense of isolation (in the manner of most other poets of the day) than with the hardships of the farmers' lives. But to the end he remained religious, rather than political, in face of the inequalities and hardships he witnessed.

Only the first of the four *Spring and the Demon* collections appeared during his lifetime. It was published privately in 1924 in an edition of one thousand copies, of which barely one hundred were sold. At the time of his death, however, his name had become known to such poets as Kusano Shimpei, and *Spring and the Demon* had attracted favorable reviews. Miyazawa published his poems mainly in obscure provincial newspapers and magazines, though at the end of his life the principal poetry magazines were eager for his work. He died just as his importance was at last recognized.

THE SHŌWA PERIOD (From 1927)

IT IS DIFFICULT to decide where to draw the line between Taishō and early Shōwa poetry. Collections of Taishō poetry sometimes include Miyazawa Kenji, but sometimes leave him for the Shōwa volume of the same series. Obviously, there can be no firm rule, especially when one is considering poets whose activities extended over both Taishō and Shōwa periods. I have chosen to make a somewhat arbitrary decision, including among the Shōwa poets only those whose careers embraced the years of the Pacific War, the most traumatic experience of Japan in the twentieth century.

Many of these poets, including Takamura Kōtarō, began publishing during the Taishō period, but their most important works were composed in the 1930s. This poetry often indirectly revealed the political background of the period. It was normal, for example, for a Japanese to visit Korea, then a part of the Japanese empire, and by the late 1930s visits to Peking, in the wake of the Japanese army occupation, also became common. The poets, more so than prose writers, served during the war years as chroniclers of the achievements of the military, singing of arms and the man in the manner of poets from time immemorial. Not all poets joined in the flaring up of poetic activity during the war years, but there was little resistance. Few of the war poems were of lasting value, and they have therefore been discussed not in terms of the work of individual poets but as part of the general survey of Japanese literature during the war.

The defeat caused some poets to express publicly their shame over the poetry they had written, but others chose not to allude to their praise for now discredited ideals. The early postwar era was still dominated by these poets of the 1930s, but a new generation of unusual ability soon appeared.

TAKAMURA KŌTARŌ (1883-1956)

Takamura preferred always to think of himself as a sculptor rather than as a poet, even refusing an appointment to the Japanese Academy because the invitation was extended to him as a poet. He considered his poetry to be no more than an outlet for thoughts he excluded from his sculpture. Nevertheless, Takamura was above all a poet; his sculptures (whether in the manner of Rodin, which he learned from the master in Paris, or in the more traditionally Japanese manner of carving insects, birds, and fruits) are relatively few and not especially impressive. His poems—particularly those describing his passionate love for his wife—enjoy great popularity, both because of their moving emotional content and because (unlike the obscure work of the Symbolists) the expression is strong and clear.

Takamura was born in Tokyo, the son of a traditional sculptor of some repute. At fourteen (1897) he entered the Tokyo School of Arts, from which he graduated in 1902. In the meanwhile he had begun to publish both tanka and haiku under various pen names. His interest in Rodin was aroused in 1904 by a photograph of *Le Penseur*, and in the following year he read a biography of Rodin that impressed him so much he returned to the Tokyo School of Arts to study Western art. In 1906 he traveled to New York, where he remained about a year, studying sculpture under Gutzon Borglum. While in New York he wrote his first modern poem and published it in *Myōjō*. He left New York in

1907 for London, where he continued his art studies and made friends with the distinguished potter Bernard Leach. In 1908 he moved to Paris. His stay was less than a year, but the effects were indelible. Not only did he study Rodin's sculptures, but he learned French by memorizing large quantities of poetry, mainly by Baudelaire and Verhaeren. He absorbed the same influences as had Kambara Ariake, but directly, in the language of the original, rather than in the paraphrases of Ueda Bin. His own poetry, even when written under the influence of Verhaeren, shows none of the constriction and effort of Ariake's.[201]

Takamura's earliest poems were in classical Japanese, cast into the usual patterns of alternating phrases, five plus seven syllables, but after his return to Japan in 1909 he became acquainted with the work of Kitahara Hakushū and Miki Rofū, and decided to adopt their manner of writing free verse in the colloquial. He joined the Devotees of Pan, in part by way of reaction to the constricting life his father sought to impose on him, and for a time behaved in the dissolute manner expected of members of the society. In the April 1910 issue of *Subaru* he published four poems under the facetious title of *Les impressions des ouonnas (à ma Bien-Aimée au Caouatchi-Leau)*. *Ouonnas* was his arch way of writing the plural of *onna* (woman) and Caouatchi-Leau was Kawachi-rō, the name of a Yoshiwara brothel he frequented. He gave his favorite prostitute the nickname of Mona Lisa, or La Joconde, alleging a resemblance in the smile. His first poem of distinction, "Ushinawareta Mona Lisa" (The Lost Mona Lisa), published in the January 1911 *Subaru*, describes his loneliness after the beautiful prostitute disappeared. The poem includes these lines:

> Mona Lisa shed no tears;
> She merely smiled, showing pale-green teeth
> With the opacity of an orient pearl.
> Separated from her picture-frame,
> Mona Lisa walked away.[202]

This extract is typical of the rather casual tone of the entire poem, even though Takamura here and there hints at the intense physical pleasure he took in this woman who "threatened my soul and poured oil on the flames of my life." Another poem, published in the same issue of *Subaru*, reveals the other side to Takamura's life at this time: "Netsuke no Kuni" (The Land of Netsuke) is an almost savage caricature of the Japanese, as they looked to the poet after three years abroad. The poem, written in the colloquial, consists of a series of adjectival phrases building up to the final word they modify, *Nipponjin* (Japanese).

> Cheekbones protruding, lips thick, eyes triangular,
> Face like a netsuke carved by the Master Sangorō,
> A blank expression, as if his soul was removed,
> Ignorant of himself, fidgety,
> Cheap-lived,
> Show-off,
> Small-minded, self-satisfied,
> Monkey-like, foxlike, squirrel-like, gudgeon-like, minnow-like,
>   potsherd-like, gargoyle-faced Japanese! [203]

Takamura's distaste, despite such descriptions, was presumably less directed at Japanese physical appearances than at the Japanese way of life. He declared that in Paris he had felt completely at home, unaware (as he had been in New York or London) of being a foreigner; the shock of his return to the old-fashioned ways of Japan was therefore much greater than if he had felt like an exile while abroad, and he plunged into a life of dissolution as an escape.

Takamura's poetry, especially works like "The Land of Netsuke," bewildered contemporary readers, who found nothing poetic in the subject matter or the diction, whether of the traditional variety or the modern poetry of Kyūkin and Ariake. Most of his poems from this time on are irregular in form and deal with conspicuously "unpoetic" subjects. Sometimes his allusions are private and elude interpretation, but the language is almost always unaffected and colloquial, as in "Fuyu ga kuru" (Winter Is Coming), which begins:

> *Fuyu ga kuru.*
> *Samui, surudoi, tsuyoi, tōmei na fuyu ga kuru.*

> Winter is coming.
> The cold, sharp, strong, transparent winter is coming.[204]

The language could not be simpler or more direct. It owes its poetic effect to its underlying masculine strength, which is punctuated occasionally by thrusts of language that reveal the complexity of the poet's mind. Sometimes, however, Takamura's techniques became almost surrealistic, as in "Kyōsha no Shi" (Madman's Poem):

> Blow, come on, blow,
> Cold wind down from Chichibu,
> Blow, rolling down the mountains!
> The world's at its last gasp, come on, blow!
> Blow on my back!
> A cat is yowling inside my head.
> Somewhere somebody is serving up Rodin for bait.
> Coca-Cola THANK YOU VERY MUCH
> Ginza Second Ward, Third Ward, and Owari Street,
> Electric car, electric light, electric wires, electric power . . . .[205]

This poem, ostensibly the ravings of a madman, is in fact the expression of Takamura's disgust with the modern wilderness of Tokyo. His summoning of the cold winter wind (rather than the softer spring breezes) was typical of his poetry; for him winter was the time of purity, of spiritual tension and physical activity. Takamura wrote:

> The shrubs and tall trees have lost their leaves, the bushes and their fruits stand withered. What was to fall has fallen, what was to be prepared has been prepared; the clean beauty exposed plainly before one's eyes, beyond confusion, is surely the beauty within beauty. They have no perfume; they do not wink. They consider it only natural to display the bare minimum of attention to appearances. I have always felt at heart that the ultimate reaches of the most advanced art were to be found in the beauty of winter.[206]

A famous poem, "Fuyu ga kita" (Winter Has Come), contains the lines:

> Winter!
> Come to me, come to me!
> I am the winter's strength; the winter is my nourishment.[207]

The poems above were included in Takamura's first collection, *Dōtei* (The Road Ahead, 1914). The title poem gave its imprint not only to this book but to the image of Takamura presented to the Japanese public during the next forty years:

Ahead of me is no road;
Behind me a road has been made.
Ah, Nature!
Father!
Vast father who has set me on my own two feet!
Protect me, and never let me from your eyes!
Fill me always with your fatherly spirit!
For the long road that lies ahead,
For the long road that lies ahead.[208]

The expression of resolute determination to forge his own way is given peculiar force by his addressing nature as a stern father, rather than as a benign and generous mother.

In 1911 Takamura, enamored as ever of the winter and the cold, moved to Hokkaidō, but things went badly and he returned to Tokyo. Soon afterward he met Naganuma Chieko, whom he married in 1914, the year he published (at his own expense) the collection *The Road Ahead*. His passionate love for Chieko provided the subjects for the poetry in *Chieko-shō* (Chieko's Sky, 1941), his second book of poems. *Chieko's Sky* is unique in the history of modern Japanese poetry in its tracing of a man's love for his wife from their first meeting, through their life together with its strong physical aspects, to the first signs (in 1931) of the breakdown that eventually destroyed Chieko's mind, and finally to her death in 1938. The directness and strength of these poems bring to mind the *Manyōshū*, even though the language is entirely modern. The lines are of irregular length and do not observe the rules of conventional prosody. If they lack overtones or symbolic import (in the more traditional Japanese manner), they succeed in the way of many European poems, conveying with great force the poet's deepest feelings in language totally unlike that of the Symbolists. "Bokura" (The Two of Us, 1913) begins:

Whenever I think of you
I feel eternity closest;

I exist and you exist—
That is all that needs to be said about me.
My life and your life
Intertwine, tangle, melt,
Return to their primeval beginnings.
All discriminations lose their value between us;
For us everything is absolute.
The war of the sexes people talk about doesn't exist for us;
We have faith, respect, love and freedom
And a great power and authority . . . .

You are fire
The longer I know you the more I feel your freshness:
You are an inexhaustible treasury, always new;
You are a core of reality, stripped of branches and leaves;
Your kisses moisten me;
Your embraces give me extreme nourishment.
Your cold hands and feet,
Your heavy, rounded body,
Your phosphorescent skin,
The strength of a living creature running through your limbs:
These are the best nurture for my life.[209]

Takamura's poems reach their peak of intensity after Chieko has gone insane. "Kaze ni noru Chieko" (Chieko Rides the Wind, 1935) describes her wandering along the shore, signaling to the birds but not addressing a word to her husband. "Aigataki Chieko" (Incalculable Chieko, 1937) tells us:

Chieko sees the invisible,
She hears the inaudible.

Chieko goes where no one can go,
She does the impossible.

Chieko does not see the real me,
She yearns for a me beyond myself.

Chieko has now thrown off the weight of pain
And wandered out into a vast, boundless, imagined beauty.

Again and again I hear her voice calling me,
But Chieko no longer holds a ticket for the world of men.[210]

The poet Yoshimoto Takaaki pointed out in a brilliant essay the hidden meaning behind these poems: first of all, the love between Takamura and Chieko is described entirely from his point of view, making the reader wonder how Chieko responded to such intense adoration. Yoshimoto suspected, moreover, that despite the apparent sincerity (or even artlessness) of the poems about Chieko, Takamura was inspired less by direct personal experience than by Émile Verhaeren's *Les heures claires* (1896), a sequence of poems describing the poet's love for his wife.[211] Yoshimoto's theory is substantiated by letters in which Takamura described his agony at having to watch over the raving Chieko, whose insanity was so far advanced that the windows and doors of the house where she lived had to be nailed shut, lest she wander outside and cause trouble; these letters by no means correspond to the tones of the poems describing Chieko running after plovers on the shore, free of the ties of the world of human beings.[212] Perhaps Takamura, as he himself suggested years after her death, discovered the eternal Chieko only after the mortal Chieko had vanished; perhaps also *Chieko's Sky* was a desperate attempt to discover a relationship that had really never existed. Whatever the facts, the poems are completely convincing, and the biography of Chieko, which Takamura appended to the collection, provides further testimony to his love.

There was another side to Takamura's emotional life: his increasing awareness of himself as a Japanese is revealed in writings that paralleled his descriptions of his love for Chieko. These poems recall, years later, how alienated he had felt while abroad. Despite his declaration that he had felt at home in Paris, if nowhere else in the West, Takamura seems to have been acutely aware of the racial differences separating himself and the French people he knew—even the French prostitute he regularly visited while he was living in Paris. His recollections of racial discrimination experienced abroad resulted now in some bitter poems like "Shirokuma" (Polar Bear, 1925), in which he recalled a visit to the Bronx Zoo some eighteen years before. After paying the rent, there had not been much left of the seven dollars a week he received from Gutzon Borglum as his assistant, and he would spend his Sundays cheaply, at the zoo. His poem concludes:

> The polar bear is not to be tamed;
> Alone he breathes Arctic air outside New York.
>
> A contemptible, instructive friendliness pervades his surroundings;
> A wonderful Christian materialism that all but chokes him
> Attempts to kill a dreamer-Jap.
>
> The polar bear silently gazes from time to time at the man.
> For the first time this week the man doesn't hear the voices of the
>   street.
> Washed in silence, he too stands motionless before the great polar
>   bear.[214]

Another poem, "Zō no Ginkō" (Elephant's Bank, 1926), concludes:

> As I walk through Central Park, bathed in evening light,
> The obelisk from the river Nile looks down at me.
> Ah, there's somebody here just as resentful as you:
> Returning to his attic room, "their" Jap feels his blood boil.[215]

Takamura saw himself as being alienated from his surroundings, like the polar bear in the zoo or the obelisk from Egypt standing in a park in New York, and he shared their imagined contempt for their surroundings. However, Takamura's impressions of New York were not totally unfavorable. He recalled many years later (in 1954):

> I suppose that what I gained from America was a release from the Japanese system of ethical values. Having been brought up in an atmosphere that was an extension of the old Edo ethics that had surrounded my grandfather, my father, and my mother, I was astonished by the basic differences in everyday human activities in America. I was struck first of all by the youthful human spirit Americans displayed in ignoring—so completely it never even came into question—the virtues of humility or immaculateness we are taught with respect to money. As a socially insignificant little Jap-

anese, I resisted their peculiarly religious, goodwilled pressure, which probably should not be labeled as hypocrisy; but at the same time I was fascinated by the openness of the Americans' humanity.[216]

Shortly before composing the poems that described the sense of alienation he had felt years before in New York, not only because he had been called a "Jap," but because he disliked the missionary goodwill directed at him, he published his translation of Walt Whitman's *Specimen Days* in 1921. Takamura knew Whitman's poetry well, and his characteristic style, unlike that of the French Symbolists who influenced so much Japanese poetry, seems to owe much to Whitman.[217]

In London he made friends with Bernard Leach (1885–1979) when both were students at the art school of Sir Frank Brangwyn. He addressed several important poems to this valued friend. "Haitaisha yori" (From a Reprobate) opens:

> Generous and serious friend!
> My friend of the Anglo-Saxon race I respect and love!
> When I think of your warm friendship I all but want to weep.
> I remember that day when, as a rare evening shower
> Fell on Chelsea, raising white smoke,
> I first shook your hand.[218]

In this poem Takamura imagines how grieved Leach would be to learn of the life of dissipation to which he abandoned himself after returning to Japan in 1909, but he promises to change, so that he can again shake Leach's hand in the same spirit as in Chelsea. Another poem, "Yorokobi wo tsugu" (Announcing My Joy, 1914) describes how happy he is to have shaken off his dissolution, thanks apparently to Leach's visit to Japan. The poem opens:

> My friend of the Anglo-Saxon race I respect and love!
> My friend of the race
> That produced Shakespeare and Blake,
> Newton and Darwin,
> Turner and Beardsley,
> And now has produced Augustus John!

Later in the poem he declares:

> My friend, my friend!
> Please do not too easily make up your mind about the soul of this
> country,
> But please inform the Anglo-Saxon people I esteem and love
> That you have now heard the true voice of a people at the other end
> of the world,
> And that there, at the end of the world, a new strength is boldly
> gushing forth.
> Ah, my foreign friend!
> This strength is small now, but with life it must grow.
> Its roots will stretch deeply, as far, finely and broadly as they can;
> They will seek the fertilizer of life from all living things
> And, extremely slowly, extremely surely, will put forth shoots and
> grow.
> A life that never before has been seen will show itself.
> Wait and see! [219]

Despite Takamura's professions of respect and love for the Anglo-Saxon race, he felt a stranger in London, and even his personal affection for Leach never blotted out his awareness of their difference in race. In "Announcing My Joy" Takamura expressed confidence that Japan would grow, taking nourishment from everywhere, and produce a new culture.

Years later Takamura recalled his impressions on arriving in Paris from London: "Paris was the West, beyond any doubt, but a West in which something of myself was mingled, and in which I therefore felt no sense of strangeness; in other words, it was an international West. I felt marvelously relaxed. In New York or London I had never been able to cease being aware I was a Japanese, but often in Paris I completely forgot my nationality." [220] A poem on Paris expressed his gratitude:

> I became an adult in Paris.
> In Paris too I first touched the opposite sex,
> And in Paris first found a liberation of my soul.
> Paris accommodates every species of human being
> With an air of taking this for granted. . . .

The modern age began in Paris;
Beauty was born and blossomed in Paris.
My eyes were opened to the truths of poetry;
I observed what culture meant
In each of the common people I encountered.
Sadly, but inescapably,
I became aware of an incomparable gap:
Even amidst my nostalgia for the things and ways of Japan
I rejected them all.[221]

Despite his professions of having found himself in Paris, we can gather from accounts of Japanese friends of his that his behavior while in Paris was most erratic. On one occasion he rose in the middle of the night, without realizing what he was doing, to work on the clay bust of his father. The next morning he was surprised to discover his hands were coated with mud.[222] Moreover, he published in 1910, soon after his return from France, works that indicated his conviction that even if understanding between Japanese and foreigners is possible with respect to art, a wall between the races makes communication a delusion.[223]

In one of his "unsent letters," written at this time, he declared, "Alone. Alone. Why, I wonder, am I in Paris? The tremendous crimson smile of Paris fills me with infinite loneliness. The joyous shouts in the Paris streets are about to plunge me into a bottomless pit of melancholy." He compared his loneliness to that of animals, who cannot communicate with human beings:

> That is why, even amid the shouts of joy of Paris, I suffer every day an anguish that is bone-deep. The white people always say of orientals that they are inscrutable. The white race is also an insoluble riddle. I cannot comprehend even the little movements of their fingers. Even while I am embracing a white woman I cannot help wondering if I am not embracing a stone, hugging a corpse. I have often longed to drive a knife deep into a pure-white, waxen breast.[224]

Elsewhere he described spending the night with a French woman. The next morning when he washed his face, he noticed with great surprise and distaste, a strange, dark man standing before him. He looked more carefully and realized it was himself, reflected in a mirror. "Ah, I am, despite everything, a Japanese! *Un Japonais. Un Mongol.* I am *Le Jaune.*" [225] Yoshimoto Takaaki believed that "this experience determined the rest of Takamura's life." [226]

The rejection of Japan so harshly stated in "The Land of Netsuke" was given more personal expression in "Oya Fukō" (An Unfilial Son), which described his return to Japan:

> Kobe appeared, looking like a tight little cage.
> "Fujiyama" was pretty but small.
> Before my overjoyed father and mother
> I apologized in my heart:
> "You don't know what's going on now in the head
> Of that fellow who was so famous for thinking of his parents."
> I have become an unfilial son,
> But in my name as a human being, it can't be helped.
> I want to live as an individual human being.
> That, no doubt, is treason
> In this country where everything rejects the human being.
> The dream of my starting a family, that my parents have happily
>   waited for,
> Will probably be the first to be destroyed.
> I don't even know myself what will happen.
> The one thing certain is that it will be at variance
> With good customs and beautiful manners.
> —"Look at his face as he sleeps!"—
> My mother, by my pillow, murmurs in a small voice.
> How am I going to face such love? [227]

The conflict within Takamura between his admiration for the artistic achievements of the West and his conviction that basically East and West were incompatible, gradually grew stronger. "Hi Yoroppateki naru" (Un-European, 1932) contrasted the blunt explicitness of the West with the indirection of the East, where deep feelings are evoked through understatement:

> —Where does spring come from?
> —Spring comes from the direction of spring.

—When does spring come?
—Spring comes when it is spring.
Love ignores love,
The deep pool of Asian love that no longer needs a dictionary of
    love.[228]

Yet in one of his most deeply felt poems, "Tsuyu no Yofuke ni"
(Late One Night in the Rainy Season, 1939), he wrote of Michelangelo as if about himself. Instead of contrasting East and West,
he described Michelangelo's patriotic activities as if they had peculiar relevance to the decisions he himself faced:

With ten times the effort he poured into the David and the Pietà
He built the fortress at the San Miniato gate south of the city.

The poem concludes:

In Tokyo, at the end of Asia, the summer rains are falling now.
The rain strikes against the late night roofs.
I, as I write this poem that is not a poem,
Groan over the anger, the grief, the strength and the prayers of a
    man who lived four hundred years ago.[229]

Not long after his father's death in 1934 Takamura began to
display a pronounced interest in the war between Japan and
China. Until then he had felt antipathy for anything reminiscent
of his father's uninformed, old-fashioned prejudices, but his own
writings now began to hint at his anti-Western feelings (hitherto
voiced mainly in "unsent letters"). Sometimes they were expressed by support for pan-Asianism, sometimes by an advocacy
of the innate simplicity and decency of the Japanese common
people. He identified himself more and more closely with the
actions of the militarists in the late 1930s. With the declaration of
war against the United States and England, he became the most
articulate of patriotic poets, urging wholehearted support for the
war and devoting his every thought to the emperor. Yoshimoto
Takaaki, who during the war shared Takamura's sentiments, later
wrote, "The war provided him with his first opportunity to free
himself completely from the tragic conflict in his heart that went

back to his student days in America and Europe." [230] Love for the
West disappeared from Takamura's poetry, which emphasized instead the bonds between fellow Asians. He declared that the war
would bring Asians release from the tyranny of European imperialism. In a poem addressed to Chiang Kai-shek he stated:

> My country, Japan, is not destroying yours, sir;
> We're only destroying anti-Japanese thought.
> If you, sir, persist in your anti-Japanism, you will also perish.
> My country, Japan, has now attacked America and England.
> America and England have been rejected by the Heaven and Earth
>   of East Asia.
> Their allies will be crushed.
> Does this bode good or ill for your country, sir?
> Reflect, sir, reflect! [231]

An assertion of racial solidarity with the Chinese, even though
their leader, Chiang Kai-shek, was misguidedly pursuing anti-
Japanese policies, is found in other poems too; but above all Takamura's wartime poetry expressed his identification with the
unquestioning worship of the emperor and the sense of racial
solidarity of the common people. As Japanese military reverses
grew more frequent and more serious, instead of withdrawing
from the arena of letters like many other writers, Takamura demanded greater and greater sacrifices from the Japanese people.
Even after the war ended in defeat, his tone did not at once
change. In a poem written on August 18, 1945, three days after the
surrender, he declared:

> Sanctity must not be violated.
> We Japanese, surrounding that one Man,
> Will form a wall of people manifold in depth.
> If anyone tries to lay a finger on that Sanctity,
> We Japanese, without exception, will lay down side by side,
> And defend Him to our last extremity. [232]

In December 1945 he expressed his hatred for those "who had
caused the Dragon Countenance to become clouded," but he took
comfort from the thought that even in defeat the endurance of the

people would persist, "and the spirit of the race will be solemn in the woodlands." [233] Not until June 1947 did his poetry reflect a change in attitude:

> We were saved from starvation by the Occupation Army,
> And barely enabled to escape with our lives.
> At that time the Emperor himself came forward
> And explained he was not a living god.
> With the passage of time
> The beam has been removed from my eye;
> Before I knew it a heavy weight of sixty years had melted away.[234]

A poem written later that year declared that the "libido for the sacred" he formerly nurtured inside himself had dropped away. He was especially tortured by the fear that his wartime poetry might have inspired men to go to their deaths for a cause that now appeared to have been misguided. This is the subject of the poem "Wa ga Shi wo yomite Hito shi ni tsukeri" (Men, Having Read My Poems, Went to Their Deaths):

> To save myself from the fear of death
> I became desperate about the "desperate times" and wrote.
> My countrymen at the front lines read those poems.
> Men read them and went to their deaths.
> The submarine captain who wrote his family
> That he reread my poems each day soon afterward went down with
>   his ship.[235]

Takamura's studio in Tokyo was destroyed during an air raid, and he went to live in Hanamaki in Iwate Prefecture with Miyazawa Kenji's relatives. When their house was also destroyed he took refuge in a hut in the remote countryside. He remained in this hut from October 1945 until 1952, apparently choosing this solitary life as a means of expiating his wartime guilt. He continued, however, to compose poetry and to sculpt. The poems include some of his most deeply felt works. "Ore no Shi" (My Poems, 1949) [236] sought to define the differences between his poems and those of Europeans; this time he found the fundamental distinctions not in their races but in their outlook on life and even in the food they ate. Perhaps the best of the postwar poems was "Yuki shiroku tsumeri" (The Snow Piled Whitely), written in December 1945. It concludes:

> With the fallen pine-needles I have gathered
> Tonight at my hearth I will warm a bowl of rice gruel.
> The defeated, you know, are peaceful at heart.
> Something like phosphorescence glitters in their souls.
> It is beautiful
> Beautiful, but in the end elusive.[237]

In this and other late poems Takamura used the classical language, as if in repudiation of the colloquial style he had established during the preceding thirty years, perhaps in the hope of achieving absoluteness through fidelity to old traditions.

Takamura's wartime poetry enjoyed great popularity because it seemed to come from the heart of a man of great personal integrity. His doubts about European civilization struck a responsive chord, not only because the nation was engaged in a bitter war with Western peoples, but because many Japanese, especially artists, had like Takamura passed through a period of infatuation with the West, only to end with the discovery that the West was fundamentally alien, and that there was something peculiarly Japanese within themselves. This discovery seems to have driven such admirers of Western literatures like Susukida Kyūkin and Kambara Ariake to silence in middle years; and during the war even the most enthusiastic worshipers of the West suffered a change of heart.

Takamura's poetry seemed fated to lose its popularity when the ideals he believed in were discredited, but the strength and honesty in his writing continued to find new readers. Postwar editions of his poems generally omitted those of a controversial nature, giving prominence to works of a straightforward masculine expression. Above all, his poems about his wife retained their hold on readers; baffled by the complexities of more specifically modern poetry, they preferred poems that seemed to come directly from the heart and were so poignantly expressed. No doubt it is for these poems that Takamura will be remembered.

MIYOSHI TATSUJI (1900–1964)

Miyoshi was certainly one of the two or three finest Japanese poets of the twentieth century. It is tempting to link his work with that of Hagiwara Sakutarō, not only because of its excellence but because Miyoshi frequently, and with unmistakable sincerity, expressed his admiration for the older poet. In an essay written in 1943, not long after Hagiwara's death, he recalled the powerful impressions a reading of Hagiwara's "Short Songs of Pure Feelings" and Murō Saisei's "Kōrai no Hana" (Flowers from Korea, 1924) produced in him about 1925: "For the first time I experienced the sensation of having come into contact with a literary awakening, a poetic revelation. That is why I have long (but secretly) felt something that might be described as 'indebtedness to my teachers.' Later I was fortunate enough to have the opportunity of long and close association in life as well as in literature with Hagiwara Sakutarō especially, and it very often happened that I was enlightened by his influence." [238] He also wrote at this time the long poem *Shi yo, Hagiwara Sakutarō*, which begins:

> Dark mass of melancholy,
> That character of yours I loved, formed of
> Doubt and pessimism, speculation and wanderlust,
> Immortal crystallization of a strange music
> Like still-warm lava,
> Gray shadow that eluded every hand . . . .

Later Miyoshi declared:

> You were truly, in this holy age, a poet without peer on earth,
> The sole supreme poet, irreplaceable, without rival.
> Only you could describe human life as it is, directly, without
>   adulteration;
> You sang at exactly the right pitch, without the professional writer's
>   overcharge.
> You possessed amazing language, amazing technique, amazing
>   wisdom.
> You first plotted on your navigator's chart, with the compass of your
>   poetic language

Our American continent, in exact, precious, vivid, mint-new
   semblances of human life.
You truly were the Columbus of poetry.[239]

Despite this extreme praise, Miyoshi was by no means an imitator of Hagiwara; on the contrary, their dissimilarities are even more striking than their common features. Their contrasting backgrounds may account in part for these differences.

Miyoshi was born in the city of Osaka and received most of his early education there. When he was fifteen he entered a military academy, both because straitened family finances dictated the choice of a free school, and because Miyoshi's father worshiped the army. On graduation from the academy he was sent in 1919 to join a battalion of engineers in northern Korea. He secretly pursued his studies of French and even read some socialist literature. Two years later the precarious state of the family business required him to leave the service. After an unsuccessful attempt to restore the business he resumed his schooling in 1922, with the financial assistance of a relative. He entered the celebrated Third High School in Kyoto. Though older than most of the students, he made valuable friendships, notably with the poet Maruyama Kaoru. The two young men read avidly in modern poetry, especially in the works of Kitahara Hakushū.

In 1925, on graduation from high school, Miyoshi entered the French Literature Department of Tokyo University, and soon was associating with various literary groups. His first published poems appeared in 1926 in the little magazine of one of these groups. They were highly praised at the time by the influential critic Momota Sōji (1893–1955) and still rank among the most popular of all his many works. The earliest poem, "Ubaguruma" (Baby Carriage), exhibits the combination of traditional expression and modern intelligence that characterizes Miyoshi's mature work:

Mother—
Something pale and sad is falling,
Something hydrangea-color is falling.
Beneath the endless row of trees
The wind is coldly blowing.

The dusk is gathering.
Mother, push my baby carriage

Toward the tear-stained evening sun,
Push my creaking baby carriage. . . .[240]

This evocation of the impressions of infancy succeeds because of the flawless choice of words, the sounds reinforcing the meaning. Each line consists of two hemistiches of seven syllables each. The language is classical Japanese, emphasizing the formality of the expression. It would be true in general of Miyoshi's future poems of nostalgia, whatever the period of composition, that he used the classical language; his poems of observation or comment were generally in the modern language. Perhaps by way of reaction against the formlessness of the experimental poems of the 1920s, Miyoshi's poetry from the beginning was severely disciplined and perfectionist. The mood of "Baby Carriage" is established by the plaintive sounds of the second line, *awaku kanashiki mono no furu*, with its repeated doubling of the vowels, impossible to reproduce in translation. The poem describes an infant's perceptions of the coming of autumn, but the atmosphere, rather than the content, gives the poem its distinction. The concluding two lines, as often in Miyoshi's poetry, lift the expression to another dimension:

Haha yo watashi wa shitte iru
Kono michi wa tōku tōku hateshinai michi.

Mother, I know this road
Is a road that goes on and on forever.

It is not clear whether the road is the imagined one of the infant being pushed in his perambulator, or the road of memories the poet travels back into the past, or the road that lies ahead of the poet now; perhaps all three meanings were intended.[241] In any case, the overtones go far beyond the infant's sensual impressions.

"Yuki" (Snow), another early poem, is probably Miyoshi's most popular:

Tarō wo nemurase, Tarō no yane ni yuki furitsumu.
Jirō wo nemurase, Jirō no yane ni yuki furitsumu.[242]

Snow falls and piles on Tarō's roof, sending Tarō to sleep.
Snow falls and piles on Jirō's roof, sending Jirō to sleep.

No translation could match the magic of Miyoshi's language, at once utterly simple and filled with nostalgic evocations. Tarō and Jirō are extremely common boys' names; the poem as a whole suggests that after a day of playing the two tired boys are put to sleep by the slow, regular fall of the snow on the roofs of their houses. Miyoshi seems to have felt nostalgia for a rural world he never knew as a child; unlike Hagiwara, who constantly expressed longing for the city, the city-bred Miyoshi wrote most affectingly about the countryside, and through much of his life he was a traveler, visiting remote parts of Japan.

Miyoshi's studies of French literature at Tokyo University influenced his early writings especially. His graduation thesis, written in French, was a study of Verlaine's *Sagesse*, and his first publication (in 1929) was the translation of Baudelaire's prose-poems *Le spleen de Paris*. During the ten years after his graduation from Tokyo University in 1928 his chief source of income was his translations from the French; it is estimated that he translated twenty thousand pages of manuscript during this time.[243] Of course, much of this was hack work, but the influence of French poetry on his own is undeniable, and his translations of Baudelaire, Jammes, and Mérimée were especially well received.

Miyoshi's first collection of his own poetry, *Sokuryōsen* (The Surveying Ship), appeared in 1930. In later years he recalled that many of the poems were written under the influence of *A Moonlit Gathering*, Horiguchi Daigaku's translations of modern French poetry. The influence of Jules Renard is particularly apparent, and among Japanese poets Murō Saisei (rather than Hagiwara) contributed most to the formation of his style, especially of the lyric poems composed in an archaic vocabulary.[244] These influences from Europe and Japan can easily be detected, but they do not detract from the importance of *The Surveying Ship*, which was Miyoshi's most popular and most often quoted collection.

Many poems in *The Surveying Ship* had previously appeared in poetry magazines. In 1928 Miyoshi joined the group that began to publish *Shi to Shiron* (Poetry and Poetics), the most influential organ of Modernism in Japan at the time. The editor, Haruyama Yukio, labeling the Taishō era as an age without poetics, determined to create a Japanese poetic criticism that would "recover" the purity of poetry, adapting the techniques of French Symbolism and the poetics of the "New Country" school in England.[245] He was attempting, in other words, to free poetry from social, political, and other preconceptions, and to promote a more intellectual approach to the artistic problem of how to compose poetry. Murano Shirō (1901–1975), a distinguished advocate of Modernism in poetry, described the movement associated with *Shi to Shiron* as "the literary renaissance that produced the basic poetical philosophy of modern Japanese poetry." [246] This magazine became the "laboratory" of Japanese poetry of the early 1930s, and attracted contributions from all the best poets. After a few years, however, basic differences in poetic outlook led to a fragmentation of the original group, some poets taking a more active interest in politics, others turning to pure surrealism, still others to lyricism. Each group came to publish its own organ, which reflected the ideas of its central figures.

Miyoshi was a founder of the *Shiki* (Four Seasons) group in 1934. The other members included such important poets as Maruyama Kaoru (1899–1974), Tachihara Michizō (1914–1938), Nakahara Chūya (1907–1937), and Tanaka Fuyuji (1894–1980). The *Shiki* poets advocated a combination of traditional Japanese lyricism with European intellectualism. Their involvement with Japanese tradition often took the form of using the classical language, even when describing contemporary scenes; often too it led to rightist political views that exalted the "Japaneseness" of their poetic expression, although this was true less of the *Shiki* group than of the later *Kogito* (Cogito) and *Nihon Rōman-ha* (Japanese Romanticist) schools.

Miyoshi's poetry reveals everywhere its connections with Japanese poetic traditions, whether the emotional intensity of the tanka or objectivity of the haiku; to these he added the intellectuality of the French poetry he deeply admired. Above all, the perfection of his expression compels admiration. Two poems written about Mount Aso illustrate his different uses of the colloquial and classical languages. The first, "Ō Aso" (Great Aso), appeared in 1937. It begins:

Ame no naka ni, uma ga tatte iru
Nitō santō kouma wo majiete uma no mure ga ame no naka ni tatte
  iru

Ame wa shōshō to futte iru
Uma wa kusa wo tabete iru.[247]

The horses are standing in the rain,
Two or three horses and some colts, standing in the rain.
A bleak and dreary rain is falling.
The horses are eating the grass.

This English translation, as close to a literal version as possible, does not remotely suggest either the rhythm of the original (each line ends with the present progressive *-te iru*) or the relation in sound between *ame* (rain) and *uma* (horse), repeated in parallel constructions. The whole of this long poem, related in the colloquial, evokes the solitude of the vast landscape of grassy hillsides leading up to the great volcano and the silence of the cluster of horses soaked in the steady, gloomy rain, pasturing in the fields. The poem concludes:

Gusshori to ame ni nurete, itsu made mo hitotsutokoro ni karera wa
shizuka ni atsumatte iru
Moshi mo hyakunen ga, kono isshun no aida ni tatta to shite mo, nan
no fushigi mo nai darō
Ame ga futte iru ame ga futte iru
Ame wa shōshō to futte iru

Soaking wet in the rain, they stay quietly clustered in the same
   place.
It would not be surprising even if a hundred years had elapsed in
   this single instant.
The rain is falling. The rain is falling.
A bleak and dreary rain is falling.

The timelessness of the scene, emphasized by the repeated use of the progressive tense, is the real subject of the poem; it was in this objective mood that Miyoshi tended to use the colloquial. The shadings of his Japanese expression are exceedingly fine; probably it would be impossible in any other language to convey the distinction between *ame ga futte iru* and *ame wa futte iru*, yet this is very much a part of Miyoshi's "Japanism."

The second poem on Mount Aso, "Kusa Senri Hama" (A Thousand Leagues of Grass), was first published in 1936. The title refers to the stretch of grassland where Miyoshi observed the horses grazing in the previous poem. It opens:

Ware katsute kono kuni wo tabi seshi koto ari
Akegata no kono yama ue ni ware katsute tachishi koto ari

I have traveled in this country before.
I have stood before atop this mountain at daybreak.

Not only is the mood much more subjective, but the contours of the poem are quite different: the mood evoked is not one of time-lessness but of time remembered, of the changes in the poet even as he gazes on an unchanging landscape. The use of the classical language, generally divided into units of five plus seven syllables, associates the poet not only with his own past but with the past in Japanese poetry. The poem continues:

In the fields skirting the Great Aso Mountain,
In the land of Hi, the green grass flourishes;
At the crest smoke drifts and blends; the mountain
Looks no different from that long ago day.
The outer ring of mountains, forming a circle,
Today too
Is hazed over by the indigo of memories.
How unreal a landscape this is!
And yet
My hopes of youthful days
And the months and days of twenty years and my friends—
Where have they all gone, leaving me behind?
The women I loved long ago?
This cloudy day in late spring
I alone, bent with age,
Have come here again, a long journey.
Leaning on my stick, I survey the scene round me:
The Great Aso Mountain in the land of Hi,
The upland pastures where colts frisk,
The Thousand Leagues of Grass of doleful name.[248]

Miyoshi was only thirty-six when he wrote this poem, surely not old enough to speak of himself as being bent; but he was following the traditions not only of Japan but of China, where Tu Fu, about the same age, spoke figuratively but with essential sincerity of his sparse white hair. The poem is deeply moving, and the diction imparts its own timelessness.

Miyoshi's relationship to the Asian past is even more evident in the poetry written during his visit to Korea in 1940. "Fuyu no Hi" (Winter Day) describes the Pulguksa (Bukkoku-ji) monastery in Kyongju. This long poem begins:

> Ah, wisdom comes, quite unexpectedly,
> On such a calm winter day:
> Here, where no one is to be seen,
> In a mountain forest,
> For example, in the garden of just such a monastery,
> Without warning, it comes before you;
> At such times, have faith in the words it whispers:
> "Untroubled eyes, a heart at peace—what other treasures are there
> in the world?" [249]

Another poem written during the same journey, "Keirin Kōshō" (A Song of Silla), was inspired by a visit to the Silla royal tombs. One section contrasts their present aspect with how they must have looked in the past:

> Outside, in the sunlight, the stone lions crouch in the earth;
> The stone men bend their bodies as in salutation.
>
> Ah, when will those who have gone return here again?
> Kings, queens and commoners, crossroads and stately houses?
>
> Mottled clouds fly over the forest crests—the phantoms
> Of singing girls who danced here once, heads covered with silks
> lighter than dreams? [250]

It was an anachronism as far as the Modernist poets were concerned for Miyoshi to write a poem on such a theme, using the classical language in alternating phrases of five and seven syllables, but Miyoshi, from early in his career, had feared for the future of Japanese poetry if traditions were totally discarded in the name of poetic freedom.[251] He was dissatisfied also with the expressive capability of the modern Japanese language, and when writing in this elegiac mood he chose to employ the richer expression made possible by the overtones of the classical vocabulary. Miyoshi was proud to think his poems were anachronistic.[252]

The brilliance of Miyoshi's poetry both before and after the war years has induced commentators to draw a veil over what they consider his unfortunate activities during the war years 1941–1945. Even the names of his wartime collections are usually omitted from otherwise detailed chronologies, and the poems are not quoted. His commitment to the war, whether it took the form of elation over the capture of Singapore or snarls of anger at the approach of enemy forces to the Japanese island, was total. This attitude may have originated in his early background as an officer-candidate in the Japanese army, but it was reinforced by his devotion to the Japanese language. His wartime "Japanism" was quite dissimilar to Takamura Kōtarō's; his love for Japan was absolute and did not imply a rejection of the West for personal or other grievances. Unlike Takamura, he did not recant after the defeat.

Miyoshi continued to deepen his art in the years after the war. His immediate postwar composition has the elegiac tones of Tu Fu; indeed, "Yokobue" (The Flute, 1945) even quoted the famous line by Tu Fu: "The country has fallen but its rivers and mountains remain." This long poem in classical Japanese is filled with a marvelously somber and beautiful music as it evokes the sounds of the now silent flute of a soldier who went to the South Pacific and did not return.[253] His collection *Suna no Toride* (Sand Castle, 1946) consists mainly of poems in the colloquial, some descriptive of the hardships the Japanese had borne during the war, others, like "Namida wo nugutte hatarakō" (Let Us Wipe Away Our Tears and Get to Work), encouraging others (and himself no doubt) to take hope:

> The eye of the typhoon of the worst fate has passed;
> The time of the worst fever has passed and gone.[254]

Some poems are almost unbearably intense, like "Kōri no Kisetsu" (The Season of Ice):

> Now is the painful time.
> Now is the most painful time.
> After a long and bitter war

Our soldiers on every front are defeated.
Our houses are burnt,
Our ships are sunk,
Our forests and fields ravaged:
We enter an age of poverty. . . .
Seventy millions of us,
And each one
Bears a heavy burden of grief too great for any man's strength.
The burden breaks our flesh;
And on our weary shoulders
The burden crushes our bones.
Now is the painful time. . . .[255]

The poem concludes with an appeal to have humble faith in the future:

With the courage of those who believe in tomorrow
—With courage,
With the most tragic and gravest courage endurable,
We shall go forward.

In this time of hardship Miyoshi became truly a "poet of the people," expressing in the purest Japanese the feelings of the entire nation.[256] Miyoshi's personal emotions, as before, tended to be voiced in the classical language, as in the moving "Yuki wa furu" (It Is Snowing), which suggests a farewell to the world, or even a deathbed verse.[257] The long poem "Sand Castle" describes his art, as he now conceived it:

My poems are a castle of sand
The sea comes
And with one soft blow crumbles it away.

Unchastened, I build it again,
I erect the walls,
My poems are a castle of sand.

I build it facing the infinite sea
This castle is easily broken,
Fragile by its very nature.

Under the blue sky,
In burning sunlight,
My castle stands solitary.

No reinforcements are needed:
This castle of sand is
Isolated, unaided. . . .[258]

The tone is light, almost self-mocking, but Miyoshi is affirming his intention of persisting in his art, fragile through it is.

The poems of Miyoshi's last period, though not among his most popular works, reveal his maturest skill. There is humor in some, though often mingled with bitterness. "Kōjin yo kutsu idase" (Passerby, Put Out Your Shoes!, 1948) describes the streets of postwar Tokyo, where shoeshine boys call to passers, urging them to have their shoes dusted, waxed, and polished. Despite the presence of American army jeeps and the black market, however, the atmosphere in Miyoshi's poem is not one of despair. Kawakami Tetsutarō, for many years a close friend of Miyoshi's, wrote:

> He describes here spring scenes in Tokyo after the defeat, evoking memories that are still fresh. The tone of the poem is elevated, as if by way of reaction to the subject matter. Focusing his attention on sidewalk shoeshine boys, a sight unknown before the war, he places them in a setting of burned-out ruins, composing his picture with his inborn skill. But the principal figure is in fact the poet himself, leaning on a stick at the crossroad. His attitude seems to be dejected, in keeping with the landscape of ruins, but this may be no more than pretense; he is, in fact, by no means a broken man. Proudly, unruffled, his eyes contemplate the scene, taking in every feature of the burned-out landscape that stretches beyond the horizon.[259]

Miyoshi's finest postwar work was in the collection *Momotabi no nochi* (After a Hundred Times). It appeared in 1962 as part of a complete edition of his works, and consisted of seventy-two poems written during the preceding decade. The poems have a depth and maturity comparable to that of other great artists at the close of their careers. The inherent loneliness of the artist is compounded by the loneliness of the aging man parted by death from his closest friends. "Zanka" (Remaining Fruit, 1955) refers to the Japanese custom of leaving one persimmon on the tree after the others have been picked to "guard" it:

> Its friends have all left the treetop;
> They've been carried to the market and sold.
>
> The one remaining survivor
> Is what they call the tree-guardian.
>
> Against the deep blue of the sky
> Its crimson form is radiant.
>
> On the withered persimmon tree with arms akimbo,
> It paints the pupil in a scrawny dragon's eyes.
>
> The tree guardian
> Is guarding the tree.
>
> Crows and woodpeckers,
> Respecting it, leave this fruit uneaten.
>
> Is it waiting for the sleet, for the snow to fall,
> For the day when at last it will die?
>
> Or is it perhaps
> Flaunting its present beauty in the cold wind? [260]

Mention of the "pupil in a scrawny dragon's eye" refers to old Chinese stories of painters who refrained from giving a final stroke of the brush to the eyes of the dragons they painted lest they leap from the wall; here the painting in of the final dot suggests a career at its completion, as well as the single brilliant touch of the last persimmon against the gaunt, bare branches. The poem is in the classical language, the lines divided in traditional fashion into units of five plus seven syllables:

> *tomora mina/ kozue wo sha shite*
> *ichi ni hakobare/ urareshi ga*

The music of the old language, joined to the specifically modern intelligence of the poet, represents Miyoshi's poetic achievement at its finest. The title poem of the collection, "After a Hundred Times" (1960), is an abbreviated form of the expression "after a hundred-fold vain regrets," often used by Hagiwara Sakutarō in his last collection, *The Iceland,* to suggest the suffering endured before the poet can arrive at his distinctive realm of poetry. It has been suggested that Miyoshi used this phrase to indicate also that he had finally attained his own domain after years of feeling he was under Hagiwara's influence.[261] The poem itself recalls with poignance his solitary visit to Pulguksa in Korea twenty years before. He still remembers the stone steps, the footfalls like falling leaves, the birds, the blue of the sky, the squirrels, the brilliance of the painted rafters, the loose tiles on the roof. The last line is:

> After a hundred times, brightly, again I recall, the clarity of that morning.[262]

The unnatural word order in this poem suggests a Japanese translation from the Chinese. Miyoshi had in fact been studying Chinese poetry, and in 1952 he and Yoshikawa Kōjirō (1904–1980), a distinguished scholar of Chinese literature, had published the volume *Shin Tōshi Sen* (New Selection of T'ang Poetry). These translations enjoyed remarkable success, especially in view of the general lack of interest in classical Chinese poetry at this time. *After a Hundred Times* is a tribute to the great continental culture to which the Japanese too were heirs.

Miyoshi's last major poem, "Ushijima Kotō no Uta" (Song on the Ancient Wisteria of Ushijima), describes magnificent clusters of wisteria, said to be a thousand years old, in language that evokes specifically Japanese traditions. The final verse is typical:

> *Mētoru mari no hana no take*
> *Nioi kagayou osoki hi no*
> *Tsumorite tōki mukashi sae*
> *Nani wo Ushijima chitose fuji*
> * Hannari, hannari.*[263]

> The length of the clusters, more than a meter,
> Sparkles with brightness these slow spring days
> Piling up, taking me far away, but what is there

To regret even in the past, the thousand years of the wisteria of
Ushijima?
Bewitching, bewitching.

The language of this stanza is complex. Miyoshi deliberately used
the ugly modern word *mētoru* (meter), following it with the archa-
ism *mari* (for *amari*, "more than"). Most surprising is the use of a
kakekotoba on the word *ushi*: *nani wo ushi* (what is sad?) is followed by the place-name Ushijima, a rare twentieth-century example of this old-fashioned device of Japanese poetry. The stanza
also contains an overt reference to Buson's

osoki hi no	Slow spring days
tsumorite tōki	Piling up, take me far away
mukashi ka na	Into the past.

This reference to the past seems completely natural in the context
of the poem, which, even in its descriptions of the appearance of
the famous wisteria, suggests the larger theme of the consolation
of beauty. The refrain, *hannari hannari*, is an expression in the
Kyoto dialect meaning something like "it is charming" or "it is
bright." Miyoshi reverted to this dialect he had spoken as a youth,
giving an indefinable charm to the poem. Kawakami Tetsutarō
said of the refrain that it was like "a brilliant red robe worn by a
gagaku performer." [264]

It is customary to speak of a "return to the past" (*kaiki*) on
the part of Japanese writers who have reached middle age. This
element is definitely present in Miyoshi's last poems, but his was
hardly a voice from the past; he was a modern poet who expressed himself in modern terms but profited also by his heritage
from the past. His short lyrics have been praised by some critics as
his finest works. It is hard to accept any judgment that belittles the
achievement of his major poems, but this praise at least suggests
his success with forms closely related to Japanese tradition. Miyoshi was not only a supremely gifted Japanese poet, but a world
poet. When read in the original his poetry is perhaps the most
appealing of any written in Japanese during the twentieth century.

NISHIWAKI JUNZABURŌ (1894–1982)

Nishiwaki has been acclaimed as the founder and teacher of a modern Japanese poetry that is part of the modern poetry of the world. A typical evaluation by an admirer states: "Nishiwaki Junzaburō played a decisive role in the fate of the Japanese modern poem. Together with Rilke, Valéry, and Eliot, he is one of four great poets who represent the twentieth century." [265] He has probably exercised the greatest influence of any Japanese poet on the post-1945 generation. Some critics have claimed that Japanese poetry died at the end of the Taishō era in 1926, but many more believe that a great resurgence in Japanese poetry occurred at precisely that time, and that the central figure in the new poetry was Nishiwaki.[266]

Nishiwaki was born in the town of Ojiya in Niigata Prefecture, where his father was a bank president. He displayed a precocious interest in English language and literature while still a middle-school student, even composing some poems in English at the time.[267] He was also talented at drawing, and at one stage in his career went to Tokyo intending to become a professional artist; however, the decadent style of life expected of young artists in those days repelled him, and he gave up his plan. In 1912 he entered Keiō University in the Department of Economics, but spent most of his time reading literature and philology. He presented his graduation thesis in 1917; it was on economics considered as a form of sociology, and was written in Latin.

In 1922 Keiō University sent him as a research student to Oxford University, where he studied Old and Middle English. He associated with various young novelists and poets, and published his first poems in English periodicals. In 1925 a volume of his poetry in English, called *Spectrum*, appeared. It was well received, but it is an undistinguished collection of Georgian verse. He also wrote some poetry in French at this time. The chief significance of his stay in Europe was that his association on terms of equality with European literary figures of his own age made him "the only poet in Japan without a colonial complex toward European literature and artists." [268]

Nishiwaki returned to Japan late in 1925. The next year he was appointed to a professorship at Keiō University, and soon afterward began contributing poetry and criticism to *Mita Bun-*

gaku, the literary periodical of that university. He formed a literary salon where he exercised a strong influence as the most authoritative commentator on European Modernism. In particular, he used the journal *Shi to Shiron* as a platform for his views, especially his advocacy of Surrealism, the movement with which his name is associated.

Nishiwaki had written his early poetry in English or French because he felt it was impossible to express himself adequately in the Japanese language. In later years he recalled an experience of 1920:

> In that year I read *Howling at the Moon*, the collection of poetry by Hagiwara Sakutarō, and I felt for the first time an impulse to compose poetry in Japanese. Until then my resistance to Japanese style—to the elegant classical style—had kept me from composing poetry in Japanese. I had written poems almost exclusively in English or French, but as the result of the complete sympathy I felt with the colloquial, free verse in *Howling at the Moon*, I resolved henceforth to write in Japanese.[269]

Nishiwaki's first collection of poems in Japanese (1933) appeared under the unfamiliar Latin name *Ambarvalia*, the designation of the pagan crop processions held in the spring. Classical European influences are certainly present, but they are less prominent than that of Hagiwara, with respect to Nishiwaki's poetic language, or of Keats in the imagery. Nishiwaki also acknowledged the influence of Nietzsche.[270] "Tenki" (Fine Weather), the first poem in the section of *Ambarvalia* entitled "Greek Lyric Poems," suggests both his indebtedness and his personal vision:

> *(Kutsugaesareta hōseki) no yō na asa*
> *Nampito ka toguchi ni te dare ka to sasayaku*
> *Sore wa kami no seitan no hi*

The translation poses various problems, but this is a possible version:

> A morning like "an upturn'd gem"
> People are whispering with someone by a door
> It is the day of the god's nativity.

The quoted phrase in the first line is from *Endymion*; stained glass windows in a Gothic cathedral apparently called to the poet's mind the colors refracted in Keats's "upturn'd gem." The inclusion of this poem among the "Greek Lyrics" suggests that the word *kami* in the third line refers to one or more Greek gods, but Nishiwaki, in response to an interviewer's question, stated that the scene was observed through a church window; in that case, the occasion would be Christmas. Nishiwaki's own note indicates that the second line refers not to people talking by the church door, but to a scene in front of an ordinary house on the street outside as observed through the stained-glass window. Nishiwaki remembered having seen such an illustration to a medieval story. But here, as in many poems, Nishiwaki was not trying to make up a puzzle that had to be solved by the ingenious reader; the images he presented were intended to stir the reader into creating a new and individual interpretation of the materials.

Nishiwaki's first important publication after his return to Japan was the article "Profanus" in the April 1926 issue of *Mita Bungaku*. In it he declared that Surrealist poetry, far from being a recent novelty, was typical of the great poets of the past. He cited especially Francis Bacon as a notable predecessor, and claimed that the views on poetry presented in *The Advancement of Learning* were completely realized only by the Surrealist and Dada poets. Although he insisted that the views set forth in his essay were not merely a restatement of the theories of Surrealism of Yvon Goll or André Breton, Nishiwaki followed quite closely Breton's famous manifestos; at one point he even stated as his own opinion Breton's "C'est du rapprochement en quelque sorte fortuit des deux termes qu'a jailli une lumière particulière, lumière de l'image. . . ." [271] Nishiwaki went on:

> The Surrealism of Breton destroyed the cause and effect relationship between image and association. It did not merely evoke an obscure awareness, but attempted to raise the electric potential between the images included in the world of awareness and to produce a beautiful radiation of sparks. In short, the point of Surrealist poetry is to create a vast awareness of everything in our minds that cannot be reduced to definite cognition. Surrealist poetry constructs a world of chaotic consciousness, which consciousness itself could

never construct. This last statement is not borrowed from the French Surrealists. It is entirely my own opinion.[272]

Nishiwaki's poetry is often puzzling on first reading, and sometimes its meaning eludes to the end even the most determined annotators. This is not surprising in a poet who professed allegiance to such Surrealist principles as "automatic writing"; indeed, it is more surprising that so much of his poetry is not only easily intelligible but sensually pleasing. It is quite possible to read his poems, especially those of the later collections, without reference to any body of poetic doctrines. The surface beauty is so appealing that at times the reader may not trouble to unravel any ambiguities in the text. This is true of the early poem "Ame" (Rain):

> The south wind has brought soft goddesses.
> They have wet the bronze, wet the fountain,
> Wet the swallows' wings, wet the golden feathers,
> Wet the tidewater, wet the sand, wet the fishes,
> Gently wet the temples, baths and theaters;
> This procession of gentle, soft goddesses
> Has wet my tongue.[273]

Obviously there is humor in the statements that rain has wet tidewater, fishes, and other objects that are wet from the start, and the poetic conceit of imagining the raindrops are "goddesses" brought by the wind is also faintly comic. The scene of the poem is Mediterranean, possible Rome, as suggested by the mention of bronze statues, fountains, temples, baths, and theaters. Perhaps there is an oblique reference to the Ambarvalia processions in honor of Ceres, the goddess of agriculture, in the words "this procession of gentle, soft goddesses." But even without such elucidations the poem is immediately attractive.

Another early poem, also from *Ambarvalia*, composed of seemingly disconnected fragments, evokes the emotions of a traveler, probably the poet himself. It is called "Tabibito" (Traveler):

> You, irascible traveler!
> Your excrement has flowed into the Hibernian sea,
> You have defiled the North Sea Atlantis the Mediterranean.

May you return to your village
And bless the cliffs of your old home!
That naked soil is your daybreak.
Akebia fruits, like your soul,
Have been dangling all summer.[274]

Instead of explaining or describing the traveler's longing for home, Nishiwaki names the foreign seas he has defiled and suggests the restoration of his senses that his native soil will bring. The akebia fruits growing along the cliffs at home have dangled in the wind like his soul, all but forgotten and waiting for someone to discover them. In later years Nishiwaki wrote about this poem:

> The world of poetry is a world of faint awareness, I believe. If this were not the case, awareness would transcend the world of poetry. The world of poetry is a harmony of reality and dream. Humor and pathos must be faintly admixed to create a single, rare entity. . . . I should like to seek in poetry a faint humor and a faint pathos. That is the kind of poetry I like. Last November, in the mountains by the coast I tried sucking dockmackie (*gamazumi*) fruits with my children. They tasted like pomegranates, and stirred in me a faint pathos. I felt a faint pathos also in the red earth and the mossy boulders, the voice of a song thrush, the crooked saké bottle. Such things become poems for me in the same manner as poems made of words.[275]

Nishiwaki continued his researches in English literature through the 1930s, publishing a study of Langland in 1935 and a massive volume on modern English literature in the following year. The next entry in the chronology of his work is for 1947. This long gap has not been satisfactorily explained; no doubt to many readers it must have seemed that Nishiwaki, like other Japanese poets of the twentieth century, had exhausted himself creatively while still in his thirties.

Anyone who had prophesied that Nishiwaki's career as a poet had ended would, however, have been gravely mistaken. Full recognition came only after the end of the war when he suddenly produced a rapid succession of collections of poetry, and when a new generation of poets discovered in his works the inspiration they needed as specifically modern poets. This was especially true of the *Arechi* (Wasteland) group of poets, who derived their name both from Eliot's poem and from the bleak postwar surroundings. The impressive revival of modern poetry after the war was linked by critics directly to the republication of *Ambarvalia* in 1947.[276] This collection, which had seemed quite dead, proved to be a phoenix that guided the new men, a triumphant proof of the capability of modern Japanese to serve as a poetic language.

Nishiwaki's first new collection was *Tabibito Kaerazu* (The Traveler Does Not Return, 1947). He first began planning this collection toward the end of 1944, while evacuated to his native town in Niigata Prefecture. At this time, cut off from other poets, he read extensively in classical Japanese literature and resumed his old interest in ink drawings. Numerous commentators have noted the "oriental" cast of countenance to these poems, and some have deplored the "retrogression." However, Shinoda Hajime questioned the "Japaneseness" of Nishiwaki's later poetry; he believed that it was more accurate to say that this poetry was "a stage in the quest of the 'sensory thought' he had pursued ever since his debut as a poet." It is almost too easy when writing of a Japanese poet to note with satisfaction that, after his rebellious youth and infatuation with the West, he rediscovered in middle age the values of traditional Japan that he had hitherto overlooked. Undoubtedly Nishiwaki's long, unbroken residence in Japan after his return from Europe in 1925 made his choice of scenes for his poems more Japanese than they were in *Ambarvalia*, which consisted of poems written shortly after leaving Europe. But there is little to suggest the tanka or haiku in these poems; the "oriental" philosophical values noted by some commentators are personal, rather than traditional.

Miyoshi Tatsuji said of the collection, "In *The Traveler Does Not Return* the inscrutability of the poetic language, which had marked his previous poems, has all but disappeared, and the Surrealistic conceptions survive only vestigially."[277] Certainly there is less need for exegesis, and some of the poems are transparently clear:

> The rains of an autumn night
> Collect in the mortars of stepping stones;
> They smell of chrysanthemums,
> A far-off smell of long ago.[278]

Or, on a more complicated level of expression:

> From travel to return to travel,
> From earth to return to earth.
> If I break this jar
> It turns to eternal shards.
> Travel flows away:
> If I put out my hand and try to scoop it up,
> It turns to foam and dreams.
> Into this bamboo hat moistened by dreams
> The autumn day leaks.[279]

The prevalent themes in the collection deal with travel and eternity, as the opening poem announces:

> Wait, traveler!
> Before you moisten your tongue
> In this insignificant stream,
> Consider! traveler of life,
> You too are only a water-spirit
> Oozed from the rocks.
> Even this thinking water will not flow forever;
> At some moment in eternity it will dry up.
> What a racket the jays make with their singing!
> Sometimes from this water
> A phantom man emerges, flowers held over his head.
> "To seek eternal life is a dream.
> To discard your thoughts in the murmuring brook
> Of life flowing away, and finally to seek
> To fall from the precipice of immutability
> And vanish—that is reality."
> So says the phantom water-sprite
> Who comes to village and town from the water to play
> When waterweeds are growing in the reflected clouds.[280]

The meaning of this poem is unclear, but not because seemingly unrelated images have been brought together in Surrealist fashion; the ambiguity stems from Nishiwaki's use of a private image, the "phantom man." In the preface to the collection he explained, after describing the "modern man" and "primitive man" coexisting within him:

> But there is yet another man lurking in me. Does he belong to the mystery of life or to the mystery of cosmic eternity? He is inexplicable, not to be resolved through normal intelligence or emotions.
>
> I call him my "phantom man," and I think of him as the eternal traveler.
>
> This "phantom man" comes to me at certain moments only to disappear. He is probably a recollection, miraculously preserved, of mankind before primitive man, a memory of human beings closer than ourselves to the world of eternity. . . .
>
> I imagine this "phantom man" lurking in me is what makes me experience something like infinite recollections when I see fruit growing on a bush by the side of the road.[281]

Even with this explanation the meaning of "phantom man" is not obvious. Murano Shirō explained the term as corresponding to the "gods of the road" that stir Bashō to leave on his *Narrow Road of Oku* journey. He added, "Nishiwaki in his poetry is constantly restless, moving from one place to another, from one time to another." [282] Murano said about another poem in *The Traveler Does Not Return*, which also mentions "eternity" (*eigō*) and the "phantom man" (*gen'ei no hito*):

> For Nishiwaki God is the conception of eternity, but the existence of God is first revealed in the desolate world of cognition stirred by the pursuit of a "phantom man" through a forest of bushes drooping with fruit; to meditate on this phenomenon is to touch the secret of human existence, and is the sole way of approaching God. Nishiwaki's God, it goes without saying, is not the God of religion, but an ontological concept.[283]

Such philosophical reasoning would certainly have been out of place in the discussion of earlier modern Japanese poets, but Nishiwaki is a scholar-poet whose critical writings are complex and sometimes obscure especially if the reader is not familiar with his vocabulary. His poetry is erudite, full of references that the average reader could not be expected to understand. His admiration for T. S. Eliot may have inspired some of this richness of allusion, but this is a characteristic not only of Eliot but of much poetry of a specifically modern nature. Unless readers are familiar with all of Nishiwaki's references they cannot be said to understand a poem fully, but most readers—as might also be said of Eliot's readers—are satisfied with less than complete comprehension. Perhaps even Nishiwaki himself could not define everything that is conveyed by a poem like the following one from *The Traveler Does Not Return*:

Akanomamma no saite	I lost my way on a muddy road
iru	Where red knotweed was
Doro michi ni fumimayou	blooming:
Atarashii shinkyoku no	The start of a new Divine
hajime [284]	Comedy.

The brevity of the poem and the juxtaposition of two seemingly unrelated statements suggest a haiku, but the third line is an intellectual concept foreign to the world of haiku. The speaker, like Dante, is lost *nel mezzo del cammin di nostra vita*. He wanders onto a road, real or imagined, where he feels a helpless frustration at being bogged down in mud, even as weeds bloom insolently around him. At that moment perhaps he envisages a descent into the inferno, a private inferno with its particular torments; or it may be that he sees beyond the inferno immediately before his eyes to the creation of the poem that was the fruit of Dante's journey. No single meaning is intended. It is enough if the reader senses the anguish in the poet's heart.

Nishiwaki's mention of the red flowers may suggest the sensitivity of the Japanese poet to nature, despite the intellectual character of his thought, but his attitude toward nature was quite unlike that of the *Shiki* poets, whose sensitivity toward the traditionally admired flowers, birds, and the like fell into familiar patterns. The poet Ayukawa Nobuo stated: "Nishiwaki's nature is a nature discovered by destroying the order of the traditional sensitivity. He may be said in this respect to have discovered a new nature for modern poets. We find in Nishiwaki's world an instant of joy at the discovery of something fresh and quite different, even in the same sights of nature, because it has been freed from the spell of the old sensitivity." [285]

In Nishiwaki's poetry the familiar elements of traditional

Japanese poetry—not only the sights of nature but the awareness of the transience of the world and similar Buddhist concepts—acquired new meaning because of his fundamentally un-Japanese approach to the Japanese language itself. One critic put it: "Nishiwaki looked at the faculties of the Japanese language from the viewpoint of the European languages, rather than from within the tradition of the Japanese language itself; this enabled him to discover and open up an entirely new dimension in Japanese." [286]

Nishiwaki has sometimes been called the "Eliot of Japan." Certainly there are elements in common between the two poets, such as the use of allusion and parody; but their differences are apparent from their attitudes toward tradition. Eliot stood on a foundation of Western European culture, and drew his references from what he considered to be the body of culture common to cultivated men in a half-dozen countries; but Nishiwaki's references are mainly to sources outside his own tradition. The distant past to which he refers is not that of his ancestors, the dancers gone under the hill of Eliot's poem, but "phantom men" of no country and no ascertainable time. He refers on occasion to Japanese poets and poetry, not to establish his spiritual descent so much as to demonstrate that Japanese poets, as sensitive human beings, shared certain basic, underlying beliefs with the great poets of other countries. In an article written in 1961 called "Surrealism and Myself," he described his early readings in Baudelaire, Poe, Rimbaud, and Eliot. He wrote:

> I came ultimately to the conviction that the lifeblood of poetry was what from long ago has been called "unanticipated juxtaposition," or what Baudelaire referred to as *surnaturalisme* or *ironie*. In short, the important elements in a poem are supernatural and surrealistic; the Surrealism of Goll and Breton was only one manifestation of this spirit. My views of Surrealism were not specifically derived from either Goll or Breton. I merely attempted to explain the general principles of modern poetry. The great Japanese poet Bashō was also a pioneer of Surrealism.[287]

Nishiwaki describes Bashō as a pioneer, and no doubt he knew Bashō's works well, but he does not suggest any particular connection between himself and Bashō that is more intimate than his relationship with Baudelaire. He sees the same "phantom man" operating within Bashō, Baudelaire, and himself.

This approach to the past resulted in a different poetic stance from Eliot's. Eliot is intellectual, responding to and continuing tradition; but Nishiwaki is prevailingly lyrical, responding to the subconscious memory of "phantom men" close to the world of eternity.[288]

Nishiwaki's poetry has sometimes been attacked for its aloofness from the problems afflicting the world. His tacit refusal to write poetry during the period of Japanese militarism of the 1930s and 1940s is grudgingly admired by his critics, but they find his withdrawal into silence no substitute for genuine resistance:

> The hellish advance of nationalism did not in the least intrude into the kingdom of uncertain nationality that was Nishiwaki's world of poetry. When the insane reality had mounted to such a degree that he could no longer protect his kingdom, he gave up overt acts in the form of poetry, and chose instead the blank of silence. But we cannot call this "poetic resistance." It was no more than an expression of the concentrated crisis in Japanese poetry, as symbolized in Nishiwaki's poems.[289]

Nishiwaki's insistence on the "purity" of poetry, on the undesirability of making poetry serve any purpose other than its own, drew the fire of committed critics as early as 1930. He was denounced for harboring the escapist feelings of a man who has lost the courage to face reality, feelings he masked by his assertion that the poet must destroy humdrum reality before he can create new and fresh poetic insights.[290] But Nishiwaki's long silence, broken only after the war ended, was more than escapism, and his decision to write poetry again involved more than a mere profiting by the favorable atmosphere for new poetry. The activities of the militarists dismayed him, but he was also dismayed when, in the bleak days after the end of the war, the Japanese attempted to forget Japan. Nishiwaki is said to have described his efforts in *The Traveler Does Not Return* as "gathering the fallen ears" left after the holocaust, and as "writing with a brush on the sooty shade of a lantern in a country inn" poems suited to a typically Japanese atmosphere. The poet Kitagawa Fuyuhiko said these poems were the product of "the mental state of Nishiwaki Junzaburō, a Japanese who, as the result of defeat in the war, no longer was in a mood (and no longer had the leeway) to be an avant-garde artist." [291]

The best of Nishiwaki's postwar collections is probably *Kindai no Gūwa* (1953), to which he himself gave the English title *Modern Fable Poems*. The title poem was originally called "April Fables," and the first line was "April fables are truly sad," an obvious reference to the opening line of *The Waste Land*.[292] The collection as a whole, as Nishiwaki's preface stated, consisted of poems "written from time to time, from a single poetic viewpoint, with the object of comforting people."

The poems in the collection are marked by a stronger note of loneliness than before, but also by an irony and even a humor that gives them a uniquely bittersweet atmosphere. "Ichigatsu" (January) is especially moving:

> The season of priests is upon us.
> Who was that priest
> Who first discovered the scent of the narcissus?
> When it comes to beauty, a naked tree
> Has it over a naked goddess.
> This is the season of crystals forming in the black earth, of roots.
> A man sticks out his hand from a yellow clump of bamboos
> And snaps the jewels of fruit from the vines.
> An oak, like a broken harp,
> Lets droop a single strand of green hair.
> No bees or women to sing the tune of lonely spring.
> That man is still among the thorn bushes,
> Squatting and thinking.[293]

Murano Shirō gave this interpretation of the poem: the mention of Buddhist priests (*bōzu*) in the first line can be taken as a symbol of dignity and control of the passions, but probably it is an abstract and somewhat comic way of expressing the "nothingness" of midwinter. The priest in the second line, on the other hand, is a member of humanity, rather than an abstraction; he has sniffed out the first faint fragrance of the narcissus to comfort himself in the bleakness of winter. The winter is depicted in terms of bare branches, of frost and ice, of roots in the earth. It is not the season of woman, preserver of the seed; and even the man stretching out his hand to pick a last fruit is a lonely, small figure.[294]

"January" shows the traditional Japanese sensitivity to the seasons, but it is expressed in language that owes little to Japanese tradition, and the whole scene has been filtered through a Western sensibility. Other poems in the collection, though varied in subject and mood, confirm the general impression given by "January." The expression is indirect and sometimes even obscure, but the beauty of the imagery can be intuitively felt, and the mood of each poem is securely established. The effects achieved may suggest those of traditional Japanese poetry in the economy of means and the skillful juxtaposition of imagery, but Nishiwaki's poetic past is European rather than Japanese. Nevertheless, the language he uses is Japanese, the landscapes before his eyes or in his mind are Japanese, and he has found in such poetic features as an intense feeling for the seasons a congruence between his European tastes and Japanese tradition. He is an international poet who has exercised a profound influence on the poetry of one nation.

POETRY IN THE 1930s

The period 1928 to 1941 forms a distinct unit in the history of modern Japanese poetry. It opened with the founding of *Shi to Shiron*, the leading journal of Modernism, and closed with the outbreak of the Pacific War. The period was by no means uniform in its poetical or political coloring: during the early years Modernism in poetic techniques and Marxism in political principles won many adherents among the poets, but by 1941 the government, by censorship or threat of imprisonment, had silenced almost all opposition to the approved ideology. Such unity as the period possessed was provided by the poets and the successive groups they formed.

The poets of the Taishō period for the most part worked independently; certainly their names are not automatically associated with a single group or magazine. But in the late 1920s the familiar Japanese phenomenon of forming groups, whether or not they stood for clearly recognizable principles, asserted itself. In place of such solitary figures as Hagiwara Sakutarō or Miyazawa

Kenji, there were groups of "like-minded men" (*dōnin*). Membership in one group by no means precluded joining one or more others, and sometimes friendships or temporary expedients induced men to associate with poets with whom they shared few convictions; but on the whole it is revealing to learn of a poet that he belonged, say, to the *Shiki* or *Rekitei* group.

Two different and sometimes unrelated criteria determined which group a poet would join. The first was that of style—whether traditional, modernistic, or iconoclastic; the second was political—whether radical, liberal, or reactionary. The same man might be Modernist in style and reactionary in his political views, though it was more common for Modernism to go with liberal political views, as iconoclasm with anarchism. The Modernist periodicals were often identified with European schools: *Shi to Shiron* (Poetry and Poetics, 1928–1933) was associated especially with Surrealism; its successor *Shihō* (Poetic Methods, 1934–1935), though friendly to Surrealism, gave greater space to English intellectualism; and its successor *Shinryōdo* (New Territory, 1937–1941) owed its name and poetical philosophy to the English journal *New Country*.[295]

The conservative and reactionary journals tended to prefer German thought, whether old-fashioned Romanticism or Nazi ideology, but their emphasis was increasingly on the "Japaneseness" of the poetry presented. The radical journals for their part maintained direct or indirect contact with similar journals abroad. Regardless of the political philosophy, Japanese poetry had come to form a branch of the modern poetry of the world.[296]

SHI TO SHIRON AND MODERNISM

Shi to Shiron established new standards of poetical criticism in Japan, and for a time attracted almost all the important poets. Later poetical or political differences caused the group to split into factions, but the periodical left a lasting impression. The editor, Haruyama Yukio (1902–1994), did not inaugurate the magazine with any manifesto of principles; but in general it stood for Modernism of the European varieties, and was opposed to the Symbolism of the poets of the 1920s as well as to the diffuse and prosaic style of the "people's poets" (*minshūshi-ha*).[297] As the title of the magazine indicated, it was concerned with poetics as well as poetry; the editor referred to the previous period as a "dark age" without poetics. His object was to raise Japanese poetry to an international level of skill and sophistication.

Haruyama was a remarkable editor. Not only did he produce a four-hundred-page issue each quarter, but he was constantly uncovering fresh talent. Even though the magazine took no definite poetic stance, it published the early essays on Surrealism by Nishiwaki Junzaburō and the translation of Kitagawa Fuyuhiko of part of André Breton's Surrealist manifesto, giving an impression of commitment to this form of Modernism. However, *Shi to Shiron* also featured discussions on prose poetry and examples by Kitagawa Fuyuhiko and Anzai Fuyue (1898–1965), and carried poems in the new lyrical style of Miyoshi Tatsuji. The most characteristic feature of the magazine was its devotion to European and American poetry and theories of poetry. It published translations and introductions to such figures as Paul Valéry, T. S. Eliot, André Breton, Louis Aragon, and Ezra Pound, and seemed to accept the proposition that enlightenment in modern poetry must be sought from the West. This unspoken assumption would before long result in several important poets breaking away from the *Shi to Shiron* group.

SHI, GENJITSU AND MARXIST POETICS

The first split in the ranks occurred in 1930 when Kitagawa Fuyuhiko (1900–1990), Miyoshi Tatsuji, and others broke away to found a new journal, *Shi, Genjitsu* (Poetry, Reality). Although the chief cause of dissatisfaction with *Shi to Shiron* was its excessive reliance on European theories and formalism, *Shi, Genjitsu* also had a conspicuously political side that was not found in *Shi to Shiron*: it made a point of presenting Marxist literary and artistic thought and of introducing proletarian literature.

This was not the first Japanese advocacy of "proletarian" poetic theory. *Donzoko de utau* (Singing in the Lower Depths), the first collection of proletarian poetry, had appeared as early as 1920, and long before then, in 1903, the collection *Shakaishugishi Shū* (Socialist Poems) by Kodama Kagai (1874–1943) had been confiscated by the authorities, presumably because any work that mentioned socialism in its title was automatically suspect.[298] During the 1920s, generally considered the liberal era of Japanese politics, other collections were banned because the titles included such dangerous words as "social" (let alone "socialism"!), or because they expressed pacifist sentiments, even though their political philosophies were by no means revolutionary. The most successful of the "people's poets" of the 1920s was Shirotori Seigo (1890–1973), who probably composed more pacifist poetry than any other Japanese. His sentiments were usually laudable, but as a poet he was excessively diffuse and sometimes embarrassingly sentimental.[299]

The first specifically socialist literary organization was founded in 1925. After various reorganizations it emerged in 1928 as the *Zen Nihon Musansha Geijutsu Remmei* (All-Japan Proletarian Arts Association). One of its organs, the poetry magazine *Puroretaria Shi* (Proletarian Poetry), carried poems that conveyed the Marxist views of the members. Most of these poets experienced great difficulty in reconciling their political aims of arousing class consciousness and of attacking feudalistic capitalism with their literary purpose of moving readers with their poems. Their poems are of mainly historical interest; they usually fail to achieve anything that might be called poetic distinction.

One poet associated with this movement stands out by virtue of his unquestionable achievement and literary importance, Nakano Shigeharu (1902–1979). He was educated as a young man in Kanazawa, where he fell under the influence of Murō Saisei's poetry, attracted by its lyricism and humanism. He was also deeply attracted by the tanka of Saitō Mokichi; he seems to have been most intrigued by the possibilities Saitō revealed of conveying lyricism even in the expression of abstract thought. Although Nakano remained a convinced Marxist, even while Saitō was moving steadily to the right, his admiration for the older poet never wavered, and his finest tribute to Saitō was in the wartime volume *Saitō Mokichi Nōto* (Notes on Saitō Mokichi, 1942). Under Saitō's influence Nakano for a time composed tanka, but his reputation as a poet is based entirely on his modern poetry.

Nakano attended Tokyo University, where he associated with other literarily minded students, including Hori Tatsuo. In 1926 they founded the little magazine *Roba* (Donkey), which continued publication for only two years. During this time Nakano published his most important poetry; his later career was as a novelist and critic.

Nakano succeeded where most of the other proletarian poets failed, not because his grasp of political theory was more profound, but because of his unique lyrical gifts. Ayukawa Nobuo wrote: "In Nakano's poetry lyricism is the result, not the cause. At any rate, there is not a single lyrical poem written with the intention of writing a lyrical poem from the start. What impelled Nakano to write poetry might be called the urgency of realistic themes." [300] In a famous poem "Uta" (Song), originally published in *Roba*, Nakano wrote:

Don't sing
Don't sing of scarlet blossoms or the wings of dragonflies
Don't sing of murmuring breezes or the scent of a woman's hair.[301]

In these lines Nakano appears to be singling out for attack precisely the variety of subjects that would stir the lyricism of a poet like Miyoshi Tatsuji, though he himself denied any intent of "illegally prohibiting" poems that celebrated the wings of dragonflies or women's hair! [302] For Nakano lyricism was a means, rather than an end, but his poems nevertheless often attained a rare degree of lyricism, thanks to his intuitively sensitive use of Japanese words and sounds. A peculiarly affecting poem, "Ame no furu Shinagawa Eki" (Shinagawa Station in the Rain), written in 1928 or 1929, describes the deportation of some Korean workers from Japan. The theme is somber, and there is not one conventionally poetic touch, but the effect is strangely moving, for both its content and its flawless lyrical phrasing:

Shin yo sayōnara
Kin yo sayōnara
Kimira wa ame no furu Shinagawa eki kara jōsha suru . . . .

A translation cannot do the music of this poem justice:

Shin, sayonara!
Kin, sayonara!
You're boarding your train at Shinagawa Station in the rain.

Goodbye, Ri,
Goodbye to the other Ri,
You're going back to the land of your parents.

The rivers in your country freeze in the cold winter;
Your rebellious spirits freeze in this moment of parting.

The sea raises its rumbling voice in the twilight.
Pigeons, wet by the rain, drift down from the car-barn roof.

Wetted by the rain you remember the Japanese emperor who drove
    you out;
Wetted by the rain, you remember the moustache, the glasses.

In the splashing rain the green signal rises,
In the splashing rain your pupils sharpen.

The rain pours on the pavement, falls on the dark surface of the
    sea.
The rain evaporates on your hot cheeks.

Your black shadows cross the ticket gates,
Your white baggy trousers flap in the corridor darkness.

The signal color changes,
You get aboard.

You are leaving,
You leave.

Sayonara, Shin!
Sayonara, Kin!
Sayonara, Ri!
Sayonara to the girl Ri!

Go and break down the hard, thick, glassy ice,
Make the long-dammed water gush forth!
Rear guard and front guard to the Japanese proletariat,
Sayonara!
Until the day we weep and laugh in the joy of revenge! [303]

Itō Shinkichi wrote of this poem that it was the finest lyrical work composed in the Shōwa period; he characterized it as lyrical in poetic character, rebellious in spirit, and class-conscious in thought.[304]

Nakano's first collection of poems, published in 1931, was confiscated by the police. A second collection was published in 1935 with twenty-three pages deleted. Only in 1947 could his poems be printed as written. In the 1930s, like many other left-wing writers, he announced he had been converted from Communism and wrote stories demonstrating his change of heart, but as soon as the war ended he resumed his earlier literary and political activity on behalf of proletarian causes.

Nakano had no direct connection with the periodical *Shi, Genjitsu*. Indeed, his career as a poet was virtually ended by 1930, when *Shi, Genjitsu* first appeared. The editor, Kitagawa Fuyuhiko, though Marxist in his political convictions when he founded *Shi, Genjitsu*, had fundamentally quite different poetic tastes from Nakano's. Kitagawa began as an avant-garde revolutionary, attracted by Surrealism and other new literary movements; later he moved toward Socialist Realism. A few months before the first issue of *Shi, Genjitsu* appeared, he published his collection *Sensō* (War, 1929), his finest poetic achievement. It has been described as "the first attempt made to clarify the relation between the artistic consciousness of Modernism and the political consciousness of Socialist Realism." [305] Kitagawa tried to fuse his artistic and political ideals by stating his social criticism in highly metaphorical language that transcended the flat, prosaic use of modern speech by the "people's poets." The poems in his collection are difficult, and their criticism is therefore veiled; but the title itself and the recurring images of warfare indicated his preoccupation with this subject, even though militarism was by no means so conspicuous in 1929 as it would become a few years later. Perhaps the most celebrated poem in *Sensō* is one entitled "Uma" (Horse):

Gunkō wo naizō shite iru.

It intestines a military port.

This poem is remarkable first of all for its shortness—even shorter than a haiku. The neologism *naizō shite iru*, "to intestine," is disconcerting; the relation of the title to the peculiar statement has elicited various explanations. The poet Maruyama Kaoru interpreted the images in terms of their associations:

> horse = military horse = army
> military port = warship = navy
> intestines = anatomical drawing = classified map

Maruyama believed that behind these images there was a concealed meaning of "The navy is inside the army," and that the poem was intended as a satire on militarism.[306] Kitagawa himself related that he had adopted the imagery in recollection of a Chagall painting showing a human being inside a cow's belly. Whatever the exact implications he may have intended to impart to this cryptic poem, the general meaning was no doubt disgust over the port, a feeling he conveyed by the somehow repellent image of the horse's intestines.

Not all of Kitagawa's poems are so difficult to analyze. His hatred of militarism is suggested by another poem, "Kujira" (Whale), which begins:

No sooner does it float the huge whale than the strait is demolished.

The poem suggests a warship sailing into a strait too narrow to bear such a great burden, and by implication, the Japanese people unable to sustain the weight of militarism. The poem concludes:

Being huge is in itself evil, evil and nothing but! [307]

Shi, Genjitsu lasted exactly one year, until June 1931. Pressure against all forms of proletarian literary activity increased after the outbreak of the Manchurian Incident in September of that year, though collections of proletarian poetry continued to appear through 1932. The death in prison of the Communist novelist Kobayashi Takiji in 1933 was also the death of the movement; some poets announced they had changed their convictions; others, like Tsuboi Shigeji (1897–1975), managed during the war to publish poems with private messages of despair by employing a Symbolist idiom that baffled the censors. Proletarian poetry did not surface again until after the war ended in 1945.

SHIKI AND MODERN LYRICISM

In May 1933 Hori Tatsuo (1904–1953), who had served as the editor of *Bungaku* (Literature), the immediate successor of *Shi to Shiron*, founded the magazine *Shiki* (Four Seasons), so called because it was intended to be a quarterly. Hori did not wish to publish a monthly magazine because he disliked the pressure, but he also hoped that his new magazine, remaining on the bookshop shelves for several months, would avoid ephemeral controversies. He was also influenced by the success of the French quarterly *Commerce* in presenting in "notebook" form fiction, essays, and poetry.[308]

Originally Hori had not thought in terms of a magazine devoted exclusively to poetry, but so many of his friends were poets that the proportion of poetry to the total contents steadily increased. The magazine, printed in only eight hundred copies, discontinued publication after two issues, apparently for financial reasons, but Hori was induced by Miyoshi Tatsuji to resume publication of *Shiki* in 1934 as a monthly. Miyoshi and Maruyama Kaoru (1899–1974), his long-time friend, joined Hori on the editorial staff. The presence of these two poets undoubtedly accounted for *Shiki* soon assuming the characteristics of a poetry magazine, rather than the general literary magazine Hori had originally had in mind. In 1936 *Shiki* was again reorganized, this time as the official organ of a group that included such distinguished poets as Hagiwara Sakutarō, Murō Saisei, Nakahara Chūya, and Tachihara Michizō, as well as Hori, Miyoshi, and Maruyama.[309]

The central presence of Miyoshi and Maruyama determined the future tone of *Shiki* poetry as one of modern lyricism. Following Hagiwara and Saisei, they rejected the Surrealist and other avant-garde experimentations with the Japanese language, which, in their opinion, had threatened to destroy it. They also rejected the Socialist Realism preached by the politically committed poets. They stood for a combination of traditional Japanese sensitivity and modern forms, for strong individuality and polished sensibility.[310]

Shiki continued publication from 1934 to 1944, appearing more or less regularly each month. Even at the height of its prosperity, it did not sell more than two thousand copies, and contributors were not paid. Although *Shiki* was not considered in the 1930s to represent the mainstream of poetry—an honor that was claimed by the posterity of *Shi to Shiron* and by the more experimental journals like *VOU*—it subsequently came to seem the most attractive, and probably the most important, of the different rival schools.

Miyoshi was the most distinguished member of the *Shiki* school, but the ideals of this school were perhaps most perfectly embodied in the poetry of Tachihara Michizō (1914–1939). His death at the age of twenty-five cut short his development as a poet, but Tachihara had already achieved a lyric quality of distinction. Murano Shirō wrote that of the many lyric poets associated with the *Shiki* school, none delineated his youthful emotions as purely as Tachihara.[311] Fault can be found with his scant body of poetry, especially the sameness of his overly sensitive and sweet tone, but it is hard to reproach a man who died so young for not having achieved the maturity of diction or thought of a major poet; Tachihara merits his popularity by his success in expressing with poignance and beauty his lyrical impulses. He was a disciple of Hori Tatsuo's from 1934, when they both spent the summer near Karuizawa, and he shared Hori's delicacy and sensitivity. The same kind of readers appreciated both men's work; in this sense, if none other, Tachihara's work most perfectly fitted into the *Shiki* traditions.

All the poems in Tachihara's first collection, *Wasuregusa ni yosu* (To the Day-Lilies, 1937), were cast in the "sonnet" form; that is, a poem in fourteen lines, though each line was irregular in length. Rhyme was unobtrusively employed. Perhaps the most successful example was "Nochi no Omoi ni" (Later Remembrances, 1936):

> The dream always returned to the lonely village at the foot of the
>   mountain—
> The wind rose in the knotweed,
> Crickets shrilled without break
> —Along the road through woods stilled by early afternoon.
>
> The sun shone in the brilliant blue sky, the volcano was asleep.
> —And I,
> Though I knew no one was listening, went on talking
> About things I had seen, islands, waves, headlands, sunlight and
>   moonlight.
>
> The dream does not go beyond that point.
> I would like to forget everything completely,
> And when I have forgotten even that I have completely forgotten.

The dream will freeze in midwinter remembrances,
And it will open a door, and in the loneliness
Go off along a road lighted by sprinklings of stars.[312]

Critics have seen premonitions of death in Tachihara's statement
that his dream did not go beyond a certain point, but perhaps this
was more a farewell to his youth than an awareness of a world
beyond death.

Tachihara's name is sometimes linked with that of Nakahara
Chūya (1907–1937), if only because both died young and both
associated with the *Shiki* group. But Nakahara's relations with
this group were far more casual than Tachihara's, and his poetry is
quite dissimilar. He is properly called a lyric poet, but his lyricism,
sharing little with the fragile evocations of Tachihara's expression,
threatened often to explode with fierce emotions; and he employed a biting irony foreign to the gentle Tachihara.

Nakahara's interest in poetry began with tanka in the vein of
Ishikawa Takuboku, but in 1923, when he was sixteen, he hap-
pened to buy a copy of the recently published *Dadaisuto Shinkichi no Uta*, a collection of poems by the Dadaist Takahashi
Shinkichi (b. 1901). Nakahara was so entranced by the daring
style that this was virtually the only modern poetry he read for a
time. In the following year, however, he met the poet Tominaga
Tarō (1901–1925), from whom he first learned about Baudelaire,
Rimbaud, and Verlaine. Nakahara was attracted especially to
Rimbaud; [313] he translated some sixty poems by Rimbaud, over
half the total of his published translations. His wayward, "bohe-
mian" life, for which he rapidly became famous (he once spent a
month in jail for having smashed street lamps while in a drunken
rage),[314] seems to have been inspired by accounts he read of Rimbaud. Kawakami Tetsutarō described Nakahara as a classic instance of an "outsider"; European post-1918 decadence, imported
into Japan in the early 1920s, created an atmosphere especially
favorable to the followers of the French *poètes maudits*. A frequently reproduced photograph of Nakahara shows a childish,
sulky face framed in long hair peeping out from under a shapeless
hat. Nakahara, who has frequently been called "the Japanese
Rimbaud," evidently felt quite at home in the role of a *poète
maudit*.

Nakahara wrote of his discovery in Rimbaud of "an intoxication of the senses that seemed capable of creating an entirely new history for mankind" and of "a principle of life" that antedated all customs and habits.[315] His readings in Rimbaud enabled him to escape the limitations of the Dadaists, though their influence was still apparent in his first collection. An even more direct influence was that of Tominaga Tarō, with whom Nakahara closely associated in Kyoto and Tokyo from February 1924 until Tominaga's untimely death in November 1925. Ōoka Shōhei, who knew both men well, contrasted their poetic styles: "For Nakahara poetry lay in a dadaistic self; for Tominaga, by contrast, poetry lay outside himself. This probably was the definitive difference between the two men, and neither was prepared to yield to the other." [316]

Nakahara's precocious maturity revealed itself also in his acquisition of a mistress at the age of seventeen. The two went to Tokyo the next year. He quickly met various young people in the literary world, including the critic Kobayashi Hideo, a friend of Tominaga's. In November 1925, the month that Tominaga died, Nakahara's mistress left him to live with Kobayashi. This painful experience proved a source of poetic creativity: Nakahara's first significant poems date from the following year. Nakahara later recalled that "Asa no Uta" (Morning Song, 1926) was the first poem he showed to anyone in Tokyo.[317] With this poem he established his poetic stance:

> On the ceiling, a vermilion color:
>   Light leaking in through a crack in the door
> Recalls a rustic military band—my hands
>   Have nothing whatever to do.
>
> I cannot hear the song of little birds.
>   The sky today must be a faded blue.
> Weary—too tired to remonstrate,
>   No word of comfort for anyone.
>
> In the scent of resin the morning is painful,
>   Lost, the various, various dreams.
> The standing woods are moaning in the wind.
>
> Flatly spread out the sky,
>   Along the bank go vanishing
> The beautiful, various dreams.[318]

The poem is in a fourteen-line "sonnet" form, and the lines are almost all composed of units of five plus seven or seven plus seven syllables. The language is the formal, classical style. The discipline involved in composing this poem had not previously been displayed by Nakahara, and he later commented that he was disgusted to discover how much trouble it was to compose a mere fourteen lines! [319] The feeling of ennui and frustration that permeates the poem suggests Nakahara's closeness to the French decadent poets: the poet, lying abed of an early spring morning, is too weary to lift his hand or to look outside at the weather, let alone concern himself with anyone else. He recalls nostalgically his dreams that seem now to be vanishing.

More than a trace of Dadaistic expression lingers in this poem, and even the most sympathetic commentator has had difficulty in analyzing the imagery.[320] The association of the patch of colored light on the ceiling with the sounds of a country military band is in the manner of the synesthesia of the Symbolist poets, but probably refers specifically to his childhood memories. The scene is apparently a lodging-house room in Tokyo where Nakahara, lonely and world-weary, contemplates without pleasure a new day. The actual sights—the patch of sunlight leaking in through a crack in the cheaply made shutters, the smell of resin from a pine immediately outside—blend with imagined scenes of woods and sky and with the poet's nostalgic remembrances.

Another poem written about the same time, "Sākasu" (Circus), was one of Nakahara's own favorites. According to Ōoka Shōhei, anyone meeting Nakahara for the first time was likely to be treated to his half-spoken, half-crooned recitation of the poem. When Nakahara came to the curious, onomatopoetic refrain yuān yuyōn yuyayuyon, he would look down, his eyes shut, and sing the meaningless sounds with pursed lips.[321] The poem begins:

How many generations ago was it?
There were sepia-colored wars.

How many generations ago was it?
In winter gales used to blow.

The nostalgic tone of the references to the Sino-Japanese and Russo-Japanese wars, preserved in faded photographs, soon gives way to the contrasting description of the tawdry excitement of the circus today. A trapeze artist is swinging from his perch:

> Upside down, his arms dangling,
>> Under the dirty canvas of the roof,
> *Yuān yuyōn yuyayuyon.*

There is not only irony but pathos in Nakahara's evocation of the loneliness of the acrobat performing for the "sardines" below, while outside:

> Outside it is pitch-black, the blackest of black,
> The night grows everlastingly darker.
> Like the nostalgia of that parachute—
> *Yuān yuyōn yuyayuyon.*[322]

The third line of this stanza is puzzling; perhaps Nakahara, contrasting the brightness inside the circus tent with the darkness outside, visualized the parachute-shaped tent as something already metamorphosed into a memory floating nostalgically in his mind. The emphasis given to the melancholy rhythm of the refrain evokes the emptiness and futility of his life at the time, but the musicality of expression was typical of the best in Nakahara. He was impressed by Verlaine's declaration that music was the most important aspect of poetry,[323] and his own poems were peculiarly well suited to public readings or to being set to music. For this reason it is difficult to appreciate Nakahara except in the original. Some lines have little value except as sound, and he frequently resorted to the device of repeating lines—even those of no great significance—for their musical effect. In "Hitotsu no Meruhen" (A Children's Story), for example, he used the onomatopoetic sounds *sarasara* five times in fourteen lines to suggest sunlight shining on a stream. The effect is undeniably musical, but it defies translation.

Nakahara's language was a curious mixture of stilted and sometimes incorrectly used archaisms along with an extremely colloquial, even vulgar language. Early in his career, apparently under the influence of Tominaga Tarō and Miyazawa Kenji, he filled his poems with Chinese-derived words and unusual characters, though his scrappy education hardly justified such a display of erudition and the use of difficult words did not come to him naturally. He insisted that the essence of poetry and art was instead something "before cognition" or "before names," the cry of "ah!" that is at once an intuition and an action.[324] A late poem, "Kotoba naki Uta" (Songs without Words, 1936), is testimony to the increasing importance he gave to melody.[325]

The only collection of poetry by Nakahara to appear during his lifetime was *Yagi no Uta* (Goat Songs, 1934), which contained forty-four poems written between 1924 and 1930. This book was printed in an edition of two hundred copies, an indication of the general lack of interest in his poetry at the time. In 1934 Nakahara also published the poem "Hone" (Bones) and the essay "Shi to sono Dentō" (Poetry and Its Traditions). In the same year his first son was born, and Nakahara began his important translations of Rimbaud. "Bones" was composed in a colloquial, almost farcical tone, though the poem conveys a nihilism that verges on a hatred for life. It consists of five stanzas of five lines each. The first is:

> Look at them! They're my bones!
> Breaking through that unclean flesh
> Filled with the suffering of when they lived,
> Washed white by the rain,
> Out they've popped, the sharp bone-tips.[326]

Nakahara made effective use of such colloquialisms as *horahora* and *nukku* to lend a sardonic humor to his lines. This is one of his most effective, unconstrained works; Murano Shirō wrote: "It is most interesting in that it is the first poem in which Nakahara Chūya gave us a glimpse of himself in something like the guise of a modern poet."[327] Kobayashi Hideo wrote shortly after the poem was published:

> Some people may say that there is nothing new about such a poem, but I, being aware that in Nakahara's earlier poetry there was an extreme outpouring of what might be termed the "techniques of new poetry," do not consider this work old. He has abandoned his complex combinations of mental images, his strongly colored adjectives and skillful use of an individual, sensuous language, his efforts to capture the elusive, and so on, and has produced instead a poem that is like the bones he describes themselves.[328]

The second tragedy in Nakahara's life, the death of his son in 1936, seems to have precipitated the nervous breakdown that occurred that year, though the moving poem "Mata kon Haru" (Spring Will Come Again), which touches on his son's death, shows no sign of disorder. His last important poem, "Shunjitsu Kyōsō" (Wild Thoughts on a Spring Day, 1937), begins:

> When somebody you love has died
> You've got to commit suicide.
>
> When somebody you love has died,
> There's nothing else you can do.[329]

The repetition of words and whole lines is extreme, but the effect of the self-mockery is cumulative.

Nakahara died in 1937 of cerebral meningitis soon after editing his second collection, *Arishi Hi no Uta* (Songs of Bygone Days), which appeared the next year. At the time of his death he was at last beginning to enjoy popularity, but his real fame dates back only to the postwar period, when his old friends Ōoka Shōhei and Kawakami Tetsutarō devoted great attention to his life and works. The poetry came to be read in close connection with the biography, and a fascination with his at once tragic and dissolute life has led some critics to voice extravagant praise of his works. Nakahara's poetry is unquestionably affecting but, as Miyoshi Tatsuji pointed out, he was deficient both in language and in poetic techniques, and seemed to begrudge the necessary efforts to improve his writings; instead, Miyoshi said, he plunged "deeply, persistently and furiously" into the agonies he had experienced." [330] Perhaps this criticism, coming from a poet who was a great perfectionist, should not be weighted too heavily; Ōoka Makoto, a poet of a different school, wrote that "In poetic techniques Nakahara possessed outstanding ability . . . but it was not in him to assume the attitude appropriate to composing a skillful poem or to establish a goal for himself and try in a craftsmanlike manner to attain it." [331]

In the end, Nakahara Chūya is apt to leave the impression of an unusually interesting second-rate poet. His violent life captures the imagination, but he unfortunately did not live long enough to achieve poetic maturity. Kawakami Tetsutarō wrote: "Strictly speaking, there was no literary development in Nakahara's case that might properly be termed 'late period,' though such a designation is almost always possible when writing of geniuses who died young." [332]

Of the other poets associated with the *Shiki* group who have not been treated elsewhere, only one requires more than passing comment, Maruyama Kaoru. He was the classmate of Miyoshi Tatsuji, who gave credit to Maruyama for having introduced him to poetry. His first collection, *Ho, Rampu, Kamome* (Sail, Lamp, Seagull, 1932), reveals in its title Maruyama's preoccupation with the sea, and the lyric style indicates what induced him to join Hori Tatsuo and Miyoshi Tatsuji in 1934 in founding a magazine that was to perpetuate the Japanese traditions of lyricism, as opposed to the nonlyrical varieties of poetry then in favor.

A poem like "Rampu ga utatta" (The Song the Lamp Şang) evokes his passion for the sea:

The anchor chain fades
   into the sea's dark face
   beyond where my eye can reach.
The rigging escapes
   into the mast's dark heights
   beyond where my eye can reach.
My feeble rays light only my sightless face.
Far in the distance past vision
A seagull fixes his eye on me and shrieks.[333]

An even superior poem in the same collection, "Hōdai" (Gun Emplacement), consists of eight lines, each treated as a separate stanza:

The shell fragments yearned to form a single whole.
The cracks yearned to smile again.
The gun barrel yearned to stand up
And sit again on its mount.
All dreamed of their evanescent original shapes.
Each gust of wind buried them deeper in the sand.
The sea beyond their sight,
The flash of a migratory bird.[334]

The imagery is neither startling nor obscure, but it was entirely new to the Japanese lyrical poem. Maruyama's vision of the abandoned gun emplacement on the shore, buried deeper in the sand by each gust of wind, yearning for its original wholeness, is compellingly expressed, but no allegorical meaning was intended. His choice of a cracked concrete gun emplacement should not suggest that either martial fervor or pacifism was in the poet's mind; Maruyama was attempting instead to suggest the inevitable breakdown and disintegration of whatever was once powerful.[335] Compared to Miyoshi, or to the totally dissimilar Nakahara, Maruyama's poetry is in a low key, but for a time, especially at the beginning of the 1930s, he enjoyed a high reputation as a lyric poet of distinction.

NIHON RŌMAN-HA AND JAPANESE LYRICISM

The poet Andō Tsuguo, writing about the development of Japanese poetry during the 1930s, said that the backbone of the modern movement was provided by two critics, Kobayashi Hideo (1901–1983) and Yasuda Yojūrō (1910–1981). It was their criticism, more than the works of other poets, that stirred impressionable young men to write poetry. These young poets, under the influence of Kobayashi or Yasuda, turned first of all to modern French poetry or to German Romantic poetry, rather than to the experimental verse that then formed the mainstream of poetic activity in Japan.

Kobayashi's role in transmitting modern French literature to Tominaga Tarō and Nakahara Chūya has been mentioned; his influence would extend during future years to many different writers, and he would be revered as the single most esteemed critic, not only of literature but of music and art. Yasuda's period of great influence was much shorter: it was terminated by Japan's defeat in 1945. Yasuda, though still only thirty-five, was so indissolubly associated with the ultra-nationalism of the war days that he withdrew from the literary world altogether, and his influence rapidly waned.

Yasuda's importance in the 1930s was due mainly to the two literary periodicals he edited, *Kogito* (Cogito, 1933–1944) and *Nihon Rōman-ha* (The Japanese Romanticists, 1935–1938), which he made the vehicles of his distinctive interpretation of Japanese literature. *Kogito* (so named after Descartes's famous formula) was founded, like *Shi, Genjitsu* and *Shiki*, by way of reaction to the excessively European—especially French—orientation of *Shi to Shiron*. Yasuda, like most of the other founding members of *Kogito*, had studied German as his first foreign language, and continued his studies of German aesthetics at Tokyo University. The magazine accordingly devoted many pages to the German Romantic poets in particular. Yasuda himself combined his interest in German literature with an appreciation of the traditional Japanese culture. In contrast to the emphasis given to French poetry by both the *Shi to Shiron* and *Shiki* groups, this fusing of the poetry of such men as Goethe, Hölderlin, and George Gruppe with Japanese lyricism going back to the *Manyōshū* and *Shin Kokinshū* created a fresh impression on readers of the scholarly looking journal.[336]

The allegiances of the Japanese Romanticists were at first by no means obvious. Kamei Katsuichirō, together with Yasuda, a founder of *Nihon Rōman-ha*, was a former theoretician for the left-wing literary movement who had been "converted" to "Japanism" in 1928 as the result of police pressure; and Dazai Osamu, by no means a "Japanist," remained a political maverick though he published several important stories in the same magazine. The poets specifically associated with *Kogito* and *Nihon Rōman-ha* included Jimbo Kōtarō (b. 1905), Tanaka Katsumi (b. 1911), and Itō Shizuo (1906–1953). These poets (and many lesser ones who wrote for the same journals) fell into disfavor after 1945 because of their wartime enthusiasm for the sacred cause of Japan, an enthusiasm that sometimes bordered on fanaticism. The pronouncements of Yasuda Yojūrō set the tone for their utterances, which did not stop at the poet's lyrical declarations of love for his country but glorified Japanese traditions to the exclusion of any others, and sometimes voiced unmasked hatred for anything alien to Japan. The wartime excesses of these patriotic poets need not detain us long; they fail as poems because they depend on an ideological concurrence that few readers are still willing to grant.

Jimbo Kōtarō, who in later years would emphasize the role of the *Nihon Rōman-ha* in fusing German Romanticism with Japanese lyricism, in 1941 published a collection of Nazi poetry, and once the war began produced at least a volume a year of patriotic poems.[337] Tanaka Katsumi wrote some of the most violent imprecations directed aginst the Americans and the British; and Itō Shizuo's wartime collection *Haru no Isogi* (The Rush of Spring, 1943) bears the author's preface stating that he desired to transmit, if only to his own children, the "vast, leaping thoughts that filled him on hearing the Imperial Rescript and the virile shouts of the imperial army." [338] But almost every poet of repute was writing similar poems at the time, even men who had hitherto been linked with literary movements extending all the way to the extreme left.[339] It should not be forgotten that these men also wrote much moving poetry. Itō especially is remembered for the beauty of his prewar lyrics. His first and best collection, *Wa ga Hito ni atauru Aika* (Laments Addressed to My Beloved, 1935), was acclaimed by Yasuda Yojūrō, who declared in *Kogito* that Itō's poems were the only ones being written that deserved to be called "lyric." He quoted Hagiwara Sakutarō's comment, "I felt a surge of joy and courage when I realized there was still one poet in Japan." [340] Hagiwara thought that Itō's poetry was reminiscent of Shimazaki Tōson's, but noted that in place of Shimazaki's youthful ardor a strain of pathos, in no way suggestive of the high spirits of youth, ran through Itō's work.

In Itō's early poetry especially it is easy to detect the influence of J. C. F. Hölderlin's *Menons Klagen um Diotima*. The name "Menon" itself was that of "one who patiently endures," the role in which the stoical Itō pictured himself.[341] The title poem of *Laments Addressed to My Beloved* describes the poet's imagined walk with his beloved under a brilliant sun, accompanied by the infinite song of praise of the birds and the wind through the trees; but in fact the poet is alone, and the sun shines coldly on the "soundless void" before him. The "song of praise" has been transformed into a lament.[342]

Itō's early poems are often obscure in expression and sometimes employ archaic vocabulary and diction. A frequent theme is the "eternal return" to some lost home, in the manner of Hölderlin. Ōoka Makoto wrote of the "timelessness" to which Itō aspired: "Itō Shizuo's poems, at least those composed at the time of *Laments Addressed to My Beloved*, came into being at the point where the poet is thrust back from the world of 'timelessness' into the time of reality. These poems are intrinsically metaphysical, and at the same time attached extremely closely to reality, the reality of the poet's spirit." [343]

The grief and despair that marked Itō's early poems gave way in later years, under the influence of Rilke, to an awareness of material things, and to something like a conversion to nature. He came to recognize, also thanks to Rilke, the importance of the metaphorical spirit in poetry, and this led him to make a reevaluation of the "artifice" of the *Kokinshū*, decried by modern poets ever since Masaoka Shiki.[344]

Perhaps the best poem in his second collection, *Natsuhana* (Summer Flowers, 1940), is "Tsubame" (The Swallow), written in the previous year, and dedicated to Hasuda Zemmei (1904–1945), a close friend who had gone to the front in China as an army officer.[345] Although nowhere explicitly stated, the arrival of the first swallow must have stirred nostalgic thoughts of his distant friend:

> A swallow is singing somewhere high up in the dazzling sunshine
>   outside my gate,
> A single note, sharp, unclouded.
> The swallow singing now is the first to reach this country.
> You, having traveled all the way from the sky
> Over the distant Moluccas, New Guinea or even farther,
> Your wings fluttering, your little legs trembling—
> I look up and listen to your frantic singing:
> You say nothing of the many nights you endured in the dark of
>   night,
> Beating your wings over the numberless waves of the sea.
> On your perch high in the blinding light by my gate,
> Your song is monotonous, sharp, unclouded.
> The first swallow to reach Japan is singing now.[346]

Itō's last collection, *Hankyō* (Echoes, 1947), was written in a much simpler style than his earlier poetry, so simple indeed that the poems have been faulted for their prosiness. The hardships of the war and of the years after the defeat exhausted him, and he died prematurely at forty-seven of tuberculosis.

In 1935 Kusano Shimpei (1903–1988), known hitherto mainly as an extremely unconventional poet with anarchist leanings, founded the magazine *Rekitei* (Course of Wanderings), which quickly established itself as one of the three or four most important poetic journals. The distinctive feature of the *Rekitei* poets was that they never stood for any single poetic ideology such as might be easily discerned in the *Shi to Shiron* or *Shiki* group. Members of the group denied it lacked characteristics of its own, claiming that it was a many-sided "society" of poets who found stimulation in one another's company and respected individualism and even eccentricity. Unlike other groups, moreover, these poets did not attach great importance to the regular publication of their magazine as their sole medium of expression; *Rekitei* appeared irregularly, but there were instead frequent meetings of the group at which poetry was declaimed. Much modern Japanese poetry is virtually incomprehensible unless read, and makes only a limited appeal to the ears, but the typical *Rekitei* poets—Kusano Shimpei, Nakahara Chūya, and Miyazawa Kenji [347]—were conspicuously interested in the effects of sound, even meaningless sound, as in the instance of Nakahara's "Circus."

The anarchism of Kusano Shimpei or of Takahashi Shinkichi, another founding member of *Rekitei*, was essentially an expression of dissatisfaction with existing social conditions, rather than an affirmation of revolutionary belief. Kusano was known especially for his poems about frogs; these harmless, defenseless creatures came in his poetry to represent common, suffering humanity. Sometimes his frog poems consist entirely of meaningless repeated sounds, like the string of alternating lines *rururi,/ririri* in "Ore mo Nemurō" (I'm Going to Sleep Too) or the nineteen repetitions of the single syllable *ru* in "Shunshoku" (Spring Propagation),[348] or in unpronounceable combinations of consonants in roman letters; or he may even present as an entire poem a large black dot, with the title "Tōmin" (Hibernation). These may have represented Kusano's attempts to reach beyond language to more ultimate expression, or they may have been mere playfulness, but such poems do not suggest the humanity revealed in his poems written in more conventional idioms, like "Gurima no Shi" (The Death of Gurima, 1928):

Gurima was caught by a kid and beaten to death.
Rurida, left all alone,
Took a violet
And pushed it into Gurima's mouth.

She stayed half a day by his side until it began to hurt, when she
    crawled into the water.
When she had buried her face in the mud
Voices of pleasure went numb in her stomach
And tears beat at her throat like a fountain.

The violet still in his mouth,
Violet and Gurima both
Shriveled in the broiling summer sun.[349]

Kusano's collection *Daihyaku Kaikyū* (The Hundredth Social Class, 1928), in which this poem appeared, consisted entirely of poems about frogs. He returned to this favorite subject again and again in later years, but he also wrote a quite different kind of poetry in which he expressed his longing for the mystery and grandeur of the universe. The sweep of waves beating against the shore, the fierce illumination of the sky, the eternity of a stone, or the tracks of a mammoth stirred wonder in him at the strength of the universe, a strength he felt even in the easily destroyed frogs he depicted.

Kusano's poetry has sometimes been compared to that of Takamura Kōtarō. Both men wrote positive, nonintrospective poetry in a "healthy" (as opposed to decadent or artificial) style, but the resemblances are otherwise slight. Kusano nowhere suggests Takamura's characteristic sensuality and explosive virility; on the other hand, he is more experimental and varied, ranging from the simplest, clearest statement to extreme avant-garde expression. The influence Kusano himself recognized was that of Carl Sandburg, whose "Chicago poems," written in everyday language about ordinary scenes and people, deeply impressed him.[350]

Kusano also composed poetry celebrating Mount Fuji, whose grandeur seemed to him during the war years to stand for the essential nature of Japan, and poems about various temples and gardens that suggested not only tradition but timelessness beyond the created works of man.

He was known as the discoverer of various poets, especially Miyazawa Kenji and Yagi Jūkichi (1898–1927). Yagi associated with members of the future *Rekitei* group, but his delicate, brief poems, often colored by his Christian faith, had little in common with Kusano's style or convictions.

The *Rekitei* poets included, nominally at least, the most fiercely independent of modern Japanese poets, Kaneko Mitsuharu (1895–1975), who went his solitary, cantankerous way unaffected by shifting poetic tastes. One of his early works, "Hantai" (Opposition), written about 1917, opened with the lines: "As a child I was against school,/ And now I'm against work./ I loathe above all wholesomeness, principles and everything of the kind./ Nothing makes people so hardhearted as wholesomeness and principles./ Of course I'm against *Yamato-damashii;*/ *Giri* and *ninjō* make me want to vomit . . . ." The poem concludes: "I am convinced that opposition is the one decent thing in human life./ To oppose is to live./ To oppose is to take hold of yourself." [351]

Although this poem is crude and immature, it foreshadows exactly the cranky spirit of resistance that characterized Kaneko through his many changes of poetic stance. His fame today rests largely—but by no means exclusively—on the fact that he alone of the Japanese poets expressed opposition to the policies of the militarists in the 1930s; he moreover managed to get his seditious poems published, despite the dangers, rather than discreetly putting them away for the future. Various theories have been advanced as to why Kaneko alone resisted, when other poets who were opposed to the war were reduced to silence or else capitulated and wrote poetry that accorded with the wartime aims of the nation. Some critics attribute his resistance to his ingrained opposition to whatever was accepted, the spirit expressed in his youthful poem "Opposition." This factor cannot be disputed, but Kaneko's long residence abroad, both in Europe and in Asia, has suggested to other critics that he was able to make his scathing criticism of Japan in the 1930s because he looked at his country with the eyes of a foreigner. Still other critics have pointed to the strongly nihilistic streak running through Kaneko's poetry as the source of his refusal to accommodate himself to the world.[352] The writings of Max Stirner, whom he read in Japanese translation, had a profound effect on Kaneko, inducing in him a nihilism that rejected everything for the sake of the poet's self-assertion; Kaneko's anarchism was thus not the political variety of Takahashi Shinkichi or Kusano Shimpei, but closely derived from Stirner's profession of egotism.[353]

No doubt each of these three explanations of Kaneko's resistance is valid, if incomplete. Kaneko's refusal to associate himself with any political ideology eventually meant that his heroic resistance to militarism would be accorded only grudging praise by postwar critics committed to more "positive" action.[354] He unquestionably ranks among the important poets of the 1930s, though his fame as a resister has tended to eclipse his purely poetic merits.

Kaneko inherited a fortune in 1917 (200,000 yen, worth about twice that many dollars in 1980), which he ran through with incredible rapidity. One large chunk of this inheritance paid for his journey to Europe in 1919, the same year he privately published his first collection of verse. Most of his time was spent in Belgium, near Brussels, and it was the most decisive and fruitful period of his entire life, according to his later testimony.[355] Unlike Takamura Kōtarō, whose stay abroad led to mixed feelings of admiration and alienation, Kaneko fitted in completely with his surroundings; the poetry written as the result of his year in Europe was definitely not marked by a sense of estrangement.[356] While in Belgium he read French poetry, ranging from Gautier and Musset to Baudelaire, Leconte de Lisle, and Émile Verhaeren. The product of this study was his collection *Kogane Mushi* (The Gold Bug, 1923), his first work of distinction. The tone is elevated, even Parnassian, and the influence of Verhaeren especially can be traced in the long lines. The imagery is "poetic," and rather conventional, and the atmosphere is of dreams and fantasies; at the time he was fascinated by the rich, mysterious world of the paintings of Gustave Moreau and of the Bengal miniaturists.[357] Some poems are "oriental" in the manner of Leconte de Lisle, rather than of any Japanese poet. The collection is minor, rather shallow, but it represented a necessary first step in the attainment of poetic techniques through imitation and practice.

Kaneko returned to Japan in 1921, and spent two years polishing *The Gold Bug* before publishing the collection. In 1925 he produced two volumes of translations of French poetry. His next collection, *Mizu no Rurō* (Wandering over Water), appeared in 1926. It represented a distinct stage of Kaneko's development as a poet, both in the incorporation of the nihilist thought of Stirner and in the choice of familiar, even repulsive materials (as in a poem describing worn-out shoes for sale at a second-hand dealer's) in place of the elegant, Parnassian subjects of *The Gold Bug*; but Kaneko still had not found his characteristic, bitterly mocking style. The title of the collection *Wandering over Water* proved to be prophetic: Kaneko's wanderings to China and Europe began the next year, and he did not return to Japan until 1932.

Kaneko's travels were inspired not by love of foreign countries so much as by a powerful desire to escape from Japan. This impulse seems to have originated when he discovered his wife had been unfaithful to him during his absence in China. He took his wife along on his peregrinations, and they lived together abroad in great poverty, mainly in Paris. During this time Kaneko, reduced to performing menial labor, gave up literature altogether. It was on his return to Japan, while in Singapore, that he felt an impulse to write poetry again.[358]

In 1935 Kaneko began to publish his new poems, mainly in the magazine *Chūō Kōron*. In December his controversial poem "Tōdai" (The Lighthouse) appeared in that magazine. During the next two years, at a time when almost all other writers, apprehensive about the increasing pressure from the militarists, refrained from making any direct or indirect criticism, Kaneko continued to publish his attacks. He became more radical in his political views. The approach of the second China Incident was heralded for him when, late one night hearing a strange rumbling outside his house, he opened the window and saw a procession of tanks rolling by; this sight inspired in him an antipathy that soon found expression in poetry.

Kaneko's new collection *Same* (The Shark) was ready in 1937, but he was urged to delay publication until the situation—the war in China—had calmed. He was persuaded by these arguments, but just at this time the editor of *Jimmin Bunko* (People's Library), a left-wing magazine, urged Kaneko to publish his book immediately, precisely because of the particular importance it would have under the tense circumstances.[359] Kaneko at once agreed, and *The Shark* appeared that year. It may be wondered how such a book managed to evade censorship, especially considering that it was published by a left-wing company. Probably the traditional stupidity of censors accounted for this lapse. Because the poems did not overtly express Kaneko's attacks on the emperor, the atrocities of the Japanese army, or Japanese feudalistic morality, but concealed his views under the imagery, transparent though it was, *The Shark* was published without incident.

The most striking poem in the collection is "The Lighthouse." This is the first section:

> You're not allowed to look too deep into the sky:
> The depths of the sky
> Are swarming with gods.
>
> In the ether, sticky as jelly, floats
> Hair from an angel's armpits,
> Moulten hawk feathers.
>
> An immense smell from the gods' skins, like burning bronze—
> You mustn't look too deep into the sky,
> The light would burn your eyes out.
>
> Down from the depths of the sky comes the everlasting authority.
> Anyone who violates the sky
> Will be punished.
>
> A single white candle
> Stands bolt upright in the middle of the sky
> To which only pious souls ascend—
> The lighthouse.[360]

In the above section of the poem the sky represents the sacred atmosphere surrounding the emperor, the source of "everlasting authority." Ordinary mortals are not permitted to look into this forbidden world, which gives off a terrible stench of burning bronze; whoever transgresses the law is punished. Yet occasionally ugly hair and feathers drift down, revealing the true nature of the gods. The poem concludes:

> But instantly divine punishment strikes us, the profaners of the
>   conceited gods, the seekers of freedom.
> A roar of thunder.
> No—those were only nagging flies

Buzzing around, directly before the lighthouse.
They circle abreast, intimidatingly,
Then flop over, baring their icy teeth.

First one,
Then another,
Loaded with divine oracles,
Five seaplane bombers.

Once one has the key to the poem it is simple to unravel Kaneko's meaning, but fortunately the censors lacked the imagination to uncover the key.

Kaneko's next collection did not appear until 1946, after the war had ended. He continued, however, to write poems he could not publish. In 1944 he helped his son to evade conscription by feeding him herbs that induced an attack of asthma. In the afterword to his collection *Rakkasan* (Parachute, 1948) he described his wartime activity: "This collection consists of relatively early works chosen from among the poems written between the beginning of the war with China and the last days of the war in 1945. They were all composed with the intention of publishing them, and almost half in fact appeared, despite the dangers involved." [361]

The title poem "Parachute" could be published even during the war because Kaneko cleverly parroted the approved sentiments in the course of the poem, even though any reader sensitive to his style would surely have realized that Kaneko was parodying rather than preaching. In the second stanza he describes his feelings as he floats down over Japan in his parachute: he notes with satisfaction the thrift and diligence of the inhabitants, the decorum of the women, the smiling acceptance of poverty, the deep mutual understanding of all Japanese, the patriotism. The catalogue continues, climaxing with:

Rows of houses of *giri* and *ninjō*,
Miniature trees,
Fuji a figurine.[362]

It is hard to imagine anyone not detecting the irony. Kaneko knew he was taking a serious risk, but he felt he had to do something to "keep the flame of liberty from flickering out." [363] At a time when almost all poets of repute had joined the Bungaku Hōkoku Kai (Patriotic Writers' Association), and quantities of patriotic rubbish was being turned out even by first-rate poets, Kaneko's solitary resistance cannot fail to stir us. His collection *Ga* (Moths, 1948) contained some of his most impressive writing, still in the spirit of resistance, but his later poetry, lacking the burning urgency of his wartime attacks, seemed weaker and less interesting; some critics even felt that there had been a retreat to the Symbolism of Kaneko's first period. His reputation will depend on the poems composed under stress and filled with intense feelings, rather than on his quieter works. His was a unique, solitary, totally independent voice.

OTHER POETS

The poets discussed above were probably the most important of the 1930s. Those who lived into the 1940s and 1950s continued to play an important part in the world of modern Japanese poetry. Other poets, some famous in the 1930s but since relegated to a minor place, some who achieved belated recognition, deserve at least brief mention.

Kitazono Katsue (1902–1978) was described as the "purest and most uncompromising" of the Modernist poets.[364] His poems, whether of the 1930s or the 1950s, are abstract, often consisting of a series of images, one to each short line, carefully disposed but providing no single thread of meaning. Kitazono (known to Ezra Pound in the 1930s as Kit Kat) founded the journal *VOU* (the title was meaningless) in 1935, and kept it going until 1940, despite the unfriendly atmosphere. Various poets who would achieve fame in the postwar period were associated with this magazine, even though they were basically uninterested in abstract poetry, because they found Kitazono's devotion to poetry more congenial than the approved "Japanism" of other schools. *VOU* was revived in 1947 by Kitazono and Nishiwaki Junzaburō, but it no longer enjoyed the popularity it had in the 1930s, when it stood for the most modern approach to poetry.

Murano Shirō during the war joined with Kitazono in publishing the periodical *Shin Shiron* (New Poetics) until the government in 1944 ordered all poetry magazines consolidated into

Nihon Shi (Japanese Poetry) and *Shi Kenkyū* (Poetry Studies). He belonged to the *Shi to Shiron* school of Modernism, but was known especially for his advocacy of *Neue Sachlichkeit*, the dominant literary thought in Germany during the decade before the Nazis seized power. Murano's preoccupation with "things," as opposed to abstract conceptions, is best exemplified by his collection *Taisō Shishū* (Gymnastic Poems, 1939), which describes sports of every kind in a totally objective manner. After the war Murano wrote both original poetry and numerous books of poetical criticism.

Yoshida Issui (1898–1973) is another solitary figure of modern Japanese poetry. Yoshida for many years made his living by writing children's songs and stories, but there is nothing simple or disarming about his poetry or poetic criticism. Yoshida was at first attracted to the Symbolism of Miki Rofū. His maiden published collection, *Umi no Seibo* (Holy Mother of the Sea, 1926), contained poems ranging in tone from romantic lyricism to a deeply philosophical, Parnassian vein. The opening poem, "Haha" (Mother), prefigures the concision and evocativeness of his mature work:

> Ah, the lovely *distance*,
> A landscape forever moving farther away.
>
> Beyond sadness, a midnight *pianissimo*
> Struck in search of my mother.[365]

The poet's recollections of his mother grow fainter, like a landscape receding into the distance, or like a softly struck note fading away. This is not lyricism in the normal sense, but something more austere and conceptual, and the poetry has an elegance exceptional in modern Japan.

Yoshida's finest work was in his series of fifteen three-line poems, *Hakuchō* (The Swan), composed during the war years but first published in 1950 in his collection *Raten Sōbi* (Latin Roses). These poems compress into an absolute minimum of words a great richness of content. Although little known even to most Japanese readers, Yoshida is highly rated by connoisseurs; Shinoda Hajime considered the works of Yoshida Issui, together with those of Nishiwaki Junzaburō and Kaneko Mitsuharu, to be the central achievement of modern Japanese poetry.[366]

POSTWAR POETRY

Hardly had the war ended in August 1945 than various literary periodicals, which had been forced by the government to suspend publication, began to appear once again. The first new magazine devoted to poetry was published in October 1945, and in 1946, when the tides of the new literature began to flow in earnest, a dozen or so new or revived poetry magazines appeared, most fated to perish after a year or two. The editors of these new magazines were for the most part men who had long since established their reputations—Kaneko Mitsuharu, Kitazono Katsue, and the like—but new names were also prominent. Most of the younger poets had belonged to prewar Modernist groups, such as those associated with *VOU* or *Shin Ryōdo*, but had been forced to give up poetry when conscripted into military service. They returned to Tokyo to find the city devastated by war and pervaded by an atmosphere of nihilism and despair. But there were also glimmerings of hope: one of the earliest postwar magazines, *Nihon Mirai-ha* (Japanese Futurism), was so called not after the Italian Futurists but out of a belief that Japan still had a future; its publication was heralded by an appeal to all poets who believed in the future of Japan to rally round.[367]

ARECHI, THE POETS OF THE WASTELAND

The first important postwar group were the *Arechi* (Wasteland) poets. The magazine *Arechi* began to appear in September 1947. The members were described by Yoshimoto Takaaki as being "extremely internal in their attitude toward poetry, ethical in their attitude toward reality, and classical in their techniques."[368] They were typified by Tamura Ryūichi (b. 1923); his conviction, as the result of witnessing the devastation of the war, was that in a world where everything had been laid waste there was nowhere left for him and his fellows either to live or to die. His preoccupation was with death, and with lives that have no possible fulfillment.[369] The gloom of Tamura's outlook suggests at least indirect association with the quite different T. S. Eliot of *The Waste Land*. The *Arechi* poets were described as having been disillusioned by war even before they themselves experienced it, from their knowledge of Europe after World War I.[370] They turned not only to Eliot but to Auden, Spender, and C. Day Lewis in the hopes of finding guidance for their imaginative powers in a chaotic world.

Tamura and the other *Arechi* poets, though still under the influence of such Modernists as Nishiwaki Junzaburō, Murano Shirō, and Kitazono Katsue, felt that they had to reject a poetic stance that insisted on artistry in language and form, almost to the exclusion of any expression of concern with society. After the war the Modernists returned to their accustomed manner, almost unchanged, but the younger poets could not be satisfied with such lofty indifference to the world around them.

Five monthly issues of *Arechi* appeared by January 1948; then, following a lapse of some months, the sixth and final issue was published. In 1951, however, the *Arechi* poets began to publish an annual anthology of their works. The 1951 volume contained a manifesto stating the special beliefs and aims of the group. It opened with the sentence "The present is a wasteland." After describing the kind of "salvation" obtainable through protests against and escape from destruction, it stated the distinctive features of their school: "We dislike most of all the cultural anemia involved in leaving out of consideration simple, unadorned life and prating on instead about acquired skills or polished intelligence and the like; and we consider that to reject fantasy and to make words exclusively subordinate to narrow articles of faith or to a political means is even more to be avoided." [371] With these words they rejected both the Modernism and the Socialist Realism of the prewar poets.

The poets of the initial *Arechi* group, in addition to Tamura, were Ayukawa Nobuo (1920–1986), Miyoshi Toyoichirō (1920–1992), Kitamura Tarō (1922–1980), and Kuroda Saburō (1920–1984). The opening poem in the 1951 *Arechi* anthology, *Bochi no Hito* (Man from the Graveyard) by Kitamura Tarō, contained the lines:

Who is it tapping on the iron rails?
It's useless

Trying to bring him back to life with your magic wand.
He died in the summer of 1947,
Vomiting sausage-like parasites.
(So many fallen gravestones have been drenched
By the bitter-cold fog.)
He died, his eyes turned up with hope, torn apart
By pain,
By humiliation.[372]

The poem "Shinda Otoko" (The Dead Man) by Ayukawa Nobuo, in the same collection, is addressed to a poet who died in Burma. It concludes:

The day you were buried, nobody spoke at the grave,
There were no witnesses.
There was no indignation, no pathos, no soft chair of discontent.
Lifting up your eyes to the sky,
You just lay there quietly, your feet encased in heavy boots.
"Good-bye. Neither sun nor sea is to be trusted!"
M! M, sleeping in the earth,
Does the wound in your chest still hurt, even now? [373]

His long poem *Kyōjō no Hito* (Man on the Bridge) powerfully evoked the loneliness and the gray cold of an "unreal city," no doubt Tokyo just after the war.

Man on the bridge!
Cigarette stuck carelessly in your mouth,
You have returned to the destroyed landscape.
The blood of fresh hopes
Halts your feet, in a "present" that commands you to wait.[374]

But hope, like the remembrances of times past when "once there were springs, brimming with life-force and nourishment, that formed pools in the fields and overflowed onto the earth," is illusory:

Man on the bridge!
The night has come, inside you
And outside you both.

The shadows of death have multiplied.
Night has come when the living dead walk round the sky.[375]

The *Arechi* poets described their anxiety over such postwar
events as the outbreak of the Korean War, not in overt terms of
protest or despair, but in terms of an internal sense of danger and
of the presence of death. Tamura, the most accomplished of the
Arechi poets, typified the feelings of emptiness of a whole lost
generation in his poem "Maboroshi wo miru Hito" (The Visionary):

A little bird drops from the sky.
To receive the bird shot down in a deserted place
There is a field.

A scream is heard from a window.
To hear this single scream, shot to death in an empty room,
There is the world.

The sky is for the bird's sake; birds drop only from the sky.
The window is for the scream's sake; screams are heard only from
    windows.

Why should this be so? I don't know
But I feel why it must be so.

There is height so little birds can fall. Something is shut
So screams can be heard.

Just as there are corpses of little birds in the field, my head is filled
    with death;
And as there is death in my head, in all the windows of the world,
    there is nobody.[376]

The poem is filled with an intense sense of loneliness, but it is not
expressed in the lyrical terms that loneliness usually evoked from
Japanese poets. The emotions of the poet have been desiccated
and crystallized by his intellect, making for a totally unsentimental presentation of his excruciating awareness of reality.[377] Another well-known poem by Tamura is "Yonsen no Hi to Yoru"
(Four Thousand Days and Nights):

In order for a single poem to be born
We must kill
We must kill many things;
We shoot, assassinate, poison most of what we love.

Look!
Just because we wanted the fluttering tongue of one small bird,
From the skies of four thousand days and nights
We have shot down and killed
Four thousand nights of silence and four thousand days illuminated
    from behind.

Listen!
Merely because we need the tears of one hungry child
From the blast furnaces, midsummer wharfs and coal mines
In every city where it rains
We have assassinated
Four thousand days of love and four thousand nights of pity.

Remember!
Merely because we wanted the terror of one mongrel dog
Who sees things invisible to the human eye,
Who hears things inaudible to the human ear,
We have poisoned
Four thousand nights of imagination and four thousand days of icy
    remembrance.

In order to beget one poem
We must kill the things we love;
That is the one way of bringing the dead back to life,
The road we must travel along.[378]

In this poem, written some eleven years (4,000 days) after the
end of the war, Tamura revealed great emotional strength, but it
was controlled and understated. The poet must destroy in order to
appreciate what is most important and to express his discoveries
in poetry. He must destroy conventional love and pity in order to
understand the truth of a hungry child's tears. In order to appre-
hend the terror of a dog who instinctively senses things we cannot
perceive, we must rid ourselves of our conventional imagination
and knowledge based on memory. Only in this manner can we

raise the dead, by seeing afresh, uncorrupted by traditional ideas of order.[379]

The *Arechi* poets were gloomy and destructive, but they command respect. They were attacked especially by the Communist poets for their defeatism, and they were labeled "reactionary." The Communist poets in the postwar period assumed that literary and political values were the same, and wrote antiwar, resistance, and other poems in which they subordinated purely literary standards to political expedience. Ayukawa Nobuo, the leading theorist of the *Arechi* group, endeavoring to free poetry from its possible political utility or educational value, wrote that he would "like to consider poetry as the bearer of metaphysical values connected to the salvation of the spirit." [380] This view, shared by Tamura, was expressed in the last lines of "Four Thousand Days and Nights," and helps to explain the strong interest in Catholicism shown by some of the *Arechi* members. Their insistence on the internal nature of poetry, as opposed to its possible uses or misuses, no doubt accounted for the bitterness with which they were attacked by the proponents of more doctrinaire views.

RETTŌ AND COMMITTED POETRY

The magazine *Rettō* (Island Chain), which appeared from 1952–1955, was characterized by its attempt to join the ideals of Socialist Realism with the techniques of Surrealism. The leading figure, Sekine Hiroshi (1920–1994), was determined that the new left-wing poetry would avoid the banality or even childishness of much prewar "proletarian" poetry by being advanced not only in its political views but in its poetic techniques. "Fuyu no Tabi" (A Winter's Journey) by Kuroda Kio (1926–1984), a member of the *Rettō* and other left-wing literary groups, indicated the new complexity and artistry possible in the expression of revolutionary beliefs:

A swarm of fish
Unable to escape
From the onrushing icy water
From the turbulence of the waves,
Heads for the deep pools.
From the banks of the lake in winter

Hiding deep inside the flashing scales
Of the hundreds of dace, a swarm
Of thousands of metacercariae, liver flukes,
Also move out
On a journey of negation and action.[381]

Obviously the expression in this poem is a far cry from the denunciations of the capitalist system or the shouts of embattled workers that filled the old-style proletarian poetry. The poem is metaphysical, intended to suggest through its somehow repulsive imagery the activity of the parasites attaching themselves to fugitive guerrillas as they flee to escape the cold.[382]

In the works of other left-wing poets, not necessarily connected with the original *Rettō* group, there is an even more complex range of expression. The poetry of Tanigawa Gan (1923–1996) has been described as "neo-Symbolist"; it is certainly an obscure vehicle for revolutionary thought, though the poet's mastery of technique is everywhere apparent.[383] Andō Tsuguo (b. 1919), sympathetic in ideology to the *Rettō* group though not a member, combined left-wing political convictions with an acute understanding of traditional Japanese poetry, especially the haiku of Bashō and Buson, and of modern French poetry. In his poems one senses a maturity that is the fruit of a poetic vision nurtured equally by tradition and modern intelligence. It is not necessary to accept Andō's political views to appreciate his poetry, any more than it is necessary to share Buson's religious beliefs or Hagiwara Sakutarō's dandyism to enjoy theirs, though undoubtedly Andō hoped in some sense to stir readers into agreement with his outlook. His finest poetical work is probably "Calendrier" (1960), in which he combined the haiku poet's concision and sensitivity to the seasons with the modern poet's use of language.

Andō's appreciation of the Japanese poetry of the past would be shared by many modern poets. After a long period when the Japanese poetic heritage was either rejected or utilized only to the extent of borrowing archaisms in the attempt to enrich the modern vocabulary, Andō and others of his generation became deeply interested in the aims and achievements of the creators of Japanese poetry. It would have been most unlikely, for example, for modern poets like Ōoka Makoto (b. 1931) and Yoshimoto Takaaki (b. 1924) to have written full-length studies of Ki no Tsurayuki and Minamoto Sanetomo if they had been active thirty years earlier. On the other hand, the postwar poets no longer turned on occasion to the composition of poetry in classical Japanese. The younger writers, as the result of their modern education, no longer can write the literary language easily, but they are able to approach the Japanese classics with the confidence born of a wide acquaintance with the poetry of the entire world.

Anzai Hitoshi (b. 1919) not only rendered translations into modern Japanese of classical poetry going back as far as the *Kojiki.* In his original poems he wrote about such figures as Fujiwara Teika, Minamoto Sanetomo, and Saigyō,[384] deliberately mixing imagery reminiscent of the past with exceedingly modern language. In "Shin Kokinshū Dansō" (1955), for example, he had Teika say: *Non! ore no me ni wa hana mo momiji mo mienu ("Non!* I can't see either cherry blossoms or crimson maple leaves"). He parodied Teika's famous poem by mingling a French word, coarse modern Japanese, and hackneyed terms of elegance. But Anzai's intent was not merely to thumb his nose at a courtier of the distant past, but to give new vitality to ossified traditions. The last line of the poem is:

Kakumei wa kisaragi ni mo minazuki ni mo okorō to shite ita.

The revolution seemed likely to start in the second or sixth moon.[385]

The combination of the modern word *kakumei* (revolution) with the old poetic names of the months *kisaragi* and *minazuki*, was certainly not for comic purposes, but poignant, giving vividness to events of 750 years before.

KAI AND LATER POETRY

In 1953 the magazine *Kai* (Oars) was founded by a group that included Tanikawa Shuntarō (b. 1931), Ibaragi Noriko (b. 1926), and Kawasaki Hiroshi (b. 1930). These poets, conspicuously more cheerful than either the *Arechi* or *Rettō* groups, were interested also in nontraditional poetic activities, such as giving public readings of poetry or writing poetic dramas for broadcasting and television. Tanikawa especially gained a wide following for his fresh, affirmative poetry that acquired its full impact only when read aloud. The *Kai* poets, perhaps because they were spared the ordeal of participating in the war, tended not to dwell on the dark subjects treated commonly by somewhat older poets. They were by no means uniform in their outlook—Kawasaki's lyricism has been likened to that of the *Shiki* poets, Ibaragi was known for her social concern, and Tanikawa was sometimes criticized for his readiness to compose poetry that amused, rather than moved, his readers. The best works of these poets, even though light by comparison to the *Arechi* or *Rettō* poems, succeeded by their combination of expansiveness and joy in poetical composition.

Another important group of modern poets was associated with the magazine *Wani* (Crocodile), published 1959–1962. These included Yoshioka Minoru (1919–1990), an exceptionally difficult but impressive writer; Iijima Kōichi (b. 1930) and Kiyooka Takayuki (b. 1922), devoted students of Surrealism; and Ōoka Makoto, much admired as a critic as well as poet. The *Wani* group, more intellectual than the *Kai* group, was noted especially for its articulate criticism.

New groups kept forming in the 1960s, some associated with "underground" theater movements or popular forms of music, most iconoclastic, and a few with specifically revolutionary messages. Most studies or anthologies of modern Japanese poetry stop with Tamura Ryūichi or earlier, as if hesitating to grant recognition as important poets to men still in their thirties or forties. This is in itself significant: most of the prewar Japanese poets had completed their work as poets before they were forty, and the ripeness of expression that comes with years is relatively scarce. The new poets have the vitality of youth but also the promise of creative activity lasting through their lives. This no doubt is thanks to the completion of the long, painful process of absorbing Western influence, which for so many years haunted the Japanese modern poets. Shinoda Hajime stated that the postwar Japanese poetry compares favorably to that being written anywhere in the world, though he added the caveat that poetry itself, regardless of the country, no longer enjoys its former importance, having been replaced by the novel as the principal vehicle of literary expression.[386] Nevertheless, it is remarkable that Japanese modern poetry, in the sixty or seventy years after Shimazaki Tōson, was able to secure for itself so high a place. It had emerged at last from its long apprenticeship to the West, and discovered how its own traditions could contribute to specifically modern expression of the world.

NOTES

1. The journal was the March 1882 issue of *Tōyō Gakugei Zasshi*. For a detailed account, see Yamamiya Makoto, "Kaisetsu," in *Nihon Gendaishi Taikei*, I, p. 446.
2. Inoue apparently did not recognize that the poem attributed to Cardinal Wolsey was in fact a soliloquy in Shakespeare's *Henry VIII*, Act III, Scene 2, beginning "So farewell to the little good you bear me." The translation was perhaps Toyama's finest. The choice of this particular speech suggests his intuitive awareness of what in Shakespeare could be most effectively rendered into Japanese. The two translations of the "To be or not to be" soliloquy from *Hamlet* are discussed by Yoshitake Yoshinori in *Hon'yaku Kotohajime*, pp. 126–29.
3. *Nihon Gendaishi Taikei*, I, pp. 34–35.
4. *Ibid.*, I, p. 30.
5. *Ibid.*, I, p. 40.
6. *Ibid.*, I, p. 105.
7. *Ibid.*, I, pp. 43–45.
8. It has been pointed out that Toyama's lengthy poem was indebted to Fukuzawa Yukichi's *Sekai Kunizukushi* (All the Countries of the World), a geography of the world published in 1869, which occasionally rises to poetic heights as, for example, in its description of the American Revolution. The chief influence, however, was Toyama's study of the writings of Herbert Spencer. See Suzuki Tōru, "Meiji Shishi," pp. 44–49.
9. Hinatsu Kōnosuke, *Meiji Taishō Shishi*, I, p. 32.
10. *Ibid.*, p. 42.
11. *Nihon Gendaishi Taikei*, I, p. 49. See also Donald Keene, *Landscapes and Portraits*, p. 135.
12. *Nihon Gendaishi Taikei*, I, p. 24.
13. *Ibid.*, I, pp. 53–54. G. B. Sansom's translation of the opening lines (in *The Western World and Japan*, p. 428) delightfully emphasizes the ludicrous aspects of the poem.
14. The translation, by Mori Ōgai himself, is discussed by Yoshitake, *Hon'yaku*, pp. 154–57.
15. Homma Hisao, *Meiji Bungaku Shi*, II, pp. 138–46.
16. For a full account of the heroic bugler, see Keene, *Landscapes*, pp. 275–79.
17. Homma, *Meiji Bungaku*, II, p. 433.
18. Kubo Tadao, "Shiron no Hatten to Ryūha no Tenkai," in Nakajima Kenzō, Ōta Saburō, and Fukuda Rikutarō, (eds.), *Nihon Kindaishi*, pp. 8–9.
19. *Ibid.*, p. 9. Coleridge's *Shakespearian Criticism* was translated into Japanese as early as 1892 by Uchida Roan.
20. *Ibid.*, p. 11.
21. *Ibid.*, p. 13.

22. See the remarks of Ōmachi Keigetsu, quoted by *ibid.*, pp. 14-15.

23. *Ibid.*, p. 18.

24. Fukuda Kōji, "Shimazaki Tōson," in Nakajima, et al., *Nihon Kindaishi*, p. 96.

25. Quoted in *ibid.*, p. 104, from an essay written in 1921.

26. Momota Sōji, quoted in *Shimazaki Tōson*, p. 113.

27. Yoshida Seiichi, *Tōson Meishi Kanshō*, p. 14.

28. Seki Ryōichi, *Kindaishi*, p. 52.

29. Seki, *Kindaishi*, p. 53, thinks so; but Fukuda, "Shimazaki Tōson," p. 113, is doubtful.

30. Fukuda, "Shimazaki Tōson," p. 113.

31. Yoshida, *Tōson Meishi*, p. 20.

32. Translated in part by Hirata Tokuboku in 1896 from the English version by Stuart Merrill, which begins, "I had my birth in the caverns of these mountains." (Quoted in Shimada Kinji, *Kindai Hikaku Bungaku*, p. 385.)

33. Yoshida, *Tōson Meishi*, p. 27.

34. Yoshida Seiichi, *Kanshō Gendaishi*, I, p. 40.

35. *Shimazaki Tōson*, p. 61.

36. *Ibid.*, p. 133.

37. Edwin McClellan, *Two Japanese Novelists*, p. 75. McClellan gives, on pp. 76-77, a translation of part of the poem "Kusamakura" (Pillow of Grass).

38. By Komiya Toyotaka among others; see Yoshida, *Tōson Meishi*, p. 137.

39. *Ibid.*, p. 123.

40. Statement published in 1908. Quoted in *ibid.*, p. 124.

41. Translation by Donald Keene, *Modern Japanese Literature*, pp. 201-2. Another translation (of the second part only) is included in Hiroaki Sato and Burton Watson, *From the Country of Eight Islands*, p. 430.

42. Seki, *Kindaishi*, p. 65, compares this verse to Psalm 90. He finds other biblical sources for passages in the poem and references to *Manyōshū*, Bashō, and Buson, as well as to Tu Fu and Byron.

43. *Shimazaki Tōson*, p. 6.

44. Quoted by Fukuda, "Shimazaki Tōson," p. 94.

45. His surname was originally pronounced Tsuchii, but he officially changed the pronunciation of his surname to Doi in 1932, not only because this was the common reading of the characters, but because Tsuchii was frequently confused in the Tōhoku dialect with Tsutsui. See Seki, *Kindaishi*, p. 334.

46. Quoted by Homma, *Meiji Bungaku*, II, p. 169.

47. Quoted in *Doi Bansui, Susukida Kyūkin, Kambara Ariake, Miki Rofū*, p. 24, from an article that originally appeared in *Taiyō* for June 1899.

48. *Ibid.*, pp. 21-22.

49. *Ibid.*, p. 9.

50. Quoted by Kubo, "Shiron no Hatten," p. 19, from an article published in *Teikoku Bungaku* for January 1899.

51. Yoshida Seiichi, *Nihon Kindaishi Kanshō*, I, p. 62.

52. *Doi Bansui, et al.*, p. 94.

53. Matsumura Midori, quoted in *ibid.*, II, pp. 176-77.

54. *Ibid.*, p. 97.

55. *Ibid.*
56. Matsuura Tōru, "Susukida Kyūkin," in Nakajima, et al., *Nihon Kindaishi,* pp. 122–23.
57. The other was *Ariake Shū*; see Yoshida, *Kanshō Gendaishi,* I, p. 128.
58. In *Yaburegame no Fu,* a more advanced example of his prosody, the lines are often in eleven syllables divided into units of six plus five or seven plus four syllables. See *ibid.,* p. 121.
59. Shimada, *Kindai Hikaku,* p. 225.
60. Yasuda Yasuo, *Ueda Bin, Kenkyū,* p. 20.
61. Quoted by Yoshida in *Nihon Kindaishi Kanshō,* I, p. 125.
62. Quoted by Yasuda, *Ueda Bin,* p. 50.
63. Shimada, *Kindai Hikaku,* pp. 292–97.
64. Yasuda, *Ueda Bin,* p. 49.
65. Shinoda Hajime, *Shiteki Gengo,* p. 39.
66. Shinoda Hajime, "Kaisetsu," in *Gendaishi Shū,* II, p. 487.
67. Quoted from the preface to *Ariake Shū,* in *Doi Bansui, et al.,* p. 211.
68. Mori Ryō, "Kambara Ariake," in Nakajima, et al., *Nihon Kindaishi,* p. 141.
69. See Muramatsu Takeshi, "Shijin no Shōzō," in *Doi Bansui, et al.,* for a description of the contents.
70. Quoted in part in *Doi Bansui, et al.,* pp. 204–05.
71. *Ibid.,* pp. 206–08.
72. Mori, "Kambara Ariake," in Nakajima, et al., *Nihon Kindaishi,* pp. 139–40.
73. *Ibid.,* p. 151.
74. From the preface to *Ariake Shū.* See *Doi Bansui, et al.,* p. 218.
75. Mori, "Kambara Ariake," in Nakajima, et al., *Nihon Kindaishi,* pp. 147–48.
76. From *Ariake Shishū.* Quoted by Mori, p. 149.
77. *Doi Bansui, et al.,* pp. 221–23.
78. *Ibid.,* pp. 247–50.
79. *Ibid.,* p. 230.
80. Some images seem to have been suggested by Rossetti's sonnet "Lost Days" in the sequence *The House of Life,* in which the phrases "ears of wheat" and "drops of blood" occur; and the theme may have been borrowed from another Rossetti sonnet, "Winged Hours." Matsumura Midori insisted on the importance of the appearance of this poem in the New Year's Day issue of a newspaper; the pressing importance of time would naturally suggest itself as a theme when writing at the end of the year.
81. Variants are given by Seki, *Kindaishi,* p. 318. Among the critics who were baffled by the poem were Yosano Tekkan and Baba Kochō. See Yoshida, *Kanshō Gendaishi,* I, p. 159.
82. *Doi Bansui, et al.,* pp. 232–35.
83. Seki, *Kindaishi,* p. 135, interprets *mune* as meaning *ishiki,* or "consciousness" rather than "mind."
84. Quoted in Yoshida, *Kanshō Gendaishi,* I, p. 162.
85. *Doi Bansui, et al.,* pp. 278–79.
86. *Ibid.,* p. 265.
87. Quoted in Yoshida, *Kanshō Gendaishi,* I, p. 168.
88. *Doi Bansui, et al.,* pp. 272–73.

89. Yoshida, *Nihon Kindaishi Kanshō*, I, p. 176.
90. Shinoda, *Shiteki Gengo*, pp. 35-36.
91. *Ibid.*, p. 37.
92. Onda Itsuo, *Kitahara Hakushū*, p. 27.
93. Hiraide Osamu, quoted in *ibid.*, p. 34.
94. *Ibid.*, p. 43. The italicized word is in English in the original.
95. *Kitahara Hakushū*, pp. 7-8.
96. Murō Saisei, *Wa ga aisuru Shijin no Denki*, p. 9.
97. *Kitahara Hakushū*, pp. 9-10. For a complete translation, see Keene, *Modern Japanese Literature*, pp. 204-05.
98. Quoted by Onda, *Kitahara Hakushū*, p. 118.
99. *Kitahara Hakushū*, p. 101.
100. *Nikushimi*, quoted by Onda, *Kitahara Hakushū*, p. 145. Japanese believed that powder from the wings of the butterfly or moth was dangerous.
101. See section on "The Modern Tanka."
102. *Kitahara Hakushū*, pp. 137-40.
103. Yoshida, *Kanshō Gendaishi*, I. p. 255.
104. *Kitahara Hakushū*, pp. 226-27.
105. *Ibid.*, p. 239.
106. *Ibid.*, p. 241.
107. Yoshida Issui, "Shijin no Shōzō," in *Kitahara Hakushū*, p. 404.
108. Yoshida, *Kanshō Gendaishi*, I, p. 271.
109. *Doi Bansui, et al.*, p. 319.
110. Quoted by Yoshida, *Kanshō Gendaishi*, I, p. 299.
111. Muramatsu, "Shijin no Shōzō," in *Doi Bansui, et al.*, p. 396.
112. *Doi Bansui, et al.*, pp. 328-29.
113. Fukunaga Takehiko, "Shijin no Shōzō," in *Hagiwara Sakutarō*, p. 387.
114. *Ibid.*, pp. 387-88.
115. Quoted by Kubo, "Shiron no Hatten," p. 20.
116. *Hagiwara Sakutarō Zenshū* (henceforth abbreviated *HSZ*), II, p. 497.
117. Kubo, "Shiron no Hatten," pp. 23-24.
118. Quoted by *ibid.*, p. 28. However, according to Remy de Gourmont, Gustave Kahn's "most noteworthy contribution to French metrics [was] the symbolist poet's recognition that French, unlike other languages, has syllabic accent, a fact which has long been overlooked." Anna Balakian, *The Symbolist Movement*, p. 91.
119. Chiba Sen'ichi, "Shiron no Hatten to Ryūha no Tenkai," II, in Nakajima, et al., *Nihon Kindaishi*, p. 37. I have in this instance translated *kindaishi* as "modern poem" and *gendaishi* as "contemporary poem."
120. *Ibid.*, p. 37.
121. Itō Shinkichi, *Kanshō Gendaishi*, II, p. 337.
122. *Ibid.*, p. 313.
123. See, for example, *Kashi oyobi kodomo*, in *ibid.*, pp. 318-19.
124. *Ibid.*, pp. 63-64.
125. Seki, *Kindaishi*, p. 265.
126. Watanabe Kazutami, quoted by Kokai Eiji, "Gekka no Ichigun," in Nakajima, et al., *Nihon Kindaishi*, p. 394.

127. Fukunaga, "Shijin no Shōzō," in *Doi Bansui, et al.*, p. 384.
128. *HSZ*, I, p. 325.
129. *Ibid.*, p. 43.
130. *Hagiwara Sakutarō*, p. 20. These comments were made by Itō Shinkichi.
131. *HSZ*, I, pp. 59–60.
132. *Ibid.*, p. 33.
133. Preface to the first edition of *Tsuki ni hoeru*. *HSZ*, I, p. 25.
134. *Ibid.*, pp. 25–26.
135. *Ibid.*, p. 38.
136. Translation in Keene, *Modern Japanese Literature*, p. 375; also, in Sato and Watson, *From the Country of Eight Islands*, p. 474.
137. *HSZ*, I, pp. 38–39. Also translated by Hiroaki Sato, in *Howling at the Moon*, p. 7.
138. *Hagiwara Sakutarō*, p. 30.
139. *HSZ*, I, p. 48. Also translated by Sato, *Howling*, p. 19.
140. *HSZ*, I, pp. 76–77. Complete translation by Sato, *Howling*, p. 48.
141. *HSZ*, I, pp. 86–87. Complete translation by Sato, *Howling*, p. 50.
142. Itō Shinkichi, in *Hagiwara Sakutarō*, p. 63.
143. *HSZ*, I, pp. 185–87.
144. *Ibid.*, pp. 151–53.
145. *Ibid.*, V, p. 402.
146. *Ibid.*, III, pp. 439–40.
147. *Ibid.*, I, p. 68. Also translated by Sato, *Howling*, p. 40.
148. *HSZ*, I, pp. 39–40. Complete translation by Sato, *Howling*, p. 36.
149. Fukunaga, "Shijin no Shōzō," in *Doi Bansui, et al.*, p. 393.
150. *Hagiwara Sakutarō*, p. 57.
151. *HSZ*, I, p. 27.
152. Quoted by Naka Tarō in Itō Sei, *Hagiwara Sakutarō*, p. 59. Hagiwara made this statement in 1918.
153. *HSZ*, I, p. 299.
154. Fukunaga, "Shijin no Shōzō," in *Doi Bansui, et al.*, p. 394.
155. *Ibid.*, p. 395.
156. *HSZ*, I, pp. 134–35. Complete translation by Sato, *Howling*, p. 85.
157. Miyoshi Tatsuji, *Hagiwara Sakutarō*, p. 126.
158. *HSZ*, I, p. 147. Complete translation by Sato, *Howling*, p. 94.
159. Quoted in Balakian, *The Symbolist Movement*, p. 90.
160. Naka, in Itō, *Hagiwara Sakutarō*, p. 143.
161. *Hagiwara Sakutarō*, pp. 249–50. See Keene, *Modern Japanese Literature*, p. 376. Also translated by Sato and Watson, *From the Country of Eight Islands*, p. 484.
162. *HSZ*, V. p. 399.
163. *HSZ*, IV, p. 71.
164. See Naka, in Itō, *Hagiwara Sakutarō*, p. 144.
165. *HSZ*, IV, p. 162.
166. See Itō Shinkichi, *Kanshō Gendaishi*, II, pp. 137–38.
167. Miyoshi, *Hagiwara Sakutarō*, p. 79.
168. This line has been interpreted quite differently. I have followed Seki, *Kin-*

daishi, p. 237, but Kokai Eiji (in *Gendaishi no Kaishaku to Kanshō*, p. 63) gives the line precisely the opposite meaning: "To be in my native place and not be able to go away."

169. *Hagiwara Sakutarō*, p. 308.

170. Tsukimura Reiko, "Hagiwara Sakutarō," in Nakajima, et al., *Nihon Kindaishi*, pp. 182–89, discusses in detail the influence of Nietzsche on Hagiwara's poetry.

171. *HSZ*, I, pp. 360–61.

172. Miyoshi, *Hagiwara Sakutarō*, p. 200.

173. Naka, in Itō, *Hagiwara Sakutarō*, p. 170.

174. Shinoda, *Shiteki Gengo*, p. 126.

175. Murō, *Wa ga aisuru Shijin*, pp. 56–57, relates details of the visit.

176. Quoted by Ōoka Makoto, in *Meiji, Taishō, Shōwa no Shijintachi*, p. 86.

177. Itō Shinkichi, *Kanshō Gendaishi*, II, pp. 107–08.

178. *Ibid.*, p. 100.

179. Itō Shinkichi, *Gendaishi no Kanshō*, I, pp. 273–74.

180. Itō Shinkichi, *Kanshō Gendaishi*, II, p. 107.

181. Ōoka, *Meiji, Taishō, Shōwa*, p. 87.

182. Itō Shinkichi, *Kanshō Gendaishi*, II, pp. 112–13.

183. *Ibid.*, pp. 115–16.

184. Translated by Edward Seidensticker, in Ivan Morris, *Modern Japanese Stories*, pp. 145–61.

185. Seki, *Kindaishi*, p. 224.

186. Itō Shinkichi, *Kanshō Gendaishi*, II, p. 75.

187. Hinatsu, *Meiji Taishō*, II, p. 98.

188. *HSZ*, III, p. 93.

189. *Ibid.*, pp. 94–96.

190. Kushida Magoichi, "Shijin no Shōzō," in *Miyazawa Kenji*, p. 385.

191. *Ibid.*, p. 386.

192. Seki Tokuya, *Kenji Zuimon*, pp. 96–97.

193. *Ibid.*, pp. 130–32.

194. Nakamura Minoru, *Miyazawa Kenji*, p. 173, says that Miyazawa was of the same opinion.

195. Keene, *Modern Japanese Literature*, p. 377.

196. Nakamura, *Miyazawa Kenji*, p. 205.

197. *Miyazawa Kenji*, pp. 311–14.

198. Kushida, "Shijin no Shōzō," in *Miyazawa Kenji*, p. 393.

199. *Miyazawa Kenji*, pp. 370–72.

200. For a sharp exchange of views on the value of this poem, see Nakamura, *Miyazawa Kenji*, pp. 211 ff.

201. Yamamoto Kenkichi, "Shijin no Shōzō," in *Takamura Kōtarō*, p. 407.

202. *Ibid.*, p. 7.

203. A variant text gives "Shūzan" as the name of the master netsuke carver. Text in *ibid.*, pp. 9–10.

204. *Ibid.*, pp. 45–46.

205. *Ibid.*, pp. 48–51.

206. Quoted in *ibid.*, p. 61.

207. *Ibid.*, p. 58. For a complete translation, see Keene, *Modern Japanese Literature*, p. 206.

208. *Takamura Kōtarō*, p. 77.

209. *Ibid.*, p. 297. There is a complete translation of *Chieko-shō* by Soichi Furuta, published under the title *Chieko's Sky*.

210. *Takamura Kōtarō*, pp. 315–16.

211. Yoshimoto Takaaki, *Takamura Kōtarō*, p. 705, pointed out that in Takamura's essay on Verhaeren he identified himself completely with the Belgian poet, expressing gratitude for deliverance from "decadence," thanks to a happy marriage like Verhaeren's.

212. *Ibid.*, pp. 76–80.

213. *Ibid.*, p. 127.

214. *Takamura Kōtarō*, pp. 148–49.

215. *Ibid.*, pp. 156–57.

216. *Ibid.*, pp. 148–49.

217. *Ibid.*, p. 363.

218. *Ibid.*, pp. 23–28.

219. *Ibid.*, p. 56.

220. Quoted in *ibid.*, p. 350.

221. *Ibid.*, pp. 349–50.

222. Umehara Ryūzaburō, quoted in Yoshimoto, *Takamura Kōtarō*, p. 69.

223. See *ibid.*, p. 127. The works published by Takamura at this time were *Dasazu ni shimatta tegami no hitotaba* (A Bunch of Unsent Letters, 1910) and *Kafue yori* (From a Café, 1910).

224. Quoted in *ibid.*, p. 15.

225. *Ibid.*, p. 33.

226. *Ibid.*, p. 34.

227. *Takamura Kōtarō*, pp. 351–52.

228. *Ibid.*, pp. 204–05.

229. *Ibid.*, p. 210.

230. Yoshimoto, *Takamura Kōtarō*, p. 128. See also Takamura's "The Day of Pearl Harbor," translated in Sato and Watson, *From the Country of Eight Islands*, p. 473.

231. Quoted in Yoshimoto, p. 129.

232. Quoted in *ibid.*, pp. 143–44.

233. *Ibid.*, p. 144.

234. *Takamura Kōtarō*, pp. 364–65.

235. Quoted in Yoshimoto, p. 147.

236. Translation by T. Ninomiya and D. J. Enright, in *The Poetry of Living Japan*, p. 39.

237. *Takamura Kōtarō*, p. 338.

238. Quoted in *Miyoshi Tatsuji*, p. 220.

239. *Ibid.*, pp. 219–22.

240. *Ibid.*, pp. 7–8.

241. For different interpretations, see Kokai, *Gendaishi*, p. 130.

242. *Miyoshi Tatsuji*, p. 9. There has been some debate as to whether Tarō and Jirō sleep under the same roof or in different houses.

243. *Ibid.*, p. 412.
244. Murano Shirō, "Kaisetsu," in *Miyoshi Tatsuji Shishū*, p. 229.
245. Murano Shirō, *Kanshō Gendaishi*, III, p. 2.
246. *Ibid.*, p. 3.
247. *Miyoshi Tatsuji*, pp. 142–43.
248. *Ibid.*, pp. 155–56.
249. *Ibid.*, pp. 208–12.
250. *Ibid.*, pp. 203–06.
251. Shinoda, *Shiteki Gengo*, p. 177.
252. Murano, *Miyoshi Tatsuji Shishū*, p. 145.
253. *Miyoshi Tatsuji*, p. 271.
254. *Ibid.*, p. 279.
255. *Ibid.*, pp. 276–77.
256. So opined by Anzai Hitoshi, quoted in *ibid.*, p. 278.
257. *Ibid.*, pp. 284–85.
258. *Ibid.*, pp. 285–88.
259. Kawakami Tetsutarō, *Nihon no Autosaidā*, pp. 67–68.
260. *Miyoshi Tatsuji*, pp. 365–66.
261. *Ibid.*, p. 379. The suggestion was made by Sakamoto Etsurō (1906–1969).
262. *Ibid.*, pp. 380–81.
263. *Ibid.*, p. 382.
264. Quoted in *ibid.*, p. 382.
265. Chiba Sen'ichi, *Gendai Bungaku no Hikaku Bungakuteki Kenkyū*, p. 163.
266. Murano Shirō, "Nishiwaki-shi no Shiteki Sekai," in Murano Shirō, Fukuda Rintarō, and Kagiya Yukinobu (eds.), *Nishiwaki Junzaburō Kenkyū*, p. 3.
267. Fukuhara Rintarō, "Nishiwaki Junzaburō no Eibungaku," in *ibid.*, p. 223.
268. Chiba, *Gendai*, p. 173.
269. Quoted in Shinoda, in *Shiteki Gengo*, p. 186. The statement was made in 1963.
270. For the influence of Keats on Nishiwaki, see Andō Ichirō, "Nishiwaki Junzaburō," in Nakajima, et al., *Nihon Kindaishi*, pp. 235–41.
271. Quoted in Chiba, *Gendai*, p. 86.
272. *Nishiwaki Junzaburō Shiron Shū*, pp. 75–76.
273. *Kinoshita Mokutarō, Hinatsu Kōnosuke, Noguchi Yonejirō, Nishiwaki Junzaburō* in Nihon no Shiika series. Chūō Kōron Sha, p. 294.
274. *Ibid.*, p. 297.
275. Quoted in Murano, *Kanshō Gendaishi*, III, p. 189.
276. Shinoda, *Shiteki Gengo*, p. 188.
277. Quoted by Kitagawa Fuyuhiko, in "Nishiwaki Junzaburō," in Murano, et al., *Nishiwaki Junzaburō Kenkyū*, p. 138.
278. *Nishiwaki Junzaburō Zenshi Shū* (henceforth abbreviated as *NJZS*), p. 143.
279. *Ibid.*, p. 139.
280. *Ibid.*, pp. 69–70.
281. *Ibid.*, pp. 67–68.
282. Murano Shirō, *Gendaishi no Kokoro*, pp. 191–92.

283. *Ibid.*, p. 194.

284. *NJZS*, p. 119.

285. Ayukawa Nobuo, quoted in Murano, *Kanshō Gendaishi*, III, p. 194.

286. Kagiya Yukinobu, quoted in *ibid.*, p. 195.

287. Quoted in Chiba, *Gendai*, p. 171.

288. Kagiya Yukinobu, "T. S. Eliot," in Murano et al., *Nishiwaki*, pp. 455–57, contrasts the two poets.

289. Kitagawa Tōru, *Shi to Shisō no Jiritsu*, p. 240.

290. *Ibid.*, p. 241, quoting Kambara Yasushi, a theorist of the Nihon Mirai-ha. Nishiwaki's remark occurs at the beginning of his essay *Chōgenjutsu Shugi Shiron*: "The reality of human existence is in itself boring. . . . When we speak of poetry we refer to the means of cognating with a special kind of interest (or strange pleasure) this boring reality." (*Nishiwaki Junzaburō Shiron Shū*, p. 9.

291. Kitagawa Fuyuhiko, "Nishiwaki," in Murano, et al., Nishiwaki Junzaburō Kenkyū, p. 139.

292. Chiba, *Gendai*, p. 193.

293. *NJZS*, p. 155. For another translation, see Sato and Watson, *From the Country of Eight Islands*, p. 513.

294. *NJZS*, p. 202.

295. Chiba, *Gendai*, pp. 91–96.

296. It would be all too easy to present a bewildering array of names of literary groups and of founding or contributing members, but only a specialist in the poetry of the period could retain such information. I have therefore limited the discussion to the main journals and poets; works cited in the notes supplement this information.

297. Ōoka Makoto, *Gendai Shijin Ron*, p. 24.

298. Itō Shinkichi, "Nakano Shigeharu to Puroretaria Shi," in *Nihon no Kindaishi*, p. 164.

299. See Itō Shinkichi, *Gendai Meishi Sen*, I, pp. 227–31, for samples.

300. Quoted by Murano, in *Kanshō Gendaishi*, III, p. 143.

301. Full translation in Keene, *Modern Japanese Literature*, p. 378. For another translation, see James Kirkup, *Modern Japanese Poetry*, p. 115.

302. Murano, *Kanshō Gendaishi*, III, p. 144.

303. Itō, *Gendai Meishi Sen*, II, pp. 242–43.

304. Itō, "Nakano Shigeharu," in *Nihon no Kindaishi*, p. 170.

305. Murano, *Kanshō Gendaishi*, III, p. 204.

306. *Ibid.*, pp. 205–06.

307. *Ibid.*, pp. 207–09.

308. Nakamura Shin'ichirō, "Hori Tatsuo to Shiki-ha," in *Nihon no Kindaishi*, pp. 268–69.

309. Other members included Ibuse Masuji, Takenaka Iku, Tanaka Katsumi, Tsumura Nobuo, and Jimbo Kōtarō.

310. Nakamura Shin'ichirō, "Hori Tatsuo," in *Nihon no Kindaishi*, p. 274.

311. Murano, *Kanshō Gendaishi*, III, p. 62.

312. *Ibid.*, p. 66. For another translation, see Sato and Watson, *From the Country of Eight Islands*, pp. 547–48.

313. He read about Rimbaud in *The Symbolist Movement in Literature* by Arthur Symons, which had been translated into Japanese by Iwano Hōmei in 1913.

314. Kawakami, *Nihon no Autosaidā*, pp. 26–27.

315. Kamayama Ken, "Nakahara Chūya," in Nakajima, et al., *Nihon Kindaishi*, pp. 253–54.

316. Ōoka Shōhei, *Asa no Uta*, p. 43.

317. *Ibid.*, pp. 122–23. Ōoka Shōhei doubts the veracity of this statement. Nakahara said that he showed the poem to Kobayashi in July 1926, but at the time they were not on speaking terms.

318. *Nakahara Chūya, Itō Shizuo, Yagi Jūkichi* in Nihon no Shiika series. Chūō Kōron Sha, pp. 9–10.

319. *Ibid.*, p. 10.

320. Ōoka Shōhei, *Asa*, pp. 143–44.

321. *Ibid.*, p. 138.

322. *Nakahara Chūya, et al.*, pp. 7–8.

323. Ōoka Shōhei, *Asa*, p. 178.

324. Ōoka Makoto, *Gendai Shijin Ron*, p. 66.

325. Shinoda, *Shiteki Gengo*, p. 229. Text in Itō, *Gendai Meishi Sen*, III, p. 158.

326. *Nakahara Chūya, et al.*, p. 85.

327. Murano, *Kanshō Gendaishi*, III, p. 83.

328. Quoted in *Nakahara Chūya, et al.*, p. 86.

329. *Ibid.*, p. 124.

330. Murano, *Kanshō Gendaishi*, III, p. 81.

331. Ōoka Makoto, *Gendai Shijin Ron*, p. 64.

332. Kawakami, *Nihon no Autosaidā*, p. 27.

333. Translated by Robert Epp, in *The Poetry of Kaoru Maruyama*, p. 5.

334. See also *ibid.*, p. 8.

335. Murano, *Kanshō Gendaishi*, III, p. 31.

336. Andō Tsuguo, *Gendaishi no Tenkai*, pp. 23–27.

337. Tsuruoka Yoshihisa, *Taiheiyō Sensōka no Shi to Shisō*, pp. 346–49.

338. Quoted by Kitagawa Tōru, *Shi to Shisō*, p. 270.

339. See Tsuruoka, *Taiheiyō*, pp. 342–70, for a list of collections of poetry published between 1941 and 1945.

340. *Nakahara Chūya, et al.*, pp. 408, 412.

341. *Ibid.*, pp. 163–64.

342. *Ibid.*, pp. 178–79.

343. Quoted by Murano, *Kanshō Gendaishi*, III, p. 95.

344. *Nakahara Chūya, et al.*, pp. 180–81.

345. Hasuda was a *Nihon Rōman-ha* critic of extreme nationalist convictions. After the war ended he killed his commanding officer because of a defeatist statement, then committed suicide.

346. *Nakahara Chūya, et al.*, p. 203.

347. Nakahara, though associated with the *Shiki* group, read his poetry at *Rekitei* gatherings. Miyazawa never formally joined the group, but was associated through his admirer, Kusano Shimpei.

348. *Kaneko Mitsuharu, Yoshida Issui, Murano Shirō, Kusano Shimpei* in Nihon no Shiika series, p. 296.
349. *Ibid.*, p. 297. For another translation, see Kirkup, *Modern Japanese Poetry*, p. 117.
350. Yoshida, *Nihon Kindaishi Kanshō*, III, p. 162.
351. Quoted by Shudō Motosumi, *Kaneko Mitsuharu Kenkyū*, pp. 22–23. *Yamato-damashii* was the mystic "Japanese spirit" exalted by the nationalists; *giri* (obligation) and *ninjō* (human feelings) were extensively discussed by Ruth Benedict in *The Chrysanthemum and the Sword*.
352. Shudō, *Kaneko*, pp. 15–17.
353. *Ibid.*, pp. 42–45. Stirner's *Der Einzige und sein Eigentum* (The Unique Man and His Own) was translated into Japanese in 1921.
354. *Ibid.*, pp. 10–11, quotes Yoshimoto Takaaki and Ōoka Makoto as saying that Kaneko's Parnassian collection *Kogane Mushi* contained his best work.
355. Quoted in *ibid.*, p. 28.
356. Andō, *Gendaishi no Tenkai*, p. 85.
357. Shudō, *Kaneko*, p. 32.
358. The special significance of Southeast Asia in Kaneko's poetry is discussed by Andō, pp. 89–92.
359. *Kaneko Mitsuharu, et al.*, p. 27.
360. *Ibid.*, pp. 28–29.
361. Quoted in *ibid.*, p. 46.
362. *Ibid.*, pp. 51–52.
363. *Ibid.*, p. 53.
364. Murano, *Kanshō Gendaishi*, III, p. 258.
365. *Kaneko Mitsuharu, et al.*, p. 105. Italicized words are in French in the original.
366. Shinoda, "Kaisetsu," to *Gendaishi Shū*, p. 497.
367. Kihara Kōichi, "Sengo no Shidan," in *Nihon no Kindaishi*, p. 313.
368. Quoted in Ōoka Makoto, *Gendai Shijin Ron*, p. 236.
369. Itō Shinkichi, *Gendai Meishi Sen*, III, p. 305.
370. Ayukawa Nobuo, quoted by Kitagawa Tōru, p. 12.
371. *Gendaishi Shū*, in Nihon no Shiika series, p. 388.
372. Quoted in Kitagawa Tōru, *Shi to Shisō*, p. 17.
373. *Gendaishi Shū*, in Gendai Bungaku Taikei series, pp. 424–25.
374. *Ibid.*, p. 431.
375. *Ibid.*, p. 434. Other translations of poetry by Ayukawa are found in Harry and Lynn Guest and Kajima Shōzō, *Post-War Japanese Poetry*, pp. 63–68.
376. *Gendaishi Shū*, in Nihon no Shiika series, pp. 106–07. Other translations of poetry by Tamura are found in Sato and Watson, *From the Country of Eight Islands*, pp. 551–61, and Guest and Shōzō, *Post-War Japanese Poetry*, pp. 90–93. Prose poetry by Tamura (and other modern poets) is found in Dennis Keene, *The Japanese Prose Poem*.
377. *Gendaishi Shū*, in Nihon no Shiika series, p. 108.
378. *Ibid.*, pp. 109–11. Another translation of this poem is in Yukio Mishima and Geoffrey Bownas, *New Writing in Japan*, pp. 208–09.
379. Murano Shirō, in *Gendaishi Shū*, in Nihon no Shiika series, pp. 110–11.

380. Quoted by Kitagawa Tōru, *Shi to Shisō*, p. 27.
381. *Gendaishi Shū*, in Nihon no Shiika series, pp. 324–25.
382. Such is the opinion of Murano Shirō, in *ibid.*
383. See *ibid.*, pp. 319–23; also, Kihara, "Sengo no Shidan," in *Nihon no Kindaishi*, pp. 319–20. A translation of the poem "Mao Tse-tung" by Tanigawa is given in Guest and Shōzō, *Post-War Japanese Poetry*, p. 94.
384. See the translations of poetry by Anzai in Graeme Wilson and Atsumi Ikuko, *Three Contemporary Japanese Poets*, pp. 18–21; also, Mishima and Bownas, *New Writing*, pp. 205–07.
385. *Gendaishi Shū*, in Nihon no Shiika series, pp. 212–13.
386. Shinoda Hajime, "Sengoshi no Hōkō," in *Nihon no Kindaishi*, p. 330.

BIBLIOGRAPHY

Note: All Japanese books, except as otherwise noted, were published in Tokyo.

Andō Tsuguo. *Gendaishi no Tenkai*. Shinchōsha, 1967.
Anzai Hitoshi. *Watakushi no Nihonshi Nōto*, I. Shinchōsha, 1965.
Balakian, Anna. *The Symbolist Movement*. New York: Random House, 1967.
Bownas, Geoffrey, and Anthony Thwaite. *The Penguin Book of Japanese Verse*. Baltimore: Penguin Books, 1964.
Chiba Sen'ichi. *Gendai Bungaku no Hikaku Bungakuteki Kenkyū*. Yagi Shoten, 1978.
Doi Bansui, Susukida Kyūkin, Kambara Ariake, Miki Rofū in Nihon no Shiika series, Chūō Kōron Sha, 1969.
Epp, Robert. *The Poetry of Kaoru Maruyama*, in *The Beloit Poetry Journal*, Summer 1972.
Furuta, Soichi. *Chieko's Sky*. Tokyo: Kodansha International, 1978.
Gendaishi Shū, in Gendai Bungaku Taikei series, vol. 67. Chikuma Shobō, 1967.
Gendaishi Shū, in Gendai Nihon Bungaku Taikei series, vol. 93. Chikuma Shobō, 1973.
Gendaishi Shū, in Nihon no Shiika series, vol. 27. Chūō Kōron Sha, 1970.
Guest, Harry and Lynn, and Kajima Shōzō. *Post-War Japanese Poetry*. Harmondsworth, England: Penguin Books, 1972.
Hagiwara Sakutarō, in Nihon no Shiika series. Chūō Kōron Sha, 1968.
Hagiwara Sakutarō Zenshū, 5 vols. Shinchōsha, 1959–60.
Hibbett, Howard (ed.). *Contemporary Japanese Literature*. New York: Alfred A. Knopf, 1977.
Hinatsu Kōnosuke. *Meiji Taishō Shishi*, 3 vols. Sōgensha, 1951.
Homma Hisao. *Meiji Bungaku Shi*, I, II. Tōkyōdō, 1937.
Itō Sakio. *Nihon Rōman-ha*. Ushio Shuppansha, 1971.
Itō Sei (ed.). *Hagiwara Sakutarō*, in Kindai Bungaku Kanshō Kōza series. Kadokawa Shoten, 1960.
Itō Shinkichi. *Gendaishi no Kanshō*, 3 vols., in Shinchō Bunko series. Shinchōsha, 1954.

————. *Hagiwara Sakutarō Kenkyū*. Shinchōsha, 1966.

————. *Kanshō Gendaishi*, II. Chikuma Shobō, 1966.

————. *Shi no Furusato*, in Shinchō Bunko series. Shinchōsha, 1968.

———— (ed.). *Gendai Meishi Sen*, 3 vols., in Shinchō Bunko series. Shinchōsha, 1969.

Kai, Renshi. Shinchōsha, 1979.

Kaneko Mitsuharu, Yoshida Issui, Murano Shirō, Kusano Shimpei in Nihon no Shiika series. Chūō Kōron Sha, 1968.

Kawakami Tetsutarō. *Nihon no Autosaidā*, in Shinchō Bunko series. Shinchōsha, 1965.

Keene, Dennis. *The Japanese Prose Poem*. Princeton, N.J.: Princeton University Press, 1980.

Keene, Donald. *Landscapes and Portraits*. Tokyo: Kodansha International, 1971.

———— (ed.). *Modern Japanese Literature*. New York: Grove Press, 1956.

Kijima, Hajime. *The Poetry of Postwar Japan*. Iowa City: University of Iowa Press, 1975.

Kinoshita Mokutarō, Hinatsu Kōnosuke, Noguchi Yonejirō, Nishiwaki Junzaburō in Nihon no Shiika series. Chūō Kōron Sha, 1969.

Kinoshita Yūji. *Treelike*, trans. by Robert Epp. Rochester, Mich.: Oakland University, 1982.

Kirkup, James (trans.). *Modern Japanese Poetry*. St. Lucia, Queensland: University of Queensland Press, 1978.

Kitagawa Tōru. *Nakahara Chūya no Sekai*. Kinokuniya Shoten, 1968.

————. *Shi to Shisō no Jiritsu*. Shinchōsha, 1970.

Kitahara Hakushū, in Nihon no Shiika series. Chūō Kōron Sha, 1968.

Kokai Eiji. *Gendaishi no Kaishaku to Kanshō*. Yūseidō, 1965.

Kōno, Ichirō, and Rikutarō Fukuda. *An Anthology of Modern Japanese Poetry*. Tokyo: Kenkyusha, 1957.

McClellan, Edwin. *Two Japanese Novelists*. Chicago: University of Chicago Press, 1969.

Mishima, Yukio, and Geoffrey Bownas. *New Writing in Japan*. Harmondsworth, England: Penguin Books, 1972.

Miyazawa Kenji, in Nihon no Shiika series. Chūō Kōron Sha, 1968.

Miyoshi Tatsuji, in Nihon no Shiika series. Chūō Kōron Sha, 1967.

Miyoshi Tatsuji. *Hagiwara Sakutarō*. Chikuma Shobō, 1963.

Morris, Ivan (ed.). *Modern Japanese Stories*. Tokyo: Tuttle, 1962.

Murano Shirō. *Gendaishi no Kokoro*, in Kyōyō Bunko series. Shakai Shisō Sha, 1966.

————. *Kanshō Gendaishi*, III. Chikuma Shobō, 1966.

———— (ed.). *Miyoshi Tatsuji Shishū*, in Ōbunsha Bunko series. Ōbunsha, 1969.

Murano Shirō, Fukuda Rintarō, and Kagiya Yukinobu (eds.). *Nishiwaki Junzaburō Kenkyū*. Yūbun Shoin, 1971.

Murano Shirō, Seki Ryōichi, Hasegawa Izumi, and Hara Shirō (eds.). *Kōza Nihon Gendaishi Shi*, 4 vols. Yūbun Shoin, 1973.

Murō Saisei. *Wa ga aisuru Shijin no Denki*, in Shinchō Bunko series. Shinchōsha, 1966.

Nakahara Chūya, Itō Shizuo, Yagi Jūkichi, in Nihon no Shiika series. Chūō Kōron Sha, 1968.

Nakajima Kenzō, Ōta Saburō, and Fukuda Rikutarō, (eds.). *Nihon Kindaishi.* Shimizu Kōbunkan, 1971.

Nakamura Minoru. *Chūya no Uta*, in Gendai Kyōyō Bunko series. Shakai Shisō Sha, 1970.

————. *Miyazawa Kenji.* Chikuma Shobō, 1972.

Nihon Gendaishi Taikei, 10 vols. Kawade Shobō, 1950–51.

Nihon no Kindaishi, ed. Nihon Kindai Bungakkan. Yomiuri Shimbun Sha, 1967.

Nihon no Shiika, 31 vols. Chūō Kōron Sha, 1967–70.

Ninomiya, T., and D. J. Enright. *The Poetry of Living Japan.* London: John Murray, 1957.

Nishiwaki Junzaburō Shiron Shū. Shinchōsha, 1967.

Nishiwaki Junzaburō Zenshi Shū. Chikuma Shobō, 1963.

Ogawa Kazusuke. *Shiki to sono Shijin.* Yūseidō, 1969.

Onda Itsuo. *Kitahara Hakushū.* Shimizu Shoin, 1969.

Ōoka Makoto. *Gendai Shijin Ron.* Kadokawa Shoten, 1969.

————. *Hagiwara Sakutarō.* Chikuma Shobō, 1981.

————. *Meiji, Taishō, Shōwa no Shijintachi.* Shinchōsha, 1977.

Ōoka Shōhei. *Asa no Uta.* Kadokawa Shoten, 1972.

Sansom, G. B. *The Western World and Japan.* New York: Alfred A. Knopf, 1950.

Sato, Hiroaki (trans.). *Howling at the Moon.* Tokyo: University of Tokyo Press, 1978.

———— and Burton Watson (eds.). *From the Country of Eight Islands.* Garden City, N.Y.: Doubleday Anchor Books, 1981.

Seki Ryōichi. *Kindaishi.* Yūseidō, 1963.

Seki Tokuya. *Kenji Zuimon.* Kadokawa Shoten, 1971.

Shimada Kinji. *Kindai Hikaku Bungaku.* Kōbunsha, 1956.

————. *Nihon ni okeru Gaikoku Bungaku*, 2 vols. Asahi Shimbun Sha, 1975.

Shimazaki Tōson, in Nihon no Shiika series. Chūō Kōron Sha, 1967.

Shinoda Hajime. *Shiteki Gengo.* Shōbunsha, 1968.

Shiraishi Kazuko. *Seasons of Sacred Lust*, trans. by Itsuko Atsumi et al. New York: New Directions, 1978.

Shudō Motosumi. *Kaneko Mitsuharu Kenkyū.* Shimbisha, 1970.

Suzuki Tōru. "Meiji Shishi," in Itō Shinkichi et al. (ed.).

Meiji Taishō Shōwa Shishi, in Gendaishi Kanshō Koza, XII. Kadokawa Shoten, 1969.

Takamura Kōtarō, in Nihon no Shiika series. Chūō Kōron Sha, 1967.

Tanikawa Shuntarō. *At Midnight in the Kitchen I Just Wanted to Talk to You.* Trans. William I. Elliott and Kazuo Kawamura. Portland, Oregon: Prescott St. Press, 1980.

Tsuruoka Yoshihisa. *Taiheiyō Sensōka no Shi to Shisō.* Shōrinsha, 1971.

Wilson, Graeme, and Atsumi Ikuko. *Three Contemporary Japanese Poets.* London: Magazine Editions, 1972.

Yamamoto Kenkichi. *Kindai Nihon no Shijintachi.* Kōdansha, 1976.

Yano Hōjin. *Kambara Ariake.* Tōkō Shoin, 1959.

Yasuda Yasuo. *Ueda Bin Kenkyū.* Yajima Shobō, 1958.

Yoshida Seiichi. *Kanshō Gendaishi,* I. Chikuma Shobō, 1966.

———. *Nihon Kindaishi Kanshō,* 3 vols., in Shinchō Bunko series. Shinchōsha, 1954.

———. *Tōson Meishi Kanshō,* in Kadokawa Bunko series. Kadokawa Shoten, 1961.

——— (ed.). *Hikaku Bungakuteki Kenkyū.* Shimizu Kōbundō, 1971.

Yoshikawa Kōjirō and Miyoshi Tatsuji. *Shin Tōshi Sen.* Iwanami Shoten, 1965.

Yoshimoto Takaaki. *Takamura Kōtarō.* Shunjūsha, 1965.

Yoshitake Yoshinori. *Hon'yaku Kotohajime.* Hayakawa Shobō, 1967.

PART THREE

THE MODERN DRAMA

INTRODUCTION

AT THE TIME OF THE Meiji Restoration, as we have seen, the quality of Japanese literature as a whole had dropped to such a low level that a need for reform was felt by all writers who had become acquainted with the literatures of Europe. The creation of a new kind of poetry and fiction in the 1880s was stimulated by the belief that the traditional literature was exhausted and incapable of expressing the thoughts and hopes of a new generation of Japanese. It is easy, however, to exaggerate the impact on the general public of such works as *The Essence of the Novel* or *Selection of Poetry in the New Style*. Although these books were seminal in their influence, their immediate effects were restricted to a small number of aspiring writers, and the mass of readers continued to enjoy the romances of the Tokugawa era or the kind of poetry that was repudiated by the self-aware Meiji men. The translations and imitations of European novels and poetry were published in small editions, and the booksellers were able to wait for the public to catch up with the new literary tastes. Even though Tsubouchi Shōyō's *The Essence of the Novel* at first sold only a few hundred copies, it could be reprinted easily when the demand arose.

The situation in the theater was strikingly different. Drama suffered the least immediate impact from the Meiji Restoration. Kabuki was flourishing at the time, thanks largely to the playwright Kawatake Mokuami (1816–1893), the one important literary figure whose works straddled the Restoration. The Japanese novelists and poets of the 1860s and 1870s could not stand up to comparison with those of Europe, but Mokuami was a fair rival to any European dramatist of the time. Before long calls for reform of the Kabuki theater, both from the government and the actors, obliged Mokuami to modify his accustomed manner of writing plays, but even if he had wished to stand in the vanguard of the new Meiji culture, practical considerations would have made this impossible. The audiences that flocked to the Kabuki theaters in Tokyo and elsewhere still wanted spectacles of the kind that existed before the Restoration and resisted innovations. The theater owners, unlike the publishers of books of poetry, could not wait for a new play to win audiences eventually; if it did not immediately succeed, they had no choice but to change the play and stage one that would enable them to pay the salaries of the actors.

Experiments with new kinds of theater were made even in the early Meiji era, but they failed because the enthusiasts for modern drama were too few to fill a theater. Some plays written by Mokuami distinctly revealed their time, whether because they treated contemporary events, employed European techniques or themes, or glorified virtues that the new government was eager to promote. But Mokuami's habits were formed during the old regime, and the surface modernity of some works did not conceal their basically conservative nature. Indeed, it was because Mokuami gave the public exactly what it wanted that Kabuki not only remained the most important form of drama during the Meiji era but was able to survive competition from modern forms of theatrical entertainment, in both the theater and the films. It might also be argued that Mokuami's successes artificially prolonged the life of Kabuki, to the detriment of the growth of a modern theater.

At the time of the Restoration, Kabuki and Bunraku (the name that the theater of puppets had been given early in the nineteenth century) shared a repertory consisting mainly of eighteenth-century plays, some always performed in revised versions made in the early nineteenth century. These plays, regardless of the period in which they were ostensibly set, reflected the customs and ways of thought of people of the Tokugawa period, and a morality that writers of the twentieth century would often call "feudal." People enjoyed seeing the standard works of the repertory performed by different actors, noting the slight differences of interpretation that each brought to his parts. They also welcomed new Kabuki plays by such writers as Mokuami, which, regardless of their subject matter, gave the actors many opportunities to display their command of traditional histrionics. The Japanese of the early Meiji era required no special preparation to understand the language of the old plays; and the sentiments voiced by the characters, familiar to them from childhood, were those that they themselves would have uttered if by some accident they were ever involved in heroic actions. The audiences for both Kabuki and Bunraku were mainly plebeian, drawn from the *chōnin*, or townsman class, as it formerly had been called. The beginning of a new Kabuki season was eagerly anticipated especially by the wives and daughters of the townsmen, who normally had few opportunities to leave the immediate vicinity of their houses and enjoyed the break in the routine of their lives provided by the theater.

The audiences for Nō, by contrast, had traditionally been drawn from the samurai class and (in Kyoto) the nobility. Performances were only rarely open to the general public. The last such occasion prior to the Meiji Restoration had been, twenty years earlier, in 1848, when the start of a particularly important series of performances had induced the government to change the reign name (*nengō*) to Kaei, meaning "celebration of eternity," referring to the unending glory of art. From time to time during the following years Nō was performed on private stages within the shogun's castle, notably in 1858 in conjunction with the inauguration of a new shogun.

Nō had been patronized by the shogunate since the beginning of the Tokugawa regime, and by the Muromachi shoguns much earlier. The collapse of the shogunate in 1868 inevitably had disastrous repercussions on Nō. Some actors accompanied the last shogun to Shizuoka after he left his castle in Edo, but there were no audiences for them in that provincial town, and they had to take odd jobs to make ends meet. The Nō actors who remained in Tokyo fared no better. Many were reduced to selling their possessions, one became a ferryman and another joined the police. Nō might well have gone down with the shogunate but for the accident that Iwakura Tomomi (1825–1883), a prince and leader of the new Meiji government who led a mission to the West in 1871–1873, discovered that it was the custom abroad to entertain foreign dignitaries with performances of opera and similar works of the theater. This led him to reconsider the possible functions of Nō as the official state music of the regime.

There were two turning points in the post-Restoration fortunes of Nō. The first occurred in April 1876 when performances were staged at Iwakura's residence as part of his welcome to the Emperor Meiji, the Empress, and the Empress Dowager, who had paid him an official visit, setting a precedent for other persons who would entertain members of the imperial family. The second occasion was the visit of U. S. Grant, the former American president, ih July 1879. Iwakura invited him to a performance of Nō, and Grant, at the conclusion, urged his host to preserve the art. His words were taken to heart.

Preservation might easily have led to a mummification of Nō into ritual ceremonies performed on state occasions. It was saved from this fate by the consecration of the actors, who persevered in their art despite the adverse circumstances, and by the generosity of influential patrons. The brilliant performances of Nō staged in 1915 to commemorate the coronation of Emperor Taishō represented the culmination of many efforts to save Nō during its period of peril.

Nō was not only saved but established for the first time as an art accessible to the entire Japanese people. Many thousands of amateurs learned for their own pleasure to sing the roles of Nō, even if they had no ambition of ever appearing on the stage. Natsume Sōseki was an enthusiastic, if not especially gifted, amateur, and he passed on this enthusiasm to his disciples. The revival of Nō is an interesting page in the cultural history of modern Japan, and it was not deterred either by the Pacific War, when most of the major theaters were burned in the bombings, or by the postwar reaction against Japanese traditions. But there were hardly any new plays written for Nō, and most of these were performed only once on a particular occasion.

Bunraku had also attained its full growth well before the

Meiji Restoration. Unlike Nō, however, new plays were constantly being written, in the hopes of persuading the public that a theater of puppets had a place in modern Japan. With the exception of *Tsubosaka Reigenki* (Account of the Miracle at Tsubosaka, 1887) none of the new works maintained a place in the repertory, and even this play is only of slight literary worth. There was a sharp revival of interest in Bunraku during the Meiji era, especially after 1890, thanks to the substitution of attractive young women as the narrators of the play, in place of the usual grizzled old men. Many intellectuals at the turn of the century attended Bunraku not for the puppets or the plays but for the pleasure of seeing young women earnestly declaiming the lines.

This fad did not last long, and Bunraku was reduced to being a provincial entertainment, popular still in Osaka, but looked down on by Tokyo audiences, who found the puppets childish. The occasional attempts of the Bunraku theater to attract attention with topical new plays were all failures. They were typified by such war plays as *San'yūshi Homare no Nikudan* (Three Heroes, Glorious Human Bullets, 1932), which introduced the bugle to the musical accompaniment of Bunraku, and *Mizu Tsuku Shikabane* (The Water-Soaked Corpse, 1942), which lived up to its title.

The only traditional form of theater that was still capable of growth after the Meiji Restoration was Kabuki. The texts of the new Kabuki plays, beginning with those of Mokuami, constitute a distinctive part of modern Japanese literature because they continued to employ the old language, and because the prevailing sentiments belonged to another age. Kabuki, at least until the time of the Sino-Japanese War of 1894–1895, had served as a mirror of the age, and plays were frequently rewritten so that they would be up-to-date; but the disastrous inability of the Kabuki actors to cope with the specifically modern situations of the war led critics to suggest for the first time that Kabuki plays should be limited to re-creating the past. Many new Kabuki plays, including some of considerable literary value, were written during the twentieth century, but all followed this prescription and dealt with historical subjects only, even though their interpretations of the past were often untraditional.

During the 1890s, when Kabuki showed itself to be incapable of treating contemporary subjects, *Shimpa* (the new school) first captured the public fancy with its vivid evocations of the war in

Korea. On August 12, 1894, just two weeks after the Japanese declared war on China, Kawakami Otojirō (1864–1911), one of the founders of Shimpa, announced that he would present *Sōzetsu Kaizetsu Nisshin Sensō* (The Sublime, Exhilarating Sino-Japanese War) by Fujisawa Asajirō (1866–1917), a member of the Shimpa troupe. The play opened on August 31 and was an immediate success. As Kawakami had promised, the naval battle in the play was staged most realistically, with electrical machinery and fireworks. The text, though devoid of literary pretensions, supplied the actors with suitably impassioned speeches.[1]

The popularity of *The Sublime, Exhilarating Sino-Japanese War* induced Kawakami to stage a succession of other war dramas, including one in which Kawakami played himself as a front-line observer. By contrast, the Kabuki actors' attempts to ingratiate themselves with the public by performing war plays of their own were failures. Kawatake Shigetoshi, the historian of Japanese theater, analyzed the failures in these terms:

> It would seem that at this point Kabuki realized that new works . . . should be left to the modern drama, and resigned itself to the fact they went beyond the limits of its own possibilities. Of course, new works derived from modern life were presented any number of times in later years, but they represented experiments of a collateral nature or special entertainments, and not new developments in the main stream. . . . At this juncture Kabuki, though appreciated by the public of the time, seems to have lost its contemporary quality which was capable of closely reflecting the present day, and to have become an increasingly classical and non-contemporary drama.[2]

Shimpa in its early days shared many features with Kabuki. All roles, including those of women, were usually taken by men, and the exaggerated posturing and heroic style of declamation were borrowed directly from the older art. However, Shimpa developed along different lines in the twentieth century and became a theater known for its treatment of contemporary but extremely melodramatic situations, which were generally borrowed from recent works of fiction. Ozaki Kōyō's *Demon Gold* and various stories by Izumi Kyōka provided the backbone of the Shimpa repertory. The new plays written specifically for Shimpa enriched the dramatic literature of modern Japan very little. The survival of Shimpa depended more and more on the popularity of a few performers, including actresses, who could not have appeared in Kabuki.

One more form of drama must be considered, *Shingeki* (new drama), the only one that merits the appellation "modern." The earliest examples of Shingeki plays go back to the 1890s when some authors, under Western influence, began to write in an idiom distinctly unlike that of either Kabuki or Shimpa. Such plays tended to remain unperformed, though they might be read for the beauty of their language or their elevated thoughts. This was probably the first time in Japanese literary history that plays were thought of as a form of literature that existed quite apart from whether or not they were performed. The recognition of the literary value of drama clearly represented Japanese acceptance of Western aesthetic judgments, though the beauty of the Nō plays or the works of Chikamatsu had of course been appreciated much earlier. The specific task of writers of Shingeki was to create works of theatrical value that could appeal to a modern intelligence.

The task of the Shingeki dramatists was complicated by an understandable reluctance to jettison Japanese traditions. The Meiji novelists and poets did not hesitate to turn their backs on the works of their predecessors, if only because of the abysmal state of fiction and poetry at the time of the Restoration, but Kabuki was still flourishing and satisfied the spectators. It was difficult to sacrifice the brilliance of the staging and costumes, the occasions for exaggerated but overpoweringly dramatic acting, the music, and the dance, in favor of plays in which people sat around discussing their problems in prosaic language against a setting devoid of charm.

The advent of the films early in the twentieth century was another stumbling block in the path of the development of a modern theater. Finally, the competition from translated plays seems to have inhibited Japanese dramatists. The first popular success of Shingeki was with Tolstoy's *Resurrection*, and translations of plays by Shakespeare, Ibsen, Chekhov, Gorki, and others continued to be mainstays of Shingeki even after modern Japanese plays of distinction had been written. A person planning to attend the theater was more likely to go to a performance of *The Cherry Orchard* or *The Lower Depths*, which he knew would move him, than to a new play by an unknown and probably difficult Japanese dramatist. Only since 1945 have plays measuring up to international standards been written and performed in Japan; even so, the audiences for serious modern works have been relatively small, and the rare plays that have won general favor have either been old-fashioned in conception or else vehicles for a popular actress.

Almost every form of theatrical performance that has ever existed in Japan still survives today, ranging from the stylized *bugaku* dances of the eighth century to the latest "underground" happening. The attempt here will not be to trace the development of theater in the modern period, though this is of course a subject of great interest, but to discuss the plays as one element in the mosaic of modern Japanese literature. The works to be considered are new Kabuki plays, most of them written before 1920, and Shingeki plays, some from the early 1900s but most from the 1920s and later.

THE LITERATURE OF MODERN
KABUKI

THE KABUKI THEATERS in Edo continued operating with only brief lapses at the time of the Meiji Restoration, even while fighting was going on elsewhere in the city. The new government, unlike the Tokugawa shogunate, which had tolerated theater as a necessary evil—much as it tolerated brothels—soon showed interest in utilizing the theater to improve public morals. In 1872 the government placed the actors under the control of the newly established Ministry of Religious Instruction (*Kyōbushō*), and in the following year organized an educational movement that was intended to instill spiritual values in the populace, enlisting the aid of Shinto and Buddhist priests as well as dramatists and actors.[3] An article published in an 1874 newspaper discussed the possibility of using actors as preceptors to the public. The editorialist, after noting that the public worshiped the actors as children worship their parents, asked, "If we borrow the actors' mouths, what will the public not obey?"[4]

The government's first concrete steps toward realizing the potential functions of the theater in the new Japan took the form of summoning the leading actors and dramatists of the three Kabuki theaters in Tokyo to the Municipal Office in 1872. They were warned that plays must not be obscene but educational, and the dramatists were urged to write plays that could be witnessed without embarrassment by members of the nobility, foreigners, and families with children.[5]

Japanese who had traveled abroad at this time reported that Western theaters, unlike Kabuki, were refined and appealed to the tastes of the upper classes. The men in the Meiji government were well aware that any attempt to deprive Kabuki of its colorful, humorous elements would probably alienate the general public, but it was determined to avoid giving foreigners who went to see Kabuki the impression that the Japanese were backward or uncouth. Later in 1872 the producer Morita Kan'ya and the dramatists Kawatake Mokuami and Sakurada Jisuke were once again summoned to the Municipal Office, where they were directed to make the time-tested principle of *kanzen chōaku* (encouragement of virtue and chastisement of vice) the central themes of the plays they presented. The encouragement of virtue and chastisement of vice were hardly new ideals for Kabuki; even the most cynical playwrights had paid them lip service. But by reminding these men of their responsibility toward society the Meiji government was indicating its intention of using the theater to disseminate its own philosophy. The playwrights were further urged to make their works historically accurate lest they perpetuate the misconceptions of the past, and to embody in their works the Confucian virtues of loyalty and filial piety, the cornerstones of Meiji morality.

The actors and playwrights, far from being offended by this seeming interference, were delighted to be taken so seriously. The ninth Ichikawa Danjūrō (1838–1903) [6] was particularly enthusiastic about the importance of historical accuracy, and in 1883 joined with various scholars to found a society that was dedicated to the composition of Kabuki plays of impeccable fidelity to the facts. Although such developments contributed few important works to the repertory, they enhanced the prestige of the Kabuki actors, who had officially been considered to be outcasts during the Tokugawa period. This change in their status was tacitly recognized in 1887 when the Emperor Meiji became the first emperor ever to attend a performance of Kabuki. The emperor, who had no prior knowledge of Kabuki, was intrigued, rather as a foreign visitor might have been, and commented, "I have witnessed a most unusual spectacle" (*Chikagoro mezurashiki mono wo mitari*).[7]

KAWATAKE MOKUAMI

The first new development in Meiji Kabuki was the creation of *katsureki*. The term originated in October 1878 with the satirist Kanagaki Robun who, when a new play by Mokuami was presented, sarcastically drew attention to its painstakingly historical accuracy by referring to it as "living history" (*katsureki*). The play, set in the late twelfth century, was indeed closer to the historical facts than previous plays set in the same period, and the costumes of Danjūrō and the other actors carefully reproduced those actually worn at that time, but many typical Kabuki implausibilities lingered on.[8]

Although this play was the first to have been labeled as katsureki, Danjūrō had earlier introduced elements of historical realism into his performances of both standard works of the repertory and new plays—much to the bewilderment of the audiences. The katsureki plays were not only historically accurate, at least in surface details, as the government had requested, but they glorified Confucian ideals, also in keeping with governmental policy, unlike the Kabuki plays written before the Restoration which had more often exhibited a perverse delight in immorality. On the whole the katsureki plays were unpopular, but Danjūrō, relying on his personal following, persisted in presenting them.

Mokuami, a thoroughly professional craftsman who had established his reputation over thirty years before, turned out a dozen or so katsureki plays for Danjūrō, though his heart was obviously not in them. Only one, *Hōjō Kudai Meika no Isaoshi* (The Glory of the Great Men of Nine Generations of the Hōjō, 1884), won a place in the Kabuki repertory, and the first act, known as *Takatoki*, is still frequently performed. Mokuami depended on information supplied by Danjūrō's antiquarian friends in his effort to make the play correspond to historical facts. At one point he complained of feeling so constricted by the facts that he could no longer write a decent Kabuki play, but Danjūrō insisted.[9] The performance was staged in an untraditional manner in the hopes of convincing the spectators that they were witnessing real people and events.

Takatoki opens as Hōjō Takatoki (1303–1333), the last of the Hōjō regents, is dallying with his mistress. The descriptive passages are in Mokuami's familiar poetic style, but the spoken sections were closely modeled on the speech of the aristocracy at the end of the Kamakura period and did not resemble the conventional Kabuki stage language. Word is brought to Takatoki that a *rōnin* (masterless samurai) has killed his favorite dog. The enraged Takatoki at once orders the man's execution; but two advisers urge him to spare the rōnin, pointing out that if it became known that Takatoki had killed a man to avenge a dog it might lead to disorder. Takatoki, at length persuaded by these counselors, spares the man's life, though only after he has changed his mind several times as his anger flared up anew. The clinching argument that the advisers use is that if he executes a man on the anniversary of the death of the second Hōjō regent, he will be guilty of a breach of filial piety. Having finally made this decision, Takatoki resumes his drinking. His mistress dances for him, and Takatoki himself is induced to sing a *saibara* song.[10] Suddenly the wind begins to howl and the lamps flicker out. Several *tengu*—winged goblins—fly into the room. At first Takatoki supposes that they are *dengaku* performers merely pretending to be tengu, and he cheerfully accepts when they offer to teach him a new dance. They make him dance until he is groggy, and by the time they eventually disappear he is in a state of collapse. Takatoki's mistress and advisers, rushing to his side, realize that the mischief was the work of real tengu. The laughter of the tengu is heard as the play ends.

Takatoki is not an impressive drama, though a great actor might find it a congenial vehicle for him to display a virtuoso range of acting as he successively dallies with his mistress, harshly orders a man's death, is recalled to a sense of propriety and decency, dances with the goblins, and finally becomes aware that he, the ninth of the Hōjō regents, has been made a fool of. Confucian doctrines pervade the speeches of his loyal advisers, and the authenticity of the period atmosphere is underlined by the performance of two characteristic arts, saibara songs and dengaku dancing. Perhaps this was as far as Mokuami could successfully go

with historical realism. In another katsureki play, presented by
Danjūrō in 1878, Mokuami's stage directions called for the actors
playing the roles of retainers of Hideyoshi to receive swords from
him in the authentic manner of the late sixteenth century, crawling forward on their knees; but to audiences accustomed to seeing
retainers in Kabuki plays walk rather than crawl, the actors
looked like caterpillars![11] Danjūrō continued to perform katsureki plays for about twenty years; and after Mokuami stopped
writing for him in 1889 he went on making "corrections" of historical fact in the plays he revived from the old repertory.

Mokuami, even as he was busily turning out katsureki plays
for Danjūrō, wrote quite different works at the request of the fifth
Onoe Kikugorō (1844–1903), Danjūrō's rival. They were called
zangirimono, a reference to the Western-style haircuts adopted by
Japanese men after the Restoration, and dealt with contemporary
events, especially those that revealed the effects of the Enlightenment. Mokuami was basically untouched by the Restoration. He
was fifty-two at the time, too old to change much, and his assistants, the men who collaborated on the plays and wrote the less
important sections, were also products of an earlier society. It is
nonetheless true that Mokuami's zangirimono included scenes
and situations that were unimaginable before the Restoration.
The characters wear Western clothes and speak familiarly of
banks, railways, post offices, and diamond rings, and the former
samurai are eager to get ahead in the world by self-help, in the
Meiji manner. Mokuami moreover threw his energies into the
task of accommodating himself to the new regime, distasteful
though some of its ideals must have been to a conservative, unbending old man. For all the problems created by the necessity of
representing contemporary, untraditional ways in his plays, it was
probably easier for Mokuami to write the zangirimono than the
katsureki plays, which hamstrung his imagination by not allowing
him to tamper with historical facts. In order to depict the new
Tokyo with convincing realism, Mokuami walked through the
streets, observing people and their ways, providing authentic
touches to the zangirimono, though the plays were essentially old-
fashioned.

Mokuami wrote altogether twenty-eight zangirimono, beginning with *Tōkyō Nichinichi Shimbun*, staged at the newly constructed Morita Theater on October 31, 1873. The play was based

on an article in the newspaper which lent its name to the title. Frequent mentions of newspapers in the dialogue gave such prominence to this new institution in Japanese life as to make one suspect that the purpose of the play was publicity. The basic plot, a tale of murder and revenge, differed little from those of the late Tokugawa period, but the characters and situations were new.

The central character, Torigoe Jinnai, is a rōnin who has led a dissolute life ever since the changes brought about by the Meiji government ended his usefulness as a samurai. One day the prosperous townsman Chichibuya Hanzaemon, a man well known for his charitable deeds, accidentally overhears a young couple who are planning to kill themselves because of their desperate financial circumstances. He gives them seventy yen to surmount the crisis. After the young people happily depart Jinnai drunkenly stumbles onto the scene, and for no good reason kills Hanzaemon. The young couple are traced by the serial numbers on the bills given them by their benefactor, and are arrested on a charge of having killed him. Jinnai learns of their predicament from the *Tōkyō Nichinichi Shimbun* and, moved to contrition, sends a telegram to the authorities confessing his guilt. After killing Hanzaemon he had fled to Kobe, but he now intends to surrender to the Tokyo police as soon as possible. He tells an acquaintance: "Fortunately I have the money I raised by selling my swords. If I take a steamship from Kobe, I'll be in Yokohama in three days. I'll take a train as soon as I arrive, and on the same day I'll give myself up in Tokyo and accept the punishment I deserve for having killed a man." [12]

Jinnai's shame over his crime was inspired by hearing a Buddhist sermon on the evils of alcohol, and his decision to save the lives of the young couple was worthy of a Confucian samurai, but the props of his speech were entirely new. He decides to inform the authorities by telegram, and to take a steamship and train on his way from Kobe to Tokyo. Moreover, Jinnai was able to make the journey only because, as the result of an edict issued in 1871, samurai were no longer required to wear swords, and he could therefore sell his. He had in fact originally planned to use the money raised by selling his swords to set himself up in business.

Tōkyō Nichinichi Shimbun was not a success, but it is of historical significance as the first Kabuki play to portray the Meiji era. The settings were deliberately chosen to emphasize the distance from the world traditionally depicted in Kabuki: the prologue takes place before a stone and brick telegraph office, and each of the following acts is set in equally unfamiliar surroundings, down to the final scene on the Kobe docks. Nor is the world bounded by Japan: in the prologue one character announces his intention of going abroad: "to France or England, wherever my feet carry me." [13] In the last act Jinnai, expressing his admiration for the newspapers, which have been instrumental in his decision to act in the manner expected of a man in the Meiji era, reveals that he no longer hates foreigners, for they have brought the Enlightenment to Japan.[14]

Mokuami's most impressive achievement in *Tōkyō Nichinichi Shimbun* was to depict the new era with reasonable fidelity while remaining within the traditional Kabuki idiom. No doubt he would have been happier to write about the Edo he knew so well, and the majority of the plays he wrote in the 1870s and 1880s were in fact set in the past, including works that dealt with such time-tested subjects as the night attack of the Soga brothers or the warfare between the Taira and the Minamoto. His most popular plays of the period were about murderers, pickpockets, prostitutes, and other denizens of the Edo underworld, in the manner that had earned him his reputation before the Restoration.

The best of Mokuami's zangirimono were probably *Kanzen Chōaku Kōshi no Homare* (Encouragement of Virtue and Chastisement of Vice: The Glory of a Filial Son, 1877) and *Shima Chidori Tsuki no Shiranami* (Plovers of the Island, White Waves in the Moonlight, 1881). Both plays dealt with criminals, and their high points were scenes in which a seemingly unregenerate man is led by a lingering spark of decency to renounce his life of crime and accept the punishment that the new, enlightened regime in its wisdom ordains. Such plays fitted exactly the specification of the government that filial piety and loyalty were to be encouraged in the theater, and the dialogue was dotted with expressions of gratitude for the great good fortune of living under so compassionate a government.

In the last act of *Plovers of the Island* the unrepentant Senta rejects the appeal of his old friend Shimazō, who urges him to surrender to the police. He declares that he would rather fight to the death than spend ten years at hard labor. Shimazō counters with: "Ten years at hard labor? That shows how little you understand things. The government will show special clemency if you return the money you stole and give yourself up. They'll reduce a ten-year sentence to seven, or even five years. And once you've served out your sentence, the crimes you committed will all be washed into the sea and completely forgotten." [15]

Not content with observing the effects of Western influence on Japan, Mokuami on occasion turned to the West for inspiration. In 1879 he wrote *Ningen Banji Kane no Yo no Naka* (Money Is Everything in This World), a comedy in two acts based on Bulwer-Lytton's *Money*, first performed in London in 1840. Mokuami learned the story from the journalist and sometime playwright Fukuchi Ōchi (1841–1906), who had visited Europe and America in 1871 as a member of the Iwakura Mission.

Mokuami transferred the scene of the play from London to Yokohama and changed the names of the characters: (Alfred) Evelyn became Efu Rinnosuke, his fiancée Georgina became Oshina, and his faithful cousin Clara became Okura. The story is of a poor young man who is badly treated by relatives and acquaintances until he inherits a fortune, when their attitudes abruptly change. He tests the sincerity of their affection by pretending that he must use the inherited money to pay his father's debts. His fair-weather friends at once melt away, and only his cousin Okura, who has herself endured similar hardships, remains loyal. The play's moral, that goodness is better than money, was hardly revolutionary, but it made a noteworthy departure from more typical Confucian themes, and the consuming interest in money was particularly relevant to the commercially minded society of early Meiji Japan.[16]

Comparing Bulwer-Lytton's original play with Mokuami's adaptation, one cannot but be struck by the superiority of the latter. Mokuami used the original freely, adding or subtracting characters as he saw fit. On the whole, the transformation into a Japanese play was completely convincing, even to small details of the characterization. For example, in Bulwer-Lytton's *Money* the hero inherits a fortune from a bachelor uncle, but in Japan a bachelor uncle would have been such an oddity that Mokuami changed the uncle into a childless widower. At some points, however, Mokuami unaccountably gave the characters an exotic touch: for example, one man who does not appear in Bulwer-Lytton's work is called Garada Usuemon, an improbable name for a Japanese. But his sentiments are exactly right for a grasping entrepreneur of the period. He reveals his mercenary bent in such terms as these: "Every year Hakone and Atami in Izu are crowded with summer visitors. My idea is to open a hot spring closer by, and to round up all the whores in Tokyo and put them to work as prostitutes, only calling them bath-girls. I'm sure I can make a pile of money as the manager of the hot-spring brothels. What do you think of my plan?" [17]

Running a brothel at a hot spring was not one of the ways of getting rich described by Bulwer-Lytton. But even when Mokuami is fairly close to his model, as in his portrayal of Oshina (Georgina), the sentiments are translated into the natural language of Kabuki: "I'd rather marry a man with money, no matter how ugly he is, than have to struggle to make ends meet with a handsome husband. I may fall in love with money, but I'll never fall in love with a man." (*Watashi ya okane ni ya horeru keredomo, otoko ni hore wa shimasenu wai na.*) [18]

Mokuami's play owed some of its effectiveness to an underlying strain that only occasionally surfaces in the dialogue, his belief that the mad pursuit of money was symptomatic of the heartlessness of the times, a heartlessness that had grown more pronounced with each advance in the Enlightenment.[19] Mokuami was certainly not using the play as a vehicle to express his grievances, but the note of personal involvement that creeps into the utterances of the admirable characters probably evoked a sympathetic response in his audiences. *Money Is Everything* ran for two months, an unusually long run, and the foreign community of Yokohama, touched by this interest in Western drama, presented the theater with a curtain, a traditional mark of respect.

The year of *Money Is Everything*, 1879, was the high point of Mokuami's experiments with introducing foreign theatrical materials into his plays. He seriously considered Fukuchi Ōchi's suggestion that he make a Kabuki adaptation of *Hamlet*, and even made a detailed outline of the plot of Shakespeare's play. He eventually abandoned this plan, but some elements in later works can be traced to *Hamlet*.

On September 1, 1879, Mokuami's play *Hyōryū Kidan Seiyō Kabuki* (Strange Tales of Wanderings Abroad, a Western Kabuki) was presented at Morita Kan'ya's theater in Tokyo. This is the story of a Japanese father and son who are separated when their fishing boat is shipwrecked. The father, rescued by a British ship and taken to London, is informed there that his son was killed by Indians in America, and in despair throws himself into the Thames and drowns. But the son is actually alive. He was saved by a Frenchman who took him to Paris. When he learns of his father's death he declares his intention of killing himself. A friend, hoping to distract him, takes him to a "Western Kabuki." At this point a play within the play was performed, a musical drama acted and sung by an English troupe imported from Hong Kong. Summaries of the foreign work were distributed to the spectators, but they were baffled by the undramatic acting techniques, and the English language sounded to them like the noise a chicken makes when its neck is wrung. *Strange Tales* was a disaster. The theater lost twenty thousand yen, and Morita Kan'ya's enthusiasm for foreign innovations rapidly dissipated.

Mokuami's last venture on a foreign subject was *Fūsen-nori Uwasa no Takadono* (The Balloonist: The Palace on High People Are Talking About, 1891), which had for its climax the descent from a balloon by an Englishman named Spencer, based on an actual occurrence of the previous year. Kikugorō, who had watched with fascination Spencer's descent, asked Mokuami for a play on the subject. The completed work included a speech in English written by a Japanese: "Ladies and Gentlemen, I have up at least three thousand feet. Looking down from that fearful height, my heart was tilted with Joy to see so many of my friends in this Kabukiza, who had come to witness my new act. Thank you, Ladies and Gentlemen, with all my heart, I thank you." [20]

Mokuami wrote various other topical plays. An early example was *Okige no Kumo Harau Asagochi* (The Morning East Wind Clears the Clouds of the Southwest), presented in March 1878 and based on events of the Satsuma Rebellion in the previous year. Danjūrō in the role of Saigō Takamori, the leader of the Satsuma forces, scored a personal triumph, and the play ran for more than eighty days.

An even more unusual topical play was *Gosannen Ōshū Gunki* (Chronicles of the Later Three Years War in the North), staged in July 1879 in honor of General U. S. Grant's visit to Japan. Grant was portrayed in the guise of Hachiman Tarō (a nickname for Minamoto no Yoshiie), an eleventh-century general. Grant may have had some trouble in following the parallels between the actions on the stage and his own triumphs, especially because Hachiman Tarō, a general from the south, was victorious in the north. But he was pleased all the same, and presented a curtain to the theater. Color was otherwise lent the performance by sixty-seven geishas dancing in kimonos of red-and-white striped material with one sleeve off the shoulder to reveal stars on a field of blue.

The new ways were hard for Mokuami to understand, but as a professional man of the theater he could write whatever the actors or the public desired. In 1881 he announced his retirement from Kabuki, writing *Plovers of the Island* as his farewell to the theater. Contrary to his usual practice, he wrote every word himself, without assistants, but despite his announced retirement, he continued to turn out new works. His last period was important especially for the plays adapted from Nō. His first work of this genre was *Tsuchigumo* (Earth Spider), written for Kikugorō in 1881—a few months before *Plovers of the Island*. Earlier adaptations of Nō by Kabuki dramatists had usually altered the plots considerably, to suit the dissimilar acting techniques; but there had been such exceptions as *Kanjinchō*, a fairly close rendering of the Nō play *Ataka*. Mokuami's versions exploited the special possibilities of Kabuki while remaining respectful toward the Nō traditions. He also wrote some Kabuki versions of Kyōgen.

Mokuami left behind one unfinished play, which was being serialized in a magazine when he died in 1893 at the age of seventy-seven. A zangirimono written in 1879 was the first Kabuki play to be printed before production, and people continued to value Mokuami's plays as literature, wanting to read as well as see them. Certainly he devoted far more attention to his dialogue than his immediate predecessors,[21] and he revived the sung narratives. This seeming throwback to the past kept his works from developing into a more modern kind of theater; but operating within the traditional framework, he single-handedly revived Kabuki, imparting to the texts a distinction they had never before possessed. Even the openings of the plays, normally left to assistants to compose because the bustle of latecomers tended to make the dialogue inaudible, were carefully written so as to create the desired atmosphere for the events that followed.

Mokuami wrote a total of some 360 plays, long and short, and even though he relied on assistants, the conception and final execution of the plays were his own. He wrote many failures, but more successes. The worth of these plays can be fully appreciated only in performance, and perhaps only as they were performed by the particular actors for whom he wrote them, but they retain their interest. Mokuami considered that his function was to serve the actors, and he probably never thought of himself as a literary man. He was obviously happier describing the familiar world of Edo than the brash new world of Tokyo, but his later achievements were also considerable. With Mokuami, however, Edo Kabuki came to an end. The works of his disciples, though still performed, did not compare with his own. Kawatake Shinshichi III (1842–1901) is remembered for such works as *Kagotsurube Sato no Eizame* (Kagotsurube: Sobering Up in the Quarter, 1888); and Takeshiba Kisui (1847–1923) wrote some popular plays that were inspired by Kyōgen, including *Sannin Katawa* (Three Cripples, 1897). But neither man enjoyed anything like Mokuami's authority. His death, followed by those of the actors Kikugorō and Danjūrō in 1903 and Sadanji in 1904, brought an end to an era.

TSUBOUCHI SHŌYŌ [22]

The most striking feature of the Kabuki plays produced during the years immediate!y after the death of Mokuami is that so many were by amateurs, men of letters who dabbled as Kabuki playwrights. In 1904, for example, works by Tsubouchi Shōyō, Mori Ōgai, Ozaki Kōyō, Tokutomi Roka, Kōda Rohan, and Oguri Fūyō—none of them professional dramatists—were staged at Tokyo theaters. Kabuki was enriched also by foreign works with the adaptation in 1905 of Hugo's *Hernani* and Schiller's *Wilhelm Tell*.[23] Such novelties bespeak the confusion and even desperation in the world of Kabuki.

The Kabuki play by Shōyō performed in 1904, *Kiri Hitoha* (A Paulownia Leaf), had been written in 1894–1895 and published in the journal *Waseda Bungaku*. Shōyō had particular actors in mind when he wrote the leading roles, and undoubtedly hoped that this play would be staged, but although it was favorably reviewed when first published, it took the deaths of three great actors to persuade the manager of the Kabuki theater to risk a play by an outsider.[24]

A Paulownia Leaf was the fruit of Shōyō's studies of both Chikamatsu and Shakespeare; he attempted to combine the stylization of the traditional Japanese theater with the consistent characterization of the Western drama, especially the history plays of Shakespeare.[25] The earliest expression of Shōyō's views on the theater are found in the long essay "Wa ga Kuni no Shigeki" (The Historical Plays of Japan, 1893–1894), in which he discussed the *jidaimono* (historical dramas) of Chikamatsu, Mokuami, and later men. The essay opened:

> The literature of the Japanese theater world has never suffered from a deficiency of good writers, whether Chikamatsu Sōrinshi in the past or Furukawa Mokuami more recently.[26] There are not a few plays, at least if one restricts one's vision to the domain of the *sewamono*, which by virtue of superior texts written by men of superior skills almost approach the Elizabethan drama, at any rate in my opinion. However, when it comes to the various examples of jidaimono, they scarcely merit being considered as historical dramas; those written long ago are, generally speaking, nonsensical, and those of more recent times are for the most part superficial and unrefined. Some of Chikamatsu's historical plays, if considered as dream-fantasies of a kind, spectacles that appeal exclusively to the eyes, are remarkably skillful, but the incidents are too implausible, the characters too uncomplicated for them to be called historical plays in the strict sense, and it is difficult for a contemporary spectator to experience an illusion of historical reality. In general, one may say of Chikamatsu's jidaimono that they are tales of a dream-fantasy land, which borrow from reality hardly more than the names of places and people.[27]

Shōyō repeatedly used the words "dream-fantasy" (*mugen*) to describe the traditional Japanese historical drama. He explained the term:

> In what way do these plays resemble dream-fantasies? In their absurd plots, their incidents which have not the least basis in fact, their unnatural characters, their illogical construction, their diffuse

relationships or, again, their plethora of metamorphoses and inconsistencies, their lack of unity of interest, their unexpected complications and their exaggeration of the materials—in every respect they are fantasies within a dream.[28]

These were harsh words from the man who had dubbed Chikamatsu "the Japanese Shakespeare." They were based on Shōyō's readings in the British Shakespeare, whose works he unconditionally admired. When he read Chikamatsu's jidaimono, they gave him the feeling of *A Midsummer Night's Dream*.[29]

Shōyō.did not, however, favor a complete jettisoning of Japanese drama. He believed that it could be successfully revived providing (1) a distinction was observed between narrative poetry and dramatic poetry; (2) the action of the plays was unified; and (3) the actions were made to stem from the characters of the persons in the plays.[30] Kawatake Shigetoshi, the historian of the Japanese drama, described Shōyō's essay as the first systematic discussion by a Japanese of the text of plays, as opposed to their performance, but more recent critics dismissed one or all of Shōyō's points as "commonplace" and "unimaginative."[31] Shōyō's efforts were directed at eliminating the illogicality, the indecency, or the sadism of the old plays in order to raise the level of Kabuki; but it might be argued that he was unwittingly trying to rob Kabuki of its vitality, which resided in precisely the places he was attacking. In a sense Shōyō was following to their logical conclusions the attempts of reformers since 1886 to make Kabuki fit entertainment for ladies and gentlemen, but he wrote more persuasively than his predecessors.

Shōyō had followed his theoretical work *The Essence of the Novel* with *The Characters of Modern Students*, a novel that was intended to embody his ideals. But he failed to achieve his.purpose, both because of his deficiencies as a novelist and because his attempts at modernization were only halfhearted. He followed "The Historical Plays of Japan" with *A Paulownia Leaf*, a more successful work than any novel by Shōyō, and one that established the future course of the Japanese historical play. The main subject was, in Shōyō's words, "the decline and fall of the House of Toyotomi, gradually brought about by complex and inevitable forces."[32] The action is centered on the sufferings of Katagiri Katsumoto as he struggles to preserve Toyotomi Hideyoshi's family after the defeat at the Battle of Sekigahara. Complexity is provided by a subplot involving the tragic love of Katsumoto's daughter, and by the depiction of the reactions of Hideyoshi's family inside Osaka Castle to the struggles outside. The play is long (originally seven acts and fifteen scenes), and each of its many characters is endowed with some distinguishing trait, in the Shakespearean manner.

With the passage of time *A Paulownia Leaf* came to be recognized as a classic of modern Kabuki, and certain scenes were frequently performed, but when first published it was subjected to severe criticism. Mori Ōgai, for example, found fault with it for failing to live up to the author's own prescriptions for drama, and claimed that too much of the action developed externally, rather than in response to conflicts within the characters.[33] Other critics deplored the excessive influence of Shakespeare.[34] Shōyō did not deny he had been influenced by Shakespeare; in fact, he recalled some years later:

> At the time I tried examining plays written abroad, thinking they might help me in reforming Japanese drama, but I discovered that most were basically incompatible with Kabuki. Only the plays of Shakespeare bore curious resemblances to Kabuki in their dramatic form, though there was no comparison in literary value. It occurred to me that, if this was indeed the case, much could be fused together. I came to feel that research into Shakespeare might be the most useful means of improving the Japanese drama, not only for me personally, but for the Japanese as a whole.[35]

Combining the best of East and West was a frequently voiced Meiji ideal, but Shōyō was more successful than most exponents of this formula. Whatever influences from Shakespeare were incorporated into *A Paulownia Leaf* might easily pass unnoticed if we were not alerted by Shōyō himself: they have been woven imperceptibly into what seems to be a purely Japanese story. For example, the death of Ginnojō, the suitor of Katsumoto's daughter, was apparently modeled on the death of Ophelia in *Hamlet*: both characters lose their minds under the strain of unbearable grief, throw themselves into a pond and drown. But even if the situation was borrowed from *Hamlet*, it does not seem un-Japanese. Again, Shakespearean influence has been detected in the scene toward the end of the third act when Ishikawa Izu-no-kami Sadamasa, who has been tricked into believing that Katsumoto is secretly plotting to turn over Osaka Castle to the enemy, goes to Katsumoto's house intending to kill him. He overhears a conversation that makes it plain to him that Katsumoto is utterly loyal. In shame over his blindness to Katsumoto's virtue, Sadamasa gouges out an eye and begs forgiveness. He prepares to commit suicide, but Katsumoto stops him, and henceforth Sadamasa is his most trusted ally.

The gouging out of the eye may recall *King Lear*, but it can equally recall Chikamatsu's *The Battles of Coxinga*. Shōyō, for all his professed consecration to the ideal of improving Kabuki, was faithful to its traditions of theatricality; that was why he disliked katsureki, which gave greater weight to historical truth than to drama. This meant that in practice he tended not to make the actions evolve naturally from the characters but from arbitrary developments in the plot. The language of *A Paulownia Leaf* is also a conventional stage language, similar to that of the jidai-mono of the previous century. There is even a musical accompaniment to some scenes, including the last, in which Katsumoto and his faithful friend Kimura Nagato-no-kami part for life on the embankment of the Nagara River. This scene, the most celebrated of the entire work, was composed in the customary dramatic verse with alternating lines in seven and five syllables.

Despite the failings in the text, which were pointed out by such critics as Mori Ōgai and Ueda Bin, the fact that they devoted such attention to a Kabuki play signified that they implicitly recognized its literary worth. Indeed, *A Paulownia Leaf* was the work that established the literary importance of Kabuki texts,[36] though plays like those of Mokuami had earlier been read for their entertainment value. The characters, it is true, were not fully rounded, and the dialogue often sounded old-fashioned, but compared to other works in the Kabuki tradition *A Paulownia Leaf* was not only conspicuously well written but intellectually satisfying. It is surprising that Shōyō, whose education after he reached maturity was mainly in English literature, and who was so passionate an admirer of Shakespeare, could have handled so adroitly the Kabuki conventions. His play was in fact attacked not by defenders of the traditional Kabuki but by men familiar with Shōyō's writings on drama who had hoped that *A Paulownia Leaf* would be closer to modern Western theater.

Shōyō's later Kabuki plays, including *Maki no Kata* (1896) and *Hototogisu Kojō no Rakugetsu* (The Sinking Moon over the Lonely Castle Where the Cuckoo Cries, 1897), were more skillfully structured than *A Paulownia Leaf,* but more prosaic; the latter play, though a sequel to *A Paulownia Leaf,* which describes the death of Katsumoto, was stripped of a Jōruri narrator,[37] and the language is close to contemporary speech.

Shōyō continued to write plays until late in life, not only for Kabuki but for dance companies, child actors, and even the films. Two works are of special importance, *Shinkyoku Urashima* (The New Urashima, 1904) and *En no Gyōja* (En the Ascetic, 1916). *The New Urashima* was a modern drama that included traditional dance and music. Shōyō confined himself to expressing the hope that the work might advance to some small degree the improvement he desired in Japanese drama, but the play was greeted with extraordinary enthusiasm. Probably no other work of all Meiji literature was so widely reviewed.[38] The Naturalist critic Hasegawa Tenkei, for example, found in Urashima's torments a symbol of Japanese living in the Meiji era and declared, "I do not hesitate to say that this work speaks for the first generation of the twentieth century. At the same time, it is an expression of the spiritual fate of our Japanese empire as it plays an ever more active role on the great stage of the world." [39] An anonymous critic compared *The New Urashima* to *Tannhäuser,* noting that Wagner's hero returned to the mortal world from the pleasure-world of Venusberg because of his love for Elisabeth, but Urashima returned to this world because he missed his parents: "The play is characteristically Japanese in its portrayal of the love between parents and child, a love based on ties of blood that cannot possibly be severed." [40] Comparisons were also made between *The New Urashima* and Gerhart Hauptmann's *Sunken Bell*: both treat the agonies suffered by a twentieth-century intellectual.

Shōyō's own explanation of the play, published in 1905, was almost entirely devoted to the effects produced by the different varieties of traditional Japanese music, and did not refer to the symbolic meanings that the critics had discovered. He wished to continue the Kabuki tradition of including music and dance in works for the theater but to impart greater content to the plot. He referred to the new genre of theater he had created as *gakugeki*, or music-drama, a plain indication of how carefully he had studied Wagner.[41] The familiar old tale of Urashima, a Japanese Rip Van Winkle, intrigued even the intelligentsia, and the critics were impressed by the grand scale of Shōyō's music-drama.[42] The success was, however, short-lived; for all the initial acclaim, the play was seldom revived.

En the Ascetic, written twelve years later, has been described as a work that inescapably recalls Shakespeare's *Tempest*.[43] Shōyō was still under the influence of Shakespeare, but his use of a language close to the contemporary colloquial suggests he intended his play to be modern as well as grand. The central character, En the Ascetic, was the legendary founder of the *yamabushi*—priests who live in the mountains and are able, because of their rigorous discipline, to effect miraculous cures. In the play En subdues the wicked god Hitokoto-nushi, who has been causing grievous harm to people in the Yamato mountains. En, however, is betrayed by a disciple, tempted (with his mother's connivance) by a beautiful woman, and finally arrested by military officials who accuse him of spreading heterodox teachings as a prelude to seizing power. His mother is held as a hostage to induce him to surrender, but En does not waver. The high point of the play is En's monologue in which he spurns temptation:

> In all the wide heavens and the world under heaven there is only this one great I! Only this undiminishing, never increasing, absolute, eternal I! This I is not opposed to anyone else. Before me are no human beings, no animals, no gods, no demons. I have no mother, no child. I recognize no man, no woman, no good, no evil. There is no life, no death. All that exists is the strength of the great I.[44]

En is the incarnation of strength, and not even the threat that his mother will be beheaded swerves him from his self-appointed destiny. He conquers anything that stands in his path and transcends all internal conflict to achieve an absolute self of incomparable magnitude. Homma Hisao, a distinguished authority on Meiji literature, proclaimed that *En the Ascetic* "in the boldness of its conception, the wealth of its philosophical insights, the richness of its poetic feeling, and the beauty of its language is the supreme masterpiece of the dramas of the Meiji and Taishō eras." [45] But, Homma admitted, the conception was so grandiose and the characters towered so much above ordinary human beings that the play was virtually impossible to perform. It was not staged in Tokyo until 1926, and it was never performed to Shōyō's satisfaction.

When *En the Ascetic* was published in 1915 people in the world of the theater conjectured that, behind the fanciful plot, Shōyō had been describing himself in the disguise of En, Shimamura Hōgetsu as En's unfaithful follower Hirotari, and Matsui Sumako as the temptress-witch.[46] This interpretation lent piquance to the play, but for a contemporary reader it is heavy going, and the Nietzschean message has dated badly. Whatever the effects might be in performance, some of the most admired scenes are comic when read.[47]

Shōyō's most lasting contribution to the development of the modern Japanese theater was probably his complete translation of Shakespeare, the last volume of which appeared in 1928. It is in the old-fashioned language of Kabuki, which conveys the poetic qualities of Shakespeare better than modern-language versions but imposes a barrier between the works and contemporary audiences. His original plays and translations were not meant merely to be read but to be performed and to enrich the Japanese theater. His ambition in the drama, as in the novel, was to enable the Japanese to rival their contemporaries anywhere in the world. The results of his efforts were less immediately apparent in the theater than in literature, no doubt because most Japanese were unconvinced of the need to reform a theater that was still triumphantly successful.

MORI ŌGAI (1862–1922)

Mori Ōgai, a self-proclaimed dilettante, wrote not only fiction, criticism, and historical studies but original plays in both traditional and modern styles. As was true of Shōyō, his most important contribution to the modern theater was probably his translations—of Ibsen especially—but some of his own plays have been praised highly by the critics.[48]

Ōgai's first play, *Tamakushige Futari Urashima* (The Jeweled Casket and the Two Urashimas), was written in 1902, the year that he returned to Tokyo from an army post in Kyushu and resumed his life as a literary man after an interruption of nearly ten years. His interest in the theater went back to his stay in Europe; in 1892 he published serially in a Kabuki magazine his impressions of European theaters, and he had even earlier translated a play by Lessing. In 1900 Ōgai's younger brother, a physician, as a side line founded the magazine *Kabuki*, and it was in this magazine that Ōgai published his first play.

The Jeweled Casket was based on the same legend that had inspired Tsubouchi Shōyō's *The New Urashima*. Ōgai had been asked to write a short play on the Faust legend, but, deciding this was beyond his powers, he wrote a play that was exactly the opposite in character, about a young man who suddenly and miraculously turns old. The work was composed in metrical, old-fashioned Japanese with hardly a suggestion of European influence. It opens as Urashima expresses boredom with the pleasures of the palace of the dragon under the sea. He decides to return to earth and his parents. The fair princess, unable to dissuade him, gives him a precious casket as a keepsake. In the second act Urashima returns to his old home. A group of men have gathered nearby, and the leader of the group, his suspicions aroused by Urashima's jeweled casket, insists on opening it: at once a cloud issues forth, which turns Urashima into an old man. Only then does he learn that the leader of the group is his descendant three hundred years removed, and that the group is about to set sail for foreign parts intending to extend Japanese overseas territories. Urashima offers the young men the pearls from the casket and his prayers for success in their mission, then announces his intention of secluding himself in the mountains.

If this play contains a message for modern audiences, it would seem to be Ōgai's approval of Japanese imperialism, a sentiment quite in keeping with the Japan of 1902.[49] But the play is exceptionally undramatic and has little to recommend it as literature.

Purumûla (1909), set in the kingdom of Sind in the seventh century A.D., was composed mainly as an exercise in stylistics. Ōgai tried to strike a balance between the archaic language of his Urashima play and a more colloquial idiom. The result was fairly close to the Jōruri style, the lines often falling into cadences of alternating groups of seven and five syllables. An exotic perfume, reminiscent of Wilde's *Salome*, hovers over the world of Purumûla, who in one speech says, "I am the Princess Purumûla. Am I not fair to behold?" [50]

Ōgai's most important original play was the one-act *Kamen* (The Mask, 1909), performed that year by the Shimpa actors. This was an unusually sober and restrained play for Shimpa, which normally staged wildly melodramatic works. The actors were baffled by the meaning, and the audiences for the first performances greeted it with catcalls; from the fourth performance it was staged at the head of the bill to get it out of the way.[51] The play is nevertheless so convincing and so skillfully constructed that one authority called it a "truly modern drama." [52] Obviously, Ōgai chose the wrong company to perform his play. But any group of Japanese actors of that time would have had trouble with a play that provided so few opportunities for displays of virtuoso acting. One enthusiast said of *The Mask* that "*as a play*, it is the greatest masterpiece of modern drama." [53] This is high praise, indeed, but by qualifying his remark by saying "*as a play*" he was obviously distinguishing the literary quality from its effectiveness in performance, pointing the way to the armchair drama of future years.

The Mask is written throughout in a natural colloquial style, which is devoid of conventional literary flourishes. The reluctance of Japanese dramatists to abandon the traditional stage language had at last been overcome; here was a play that not only portrayed contemporary Japanese living in Tokyo but included quotations from Nietzsche and ended with the anticipated pleasure of a piano recital. Ōgai had left behind the implausible situations of the old dramas, but the characters are hardly more than stereotypes and there is insufficient dramatic interest. Perhaps the meaning of *The Mask* was essentially personal: Ōgai himself wore a mask before the world and led a life that the average man of his day found incomprehensible. Perhaps also the death of the brother who had founded the magazine *Kabuki* gave another dimension to this play about a dying man.[54]

Ōgai did not choose to continue writing in the modern vein he had explored. His only other important work for the theater, *Ikuta-gawa* (The River Ikuta, 1910), was derived from a story found in the *Manyōshū* and *Yamato Monogatari* about a maiden who is sought by two equally desirable suitors. The play, unusual for a work on a historical subject, was written in the colloquial, but it has an atmosphere of unreality, of otherworldly indefiniteness that is reminiscent of Maeterlinck. In this sense *The River Ikuta* might be said to be modern, but its thematic material represented a turning back from the contemporary themes of *The Mask*.

OKAMOTO KIDŌ (1872–1932)

During the five or six years after the Russo-Japanese War, Kabuki was in the doldrums. No actor of prominence had emerged to replace in the affections of the public the major figures who had recently died, and the new plays written for Kabuki had little appeal. The nontraditional forms of theater, Shimpa and Shingeki, stepped in to fill this void and for a time acquired a considerable following,[55] but it did not take long for Kabuki to regain its hold on the Tokyo audiences.

In 1908 a newspaper reporter named Okamoto Kidō, who had been publishing unperformed plays in theater magazines since 1896, and who had had one notably unsuccessful play performed by the Kabuki actors in 1902, was asked by Kawakami Otojirō for a new play. It was to be for the second Ichikawa Sadanji (1880–1940), a young actor who enthusiastically favored reform of Kabuki. The play, *Ishin Zengo* (Before and After the Restoration), was successfully performed in September of that year, the beginning of the collaboration between Kidō and Sadanji, which would be a central force in the revival of Kabuki.

The new Kabuki of Kidō and Sadanji would be marked by greater realism in the dialogue and story than the standard works of the repertory, but it was still definitely a theater of actors, for whom the dramatists supplied vehicles that displayed to fullest advantage the particular talents of different men. The plays were almost all historical dramas, and the situations were familiar from other works about the same figures; but generally some unexpected psychological development would call attention to the modernity of the play. The elimination of the Jōruri musical accompaniment and the customary mimed dancing brought the new

Kabuki much closer than the old to realistic drama; some of these plays were in fact successfully staged by Shingeki actors.

The first major triumph of the combination of Kidō and Sadanji came in 1911 with *Shuzenji Monogatari* (A Tale of Shuzenji), a one-act play. This is the story of the mask-carver Yashaō who lives at the Shuzenji, a Buddhist temple on the Izu Peninsula. He has been commanded by the shogun Minamoto Yorie, who is in seclusion nearby, to carve a mask of his face. Early in the play Yorie visits Yashaō to complain of the inordinate time it has taken to fulfill his commission. Yashaō explains his difficulty: no matter how carefully he has delineated the features, the mask always looks like a corpse's, not that of a living man's face. He shows Yorie his most recent effort. Yorie is delighted with it. He also demonstrates his interest in Yashaō's daughter, Katsura, who has upset her family by announcing that she has no intention of ending her days as an artisan's wife. Yorie enables her to realize her dream of becoming a great lady.

In the second scene Katsura describes her joy at being able to serve so great a prince, but Yorie bitterly answers that although he is the shogun, real power rests in the hands of the Hōjō family. As they talk a Hōjō messenger appears. Yorie intuitively suspects that the man has been sent to kill him, but the man denies the accusation. Later, after Yorie and Katsura have left, the messenger and his two accomplices discuss their forthcoming attack.

The third and last scene takes place at Yashaō's house. Reports reach him of fighting at the shogun's mansion. Presently Katsura returns. She tells how she attempted to protect Yorie by disguising herself in his armor and covering her face with the mask her father carved, but to no avail. Yorie was killed and the wounded Katsura has not long to live. She has no regrets; she rejoices that, instead of leading a humdrum life, she will die as the mistress of the shogun. Yashaō is also pleased: he knows now that his inability to impart a living expression to the mask was caused by an unconscious awareness that Yorie had not long to live. He cries out in joy that he is indeed the finest mask-carver in the country. Then he sets about sketching the face of his daughter as she writhes in her final agonies. The play ends as a priest intones the invocation to Amida Buddha.[56]

A Tale of Shuzenji has enjoyed uninterrupted popularity ever since its first performances, and it exercised considerable influence over the development of the new Kabuki; but it has little value as literature. The characters are types, they speak a vaguely archaic and poetic language, and the entire plot can be guessed from the revelation in the first few minutes of Katsura's determination to rise in the world and Yashaō's disappointment in the mask he has carved of Yorie. The play's success stemmed from its suitability as a vehicle for great actors. This is of course proper in a work intended for performance, but anyone who searches *A Tale of Shuzenji* for evidence of the reform movement in Kabuki is likely to be unimpressed. It is true that the main characters, Yashaō and Katsura, are somewhat unconventional: Yashaō is a consecrated artist who refuses to bow to authority and does not forget his art even when his daughter is dying; and Katsura, unlike the usual swooning Kabuki princesses, is a woman of determination. But it is hard to believe that at this time other Japanese dramatists were being influenced by Ibsen and Maeterlinck. Kidō and Sadanji clearly were aiming at a different, more traditional public from the intellectuals attracted by Shingeki. *A Tale of Shuzenji* offered a mixture of familiar Kabuki elements—swordplay, scenes of amorous dalliance, dying utterances, shouts of defiance, and so on. It made only minimal concessions to the new age, but they were enough to persuade audiences that Kabuki had been revivified.

Kidō's next important play, the three-act *Minowa no Shinjū* (Love Suicides at Minowa, 1911), dealt with love suicides, a theme rarely treated since Chikamatsu's day. The story, tracing the passionate attachment formed by the high-ranking samurai Fujieda Geki for the courtesan Ayaginu, was based on actual events of the eighteenth century, but Kidō manipulated the facts to fit his dramatic conception. The distinctly modern elements in the play are not, however, the departures from historical fact but the attitudes displayed by the characters. Geki is opposed to "feudal morality," and is not in the least concerned about besmirching the honor of his family or ruining his own reputation. When pressed for money by a creditor, he does not hesitate to pawn the armor that has been a hereditary treasure of his family for generations, and when his sister tries to stop him, he retorts:

> We've had over a hundred years of peace. Things are different today from what they were in the bloodthirsty old days,[57] and people

have also changed. People used to pride themselves on their armor and swords and say they were a samurai's soul, but those days are gone forever. I myself used to be a fanatic about the martial arts, and I sweated myself sick over fencing and judo, but it all seems pretty silly when I think of it now. Some samurai, of distinguished families too, don't even know how to hold a bamboo sword or to draw a bow. They abandon themselves to music and dance and devote more of their energies to practicing popular songs and the samisen than to the martial arts. Yet all the same, everybody considers they are performing their duties in the manner expected of them, and their families prosper. In times like these, armor and swords have no meaning. They're just like the armor they put on dolls for the Boys' Festival or the swords made of iris stalks that the dolls carry. I'll be glad to sell our treasures to the first buyer, providing the price is right.[58]

Toward the end of the play, when Geki is about to commit suicide with Ayaginu, he expresses even more surprising views:

In our constrained society, which torments people with family pride, social position, and every other kind of handcuffs and shackles, we are like butterflies or dragonflies caught in a spider's web, and cannot even drink dew from the flowers that might sustain us. We struggle until we die with fettered wings. Ah, what curse was it that predestined me to be born a samurai? In the other world, to which we go, there will be no family pride or social position. Samurai and townsmen are equals there. Surely it will be a more agreeable place than this bothersome world.[59]

Geki declares that when he has broken through the restrictions of this confining world to die for love, of his own free will, his face will wear the same look of triumph that graced the faces of his ancestors when they were victorious in war. He believes in democracy, the equality of all men, and the supreme importance of love.

These were novel attitudes for a samurai in a Japanese play, but they are hardly convincing. It may even seem vulgar for Kidō to have put in the mouth of a character who lived two hundred years before, sentiments that belonged to twentieth-century Japan. This was the manner of popular historical fiction, and no doubt accounted for the success of this and similar plays by Kidō with mass audiences; but as literature such a play cannot be taken seriously.[60]

Kidō's drama *Onoe Idahachi* (Onoe and Idahachi, 1915) was in every way superior. It too was unconventional, but in the manner of Tsuruya Namboku (whose plays were enjoying a revival at the time), not in its defiance of repudiated samurai ideals. The play opens (rather than closes) as the courtesan Onoe and her samurai lover Idahachi decide to commit a lovers' suicide. Idahachi, who has given himself to pleasure and neglected his samurai duties, knows that dying in the Yoshiwara Quarter will disgrace him, but he is resigned to the contempt of later men. Onoe is happy to die with the man she loves. Their language is familiar, and the dialogue is interspersed with offstage songs in the Jōruri manner. Almost every remark seems to echo the words of some love-suicide drama of Chikamatsu. But even as Idahachi is composing his farewell note, a man enters and relays the gossip that a couple who failed in their attempted suicide have been subjected to public exposure in the marketplace. The lovers are distressed, but set out all the same on their journey to death.

So far everything has been so conventional, so typical of scores of earlier plays, that the first audiences probably thought they could guess the rest, but Kidō deals not with the triumph of a love death, in the accustomed manner, but with the misery of a botched lovers' suicide. Borrowing perhaps from Edith Wharton's *Ethan Frome* (1911), Kidō describes what happens to a couple when they must live on with their disgrace.

The next scene takes place five years later. We see Idahachi lying asleep under a tree outside a teahouse. Customers and shop assistants comment with distaste on his presence, and we learn that he has become a public executioner. Someone wakens Idahachi, and we see his face plainly for the first time; it is so disfigured as to be repulsive, and there is a conspicuous scar on his throat, no doubt a memento of his attempted suicide. His younger brother appears, and Idahachi briefly describes the unsuccessful love suicide and the ensuing humiliation. The brother, now head of the family in place of the disgraced Idahachi, is searching for the criminal who stole one thousand ryō in gold from the mansion of the lord whom Idahachi once served. As the brother leaves the teahouse he is told that Idahachi, despite his mean appearance and base profession, is rolling in money.

The first act concludes at this point. Although it opened with a scene that seemed to promise a conventional love suicide, it surprised the audience by revealing that the attempt had been unsuccessful.[61] The transformation of the handsome samurai of the first scene into the brutal-looking outcast of the second was another surprise, and there is a hint at the close of the act that Idahachi is now so depraved that he has stolen his master's money. As yet we have not learned Onoe's fate, and the change in Idahachi has been so complete that we might suspect that (in the traditional Kabuki style) his disreputable appearance is feigned so as to throw enemies off the track.

The second act shows us the wretched hut where Idahachi lives with a gang of outcasts. He describes to the others his part in the execution of a woman who was convicted of killing her husband. First she was crucified, then he and his fellows ran her through with spears. But, Idahachi adds, to the end she laughed at her executioners. He relates how he was "reborn" five years ago to the day. He now feels completely at home among the outcasts and marvels that he was ever able to endure the constricting life of a samurai. "It's like shutting up a human being inside a box." [62]

We realize now that the changes in Idahachi have not been merely on the surface; he has become exactly the hardhearted monster he seems. This impression is confirmed by his coarse abuse of Onoe, who is now known as Osayo and who makes a living as a street musician. She enters soon afterward, complaining of the wound in her neck, which hurts in cold weather. She and Idahachi exchange a few words. We discover that she still loves him and worries about his dissolute ways, but he snarls back: "I have you to thank for that. A distinguished samurai has been reduced to these miserable circumstances all because somebody named you was around. Considering all that's happened, I'm under no obligation to listen to your complaints." [63]

In the next act we see Osayo helping a girl escape whom Idahachi has forced to be his "bride." When Idahachi learns what has happened he beats Osayo and, finally, in a paroxysm of rage runs her through with the spear he uses for executions. He comments, "What a curious stroke of fate I should now have killed the same woman I intended to commit suicide with five years ago!" [64]

His reveries do not last long. Learning that he is suspected of the theft of the one thousand ryō, he tries to escape with the money, only to be apprehended by his brother. The brother offers him the privilege, as an ex-samurai, of committing *seppuku*, but Idahachi refuses. His last words as he is dragged off are the curse he flings at his captors, "*Baka yarōme!*"

Idahachi, like the woman who killed her husband, is defiant to the end, a refreshing note after all the Mokuami villains who repent of their sins; but Kidō's disregard of the humanitarian ideals of the enlightened Meiji regime distressed audiences, and the play soon ran afoul of the censors. It could not be staged in Osaka until after 1945, and it has seldom been performed elsewhere, though it was one of Sadanji's ten favorites among the plays Kidō wrote for him.[65]

Onoe and Idahachi is intelligently conceived and absorbing throughout, but neither the characterization nor the dialogue is entirely satisfying. Onoe changes her name but remains the same; Idahachi, on the other hand, is abruptly transformed from the pleasure-loving son of a distinguished family—a familiar Kabuki figure—into a merciless executioner. His defiance of the samurai code is attractively individual, but his actions are uniformly despicable. Perhaps the most intriguing aspect of the play is that it makes readers wonder what might have happened to Chikamatsu's heroes and heroines if they too had failed in their suicides. Certainly Onoe and Idahachi would have been much better off dead.

One feature of *Onoe and Idahachi* that cannot easily be conveyed in a summary is the skill with which Kidō drew the minor characters. They are not simply types—a defrocked priest, a stutterer, a shrewish wife, and so on—but are provided with effective scenes. Moreover, as Kubota Mantarō pointed out, the stage effects are superbly handled: the cloudy sky of a late spring day, the cries of frogs, the sound of rain falling softly on blossoms, and other effects prescribed in the stage directions help to create an atmosphere exactly appropriate to the action of the play.[66] Kidō was a master of the theater, and to discuss his plays in terms of their literary value is to do him an injustice; but even in literary terms *Onoe and Idahachi* was perhaps his best work.

Two one-act plays of the same period have maintained their

popularity, *Toribeyama Shinjū* (The Love Suicides at Toribeyama, 1915) and *Banchō Sara Yashiki* (The Mansion of the Dishes in Banchō, 1916). Neither play is of much literary distinction, but both provide actors with many opportunities to perform in the grand manner. *The Love Suicides at Toribeyama* is written in a deliberately old-fashioned style. A chanter sings Jōruri descriptions in the traditional manner, and the concluding scenes fall into the familiar pattern of alternating phrases in seven and five syllables. It is a pastiche of an old drama, but an effective one. A modern reader will have more trouble understanding the popularity of *The Mansion of the Dishes in Banchō*, though it is always successful in performance. The story of the dishes, a family treasure so precious that anyone who broke a dish might be put to death, had been written and rewritten since the eighteenth century,[67] but Kidō's version departed radically from earlier versions.[68] Although set in the past and based on traditional materials, his play is unmistakably modern. It would be rare indeed to find in a work of the Tokugawa period a samurai who was so faithful to his beloved that he never once visited the Yoshiwara Quarter, not even to be sociable, and his determination to marry a servant girl was equally unusual. But there are also elements in the play that are distinctly not modern, such as the man's readiness to kill the woman he loves. This unpleasant mixture of new and old will distress readers of *The Mansion of the Dishes in Banchō*, but it seems not to have bothered audiences, which enjoy Kidō's twists to a familiar old story.

Kidō wrote 196 plays and so many other works (including novels and essays) that it has never been attempted to count them all.[69] Most of the plays were set in the middle of the Tokugawa period, the typical background for Kabuki, but a few describe events during the last days of the shogunate or the early Meiji era. *Amerika no Tsukai* (The American Envoy, 1909), written for the fiftieth anniversary of the opening of the port of Yokohama, sympathetically portrays Townsend Harris as an advocate of good relations between Japan and the United States. Unfortunately, this early work, for all the laudable sentiments attributed to the forces of Enlightenment, is clumsily executed and unbelievable.[70] *Seinan Sensō Kikigaki* (Memorandum on the Southwest War, 1922), a long play in six acts, shows us Saigō Takamori in an unfamiliar guise, as a hesitant and even tormented man who is worried because his army is opposed to the imperial forces and because so many young soldiers have died for his sake. This play, though not a great favorite of the public, represented perhaps Kidō's most conscious attempt to delineate character, instead of merely depicting people as they respond to situations of his devising.

Kidō's most successful work (though not necessarily his best) was unquestionably *A Tale of Shuzenji*. Some critics have praised *Gonza to Sukejū* (Gonza and Sukejū, 1926), a suspense comedy set in a tenement, which evokes life among the lower classes in Edo; others prefer *Shinjuku Yawa* (Night Tale of Shinjuku, 1925), unusually constructed, with two scenes set in the present sandwiching a scene of forty years before. *Tempō Engeki Shi* (A History of Drama in the Tempō Era, 1929), despite its forbidding title, is an effective account of the attempts to preserve the theaters in Edo when they were threatened by the government. No doubt Kidō, after a lifetime devoted to the theater, felt personally involved in this play, which was produced in 1930, at a time when he may have feared that the theater was again endangered.

But Kidō was otherwise without a message or even a consistent view of the world. His plays have retained their popularity with Kabuki audiences, but Kabuki in his day had become something of an anachronism, and his works have therefore been little discussed by critics of Japanese literature.

MAYAMA SEIKA (1878-1948)

The other important writer of twentieth-century Kabuki plays was Mayama Seika. He began his career as a novelist. In 1904 he went to Tokyo from his native Sendai in the hopes of studying under Tokutomi Roka, but Roka modestly refused to take him as a disciple, saying he was not qualified to teach anyone. Seika turned then to the Ken'yūsha novelist Oguri Fūyō, a strange second choice, considering his writings were totally unlike Roka's. Fūyō seems in any case to have exerted little influence on Seika, whose first novel to attract attention, *Minami Koizumi Mura* (South Koizumi Village, 1907-1908), was an account of the lives of poverty-stricken farmers in the northeast region. The descriptions are mercilessly objective, with no noticeable sympathy for the afflicted farmers. It was, in short, in the Naturalist vein, and Seika's name was accordingly linked with that of Masamune Hakuchō as a promising new writer of that school. Most of his works before 1913 were novels, but he also wrote two one-act Shingeki plays of importance, *Daiichininsha* (The First Man, 1907) and *Umarezarishi naraba* (If He Had Not Been Born, 1908). Both plays were unmistakably influenced by Ibsen, but the settings and characterization were Japanese.

Almost every critic who has discussed *The First Man* has pointed out the influence of Ibsen's *John Gabriel Borkman*. This gloomy example of late Ibsen was curiously popular in Japan at the time. Not only was it the first play performed by the Jiyū Gekijō (Free Theater) in November 1909, but it profoundly stirred a largely young audience, who sympathized with Erhart, Borkman's son, when he cried, "I am young. . . . I want to lead my own life!" The misinterpretation of the play, which made Erhart the central figure and Borkman a cold and "feudalistic" father unresponsive to his son's desires, was corrected before long, but it left an indelible impression of having been a plea for the rights of the younger generation.[71] It was partly accidental, the result of the unsystematic arrival of European books in Japan, that *John Gabriel Borkman*, rather than one of Ibsen's better-known plays, had attracted such attention; but it may also have been because of the scarcity of capable actresses that the Free Theater chose a work with only a few roles for young women.[72]

The parallels between *Borkman* and *The First Man* are obvious but not especially important: both heroes are obsessed with the rightness of their actions, despite the condemnation of society. Other resemblances, which have been dutifully noted, include the fact that in both plays there are sisters of contrasting characters.[73] The dissimilarities are far more striking.

The First Man is the story of Narazaki Genjō, who has returned to Tokyo after eight years spent exploring the North Pole. Nobody believes his account of reaching the Pole; even his two daughters (one outspokenly and the other hesitantly) express doubts. Nor is anyone willing to publish the immensely detailed narrative of his travels. The experts who have read the manuscript declare that it is full of contradictions. Narazaki decides to publish the book privately, though he will have to sell his house to raise the money. His daughter Michiko expresses strong opposition to his plans, pointing out that her sister Toshiko will be unable to find a decent husband without the house as her dowry. Narazaki's old servant, bitter because her son was lost on the expedition, deliberately lets the only witness to Narazaki's conquest of the Pole, his dog, escape. Narazaki is beside himself with rage when he learns that the dog is missing and rushes out to find him, but the dog is shot after biting someone.

Narazaki returns home a changed man. He admits now that he was mistaken and apologizes. He realizes that he should never have revealed the secrets of the North Pole, and that nature punishes those who divulge her mysteries: "Ah, it was surely no accident that the other twelve men all died, that nobody believes my story, that my eyes are bad and I cannot speak easily. Heaven does not wish human ears to hear the great secrets of freedom on which I intruded. Now at last I understand why my explanations have remained a riddle to everyone else." [74] Narazaki understands that the "first man" is always doomed to be a victim, and his ultimate revelation is that his life has been a meaningless void. He burns the manuscript. At the end the father and two daughters, reunited, gaze in wonder at a magnificent sunset.

The accommodation that Narazaki makes with his family and society, in the name of preserving the inviolable mysteries of nature, was in no sense influenced by Ibsen's play, which concludes with Borkman dying in the snow, an icy hand clutching his heart.

Perhaps the most important resemblance between Seika's play and Ibsen's was the creation of a character who demands the attention of society. Others of Seika's early plays and works of fiction also contain characters who insist on the correctness of their beliefs, regardless of what other people think, only to crumble in the end before their own self-doubts and loneliness. *The First Man* is not wholly successful, but compared to the plays of Tsubouchi Shōyō or Okamoto Kidō it belongs to a later stage of the evolution of Japanese drama. It was clearly intended for the modern theater: no appeal is made to the eye or ear by brilliance of presentation or beauty of language. Unlike the dramas of Mori Ōgai, moreover, the characters are human beings and not ideas given visible presence.

Seika undoubtedly learned much from Ibsen, but so did most of the best European dramatists of the time. His play is weakest in its basic premise: the story of a Japanese explorer who has reached the North Pole but is doubted by his compatriots is somehow unconvincing. To the end we are not sure about Narazaki. Perhaps he reached the Pole and the doubters are merely jealous of him. But how are we to interpret the conclusion when, overcome by a mystic vision of nature, Narazaki yields his pride as an explorer, and assumes the more traditional Japanese role of being a father and grandfather? Seika may have felt an obligation to accommodate the play to the tastes of his audience. The conclusion has been described as "oriental," signifying that Narazaki, like a good Japanese, has found spiritual guidance in nature, but the destruction of the manuscript seems not acquiescence before nature but the abandonment of a futile dream. Narazaki is less heroic than Borkman, who never wavers, even when he is totally in the wrong.

The First Man was a superior work of Naturalist drama, and its conflicts apparently resembled those that beset Seika himself. He borrowed from Ibsen (and Hauptmann) not merely to be abreast of the times but because their themes revealed to him truths about himself. In 1914 Seika wrote for the Shimpa actors the play *Sasori* (The Scorpion), a study of a poet, his wife, and the wife's younger sister, directly derived from Hauptmann's *Einsame Menschen*, but the play is at the same time partly autobiographical; the European work and the Japanese experience coincided.

The influence of Ibsen was also apparent in *If He Had Not Been Born*. The story of the victim of a hereditary bone disease seems to have been modeled on *Ghosts*, though heredity was a theme much beloved by the Naturalist writers. The title refers to the passage in Matthew 25: 24: "Woe unto that man by whom the Son of man is betrayed! it had been good for that man if he had not been born." Reference to Judas Iscariot is made in the play by Tsuki Ryūsaku, the father of a young man whose leg is about to be amputated. Tsuki, in an apparent drunken frenzy, takes down the painting of the Madonna from the wall of his son's hospital room and replaces it with one of Judas. He shows the son, Kiyoshi, the painting.

> KIYOSHI: It's a painting of Judas Iscariot, isn't it? What gloomy
> colors! It depresses me just to look at it. I suppose it's
> from the Middle Ages or even earlier. Is it Dutch?

TSUKI: It's not the picture I'm showing you. Read what it says on the label. Here, under the picture.

KIYOSHI: *If he had not been born.* That's from the Gospel according to St. Matthew.

TSUKI: . . . Yes, it means that such a man would have been better off not to have been born. He sinned because he was born. His sins came from the fact of his birth. Don't you think this one phrase sums up the deep, strong feelings of the Lord's compassion? Every time I read it, I am overcome by God's immense mercy.[75]

Word comes that the kimono, which Mrs. Tsuki ordered, is ready. She is so impatient to see how it looks on her that she rushes from her son's sickroom. Tsuki drunkenly reveals to Kiyoshi that he, like Borkman, married in the hopes of worldly advancement, not love. A nurse enters to say that everything is ready for the operation. Kiyoshi, who has not known his leg was to be amputated, cries out that he is sure something terrible will occur. At that moment his mother enters carrying her new kimono. As she tries it on, a blind old man gropes his way to Kiyoshi's bed and mutters that great danger threatens him. The atmosphere, no longer Naturalist, suggests Maeterlinck. Kiyoshi is wheeled out to the operating room. When he returns his father sadistically torments him by calling him a weakling and a cripple, and by repeatedly insisting that Kiyoshi look at the portrait of Judas. He opens the window to let Kiyoshi hear the ominous roar of thunder. The conclusion is unconvincing, but it is clear that Seika was valiantly attempting to create three rounded, complex characters in the European manner. The conflicts, expressed verbally rather than with swords, would be typical of his best plays.

Seika's career was interrupted in 1908 when he published the same manuscript in two different magazines. He admitted his guilt and announced that he "hoped to be abandoned by the literary world. . . . I intend to live as inconspicuously as possible, somewhere out of its sight and hearing." [76] But in 1911 he repeated the same offense! This time the newspapers demanded that he give up writing. Articles in his defense were written by some prominent members of the literary world, but most people were shocked by Seika's money-grubbing deceit, and he apparently decided to write no more. He immersed himself instead in the study of Tokugawa literature, especially the works of Saikaku.

In the spring of 1914 he was asked to write for the Shimpa company, and during the next ten years he turned out many melodramas, using a pseudonym. Some of these plays, however, prefigured his mature achievement as an author of historical dramas, notably *Gemboku to Chōei* (Gemboku and Chōei, 1924), which he published under his own name, apparently confident of its worth. The play was greeted with acclaim.

There are only two characters in *Gemboku and Chōei*, the successful physician Itō Gemboku and his former schoolmate Takano Chōei, who has recently escaped from prison. Chōei asks for money so that he can avoid the police, but Gemboku refuses, taunting Chōei, "I'm sure that at the bottom of your heart you're really hoping I won't lend you the money." He recalls how, when they were students together, he had disliked Chōei's ostentatiously independent behavior. The two men exchange barbed remarks about each other's family. As the dispute grows heated, Chōei accuses Gemboku of having betrayed their teacher Siebold, the German scientist who instructed many Japanese physicians in the 1820s before being expelled from the country. Gemboku declares that he considers it his duty to minister to the sick, one at a time, and that he has no ambition, like Chōei, of serving as a doctor to the whole nation. At the end, after Gemboku has refused a last time to give any money, Chōei leaves. Gemboku says sadly, "I like that man. And yet, at the same time, I hate his guts." [77]

The conflict between Gemboku and Chōei was essentially one within Seika himself. One critic wrote:

> As people are well aware, the prototype of his plays is found in *Gemboku and Chōei*. The theme is always the conflict and struggle between people of two different natures. No matter how many people may appear in a play, the substance is the same. It is the configuration of the two opposing forces that dwelled in the mind of Mayama Seika himself. In the end, no matter whom he portrayed, he wrote about himself, for he imparted to the heroes of his plays, to the degree that he treated them in depth, the two alter ego personalities of himself. [78]

Seika was not a systematic thinker, but we often find in his plays conflict between different systems of thought, for example, between humanitarian and feudalistic beliefs. His nationalism, which mounted after the outbreak of war in China, colored his writings of the 1930s, but even the most extreme examples of wartime plays, such as *Tatakai wa kore kara da* (The Fight Has Just Begun, 1933), present a conflict between nationalism and love of fellow man, in both of which Seika believed. In this play the conflict is between a Japanese colonist in Manchuria, who has tried to accommodate himself to the ways of the Chinese, and his high-strung son who denounces compromise between Japanese and Chinese ways as iniquitous. Not until the atypical, rather hysterical ending does Seika make a choice, when the father, provoked beyond endurance by the obdurate Chinese refusal to listen to reason, dons a military uniform to lead the fight against them.[79]

Seika's best-known works are his historical dramas, which cover a span ranging from *Taira no Masakado*, set in the tenth century, to the Meiji Restoration. He imparts to his characters a self-awareness that was the product of painstaking research into the historical backgrounds. After winning rehabilitation in the literary world with *Gemboku and Chōei*, Seika wrote over sixty plays. Most of them have an unmistakable literary bias; although they were successfully staged and not infrequently revived, they tend to be rather static in performance. Among his important history plays were *Edo-jō Sōzeme* (All -Out Attack on Edo Castle, 1926), an account in grandiloquent language of the attempts made by supporters of the shogunate to save the life of the last shogun; *Ōshio Heihachirō* (1926), about the leader of a rebellion against the government in 1837; and *Sakamoto Ryōma*, the memorable study of a late-Tokugawa figure. About this time Seika revealed to members of his family that he had been converted to Marxism and was reading books on socialism and economics, but this may have been something of a pose, considering the nationalistic tone of his later plays. He introduced bits of quasi-Marxist philosophy into the dialogue of some plays, but the interest was always focused on the character of Tokugawa Yoshinobu, Saigō Takamori, Ōshio Heihachirō, or whoever was the subject, and the conflicts were not the result of class warfare but of internal contradictions within the characters themselves.

In Seika's own opinion his finest achievement was the immensely long, nine-act *Genroku Chūshingura*; but although this work was written with obvious dedication, the pace is slow, at least for a Western reader. Seika devoted pages to overpowering displays of pedantic information; in the stage directions, for example, he described the costume and crest of every samurai who appears, and even stated his annual salary. However, he neglected to supply the background of the quarrel between Asano and Kira, which sets the tragedy in motion; for that matter, the villain Kira does not make a single appearance in the course of the long play. Perhaps Seika assumed that his audiences were thoroughly familiar from the original *Chūshingura* with the circumstances of the dispute, but one critic has stated that Seika wished to show that the hero, Kuranosuke, was indifferent both to the nature of the quarrel and to the enemy: his only concern was to act as his loyalty to his master commanded.[80]

The political background of *Genroku Chūshingura* is definitely not Marxism but the nationalism of the late 1930s. At the close of the second act, for example, a member of the Asano clan who has been serving in Kyoto reports the rumor that the emperor himself has been heard to murmur from behind his screen of state that Asano was to be pitied because he failed to kill Kira. Kuranosuke, whose chief concern all along has been that Asano's rash action in the palace, where an imperial envoy was being entertained, might have been interpreted as lèse-majesté, is overcome with emotion. His fears have been alleviated, and though Lord Asano is dead, he has been saved by the words vouchsafed by the emperor.[81]

The final act of *Genroku Chūshingura* is devoted to Kuranosuke's last day, before he receives the command to commit seppuku. The act impressively lends the solidity and weight of history to Seika's play. Of all the many dramas written about the loyal forty-seven retainers of Asano, both before and after *Chūshingura*, Seika's is the only one that stands comparison with that masterpiece of Japanese theater, though his methods are strikingly dissimilar.

Seika's plays are almost uniformly dark in tone. He seems to have had little sense of humor, and his attempts at comic relief are unconvincing. Romance figures infrequently as a theme, perhaps because he was aware that he did not excel at portrayals of women. His plays are distinguished instead by the "heroic sentimentalism" (as one admirer put it [82]) of the male characters. This, of course, was in the Kabuki tradition, but it was surprising in

Seika, a playwright who had demonstrated a mastery of Naturalism. The roar of contemptuous laughter, the tears concealed by a feigned rheum, the mute look of determination on the face of the man who fights for a doomed cause are typical highlights of his plays, though his heroes at times remind readers that the author was a twentieth-century writer by expressing such sentiments as distaste for the carnage of war, sympathy for the common man, and so on. At best, Seika's works demonstrated that Kabuki was still a vital tradition in a changed Japan; at worst, they lead into the samurai films of the 1930s and afterward. At first his plays were performed only by Kabuki or Shimpa actors, and only after some years were the Shingeki actors given their chance to interpret them.[83] It was in fact because of the successes of Mayama Seika and Okamoto Kidō that the new Kabuki was able not only to retain its audiences but to block the growth of nontraditional theater after its promising start at the beginning of the century.

THE LITERATURE OF SHIMPA AND SHINGEKI

TOWARD THE END of the Meiji era Kabuki was threatened by competition from two nontraditional forms of theater, Shimpa and Shingeki. This was particularly true during the early years of the century, when Kabuki was crippled by the deaths of leading actors and the lack of outstanding dramatists.

Shimpa, which had originated about 1890 with plays on political themes, had won popular favor initially because of its novelty and the appeal to patriotic sentiments. Kawakami Otojirō, the guiding spirit of Shimpa for its first twenty years, appeared in a play staged in 1891, which had for its high point the song he sang, dressed in the garb of a Restoration patriot, a rising-sun flag in his hand.[84] The plays performed were mainly dramatizations of recent political events, such as the stabbing of Itagaki Taisuke, the leader of the popular rights movement, in 1882. When attendance was poor, Kawakami resorted to exploding ammunition onstage or to galloping on a horse around the theater in order to attract attention. The use of actresses, breaking the ban imposed by the

Tokugawa Shogunate in 1629, was favored by the Shimpa troupe and tolerated by the new government.

The success of the Shimpa actors in treating the Sino-Japanese War of 1894–1895 established the fortunes of the theater. Shimpa plays were performed on the stage of the Kabuki Theatre in Tokyo and in the hinterland. Intoxicated by success, Kawakami, his wife Sada-yakko, and a troupe of eighteen other Shimpa actors traveled in 1899 to Europe and America, where they were acclaimed. Sada-yakko in particular was admired; Max Beerbohm declared that if, like Paris, he was forced to choose among the goddesses Bernhardt, Duse, and Sada-yakko, he would award Sada-yakko the golden apple. Kawakami's troupe performed in Japanese, a language that extremely few people in Europe understood; its triumphs were obviously the result of the displays of emotive talent, rather than of subtlety in interpreting the texts.

After Kawakami's troupe returned to Japan in 1902, the Shimpa repertory was expanded to include plays by Shakespeare, and before long by Maeterlinck and Sardou. The Russo-Japanese War of 1904–1905 also inspired a series of successful works, and various European literary masterpieces, including *The Divine Comedy* and *The Count of Monte Cristo*, were adapted for the Shimpa stage. The dramatization of Tokutomi Roka's novel *Hototogisu* was so successful that three rival theaters in Osaka simultaneously produced it, including one that featured Kabuki actors in the leading roles.[85] Shimpa seemed to be conquering all before it, but the rise of Shingeki and the increasing difficulty of obtaining new plays checked its development. It was preserved, as almost every theater art ever known in Japan has been preserved, but it had lost its vitality and its audiences tended to be restricted to people with nostalgic memories of the Meiji era.

Shingeki, a far more important theater, was originally inspired chiefly by translations of the plays of Shakespeare and Ibsen. The early translations had not been intended for performance because there was so little likelihood that audiences accustomed to Kabuki would welcome such plays; but in 1905, with the foundation of the Bungei Kyōkai (Literary Society), the Japanese attempted to create a new kind of theater, which would have for its objective the presentation of texts of literary importance. Two years later an even more effective group in the creation of literature for the stage, the Ibsen Society, was organized by a group consisting mainly of Naturalist authors, plus Osanai Kaoru (1881–1928), the founder in 1909 of the Free Theater. The works of Ibsen had first been made known to the Japanese when Takayasu Gekkō (1869–1944) published partial translations (from the English) of *An Enemy of the People* in 1893 and of *A Doll's House* in 1901; but only after Ibsen's death in 1906 did the craze for his works reach fever pitch.[86]

The Japanese of the time were impressed above all by the strength of the individual, as displayed in Ibsen's plays, and they applauded the will to resist social pressure even of such characters as Hedda Gabler. This was the first time that the theater had provided Japanese audiences with the vicarious pleasure of asserting themselves and their individuality. The creation of the individual would be the chief problem faced by the new Japanese dramatists of the Shingeki school. The success of *John Gabriel Borkman*, the first production of the Free Theater in 1909, owed much to Mori Ōgai's translation, but even more to its portrayal of a strong-willed man. The failings of the character Borkman—the loveless marriage he made in order to advance his career, his speculation with the deposits of customers of his bank, his deluded belief that his successors would eventually come on their knees to beg his guidance—apparently struck the Japanese as being no more than minor flaws in a man of tragic stature. Perhaps Borkman's worst failing (in their eyes, at least) was his lack of sympathy for his son, a man of equally passionate emotions.

The influence of Ibsen revealed itself in the works of the Shingeki playwrights, including Mayama Seika (in his first period), Satō Kōroku (1874–1949), Nagata Hideo (1885–1949), and Nakamura Kichizō (1877–1941).[87] Nakamura's enthusiasm for Ibsen, fostered by his study under Brander Matthews and William Archer at Columbia University in 1907–1908, was so extreme that people took to calling him Henrik Nakamura, especially after he had published a study of Ibsen in 1914. Nakamura attended many performances of Ibsen in New York, London, and Berlin. It is not surprising that his play *Bokushi no Ie* (A Vicarage, 1910) revealed many traces of borrowing, though he himself in later years would refer to this play as the first "war cry" of the Shingeki movement.[88]

Both Shimpa and Shingeki enjoyed a relatively brief period

of prosperity before Kabuki reasserted itself as the chief Japanese theater. It is common to speak of a "period of stagnation" in the nontraditional theater arts, but it would perhaps be more accurate to refer instead to the revival of Kabuki, thanks to new playwrights and actors. In any case, the 1920s were hard times for Shingeki. The audiences were small for the plays of Wedekind, Gorki, Maeterlinck, or Andreev presented in translations, or for such original works as Mori Ōgai's *The River Ikuta*, and consisted mainly of Western-oriented intellectuals; only with the rise of the "proletarian" theater were other segments of society attracted. Despite these unpropitious circumstances, there was a considerable volume of new plays written in the Shingeki manner, especially by novelists, though they had little hope of seeing their plays performed. The situation led to a heated controversy on the merits of *Lesedrama*; many exceedingly obvious distinctions between writing plays and writing novels were put forward with the utmost solemnity. But even severe criticism did not deter such novelists as Tanizaki Jun'ichirō, Masamune Hakuchō, and Kikuchi Kan from writing plays, and when these plays were in fact performed they were sometimes very successful. As might be expected, however, more plays failed than succeeded, if only because the authors were insufficiently familiar with the special requirements of the stage. As yet Shingeki was unable to sustain playwrights who would devote their full energies to the theater.

OSANAI KAORU

A key figure in the creation of a specifically modern theater in Japan was Osanai Kaoru. As a young man he studied English literature at Tokyo University. His interest in the theater was aroused by meeting such famous literary figures as Mori Ōgai, and he was introduced by Miki Takeji, Ōgai's younger brother, to Ii Yōhō (1871–1932), a pioneer figure in the Shimpa movement who had actively promoted the use of actresses on the stage. Osanai took a job at Yōhō's theater, the Masago-za, in 1904, and soon afterward began making the adaptations and translations of European dramas and novels that would establish his reputation as a genius at imitation, though not at creation.[89]

In 1909 Osanai and the second Ichikawa Sadanji founded the

Free Theater which, together with Tsubouchi Shōyō's Literary Society, stood in the vanguard of the new movement in Japanese theater. He traveled to Europe in 1912 to study techniques of production and the training of actors. After his return the following year he staged plays for the Free Theater and wrote some of his own. The Free Theater did not prosper, and Osanai drifted from one organization to another. His life and the entire Shingeki movement was changed, however, in 1924 when, at the urging of the young nobleman Hijikata Yoshi (1898–1951) he helped to found the Tsukiji Shōgekijō (Tsukiji Little Theatre), the first modern theater of Japan.[90]

At first the Tsukiji Little Theatre staged only translations of European plays, including works by Chekhov, Čapek, Bjørnson, Ibsen, O'Neill, Pirandello, Strindberg, and Shaw.[91] Osanai declared at a lecture meeting in 1924 that for the time being the theater would continue to produce foreign plays exclusively because the works of Shingeki playwrights did not excite him. This statement caused a furor within Japanese theatrical circles,[92] but eventually Osanai modified his stand and the theater came to serve as a valuable training ground for young Japanese dramatists. Osanai insisted, however, on the distinction between theater and plays; a declaration issued in August 1924 opened with these remarks:

> The Tsukiji Little Theatre, like all other theatres, exists for drama. . . . It does not exist for plays.
>
> Plays are literature. Literature has its own organs—newspapers, magazines, books—things that are printed.
>
> Theatres do not exist for literature.[93]

The emphasis on the presentation, rather than the texts, inspired rigorous training for the actors in voice production and eurhythmics, and the success of the company with the public owed much to the cyclorama and lighting, which rivaled that of many theaters in Europe, rather than to the plays.[94] The theater, however, lost money from the start, and by 1926 was divided into two factions centered around Hijikata and Osanai. The rise of the proletarian theater presented another threat to the Tsujiki Little Theatre, whose artistic tendencies were progressive, but which was not committed to socialist thought.

Osanai wrote the first Japanese radio drama in 1925, and two years later the first talkie for the Japanese films. He was invited to the Soviet Union in 1927 as part of the celebrations of the tenth anniversary of the revolution, and studied the new drama there. His travels, however, aggravated his failing health, and he died in 1928, not long after his return to Japan.

Despite his insistence on drama, rather than plays, Osanai himself wrote several plays that contributed to the Shingeki repertory. *Daiichi no Sekai* (The First World, 1921) was probably the best; it demonstrated both his expert knowledge of the requirements of the theater and a feeling for literary expression. Osanai spoke of *The First World* as his "maiden work," though he had in fact composed several plays during the previous decade; no doubt he meant that it was the first play that he was proud to have written.

The First World is a study of the recluse Yamanaka Shin'ichi, who has taken refuge from the real world in a "second world" of mystical experience. He lives in a towerlike retreat with his daughter Toshiko and a young man named Shimamura whom he took from an orphanage. Shimamura, a devoted disciple of Yamanaka's, is in love with Toshiko, but she loves another man. The Italian government awards Yamanaka a prize for his researches on Dante's *Purgatorio*. As word of the prize gets around, outsiders from the "first world" intrude on Yamanaka's privacy: there are newspaper reporters eager for details, and also an old friend, Tanimura, and his wife who, as we gradually discover, formerly loved Yamanaka. They are the parents of the young man whom Yamanaka's daughter Toshiko wants to marry, and they obtain Yamanaka's consent. Shimamura, disappointed in love and in the seeming change of his master's attitude, leaves the tower to try his luck in the "first world." Yamanaka, alone, returns to his windowless study. He declares, "My real life is just beginning." [95]

The First World was enthusiastically received in December 1921 after the performances by Sadanji and his troupe. The dramatist Ikeda Daigo (1885–1942) declared that he would not be ashamed to see this play performed in "the marketplace of the world." The novelist Minakami Takitarō (1887–1940), who had thought the work a failure when he read the text, changed his mind when he saw it performed. Naturally, the influence of Ibsen and Maeterlinck was pointed out by the usual industrious seekers of influences, but whatever influences were present, it is clear that Osanai felt some internal compulsion to write this play.[96] Mysticism attracted him; after he had abandoned the Christian faith he had absorbed from Uchimura Kanzō as a young man, he found solace in liquor and women, but eventually, like Yamanaka in the play, he sought refuge beyond the confines of the "first world."

Osanai's political and social outlook shifted frequently. He was attracted to socialism, as he unobtrusively revealed in two short plays, *Teishu* (The Husband, 1925) and *Naraku* (The Trap-Cellar, 1926), both of which treated the lives of people of the lower classes. In *The Husband* a woman, enraged over her husband's inability to support the family, orders him from the house, then asks a lodger to become her "husband" in his place. *The Trap-Cellar* is the story of men who work in the cellar of a theater, spending their days in a sunless hole where they turn the revolving stage. The atmosphere is oppressive, but there is also a camaraderie among the men who fight and gamble together; the play may have been Osanai's symbol for life in this world.[97] These short plays, though slight in content, are both convincing in language and characterization and effective as theater, as performances at the Tsukiji Little Theatre proved.

Osanai also wrote several plays about persons from recent history whom he particularly admired. *Mori Yūrei* (1926), about the minister of education who was assassinated by a fanatical opponent of his enlightened views on the day that the Meiji Constitution was proclaimed in February 1889, and *Kin Gyokkin* (1926), about the Korean patriot Kim Okkyum who was assassinated in Shanghai in 1894, are the best of his plays in this vein. Osanai, however, denied that these were "tragedies of character":

> I treated Mori Yūrei as the central figure of my drama for convenience's sake, but it was definitely not my intention to write a tragedy about a particular individual. I wanted instead to reexamine calmly each of the periods between the early years of Meiji and the time when, after the Russo-Japanese War, capitalism reached full maturity. *Mori Yūrei* constituted one section of this plan, *Kin Gyokkin* another. . . . If *Mori Yūrei* is a tragedy, it is the tragedy of an age, the tragedy of the culture of an age. I therefore consciously

rejected individual characterization, psychological description, and what are known as the tender emotions.[98]

Osanai never completed his proposed cycle of ten or twenty plays. Instead, apparently as the result of a change in his political views, he wrote in 1927 *Shina no Gōzun* (Chinese Gordon), a play glorifying the Englishman who tried to fight a "civilized" war against brutal Chinese. Osanai's play *Mussolini*, performed by Sadanji's troupe in May 1928, represented Mussolini as the unwavering ally of the common people, and his ideals of power and will were admiringly described.[99] Finally, Osanai wrote several adaptations of plays by Chikamatsu, including his own *The Battles of Coxinga* (1928), in which he attempted to create a "national theater" (*kokugeki*) for the Japanese by modernizing and making more spectacular the classics of the Japanese tradition.

Osanai was a figure of the greatest importance in the history of the development of the modern Japanese theater. As a playwright, however, his achievements were modest; his plays soon slipped from the repertory and seem unlikely ever to be revived.

THE *SHIRAKABA* DRAMATISTS

Shiga Naoya was the only well-known member of the *Shirakaba* group who did *not* try his hand at writing plays. Mushakōji Saneatsu, Arishima Takeo, Satomi Ton, Nagayo Yoshirō, and Kurata Momozō all wrote successful works, which are generally labeled as "idealist" or "humanitarian," terms that come easily to the critics when discussing the *Shirakaba* group. Time has not dealt kindly with these plays; a critic writing in 1972 dismissed them as "accidental products of a transitional period" before the modern drama was firmly established.[100] The *Shirakaba* dramatists nevertheless deserved credit for having broken the oppressively gloomy atmosphere that had permeated the Naturalist theater; and, in place of determinism and nihilism, they advocated ideals of mankind which reflected the influence of Tolstoy.

Plays by Mushakōji and Arishima appeared in the magazine *Shirakaba* during its first year of publication, 1910. Despite their devotion to ideals, their plays reveal that they were by no means immune to Ibsen. Arishima was in fact one of the first to praise *Hedda Gabler* (in 1910):

> She never complains about her internal contradictions. These extraordinary contradictions are quite natural to her. The one thing she dreads and frets over is the possibility that Hedda, the individual, may be crushed by external pressure. For this reason Hedda fights out her battle to the point where she has no choice but to destroy herself. She is a magnificent martyr.[101]

Arishima's own plays, even when not dealing with such biblical personages as Samson or Noah, were permeated with a religiosity that owed little to Ibsen. Perhaps his most effective play was *Shi to sono Zengo* (Death and Its Consequences, 1917), a dramatization of the last hours of his wife, who had died in the previous year. The mixture of touching realism in the evocation of Arishima's love for the dying wife, and religious fantasy in the person of Death, who appears at the beginning and end of the work, gave the play a depth beyond its rather slight materials.[102]

The modest successes scored by the *Shirakaba* dramatists came from their treating, in a quite ordinary manner, the ordinary events of life; they made no attempt to create memorable individuals like Hedda Gabler or John Gabriel Borkman. The language was relaxed, closer to the conversations in novels than to the heroic declamation customary in the traditional Japanese theater. In Mushakōji's plays, whether on traditional subjects or modern life, the language is so unassertive that they often seem like armchair dramas or even novels without the connecting descriptions. His plays were nonetheless the most successful of those by the *Shirakaba* group. *Aru Katei* (A Family Affair, 1910),[103] an early work, was described years later by the author as "plainly revealing his special qualities." [104] It is a slight play, interesting mainly because of the glimpses it gives of the lives of the upper class at the time. The self-sacrifice of the younger brother, who renounces his love for the beautiful maidservant because he knows how deeply his brother loves her, was typical of similar acts of self-sacrifice in Mushakōji's later plays, but there is hardly anything else worth noting.

Sono Imoto (The Younger Sister, 1915), a much longer and

more involved play, has kept its high reputation, mainly because of an extraneous factor: the central character, Nomura Hiroji, is a promising painter whose career has been ruined because he was blinded in a war, and this circumstance occasions expressions of antiwar sentiments. Such sentiments, which must have startled the first audiences, who were accustomed to panegyrics of Japan's military traditions, have been acclaimed in recent years as instances of Mushakōji's "resistance" to militarism. Unfortunately, Hiroji's tirade against the cause of his misfortune is voiced in an embarrassingly inept manner. He asks Shizuko, his devoted sister and amanuensis, to write down the speech that he has composed in his head. No reason is offered either why he chooses this particular moment to utter such sentiments, which surely must have occurred to Hiroji many times before, or what purpose he has in mind when he asks that they now be recorded. He begins:

> I am blind. I was blinded in the war. Perhaps you gentlemen, hearing this, will say that I should consider myself lucky not to have been killed. Precisely so. I do indeed consider I was lucky not to have died. But the loss of my eyesight was a calamity rather more painful than I could bear. You may think this is obvious, even without my saying so, but the loss of sight was a far crueler blow than you can imagine. Gentlemen, I was a painter. . . .[105]

Hiroji's long speech, full of self-pity and regret for the career he has been denied, acquires its only dramatic quality with the pacifistic remarks at the conclusion:

> I went to war, I who was a convinced pacifist. I am a man who hates killing and detests the thought of being killed. I was unhappy when my country went to war. I discussed this with friends. My career as an artist had been delayed because I had been conscripted for military service and now, just when I thought I had at last caught up, I was sucked into a war. I went to war. I carried a gun. I was even in the firing squad that shot some poor devil of an enemy soldier who had been caught spying. In my heart I asked his forgiveness, and as I prayed for him, I deliberately aimed my gun away from the target. But I could not save his life, nor could I shake off the terror of death. Why was it necessary for me to do such a thing? Even now, I can see the man's face before me.[106]

Hiroji, unable to paint because of his blindness, attempts to make a living as a writer. His friend Nishijima sympathizes with him, and arranges for publication of a story Hiroji has written, but it attracts no attention. Nishijima, though a moderately successful author, cannot support Hiroji and Shizuko without great sacrifice. He nevertheless continues to provide money, apparently because (as his wife correctly suspects) he has unwittingly fallen in love with Shizuko. Rumors spread that he and Shizuko are lovers. Shizuko, despairing of any other solution, consents to marry a rich but odious man. At the end Hiroji, resigned to Shizuko's leaving him, cries out, "I must be strong!" [107]

The play is not only static but repetitious, and the situations are patently contrived. People constantly arrive at unlikely moments, overhear rumors under implausible circumstances, and make speeches that do not fit the fabric of the play. Hiroji's blindness is affecting, but in the absence of any other theme it becomes monotonous, and the play stretches to an inordinate length, considering the thinness of the material. It has nevertheless been acclaimed as "an epoch-making masterpiece, one of the powerful 'life-works' of Mushakōji . . . a grand summation of the plays of the 1910s and the splendid point of departure for the next period." [108] Perhaps such praise reflects the sympathy of the critic with Hiroji's predicament and his courage in the face of disaster, but apart from the naturalness of the dialogue, the play has few attractions. Mushakōji was incapable of creating a dramatic scene; each section tends to become a debate between two characters. Hiroji's repeated assertions that he is a man, no less than any other, is vitiated by lachrymose passages in which brother and sister sob together. *The Younger Sister* was an exceptionally influential play, but it was appreciated more as a work of literature than of theater. It led the way to *Lesedrama* by novelists who enjoyed writing dialogue.

Mushakōji wrote one other play of interest, *Aiyoku* (Desire, 1926). This melodramatic work was acclaimed in its day, and even those who were unmoved when they read it were deeply impressed by the performances later that year at the Tsukiji Little Theatre. When read today, however, it is unconvincing in the extreme. Nonaka Eiji, a brilliant painter, is tormented because he believes that his wife, Chiyoko, loves his older brother. Eiji is a hunchback, and this affliction makes him doubt that his wife has ever really loved him. He goes so far as to declare that he will never know peace until he has killed the wife, the brother, or himself. His jealousy drives his wife into announcing that she intends to leave him. Eiji kills the wife and stuffs her body into a trunk. The brother and a friend arrive to find Eiji in a trance. They promise not to desert him.

Desire displays all the faults of dramaturgy that marked Mushakōji's earlier plays, though the character Eiji is intermittently interesting, if only because of his bitter humor, a quality not often encountered in Mushakōji's deadly serious works. *Desire* is enlivened also by a curious scene in which Chiyoko reappears before Eiji after he has killed her, in the manner of traditional ghost plays. The ending is probably the worst part, but the note of hope and trust may have been necessary for this author.

Mushakōji also wrote several short plays about Buddhist priests,[109] though the *Shirakaba* authors were usually more attracted to Christianity than to Buddhism. The most famous play to have been written by a member of the group, however, was specifically Buddhist: *Shukke to sono Deshi* (The Priest and His Disciples, 1916) by Kurata Hyakuzō (1891–1943). This extremely long play was intended primarily as a *Lesedrama* and sold so well as a book that, in the old phrase, "the price of paper rose." When staged it was immensely successful, and translations were made into various foreign languages.[110]

The Priest and His Disciples is the story of Shinran, the founder of the Shin sect of Jōdo Buddhism, and of the different disciples he gathered around him. Yuien was the son of a man who once reviled Shinran when he sought shelter on a snowy night, and though he is a devoted disciple of Shinran, he is attracted by a prostitute and tormented by the propriety of becoming intimate with her. Shinran, who always insists that he is the most sinful of men and can gain salvation only by throwing himself on Amida's mercy, is indulgent toward Yuien's love, providing it is not selfish. The other priests at first condemn Yuien, but eventually recognize that it was precisely to help such persons gain salvation that their sect was founded. Shinran's one failure was with his son Zenran, who to the end remains agnostic and cannot comfort his dying father by saying he believes in the Buddha.

The play is full of noble sentiments, Christian as well as Buddhist, but at times it is perilously close to sentimentality. The play aroused new interest in Shinran, and excited the admiration of Romain Rolland, who declared that it contained the purest expression of faith in contemporary literature. But for all its earnestness and the persuasive presentation of Shinran's beliefs, its literary merit does not seem nearly so impressive now as when it first appeared.

Kōu to Ryūhō (Hsiang Yü and Liu Pang, 1915–1916) by Nagayo Yoshirō (1888–1961) is another work of unusual length and seriousness, and it has been acclaimed, along with *The Priest and His Disciples*, as the play that best represents the Taishō era. It is set in China during the period immediately before Liu Pang founded the Han Dynasty, and has two clearly defined characters, Hsiang Yü, a hero of strength, and Liu Pang, a hero of wisdom. The dramatist's sympathies clearly lie with the latter, but he manages to make a tragic fiugure of the defeated Hsiang Yü.

The plays of the *Shirakaba* authors gave Shingeki intellectual distinction, but they tended to be remote from the problems facing Japanese of the time. The plays were composed mainly by way of diversion from other literary activities, but the philosophical convictions they expressed imparted a solidity to the works, which attracts readers even now when they are no longer performed. The *Lesedrama*, for good or ill, began with these writers.

THE *SHINSHICHŌ* DRAMATISTS

Shinshichō (New Tides of Thought) was a magazine founded in 1907 by Osanai Kaoru chiefly as an organ for introducing Western dramatic theory and translations of European plays. The first series of this magazine lasted only a year, but it was revived no less than seventeen times, dying whenever funds and enthusiasm flagged, reviving whenever a small group of writers felt confident they could make it succeed. It drew its authors chiefly from graduates of Tokyo University, and was distinguished by the high quality of the works it printed. Such writers as Tanizaki Jun'ichirō first gained recognition from stories published in *Shinshichō*, and among the playwrights Kikuchi Kan, Yamamoto Yūzō, and Kume Masao (all three of whom were, however, even better known as novelists) were long associated with the magazine.

These dramatists used *Shinshichō* as the forum for their particular views on the theater, which they characterized as *shin genjitsu shugi* (new realism) or *shin gikō-ha* (new technique school), to distinguish themselves from the idealism of the *Shirakaba* writers or the romanticism of others. In practice, however, the *Shinshichō* dramatists stood for little more than writing plays that would be effective with the public; though the influence of Ibsen is apparent in many works, the writers were careful always to anchor their plays in the realities of contemporary Japanese life.

The best known of the *Shinshichō* dramatists was Kikuchi Kan (also known as Hiroshi, 1888–1948).[111] He began writing plays while still an undergraduate in the English Department of Tokyo University, and was instrumental in organizing the third and fourth series of *Shinshichō*. He became interested especially in the Irish playwrights, an influence apparent in his later works. Although Kikuchi's published plays attracted praise from readers as early as 1916, not until 1920 was a play of his, *Chichi Kaeru* (The Father Returns), produced. It caused a sensation, and Kikuchi was launched as a dramatist. *The Father Returns* has been described as being "not only the outstanding work of the author, but a work that has maintained its long life to this day." [112] The first performance was the equivalent, for a modern Japanese play, of the success of *John Gabriel Borkman*, but it affected the audience even more deeply, if only because Japanese, seeing other Japanese on the stage, could identify more easily with them than with characters in a foreign play. The author related that he himself wept uncontrollably at the first performance, and Akutagawa Ryūnosuke, who was seated beside him, also wept. Kikuchi remembered this as the most dramatic and joyful occasion of his entire career.[113]

The Father Returns tells of a man who has deserted his wife and three children twenty years before the action begins. The family has survived without him, though at one point the mother thought of committing suicide with the children. Since then she and the older son, Ken'ichirō, have struggled to keep the family going. The play opens as the family learns that the father has returned to town. Soon afterward he comes to the house. The older son rejects him, recalling all the hardships they suffered because of his irresponsibility, but the others are moved to pity for the old man, who has nowhere else to go. At the end even the older son, relenting, asks his brother to run after the father and bring him back to the house.

The dialogue, tinged with dialect, is natural, and the conflict between the cold rationality of Ken'ichirō, who repudiates the sentimentality of his mother and brother, and the generous feelings of the others, gives way to his natural affection for his father and to the basic truth that "blood is thicker than water." The intellectual content of the play is close to zero, but it was remarkably effective in presentation. Kikuchi was apparently inspired to write this typically Japanese drama by reading *The Prodigal Son* by St. John Hankin (1860–1909), a minor English playwright. Kikuchi changed the story to make it the father, rather than the son, who returns home after a life of dissipation. The influence of Irish drama is apparent in the treatment of the relationships within the family, but Kikuchi naturalized the foreign elements to create a work that has not lost its appeal.

Okujō no Kyōjin (The Madman on the Roof, 1916) was Kikuchi's second most popular play. It is more artistic, if only because of the theme: a madman who enjoys the beauty of a sunset is better off than a sane man. The madman's younger brother opines: "Nobody in the whole country is as happy as he is—perhaps nobody in the world. Besides, if you cure him now, what can he do? . . . If he were cured he would be conscious of being crippled, and he'd be the most miserable man alive." [114]

One other play by Kikuchi Kan is still performed, *Tōjūrō no Koi* (Tōjūrō's Love, 1919), a one-act play about a famous Kabuki actor of the Genroku era, Sakata Tōjūrō. In order to portray a secret lover convincingly, he makes advances to the wife of the proprietor of a teahouse. When the woman discovers that his amorous professions were insincere, she commits suicide, but Tōjūrō remains unruffled; the sacrifice of a woman means nothing to a great artist. The theme of the artist who must himself experience what he portrays, whether a role in a play or a painting, was not uncommon at the time (Okamoto Kidō's *Tale of Shuzenji* and Akutagawa Ryūnosuke's *Hell Screen* come to mind), but the play provided an actor with the opportunity to perform like a virtuoso. *Tōjūrō's Love* is inconsequential, but it has been a mainstay of the repertories of amateur theater groups for generations.[115]

Kume Masao (1891–1952), another member of the *Shinshichō* group, was a popular, though superficial writer. The distinguishing quality of his plays is the same kind of pastoral beauty found in his fiction. He was a competent technician who occasionally revealed flashes of more distinguished capabilities. Perhaps his best work was *Jizō-kyō Yurai* (The Origins of the Jizō Cult, 1917), a play inspired by Lord Dunsany's *The Gods of Pegana* (1905) but skillfully adapted to the Japan of the late Meiji era.

Yamamoto Yūzō (1887–1974), like other *Shinshichō* authors, was known chiefly as a novelist, but he had a greater acquaintance with the theater than most, and this enabled him to write with professional competence even in his early works. His interest in Hauptmann (the subject of his graduation thesis at Tokyo University) is apparent in his first play, *Ana* (The Hole, 1910), the story of some miners. The play was the outgrowth of Yamamoto's visit to the copper-mining town of Ashio where there had been a celebrated strike in 1907. The play, however, does not describe this conflict, but is a rather superficial sketch of daily life among the miners.

Yamamoto gained fame as a dramatist with *Seimei no Kammuri* (The Crown of Life, 1920).[116] The hero of the play, Arimura Tsunetarō, seems to come straight out of Ibsen: his insistence on absolute honesty and integrity in his actions, regardless of the painful consequences, makes him a heroic though unsuccessful figure. His refusal to compromise, either with the quality of the crabs he has contracted to send to England or with the boatowner who is willing to help Arimura fulfill his contract providing he obtains Arimura's sister as his bride, is clearly in the Ibsenian vein; but the note of quiet resignation at the end has a Japanese quality. Undoubtedly this play was for Yamamoto an expression of his own idealism. Although it has unnecessary scenes and characters, and we may not be persuaded that all the crises in Arimura's life are absolutely inevitable, it is Yamamoto's most impressive work; the echoes of Ibsen do not detract from his success at depicting Japanese living in the cold, unfriendly region of Karafuto.

Eiji-goroshi (A Case of Child Murder, 1920)[117] has been described as being the antithesis of *The Crown of Life*.[118] Unlike Arimura, who refuses to transgress his code of ethics, regardless of the circumstances, Asa kills her child out of desperate poverty, physical exhaustion, and illness. The policeman who discovers the crime, though committed to carrying out the law, realizes that in a sense he has been guilty of the same crime: he was too poor to buy medicine for his wife and son, who died as a result. The fault lies with society, we may decide, but the author does not state this as his conviction; he merely presents the evidence.

Yamamoto turned about this time from plays describing contemporary life to historical plays. It has been suggested that he had reached an impasse in his social dramas where he had to offer some solution to the problems he treated, or at least call for a solution, but he was not prepared to go that far; instead, he abandoned such problems and turned to historical subjects. At the request of Onoe Kikugorō VI he wrote *Sakazaki Dewa-no-kami* (Sakazaki, Lord of Dewa, 1921) [119] and it was performed by Kabuki actors. The story is simple: Sakazaki, who had been promised the hand of Lady Sen, the granddaughter of Tokugawa Ieyasu, charges through the flames of Osaka Castle to rescue her. His face is disfigured by burns, but he is sure he has proved his right to marry her. Lady Sen, however, is not in the least attracted by this doughty but boring warrior, preferring the handsome young Honda Heihachirō. Ieyasu is unable to persuade Sen to accept Sakazaki. As a last resort, Ieyasu's Buddhist adviser deceitfully informs Sakazaki that Sen has decided to become a nun. Sakazaki believes this, only to discover that he has been the victim of a ruse. At the end he attempts to break into the marriage ceremony of Lady Sen and Honda, but is restrained by his retainers. He thereupon commits suicide in the traditional manner.

Only one other play by Yamamoto is of importance, *Dōshi no Hitobito* (The Comrades, 1923). This too was written for Kikugorō, and the cast included (at Kikugorō's request) another great actor, Nakamura Kichiemon. The entire play takes place during a single day in the summer of 1862 aboard a ship. Some men of the Satsuma clan have participated in an unsuccessful attempt to overthrow the shogunate. Two rebels are aboard the ship. The leaders of the clan plan to have them killed before the ship reaches port. Koreeda, a close friend of one of the men, opposes this action, but in the end, realizing there is no way to save the two men, he accepts the task. He tries to persuade his friend to commit suicide, but the latter stubbornly refuses; in the end Koreeda kills him, and the other man commits seppuku.[120]

The success of *The Comrades* depended on the tightness of its construction and the author's ability to depict within the limitations of time (one evening) and space (aboard a ship) the conflicting emotions of the different persons involved in the conspiracy. The play displayed the best in Yamamoto Yūzō as a dramatist, but when one compares it to the plays that were being performed in Europe and America about the same time it is obvious that it belongs to another stream of theatrical development. The Kabuki actors were masters at expressing the kinds of psychological realism called for in this work—suppressed rage; stubborn, uncompromising resistance; the reluctant assumption of the onerous task of killing a comrade—but this was a far cry from the prevailing realism of European drama or of Yamamoto's earlier plays. The historical plays tended to involve heroic attitudes and larger-than-life declarations; and although Japanese audiences responded to such histrionics more readily than to the European plays presented at the Tsukiji Little Theatre, these plays did not lead forward in any direction, but were little more than a modernization of familiar patterns.

Two kinds of more modern theater were important in Japan during the 1920s: the specifically modern theater of Kishida Kunio, who had studied in France, and the proletarian theater, written by men who conceived of the theater as a forum for presenting Marxist ideology. Kishida's works surprised Japanese audiences with their sophistication, but those by the proletarian writers struck at the audiences with both fists, appealing to their sense of justice in the attempt to foster resistance to the existing order.

THE PROLETARIAN THEATER

Japan was torn after the end of World War I by confusion and social unrest. Prices rose markedly and there were rice riots. This discontent was accompanied by a new sense of self-awareness on the part of the working classes. The various labor and social movements came to exercise a strong influence over many aspects of culture; one product was the proletarian theater. The earliest proletarian dramas date back to some performances staged in 1919, which were inspired by strikes at the Kobe and Kawasaki shipyards. Two years later a group was formed in Tokyo to arouse through live drama the workers' consciousness of the inequalities they were suffering. About the same time some intellectuals formed a company to stage plays of "progressive" tendencies by Japanese and by such foreign dramatists as August Strindberg and Eugene O'Neill. Other companies were founded in the early 1920s as part of the wider cultural struggle to achieve the liberation of the proletariat. The Zen'ei-za (Avant-Garde Theatre) was the first troupe of professional competence, and its members included such critics and writers as Aono Suekichi, Senda Koreya, Hayashi Fusao, Maedakō Hiroichirō, and Hayama Yoshiki. The announced principles of the Avant-Garde Theatre stated that the purpose of the company was to present "healthy" plays that would guide the people toward a brighter future. The members rejected the decadent view of the world prevalent in some circles, and promised to explore areas never before trodden by their predecessors both in the contents of the plays and in the forms of expression.[121] The first performance of this group took place in December 1926 with the play *Don Quixote Liberated* by A. V. Lunacharsky (1875–1933), the Russian dramatist and theoretician of proletarian literature. The performances at the Tsukiji Little Theatre were well received, and the play ran for three days, a fairly long run for a work of the modern theater. Hayashi Fusao, later to be known for quite different political views, declared that the play made it possible for the audience to see reality; each action on the stage was immediately linked in the minds of the spectators with some occurrence in their own lives, and when the performance ended they discussed it in terms that suggested that they had had a real experience.[122] But on the whole, despite the interest not only the working classes but the intelligentsia displayed in such plays, the performances by the different proletarian companies were distinguished neither by the artistic value of the plays nor by the abilities of the actors; their primary function remained agit-propaganda.

Extremely few works of proletarian drama were written by members of the proletariat. Almost all were the work of intellectuals eager to promote social consciousness and to expose the "contradictions" in capitalist society. The few works written by true members of the working class were devoid of artistic interest, but they gave no thought to creating works of lasting literary quality. The intellectuals who wrote proletarian dramas were more literary, but also more remote; it has been pointed out that although genuine proletarian writers felt free to criticize the workers, the intellectual writers almost never wrote a word criticizing anyone except the capitalists.[123] In such plays the capitalists are quite naturally the villains, and the workers are unqualifiedly admirable, and there is certainly no suggestion offered as to how workers and capitalists might get along more harmoniously.

Nakamura Kichizō (1877–1941) is generally classed with the proletarian dramatists although he belonged to a consciously literary tradition. His early plays were written under the strong influence of Ibsen, and his later works included historical dramas that bore no apparent relationship to proletarian literature but were written for general audiences—seemingly to make money.

Nakamura first gained fame with *Kamisori* (The Razor, 1914),[124] a one-act play with a rather implausible plot. Tamekichi, though he graduated first in his class from elementary school, was obliged by the dire poverty of his family to become a barber. His classmate Okada was rich enough to attend a higher school, and now he has been elected a Member of the Diet. Okada returns to his hometown after some absence and stops at Tamekichi's barbershop for a haircut. Tamekichi's wife, Oshika, was formerly a geisha, and as Okada banters with her she begins to yearn again for a more amusing life than as a barber's wife. Tamekichi, angered because of the inequality of the lots that fate has dealt Okada and himself, and jealous of the interest Oshika shows in his rival, kills Okada with his razor. The author obviously sympathized with Tamekichi, frustrated in his hopes of advancement by an accident of birth, and the audiences no doubt shared his view. The play was performed 335 times, proof of its remarkable popularity.

The comedy *Hakuin Oshō* (The Priest Hakuin, 1917) marked Nakamura's first essay at historical plays. The story is simple and rather touching, but the priest who accepts a charge of which he is innocent—being the father of an unwed girl's baby—has little about him of the proletarian hero. Nakamura turned, in this work, from revealing social injustice to a more bourgeois concern with the individual foibles and virtues of the characters he portrayed. The best of his historical dramas, *Ii Tairō no Shi* (The

Death of Ii Tairō, 1920),[125] is a long, rather confused account of the circumstances leading up to the assassination of Ii by men outraged that he has opened the country to foreigners. The play satisfied the usual craving for a popular retelling of history, and Nakamura presented Ii with sympathy as a brave man forced to make harsh decisions in the interest of his country's safety. Occasionally he had Ii voice sentiments that seem out of place, as when Ii expresses sympathy with the rōnin attempting to destroy the "feudal, hereditary system that has already begun to crumble," but there is otherwise little overt expression of political views.

Akita Ujaku (1883–1962) was more open in his advocacy of socialism. Two one-act plays, *Kokkyō no Yoru* (Night at the Border, 1920) and *Gaikotsu no Butō* (The Skeletons' Dance, 1924), were perhaps his finest achievements. The former takes place in northern Hokkaidō. Ōno Sanshirō, a pioneer cultivator of the region, has developed over the years a philosophy of self-reliance, which is never to ask favors of others or do favors for them. Late one night, amid a terrible blizzard, a couple with a small child knock on his door asking for shelter. Ōno pretends not to hear them. That night he has a dream of a robber breaking in, stealing his money, and strangling his wife and children. When he awakens, he is informed by a faithful Ainu employee that the bodies of a couple and a child are lying dead in the snow. Ōno realizes for the first time the enormity of his crime and rushes out to find the bodies. The play is melodramatic and unconvincing, but it has frequently been performed by amateur groups.[126]

The Skeletons' Dance is rather more interesting. It takes place somewhere in the north of Japan in a large tent that has been erected at a railway station to treat the victims of the Tokyo earthquake of 1923. The facilities are wretched, and the army doctor who tends the victims is callous. A group of men fantastically garbed in medieval armor and other items of battle-dress burst in. They have heard reports that a Korean is among the evacuees. They choose a likely looking man and determine that he is indeed a Korean, both by his accent and by his inability to remember the Japanese designation of the year in which he was born.[127] They intend to lynch him, but the Korean is saved by a young Japanese who shows him the warmth of a fellow human being. The Japanese then transforms the attackers into skeletons and makes them waltz to his tune. The fantasy in this play gives it a beauty not typical of Akita Ujaku's works; but the magazine that printed *The Skeletons' Dance* was banned, and the play could be published later on only after passages identifying the intended victim as a Korean were expunged. The rumors that Koreans had taken advantage of the earthquake to kill Japanese, poison the wells, and so on had brought about a wholesale killing of Koreans, which the government wished to conceal. The play was an honest attempt to protest, but rigid censorship inhibited the expression.

These early examples of proletarian drama are on the whole unimpressive, but in a sense they are more compelling than the historical plays by Okamoto Kidō and similar masters, if only because they treated real problems of real people. Even though the 1920s are often thought of as a period of liberalism, the left-wing dramatists were certainly not free to publish and produce what they chose. Hirasawa Keishichi (1889–1923), a labor organizer and playwright, was arrested and shot by the police. Nevertheless, the proletarian movement in the late twenties became the dominant form of Shingeki; it was even averred that Shingeki that was not proletarian should not be called Shingeki at all.[128]

The purpose of these plays was didactic, to instruct audiences about the course of action that the dramatists believed the workers must take. When they succeeded they aroused spectators to a sharp awareness of their problems. Even plays totally devoid of literary merit might justify their crudity by the strength with which they depicted a group of "comrades" challenging authority and demanding revolution. The orthodoxy of the ideology of these plays was sometimes questioned by the Communist party, then underground, but the theaters of the time were a "crucible of agitation," and the participants in the plays were convinced of the revolutionary significance of their actions.

The similarities between the proletarian movement in the theater and in other genres of Japanese literature are obvious. The only recognized function of literature was to promote the liberation of the working classes. Any work that advanced this cause was praiseworthy, but works that wandered off into other subjects were condemned as frivolous or useless. Similar arguments were common in Europe. Literary criticism, even in Czarist Russia, "not only ceaselessly demanded that all writers be topical, obviously relevant and socially critical, but also prescribed rigid formal and aesthetic criteria to which all literature was supposed to conform." [129] The "radical utilitarian" critics in Russia decried works like *Anna Karenina* as being "socially irrelevant" and attacked Chekhov bitterly as a "mindless literary clown" because he failed to incorporate in his works their own ideals.

The Japanese proletarian theaters of the 1920s were for the most part firmly and avowedly Marxist in their ideology. The troupes were organized along party lines, and the plays they acted were primarily concerned with the struggles of workers, tenant farmers, and other oppressed classes. The actors performed not only plays but *Sprechchor*, sang poems, and chanted slogans like "Theater for the factory workers and the peasants!" [130] The plays written for these troupes naturally reflected these ideals. Murayama Tomoyoshi (1901–1977) began his career as a dramatist with *Skāto wo haita Nero* (Nero in Skirts, 1927), a play describing the lascivious love life of Catherine the Great. It concludes as a group of Russian soldiers, disgusted with the war against the Turks, which Catherine started, fraternize with their nominal enemies, a party of Turks who killed their commanding officer; their solidarity as oppressed members of society counts for more than their different nationalities. Catherine herself is a monster who laughs cheerfully when the severed head of her ertswhile lover, gushing blood, rolls at her feet.[131]

Murayama's best-known work, *Bōryokudan Ki* (Account of a Terrorist Gang, 1929), chronicles the brave struggle of the Chinese railway workers in 1923 to unionize in face of the opposition of the military. There is no hero in this play; instead, Murayama attempted to suggest a mass of men acting almost anonymously toward a common goal. Many lines are assigned to unspecified persons, including the last speaker, identified merely as "a voice in the darkness," who cries out as the military police charge,

> Comrades! Why has it failed? You've seen the cause with your own eyes. We must overcome that cause. But we have succeeded in establishing solid foundations for a nationwide Mass Assembly of Workers. We have succeeded also, as the result of our bloody struggle, in implanting certain slogans in the hearts of the masses. These were the shouts uttered as by one man from the mouths of the

members of our united strike front: Down with the military clique!
Down with imperialism! Long live the government of the workers
and peasants! [132]

Account of a Terrorist Gang, despite many structural and literary
failings, has undeniable power, and it has been acclaimed as the
finest work of the proletarian theater of the 1920s.[133]

Kubo Sakae (1901–1957) is usually considered to have been
the outstanding author of proletarian drama. After his graduation
from the German Literature Department of Tokyo University in
1926 he became a member of the Tsukiji Little Theatre, studying
under Osanai Kaoru. He was particularly interested in German
Naturalism and Expressionism, and rendered some translations of
modern European plays. In 1928 he defined the role of the Tsukiji
Little Theatre as being an artistic and not a political organization;
but he himself by that time had moved far to the left and believed
that men of the theater should adopt the Marxist view of the
world, recognize the historical mission of the proletariat, and by
means of their work in the theater participate in the movement of
liberation of the exploited classes.[134] His theoretical writings as
much as his plays gave Kubo a central position in the movement.

In 1930 he moved to the Proletariat Theatre League, and in
1934 joined still another left-wing theater group. During this period he wrote several of his best-known plays including *Goryō-
kaku Kessho* (Writing in Blood at the Five-Cornered Fort, 1933),
based loosely on the resistance in 1868 of Enomoto Takeaki and
his forces to the central government's armies at Hakodate in Hokkaidō. Kubo, a native of Hokkaidō, revealed in this and several
later works his special interest in the history of the island, less as a
native son than as an exponent of Marxism. He wrote:

> The Meiji Restoration was an important era when the foundations
> of the present power structure were laid, and it has furnished mate-
> rials that the conventional theater has gladly adopted in the inter-
> ests of its reactionary purposes; however, an artistic elucidation of
> the Restoration from our point of view has rarely been attempted to
> this day. *Writing in Blood at the Five-Cornered Fort* is a first little
> spade dug into this untilled land. I took up my pen with the inten-
> tion of delineating concretely the truth with respect to such points
> as: by means of what political and economic factors, combinations

of different forms of authority, and sacrifices of certain things was the present structure erected seventy years ago; and how were the actions taken by various foreign countries, which looked on the struggle between the government and the "bandits" as a Japanese Civil War, reflected inside the country.[135]

His intention, Kubo stated, was not merely to make a historical re-creation of the past; he wished to achieve an artistic meaning and effect no less immediate as a study of the development of mankind, treated in accordance with the principle of historical determinism, than his works based on contemporary themes. The play is the tragedy of a samurai of the Hakodate region who deplores the cruel treatment of the common people, exploited by both the Meiji government and an English trading company. He joins forces with Enomoto, only for Enomoto to conclude peace secretly with the central government. At the end the samurai realizes that he has been betrayed, and that the blood shed on behalf of Enomoto's "Republic of Hokkaidō" was shed in vain; the only way for the people to eradicate the injustices and inequity afflicting them is to rely on their own strength and not that of people at the top.

Unlike some proletarian dramatists, who showed little concern for theatrical effects, Kubo employed the resources of Kabuki and other traditional forms of theater in the effort to appeal to mass audiences. His theatrical criticism will be familiar to anyone who has read works by European advocates of Socialist Realism; it was a presentation of existing rather than original ideas. He insisted that the political values of works for the theater were more important than any others, but he tried always to bolster his political message with artistic excellence. His use of historical materials typified his stand: "The important thing for us is not to twist or improve facts by our subjective views—the class views of the proletariat—but to discover facts that conform to our views." [136]

Kubo's extremely long play *Kazambai-chi* (Region of Volcanic Ash, 1937) has been acclaimed as a masterpiece by some critics.[137] Kubo himself was convinced that he had created a work of seminal importance: "The dramaturgy embodied in *Region of Volcanic Ash* is the definitive method of apprehending contemporary Japan. . . . It is the only logic that can fill the young who are seeking to bring about a renaissance in Japan." [138] But despite the self-acclaim, the play has dated badly.

Clearly Kubo learned much from the epic theater of Germany. *Volcanic Ash* opens with a film presenting the title, theme-song music, and the voice of a "reader" emitted by a loudspeaker. Although a few individuals stand out in this play, especially Amemiya, the humanitarian who directs a research laboratory, the prevailing impression is of epic theater in its impersonality. "Epic writing looks beyond personal comedy or tragedy to the relationships which are bigger than people. These sociological—sometimes even technological—relationships are the fundamental cause of comic or tragic events." [139] Although this international aspect of Kubo's plays has not been given much attention, clearly he was influenced by Soviet as well as German theater. Kubo conceived of his work as "anti-capitalist realism," a term that seems to hark back to the Socialist Realism that had been adopted in 1934 by the Soviet theater as "the style which it considered best suited to its audiences and theatre workers." [140]

The performances of *Volcanic Ash* were highly successful, even though many people later complained of the difficulty of understanding the play, the excessive number of characters, and the slowness of the tempo. The critic of the *Tōkyō Asahi Shimbun* wrote in July 1938:

> This work depicts reality with complete sincerity. There is no make-believe, nor is there any meaningless excitement. The author's design is correct, and his techniques are extremely precise. . . . His single-minded spirit and unflagging convictions are fully worthy of our respect; but the play, it must be admitted, is too long. It talks about too many things. And the methods and conceptions are so lacking in dramatic tempo and rhythm as to be novelistic. . . . It is by no means to the credit of the author that even after one has seen the whole play, the various relationships are still confused. Of course, if one goes back over the play and painstakingly pieces together the broken utterances of each character and reviews the relationships, it would not be impossible to grasp them sufficiently well, but this is to make excessive demands on the spectators.[141]

Kubo in later years explained the causes of the undeniable obscurity in the play. He began writing it just as the China Inci-

dent of 1937 was beginning, and if he had been somewhat slower
in completing it, the work might never have seen the light of day.
He had to worry about possible interpretations by the censors,
and as a consequence "what should have been the principal
theme was, by force of circumstances, made secondary" and various characters who appeared early in the play could not be allowed to reappear. Important dialogue was buried in the midst of
passages of complicated action. But Kubo was determined not to
yield one step in the basic content of the play, however he cam-
ouflaged the meaning. His hero, the scientist Amemiya, is not
portrayed specifically as a socialist, but he realizes that an improvement in agricultural techniques alone will not solve the
problems of the farmers. When he spoke of "hidden hints" of
great importance that Japan might learn from abroad, the audience knew what he meant, and there were regularly shouts of
approval and applause.[142]

In August 1940 the government ordered two left-wing theater
groups to disband, and their principal figures, including Kubo,
Akita Ujaku, and Murayama Tomoyoshi, were simultaneously arrested. Kubo was not released until the end of 1941, after the war
in the Pacific had broken out. During the war he was unable to
publish anything, but he began work on *Ringoen Nikki* (Diary of
an Apple Orchard), completed in 1946. He also worked on a new
translation of *Faust* and on a study of his mentor, Osanai Kaoru.
His postwar works have their admirers, but they are smaller in
scale and weaker in impact than *Region of Volcanic Ash*. His last
play, *Nihon no Kishō* (Weather Conditions in Japan, 1953),
treated postwar Japan, describing with Socialist Realism the hardships suffered by scientists at a meteorological station because of
the rapidly changing, confused conditions. Kubo committed suicide in 1957 while at a hospital suffering from a long illness.

One other dramatist, though later associated with quite different ideology, originally belonged to the proletarian drama
movement, Miyoshi Jūrō (1902–1958). While a student at Waseda
University he was attracted to Marxism. In 1923 he published his
first play, a comedy, and followed this with a play more obviously
in the proletarian tradition, *Kizu darake no Oaki* (The Much-
Maimed Oaki, 1927). Miyoshi at the beginning threw himself into
the proletarian movement, but he gradually became disenchanted
with the hard-line emphasis placed on politics by the principal

proletarian drama groups and broke off his associations. In 1934 he published *Kirare no Senta* (The Stabbed Senta), a work set at the end of the Tokugawa period when samurai and peasants joined in an attempt to overthrow the oppressive local regime. The refusal of the main character, Sentarō, to cooperate any further with the samurai, convinced as he is that the lower ranks of society (whether farmers or townsmen) must fight their own battles, was an implicit rejection of the cooperation between intellectuals and workers on which the orthodox left-wing theater was based. His use of Kabuki techniques and other traditional elements of production, intended to give the play general appeal, also displeased other proletarian writers.[143]

There could no longer be any doubt that Miyoshi had shifted away from the proletarian theater when his most important work, *Bui* (Buoy, 1940), appeared. It revealed both his concern with the lower classes and his independence of party dogma. This play had a special meaning for Miyoshi: he realized that being a dramatist was his "heaven-appointed profession," and the work is closely autobiographical, an *Ich Drama*, devoted mainly to an evocation of the circumstances surrounding the death of his wife.[144] Some critics have hailed it as a monument of modern Japanese dramatic literature. The dialogue is unaffected and believable, and even the minor characters are skillfully drawn. The central figure, the painter Kuga, is the alter ego of Miyoshi, and his anguish after his conversion (*tenkō*) away from party ideals is especially compelling.

Miyoshi's break with the party was perhaps the most crucial event of his career. He referred often to his dissatisfaction with orthodox Marxist theory, insisting, for example, that for the artist, at least in his creative life, all elements of reality must be portrayed with the same attitude; he must treat with the same detachment a bourgeois and a member of the proletariat. If politics is considered something like soy sauce for art, enabling the diner to eat an otherwise insipid dish, not only will the art die, but the true political quality, which only art can display, will also die.[145] Miyoshi refused to accept the reduction of all elements to political ones in the schematized, mechanical, conceptual manner of the Materialist Dialecticians. He found the usual division of the characters in proletarian dramas into wholly good or wholly evil characters absurd, and even in his specifically proletarian works did not conform to such stereotypes.

After his "conversion" he pursued with an even greater intensity his search for the truth about human life, culminating in *Buoy*. He felt a deep love for ordinary people, especially the farmers. In an essay relating to his play *Shishi* (The Lion, 1943), Miyoshi stated that the most conspicuous characteristics of the Japanese were that they ate rice as their staple food and lived in an agricultural country. But he was aware how the conditions of modern life had distorted and even perverted the essentially good nature of the farmers, and this inspired in him an anger that dominated some of his later works.

After the end of the war in 1945 Miyoshi did not stage an about-face conversion in the direction of the now acceptable Marxist ideology, but continued to wage his solitary battle to depict the lives of the common people in their true colors, without admixture of political propaganda. *Sono hito wo shirazu* (I Know Not the Man, 1948) is about a factory worker, Katakura, who has become a devout Christian and refuses to be conscripted. He is tortured by the military police (*kempeitai*), but does not budge from the Christian teaching that forbids the taking of life even in times of war. He is accused of being a traitor, his mother falls ill under the strain, and his brother (who had been working at the same factory) is fired because of Katakura and sent to the front, where he dies. Even when the pastor who baptized Katakura urges him to change his mind, he refuses. He is imprisoned. His father visits him daily, begging him to recant, but he refuses. When the war ends Katakura is released. By this time his family has been virtually destroyed by his unbending faith. His sister is blinded by an explosion at the factory where she works, and his father has committed suicide. Another sister has become a streetwalker. But at the factory where Katakura was formerly denounced as a traitor, he is now treated like a hero. Obviously Miyoshi was expressing his indignation with the fecklessness of society, but the hero, who has withstood all pressure during the war, is later torn by doubts as to the wisdom of his intransigence; he even wonders about the existence of the God for whom he sacrificed so much.[146]

Other works that describe the postwar world include *Haikyo*

(Ruins, 1947), *Tainai* (Inside the Womb, 1949), and *Okashita Mono* (The Desecrated, 1952). These works are prevailingly dark and depressing. The characters live in houses that have been broken by the war, and memories of the war, together with present poverty, dominate their thoughts. In the afterwords he wrote to various plays Miyoshi insisted on the factual truth of the incidents he had dramatized; for example, the hero of *The Desecrated* was a friend who had committed suicide the year before, and none of the other characters was invented. These plays are so close to the events they re-create that they do not escape the danger of becoming dated; but we can still sympathize, say, with Shibata, the professor in *Ruins* who has resolved to live strictly within the rations, even though he knows that the meager allotments are insufficient to keep a man alive, because of the guilt he feels at having loved his country and prayed for its success during the war.[147] Miyoshi was able to transcend the limitations of a particular time by discovering the humanity in the characters and imparting to their predicaments something of universal significance. For this reason his plays seem likelier to retain their value longer than those of other dramatists of the proletarian school.

THE ARTISTIC SCHOOL

The name "Artistic School" (*geijutsu-ha*) is a catch-all appellation for a variety of Shingeki dramatists who were alike only in that they were not Naturalists, idealists, humanists, or socialists. Most were also known for their novels and a few for their poetry. Their plays otherwise had little in common, and even within the works of a single dramatist there was no unifying manner. These dramatists were attracted to the theater for its own sake, but their preferred form of expression ranged from intensely romantic dramas to unadorned descriptions of daily life.

Among the Romantic dramatists none was more extreme than Kōri Torahiko (1890–1924), a minor but interesting figure. He began his career as a novelist and was associated with the *Shirakaba* writers from the beginnings of their movement. His first play, *Fuhai subekarazaru Kyōjin* (The Incorruptible Madman, 1911), is set at the time of the French Revolution, and depicts Robespierre as he is tormented by the ghost of Danton, whom he sent to the guillotine. This short play is a perfect example of the weird, ominous atmosphere that was Kōri's forte. In the following year he wrote *Dōjōji*, the first of his modern versions of Nō plays. The atmosphere is heady and decadent, rather in the manner of Wilde's *Salome*.

Although Kōri's play follows approximately the familiar story of the priest who was roasted alive in the bell of the Dōjōji by the vengeful spirit of a woman whose love he had spurned, the plot as such is less important than the murky atmosphere. It opens as a young priest wanders through the mist to the temple. He sees the moonlight climb the temple steps "like a horrible spider, one step at a time." Later he learns from another priest about the girl whose vengeful fury had turned her into a serpent who pursued a priest to this temple. "Vomiting forth sulphur-colored flames, she coiled her body around the bell again and again, and before we knew it the bell and the man had dissolved into a muddy, leaden liquid." The color of the moonlight, the sinister odor of leaves in the dark, and the faces of ghosts with blood-red lips are evoked. The play concludes with the coming of a baleful dawn: "A mist powdered with blood has crept up from the valley bottom—a weird break of day has come. Even the breast of the sky is a raw red, like a human body from which the epidermis has been stripped, and it breathes painfully in the morning wind." [148]

Lush writing was typical of Kōri, and the language in places is so obscure that the play is difficult to follow. Kōri wrote other Nō plays imbued with much the same atmosphere, insisting always on the great distance separating his scene from the ordinary world of today. Kōri went to Europe in 1913 and spent most of the rest of his short life there, dying in a Swiss sanatorium. He wrote several plays in English, including *Saul and David* (1918) and *The Toils of Yoshitomo* (1922), an account from the *Hōgen Monogatari* dramatized in the form of a Greek tragedy.[149]

The plays of Tanizaki Jun'ichirō (1886–1965), though by no means comparable in importance to his novels, are often effective in the sinister vein exploited by Kōri Torahiko. His plays have been characterized as decadent because they were largely concerned with the obsessions of people with distorted minds, and revealed virtually no trace of social or moral awareness, emphasizing the quest for beauty rather than any desire to improve human life. Some of Tanizaki's plays treated the distant past, like

Hōjōji Monogatari (1915), set in the times of Fujiwara no Michinaga. His interest in the past was unlike Mayama Seika's; Tanizaki's historical characters, far from suggesting heroic fortitude, find meaning in beauty alone. In *Okuni to Gohei* (Okuni and Gohei, 1921) the cowardly Ikeda Tomonojō, in love with the beautiful Okuni, kills her husband, but is too ineffectual to fight for her hand with Gohei, the husband's retainer who has sworn to avenge his master's death. Tomonojō covertly follows Okuni and Gohei around the country, craving only to be near her. The play is interesting especially because of its close connections with the novels in which Tanizaki described, in much greater detail, the slavish devotion of men to beautiful women.[150]

Tanizaki's best-known play, *Aisureba koso* (Because I Love Him, 1921), is set in the contemporary world. The beautiful Sumiko is in love with an opera singer named Yamada who mistreats her brutally; but although she is grateful for the love of the noble-minded youth Miyoshi, she is magnetically drawn back to Yamada and his corrupt ways. She finally decides, "The real way for me to love Yamada is not to try to save him, but to join him in his depravity." In *Mandorin wo hiko Otoko* (The Man with the Mandoline, 1925) a blind man drugs his wife each night because he is afraid that a rival will somehow make his way into the fortress where he keeps the wife a prisoner.[151]

It need hardly be said what a gulf separates these plays from those of the *Shirakaba* or proletarian dramatists written about the same time. Tanizaki's main period of activity as a playwright corresponded to a slump as a novelist, and once he resumed his brilliant career as a novelist in the mid-1920s, he wrote no more plays.

Kubota Mantarō (1889–1963) was another prominent member of the "artistic school" of dramatists as well as a novelist and haiku poet. He was born and bred in Tokyo and attended Keiō University, where he helped to found the literary magazine *Mita Bungaku* in 1910, under the aegis of Nagai Kafū, then teaching at the university. This periodical, opposing the Naturalism espoused by *Waseda Bungaku*, the literary organ of the rival university, became the bastion of "anti-Naturalism" and as such published works by Izumi Kyōka, Kitahara Hakushū, and Tanizaki Jun'ichirō. Among the writers who gained recognition in *Mita Bungaku*, none showed greater promise than Kubota Mantarō. His first story appeared in the magazine in 1911, and he followed this the next year with his first play. From then on, through the long career that lasted almost until his death, he wrote plays for Kabuki, Shimpa, and Shingeki.

Even in his early play *Kuregata* (Twilight, 1912) Kubota's characteristic manner is apparent. Although this (and his later plays) lacked normal dramatic conflict and complications, and expounded no view of the world, let alone ideology, it succeeded thanks to its perfect evocation of an atmosphere. The scene of Kubota's plays was most often Asakusa, the old-fashioned district of Tokyo where he grew up. The people are generally quite ordinary members of the lower middle class who are often almost inarticulate, unable to express deeply seated feelings that they do not fully understand themselves. It is difficult to summarize the plots of most of these plays: the lack of dramatic tension has suggested to some critics that the plays were meant to be read, rather than performed; but the silences, the offstage noises, the feeling of the seasons pervading the plays give them a unique appeal.

The one-act *Mijikayo* (Short Night, 1925), one of Kubota's best plays, opens as a group of people sit around on a summer night in Senzō's house in Asakusa. They talk indirectly, with many pauses, about a subject that only gradually becomes apparent—their decision to break up the marriage between Ofusa and her husband, Isaburō, a young man who has taken to drink. Only once in the play does Ofusa utter a word, merely to confirm that she has been married for five years. The rest of the time she remains silent, even when directly questioned. But toward the end, after Isaburō (who has also been silent through most of the discussion) has been informed that he will not be allowed to meet Ofusa again, she suggests by silent tears her reluctance to lose her husband. The play ends as Senzō, looking out the window, comments, "That's good. The sky's already become light." But Kubota appended a stage direction that undercut the seeming hopefulness of the final line: "He speaks with a suggestion of the tears of anguish that spread out, filling his heart. The three women continue to weep." [152] The traditional Japanese ability to make a conventionally polite or even cheerful remark when in spiritual anguish has rarely been employed so tellingly by a dramatist.

Short Night is peculiarly successful in its evocation of old-fashioned Japanese people. Chikamatsu wrote: "If a playwright were to model his characters on the ways of real women and conceal their feelings, such realism, far from being appreciated, would permit no pleasure in the work." For this reason the female characters in Chikamatsu's plays openly express feelings that real women would conceal. Kubota's female characters, by contrast, tend to remain wordless; they reveal their emotions through their silences or their unexplained tears. The most common indication of dialogue in *Short Night* is a string of dots, indicating that the character has failed to respond. Even when the character speaks, he or she does not necessarily say what he or she really means, but for a Japanese audience (at least one of 1925) explanations were unnecessary; they could empathize totally with the people on the stage.

Kubota's most ambitious play was *Ōdera Gakkō* (The Ōdera School, 1927), set in the Asakusa district toward the end of the Meiji era. Ōdera Sampei, the principal of a private school that bears his name, is an old-fashioned teacher who has no understanding of the changes that have occurred in recent years. His school, founded at the time of the proclamation of the Meiji Constitution, is celebrating its twentieth anniversary, and a party has been arranged. Several days later Ōdera learns that a public school will be erected in the neighborhood. He refuses to believe the news, knowing that the free public school will drive his private school out of business. He drinks more heavily than usual and, at the end, distracts himself by singing the Ninokuchi Village scene from Chikamatsu's *Courier for Hell*, an expression of an old-fashioned morality that has seemingly been repudiated in the new era.[153] The gradual disappearance of the old Tokyo, a familiar theme in Kubota's plays, is stated here with poignance. But though the audience sympathizes with Ōdera, it is obvious that the kind of education for which he stood was doomed, and that it no doubt was inferior in quality to the education the new public school will provide. Bittersweet nostalgia for the old Tokyo is typical of Kubota's work, but he was not blind to the shortcomings of life in the past, though the harshness of the new world repelled him. The production of *The Ōdera School* at the Tsukiji Little Theatre in 1928, just a month before Osanai Kaoru's death, marked the highest artistic level that theater achieved.

Iwata Toyoo (1893–1969), who himself wrote a successful play, the brilliant farce *Higashi wa Higashi* (East Is East, 1933), wrote of Kubota,

> I wonder if Kubota has been properly appreciated as a dramatist. I have seen numerous instances when he was considered as a dramatist of mores, or as a dramatist who specialized in sketches from life. But even though people admire his admirable *paroles*, few have noticed his *solide* dramaturgy. It goes without saying that a drama of mores or a drama that is a slice of life does not require true dramaturgy. I believe that an examination of, say, *The Ōdera School* will reveal that the composition, structure, development, and conclusion are all incredibly skillful. Masamune Hakuchō was overcome with admiration when he read *The Tale of Genji* in an English translation; in the same way, I feel sure that if such a work as *The Ōdera School* were translated, it would set off in high relief the author's dramatic framework. In this sense there is no more extraordinary author than Kubota. He is the most Japanese of authors in his lyricism, vocabulary, and materials, but his dramaturgic lineage may be said to be purely Western. He reminds one of the style of the French writers of the *école de silence*. One senses an extraordinary resemblance in the spirit of the dramaturgy, even more than in the techniques.[154]

The similarities between Kubota's plays and European drama could have resulted from his readings or from the years he spent as the chief of the drama division of the Japanese National Broadcasting Company (NHK). But possibly they were accidental, the unconscious effect of the new atmosphere in Japan, which Kubota breathed in even as he nostalgically recalled the Japan of the past.

In 1937 Kubota, Iwata, and Kishida Kunio (1890–1954) founded the Bungaku-za (Literary Theatre).[155] As its name indicated, this theater gave special attention to works of literary value. It was opposed to popular stage entertainments, devoid of intellectual content, but also to the various proletarian theaters, which expounded political doctrines at the expense of artistry. Kishida was the most qualified of the three men to create such a theater; indeed, he was the first Japanese to have acquired a systematic knowledge of the European theater through experience abroad, and he attempted to create in Japan a theater similar in both literary and dramatic quality to those he had frequented in Paris.

Kishida entered the French Literature Department at Tokyo University in 1917. Two years later he went to France, and for three years studied intensively, mainly under Jacques Copeau. He returned to Japan late in 1923, and the next year his play *Furui Omocha* (Old Toys) was published in the newly founded magazine *Engeki Shinchō*, on the recommendation of Yamamoto Yūzō. This first play had earlier been written in French for Georges Pitoëff's company, and was subsequently rewritten in Japanese.[156] It is the story of Tomeo, a young Japanese artist who goes to France to study painting. He is disgusted with the Japanese feudalistic mentality and enjoys the freedom of the West. Although he experiences feelings of inferiority as an outsider and especially as a Japanese, he falls in love with a French girl, Louise, who is also a painter. Tomeo's father urges him to return to Japan, but he has absolutely no intention of returning to a country he despises. In the meantime he learns from a Japanese woman with whom he formerly was involved that she still loves him. She has decided to break with her husband and join him. But Tomeo rejects her and marries Louise instead. Problems arise, largely because of Tomeo's inferiority complex. Louise wishes to go to Japan but he refuses to take her. She leaves him and he falls ill. Fusako, his old lady-friend, comes to tend him in his loneliness.

One Japanese critic has suggested that Tomeo is a portrait of Kishida himself, a man who rebelled against life in Japan typified by his father, an army officer, and sought freedom in Europe, only to feel loneliness and an awareness of being a stranger.[157]

Kishida's next important play, the one-act *Chiroru no Aki* (Autumn in the Tyrol, 1924), marked a great advance in his development as a dramatist. It too is about a Japanese in Europe, at a resort hotel in the Tyrol, but instead of the flat realism of the earlier play, a poetic atmosphere is created. Amano meets a mysterious woman named Stella on the last day of the hotel season. They must leave the next day. In the course of their conversation he asks her nationality, but she evades the question, suggesting he consult the hotel register if he really wants to know. He answers:

I'm not all that conscious of being a Japanese. That's why I'm
not especially interested in what country a person comes from.

I imagine that the lives we two are leading are not so different.[158]

We never learn who these two people are, nor why they are
constantly traveling. Amano remarks: "It's a strange thing, isn't it,
the way people feel when they travel. They become almost terri-
fyingly sensitive about friendships. . . . But all the same, in the
face of stronger emotions they are almost comically timid."

The two speak politely, ironically, in unfinished thoughts.
Amano recalls: "This summer a German officer told me that during the war, when his company, which had been occupying a
French village, was about to withdraw, the girls in the village all
turned out that day and stood weeping and wailing along the
roads." Stella answers: "What a disagreeable story!" [159]

The conversation blurs. Amano at length induces Stella to
join in a dream fantasy in which their hidden thoughts might
coalesce. Each speaks, only half aware of the other, until Stella
suddenly blurts out, "My mother was born in Japan. . . . Her
name was Hama. . . ." Amano now begs her with urgency to tell
him who she is, but again she drifts into reveries, speaking as if to
a long-ago lover. They separate with a final promise to say goodbye the next day, "dreams permitting."

A summary cannot do justice to the atmosphere of *Autumn in
the Tyrol*, but even these excerpts should indicate how little it
resembles the Japanese plays we have been considering. The language is vague, the world evoked dreamlike, and the place ambiguous. There is no resolution, nor even a continuity in the plot.
Kishida once praised the "southern" style of drama, as opposed to
the "northern" drama of Ibsen, and regretted that the "southern"
drama—by which he meant mainly the French—had influenced
very few Japanese writers, though many had been inspired by
Ibsen. He said of the "southern" style: "Authors who write in this
style prefer fragrance to strength, nuance to depth. Instead of
treating human anguish head-on as anguish, these dramatists create comedies through the use of fantasy." [160]

Autumn in the Tyrol is not comic, but Kishida's most popular
plays closely approximated this "southern" style. *Buranko* (The

Swing, 1925) was the first in a series of two-character plays about a husband and wife. Their dialogue is whimsical, and no attempt was made to achieve an orderly plot, let alone to deliver a message. The plot involves the balance between the dream world of beauty envisioned by the husband and the practical realities of life on which his wife insists. The husband succeeds in drawing his wife into his dreams for a moment, only for the husband's friend, the man with whom he goes to work each morning, to knock on the door and bring the couple back to reality.

Kishida's most popular play was the one-act *Kami Fūsen* (Paper Balloon, 1925). Again the characters are an unnamed man and wife. It is Sunday, and they are bored. The wife urges the husband to go visit a friend, but he is uninterested. He reads the newspaper. They drift into a discussion of the proper behavior for a new and enlightened woman. The wife imagines going out and leaving the husband behind for a change. Then they plan an imaginary trip to Kamakura, lovingly enumerating all the proper things to see and do. The fantasy breaks off. After a long silence the dialogue resumes:

HUSBAND: I wonder if we aren't doing pretty well, considering.
WIFE: I wish things were just a little bit better.
HUSBAND: You mean money?
WIFE: That's not what I mean.
                (*Long silence.*)
HUSBAND: Shall we get a dog?
WIFE: Wouldn't a canary be better?
                (*Long silence.*)
HUSBAND: (*Yawns.*)
WIFE: (*Yawns.*) [161]

The ennui is broken when a paper balloon is batted into the garden by the little girl from next door. Husband and wife fight for the privilege of batting the balloon back.

Nothing of consequence occurs in the play. We are left with an impression of a lazy, uneventful Sunday in the life of a couple of the kind the world calls happy. The intrusion of fantasy relieves their boredom for a moment, but there is basically nothing to say. In *Ashita wa Tenki* (It Will Be Fine Tomorrow, 1928) [162] a husband and wife have saved money to go to a seaside resort, but it rains every day. The wife writes picture postcards describing how much they have been enjoying the water and the sunshine; the husband practices swimming on the tatami of his room at the inn. They learn to their disappointment that it has been cool in Tokyo. The husband imagines journeys to distant places and describes the glorious scenery, but the wife fails to respond. He then tries to stir her with an account of meeting an old sweetheart, but she dozes off. At last he makes up his mind that they will return at once to Tokyo, though the maid assures them that it will definitely clear tomorrow.

These plays are slight but effective vignettes of the lives of ordinary people. Little in the expression is traditionally Japanese, even though the characters wear kimonos and sit on the tatami. Kishida seems to be suggesting that this is what life in Japan during an unheroic age is really like, and his superb control of the dialogue makes the characters wholly believable.

Kishida was criticized for not having dealt with social problems. Only in one play, *Okujō Teien* (Roof Garden, 1926), did he even venture into suggesting the differences that separate the social classes. Two school friends accidentally meet after some years and discover that the present difference in their financial situations makes it impossible to regain their old intimacy.[163] For the most part, however, the unhappiness of Kishida's characters arises from within themselves, rather than as an effect of society or heredity. His early plays managed to sustain a mood of bittersweet comedy, but in the later, longer plays the tone was darker. The five-act *Ushiyama Hoteru* (Ushiyama Hotel, 1929) is considered by some to be Kishida's major work. It is set in Haiphong in French Indochina in the early 1920s, and the hotel apparently was closely modeled on the one where Kishida made a fortune playing bridge while on his way to France. Unlike the earlier plays, *Ushiyama Hotel* has a plot with dramatic incidents and clearly defined characters. A group of Japanese businessmen, their wives or mistresses, and various others of the Japanese community live in a small hotel near the port. Some Japanese women, prostitutes from Kyushu, live in the same hotel. The plot is involved, but the play successfully depicts the different effects on Japanese of their exotic surroundings. Some are determined to retain their Japanese qualities, others (especially the hero, a self-proclaimed cosmopolitan) seem gradually to have lost their Japanese identity.

Kishida, disappointed by the failure of some of his plays to be produced at all, and by the unsatisfactory productions given to others, tried for a time to write plays that the actors and directors could handle more easily.[164] The dialogue in such works is prosier and the situations more familiar, but he failed to win a following for his plays.

He returned to his best form in two long plays published in 1935: *Sawa-shi no Futari Musume* (Mr. Sawa's Two Daughters) and *Saigetsu* (A Space of Time). Both plays are tragic in tone and possess genuine distinction.[165] Kishida created a memorable character in Mr. Sawa, an ex-diplomat whose undistinguished career was marked by an official reprimand for dereliction. He returned to Japan after years abroad on receiving word that his unloved wife was dying, and ever since he has raised two daughters on his meager income as the business manager of a small Catholic sanatorium. An old crony, Kamitani, visits Sawa and they indulge in reminiscences of the past. Sawa produces a bottle of white wine for the occasion, and his speech is dotted with French words, evidence that the years abroad have not been forgotten. But when Kamitani relays the information that a titled Frenchman with vast estates wishes to marry Sawa's younger daughter, Sawa is indignant at the thought of allowing a foreigner to take his daughter into his arms.

The characters—Sawa, Kamitani, and the two daughters—are convincingly drawn, but Sawa alone compels our attention. Although early in the play he tells his daughters that Western food no longer agrees with him, and he refuses to allow his daughter to marry a foreigner, he is a *dépaysé*, incapable of living either as a Japanese or as a foreigner. At the end of the play, left all alone, he removes his jacket and "taking a crust of bread from the cupboard in one hand, he holds a piece of cheese in the other. He paces back and forth, taking a bite now of the bread, now of the cheese." [166] At this point the curtain falls.

A Space of Time describes three stages in a woman's life: shortly before she gives birth to her lover's child; seven years afterward when her lover (who has been forced to marry the woman, though they do not live together) demands his freedom, even if this means she will kill herself; and then years later when the lover finally asks the woman to live with him, but she refuses, realizing that he is no longer the man she loved. The lover never appears, giving maximum emphasis to the woman's reactions.

Kishida virtually stopped writing plays between 1936 and 1948. Ironically, it was the novels written during this period, especially *Danryū* (Warm Current, 1938), which established his reputation with the general public.[167] During the war Kishida served as the head of one of the main patriotic organizations of writers. These activities led to his being purged for three years after the war, and his postwar production was scanty.

Kishida was also an important critic of the theater, serving especially to introduce to the Japanese the latest developments in France. He stood always for Modernity, and although he also recognized there was Modernity in "the style of Kubota, the themes of Kikuchi and the construction of Yamamoto," [168] Modernity obviously meant something different to him from what it had meant to these three dramatists. Kishida's plays are about Japanese people, usually living in Japan, but he did not dwell on the conflicts between the old morality and the modern world, in the manner of other playwrights. He was moreover totally uninterested in costume dramas or in the fading remnants of old Tokyo. He wrote plays that accorded with his understanding of the most advanced Western theaters of the day. He was handicapped by the scarcity of Japanese actors who could successfully perform in this style, and by the slowness of audiences to respond to plays that were so unlike Okamoto Kidō's or Yamamoto Yūzō's. His refusal to "combine the best in East and West," the chimerical illusion that had led so many promising Japanese writers astray, bore fruit only after 1945 when some Japanese resolutely turned their backs on the old theatrical traditions and wrote plays that asked to be judged in absolute terms alongside those being written anywhere in the world, whether or not they expressed the Japanese psyche.

Kishida succeeded singlehandedly in creating a modern theater for Japan, but his success was of esteem, not of general acclaim. His best plays were rarely performed, and have enjoyed only sporadic revivals even in recent days. Other men benefited by his integrity and devotion to the ideals of European theater, but neither Kishida nor any of his successors were able to create an adequate audience for their plays. But inasmuch as Kishida insisted on the literary aspects of the theater, it was not an unmitigated disaster that his plays have tended to be read rather than seen. He hoped that his plays would please large audiences, and tried to educate the Japanese of his time to understand such works, but serious modern plays, despite his efforts, were of interest to far fewer Japanese than Kabuki or the films.

One of the few writers who was able to continue writing plays effectively during the war was Mafune Yutaka (b. 1902). He studied English literature at Waseda University, and was especially attracted by the plays of John Millington Synge and Strindberg. As an undergraduate he published a few short stories, but having become converted to Marxism in the meanwhile, he left the university without graduating and went to work as a cowherd in Hokkaidō. During the next eight years he wandered around the country, at one time throwing his efforts into a farmers' movement in Shikoku. After his return to Tokyo in 1934 he published the three-act play *Itachi* (The Weasels) in a coterie magazine. It was produced in the same year and met with extraordinary success, establishing this previously unknown playwright as a major figure. Just about this time the proletarian companies were forced by the government to disband, and there was a general reorganization of Shingeki. The surviving companies either stood for artistry in the manner of Kishida and the group associated with his magazine *Gekisaku* (Playwriting), or else attempted to preserve realism, if not Socialist Realism.

The Weasels was produced by the Sōsaku-za (Creative Theatre), one of the latter groups. It describes a farming village in the northeast, and is written in a modified dialect, supposedly that of Aizu, but actually a composite dialect not spoken anywhere, yet generally intelligible.[169] From the first the critics praised Mafune's ability to capture the primeval passions of the villagers, especially the unbounded greed for property that divides parents and children, brothers and sisters. Mafune's portrayal of these villagers bears not a trace of sentimentality and very little compassion. His years of living and working with farmers enabled him to view them with far greater clarity than intellectuals whose knowledge of the countryside was mainly theoretical. The play, unlike the cosmopolitan works by Kishida Kunio, was peculiarly and uniquely Japanese; but it differed from the studies of the peasantry by proletarian dramatists because ideological considerations never induced Mafune to alter the truth.

The plot of *The Weasels* defies ready summary, but more important than the details of the various conflicts are the characters, who are vividly alive in every speech. Mafune described at length his determination to pursue the essential, naked nature of human beings. In practice this meant exposing the egoism of his characters in all its ugliness. Obviously, ugliness is not the whole truth about human beings, but the surface veneer of civilization did not interest Mafune. He seems to have doubted that at the most fundamental level the beauty of human nature, so often celebrated by other writers, really existed. But even *The Weasels* contains a kind of mordant humor, which prefigures the comedies and farces that Mafune was later to write.

The Weasels brought Mafune fame and he was much in demand for new plays, not only by the Shingeki troupes but by Shimpa, and even by the Kabuki actors. He wrote *Tonsōfu* (Fugue, 1937) for the second Ichikawa Sadanji, then attempting to revive the Free Theatre. However, the word "free" itself was suspect at a time when Japanese militarism was rampant, and the Free Theatre could not be resuscitated. The central figure in *Fugue*, Kabayama Gengo, is a lovable tyrant who runs his family with an iron hand. There is caricature in the portrayal, but never so much as to seem unnatural. This play is set in Tokyo, but Mafune proved that his skill with dialogue did not depend on dialect, and his theatrical instincts were unerring. Perhaps, as Nagahira Kazuo suggested, Mafune's plays were the only true examples of Naturalism in the Japanese theater since Mayama Seika's first plays; the characters, though objectively portrayed, were clearly nurtured by Mafune's own experiences and deepest feelings.[170]

Mafune was able to continue writing even during the war years, a blank period for Japanese drama. The theater, or what was left of it after the government consolidated most troupes, was intended exclusively to promote the war effort; nothing that was merely entertaining, let alone controversial, was tolerated.[171] Mafune compromised very little, but because he was so intensely personal in his expression he did not greatly upset the authorities. He traveled to China in 1942 and again in 1944, and was in Peking when the war ended. *Nakahashi Kōkan* (The Nakahashi Clinic, 1946) is the account of a group of Japanese resident in China. The central character, Nakahashi Tetsuhito, is a doctor who has spent over fifty years in China caring for opium addicts, a cranky old man who gives little consideration to his own family. Their experiences in Peking as the war ends—no doubt Mafune's too—are at once comic and touching.[172]

Mafune's later plays were mainly farces, perhaps the only outlet he could find for the complicated emotions that beset him after the defeat. His reputation will doubtlessly rest on his early plays.

THE POSTWAR DRAMATISTS

During the war years companies of both traditional and modern theater continued to play at theaters in Tokyo and in the provinces despite the extreme difficulties occasioned by shortages and the bombings. The plays performed by the traditional theaters—Nō, Bunraku, and Kabuki—were drawn almost exclusively from the standard repertory, and the level of performances remained high. The Shingeki actors were under greater compulsion to prove their usefulness during the war emergency by staging plays intended to bolster morale on the home front.

The only new dramatist of significance to emerge during the war years, Morimoto Kaoru (1912–1946), had been affiliated with Kishida Kunio's magazine *Gekisaku*, to which he began to contribute plays in 1934. His fame as a dramatist rests on two plays written toward the end of the war, *Dotō* (Angry Waves, 1944) and *Onna no Isshō* (A Woman's Life, 1945), the latter work commissioned by the Greater East Asia Congress.[173] With excisions and additions made after the war, *A Woman's Life* served for many years as a vehicle for the actress Sugimura Haruko, who played the central figure from girlhood to old age.

By the time the war had ended, most theaters in Tokyo had been destroyed. All schools of Nō had to share the one remaining stage. The Bunraku Theatre in Osaka had been badly damaged, and even after repairs had advanced sufficiently for performances to be resumed in April 1946, the dank, gloomy premises attracted few customers. Kabuki was afflicted not only by the loss of the main theater in Tokyo, reduced to a shell by the bombing, but by the decrees of the Army of Occupation, which, in its determination to rid Japan of militarism, severely restricted which plays could be performed. Such classics as *Chūshingura* could not be performed because they allegedly glorified the feudal mentality. Eventually this ban was lifted, and *Chūshingura* was again performed, without any noticeable deleterious effects.

The traditional theaters were slow in regaining their audiences, but by the 1960s enjoyed at least as much popularity as before the war. The repertories of even Nō and Bunraku were enriched from time to time by new works. The Nō actors performed such plays as the Japanese version of W. B. Yeats's *At the Hawk's Well*, itself modeled on Nō; and the Bunraku puppets were seen in *Madame Butterfly* and *Hamlet* as well as various original plays by Japanese dramatists.[174] None of these additions remained long in the repertory. New Kabuki plays were far more numerous, and included a few (notably by Mishima Yukio) that not only were well received at their first performances but were revived.

By and large, however, the only postwar dramatic works of importance were those written for Shingeki. During the period immediately after the war the Shingeki companies performed mainly translations of European and American plays. Each company was a repertory group centered around a few men—playwrights, directors, and actors—and had its special characteristics. Sometimes the characteristics—whether the political overtones of productions, the nature of the repertory, or the relative emphasis given to the literary value of the texts—were determined by the chief person in the company, as had been true with Shimamura Hōgetsu's Geijutsu-za (Art Theatre) in the 1910s.[175] At other times, as had been true of the Zenshin-za (Progressive Theatre), founded in 1931, a common philosophy of theater brought together the members of the troupe.

The two main Shingeki companies in Tokyo during the immediate postwar period were the Bungaku-za, founded (as described above) as a literary theater in 1937, and the Haiyū-za (Actors' Theatre), founded in February 1944 primarily as a training place for actors. The Bungaku-za had successfully staged Morimoto Kaoru's plays during the war. After the war the core of its repertory was translations of French theater, from Molière to

Jules Renard, but it also performed plays by Kishida Kunio and such works as William Saroyan's *My Heart's in the Highlands*. The first notable production of the Haiyū-za after the war was of Gogol's *The Inspector General* in 1946. Plays by Dazai, Mafune, and Mishima were also produced, but its biggest triumph of the postwar period was with Beaumarchais's *Le Mariage de Figaro*, which ran for fifty performances in 1949, a long run for Shingeki.

The first new playwright to make a name in Shingeki after the war, Kinoshita Junji (b. 1914), was one of the founders of Budō no Kai,[176] the group that from 1947 to 1964 staged most of his plays. Kinoshita, a graduate of the English Literature Department of Tokyo University, where he had specialized in the works of Shakespeare, had begun to write plays as early as 1939, when the first version of *Fūrō* (Wind and Waves), a full-length drama about the conflict between old and new ideologies after the Meiji Restoration, was completed. Kinoshita's plays in general fell into two distinct groups—those like *Wind and Waves*, which dealt with ideological problems, usually of modern Japanese, and those on folk themes, which attempted to give new meaning to traditional Japanese tales.

Hikoichi-banashi (The Story of Hikoichi, 1946) was the first of Kinoshita's "folktale plays" (*minwageki*) to be published, though he had written during the war a version of what would be his best-known play, *Yūzuru* (Twilight Crane, 1949). These folktale plays, based on authentic materials, were written in a dialect that incorporates features of nonstandard Japanese speech from many regions in order to suggest the common language of the entire people. Kinoshita's folktale plays are simple enough to be readily understood even by children, but they are the products of a complex mind and their overtones are certainly beyond a child's grasp.

Twilight Crane [177] is the story of a crane who turns herself into a woman out of gratitude to the farmer who saved her life when she was wounded. She becomes his wife and weaves for him a wondrous cloth of her own feathers. Yohyō, the farmer, at first accepts her gifts with humility, but later he discovers that there is a market for the cloth. Merchants from the city tempt him with tales of the pleasures that will be his if he can deliver more cloth. Tsū, the crane-woman, pressed by her husband, weaves one last piece of cloth, then transforms herself back into a crane and flies away. Out of love for her husband she used all the feathers she could spare, but now she can weave no more cloth. Only then does the husband realize what his greed has cost him.

The play shares elements with folktales known all over the world, but its great appeal lay in the womanly warmth of Tsū, whose uncomplaining sacrifice seemed especially Japanese. The play was interpreted allegorically as an illustration of how love can be corrupted by the desire for money, or of how village life can be corrupted by capitalism. No matter how interpreted, the play enjoyed extraordinary success. It was adapted as an opera and a Nō play. Audiences seemed never to have their fill of this story, which gave them the feeling of witnessing a work born from uniquely Japanese traditions.

Kinoshita in his ideological plays used incidents of the recent or distant past, but he was less concerned with fidelity to his sources than with creating works that treated subjects of universal and lasting significance. *Kaeru Shōten* (Ascension of a Frog, 1951) transferred to the world of frogs a recent incident that had arisen from the repatriation of Japanese detained in the Soviet Union after the war. *Kami to Hito to no aida* (Between God and Man), first produced in 1970, treated the war crimes trials in Tokyo in 1946–1947; by allowing that much time to elapse before writing his play Kinoshita was able to see both universal and particular meanings in one of the trials.[178]

Other important dramatists of the postwar period had begun their careers before the war, but only after the war did they win a reputation. Tanaka Chikao (1905–1995) had a play published as early as 1933, and was associated with Kishida's *Gekisaku* group, but he remained a minor figure, recognized chiefly by other playwrights for his ability to capture in dialogue the nuances of real conversation. His first success was scored with the one-act *Kumo no Hatate* (The Edge of the Clouds, 1947), a work that was acclaimed as the earliest example of Japanese Existentialism.[179] French influence, whether from the plays of Charles Vildrac, the Existentialists, or (at one remove) from Kishida Kunio is evident in Tanaka's plays. The one-act *Kyōiku* (Education, 1953) has characters with French names and there are many references to French culture.[180] His early plays depicted women so unsympathetically that he became known as a misogynist, but this phase of his career gave way to the deeply religious *Maria no Kubi* (The Head of Mary, 1959), a

play set in Nagasaki after the dropping of the atomic bomb, which
brought death to many, scars to even more, and destroyed the largest
Catholic church, leaving the heads of the stone sculptures lying in the
ruins. The play is a mixture of realism and fantasy, the language at
times approaching poetry.[181]

Another playwright who experimented with dramatic poetry was
Fukuda Tsuneari (1912–1994). His name was known to the general
public mainly for his writings on politics and his criticism, but
his most lasting work was in the theater, both as a dramatist and
as a translator.[182] Fukuda's first success was with *Kitei Taifū*
(Typhoon Kitty, 1950), which suggested a parody of Chekhov's *The
Cherry Orchard* in its portrayal of futile Japanese intellectuals
after the war. *Ryū wo nadeta Otoko* (The Man Who Stroked the
Dragon, 1952) was in the mood of T. S. Eliot's *The Cocktail Party*,
with a broad hint of the James Thurber story about the unicorn in
the garden. Fukuda made no attempt to conceal such borrowings.
At one time he even confessed to a poverty of the imagination,
which made him depend on an existing model, preferably in the
classics, when writing his plays. *Akechi Mitsuhide* (1957) owed
much to *Macbeth*, and *Arima no Miko* (Prince Arima, 1961) to
Hamlet. Fukuda's translations of Shakespeare, the most extensive
since Tsubouchi Shōyō's, were praised for their vitality and naturalness of language, which made it possible for Japanese audiences to witness a play by Shakespeare not merely with the
deference due to a classic but with excitement.

Although Fukuda's historical plays revealed his interest in
the Japanese past, and he was politically conservative, his plays do
not seem specifically Japanese. No attempt is made in the modern
plays to set them in any particular region of Japan, and the characters are often rootless intellectuals. Even the historical plays are
filled with unmistakably modern perceptions of the world. The
condition of man, rather than the fate of being a Japanese, was his
theme, even when the language was poetic or remote.

During the postwar period many novelists also wrote for the
stage, sometimes gaining almost equal recognition as dramatists.
Mishima Yukio was probably the outstanding exemplar of this
group.[183]

Mishima's absorption with the theater extended to almost
every variety current in Japan. Alone among the writers of his
generation, he had not only a connoisseur's appreciation of Bun-

raku and Kabuki but could write new plays for these theaters easily, in the appropriate stage language. His versatility in the theater ranged from translations or adaptations of Greek tragedy to a farce based on the *Arabian Nights*, which featured a genuine flying carpet. Perhaps the strongest influence on Mishima came from Racine. Unlike Fukuda, who was drawn to Shakespeare as the central figure of European culture, Mishima preferred the formality of Racine, who presented violent passions in elegant language and patterns of movement. Mishima admired Nō for similar reasons: intense emotions are conveyed despite the formal language and the lack of overt action.

Among Mishima's most successful works for the theater were his modern Nō plays. He wrote nine in all, beginning with *Kantan* in 1950. The collection *Kindai Nōgaku Shū* (Five Modern Nō Plays, 1956) contained an afterword in which he stated that he would not write other plays in this form, but he subsequently added four more. In the same afterword he explained why he had turned to Nō: "I modernized the situations in order to give new meaning to the free disposition of time and space characteristic of Nō and new life to the openly metaphysical themes." [184]

The characters in Mishima's Nō plays often have the same names as in the original plays he followed, and the plots are similar, but his settings were modern: a hospital room, a couturier's shop, a family court. The central character in *Yoroboshi*, as in the original Nō, is blind, but his blindness comes not from excessive weeping over his father's coldness but from the bombing of Tokyo during the war. In his *Yuya* Mishima burlesqued the situation of the original by having Yuya's mother, whose fatal illness was the reason Yuya gave for not wishing to accompany her patron on his excursion to see the cherry blossoms, appear in robust good health, giving the lie to the heroine's pretended grief. In *Dōjōji* the dancer enters the huge wardrobe being displayed at an auction sale (Mishima's equivalent of the temple bell of the original) after declaring that she intends to destroy her beauty. But when the door of the wardrobe opens, she is unchanged: she has decided that she must not waste the springtime of her beauty. Though the plays twist the originals and sometimes increase their complexity with added themes, Mishima undoubtedly sensed these possibilities within Nō, and his intention was certainly not parody.

Mishima turned to the Nō plays not because he lacked imaginative powers but in order to keep his extraordinarily fertile imagination under control by subjecting it to the restraints of a traditional form. He did not attempt to imbue his Nō plays with the mysterious beauty of yūgen, but the symbolic overtones of Nō were present all the same, and the plays at times attain heights not common in more realistic forms of theater. Although these plays are set in Japan, they have the timelessness characteristic of Nō, and Mishima hoped that when staged abroad the settings would be altered to one appropriate for the country of presentation. These were, in fact, the first Japanese plays to be widely performed abroad.

Mishima's most popular play was undoubtedly the four-act Shingeki *Rokumeikan* (1956). It is set in the Japan of 1886 when the fashionable people of the day flocked to the Rokumeikan, a ballroom built in the Western style, to show off their European finery and to demonstrate to foreign guests that they could waltz, eat with a knife and fork, and perform other "civilized" actions. The plot is old-fashioned, involving an unscrupulous viscount, his beautiful wife (who was formerly a geisha), and the son whom she bore to her lover, her husband's most hated political enemy. The plot accords so perfectly with 1886 that one can only assume that Mishima was writing with tongue in cheek, but the audiences who have attended the frequent revivals watch the play with the utmost seriousness. They seem unperturbed that Viscount Kageyama is a cardboard villain, that his wife, the beautiful Asako, is too self-sacrificing to be true, and that her son Hisao is guileless to the point of obtuseness. The brilliance of the costumes and sets and the skill of a well-made play seem to ensure that *Rokumeikan* will continue to be performed more often than Mishima's superior plays.

Mishima's Shingeki works include the partly autobiographical *Wakōdo yo Yomigaere* (Wake Up, Youth of Japan!, 1954), which treats a group of Tokyo University students and their fantasies just before and after the end of the war in 1945. *Shiroari no Su* (A Nest of Termites, 1955) seems to reflect Mishima's experiences during a visit to Brazil in 1952. *Tōka no Kiku* (Chrysanthemums Past Their Prime, 1961) was one of a series of stories and plays devoted to the February 26, 1936, attempted coup of the Japanese army. Mishima's best Shingeki play was probably *Sado Kōshaku Fujin* (Madame de Sade, 1965),[185] in which he employed the Racinian convention of the *tirade* to express the conflicting personalities of the characters, each embodying an aspect of French society of the late eighteenth century. *Madame de Sade* has an all-female cast; its opposite number is *Wa ga Tomo Hittorā* (My Friend Hitler, 1968) with an all-male cast, each character representing a side to Hitler's life—the devoted Röhm who remembers nostalgically his early comradeship with Hitler, the industrialist Krupp who attempts to use Hitler for his capitalistic purposes, the anticapitalist Strasser who imagines that Hitler plans to carry out a socialist revolution, and Hitler himself, who uses each of these men to achieve power.[186]

Mishima's writings for the traditional Japanese theater included the brilliant *Fuyō no Tsuyu Ōuchi Nikki* (Dew on the Hibiscus, a Chronicle of the Ōuchi Family, 1955), a one-act adaptation of Racine's *Phèdre* in the style and metrical language of the Bunraku theater, and his last work for the theater, a dramatization of Bakin's novel *Chinsetsu Yumiharizuki* (Crescent Moon), written in 1969 and subsequently performed both by the Kabuki actors and by the Bunraku puppets.

Mishima wrote in many styles and his materials were gathered from both East and West, but he was not an avant-garde dramatist. He showed little interest in contemporary theater abroad, preferring classical theater, whether the Greek plays, opera, or nineteenth-century tragedy. He had a natural, unerring feeling for the theater and could compose dialogue that was vivid but stylized. He stood at the end of several great traditions and made no attempt to guide the theater of the future.

Japanese theater, as it developed in the 1960s and afterward, was definitely a part of contemporary world theater. Plays by European and American dramatists were quickly translated and staged, sometimes with more imagination than the original productions. The Theatre of the Absurd, the underground theater, and the nonfiction drama all had their Japanese exponents. Needless to say, the Japanese dramatists were acutely aware of the danger that their works might become faceless, cosmopolitan works with no distinctively Japanese characteristics. Some playwrights deliberately used traditional materials, whether folk stories or literary works of the past, preserving their identities as modern writers by giving the old materials psychologically new interpretations. Other playwrights treated problems which, if not peculiarly Japanese, accurately evoked the lives of contemporary Japanese people. Still others, indifferent to whether or not their works were considered to be truly Japanese, wrote plays that might have been created in any country, but which were inevitably, even if unintentionally, Japanese because of the nationality of the author and the language he used. Finally, some of the plays of Abe Kōbō (b. 1924) depended for their effects on movement, lighting, and sound, suppressing the dialogue or reducing it to fragmentary utterances.

If Abe's style of drama should come to dominate the Japanese theater it might mean the end of dramatic literature in the sense in which these words are conventionally used. The exceptional quality of Japanese films, despite their literarily undistinguished scenarios, points in the same direction.[187] More likely, however, the separate streams that make up the modern Japanese theater will continue to maintain their identities, contributing to the diversity that has made of the Japanese theater as a whole a marvel of the modern world.

NOTES

1. For further details in English, see Donald Keene, *Landscapes and Portraits*, pp. 282–85; also, Komiya Toyotaka, *Japanese Music and Drama in the Meiji Era*, pp. 268–69.
2. Quoted in Keene, *Landscapes*, p. 285.
3. Ōyama Isao, *Kindai Nihon Gikyoku Shi*, I, p. 8.
4. *Ibid.*, p. 9.
5. Yamamoto Jirō, *Mokuami*, p. 14.
6. Kabuki actors, like European monarchs, succeeded to the names of important predecessors, and were known as the "fifth" or the "seventh" Danjūrō, much as Henry V and Henry VII were so called.
7. See Kawatake Toshio, "Meiji Tenrangeki no Kenkyū," p. 115; also, Komiya, *Japanese Music and Drama*, pp. 224–27. The next time an emperor viewed Kabuki was in 1953.
8. *Engeki Hyakka Daijiten*, IV, p. 311; also Komiya, *Japanese Music and Drama*, p. 198.
9. Takano Masami, *Jōruri, Kabuki*, p. 199.
10. *Saibara* was a kind of song performed to musical accompaniment that was introduced to Japan from the Asian continent early in the Heian period. It enjoyed popularity among the nobility for many years, but died out by the late fourteenth century. The use of saibara therefore set the play earlier in the fourteenth century.

11. Komiya, *Japanese Music and Drama*, p. 198.

12. *Mokuami Zenshū*, XXIII, pp. 271–72.

13. *Ibid.*, p. 173.

14. *Ibid.*, p. 265.

15. Donald Keene, *Modern Japanese Literature*, p. 45.

16. Kawatake Toshio, "Kaidai," in *Kawatake Mokuami Shū*, p. 414.

17. *Kawatake Mokuami Shū*, p. 259.

18. *Ibid.*, p. 288.

19. See *ibid.*, p. 277 ("Sekai wa kaika ni susumu hodo hito ga hakujō ni naru").

20. Quoted from Hasegawa Shin, "Gosei Kikugorō no Eigo," in Nakamura Giichi, *Shibai*, p. 13. Hasegawa himself composed the speech.

21. The characteristics of Mokuami's dialogue are discussed by Tai Shōnosuke, in *Kinsei Engeki no Kenkyū*, pp. 419–508.

22. For details of Tsubouchi Shōyō's career and contributions to the development of the Meiji novel, see *Dawn to the West: Fiction*.

23. Kawatake Shigetoshi, *Nihon Engeki Zenshi*, pp. 871–72.

24. *Ibid.*, p. 881.

25. Matsumoto Shinko, *Meiji Engekiron Shi*, pp. 228–29.

26. Tsubouchi Shōyō used alternate names for Chikamatsu Monzaemon and Kawatake Mokuami.

27. *Tsubouchi Shōyō Shū*, p. 287.

28. *Ibid.*, p. 307.

29. *Ibid.*, p. 288.

30. Kawatake Shigetoshi, *Nihon Engeki Zenshi*, p. 879.

31. Nagahira Kazuo, *Kindai Gikyoku no Sekai*, p. 33.

32. Quoted by *ibid.*, p. 33.

33. Matsumoto, *Meiji Engekiron*, p. 274.

34. Ōyama, *Kindai Nihon*, I, pp. 260ff.

35. *Ibid.*, p. 263.

36. *Ibid.*, p. 262.

37. Jōruri refers to the combination of a recited and sung dramatic text and the accompaniment, generally the samisen. See Keene, *World Within Walls*, pp. 235–38, for a description of its origins.

38. Ōyama, *Kindai Nihon*, I, pp. 370–71.

39. *Ibid.*, p. 371.

40. *Ibid.*, p. 372.

41. Matsumoto, *Meiji Engekiron*, p. 831.

42. See *ibid.*, pp. 830–47.

43. Hisamatsu Sen'ichi and Yoshida Seiichi, *Kindai Nihon Bungaku Jiten*, p. 488.

44. Ōyama, *Kindai Nihon*, II, p. 172.

45. Homma Hisao, *Tsubouchi Shōyō*, p. 207.

46. Komiya, *Japanese Music and Drama*, p. 296.

47. The most admired scene (Act II, Scene 2) opens as weird spirits declaim meaningless syllables (*Piipapiika, hatteta!*), after which a giant "eight or nine feet tall" with reddish-black hair like a lion's mane appears, his face concealed by his hair. The upper half of his body resembles that of a human being, but his

hairy legs look more like those of a wild boar, and his silver-colored heels glitter in the moonlight. The monster sends his faithful goblins on an errand, urging them: "Hurry back! I'm hungry! . . . *Uun, uun!*" (Text in *Nihon Gikyoku Zenshū*, XXXIII, pp. 549–51.)

48. For a discussion in English of the plays, see Frank T. Motofuji, "Mori Ōgai: Three Plays and the Problem of Identity."

49. Motofuji ("Mori Ōgai," pp. 420–21) interprets the pearls as being the knowledge Ōgai had obtained from the West, and likens the plays to short stories in which Ōgai expressed confidence that Japan would one day be able to return the gifts of scientific learning it had received from the West.

50. *Ōgai Zenshū*, II, p. 76.

51. Matsumoto, *Meiji Engekiron*, p. 497.

52. So stated by Mafune Yutaka; quoted by Nagahira, *Kindai Gikyoku*, p. 49.

53. Aoe Shunjirō, "Ōgai no Gikyoku," p. 22.

54. For an account of the brother, Miki Takeji, see Toita Yasuji, "Mori Ōgai to Miki Takeji," in *Geppō* 15 for *Ōgai Zenshū*, II.

55. Shimpa and Shingeki are discussed in the following chapter.

56. *Okamoto Kidō Gikyoku Senshū*, IV, pp. 7–24.

57. Geki actually gives reign names rather than "old days." He mentions Keichō (1596–1614) and Tenna (1681–1683); presumably the latter was an error for Genna (1615–1623).

58. *Okamoto Kidō Gikyoku Senshū*, VI, p. 22.

59. *Ibid.*, p. 38.

60. The one-act *Nagara no Hitobashira* (The Human Pillar of the Nagara River, 1913) similarly invokes reason agains the barbarous practice of immolating a human being in order to ensure the permanence of a bridge. No doubt it pleased the spectators to think of themselves as being more civilized than their ancestors, but the anachronisms in the thought are jarring. (Text in *Okamoto Kidō*, IV, pp. 175–92; English translation *The Human Pillar* by Zoe Kinkaid and Hanso Tarao.)

61. *Okamoto Kidō Gikyoku Senshū*, VI, p. 459. The play was loosely based on an actual occurrence of 1746.

62. *Ibid.*, VI, p. 63.

63. *Ibid.*, VI, p. 68.

64. *Ibid.*, VI, p. 81.

65. *Ibid.*, VI, p. 460.

66. See Ōyama, *Kindai Nihon*, II, p. 197.

67. *Engeki Hyakka Daijiten*, III, p. 11; also, Ochi Haruo, *Meiji Taishō no Gekibungaku*, pp. 55–56.

68. In most versions of the story the servant girl is driven wild with anxiety when she discovers that one plate is missing; it has been deliberately hidden by someone who wishes to torment or even kill her. In Kidō's play the servant, Okiku, learning that the young master, Aoyama Harima, who is her lover, is about to marry a young lady of good family, decides to test his affection by breaking one of the plates, even though she knows that the penalty is death.

69. *Engeki Hyakka Daijiten*, I, p. 418.

70. *Gendai Nihon Gikyoku Senshū*, II, p. 43.

71. Ochi, *Meiji Taishō*, pp. 480–92.
72. Akiba Tarō, *Nihon Shingeki Shi*, II, p. 159.
73. Fujiki Hiroyuki, "Mayama Seika no Gikyoku," p. 104.
74. *Gendai Nihon Gikyoku Senshū*, II, p. 43.
75. *Mayama Seika Zenshū* (henceforth abbreviated *MSZ*), XII, p. 519.
76. Yamamoto Jirō, "Kaisetsu," *Gendai Nihon Gikyoku Senshū*, IV, p. 431.
77. *MSZ*, IX, p. 336.
78. Quoted by Ochi, *Meiji Taishō*, p. 176, from the writings of Mizumori Kamenosuke.
79. *MSZ*, XII.
80. Tanabe Akio, *Mayama Seika*, p. 106.
81. *MSZ*, I, p. 80.
82. Ōyama, *Kindai Nihon*, III, p. 167.
83. Ozaki Kōji, "Mayama Seika to Geijutsu no Tankyū," p. 357.
84. Komiya, *Japanese Music and Drama*, pp. 266–67.
85. *Ibid.*, p. 279.
86. Kawatake Shigetoshi, *Nihon Engeki Zenshi*, p. 1055.
87. Komiya, *Japanese Music and Drama*, p. 287. See also Toshihiko Satō, "Ibsen Parallels in Modern Japanese Drama," for a comparison of a play by Nagata Hideo and three plays by Ibsen. Satō's article "Nakamura Kichizō's *A Vicarage* (1910) and Ibsen" also discusses influences.
88. Toshihiko Satō, "Nakamura Kichizō's *A Vicarage*," p. 450.
89. Nagahira, *Kindai Gikyoku*, p. 68.
90. The founding of this theater is discussed by Brian Powell in "Japan's First Modern Theatre: The Tsukiji Shōgekijō and Its Company, 1924–26," pp. 68–72.
91. *Ibid.*, p. 75.
92. *Ibid.*, p. 74.
93. *Ibid.*, p. 75. I have slightly modified the translation in order to accord with usage elsewhere in this chapter.
94. *Ibid.*, p. 73.
95. *Nihon Gikyoku Zenshū*, XL, p. 396.
96. Nagahira, *Kindai Gikyoku*, p. 84.
97. Texts in *Nihon Gikyoku Zenshū*, XL, pp. 290–99 and pp. 300–307.
98. Quoted in Nagahira, *Kindai Gikyoku*, p. 101.
99. *Ibid.*, p. 104.
100. *Ibid.*, p. 106.
101. Quoted by Ochi, *Meiji Taishō*, p. 478.
102. Ōyama, *Kindai Nihon*, II, pp. 340–42; English translation *Death* by Yozan T. Iwasaki and Glenn Hughes, in *New Plays from Japan*.
103. Translated in Iwasaki and Hughes, *New Plays*.
104. *Mushakōji Saneatsu Zenshū*, XV, p. 425.
105. *Ibid.*, p. 105.
106. *Ibid.*, p. 108.
107. *Ibid.*, p. 216.
108. Ōyama, *Kindai Nihon*, II, p. 348.
109. English translations by Umeyo Hirano, in *Buddhist Plays from Japanese Literature*.

110. English translation by Glenn W. Shaw (1922); French translation by Kuninosuke Matsuo and Emile Steinilber-Oberlin (1932).

111. For a discussion of Kikuchi's activities in the Japanese literary world, see pp. 546–52.

112. Nagahira, *Kindai Gikyoku*, p. 128.

113. *Ibid.*

114. Translation by Iwasaki and Hughes, in Keene, *Modern Japanese Literature*, p. 285.

115. See Ōyama, *Kindai Nihon*, II, p. 520.

116. English translation by Glenn W. Shaw, in *Three Plays*.

117. English translation by Eric S. Bell and Eiji Ukai, in *Eminent Authors of Contemporary Japan*, I.

118. *Karaki Junzō Zenshū*, I, p. 156.

119. Translation by Glenn W. Shaw, in *Three Plays of Yamamoto Yūzō*.

120. *Yamamoto Yūzō Zenshū*, I, p. 615.

121. Ōyama, *Kindai Nihon*, II, p. 103.

122. *Ibid.*, p. 104.

123. *Ibid.*, p. 109.

124. Translation by Iwasaki and Hughes, in *Three Modern Japanese Plays*.

125. There is a translation by Mock Joya, *The Death of Ii Tairo*.

126. Text in *Gendai Nihon Gikyoku Senshū*, VIII; see also Ōyama, *Kindai Nihon*, II, p. 495.

127. That is, he does not know in which year of the emperor Meiji's reign he was born.

128. Ōyama, *Kindai Nihon*, III, p. 38.

129. Simon Karlinsky, Introduction to *Letters of Anton Chekhov*.

130. Ōyama, *Kindai Nihon*, III, pp. 51–53, gives a detailed statement of the revolutionary ideals and activities of these troupes.

131. *Gendai Nihon Gikyoku Senshū*, V, pp. 443–44.

132. *Ibid.*, VIII, p. 241.

133. Ōyama, *Kindai Nihon*, III, p. 352.

134. Quoted by Nagahira, *Kindai Gikyoku*, p. 164.

135. Quoted by Ōyama, *Kindai Nihon*, III, p. 335.

136. Quoted by Nagahira, *Kindai Gikyoku*, p. 169.

137. But Nagahira, in *ibid.*, pp. 180–211, gives an extended, unfavorable critique.

138. Quoted in *ibid.*, p. 206.

139. Mordecai Gorelik, *New Theatres for Old*, p. 412. Gorelik describes (pp. 420ff) Erwin Piscator's interest in the use of motion pictures during stage performances. He also discusses (pp. 398–99) Living Theatre productions in the United States in 1935.

140. Gorelik, pp. 336–37; see also Kawatake Shigetoshi, *Nihon Engeki Zenshi*, p. 1090.

141. Quoted in Ōyama, *Kindai Nihon*, III, p. 346.

142. *Ibid.*, p. 340.

143. See the comments by Murayama Tomoyoshi quoted in *ibid.*, pp. 307–08.

144. *Ibid.*, pp. 312–13.

145. Described in *ibid.*, pp. 300–301.
146. *Ibid.*, IV, pp. 300–301.
147. Text in *Gendai Nihon Gikyoku Taikei*, I, p. 289.
148. Text in *Gendai Nihon Gikyoku Senshū*, II, pp. 290–307.
149. See J. Thomas Rimer, *Toward a Modern Japanese Theatre*, p. 37, for a sample of Kōri's English style.
150. Translation by Bell and Ukai, *Eminent Authors*, II.
151. Translation by Donald Keene, in *New Directions 24*.
152. Toita Yasuji and Takahashi Kenji, *Kubota Mantarō, Yamamoto Yūzō*, p. 215.
153. Text in *Gendai Nihon Gikyoku Senshū*, VI.
154. Quoted in Ōyama, *Kindai Nihon*, III, pp. 364–65.
155. See Rimer, *Toward a Modern Japanese Theatre*, pp. 117–22.
156. Ōyama, *Kindai Nihon*, II, p. 569; but Rimer (*Toward a Modern Japanese Theatre*, pp. 146–47) quotes Kishida as saying that he wrote the play originally in Japanese, and "with the help of a French friend" translated it into French. But the play published in Tokyo does not seem to be the same as the one Kishida originally wrote in Japanese.
157. Yasuda Takeshi, *Sensō Bungaku Ron*, p. 83.
158. *Kishida Kunio Zenshū*, I, p. 46.
159. *Ibid.*, p. 47.
160. Rimer, *Toward a Modern Japanese Theatre*, p. 142.
161. *Kishida Kunio Zenshū*, I, p. 95.
162. Translation by Bell and Ukai, *Eminent Authors*, II.
163. See Rimer, *Toward a Modern Japanese Theatre*, pp. 175–77; text in *Kishida Kunio Zenshū*, I, pp. 185–95.
164. See Rimer, *Toward a Modern Japanese Theatre*, pp. 192–210, for a discussion of the unsuccessful *Mama Sensei to sono Otto* (1930) and *Asamayama* (1931.)
165. An extensive summary of *Sawa-shi no Futari Musume* and of *Saigetsu* is given by *ibid.*, pp. 214–23.
166. *Kishida Kunio Zenshū*, VI, p. 379.
167. Fukuda Kiyoto and Takenaka Sakuko, *Kishida Kunio*, p. 157.
168. Quoted by Nagahira, *Kindai Gikyoku*, p. 143.
169. Apparently, however, Mafune's father, a native speaker of the Aizu dialect, was unable to understand the language of the play. See *ibid.*, p. 217.
170. *Ibid.*, p. 224.
171. See Ōyama, *Kindai Nihon*, III, p. 151, for a statement of the wartime principles.
172. Text in *Gendai Nihon Gikyoku Taikei*, I.
173. See Keene, *Landscapes*, pp. 312–13.
174. A more favorable appraisal of these plays is given by Stanleigh H. Jones, Jr., in "Experiment and Tradition: New Plays in the Bunraku Theatre."
175. For an account of this theater, see p. 544.
176. The meaning of this name, which was given in kana only, is not clear: Grape Society? Unreasonable Society? Or possibly Martial Arts Society?
177. Translation by A. C. Scott, in *Playbook*.

178. See Introduction to the translation by Eric J. Gangloff of *Between God and Man*.
179. So stated by the scholar of French literature Ibuki Takehiko; see Ōyama, *Kindai Nihon*, IV, pp. 188–89.
180. J. Thomas Rimer, "Four Plays by Tanaka Chikao," pp. 279–84.
181. *Ibid.*, pp. 285–86.
182. See Benito Ortolani, "Fukuda Tsuneari: Modernization and Shingeki."
183. For a discussion of Mishima's work as a novelist, see *Dawn to the West: Fiction*.
184. Mishima Yukio, *Kindai Nōgaku Shū*, p. 209.
185. Translation by Donald Keene, *Madame de Sade*.
186. Translation by Hiroaki Sato, *My Friend Hitler*.
187. Two of the best film scenarios, *Ikiru* by Kurosawa Akira and *Tokyo Story* by Ozu Yasujirō (with assistance), are translated in Howard Hibbett (ed.), *Contemporary Japanese Literature*, pp. 146–237.

BIBLIGRAPHY

Note: All Japanese books, except as otherwise noted, were published in Tokyo.

Akiba Tarō. *Nihon Shingeki Shi*. 2 vols. Risōsha, 1955–56.
Aoe Shunjirō. "Ōgai no Gikyoku," in *Higeki Kigeki*, May 1951.
———. "Ōgai to Engeki," in *Higeki Kigeki*, June 1951.
Ara Masahito. "Miyoshi Jūrō Ron," in *Higeki Kigeki*, April–May 1970.
Bell, Eric S., and Ukai, Eiji. *Eminent Authors of Contemporary Japan*. 2 vols. Tokyo: Kaitakusha, 1930.
Chatani Michio. "Mayama Seika," in Nihon Bungaku Kyōkai, *Nihon no Geki Bungaku*. Tōkyō Daigaku Shuppankai, 1955.
Engeki Hyakka Daijiten. 6 vols. Heibonsha, 1960–62.
Fujiki Hiroyuki. "Mayama Seika no Gikyoku," in *Nihon Kindai Bungaku*, May 1967.
Fukuda Kiyoto and Takenaka Sakuko. *Kishida Kunio*. Shimizu Shoin, 1967.
Gangloff, Eric J. (trans.). *Between God and Man*: A Play in Two Parts by Kinoshita Junji. Tokyo: University of Tokyo Press, 1979.
Gendai Nihon Gikyoku Senshū, 12 vols. Hakusuisha, 1955–56.
Gendai Nihon Gikyoku Taikei, 8 vols. San'ichi Shobō, 1971.
Gorelik, Mordecai. *New Theatres for Old*. New York: Samuel French, 1955.
Hanada Kiyoteru. "Mayama Seika no Taishūsei," in *Bungaku*, June 1960.
Hibbett, Howard. *Contemporary Japanese Literature*. New York: Alfred A. Knopf, 1977.
Hirano, Umeyo. *Buddhist Plays from Japanese Literature*. Tokyo: CIIB Press, 1962.
Hisamatsu Sen'ichi and Yoshida Seiichi (eds.). *Kindai Nihon Bungaku Jiten*. Tōkyōdō, 1954.

Homma Hisao. *Tsubouchi Shōyō*. Shōhakusha, 1959.

Ikuta Chōkō. "Mayama Seika-shi wo ronzu," in *Kosugi Tengai, Okamoto Kidō Oguri Fūyō, Mayama Seika*, in Gendai Nihon Bungaku Zenshū series, vol. 56. Chikuma Shobō, 1957.

Inono Kenji. "Shizen shugi sakka toshite no Mayama Seika," in *Bungaku*, June 1960.

Iwasaki, Yozan T., and Glenn Hughes. *New Plays from Japan*. London: Ernest Benn, 1930.

———. *Three Modern Japanese Plays*. Cincinnati: Steward Kidd Co., 1923.

Jones, Stanleigh H., Jr. "Experiment and Tradition: New Plays in the Bunraku Theatre." *Monumenta Nipponica*, XXXVI, No. 2, Summer 1981.

Karaki Junzō Zenshū, 12 vols. Chikuma Shobō, 1967.

Karlinsky, Simon. *Letters of Anton Chekhov*. New York: Harper & Row, 1973.

Kawatake Mokuami Shū, in Meiji Bungaku Zenshū series. Chikuma Shobō, 1966.

Kawatake Shigetoshi. *Kawatake Mokuami*. Shun'yōdō, 1925.

———. *Nihon Engeki Zenshi*. Iwanami Shoten, 1959.

——— (ed.). *Mokuami Zenshū*, 28 vols. Shun'yōdō, 1924-26.

Kawatake Shigetoshi and Yanagita Izumi. *Tsubouchi Shōyō*. Fuzambō, 1939.

Kawatake Toshio. "Meiji Tenrangeki no Kenkyū," in *Sōgō Sekai Bungei*, VIII, 1954.

———(ed.). *Kawatake Mokuami Shū*, in Meiji Bungaku Zenshū series. Chikuma Shobō, 1966.

Keene, Donald. *Landscapes and Portraits*. Tokyo: Kodansha International, 1971.

———. *Modern Japanese Literature*. New York: Grove Press, 1956.

Kikuchi Kwan. *Tōjūrō's Love and Four Other Plays*, trans. Glenn W. Shaw. Tokyo: The Hokuseido Press, 1956.

Kinoshita Junji. *Kaeru Shōten*. Miraisha, 1952.

———. *Minwageki Shū*, 3 vols. Miraisha, 1952-53.

———. *Twilight Crane*, trans. A. C. Scott, in *Playbook*. New York: New Directions, 1956.

Kishida Kunio Zenshū, 10 vols. Shinchōsha, 1954-55.

Komiya Toyotaka (ed.). *Japanese Music and Drama in the Meiji Era*, trans. Edward G. Seidensticker and Donald Keene. Tokyo: Ōbunsha, 1956.

Kurata Hyakuzō. *The Priest and His Disciples*, trans. Glenn W. Shaw. Tokyo: Hokuseido, 1922.

Matsumoto Shinko. *Meiji Engekiron Shi*. Engeki Shuppan Sha, 1980.

———. *Meiji Zenki Engekiron Shi*. Engeki Shuppan Sha, 1974.

Mayama Seika Zenshū, 15 vols. Dainippon Yūbenkai Kōdansha, 1940-42.

Mishima Yukio. *Dōjōji*, trans. Donald Keene, in Mishima, *Death in Midsummer*. New York: New Directions, 1966.

———. *Gikyoku Zenshū*. Shinchōsha, 1962.

———. *Kindai Nōgaku Shū*. Shinchōsha, 1956.

———. *Madame de Sade*, trans. Donald Keene. New York: Grove Press, 1967.

———. *My Friend Hitler*, trans. Hiroaki Sato in *St. Andrews Review*, IV, nos. 3-4, 1977-78.

Mokuami Zenshū, 28 vols. Shun'yōdō, 1924–26.

Motofuji, Frank T. "Mori Ōgai: Three Plays and the Problem of Identity," in *Modern Drama*, IX, February 1967.

Mushakōji Saneatsu Zenshū, 25 vols. Shinchōsha, 1954–55.

Nagahira Kazuo. *Kindai Gikyoku no Sekai*. Tōkyō Daigaku Shuppanbu, 1972.

———. "Kishida Kunio," in *Nihon Kindai Bungaku*, VI, 1967.

Nagai Tatsuo. *Kikuchi Kan*. Jiji Tsūshin Sha, 1961.

Nakamura Giichi. *Shibai*. Ōkōchi Shoten, 1948.

Nakamura Kichizō. *The Death of Ii Tairo*, trans. Mock Joya. Tokyo: The Japan Times, 1927.

Nihon Gikyoku Zenshū, 68 vols. Shun'yōdō, 1928–29.

Ochi Haruo. *Meiji Taishō no Gekibungaku*. Hanawa Shobō, 1971.

Ōgai Zenshū, 53 vols. Iwanami Shoten, 1952.

Okamoto Kidō Gikyoku Senshū, 8 vols. Seiabō, 1959.

Okamoto Kidō. *The American Envoy*, trans. Masanao Inoue. Kobe: J. L. Thompson, 1931.

———. *The Human Pillar*, trans. Zoe Kincaid and Hanso Tarao. New York: Samuel French, 1928.

Ortolani, Benito. "Fukuda Tsuneari: Modernization and Shingeki," in Donald H. Shively (ed.), *Tradition and Modernization in Japanese Culture*. Princeton, N.J.: Princeton University Press, 1977.

Ōyama Isao. *Kindai Nihon Gikyoku Shi*. 4 vols. Yamagata: Kindai Nihon Gikyoku Shi Kankō Kai, 1969–73.

Ozaki Kōji. "Mayama Seika to Gekijutsu no Tankyū," in Ōgochi Kazuo and Ōya Sōichi (ed.), *Kindai Nihon wo tsukutta Hyakunin*, 2 vols. Chūō Kōron Sha, 1965.

Powell, Brian. "Japan's First Modern Theatre: The Tsukiji Shōgekijō and Its Company, 1924–26," in *Monumenta Nipponica*, XXX, No. 1, Spring 1975.

Rimer, J. Thomas. "Four Plays by Tanaka Chikao," in *Monumenta Nipponica*, XXXI, No. 3, Autumn 1976.

———. *Toward a Modern Japanese Theatre*. Princeton, N.J.: Princeton University Press, 1974.

Satō, Toshihiko. "Ibsen Parallels in Modern Japanese Drama," in *Yearbook of Comparative Literature*, XI, 1962.

———. "Nakamura Kichizō's *A Vicarage* (1910) and Ibsen," in *Modern Drama*, X, February 1967.

Satō Zen'ya. "Yamamoto Yūzō no Shakaigeki," in *Nihon Kindai Bungaku*, VI, 1967.

Shaw, Glenn W., trans. *Three Plays of Yamamoto Yūzō*. Tokyo: Hokuseido, 1935.

Sugai Yukio. "Shingekishi ni okeru Seika no Ichi," in *Bungaku*, June 1960.

Tai Shōnosuke. *Kinsei Engeki no Kenkyū*. Ōfūsha, 1972.

Takano Masami. *Jōruri, Kabuki*, in Nihon Koten Kanshō Kōza series. Kadokawa Shoten, 1959.

Takaya, Ted T. *Modern Japanese Drama: An Anthology*. New York: Columbia University Press, 1979.

Tanabe Akio. *Mayama Seika*. Hokuyōsha, 1976.

Tanaka Chikao (ed.). *Gekibungaku,* in Kindai Bungaku Kanshō Kōza series. Kadokawa Shoten, 1959.

Terada Tōru. "Kubo Sakae no Buntai," in *Bungaku,* June 1960.

Toita Yasuji and Takahashi Kenji. *Kubota Mantarō, Yamamoto Yūzō,* in Nihon Kindai Bungaku Taikei series. Kadokawa Shoten, 1973.

Tsubouchi Shōyō Shū, in Meiji Bungaku Zenshū series. Chikuma Shobō, 1969.

Yamamoto Jirō. "Kaisetsu," in *Gendai Nihon Gikyoku Senshū,* IV.

———. *Mokuami,* in Iwanami Kōza Nihon Bungaku Shi series, X. Iwanami Shoten, 1959.

Yamamoto Yūzō Zenshū, 10 vols. Iwanami Shoten, 1939–40.

Yamazaki Masakazu. *Mask and Sword,* trans. J. Thomas Rimer. New York: Columbia University Press, 1980.

Yasuda Takeshi. *Sensō Bungaku Ron.* Keisō Shobō, 1964.

PART FOUR

MODERN CRITICISM

INTRODUCTION

LITERARY CRITICISM has a long history in Japan. As far back as the tenth century theories of poetry were presented in the preface to the anthology *Kokinshū*, and in the following century Murasaki Shikibu, speaking through characters in *The Tale of Genji*, expressed her views on the art of the novel. A considerable body of critical discussions of the waka was composed over the centuries, and there were many books of criticism of renga, Nō, haiku, and *The Tale of Genji* as well. Much of this criticism is no longer of interest because it deals with the minutiae of secret traditions or is exclamatory rather than analytical; but the works of Motoori Norinaga, written in the eighteenth century, are still worth reading for his remarkable insights into the nature of literature.

A new kind of literary criticism was created in Meiji Japan and developed under Western inspiration, but the writers, consciously or not, still turned to Motoori and other predecessors for guidance. Tsubouchi Shōyō's rejection of didacticism as a function of the novel, though influenced by his readings in European criticism, in effect repeated what Motoori had written about *The Tale of Genji* a century earlier. Even enthusiastic admirers of European literature usually had their tastes formed in boyhood by readings in the Japanese classics, and remembrances of these works colored their appreciation of both foreign and recent Japanese writing.

Literary criticism of many varieties appeared during the hundred years after the Meiji Restoration. If one were to include studies printed in learned journals, the quantity would be too vast to treat in a single survey. I have chosen instead to describe the works of a few critics who represent each of the three periods— Meiji, Taishō, and Shōwa—into which it is customary to divide modern writing. These men not only were outstanding critics but established themselves in the eyes of the public as literary personalities. There are, for example, so many accounts of Kobayashi Hideo in popular as well as scholarly works that he could hardly be ignored in a discussion of twentieth-century Japanese literature, let alone of literary criticism. Other critics, even some whose writings were nearly as impressive, did not emerge so conspicuously as individuals whose tastes molded those of a whole generation, and their contributions tend therefore to be only ancillary to our understanding of other people's poetry or prose. Still other important critics have dealt with folktales, children's literature, popular fiction, and other kinds of writing that are not discussed in these volumes. I have not considered them here, nor have I treated the scholars of the Japanese classics, though I have greatly benefited from their learning when writing about pre-modern literature. Most of the critics described in this chapter were principally concerned with modern writings, both Japanese and foreign, and touched on the literature of the past only when it bore some obvious relationship to the literature of the present.

Among the prominent features of modern Japanese criticism is the *ronsō*, or literary dispute. Participants in a ronsō often battle over an issue month after month in the literary journals, exchanging sharper and sharper remarks as their patience ebbs with opponents who refuse to admit defeat in face of incontrovertible arguments. So much of modern criticism took the form of ronsō that editors have found it convenient to publish collections of critical writings grouped according to the particular issues that were disputed.

The ronsō often developed over ideological, rather than purely literary, issues. The relations between politics and literature, the importance of "positive" writing in times of crisis, or the necessity for writers to abandon their private views in the interest of the people as a whole were typical themes of ronsō, but there were also notable ronsō on "pure novels" (as opposed to those of wide popular appeal) and on the merits of the modern haiku.

These ronsō (and other examples of literary criticism) were sometimes couched in easily understood, if dogmatic, terms, but at other times in complex, unidiomatic Japanese, which revealed the direct influence of the critics' readings in foreign works of literary theory. New words had to be coined to convey in Japanese the technical vocabulary of modern criticism, and these neologisms often varied from critic to critic until one or another gained general acceptance. The criticism of the 1930s was difficult to understand for other reasons: the writings of the European Surrealists, Dadaists, and other exponents of Modernism presented extreme problems of interpretation for Japanese who wished to remain abreast of their contemporaries abroad, and even Valéry was by no means easy to follow. Writers of the 1930s who were convinced of the truth of Marxist literary criticism at times deliberately chose the path of obscurity in their writings, in order to avoid the wrath of the censors. Obscurity in fact came to exert a peculiar appeal over certain intellectuals, notably university students, who used the abstract terms of the critics as the private language of their milieu.

In contrast to the density of expression found in many critical writings, the *zadankai*, or roundtable discussion, was a genre popular both with participants (because no advance preparation was required) and with the general readers, who had no trouble in following remarks made even by normally recondite critics under the special, informal circumstances. The stenographic records of zadankai were usually revised considerably before they were printed, but sometimes not; in which case, the repetitions and incoherences of convivial conversation were presented to the public in pristine form. Readers seemed to feel that this brought them closer to the critics than more formal presentations of their ideas.

Finally, there were innumerable collections of miscellaneous essays in the zuihitsu ("following the brush") tradition. Such essays, surprisingly popular with the general public, were more apt to read like homespun philosophy than criticism, but the critic in Japan has always been admired more as a purveyor of wisdom than as an analyst of literature.

THE MEIJI PERIOD (1868–1912)

SHŌYŌ AND ŌGAI

Modern Japanese literary criticism came into being in the mid-1880s with the publication of Tsubouchi Shōyō's *Shōsetsu Shinzui* (The Essence of the Novel, 1885–1886). Shōyō, needless to say, did not start from scratch; he was well aware of the criticism written in the past of the different genres, and even of the casual but penetrating observations that were a feature of the zuihitsu collections. He learned much especially from Motoori Norinaga, whose answers to many literary questions were still pertinent: Why do authors write? What makes one work better than another? What is the social value of literature?

Shōyō was also influenced by more recent critical writings, which had appeared in Japanese, especially the translation made by Nakae Chōmin in 1883–1884 of Eugène Véron's *L'esthétique* and the opinions on the functions of poetry expressed by the compilers of *Shintaishi Shō* (Selection of Poetry in the New Style).[1] Even more important to Shōyō were the works of criticism that he read in English; without them, *The Essence of the Novel* could not have been written.

Although criticism had long traditions in Japan, it had never been dignified to the extent of being recognized as a Way to which a man might devote his life. Criticism in the modern sense owed its existence to the first encounters of Shōyō and others with European criticism, and its vogue would soon be attested by the many new literary magazines and literary pages in the newspapers, which offered a forum to would-be critics.[2]

Shōyō's career has already been described; suffice it to say here that his earliest writings as a critic are found in the prefaces he contributed to his translations of works of European fiction. The first was the poetic version, called *Shumpū Jōwa* (Spring Breezes Love Story), of Sir Walter Scott's *The Bride of Lammermoor*, published in 1880. Shōyō explained the universal appeal of this novel:

> The story is based on the principle of cause and effect (*inga gahō*), and treats in a touching and delightful (*aware ni okashiku*) manner the delicate shadings of human feelings and distinctions in social usages. . . . The style of the writing also resembles that of the romances that enjoy popularity in our own country. Readers who peruse this book will consequently discover that even in countries far across the seas, despite national differences of a thousand varieties, there is nevertheless no difference in the depth of *mono no aware*, and that their novels, reflecting this truth, therefore have the same functions as our own.[3]

Shōyō's use of the most familiar terms of traditional Japanese literary criticism—the Buddhist principle of cause and effect, the importance of *mono no aware* (a sensitivity to things) as the touchstone of feeling—was in the nature of an attempt to reassure Japanese readers that although his book was a translation of foreign work it possessed universal, irresistible charm.

Shōyō reinforced these remarks in the preface to his translation of Bulwer-Lytton's novel *Rienzi, the Last of the Roman Tribunes* (1835), published in 1885 at a time when the movement to secure freedom and popular rights was at its height. Although the political background of the novel could easily have been exploited to promote this translation, Shōyō seems to have been interested in *Rienzi* solely for its literary value. He declared:

> A novel is a work of art, a variant form of poetry. For this reason, the core of a novel must be human feelings and social conditions. By human feelings I mean the passions. The passions are seven: joy, anger, grief, fear, love, hate, and desire. A true novelist's skill consists in portraying these emotions vividly, describing human feelings precisely and completely, omitting nothing; and in making imaginary characters in an imaginary world behave so convincingly that they seem like real people. But even if human feelings are faithfully portrayed, the work will still not merit being called a true novel if the author has depicted only the surface.[4]

Shōyō's insistence on the accurate evocation of the emotions in all their depth and complexity did not dispose him favorably toward the traditional Japanese novels that sacrificed verisimilitude in order to preach the "encouragement of virtue and the chastisement of vice" or any other nonliterary doctrine. Of course, some Western novels were also didactic in intent, as Shōyō realized, but he was sure that they never subordinated their portrayal of human feelings to a thesis. He wrote about Bakin's novel *Biographies of Eight Dogs*:

> The eight heroes of this work invariably act in perfect accord with the Way, and never entertain any evil thoughts; they are pictured as pure and incorruptible saints. But man is a creature of passions. Even supposing that, thanks to his education and heredity, a man has always displayed his innate good nature, it is inconceivable that he should have totally escaped the 108 causes of human suffering so successfully as to become oblivious to them. Is it possible that these eight heroes, no matter how sagacious they may have been, never knew a moment of delusion when the hounds of passion ran loose or the wild horses of desire leaped? . . .
>
> Then, it would seem that the eight heroes are what one might call "saints," free from the passions and the desires. Or was it simply that Bakin did not possess sufficient insight into human emotions? If the eight heroes are saints, one cannot very well consider them as mere human beings, and if we decide that they are not

human, it is obvious that they are not suited to be the heroes of a novel, which has human emotions as its chief subject. To narrate the biographies of the saints is the work of the theologian; it does not fall within the purview of the novelist.[5]

These observations, set down even as Shōyō was formulating the similar views he expressed in *The Essence of the Novel*, indicate how closely his theories of criticism were related to his work as a translator of European literature.

In *The Essence of the Novel*, discussed elsewhere,[6] Shōyō reached the conclusion that the "artistic" novel was the only kind of novel worthy of the name; the "didactic" novel, as exemplified by the writings of Bakin, was so implausible that it could not be taken seriously as literature. Shōyō called for a new Japanese literature that would bear comparison even with the masterpieces written in Europe. Many young Japanese responded to this call, though few had much success. In any case, *The Essence of the Novel* established Shōyō in the eyes of young writers as the prophet of a new literature, and his reputation as the outstanding critic of the time remained unshaken after he had become even more celebrated as a novelist, playwright, and translator. He continued to write literary criticism, especially for *Waseda Bungaku* (Waseda Literature), the periodical he founded in 1891 and edited until publication was discontinued in 1898.[7] Apart from *The Essence of the Novel*, his best-known critical writings were those connected with the ronsō he carried on with Mori Ōgai in 1891–1892. This dispute, though no longer of great interest in itself, is historically important as the first of many ronsō that would enliven the Japanese literary world.[8]

Shōyō surely never had any intention of engaging Ōgai in a formal dispute, for he knew that although Ōgai was three years his junior, his study in Europe had provided him with a much more solid foundation in literary criticism than he himself possessed. Indeed, one of the few unfavorable opinions expressed on the importance of *The Essence of the Novel* had been published by Ōgai in the inaugural issue of his magazine *Shigarami Zōshi* (The Weir) in October 1889. It was not that Ōgai disagreed with Shōyō's attacks on gesaku fiction or with his insistence on the artistic importance of true novels, but that he found Shōyō's methodology crude and ill-informed concerning the latest European techniques of criticism.[9] Ōgai's poor opinion of *The Essence of the Novel* is suggested also by his failure ever to refer to the work again, even in testimonials written about his old friend.[10] But although Ōgai was unimpressed, many other Japanese writers, especially Kōda Rohan and Masaoka Shiki, would declare that *The Essence of the Novel* had guided them out of the swamp of gesaku fiction.

Shōyō, continuing his activities as a critic, published articles in the *Yomiuri Shimbun* during 1890–1891 in which he refined his opinions. The first article, "Shōsetsu Sampa" (Three Schools of the Novel), classified recent Japanese fiction [11] into three categories. The first, in the traditional vein, narrated the vicissitudes of the persons of the story, but did not attempt to plumb their characters. Although greater emphasis was given to characterization by the second school of fiction, the events did not grow from the persons of the story and, in a sense, even antedated them; the characters were obliged by the authors to confront existing incidents. The characters in novels of the third school were unquestionably more important than the incidents, which develop from the characters, in the manner that the tragedy of Macbeth stems from Macbeth's ambition. One might suppose that Shōyō had presented the "three schools" in ascending order of importance, but he specifically denied any such intent. He refused to rank the three schools, declaring that it was the function of a critic to distinguish literary phenomena, but not to evaluate them.[12] This was an unexpected opinion from the author of *The Essence of the Novel*, who had clearly thought some novels were better than others.

Shōyō's second article in the *Yomiuri Shimbun*, entitled "Azusa no Miko" (The Medium's Divining Rod), was much in the same vein. He asserted: "Criticism must be objective, especially when it deals with objective poetry—that is, dramatic poetry; in other words, it must be inductive criticism. The critic, like a botanist describing plants or a zoologist writing about animals, should avoid preconceptions when writing about a work." [13]

Ōgai published in September 1891 a response to Shōyō's articles. He expressed satisfaction that Shōyō had unwittingly divided literature into the same three categories distinguished by Hartmann in his book on aesthetics, though the nomenclature was different.[14] However, he disagreed with Shōyō's reasons for refusing to evaluate the schools; Ōgai was sure that the third was superior.[15] He argued, further, that observation and study, though essential to the formation of inductive criticism, cannot be ends in themselves; even if a critic refuses to pass judgment, ideas and standards nevertheless exist.[16]

Shōyō's rejoinder, published in the inaugural issue of *Waseda Bungaku* in October 1891, is found in the article entitled "Preface to a Commentary on *Macbeth*." He declared that there were two kinds of commentary: the first elucidated the meanings of the words, grammar, and so on in a text; the second attempted to explain the *risō*, or purpose, which had motivated the author. At first he had concentrated on the latter method, but had come to prefer the former as he became aware that any literary work, but especially a play by Shakespeare, is susceptible of many different interpretations, according to the depth of understanding of the reader. Shakespeare, like nature itself, provided no explanations for his creations, no risō. His characters, unlike those in works of obvious didactic intent, are not out-and-out villains or flawless heroes, not wicked stepmothers or angelic mothers, but are as complex and indefinable as real human beings. The same holds true of any literary work that portrays nature as it really is. He cited the celebrated opening of *The Tale of the Heike* to illustrate his point:

> The sound of the bell of the Gion Monastery, if heard by the Buddha, echoes the bliss of annihilation, they say, but how does it sound to a woman who is waiting for her lover? The color of the blossoms of the twin-trunked sal trees might appear to someone who had rejected the world as the embodiment of the impermanence of all things, but how would they look to a maiden who has never known sorrow? In short, no man has ever yet discovered the purpose of creation. It is simply because one has melancholy feelings that one is aware of the pathos of autumn, or because one is in a joyful mood that the flowers and birds of the spring seem joyous. The basic characteristic of creation is no doubt indifference.[17]

When Shōyo denied that Shakespeare's plays had any more purpose than the color of a flower or the timbre of a particular bell, he may have meant no more than that Shakespeare (unlike

Bakin) did not seek to impart philosophical convictions through his creations. He may also have been recalling his experience as a university student when he answered an examination question on the character of Gertrude in *Hamlet* by denouncing her in terms of Confucian morality. He may even have thought that what he termed *botsurisō* (submergence of ideals) was a self-evident feature of Shakespeare's plays; if so, Ōgai's response must have come as a shock. Ōgai took issue, for example, with Shōyō's comments on the opening lines of *The Tale of the Heike*:

> Some people who hear the sound of the bell of the Gion Monastery will think fondly of a person they are waiting for, others will sense the bliss of annihilation, but everyone will agree that the sound is beautiful. Some who observe the color of the blossoms of the twin-trunked sal trees will experience the impermanence of all things, others will suppose that it is auspicious, but everyone will agree that their color is beautiful. The fact that a sound or a color seems truly beautiful is not because people, having ears, are able to hear or, having eyes, are able to see. It is because a preconceived notion has at this moment leaped out from the darkness to proclaim that this voice or that color is beautiful.[18]

Ōgai in this and similar articles directed at Shōyō quotes Leibnitz, Schopenhauer, Parmenides, Shaftesbury, Victor Cousin, and, above all, Eduard von Hartmann, whom he extravagantly admired. By this time it had become quite apparent that the contest was unequal between the two men, certainly when it came to a discussion of philosophic concepts; in fact, they were using the same word, *risō*, in two quite different senses. For Shōyō it meant didactic intent, a quality in literature he had rejected in *The Essence of the Novel*, but for Ōgai it meant a Platonic or universal ideal that lay behind the composition of a work of art or the appreciation of that work of art by the critic. Shōyō realized more quickly than Ōgai that they were talking about different things, and explained that botsurisō (submergence of ideals) was not the same as *murisō* (absence of ideals). No doubt he hoped to end the ronsō on this conciliatory note, but Ōgai relentlessly pursued Shōyō with more German aesthetics. In desperation, Shōyō couched his next contribution to the ronsō in the language of farce, but Ōgai could not resist restating his arguments once more. Shōyō did not respond; the ronsō thus ended in June 1892 with Ōgai's final riposte.

Nothing was settled or even clarified by the ronsō, but Shōyō had at least become aware of the problems of terminology he was likely to encounter in future literary criticism. The ronsō, though it attracted considerable attention at the time, was quickly forgotten,[19] but not before critics had become aware of the necessity of making systematic presentations of their opinions instead of merely setting down on paper whatever random discoveries flashed through their heads. Perhaps Shōyō at the end privately came to share Ōgai's conviction that the third "school" of literature was superior to the other two, and that Shakespeare, though he openly propounded no doctrine, was not devoid of "ideals."[20]

Ōgai engaged in various other ronsō, notably with Ishibashi Ningetsu (1865–1926). His exchange of views with Ningetsu chronologically preceded the one with Shōyō, but it is customary to discuss it afterward because it was focused on a later work—Ōgai's story "Maihime" (The Dancing Girl), published in January 1890. Ningetsu at the time enjoyed considerable renown; indeed, he was the first professional critic of the Meiji era. He had studied German, at first with an uncle who practiced Western medicine in Nagasaki, and later in Tokyo. Ningetsu had the distinction of having introduced Lessing to Japanese readers, and so often referred to Lessing's *Laocoön* in particular that he acquired the nickname of "Lessing Ningetsu."[21] His earliest criticism was published in 1887, while he was still a student, and impressed readers with his knowledge of European theories of criticism, which he had acquired not only from Lessing but other German critics of the first part of the nineteenth century. Ningetsu's criticism is no longer of interest. A recent scholar, after subjecting to a dispassionate examination Ningetsu's moral preoccupations, use of terminology, methodology, and so on, left him without a shred of intellectual respectability;[22] but here is what Uchida Roan (1868–1929), a noted essayist and translator, remembered about Ningetsu:

> Criticism at the time consisted exclusively of what might be termed "thrusts" (*ugachi*), nitpicking or else mere impressions, and the arguments were almost never presented in a dignified manner. That is

why Ningetsu's criticism, logically and boldly phrased, attracted such attention. We felt, at least until Ōgai made his appearance, that Ningetsu was running all by himself, a thousand miles ahead of the rest of us. It is incontrovertible that his criticism enlightened our literary world and guided our readers. For example, a work like Futabatei's *Aibiki* [23] was almost incomprehensible to the average reader of the day, and that was why Ningetsu's criticism, in which he minutely analyzed the work and traced the course of the action, point by point, rather like dissecting an ox with a butcher's knife, served as road markers for readers who had hitherto been wandering in a labyrinthine maze. It was Futabatei who introduced Turgenev to Japan, but Ningetsu who elucidated Turgenev's special qualities and importance, as revealed in Futabatei's translation.[24]

Ningetsu's review of "The Dancing Girl," which appeared in *Kokumin no Tomo* (The People's Friend) two months after Ōgai's story was published in the same magazine, contained various specific criticisms. For example, he claimed that Ōta Toyotarō, the hero of the work, was too prudent and conscientious a man to have cold-bloodedly abandoned the dancing girl—in the manner that Napoleon got rid of Josephine—in order to realize his ambitions. Ningetsu recalled also how Johann Heinrich Merck had rebuked Goethe for having made the hero of one of his youthful tragedies, a man who is otherwise portrayed as being weak-willed, commit violent actions that stem from pent-up rage. Merck had urged Goethe never again to depict such a spiritless, insincere, filthy idiot. Ningetsu did not consider Ōta in quite such terms of dispraise, but regretted nevertheless that his irresoluteness and lack of sincerity should have stunted his emotional development.[25] Ningetsu also objected to the title, which led readers to expect that the story would be about a dancer, when actually it consisted of Ōta's confessions, and the dancer was only incidental.[26] However, he concluded the review with high praise:

If the world of the novel in 1888 and earlier was the period dominated by Shōyō, and 1889 was the period of Saganoya Omuro, Bimyō and Kōyō, 1890 will probably prove to have been the period of Ōgai and Rohan. I believe that supremacy in the world of letters this year is in the hands of these two men.[27]

The points raised by Ningetsu did not reveal any deep understanding of Ōgai's story or, for that matter, of the German criticism he so admired, but they at least suggest a critical intelligence.
Other writers of the day who discussed "The Dancing Girl"
tended to express themselves in the exclamatory manner of the
kanshi poet Noguchi Neisai (1867–1905). He related how he had
taken a stroll through the deserted countryside, found a suitable
perch on a rock, and taken out his copy of Ōgai's story:

> I read with unflagging interest. By the time I was half-way through,
> I had imperceptibly turned into one of the characters in the story. I
> felt terribly frightened and red-facedly embarrassed. When I fin-
> ished reading, my face was flushed and my eyes filled with tears.
> Unaware of what I was doing, I lifted my head to the sky, and the
> sun shone on me radiantly. I wondered if the sun was the light of
> the truth. The laughter of the plum blossoms, the singing of the
> thrushes—even these somehow struck me as heartbreaking.[28]

Neisai's criticism seems very old-fashioned today, but Ōgai,
in the course of his ronsō with Ningetsu, singled out Neisai's essay
for special praise. He was especially impressed by the observation
that Ōta was a man incapable of feeling true love; Ōgai thought
that this was the most astute comment anyone had made about
"The Dancing Girl." [29] Of course, even an old-fashioned critic
was capable of perceptive insights, but Neisai probably did not
mean by his comment what we—or Ōgai—would take it to mean.
He made this observation by way of explaining why Ōta was cold
to the German girl; but Ōgai interpreted it as an analysis of the
fatal flaw in Ōta's nature, which prevented him from ever having
a satisfactory relationship with any other human being. Neisai's
statement becomes clearer when we read his opinion that Ōta was
a "modern Tanjirō" who had been drawn by Ōgai with the same
kind of skill as Tamenaga Shunsui's.[30] It is baffling how anyone
could have seen resemblances between Ōta, whom we see from
the inside, and the decorative Tanjirō, over whom various young
women fight, but whose own feelings are never revealed. It is even
more baffling why Ōgai should have praised Neisai but not
Ningetsu, whose criticism at least made sense.

Ōgai replied at length to Ningetsu in an article that he face-
tiously signed "Aizawa Kenkichi," the name of Ōta's well mean-

ing but ultimately destructive friend. He answered, for example, Ningetsu's objections to calling the story "The Dancing Girl," though it was mainly about Ōta, by citing similar instances in the works of Alphonse Daudet and Friederich Halm. His tone was ironic, but he displayed a broad knowledge not only of European literature but of the major German critics of the late nineteenth century. Poor "Lessing Ningetsu" could not withstand this avalanche of erudition, but he held out a while longer. In October 1890 he wrote a review of Ōgai's story "Utakata no Ki" (An Ephemeral Record),[31] in which, after his usual words of praise for Ōgai's style, he moved on to criticism: he declared that the story was successful only in surface terms, and lacked the yūgen (mysterious depth) of a true masterpiece.[32] Moreover, the love between the Japanese painter and the German girl was not "depicted in absolute terms as pure *rabu*" because it involved, as in "The Dancing Girl," the gratitude the girl feels toward her benefactor.[33]

The tone of Ningetsu's reviews grew sharper as he became increasingly aware of the disparity as a critic between Ōgai and himself, and one sometimes gets the impression that he was driven to extremes of nitpicking in order to find something to criticize in Ōgai's writings.[34] But although his methodology was faulty, he deserves credit for having attempted to judge literature as literature, rather than as edifying thoughts presented in a diverting manner. He was no match for Ōgai in a ronsō, but neither was anyone else in Japan at the time.

One other sometime adversary of Ōgai's was Saitō Ryokuu (1867–1904), a man who was affiliated with no school, exercised little influence, and was rarely serious, but whose writings are still enjoyable to read. Ryokuu at first intended to become a gesaku novelist and studied with Kanagaki Robun, but he left Robun behind with his satirical essays on contemporary literature, "Shōsetsu Hasshū" (Eight Sects of the Novel, 1889). In the first of his broadsides directed against the new Meiji literature (he remained to the end a partisan of gesaku writing, and has frequently been called "the last of the gesaku authors")[35] he chose for his targets Tsubouchi Shōyō, Futabatei Shimei, Aeba Kōson, Yamada Bimyō, Ozaki Kōyō, and Morita Shiken.[36] Much of the effect of his parodies depends on immediate recognition of the originals. In this treatment of the "sect" of Shōyō, for example, he not only made fun of some of the best-known passages in *The Essence of the Novel* but twitted Shōyō for his frequent invocation of European authors, including "Scott, Lytton, Dumas, Eliot, Fry, Omelet, Rice Curry" and others.[37] Not even Ōgai totally escaped Ryokuu's barbs, but for a time they (and Kōda Rohan) joined to publish anonymously reviews of contemporary writings.[38] Ryokuu was a minor figure, but he provided a welcome note of humor. The criticism associated with both the Romantic and Naturalist schools during the Meiji period—whether Kitamura Tōkoku's or Shimamura Hōgetsu's—conspicuously lacked this quality.

ROMANTICISM

Romanticism—the exaltation in literature of the individual and the emotions—is associated in Japan with the magazine *Bungakkai* (Literary World), which appeared between January 1893 and January 1898.[39] The founding members of the magazine were young men who had been much influenced by Christianity, and *Bungakkai* had grown out of the literary supplement to *Jogaku Zasshi*, a magazine intended to promote Christian education among women. The founders of *Bungakkai* were linked by a mutual dissatisfaction with the state of Japanese letters and by common enthusiasms, notably for English and American literature of the nineteenth century, but they never considered that they had started a movement or that *Bungakkai* was the organ of Romanticism.[40] The judgment of posterity that the *Bungakkai* members were the chief exponents of Japanese Romanticism is probably true, despite such disclaimers, but only a small part of the contributions printed in the pages of *Bungakkai* were of literary interest. The contents of the magazine, despite the presence of several writers of talent among the editors and the contributions of outsiders, is disappointing.[41] About all that is still read today are the essays of Kitamura Tōkoku, a few stories by Higuchi Ichiyō, and the early poetry of Shimazaki Tōson. The names of the other dōnin (associates)—Hoshino Tenchi, Hirata Tokuboku, Togawa Shūkotsu, and the rest—are buried in Meiji literary history.

Tōkoku best typified the Romanticism of *Bungakkai*. His early poetry, written under Byron's influence, is discussed elsewhere.[42] Although he wrote relatively few works of literary criticism as such, his philosophical essays influenced a generation of Japanese readers and, especially in recent years, he has been given critical attention that seems far in excess of what his modest corpus of writings requires. His tragic suicide at the age of twenty-six deprived the Meiji literary world of one of its most attractive figures, and he continues to appeal to readers because of qualities that typify his age: he was intensely earnest, full of noble though sometimes clouded ideas, ready to weep with heartfelt emotion over a line from Byron or Herbert Spencer.

Tōkoku's essay "Ensei Shika to Josei" (The Pessimist Poet and Womanhood, 1892) produced an electrifying effect on its first readers.[43] The opening words—"Love is the secret key to life. Only after love came into being did human society exist. If love were taken away, what color or flavor would life possess?"—undoubtedly owed much to Ralph Waldo Emerson, but Tōkoku was not merely borrowing; he sincerely believed every word he wrote, though for a member of the samurai class these were startling assertions. Tōkoku was not the first Meiji writer to exalt love in this manner. Iwamoto Yoshiharu (1863–1943) had written in much the same terms in 1891 during the course of a ronsō with the journalist Tokutomi Sohō (1863–1957), who, in a more typical samurai manner, had urged any young man who was obliged to choose between love and glory to reject love. Iwamoto, undoubtedly thinking specifically of Christian love, had proclaimed that love was sacred and far preferable to glory; but when Tōkoku wrote of love he meant attachments between men and women, especially of the kind that are called platonic. He was sure that love enabled a man, despite his finite limitations, to glimpse infinity.

Tōkoku esteemed especially writers of the past whose works possessed more than surface interest. Among writers of the Tokugawa period he was attracted above all to Bashō, as we know from the essay "Matsushima nite Bashō-ō wo yomu" (Reading Bashō at Matsushima, 1892). He wonders why Bashō failed to write any poetry at the most renowned scenic spot of all Japan. Gradually, as he ponders the question, he begins to understand. The wonder of creation is revealed at places of scenic beauty, and when a person of poetic disposition visits such places the godhead within him is naturally stirred, and his spirit soars. But places of scenic beauty contain only a part of the pure beauty of nature, and the poet's work is to pass from his perception of the beauty of a particular site to the "treasury of Creation." [44] The poet, after prolonged mystic communion with nature, will discover in mountains, rivers, trees, and plants the same soul as himself, but may ultimately reach a state of pantheistic accord with nature that will actually prevent him from writing poetry, as he discovers nature's beauty within himself and himself within nature. Indeed, a supremely beautiful landscape is likely to "kill" not only the kind of poetry that Japanese have habitually composed whenever they visited famous places but even the awareness of self. That is why Bashō could write no poetry at Matsushima.

Another writer of the Tokugawa period admired by Tōkoku was Bakin, though Bakin had not long before been subjected to the attacks of Tsubouchi Shōyō for his didacticism. Tōkoku revered Bakin as a "romantic idealist" and declared that he and Bashō were the two Tokugawa authors who "knew the savor of profound religion." [45] Tōkoku deplored the tendency of critics to reproach Bakin for having advocated the "encouragement of virtue and chastisement of vice" without ever discussing his philosophical ideas, notably his theory of "compensation," [46] especially as revealed in Bakin's masterpiece *Biographies of Eight Dogs.* "Compensation" (the word is sometimes translated, sometimes given in transliteration) was a concept Tōkoku had borrowed from Emerson.[47]

Tōkoku's admiration for Bashō and Bakin did not extend to many other Tokugawa period writers. He was repelled especially by the attitude toward women expressed in the works of the gesaku authors, as a passage from his essay "Shojo no Junketsu wo ronzu" (On the Chastity of Virgins, 1892) will suggest:

I have long suffered on account of our literature. Sad to say, our literary predecessors showed no reverence for the chastity of virgins. This was obviously true of the gesaku writers of the Tokugawa period; but even the poets of antiquity and our extraordinary pessimist thinkers [48] never came to revere the chastity of virgins. This makes the solitary traveler of a thousand years shed a tear of blood on his inkstone when he starts to write his criticism. Ah, can we never look forward to the appearance in our literary world of an author who shows the proper respect for the chastity of virgins? [49]

The essay "Tokugawa-shi Jidai no Heiminteki Shisō" (Plebeian Thought of the Tokugawa Period, 1892) opens with a passage
explaining the curious mixture of attraction and repulsion that
Tōkoku felt when he read gesaku writings. The works of Samba,
Gennai, and especially Ikku [50] gave him the feeling of "touching
the strings of a kind of plebeian nihilism," and he wondered if the
sin of these writers in having degraded their pleasure-loving readers and in the end themselves should not be attributed to their age
rather than to the writers alone.[51] There was no philosophy or
religion suited to the commoners; even though Confucianism was
the officially accepted source of morality, very few commoners
ever became Confucian scholars, and the prevailing varieties of
Buddhism taught subservience to the authorities and little more.
And, naturally, there was no freedom. Tōkoku continued:

> Freedom is an inborn part of man's divine spirit. It is also an ex-
> tremely natural craving. But they were forced to recognize that it
> was their fate to have lost this divine spirit from the moment when
> they uttered their first infant cries. They had been thrown into the
> cage of *time* in which they had no choice but to suppress their
> natural craving for freedom and learn an unnatural subservience.
> Who among men would find it agreeable to be imprisoned in the
> cage of *time*? Would any man consider himself to be lucky in that
> he was fated to cause his inborn divine nature to kill itself? Shake-
> speare, recognizing that man was afflicted with ineradicable afflic-
> tions of this sort, explained it:
>
> For who would bear the whips and scorns of time,
> The oppressor's wrong, the proud man's contumely, etc.
>
> Truly, man is meant to enjoy liberty. If one carefully examined
> history to the present day, one would see how great has been the
> cost in blood and in suffering which men have endured so that they
> might obtain liberty.
>
> And thus the native hue of resolution
> Is sicklied o'er with the pale cast of thought, etc.[52]

One feature of Genroku literature commended itself to
Tōkoku: it was the first in which one could hear the voices of
commoners.[53] The new culture of the commoners even contained

a kind of chivalry, but unlike European chivalry, which paired chivalrous qualities with love, the Genroku chivalry represented a kind of resistance to authority, and the love it depicted was anything but exalted. The flourishing of the licensed quarters in Genroku Japan was proof of the contemporary belief that women were nothing more than the playthings of men.[54]

Tōkoku contrasted Western and Japanese "chivalry" (a word he always gave in transliteration) with respect to the ego. In the West men were reluctant to give up their lives, but in Japan chivalry began with death. In the West, too, religion and morality were indispensable elements in chivalry, but the chivalry of the Japanese commoners tended to reject the morality of the time and to be only faintly connected with religion. The chivalrous commoner, reacting against the excessively ritualistic ways of the samurai, was likely to turn to dissolute or uncouth living.[55]

Tōkoku disliked the culture of the Tokugawa period because of the gulf separating the social classes (in Europe aristocrats and commoners worshiped together in church, but in Japan, under Indian influence, Buddhism always kept the classes apart) [56] and the lack of respect for women even on the part of the commoners. He was therefore unsympathetic to the Saikaku revival, which was so prominent a feature of literary activity in the 1890s, and could not praise new works of fiction that were written in the Genroku manner. In a review of recent novels by Ozaki Kōyō and Kōda Rohan, the best-known authors of the day, he paid tribute to their skill and expressed admiration especially for Rohan's earlier works, but the evocations of Genroku literature were distressing. Most offensive in Genroku literature was the treatment of love. Although it was not confined to the licensed quarters, the atmosphere was that of the brothels even when it dealt with the love of a man for an ordinary woman, and the love depicted could be no more than an artificial flower or at best a mean-looking plant growing in sand. He went on:

> Consider what a distance separates lust from love in literature. Lust gives free rein to man's lowest animal nature; love is the expansion of the exquisiteness of man's divine spirit. To depict lust is to drive mankind into the degenerate realm of the beasts; to depict true love is to provide man with beauty and a soul. The writer who has become an instructor in lust and its interpreter incites mankind to

become the lowest of animals and wantonly harms the most wondrous and beautiful aspect of literature.[57]

Tōkoku's comments may seem sentimental or naïve, but it should be remembered that at the time the brothels seemed to be an indestructible feature of Japanese life, and their attractions were still celebrated not only in fiction but in the Kabuki theater and the *ukiyo-e* prints. His insistence that love was an expression of "man's divine spirit" was hardly a commonplace; readers for whom a visit to a brothel was no more than an agreeable way of spending an evening were baffled or amused by such high-flown language.[58] And Tōkoku's strictures directed at Saikaku and his followers, though they fail to explain the continued popularity of these portraitists of the floating world, suggest why this world had ceased to inspire works of distinction. Saikaku had described the "artificial flowers" of the licensed quarters with such brilliance that nothing more needed to be said about them; but "true love" could always inspire the writer.[59]

Tōkoku engaged in a ronsō with Yamaji Aizan (1864–1917), a critic associated with *Kokumin no Tomo* (The People's Friend), the Christian-oriented magazine founded by Tokutomi Sohō in 1887, which played so important a role in the intellectual life of the 1890s. *Kokumin no Tomo* also published writers who were Romantics, but it became increasingly nationalistic, especially after the Sino-Japanese War of 1894–1895, and even earlier stood for a more pragmatic approach to literature than Tōkoku's.

The ronsō between Tōkoku and Aizan had at its core Aizan's belief that literature must do more than "tepidly" reflect life; it had to promote moral enlightenment.[60] From this it was only a short step to evaluating literary works in terms of their practical or didactic value, an attitude that was even more distasteful to Tōkoku than it had been to Tsubouchi Shōyō. The ronsō began with the essay by Aizan, "Rai Jō wo ronzu" (On Rai San'yō, 1893), which opened:

Writing is an enterprise. (*Bunshō sunawachi jigyō nari.*) The writer wields his pen as the martial hero wields his sword. Neither uses it to strike at emptiness; they do what they do because there is something to be done. Ten thousand bullets and a thousand sword-points are no more than an emptiness within an emptiness unless they do some good for the world. Even if one writes hundreds of volumes of brilliant words and exquisite prose and they survive in the world, unless they closely relate to human life, they too are an emptiness within an emptiness. Writing is an enterprise; that is why we should respect it. When I discuss Rai San'yō, it is in terms of his enterprise.[61]

Tōkoku was dismayed by what he took to be a grossly utilitarian attitude toward literature. Of course he did not advocate the opposite—the frivolity of gesaku fiction—but he insisted that man is born to struggle, with a pen or a sword, depending on the adversary, and the aim of a warrior is not victory but the struggle itself; striking against "emptiness" is man's challenge to the realm of lofty ideals. Above all, Aizan's assertion that literature was an "enterprise" that must be closely related to life incensed Tōkoku. He declared:

> The immaculate and inviolable dignity of literature must surely be damaged if it is brought into the close proximity of the "god" of the vulgar world known as "enterprise." The god called "enterprise" does not occupy a very lofty position among the eight myriad, myriad gods, and the goddess called literature would surely not consent to becoming the wife of so ignoble a god, even if the only alternative was ending her days as an old maid.[62]

Aizan continued the ronsō with his ambitiously entitled *Meiji Bungaku Shi* (History of Meiji Literature, 1893), of which he published only seven installments before dropping this project. After a general consideration of how the coming of the enlightened Meiji age had awakened Japan from its long somnolence in "the cradle of feudalism," and how "Men who had been imprisoned in Japanese and Chinese learning breathed the air of freedom; the chains that had seemed firm as iron melted away like mud," he discussed the work of Fukuzawa Yukichi and the other pioneers of Western learning. This recitation is interrupted by three introductory remarks. The second, entitled "Explanation of What I Mean by Literature," opens:

> I am profoundly convinced and do not doubt that writing is an enterprise. . . . A man called Kitamura Tōkoku has criticized the

statement I made at the head of my essay on Rai San'yō that writing should be respected because it is an enterprise. However, he has completely misunderstood me. He says that I mean that unless the theologian, the poet, or the philosopher engages in some activity that can be described as worldly, his writing is of no value. Why is he so cockeyed? . . . When I said that writing was an enterprise, it was because writing is thought in action, and because once thought becomes action it will affect the world. If a man exerts no influence on society or, to put it in other terms, if he does not in any way make the world better or cause it to progress toward greater happiness, he is not a poet or a man of letters. If the word "enterprise" is taken to mean a successful undertaking, or if "relating to the world" is interpreted as "touching the materialistic world," my statement that writing is an enterprise will surely seem mistaken.[63]

Tōkoku's response took the form of his "Meiji Bungaku Kanken" (Personal View of Meiji Literature, 1893). Though never completed, it was his most ambitious piece of literary criticism. In this essay Tōkoku attempted to clarify his opposition to Aizan's statement that literature must be closely related to life. Some people had praised him for making the attack, but their praise had embarrassed him because it was based on a misunderstanding of his intent. He continued:

I too believe that literature is closely related to life. Surely no one in the world is so stupid as to claim that literature should not be related to human life. What I was objecting to was the assertions (1) that its purpose was to benefit the world; (2) that it wielded a sword like a martial hero; but (3) that it had a target and did not stab into emptiness; and (4) that it was obliged to rid itself of beautiful phrases and fine language and relate closely to life.[64]

These clarifications read suspiciously like backtracking. Perhaps Tōkoku regretted the intemperance of his initial outburst or realized that he and Aizan were actually not so far apart. Nothing was proved by this ronsō, but one is left with an impression, despite the quibbling, of Tōkoku's belief in the integrity and self-sufficiency of literature; Aizan, on the other hand, was suspicious of "pure literature" that served no purpose other than to communicate the thoughts and feelings of the writer.[65]

Tōkoku's literary criticism was generally expressed in terms of philosophic issues rather than in terms of form, content, style, and so on. His "Personal View of Meiji Literature," for example, is divided into four sections: Pleasure and Utility, Freedom of the Spirit, the Age of Transition, and Transition in Politics. There are interesting observations in each section, but the unfinished essay is not satisfactory as an overall account of Meiji literature. His opinions have an appealing idealism, but they sometimes betray his immaturity. Often he appears to be an unqualified admirer of occidental thought, as in "Personal View," where he contrasted the emphasis on freedom, empirical observation, and respect for scientific principles in the West with the "patriarchal system of thought" prevailing in the East, which does not recognize the individual and allows freedom only to those at the top of society.[66] But in the same month Tōkoku also wrote these words:

I have long entertained high hopes for Meiji literature. It is about to attain its goal of many years, which is none other than the perspicacious expression of the philosophy unique to our people. Meiji thought is extremely complex, and until today it has concealed its face with a veil, like a beautiful Persian woman when she leaves her house. This is because the thought peculiar to our people has been suppressed by Western culture. Literature must be the unalloyed voice of our people. It must be the vessel into which the genius of the age is poured. Literature, the pride of a nation, must be constructed on the foundations of the special nature of that nation's people. I am not saying that Western culture must be expelled, nor that we should cling blindly to the "essence" of the East. However, we must not allow the voice of our people to become the voice of lackeys; even if our native thought should err on the side of arrogance, it should never be permitted to accept servility. I have long grieved over the absence of the genius of the East from Meiji literature. Rough and fierce though the waves of the Pacific may be, I earnestly hope that the unique philosophy of the East will not be shipwrecked in its wild surf.[67]

These are not the sentiments that won Tōkoku a following in his own day, when he was esteemed more as an advocate of the individual, freedom, love, and pacifism [68] than as a literary critic. His insistence on the importance of Japan's "Eastern" heritage suggests the lingering attachment he felt for the old traditions, which he and his contemporaries had absorbed in childhood and had retained almost despite themselves. This aspect of his thought was of less importance in forming his future literary tastes than what he had learned from Emerson, his association with Quaker missionaries, and his readings in English philosophy, but it helps to explain the periodic "return to the East" that would characterize twentieth-century Japanese tides of taste.

Regardless of the origins of his opinions, their role in forming a distinctively modern Japanese literature cannot be overlooked. Tōkoku found Japanese literature two-dimensional and provided it with a third: the depth of the individual. There are confusions and contradictions in his writings, but there is something endearing even in his failures; he lingers in the memory as a brilliant if erratic Romantic who typified Meiji idealism.

Bungakkai was left leaderless after Tōkoku, a prey to intense depression and perhaps madness, committed suicide in 1894, but the magazine thrived for another four years. A typical issue contained essays on some aspects of Romanticism, original stories and poems in the Romantic tradition, discussions of classical Japanese literature, and translations of European poetry. No doubt because it had originated as the literary supplement to the women's magazine *Jogaku Zasshi*, the editors from the first encouraged writing by women. Higuchi Ichiyō published several stories in *Bungakkai*, including her masterpiece, *Takekurabe* (Growing Up, 1895–1896). Other guest contributors included Tayama Katai, whose early works were Romantic, though he was to gain celebrity as a Naturalist. Ueda Bin, the distinguished translator of French poetry, published an essay on Dante in the October 1895 issue, and followed it with appreciations of works of European literature and art.

The last of the Romantic critics was Takayama Chogyū (1871–1902). His career began when he won a literary competition sponsored by the *Yomiuri Shimbun* with his historical novel *Takiguchi Nyūdō* (The Lay Priest Takiguchi). Chogyū was only twenty-three at the time, a student at Tokyo University. *The Lay Priest Takiguchi*, though closely based in content and manner on *The Tale of the Heike*, contains also a pleasing admixture of sentimental detail from *The Sorrows of Young Werther* and its lyrical expression. It is a noteworthy example of the richly poetic prose favored by many Japanese writers at the end of the nineteenth century and still appeals to some Japanese readers.[69]

While a student Chogyū also helped to found (in January 1895) *Teikoku Bungaku* (The Empire's Literature), the organ of the Literature Division of Tokyo Imperial University. This journal from the start (as an editorial by Chogyū stated) [70] would advocate "literature of the people"(*kokumin bungaku*), in contrast to other literary periodicals that gave great prominence to translations of foreign writing. Chogyū's first significant piece of literary criticism was an article on Chikamatsu. Unlike Tōkoku, however, he was completely uninterested in classical Japanese poetry, whether the *Manyōshū* or Bashō. He deplored especially the renewed interest in haiku among writers of his day: "I consider that the popularity of haiku is a disaster to the literary world. It is quite impossible to express within a mere seventeen syllables complicated modern thoughts." [71] He shared with Tōkoku a dislike for Saikaku, whom he dismissed as a prime exemplar of the superficiality of Genroku literature.[72] But he genuinely loved Chikamatsu, as his articles in both *Teikoku Bungaku* and *Taiyō* (The Sun), another recently founded magazine, demonstrated. He was not the first Meiji critic to express admiration for Chikamatsu. As early as 1891 Tsubouchi Shōyō had afflicted Chikamatsu with the sobriquet of "the Japanese Shakespeare" and had compared various of his works with *Macbeth* and other plays by Shakespeare.[73] Chogyū was less interested than Shōyō (a professional dramatist) in the structure of the plays than in the individuality he discovered, say, in the heroines of Chikamatsu's plays, who at first reading may seem so undifferentiated. Chogyū was able, moreover, to reach a larger audience than Shōyō because of his command of a particularly pleasing, though old-fashioned literary style.

Chogyū's career lasted only eight years, from *The Lay Priest Takiguchi* until his early death, but scholars have managed to divide these eight years into three periods. The first, from 1894 to 1895, was characterized by "abstract idealism," expressed in his very first essay, on Lao Tzu, as well as his other early writings published in *Taiyō*; his second period, lasting from 1896 to 1899, was marked by his "Japanism" (*Nihon Shugi*); and his third, from 1900 to 1902, by Modernism (*Kindai Shugi*).[74] The accuracy of this scheme of periodization is not of great importance; it is interesting, however, to note how in the course of a few years Chogyū's convictions changed, partly because of his immaturity, partly also because of the times. His shift to Japanism, for example, was undoubtedly linked to the wave of nationalistic sentiment that swept over Japan in 1895 after the Sino-Japanese War, especially after the Triple Intervention (of France, Germany, and Russia), which seemed to have deprived the Japanese of the fruits of victory.[75]

Chogyū's shift to Japanism was confirmed in May 1897 when he, along with the philosopher Inoue Tetsujirō (1855–1944) and others, founded the magazine *Nihon Shugi* (Japanism). The following month Chogyū published an article in *Taiyō* on the subject of Japanism.[76] This piece is not concerned with literature but expresses nationalistic sentiments about the unbroken lineage of the imperial family and other uniquely Japanese institutions. Chogyū sharply rejected (perhaps under Inoue's influence) all forms of religion (excepting possibly Shintō, which he did not discuss) as being incompatible with Japanism. He advocated the creation of plays and works of art that would be in consonance with this ideal.[77]

Chogyū began to move away from Japanism in 1899. No doubt he sensed that the patriotic fervor that had swept the nation was waning, and he may have come under the influence of his close friend Anesaki Masaharu (1873–1949), the noted scholar of Buddhism, whose views on religion were quite unlike those preached by *Nihon Shugi*.[78] Chogyū also became increasingly interested in aesthetics, and created something of a stir with his articles on the subject. He had few rivals in this discipline, and in 1900, when a post in aesthetics was created at Kyoto University it was informally agreed to appoint him. In the same year he was given a grant by the government to study aesthetics for three years in Europe. He bade farewell to the literary world in an announcement published in the September issue of *Taiyō*, only to be stricken with tuberculosis. He was to have traveled to Europe on the same ship with Natsume Sōseki.[79]

While recuperating from his illness, which at first he did not take very seriously, Chogyū read widely in recent European literature, and was impelled once more to take up his pen. The article "Bummei Hihyōka toshite no Bungakusha" (The Writer as a

Critic of Civilization), published in the January 1901 issue of *Taiyō*, marked the first appearance in his writings of Nietzsche, the most important influence during Chogyū's last years. The essay begins,

> I have long regretted, every time I have heard people talking about Nietzsche, that I had no time to become acquainted with his books. Recently I have profited by some leisure to read several of his works, and I have been able to grasp their essentials. My first reaction, however, was astonishment over their most unexpected contents. I wondered how it had happened that at the present time, when the theory of evolution, which places such importance on history, and socialism, which insists on equality, have permeated almost every level of the entire intellectual world, that such views— so eccentric and bold as to be at times almost unintelligible—should have appeared in Germany, the center of science and philosophy. . . . How was it possible for a man who despised science, ignored history, and arbitrarily strung together implausible fantasies as if proud of his obscurity and enigmas, to have stirred a whole generation in this way? I thought that there must be sufficient reasons for such a phenomenon and, after careful reflection, decided that Nietzsche's great fame was not hollow. Probably he should be considered as a great poet rather than as a philosopher; and the reason he was so great as a poet was because he was a supreme *Kulturkritiker*. In almost every domain Nietzsche repudiated the culture of the nineteenth century.[80]

Chogyū's appreciation of Nietzsche was not especially original, but it was of interest in terms of the subtitle to his essay, "A Sidelong Examination of the Japanese Literary Establishment," and in terms of the new ideals that Chogyū had set for himself. He saw himself as a Japanese Nietzsche who, like his master, had become aware that the nineteenth century was a record of frustrated individual liberties, of humanity reduced to banality, and of every kind of genius brought under a curse.[81] Like Nietzsche, he was ready to abandon democracy and equality in the interests of enabling people to display their individuality in purest form.[82] The greatness of Nietzsche, he was sure, lay in his struggle to liberate the individual.[83] Chogyū went far beyond Tōkoku in his glorification of the individual, but this was not entirely out of keeping with his earlier writings. In 1896 he had published in *Taiyō* an essay on genius (*tensai*), and during his period of Japanism he had displayed special respect for heroes. "In "The Writer as a Critic" he had lashed out at contemporary Japanese critics, whom he dismissed as mere flatterers, men devoid of ideals who thought of literature as merely a salable commodity; and he contrasted them with his heroes: Whitman in America, Tolstoy in Russia, Ibsen in Norway, and Zola in France, all of whom defied society in the name of principles in which they believed. Chogyū fervently hoped that similar heroes would make their appearance in Japan. In another essay, written in the same year, he denounced the "scholastics" and declared that the time had come for a Romantic movement to arise in Japan and promote liberty of thought and emotions.[84]

Chogyū's statements, reinforced with commas, circles, and triangles alongside the words to indicate varying degrees of emphasis, plainly indicate his dissatisfaction with the existing state of literature in Japan. But apart from the general observation, borrowed from Matthew Arnold, that poetry should be a criticism of life, it is difficult to obtain any clear impression of what he wanted Japanese writers to do that they had not been doing. He rarely made specific criticisms of literary works, and when he did, he usually exposed his naturally bad taste. The poems he admired were easily intelligible—he detested obscurity—but often childishly uncomplicated. He indiscriminately praised good and bad works by the same author; for example, he seemed to be equally pleased with Higuchi Ichiyō's best work, *Growing Up*, and one of her least successful stories, "Warekara" (The Hermit Crab).[85] In his own eyes, at least, he maintained his integrity as a critic by making repeated attacks on Mori Ōgai, revered by almost everyone else in Japan at that time for his scholarship; he dismissed Ōgai's writings on Hartmann, for example, with the bold assertion that Ōgai had not properly understood even the introduction to one work by Hartmann.[86]

Chogyū's harsh appraisals were not confined to Japanese literary critics. He denounced contemporary novelists with equal vigor for their slipshod and superficial treatment of their materials. He cited the example of one writer who visited Yokohama for a couple of days in order to ferret out the city's secrets. Chogyū asked ironically how many of the secrets of a great city like Yokohama could be uncovered in so short a time, and contrasted the Japanese writer with Zola, who had devoted years to preparing himself to write *La bête humaine*.[87] He urged Japanese novelists to desist from the frivolity of gesaku writers and to study instead the recent masterpieces of poetry and fiction that had been produced in the West.

Chogyū moved next in the essay "Biteki Seikatsu wo ronzu" (On the Aesthetic Life, 1901) to a proclamation of belief in aesthetic, rather than moral, ideas. He declared that the pleasure of performing such virtuous acts as helping the needy or rescuing orphans, though real, could not possibly match that of listening to music with a beautiful woman in her boudoir. To pretend that the pursuit of lofty ideals brought the highest pleasure was hypocrisy: such pleasure in no way equaled that of the flesh. If a moral philosopher could be persuaded to speak the naked truth, he would no doubt agree that the satisfaction of sexual craving was, in the final analysis, the highest of pleasures. "I have not heard of many instances of people who died for scholarship or who went mad for philanthropy, but when it comes to love, do not people in fact often place very low value on their lives?" [88] Ever since man was mistakenly styled the "lord of creation" he has come to feel ashamed of his true animal nature, and deliberately or unconsciously has led a life of hypocrisy opposed to his real nature. Chogyū concluded this section: "I wonder what use morality and wisdom are anyway?" [89]

Virtue, Chogyū insisted, must be spontaneous "like the flowing of water, the singing of the birds, the blossoming of flowers in the field, the yearning of an infant for its mother, or the way the loyal and righteous warriors of old died for sovereign and country." [90] As the last of his examples suggests, he had not quite forgotten Japanism; the spontaneity of virtue could have been learned not only from Nietzsche but from such National Learning philosophers as Motoori and Hirata.

Chogyū, no less than Tōkoku, was convinced (at this time) that the most beautiful part of the aesthetic life was love. He described the bliss of young men and young women walking "hand-in-hand along a moonlit beach, in the shadows of a fence where roses fragrantly bloom." [91] Chogyū's qualifications as a Romantic, though sometimes obscured by other enthusiasms, emerged in full strength at this time. During his last year of life he wrote with admiration of the despot Taira Kiyomori and espe-cially of the Buddhist prophet Nichiren, discovering in them Nietzsche-like characters.

A few weeks after Chogyū's essay on the aesthetic life ap-peared, Hasegawa Tenkei (1876–1940) published a rejoinder in which he questioned the applicability of the term "aesthetic" (*biteki*) to the satisfaction of animal cravings. He also emphasized the difference between inherited instincts and habits, which Chogyū had lumped together. These may seem like minor excep-tions to a thesis that cried out for fundamental questioning; but Tenkei, who would soon be associated with Naturalist criticism, was evidently only feeling his way toward the new orthodoxy.

SHIMAMURA HŌGETSU (1871–1918)

The best-known critic of the late Meiji era and of the Natu-ralist movement was undoubtedly Shimamura Hōgetsu, whose reputation was created by the influence of his writings and the sensational aspects of his private life. Hōgetsu, who was born on exactly the same day as Takayama Chogyū, represented Waseda University, much as Chogyū stood for the rival, generally more academic Tokyo Imperial University.

Hōgetsu came from the province of Iwami on the Japan Sea coast, not far from Mori Ōgai's birthplace. Japanese critics, who often write as if geography were a critical factor in character for-mation, have likened these two sons of Iwami in their remote, seemingly unemotional natures, but one would have to search for other points of resemblance, especially with respect to their liter-ary careers.

Hōgetsu came from so poor a family that he would not have been able to continue his education beyond elementary school had he not been adopted by a man who recognized his unusual scholastic ability. He eventually went to Tokyo, where he entered the Tōkyō Semmon Gakkō, the predecessor of Waseda Univer-sity, in 1891. His teachers included Tsubouchi Shōyō (History of English Literature), Ochiai Naobumi (Japanese Poetry) and Mori Kainan (Poetry of Tu Fu). In the year he matriculated, the journal *Waseda Bungaku* (Waseda Literature)—in which many of his es-says would appear—was founded.

When Hōgetsu graduated in 1894, at the head of his class, he wrote a brief autobiographical sketch in which he mentioned his favorite reading matter. It included the poetry of T'ao Yüanming, Su Tung-p'o's *Prose-Poem on the Red Cliff, Account of My Hut, Tales of Rain and the Moon*, the love poetry in *Shin Kokinshū, The Tale of the Heike*, and Goldsmith's *Deserted Village*.[92] The choice is surprisingly old-fashioned for a man who had been specializing in English literature and who would make a name for himself as the chief theoretician of Naturalist literature, but it undoubtedly reflected his tastes. His *gō* (literary name), Hōgetsu, which means literally "embrace the moon," was taken from a line in *Prose-Poem on the Red Cliff*: "If we could only link arms with the flying immortals and wander where we please, embrace the moon and grow old with it. . . ."[93]

Hōgetsu's first essay, published in 1894, was on detective stories, presumably because the works of Edgar Allan Poe were enjoying something of a vogue at the time.[94] Shortly before, he had taken a job with *Waseda Bungaku* as a reporter. The salary was miserably low, but the job provided him with opportunities to have his writings published. His first important work was an essay on Saikaku published in 1895. Saikaku had not long before been rediscovered, and influenced such writers as Kōda Rohan and Higuchi Ichiyō, but Hōgetsu's opinion of his works was by no means favorable. Consciously or not, he applied to his evaluations of Saikaku the European standards he had absorbed at Waseda. He disapproved of Saikaku especially because his works lacked the structure of true novels. Even *The Life of an Amorous Man* and *The Life of an Amorous Woman*, which seem to be focused on a single person, were made up of almost unrelated incidents arbitrarily linked together. Hōgetsu could detect no attempt on Saikaku's part to probe beneath the surface of his characters; but, he admitted, Saikaku's manner was well suited to the passionate and even maniacal temper of the Genroku era, which he likened to Elizabethan England.[95] He believed that only one work by Saikaku deserved to be called a masterpiece, *Five Women Who Loved Love*, in which Saikaku had made plain his belief, despite his reputation as an optimist, that love did not always bring happiness.[96] After recapitulating Saikaku's failures, Hōgetsu concluded:

He still had not achieved the form of a novel, at least as the term is understood today. What is valuable in Saikaku is the sharpness of his observations of people and his success in depicting vividly, without a trace of reserve, the world of passions of the Genroku era, stripping away the garments and even the skin. I believe that it is in this respect alone that Saikaku is sufficiently important to be discussed alongside Chikamatsu and Bakin.[97]

Hōgetsu's field of vision when he examined Saikaku's works was excessively narrow, but one cannot help but respect him for having applied to writings that had hitherto not been deemed worthy of a scholar's attention the same standards with which he would treat the European masters.

Most of Hōgetsu's early critical essays were devoted to Japanese literature, ranging from Jōruri by Chikamatsu to recent fiction by Kōda Rohan and Ozaki Kōyō, as well as to poetry in the new forms. He also wrote some fiction and published an adaptation of *The Woman Who Did* (1895) by the Canadian author Grant Allen (1848–1899), an early plea for women's liberation.

In 1902 Hōgetsu was awarded a fellowship by Waseda to study aesthetics in Europe. Surely no Japanese who had previously gone abroad to study was so well qualified, and the whole of the literary world seemed to pin its hopes on him to bring back to Japan the latest and most authentic developments in European criticism. In the previous year, when Takayama Chogyū's planned trip to Europe had been canceled because of his illness, his friend Anesaki Masaharu, perhaps to console him, had published an article asserting that study abroad was of no use to a Japanese, but this view was clearly not shared by the many people who attended the farewell banquet for Hōgetsu.

Hōgetsu sailed on March 8, 1902, and reached Marseilles on April 27. He went ashore to see the city, and was particularly struck by the nudes in the picture gallery; this encounter apparently first awakened his interest in art.[98]

His stay in England was unusually happy and profitable. He attended the theater in London often, beginning with a performance of *Aida* at Covent Garden, which impressed him by its similarities to Nō.[99] His second opera, *Tristan und Isolde*, confirmed the resemblances: opera, like Nō, was set in the Middle Ages, and the Middle Ages, whether in Europe or Japan, shared the same preoccupation with religion and the supernatural. However, performances in English of *Carmen* and *Faust* suggested that opera might be more like Jōruri than Nō. Later, while in Berlin, where he saw many operas by Wagner, he would decide that he had been mistaken in finding resemblances between opera and either Nō or Jōruri; it was something distinct because, even when an opera was set in the Middle Ages, the treatment and structure clearly belonged to the nineteenth century. Hōgetsu's readiness to change his conclusions in the light of further evidence was to mark all the many articles he sent back to Japan from Europe.

Hōgetsu visited museums, had dinner with foreign friends, attended church (not for religious but aesthetic reasons), and went to see Wordsworth's house at Rydal Mount. He attended lectures at the universities of London and Oxford on literature and psychology. His stay in England, infinitely more agreeable than Natsume Sōseki's, enlightened him especially about the theater, though it was a time of great actors rather than of great plays. He saw Sir Henry Irving perform and wrote articles about him, but the most important experience, at least in terms of his own career, was attending the dramatization of Tolstoy's *Resurrection*—a play that would figure prominently in the tragedy of his life.

In July 1904 Hōgetsu, fulfilling the terms of his grant, left England for Germany, to study aesthetics in Berlin. He did not enjoy his life in Germany, largely because he was constantly being made aware of people staring at him. All the same, he attended lectures delivered at the University of Berlin on nineteenth-century art by Heinrich Wölfflin, and heard no less than forty performances at the Berlin theaters and opera houses. He made no friends in Germany, but his time was well spent.

Before leaving Europe, Hōgetsu visited Vienna, Prague, Dresden, Budapest, Rome, Venice, Zurich, and Paris. He liked them all, but when he returned to England for a last brief stay he felt "like a fish in water." He wept when he left London. His ship reached Yokohama in September 1905 after an uneventful voyage; he had been away for three and a half years. There was a great banquet to welcome him home, and the guests included such celebrities as Tsubouchi Shōyō, Tokuda Shūsei, Kunikida Doppo, and Hirotsu Ryūrō. Articles about Hōgetsu appeared in the leading magazines, and the Waseda students staged celebrations. He resumed teaching at Waseda in October, but his time was soon divided between his university duties and a recently founded drama group that had been awaiting his return before commencing its activities. In January 1906 the journal *Waseda Bungaku*, which had discontinued publication in 1899, appeared in a new series, and the inaugural issue was headed by Hōgetsu's essay "Torawaretaru Bungaku" (Literature in Shackles), his first memorable work.

"Literature in Shackles" opens with Hōgetsu's description of being aboard a ship anchored in the harbor of Naples during the preceding August. He was in a melancholy mood as he reflected on the decline of civilizations: Italy was now no more than the cadaver of ancient Rome, and Greece was barely breathing. As he gazed out over the landscape toward Vesuvius, a figure who looked exactly like Dante in Giotto's painting suddenly appeared and began to explain to the young Japanese the whole of European cultural history, rather in the manner that Virgil had guided Dante on his journey. He described the great painters, religious leaders, dramatists, poets, and others of the past, and even analyzed such movements in nineteenth-century Europe as Naturalism, Pre-Raphaelism, Impressionism, and Symbolism. "Dante" related how Expressionism in France and Germany had arisen in opposition to Naturalism because literature was threatened by the "shackles" of science and Naturalism. He had kind words for Arthur Wing Pinero who, he opined, shared with Arthur Jones the distinction of being the luminaries of the world of contemporary British drama; but he did not hold out much hope for problem plays in the manner of Ibsen. He also summarized the work of Johannes Volkelt, *System der Asthetic*, which had only recently been published.

"Dante" was particularly interested in Symbolism, which he contrasted with the Naturalism of the latter half of the nineteenth century. The two qualities he distinguished in Symbolism were the romantic and the religious elements. The romantic element had come to the fore because the stress given to the intellect by the Naturalists had brought about an impoverishment of literature. A tendency had consequently developed to explore the pleasurable, feminine, mystic, and naïve elements in literature, and to pass beyond knowledge to the free realm of the emotions. He continued:

> Literature is in shackles. It has been shackled and bypassed by the extraordinary vitality of knowledge in the latter part of the nineteenth century. I light the sacred fire before the altar of the muses and in this way express my approval of the raising of a righteous army, which will do battle for literature now in shackles.
>
> Literature must first be set completely free from the bonds of knowledge, and allowed to wander over the great sea of the emotions. . . . May literature today bathe in this sea, find liberty, and wash away the dust.[100]

The views expressed here were in sharp opposition to those of the Naturalists, who emphasized the clinical treatment of the passions, but Hōgetsu (still in the persona of Dante) added:

> I am not one to abuse or belittle Naturalism. Most of the major works of nineteenth-century literature were created under its influence. The only really objectionable feature is its extremism, which is not surprising, considering that Naturalism came into being only after first having been enslaved to knowledge. But if Naturalism could return once again to nature, and be faithful to the sources of natural emotions that are neither ornamented nor falsified, there would be a whole flotilla of Naturalist works whose sails would range together as they traveled together over the sea of passions.[101]

"Dante" stresses the importance of religious literature, but is at pains to make it clear that he does not mean religion in a conventional sense; the religion he is discussing transcends the realm of knowledge and everyday emotions, and is to be attained only through a sudden enlightenment or epiphany.[102] He concludes with a remark on the lateness of the hour and bids goodbye to his Japanese friend. Hōgetsu clutches at "Dante's" sleeve, but it is too late. Before long the ship has weighed anchor and departed.

In a postscript Hōgetsu recalled "Dante's" words urging him to release the "boat of literature" from the pier of knowledge and to let it float on the sea of feelings until it reaches the shores of religion. "Dante" believed that it did not matter which course one set in one's boat, whether philosophical, mystical, symbolic, naturalistic, or realistic, as long as one's goal was the realm of the extraordinary. Hōgetsu concurred, with one reservation:

> Surely there must be some theory of literature, whether emotional, religious, or some other, which is responsive to the special conditions of Japan in the modern world. Might it be something which would give full play to the genius of Japanese or perhaps oriental literature? At present our country is flourishing; it is the time for a national self-awakening. There are basic differences in Eastern and Western emotions that are by no means easy to reconcile. Is it not natural, then, that literature, which springs from these emotions, should differ in coloration, depending on whether it is Eastern or Western? Some say that the literature of the entire world must eventually be unified, and there is nothing wrong with that. But first it is essential that the individual qualities of each be fully exploited. I visited Hungary and saw how, for a thousand years, the inferior culture of western Asia has been completely overpowered and destroyed by the stronger culture of eastern Europe. I could not keep the tears from coming to my eyes. Is it possible for Japan not to realize the importance of first establishing a Japanese or oriental civilization? [103]

These views, reminiscent of Tōkoku's declaration that "literature must be the unalloyed voice of the people," make it clear that Hōgetsu's love for the classics of Japan and China had stayed with him even while he was most eagerly absorbing European culture. He promised to write more on the subject of the relations between oriental traditions and the emotional, religious literature recommended by "Dante" but, in fact, this was not to be the direction of Hōgetsu's future criticism; he was to establish himself instead as the leading exponent of the Naturalism that he had decried as "literature in shackles." For all his insistence in this first major essay on what he called "Japanese or oriental" traditions, which doubtless had acquired special relevance while he was living in Europe, he would be remembered for his advocacy of theories of literature and drama that owed very little to the East. The realities of life as a teacher and critic in Japan soon blotted out memories of the lectures he had heard in Europe, and he found himself obliged to adopt views that were quite contrary to those he had espoused when his European experiences were still fresh.

The work crucial in converting Hōgetsu from an enemy of Naturalism to its chief proponent was Shimazaki Tōson's *Hakai* (The Broken Commandment). Hōgetsu's review, published in the May 1906 issue of *Waseda Bungaku*, opened with these words:

> *The Broken Commandment* is a strikingly new phenomenon in our literary world. I cannot help feeling that it represents a turning point for our novels. This is the first time that a Japanese creative work has succeeded in conveying with an equivalent degree of significance the vitality transmitted by the European Naturalists in their controversial works of recent years. Like the European examples, it exudes an odor of nineteenth-century *fin-de-siècle Weltschmerz*, and epitomizes the many pioneering works that have created or attempted to create a new era in the world of Japanese fiction. . . . *The Broken Commandment* is without question the major work of recent years.[104]

Hōgetsu expressed various criticisms of Tōson's novel in the light of his knowledge of European literature and theories of aesthetics, and voiced particular disappointment over the flabbiness of the happy ending. But he concluded that these faults did not mar the book's great virtues of spirit, sentiments, and descriptions.

In April 1907 Hōgetsu reviewed Oguri Fūyō's Naturalist novel, *Seishun* (Youth). He found much to praise, both in the brilliant style and in the creation of a hero whose likes had not previously been seen in Japanese fiction. He had fewer faults to find with *Youth* than with *The Broken Commandment*, regretting only that the hero was not portrayed in sufficient depth for him to occupy a dominant place against the background, the literary world of the 1890s.[105]

By this time Hōgetsu, perhaps without realizing it, had aligned himself with the creators of Naturalist fiction. In the essay "Ima no Bundan to Shin Shizen Shugi" (The Literary World Today and the New Naturalism), published in June 1907, he discussed Naturalism mainly in terms of its rejection given to the techniques of other schools; the term "Naturalism" evidently still meant "natural," as opposed to the special kind of realism later associated with the movement.[106]

In October 1907 Hōgetsu published a review of Tayama Katai's short novel *Futon* (The Quilt), which opened with a declaration of his allegiance to Naturalism:

> I accept Naturalism. At the very least, it is the newest trend in Japanese literary circles. . . . Only recently, twenty or more years later than the French, has the Japanese reading public belatedly come to want to savor for itself, in a deeply personal manner, the flavor of what the Europeans call Naturalism. These are the plain facts, and nothing can alter them: our literary world still has a long way to go, but every step forward, no matter how small, is to the good. . . .
>
> Some people say that they like Naturalism, but cannot abide the present products of Naturalism. Do they mean that these works do not accord with their tastes? Or is it that the works are badly written? If it is a matter of taste, it is worth hearing the reason, but if the works are badly executed, it has nothing to do with Naturalism itself.[107]

Turning to the prophecies of those who predicted that the public would soon tire of Naturalism, and that it would not last a year, Hōgetsu admitted that tastes were constantly shifting, and that it was of course impossible that Naturalism would remain unchanged through all time to come. Perhaps, at some future date, the Japanese might follow the French in moving from Naturalism to Symbolism or Mysticism; but it was senseless to deny the value of something new because it was likely to change. For the French, Naturalism was already "past tense," but "in Japan Naturalism is *present tense* and perhaps *future tense.*" [108]

Hōgetsu devoted so much of his review of *The Quilt* to his description of the present and future state of Naturalism in Japan that there was not much space left for discussing the book. Obviously, he admired Tayama Katai's novel, more because of what it represented within the Naturalist movement than for its intrinsic qualities. After briefly mentioning various faults in *The Quilt*, he concluded:

> This is the daring confession of a man of flesh, a naked human being. In this respect, the present work reveals in a clear and entirely conscious manner something that we have been trying, ever since the birth of the Meiji novel, to glimpse in the writings of

Futabatei, Fūyō, Tōson, and other authors. The work embodies perfectly one aspect of Naturalism in its descriptions, which present beauty and ugliness in a raw state, or which go even one step further and portray only the ugly. Ugliness is the voice of the irremediable beast-nature of the human being; *The Quilt* presents to the public gaze, so nakedly as to make us avert our eyes, a specimen of the self-conscious, modern nature of man, as illuminated by his reasonable half. Such is the work's lifeblood and its value. And yet, voices of protest would surely have been raised in the past in the name of morality; the absence of any outcry of protest is perhaps to be ascribed to a change in the times or something similar.[109]

Hōgetsu's review of *The Quilt* was the first of a series of essays that gave the Naturalist movement respectability and laid the foundations for his own reputation as the leading literary critic of the Meiji era. He himself attached greater importance to his essays on aesthetic theory, but they were little more than presentations in Japanese of the opinions of European scholars. Hōgetsu's work in the theater, though certainly of historical interest, contributed relatively little to the development of modern drama, and his academic writings are of slight importance.[110] All the same, his broad, general knowledge and his ability to write in an interesting manner about contemporary works won him a surprisingly large following, as popularity polls attested.[111]

The most important of the essays on Naturalism published by Hōgetsu in 1908–1909, at the height of his activity as a critic, was "Shizen Shugi no Kachi" (The Value of Naturalism, 1908). This work opens with a consideration of two well-known novels of the period immediately preceding the advent of Naturalism, *Tajō Takon* (Many Passions, Many Griefs) and *Konjiki Yasha* (Demon Gold), both by Ozaki Kōyō. Hōgetsu commented:

> *Many Passions, Many Griefs* contains no perceptible overtones of a philosophical nature, but one can discern in the author's depiction of certain emotional states or peculiar human quirks his intention of bringing us a little closer to the meaning of life. *Demon Gold* obviously is also meant to leave an intellectual impression of having employed particular insights in order to illuminate an aspect of the meaning of life. As it happens, the former work, for the very reason that its intellectual message is not openly communicated, is in a

sense more of a piece and more Naturalistic; but there is so little depth to the background of the emotions that the book risks being nothing more than a description of emotions. It is not impossible to find a good deal more meaning in *Demon Gold* than in *Many Passions, Many Griefs* if only because the ideas are presented on the surface; but these ideas are so exceedingly simple and self-evident that if one examines them closely they become abstract notions, which detach themselves from the work.[112]

Hōgetsu admitted that both novels by Ozaki Kōyō were interesting, but insisted that a novel without "authority" is a mere distraction without aesthetic value. He quoted passages from the novels to illustrate the point that although the surface is brilliant, they are no more than fabrications of the author, whose presence is easily detected behind the scenes manipulating the characters. Hōgetsu declared that Kōyō's inability to communicate the inner meaning of life was the respect in which he most conspicuously betrayed his inferiority to recent writers, especially the Naturalists. He quoted long passages from Masamune Hakuchō's novella *Izuko e* (Where To?) and Mayama Seika's story "Kachō-gai" (The Duck Raiser) to demonstrate that although these writings are stylistically no match for Kōyō's, they transmit a convincing sense of reality.[113]

Hōgetsu analyzed, in terms of such criteria as "aesthetic emotions" and "aesthetic mood," the philosophical foundations of Naturalist literature. He stated that "lyrical subjectivity is excluded from the surface of Naturalism because it frustrates or impedes the truth about nature."[114] Naturalist literature was properly concerned with social questions, science and reality. Such Naturalist masters as Zola and Maupassant had described the bestial, dark side of human life not merely to display their scientific detachment but in order to express their conviction that these aspects of life must not be concealed or excluded from literature; unless this side of human existence was taken into account one would not be able to understand life. The writings of the Naturalists had been attacked because they insisted on the "animal nature" of the relations between men and women, or because they favored the gratification of the instincts. It was quite true that such subjects were treated in Naturalist literature; indeed, this was the most daring feature of Naturalism, but it was definitely not the only aspect of reality that was treated.[115] Hōgetsu recognized the danger that readers of inferior intellectual capacity might be so enthralled by the sensational descriptions in Naturalist fiction as to overlook the inner meaning, but this was a danger inherent in all serious literature.

The essay "Bungeijō no Shizen Shugi" (Naturalism in Literature), published in January 1908, was a kind of history of Naturalist literature, corresponding to the history of Romantic literature he had presented in "Literature in Shackles." Naturalism offers no solutions and has no ideals, but once all pretense has been stripped away, in accordance with the Naturalist insistence on truth, and the extreme limits of realism are reached, the observer may be moved to reveries on the invisible aspects of life and to meditative thoughts that eventually lead to religious exaltation. He commented: "Naturalist literature leads us to the point where we can even touch the religious. This should be the object of one's attention when one is creating a work of literature. It is the highest reach of beauty, the true form of life itself." [116]

Hōgetsu's essay involved some bewildering intuitive leaps, but it brought delight to members of the Naturalist school, who welcomed it like "rain clouds after a drought." [117] The promise of beauty and even of religious exaltation at the end of the long, dusty road of Naturalism was comforting not only to the reading public but to Hōgetsu himself, who at this time was evidently wavering in his allegiance to the principles of Naturalism.

His last important works of literary criticism appeared in 1909.[118] In June of that year he published at the head of a work on modern literature the essay "Jo ni kaete Jinseikan-jō no Shizen Shugi wo ronzu" (By Way of Preface: On Naturalism as a View of Life) in which he admitted that he no longer possessed a "view of life" (*jinseikan*):

All existing views of life have lost their value as objects of faith in face of my knowledge. My knowledge is to be detested, I know, but there is nothing I can do about it. If some higher force were to overcome knowledge of mine I would probably be able to join the ranks of the fortunate ones who can believe.

That is why at present I am incapable of proposing any fixed view of life. As a matter of fact, the present moment is more suited for me to confess plainly my doubts and uncertainties. . . . When I look around me, taking myself as a measuring rod, I get the impression that the people who talk about their "view of life" are all more or less in the same position as myself. If this is the case, perhaps this is an age of confession for the whole world.[119]

The flaws and contradictions in Hōgetsu's arguments are obvious, and they were leaped on by such enemies of Naturalism as Gotō Chūgai (1866–1938), who denied that Hōgetsu had anything new to say. But the phrase "age of confession" was peculiarly apt, and suggested why, even after the "age of Naturalism" in its narrow sense ended, the "I novels," the most conspicuous examples of confessional literature, preserved much of the heritage of Naturalist beliefs.

Soon after publishing his doubts on the validity of Naturalism as a guide to life, Hōgetsu began to shift his interests from criticism to the theater, especially to the activities of the Bungei Kyōkai (Literary Society). The organization had originally been founded to encourage all the arts, but at this time was devoted almost exclusively to the theater, especially to the training of actors of modern drama. An evening school, which offered courses in different aspects of the theater, was started in 1909, and Hōgetsu was one of several distinguished lecturers who took part. He was charged with teaching modern Western drama, and for this purpose translated (from the English translation) Ibsen's *A Doll's House*. His activities at the school were at first only a minor part of his work, but gradually he began to neglect his other duties, both at Waseda University and as a critic. This was especially true after one of the Literary Society students, Matsui Sumako, successfully performed as Nora in a production of the first and third acts of *A Doll's House* in September 1911. (Hōgetsu read a summary of the second act, which had not yet been rehearsed.) In the following year he and Sumako became lovers. When Tsubouchi Shōyō found out what had happened, he sent for Sumako and commanded her to give up Hōgetsu, for the sake of his wife and children. He also threatened to disavow Hōgetsu as his disciple. But the two refused to sacrifice their love. In June 1913 Hōgetsu and Sumako signed an oath in which they swore that, in the interests of the nascent theater movement, they would remain true to their love, no matter what difficulties might be involved. They also promised to get married in a few years, but no mention was made of the disposition of Hōgetsu's family. This oath was repeated several times during the next few years, with more and more drastic penalties attached if either broke it.

The Literary Society was dissolved in July 1913 largely because of the dissension aroused by the romance. In the same month, however, Geijutsu-za (Art Theatre) was founded by Hōgetsu, Sumako, and others. The first program, staged in September of that year, included Maeterlinck's *Monna Vanna* in Hōgetsu's translation. This and subsequent productions of the Art Theatre were praised by the critics, but did not make much of an impression on the public, and the company was beset by resignations. The situation changed markedly in March 1914 when Sumako scored a personal triumph in the production of Tolstoy's *Resurrection*, translated and staged by Hōgetsu. It was less the play itself than Sumako in the role of Katusha, and especially her plaintive song, that made *Resurrection* so popular. Its success saved the Art Theatre. *Resurrection* was performed all over Japan, from Hokkaidō to Kyushu, and even in Taiwan, Korea, and Manchuria—444 performances in all.

Hōgetsu continued to write critical essays from time to time, none of major importance. In June 1914 he stated that he now preferred to work in silence rather than voice his opinions. Relations between him and Sumako, with whom he had been living openly since 1914, rapidly deteriorated. By 1918 her tantrums and capricious behavior had exhausted him physically and mentally, and perhaps made him susceptible to the influenza epidemic of 1918. He died of influenza on November 5, at the age of forty-seven. Matsui Sùmako hanged herself on January 5, 1919, more faithful to Hōgetsu in death than in life.

Despite Hōgetsu's high promise and undoubted talent, his works quickly lost their appeal, and he was remembered more for his stormy love affair than for his contributions to Naturalism. But he had done his work conscientiously and had given respectability to a movement that would remain a force in Japanese writing through much of the twentieth century.

In addition to the men who were known specifically as critics, many authors of the Meiji era wrote criticism, some of which has been discussed elsewhere in connection with their fiction. Special attention has been given to the writings of Shimamura Hōgetsu, but his opponents were numerous and vocal. His essays were distinguished by the presence of ideas in which he believed; but theirs consisted mainly of rejoinders and denials. Their negativity would be typical of the criticism of the early Taishō era, but before long a new and more positive criticism would emerge.[120]

THE TAISHŌ PERIOD (1912–1926)

THE MOST IMPORTANT CRITICISM written during the Taishō period—at any rate, after 1920—was by men who were primarily known as novelists, and their essays, though sometimes brilliantly effective, were less concerned with critical theory than with subjective impressions. The most typical forms of critical essays were *sakkaron* (discussions of authors) and *sakuhinron* (discussions of works), rather than extended treatments of the principles of literary expression or the historical surveys that were typical of the Meiji period. The ronsō continued to flourish as each new development in the literary world was subjected to scrutiny by opposing groups of critics.

KIKUCHI KAN AND THE BUNDAN

Perhaps the most significant change during the Taishō era was the greatly improved social status of the writer, thanks largely to one man, Kikuchi Kan (1888–1948), who earned for himself the sobriquet of *bundan no ōgosho*, or tycoon of the literary world. The word *bundan* itself, used by Tsubouchi Shōyō as early as 1889, referred originally to the closely knit group of Ken'yūsha writers who surrounded Ozaki Kōyō and looked to him not only for literary guidance but for help in getting their stories printed. Kōyō and his followers for a time controlled the literary page of the *Yomiuri Shimbun*, and even exercised a veto power over what was published by two major houses, Shun'yōdō and Hakubundō. After the death of Kōyō in 1903 the Ken'yūsha group rapidly lost importance, and control of the bundan passed into the hands of the Naturalists. Not all writers were associated with the bundan; indeed, the most distinguished novelists of the Meiji era, Natsume Sōseki and Mori Ōgai, remained aloof from the literary market-place, and several writers of the Taishō era, notably Tanizaki Jun'ichirō and Shiga Naoya, tended also to stay away from the cafés and other places where members of the bundan gathered. But all writers benefited from the improvement in fees paid for manuscripts and from the increased respect accorded to the literary profession, especially after 1920. Masamune Hakuchō, writing in 1954, attributed the improvement in the status of writers to the prosperity brought about by World War I:

> War is hateful, but the prestige accorded to literature has sometimes been completely changed by a war. After the Russo-Japanese War, the bundan, which had been languishing, was given a fresh infusion of life as the result of the rise of Naturalism and the importation of Russian literature. As the years of World War I passed, Japan suddenly became rich, and the lives of people in many walks of life seemed to enjoy more prosperity than ever before. Even the bundan, which had always made a talking-point of its poverty, shared in the overflow of the wartime boom. Magazines sold, books sold, and writers who had never before known the feel of money learned the comforting warmth of a full wallet. . . .
>
> Literary activity rose to a peak under the impetus of the war. The young authors who made their appearance at this time held quite different attitudes from those of my generation when we made our furtive entrances into the bundan. These young men said that they were writing a new page in bundan history, and I believed

them. Kikuchi Kan came to be recognized as something like the spokesman for the new bundan, and the young authors exuded confidence. . . .

Writers of my generation left payment for manuscripts entirely up to the other party, but the up-and-coming new writers, I gathered, demanded huge fees, boldly and fearlessly.[121]

Hakuchō further recalled that it had been true in the past that if ever a young man informed his parents of his intention of becoming a novelist they would be much upset, but this ceased to be true after 1918: "Previously writers had given the impression of living detached from the world, but once Kikuchi Kan appeared on the scene, writers came to be thought of as people who lived very much in the world." [122] This situation was not altered even after the Great Depression of the late 1920s; writers had no intention of returning to their former humble status. "The writers of the new era—Kikuchi, Akutagawa, Kume, Satomi, Satō—seemed to us older writers like creatures who led lives of unprecedented extravagance." [123]

The enhanced position of writers strengthened their feelings of belonging to a special, privileged group, the bundan. Masamune Hakuchō, despite his unsociability and his sporadic literary production, never doubted his importance within the bundan, and frequently wrote about other members; but the leader of the bundan during the 1920s was unquestionably Kikuchi Kan. Kikuchi's literary production is only of modest interest: a few short stories, two or three one-act plays, and a few essays constitute the bulk of his writings that are still remembered and included in "complete collections" (*zenshū*) of modern Japanese literature. However, when Kikuchi first became a prominent writer, just after the end of World War I, he was producing short stories at the rate of one a month, and seemed to be on his way to becoming a major new author. His best-known story, "Tadanao-kyō Gyōjō Ki" (On the Conduct of Lord Tadanao),[124] which appeared in the September 1918 issue of *Chūō Kōron*, was so highly acclaimed that Kikuchi was able to realize the dream of young writers of his day: the private rickshaw of the magazine would come to his door to call for him. Success seems to have gone to his head. At any rate, within a few years he deserted the world of "pure literature" and wrote instead fiction with mass appeal, publishing wherever the fees were the highest. In 1926, for example, when *Chūō Kōron* was paying seven yen a page for manuscripts, Kikuchi demanded (and received) one hundred yen a page for a story he sold to the family magazine *Kingu* (King). But he was not content with obtaining greater benefits for himself alone; in the same year he founded the Bungeika Kyōkai (Writers' Association), whose purpose was to protect copyrights and in other ways assure writers of a decent income. Kikuchi had an uncanny ability to predict what the public would want, and used this talent to promote the new magazine, *Bungei Shunjū*, which he founded in 1923 as a popular, gossipy literary journal. The initial circulation was only about 3,000 copies, but by 1927 it had grown to 180,000 copies, an astonishing figure for the time. The magazine owed its appeal largely to Kikuchi's imaginative journalism; for example, Kikuchi made the zadankai, a roundtable discussion that had hitherto served mainly as a forum for serious exchanges of opinions, into the medium for dealing in an informal way with any subject likely to interest readers. This distinctively Japanese contribution to journalism was congenial both to the participants, who enjoyed talking casually with their compeers, and to readers who preferred the relaxed manner of a zadankai to sustained arguments.

Kikuchi's own writings during this period were aimed at a mass readership, and seemed to have been composed with the motto of "livelihood first, art second." [125] His success with the public helped to obtain not only for himself but for all Japanese writers greatly improved treatment. Kikuchi was also active in promoting new writers, including the novelist Kawabata Yasunari and the critic Kobayashi Hideo.

Kikuchi's postwar reputation was harmed by the readiness with which he lent his support to the militarists both before and during the Pacific War. He died in 1948, still under a cloud because of this collaboration, but the Akutagawa and Naoki prizes, which he initiated in 1935 as marks of recognition for new writers of "pure" and "popular" literature respectively, continued to rank as the most sought-after distinctions. Above all, Kikuchi created the bundan as a major force in modern Japanese literature. The death of the bundan has more than once been solemnly pronounced, but the judges of the major literary prizes and the compilers of the various collections of modern literature continue to be drawn from the same group within the bundan—senior writers and critics whose reputations are securely established and whose opinions are constantly sought by the press and magazines.

The bundan at times has been able not only to promote but to frustrate writers by denying them outlets for their works, though its power has never been absolute; a writer's real worth is likely to be learned in time, whether or not he receives literary prizes. Kikuchi Kan wielded such great influence over the literary world of the 1920s that he secured new dignity for the writing profession, but his eagerness to please the reading public also encouraged the growth of the *taishū shōsetsu*, novels of mass appeal.

Works known as taishū shōsetsu are usually relegated to a limbo outside the realm of "pure" literature, and seldom appear in collections of modern Japanese literature. *Dai Bosatsu Tōge* (Dai Bosatsu Pass) by Nakazato Kaizan (1855–1944), though left unfinished at the time of the author's death, is surely one of the longest novels ever written. It appeared between 1913 and 1941, all but the last volumes having first been serialized in various newspapers before they were published as books. *Dai Bosatsu Pass* enjoyed a far greater readership than any work of "pure" literature written during the Taishō and early Shōwa eras, but it was rarely given serious attention by the critics. Nakazato angrily denied that he had written a taishū shōsetsu, insisting that his book was more properly called a *daijō shōsetsu*, or Mahayana novel, referring to the Buddhist inspiration for his rambling account of life in Japan during the late Tokugawa period.

The distinction between writers of "pure" and "mass" literature was not easy to make. Kikuchi once defined the difference in these terms: "A work that a writer writes because he wants to write it is pure literature; a work he writes in order to please the public is mass literature." [126] But Kikuchi was by no means consistent in his standards. He wrote about his friend Naoki Sanjūgo (1891–1934): [127] "It was because of the accidental circumstance that he began to write in the period when mass literature was at its height that Naoki was called a mass writer, but his real forte was as a great historical novelist. It is no exaggeration to say that with Naoki the historical novel first came into being in Japan." However, when Kikuchi founded a prize for popular literature he gave it the name Naoki Prize, no doubt reflecting his awareness that the kind of literature that Naoki wrote was not only different from but less important than Akutagawa's.

The period of greatest popularity of the taishū shōsetsu was after the Great Earthquake of 1923. Most works of the genre were historical fiction, and this for a time was the chief distinction between the taishū shōsetsu and the *tsūzoku shōsetsu*, popular fiction which was generally contemporary in setting. The reasons for the popularity of these works of relatively little intrinsic literary value can perhaps be understood in terms of the kinds of "pure literature" that were being published in the 1920s. The average reader who wished to pass some diverting hours with a book was unlikely to be attracted by the oblique style of the New Sensationalist writers, or by the emphasis on unexciting incidents typical of the "I novel," or for that matter by the gloomy and awkwardly constructed works of proletarian literature.

In July 1922 Kikuchi precipitated a brief ronsō with Satomi Ton when he published the article "Bungei Sakuhin no naiteki Kachi" (The Internal Value of Literary Works), in which he asked why he was sometimes moved even by a badly written story, yet left unaffected by a well-written one. He came to the conclusion that artistic excellence was not the sole value in literature. He revealed that his own story "Onshū no kanata" (The Realm Beyond, 1919) [128] had been based on an account he had read in a guidebook, which had moved him despite the clumsy expression. He continued: "I could go on indefinitely listing examples of internal values, but one more will suffice, *Shisen wo koete* (Before the Dawn) by Kagawa Toyohiko. I set about reading this work with considerable antipathy, as was normal of a member of the bundan, but even though I kept telling myself, 'He can't write, he can't write,' at quite a few places in the work I could not hold back the tears that filled my eyes." [129]

As a member of the bundan, Kikuchi felt obliged to look down on the novels of Kagawa Toyohiko (1886–1960), a Protestant minister who had won something of a reputation as a novelist. However, the content of the book, which describes the suffering of the hero who gives his life to aid the poor, made Kikuchi weep; in this respect he was no different from the mass of readers.

Yoshikawa Eiji (1892–1962), more than any other writer, can

be credited with having established taishū bungaku as the basic reading matter of most Japanese. His historical novels enjoyed incredible popularity not only when they first appeared, beginning in 1926, but for many years afterward. *Miyamoto Musashi* (Musashi, 1935-1939) and *Shin Heike Monogatari* (The New Heike Story, 1950-1957) were so popular with every class of reader that they have been styled *kokumin bungaku* (literature of the people) to indicate that their appeal has not been limited to fanciers of literature. Their place in literary—as opposed to social—history is unlikely to improve with time, but their many volumes will no doubt continue to crowd the shelves of booksellers and lending libraries.

Kikuchi Kan cannot be credited with (or blamed for) all these developments of the Taishō era, but for much of the period and later he was the emblematic figure of the bundan, and he had many devoted admirers even among discerning literary critics. His writings, by contrast, seem unlikely to survive except as documents of a life of exceptional interest.

IKUTA CHŌKŌ (1882-1936)

Among the Taishō writers who were known especially for their literary criticism, the most conspicuous was Ikuta Chōkō, a frequent and generally strident participant in many of the ronsō of the day. He attracted attention in 1906 with an article, written while still a student at Tokyo University, on the Ken'yūsha novelist Oguri Fūyō. This was the first sustained example of what would become a typical form of literary criticism during the Taishō era, the sakkaron.[130] Ikuta was also one of the first critics to deal with current Japanese literary production; earlier critics had usually discussed only foreign writers, and if an occasion arose when comparisons were to be made between foreign and Japanese authors, it was in terms of pointing out the inadequacy of the Japanese.[131] Chōkō admitted that he had chosen to discuss Oguri Fūyō because he especially admired his writings, but he insisted that it was important for all critics to study and analyze the works of contemporaries, especially fellow countrymen. This opinion, expressed in the preface to Chōkō's article, will hardly

strike a Western reader as controversial.[132] But the vehemence
with which Chōkō attacked critics of his day who devoted themselves to the literature of the past or of other countries suggests
how far from usual he considered his position to be.[133]

Chōkō's collections *Saikin no Shōsetsuka* (Recent Novelists,
1912) and *Saikin no Bungei oyobi Shichō* (Recent Literature and
Thought, 1915) contained criticism of such contemporaries as
Natsume Sōseki, Mori Ōgai, Tayama Katai, and Izumi Kyōka.[134]
The choice of authors at this distance seems so correct and even so
inevitable that we are apt to forget the difficulties of guessing
accurately which contemporaries will stand the test of time.
Chōkō made remarkably few mistakes.

Chōkō's approach to literature was much influenced by his
readings in Nietzsche, not surprising when one considers that his
translations of Nietzsche were probably his most important work.
For example, when he criticized Sōseki, an author for whom he
generally expressed only admiration, it was in terms of his failure
to make a "revaluation of all values." Chōkō continued, "Sōseki's
outlook on man and the world is not the dangerous kind of idealism professed by the patriots who fought to restore the emperor
during the late days of the shogunate; his is a safe idealism, rather
like Bakin's 'encourage virtue and chastise vice.' " [135]

None of Chōkō's contributions to many ronsō created more
of a stir than "Shizen Shugi Zempa no Chōryō" (Pre-Naturalists
on the Rampage, 1916), in which he derided Mushakōji Saneatsu
and others of the *Shirakaba* school for their immaturity; he declared that they had not yet even reached the stage of literary
development represented by Naturalism.[136] Chōkō was equally
caustic in his contributions to the ronsō on the "I novel." [137] For
that matter, the rise to prominence of the New Sensationalists did
not please him either; in his essay "Bundan no Shinjidai ni atau"
(To the New Generation of the Bundan, 1925) [138] he made fun of
the contrived metaphors, personification, and "skips" of association typical both of Paul Morand and of his Japanese followers.[139]
Chōkō's criticism of Morand's novel *Ouvert la Nuit* is by no
means inept. As he points out, descriptions of sensations tend to
be self-destructive because they foster a craving for ever more
unusual, intense sensations; moreover, the startling images in
Morand's novel seem to have been intended to hide the fact that

he had nothing to say about postwar Europe: "One cannot detect any sign of the nausea that recent Europe might arouse, nor does one find any yearning for a totally new way of life and a new society." [140]

Chōkō made his position even clearer later in the same article:

> The author of *Ouvert la Nuit* has nothing in common with Nietzsche or Tolstoy, nor with Ruskin, Morris, Whitman, Carpenter, or their followers (in whose number I am glad to count myself). As far as he is concerned, the cities, the culture, the mechanization of human beings, the disgrace to humanity called commercialism, the celebrated capitalism, socialism based on a materialistic conception of history, which is not more than the foster-brother of capitalism, suckled at the same breast—all these aspects of recent Europe can be tolerated without difficulty.[141]

Chōkō's mixture of social concern with a distinctly antisocialist bias was noteworthy at a time when proletarian literature was evolving and many writers were shifting toward the left, but his attitudes were an extension of the many abrupt changes in his thought. At one point, for example, he advocated what he called "super-Modernism" (*chōkindai*), and claimed for the founders of his school Tolstoy, Dostoevski, Strindberg, Nietzsche, William Morris, and especially Edward Carpenter (1844–1929), the English social reformer who "attempted to live exclusively in accordance with Oriental simplicity and reverence for the soil." [142] But Chōkō's prediction that the "day of the Oriental was coming" was not an expression of ultra-nationalism; although his opinions changed frequently and dramatically, he remained true to a statement of his ideals made in 1917: "The ultimate objective of human culture is assuredly to become human and individual. The race (*minzoku*) and the nation (*kokka*) are only transitional phenomena." [143] Chōkō never lost sight of this ideal, but he became increasingly a professional gadfly, ready to take on any adversary, for the sake of argument if nothing else.

MASAMUNE HAKUCHŌ (1879–1962)

Anyone who turns to the literary criticism published during the Taishō era in the hopes of finding a systematic presentation of new theories of literature will be disappointed, but the evaluations of contemporary writings are not only astute but often make enjoyable reading. This is true especially of the criticism written by three men who were also known as novelists: Masamune Hakuchō, Hirotsu Kazuo, and Satō Haruo. All three were prominent members of the bundan, but their literary careers were dissimilar: Hakuchō was a central figure of Japanese Naturalism; Hirotsu, a mediocre novelist though an impressive man, first wrote in the manner of the "I novel," but created his most lasting monument with his painstaking research on the Matsukawa Case (1954–1959); and Satō, a brilliant writer who began his career as a Modernist, is known equally for his poetry. Common to all three men was an intuitive ability to recognize literary worth.

Masamune Hakuchō's first published criticism was a review of *The Order-Book* by Izumi Kyōka, which he published in the *Yomiuri Shimbun* in April 1901. Hakuchō, then twenty-two years old, was a student at Waseda University, and probably owed the opportunity to publish a review in the outstanding literary forum of the day to his mentor at Waseda, Shimamura Hōgetsu, who was then the chief writer for the Monday literary page of the newspaper. The review was generally favorable, but Hakuchō went to pains to point out the faults of Kyōka's novel too: "The entire work has something of the eeriness and excitement of a ghost story as narrated by a skillful storyteller, but the observation is only skin-deep and does not penetrate to the real meaning of the human life hidden behind the incidents." [144]

Hakuchō's reviews for the most part were of contemporary novels. But he returned again and again to Genroku literature, especially to Chikamatsu, whose works had given him intense pleasure during his adolescence, and to Saikaku, whom he would one day call "Japan's greatest novelist." [145] Sometimes he singled out for special praise Saikaku's creation of the high-spirited, passionate women of such works as *The Life of an Amorous Woman*, but he was attracted above all by Saikaku's concise but evocative style. He often found occasion to remark that he now preferred

Saikaku to Chikamatsu, but despite the unsentimental nature of his own works, and his suspicions of anything smacking of the murkiness of the Edo past, he could not quite suppress his love for the music of Chikamatsu's language:

> I suppose it is because the plays were originally written as Jōruri, but even as I read them I can almost hear the music of samisens, and I feel my usual irritation being calmed. Whenever I hear a samisen, it is as if the soft, gentle pessimism that one generation of us Japanese has passed on to the next was agreeably soaking through my entire being. The same is true when I read Chikamatsu. The feelings are quite unlike the world-weary emotions which Saikaku's *Life of an Amorous Woman* or *F've Women Who Loved Love* arouses in me. Certain works by Maupassant plunge me into a gloom which is quite unlike the gentle melancholy stirred by a reading of Turgenev. That, more or less, is the difference between reading Saikaku and Chikamatsu.[146]

Hakuchō was especially fond of the late and posthumous works of Saikaku in which the pessimism is most pronounced. The style of these works, though still concise, is conspicuously easier to understand than in the earlier works, and this also appealed to Hakuchō, who detested obscurity almost as much as wordiness. Saikaku's descriptions of ordinary townsmen, who are threatened by creditors or driven to acts of desperation by circumstances that seem to admit no escape, share much with Hakuchō's stories of similarly afflicted Japanese of the twentieth century, and the manner of reporting the events is equally unsentimental. The hold that Chikamatsu retained on Hakuchō's heart, irrespective of literary principles, indicates that there was a side to his sensibility that he preferred not to reveal in his own works, but which colored his appreciation of other people's.

Hakuchō's reputation as a critic in his own day was based on his outspoken observations on contemporary Japanese fiction, but the two writers who seem to have meant the most to him were Saikaku and Dante.[147] His absorption with Dante was not what one might expect of an uncompromising advocate of Naturalism, but Hakuchō's interest in Christianity, formed as a student, remained with him (whether or not he himself realized it) until his death, when he asked for a Christian burial. His latent faith may account for his interest in the great Christian poet, but his praise of Dante usually contained expressions of disgust with the Japan of his own time, as in the following comparison:

> Look at our country today! It need hardly be said that it possesses none of the qualities that distinguished the Elizabethan Age or Periclean Greece, nothing that the whole people would wish to celebrate in poetry. How extremely prosaic everything is—our speech, our literary compositions, our apparel, everything down to the last detail of our behavior! No ideals can be detected in *our* people. I wonder if there is even enough intellectual activity to stir the small number of intellectuals? Religious movements, Japanism—the whole picture is depressing. . . .
>
> If Dante were born today, he would be no more than a run-of-the-mill poet who had been disappointed in love. It is hard to imagine that he would have been capable of writing an imposing work that encompassed the whole of the magnificent thought of the Middle Ages. In Japan there can be no Rousseau, no Herder, and could even Goethe achieve his greatness? [148]

With withering sarcasm Hakuchō characterized the two leading poetry magazines of the day, *Hototogisu* and *Myōjō*: "Here I have one little magazine called *Hototogisu* and another called *Myōjō*. The first is like sugar-water, and the second like lemon squash. Obviously, neither provides much excitement, but both have their little circles of readers who prize their special flavors." [149]

Hakuchō's reviews, whether of literature, art, or the theater, were noted not only for the keen intelligence they revealed, but for their acerbity, and they quickly became one of the features of which the *Yomiuri Shimbun* was most proud.[150] His irreverence was not confined to Japanese works; he once termed the Bible and the *Analects* "mediocre books that inspire no awe in me." [151] It was with seeming reluctance that Hakuchō praised works under review. He liked Natsume Sōseki's writings, initially because they were so unpretentious, even though the author was a professor at Tokyo University; [152] but he was bored by some of Sōseki's most famous novels, including *Afterward, Kokoro*, and *Light and Darkness*.[153] He praised without reservation only one novel, *Grass on the Wayside*. It is easy to see why Hakuchō should have liked

Sōseki's only autobiographical novel, the work that was closest to his own fiction, but that was not the reason he gave: he praised *Grass on the Wayside* as the only novel of Sōseki's maturity that he really wanted to write; the rest were written in fulfillment of his duties as the staff novelist of a newspaper.[154]

Hakuchō invariably addressed himself directly to the work in question and pronounced his opinions unambiguously. This was in contrast to the more pretentious criticism of the 1930s and later, when Japanese critics wrote essays in the manner of admired Frenchmen, and told the reader more about themselves than about the works under examination. Hakuchō was not only to the point but often startlingly acute.

Perhaps his most compelling review was of Arishima Takeo's novel *A Certain Woman*. This work did not fit into the mainstream of modern Japanese literature and was seldom discussed by critics when they surveyed the major works of the Taishō era; but Hakuchō unequivocally declared that it was unexampled in its natural artistic qualities, its taut, polished prose, and the precision with which the author observed the characters both externally and internally. He declared that probably no other author of modern Japan has understood women as well as Arishima. Sometimes, it is true, he wondered if the kind of woman Arishima portrayed with such earnest attention had in fact existed in Japan, "but the breath of a real human being is exhaled by each chapter, each page, each line." [155]

Writing in 1927, Hakuchō chose three novelists of the modern period who exerted a special appeal on the Japanese people as a whole: Ozaki Kōyō, Natsume Sōseki, and Arishima Takeo. He qualified this statement by putting down Kōyō's works as a continuation of the "light literature" of the Edo period, which did not go beyond commonplaces in their observations of society. Sōseki had both learning and insight, and he probed deeply into the psychology of his characters, but his novels were redolent of the study; Hakuchō often had the feeling that Sōseki's novels were no more than intellectual exercises. But Arishima's *A Certain Woman* was different: it did not smell of the lamp, nor was it the product of ordinary commonsense, but was the work of a man who, though his humanism enabled him to touch the realm of the sacred, had seen, more than normal men, both hell and purgatory.[156]

There are contradictions in Hakuchō's opinions, as one might expect in a critic who went on publishing for sixty years. The early works of Sōseki, which did not impress him much when they first appeared, by 1927 had been promoted to the ranks of "incomparable" novels.[157] On the other hand, the enthusiasm with which he had greeted the first publication of Shimazaki Tōson's novel *The Broken Commandment* dissipated in later years as he read other novels that even more powerfully embodied the seriousness of artistic purpose that Hakuchō prized. His instincts were almost always right, but he did not hesitate to admit it when he became aware that his first reactions had been mistaken. In an article published in 1922, for example, he described why he had not admired Shiga Naoya's earlier work. He took up next the recently published *A Dark Night's Passing*, and after pointing out various flaws, concluded by saying that it was "nevertheless the major work most worthy of the attention of the reading public today." [158]

Such praise was unusual from Hakuchō. It happened even more rarely that he enthusiastically reviewed a work that is no longer so admired. In 1924 he stated that if he had to choose the single work of all Meiji and Taishō literature that most deserved to be called a masterpiece, he might settle on *Suspicions* by Chikamatsu Shūkō.[159] This judgment was not repeated by Hakuchō or by anyone else; but the special importance of *Suspicions* would be emphasized by Hirano Ken some thirty years later when he termed it the first true "I novel." [160]

Hakuchō was known as a Waseda critic. This meant that he followed the traditions of Tsubouchi Shōyō and Shimamura Hōgetsu, and it also meant that he seized every opportunity to attack Tokyo University scholars. He had a particular aversion for Ueda Bin, whose polyglot abilities he mocked, and whose translations irritated him with their flowery, archaic language. In an article published in January 1905 Hakuchō compared Ueda Bin with Natsume Sōseki, entirely to the advantage of the latter. He also poked fun at Ueda Bin's lectures:

> Bin sensei's lectures on *Romeo and Juliet* are full of displays of his erudition, but his manner of delivery produces an effect of chewing on wax . . . . Sometimes he does nothing more in the course of an hour than read aloud, without explanation, five or six pages of the

Cassell edition. He frequently finds the occasion, however, to declare that a certain passage is skillfully written or that another has a profound meaning, but he provides the students with no clues for entering into his thoughts. As a consequence, extremely few students even bother to attend his lectures. . . . Sensei is a genius at languages; he has never been abroad, but he is fluent not only in English, French, and German, but in Italian and Spanish as well—or so it is reputed among his acquaintances. This, no doubt, is an achievement of which he deserves to be proud, but the manner in which he shows off his knowledge of foreign languages, even when there is not the least necessity, is unworthy of a sophisticated man.[161]

Hakuchō, praising Sōseki, quoted a lecture on *Hamlet* during the course of which he informed his students, "You can never hope to understand this great master of Western literature in the same way a Western person might. It is quite enough for you to enjoy what you yourself have actually felt. You needn't make the effort to feel what you actually don't feel, simply because of what some Western critic has said." [162] This was Hakuchō's attitude when he wrote about Dante, Maupassant, and other European authors he admired.

Hakuchō's aversion to Tokyo University appeared most blatantly in the sketches "Bunka Daigaku Daigakusei Seikatsu" (Life of a Student in the University Literature Department, 1905). He wrote with venom, aiming his barbs at the establishment. It is not an impressive work,[163] but it was typical of Hakuchō's dislike of authority, especially the academic establishment. The audacity of his attacks on authority won him enemies but also admirers, as we can gather from his admission to the Ryūdokai, the dining club that at the time was the haunt of the bundan, well before he had made a mark for himself as a novelist.[164]

Hakuchō wrote weekly columns of the variety known as *bungei jihyō* (literary chronicles) until he resigned from the *Yomiuri Shimbun* in 1910.[165] He subsequently devoted himself mainly to fiction, and only on occasion would produce a piece of criticism. He became known as a pillar of Naturalism, and after that school fell out of public favor Hakuchō's fortunes as a novelist waned, but he remained an important presence in the bundan, feared for the sharpness of his intellect and the readiness with which he lashed out at whatever he disliked.

In 1926 Hakuchō returned to criticism with the bungei jihyō he published in *Chūō Kōron*. Bungei jihyō originated in the late 1880s, when magazines and newspapers first began to carry articles, usually unsigned, about current literary production. They were most often printed in monthly magazines or else on a monthly basis in newspapers. The bungei jihyō written by Hakuchō established his lasting reputation as a critic; his best-known critical work, *Bundan Jimbutsu Hyōron* (Reviews of People in the Bundan, 1932), was a collection of bungei jihyō published mainly in the 1920s on leading literary figures of the time.[166] His comments were always of interest, though they often suggest zuihitsu, the miscellaneous jottings that formed a prominent part of the Japanese literary heritage. Even when his essays are brilliant, they are generally unsystematic and tend to be marred by a quirkiness that suggests Hakuchō considered himself to be a "character" from whom unconventionality was expected.

Hakuchō frequently participated in ronsō, especially after he resumed activity as a critic. The ronsō were not always of his making. In March–April 1926, for example, he found himself exchanging accusations with Nagai Kafū, a writer he so greatly admired that he stated on occasion that if he were to buy the complete works of only one modern Japanese author, it would be Kafū. At the time Kafū was deeply involved in antiquarian researches on literary figures of the Edo period. Hakuchō unwittingly began the ronsō by stating in an article that although he did not oppose such digging in the relics of the past, "Kafū's recent works give me the feeling of a once beautiful woman who powders a face that is now ravaged by wrinkles." [167] He regretted also that Kafū was wasting his time with the "stupid *kyōka*" (a comic variety of waka) of Ōta Nampo, and that he had "recommended with a straight face a minor bunjin like Narushima Ryūhoku, who embodied all the unpleasant qualities of the late Edo period." [168]

Such criticisms were interspersed with praise and expressions of admiration for Kafū as a "true artist," but Kafū was not easily mollified. His rejoinder was couched in an elaborate classical style and was filled with archaic phraseology. He bluntly declared that Hakuchō's writing was so unlike anything he normally read that he had trouble even grasping the meaning. For example, the phrase "an old woman's cosmetics" was used in the old haikai poetry to refer to moonlight on a cold night, as everyone knew. If that was not Hakuchō's meaning in his article, he should realize that he was not free to change the meaning of established phrases. Kafū was also irritated by the uncomplimentary references to kyōka. An understanding of kyōka was essential to a proper appreciation of the special culture of the Edo period. Besides, Kafū was personally acquainted with a fifth-generation descendant of Nampo, and grew up in the neighborhood where Nampo had lived. Was this not sufficient reason for having a special interest in the man? Kafū concluded by reporting that he had heard Hakuchō's laughing comment that he was not worried about Kafū's reactions to his article because he had heard that Kafū never read the monthly magazines. How dare Hakuchō publish criticism without giving the object of the criticism the chance to make a rebuttal? [169]

Kafū's rejoinder is unpleasantly haughty, but Hakuchō chose not to adopt a similar tone in his reply. He defended the clarity of his style and the aptness of his observation about the faded charms of Kafū's recent writings. Then, most uncharacteristically, he set about establishing his qualifications for discussing kyōka and gesaku fiction: his great-grandfather was so fond of kyōka that he had officially inscribed himself as the disciple of a well-known master, and Hakuchō had grown up in a house filled with mementos of Ōta Nampo. All the same, he was sure that Nampo, when set beside the important figures of both East and West, was only a minor writer, whose works, even judged as humor, never rose above the level of bad jokes. Hakuchō accused Kafū of an excessive fondness for the Edo past, which was apparently by way of reaction to modern literature, though Kafū seemed not to have read much of modern Japanese authors. Hakuchō was sure that "Edo literature is worthless. Even now, though I take pains to make sure that I will not be infected by its rank odor, I still feel twinges of nostalgia for childhood reading pleasures, and occasionally I sneak a glance over those old books." [170] As for Kafū's accusation that he was being slandered in secret, if that had been Hakuchō's intent he would not have published his article in a magazine so well known as *Chūō Kōron*.

The ronsō between Kafū and Hakuchō is interesting less for its content than for the sidelights cast on the two exceptionally opinionated writers. It was occasioned mainly by Kafū's disdain for Hakuchō and all the other provincials who were responsible for the deterioration of the old Edo culture.

There was no fundamental difference in approach to literature in the somewhat similar ronsō that Hakuchō conducted with Satō Haruo in 1926–1927. Satō innocently began the ronsō with an article entitled "The Literature of Mature Men" in which he expressed his dissatisfaction with the *shinkyō shōsetsu* (mental attitude novel), which had recently become prominent. At best these novels suggest prose-poetry in their delicate and even lyrical evocations of tiny subjects, but more often they are less like fiction than entries in a notebook. Satō deplored especially the lack of criticism of society in works that are single-mindedly devoted to the author's impressions. He asserted that the literature of the 1890s, typified by Kunikida Doppo and Kitamura Tōkoku, had more openly criticized Japanese society than recent works, and blamed this loss of engagement with larger issues on the excessively favorable treatment now accorded to promising young writers by magazine editors. These writers, kept under artificial, hothouse conditions, quickly exhaust their original, lyrical impulses, and have no choice but to shift to the prematurely aged manner appropriate to mental attitude novels. Satō called for a literature that was the work of mature men—neither youths nor old men but men in their prime—a literature that would provide criticism of contemporary culture.[171]

Hakuchō's response was in the avuncular manner of the man who was there when it happened and who feels obliged to set the young people straight: he denied that Doppo and Tōkoku were critics of society. Tōkoku had in fact been considered a highbrow who was untouched by the hurly-burly of current social issues. Takayama Chogyū had expressed indignation over the lack of criticism in precisely those works of Tōkoku that Satō had singled out for their possession of a critical spirit.

Satō replied in terms of hurt surprise. Like Hakuchō confessing his love for Kafū's writings, he described how much Hakuchō's fiction and essays on Saikaku and Dante had meant to him, and how much it pained him now to disagree with an old mentor.

But he has been forced to come out with it: Hakuchō's criticism has always been so nearsighted that it does not permit the reader to understand the age to which the object of the criticism belongs. The insistence on the inner life that was typical of Tōkoku's thought was a criticism of the society, a call for the awakening of the individual in a world that was given over to material advancement. Even a Parnassian might be a critic of society; indeed, both George Moore and Oscar Wilde, advocates of art for art's sake, were rigidly exacting critics, and the same might be said of Baudelaire.[172]

A more substantial difference of opinions was contained in the ronsō of 1926 between Hakuchō and Aono Suekichi (1890–1961), a leading critic associated with the proletarian literature movement. The first contribution to the ronsō was Aono's article "Ten Great Faults of Modern Literature." The first fault he listed was that literature tended to be excessively particular, dealing chiefly with individual impressions of minor events that had occurred close to the author. This was the same fault that Satō had already criticized; and the second fault, that modern literature emphasized technique and contained no ideas, was also similar to Satō's complaint about a lack of criticism of society. Other faults were the overly imitative nature of modern Japanese literature—a dig at the New Sensationalist followers of Paul Morand; the commercialization of literature; and the nihilism found in much Naturalist fiction, especially Hakuchō's. Aono deplored also the failure of modern Japanese literature to suggest that a better society is possible.

It is clear from the general tone as well as from the specific faults listed that Aono was committed to the proletarian literature movement,[173] though one of the faults he listed was the hysterical tendencies of proletarian literature, by which Aono seems to have meant crude expressions of hatred for class enemies. This caveat, together with his reference to the lack of hysteria in the Expressionist and Constructive schools of left-wing literature in Europe, indicated that Aono was concerned with literary as well as political values.

Hakuchō quickly responded. In reply to Aono's complaint about the overemphasis placed on technique, he declared that technique was essential before a writer could achieve anything in a literary career:

When one says that an author's technique is poor, it means that there is no life in what he has written, and when one says that his technique is skillful, it means that what he has written comes alive. Aono says various things about Tolstoy, but is not the portrait Tolstoy painted of Anna, devoid though it is of ideas, incomparably superior to any others drawn in past or present? It is even superior to Tolstoy's portrait of Levin. Literature is surely not an explanation of intellectual ideas.[174]

Hakuchō compared contemporary, politically motivated critics with the patriots of the time of the Meiji Restoration who used Rai San'yō's *Nihon Gaishi* (Unofficial History of Japan) for their own purposes, regardless of what Rai San'yō had originally meant. Critics like Aono, he claimed, would make Japanese literature serve as the instrument for indocrinating people with a certain political philosophy. Such critics would read Bakin not for the story but to learn from him to "encourage virtue and chastise vice"; in other words, they conceptually antedate Tsubouchi Shōyō's *The Essence of the Novel*, which had insisted on the overriding importance of human feelings. Hakuchō gave as his own credo: "I consider that the first consideration of art is that it skillfully depict human life and social conditions, and it has been my aim to advance along this never-ending path. Ideas will of course be present within the life and conditions portrayed, but one does not create works of art as means of expressing ideas." [175] Hakuchō concluded:

The author is free to write poetry or novels for the purpose of propaganda for a political cause, or to draw pictures for the sake of explaining some concept. Countless such works have been created in both East and West since ancient times, and they are by no means unusual. But it is idiotic for critics who have a preference for such works to attempt to drag over to their side people who are headed in a different artistic direction. Tolstoy's ideology has become old but his art has not; the problems with which Ibsen dealt have become outdated, but the people he depicted are still as vivid as they were. In the case of Bakin too, his feudalistic ideology has become outmoded, but his descriptions of certain social conditions still have the power to strike us to the heart.[176]

Aono explained in his reply what he had meant by ideas (*shisō*), and insisted that without some viewpoint it is impossible to criticize or even to describe life and society. This time he stated more plainly than before the kind of viewpoint that he favored: he was sure that unless one took the side of the proletariat one could not understand the true state of social conditions, and it would therefore be impossible to portray these conditions truthfully.[177]

Hakuchō's response, in a now familiar vein, compared Aono to Takayama Chogyū, quoting the latter's complaints about the failure of Meiji novelists to depict the spirit of the age as illustrative of his contention that Aono and his fellows were merely repeating worn-out old arguments. But in two respects Aono was not the equal of Chogyū: the novel *The Lay Priest Takiguchi* demonstrated that Chogyū had warm, lyrical impulses that could still touch the hearts of young people, but it was obvious that Aono had never written poetry, or any work of artistic content. Moreover, Aono's arguments all tended toward the inescapable conclusion that art was useless; why did he take the easy course of being a writer instead of resorting to direct action in the struggle with the capitalists?

Aono replied first to Hakuchō's accusation that he had taken the easy road of art, saying that he had previously encountered the same criticism from within the movement, but that most of the activists had come to recognize the value of his work. He denied Hakuchō's claim that art was the product of leisure: "Recent scientific studies have proved that art did not originate in leisure time. Art originated as work songs that accompanied the muscular rhythm of work." [178] It was difficult for him to direct such harsh words at Hakuchō, for it was reading Hakuchō at an early age that had first opened his eyes to "the dirty reality of human life." [179] Yet there was one aspect of Hakuchō's thought that he could not abide, his celebrated nihilism.[180]

Aono agreed that Hakuchō undoubtedly had individuality, but insisted that it was much less than he supposed; Hakuchō shared with most intellectuals the belief that they could carry on their activities within society and not belong to any class. This misconception was a product of the liberal thought typical of the intellectuals. But liberalism owed its inception and development to the bourgeoisie, as more and more intellectuals have come to realize; that is why there has been a steady movement of former liberals to the ranks of the proletarian movement.

Finally, in response to Hakuchō's charge that he lacked a sense of poetry, Aono related his life story in moving terms, describing how he lost both parents when a small child. His nurse, who had looked after him, lived in acute poverty and one day, yielding to despair over her illness, hanged herself. His education was many times interrupted, and he threw himself for protracted periods into drink and license. For a long time he abandoned literature, but when he became aware of its role in the struggle, he returned. At one point he had been infected by Hakuchō's nihilism, but when he resumed his work with the movement it was with the determination to hasten the collapse of the literature of the bourgeoisie, including Hakuchō's, and to promote the struggle by cultivating the literature of the newly arisen classes. Aono felt indescribable emotion at the thought that he was turning his weapons now against his teacher of many years, but he had made his choice: he would be a simple soldier in the great class enterprise of the liberation of the proletariat, and he would be content if he fell while engaged in this struggle.[181]

In terms of the ronsō Aono came off rather better than Hakuchō, who failed to make his points as effectively as he might have; it is surprising, for example, that he did not address himself to the question of the literary value of the works that had already been produced by the proletarian literary movement in Japan. Nevertheless, this ronsō is of particular interest because the conflicting views are stated unambiguously.

Aono himself seems to have become disillusioned with the progress of the proletarian literature movement as it passed through various internal crises, and by the early 1930s he was no longer considered by the authorities to be a leader of the movement; at any rate, he was not obliged to commit tenkō. During the war years he even wrote with shame of his years as a soldier in the proletarian literature movement. Hakuchō, by comparison, remained cynically aloof from the right-wing hysteria, and wrote nothing in support of the war ideals. His liberalism stayed with him to the end.

Hakuchō's criticism, not only of literature but of the theater, continued to appear in leading magazines until shortly before his death. Most of his postwar works were recollections of the bundan in the old days, including *Shizen Shugi Seisui Shi* (A History of the Rise and Fall of Naturalism, 1948) and *Bundan Gojūnen* (Fifty Years in the Bundan, 1954). He delighted especially in exploding theories advanced by scholars who were not present when the events they describe took place. For example, there was a tendency among "progressive" critics to attach great importance to the Grand Treason trial of Kōtoku Shūsui of 1910–1911 as a watershed in Japanese literary history.[182] Hakuchō, in his last work of criticism, *Hitotsu no Himitsu* (A Secret, 1962), insisted this was not the case:

> Some people grumbled to themselves or muttered angrily, but for the most part the bundan was indifferent. One might argue, I suppose, that people were only pretending to be indifferent, fearful for their lives if they inadvertently expressed dissatisfaction, but that was not the whole story; it was my impression that the response was *really* one of indifference. . . . And if someone should ask me whether, in view of the graveness of the incident, I personally did not feel secret indignation deep down in my heart, curse life itself, lose all interest in food and all capacity to sleep soundly at night, I would have to reply that I experienced nothing even remotely resembling such emotions.[183]

Hakuchō to the end remained a debunker, a man who refused to follow the herd in its unquestioning acceptance of currently fashionable beliefs. His crankiness should not, however, obscure his genuine gifts as a critic; his essays are as stimulating today as when he first wrote them.

HIROTSU KAZUO (1891–1968)

Hakuchō was undoubtedly the central figure in literary criticism during most of the Taishō era. Like two other important critics of the period, Hirotsu Kazuo and Satō Haruo, he considered himself to be primarily a writer rather than a critic, but his commonsensical essays lacked the grace one might expect of a novelist and playwright. Hirotsu and Satō, by contrast, wrote criticism that was not only effective but often moving in its expression.

Hirotsu's father was the Ken'yūsha novelist Hirotsu Ryūrō.

After the death of his mentor, Ozaki Kōyō, in 1903, the father seems to have lost his touch as a writer, and Hirotsu Kazuo was obliged to work his way through Waseda, mainly by translating (from English translations) works by various Russian and French authors, including Chekhov, Tolstoy, and Maupassant. At Waseda he fell under the spell of Shimamura Hōgetsu, about whom he would write several essays, but he was influenced less by Hōgetsu's advocacy of Naturalism than by the nihilism that Hirotsu detected in his attitude toward life.[184] Hirotsu became something of a nihilist himself, despite his strong sense of social responsibility. He was also attracted to Masamune Hakuchō, whose stories, beginning with "Where To?" were filled with the kind of nihilism he had admired in Hōgetsu. Hirotsu's sense of decency was outraged, however, when he read Hakuchō's story "Clay Doll," written shortly after his marriage, which described his bride with unveiled contempt.[185] But even this disillusion did not destroy his respect for Hakuchō.

Hirotsu began his career as a critic in 1916 with the publication of monthly bungei jihyō in the magazine *Kōzui Igo* (After the Deluge), which were praised by such notables as Ikuta Chōkō. Later that year Hirotsu published his first studies of Tolstoy. At the time Tolstoy was worshiped in Japan not only as a great novelist but as the supreme humanist, and it took courage for Hirotsu to publish criticism of this idol. "Ikareru Torusutoi" (The Wrathful Tolstoy, 1916) and "Shiga Naoya Ron" (On Shiga Naoya, 1919), Hirotsu's two most admired pieces of literary criticism, have been described as "monuments" of the Taishō era.[186]

Hirotsu listed at the head of "The Wrathful Tolstoy" the five commandments that Tolstoy had formulated from the teachings of Christ: do not be angry; do not lust; do not bind yourself by oaths; do not resist evil with evil; do not become an enemy to others. Tolstoy had given greatest emphasis to the fourth of these commandments, but Hirotsu believed that the first was the most basic because it not only subsumed the fourth, which deals with the relations between man and man, or between the individual and society, but also the relations between man and God.[187] He was convinced that nothing harmed the spirit so much as wrath, because it impaired the life-force that God has bestowed on the individual. Wrath is an act of blasphemy directed at both God and infinity.[188]

As these remarks indicate, Hirotsu was not simply introducing Tolstoy's ideas, in the manner typical of Meiji writers when discussing foreign authors, but critically examining them; and the condemnation of wrath, together with the title "The Wrathful Tolstoy," demonstrated that his attitude was by no means worshipful. Hirotsu modestly disclaimed any special knowledge of the Bible, but obviously he had read it carefully, and he quoted a wide variety of Russian authors from published Japanese translations. The judgments he pronounced on Tolstoy's works and beliefs bespoke an assurance born of careful preparations, unlike the flashes of intuitive understanding more common in criticism of his day. Hirotsu was sure that Tolstoy's unhappiness originated in his inability to restrain his wrath, and that this poisonous element in his disposition revealed itself in his works, especially *The Death of Ivan Ilyitch* and *The Kreutzer Sonata*:

> Tolstoy stated in his diary that he was confident that *The Kreutzer Sonata* had in some way benefited mankind. Probably it was of some benefit in that it exposed and described the falsehood of modern civilization, especially the falsehood of married life. But it actually brought mankind more irritation than benefit. *The Kreutzer Sonata* is of no significance to the possessor of a tranquil soul. It is nothing more than an extremely annoying and boring story.[189]

Hirotsu summed up his impressions of Tolstoy in the following terms:

> What does Tolstoy's life have to teach us? Or, at any rate, what does it have to teach me? Tolstoy received from God the greatest life-force possessed by any human being, but he controlled it with an intelligence than was less than ten percent of the life-force. When the huge, elephantlike life-force tried to crawl through the truth, no bigger than the eye of a needle, which his intelligence had taught him, it struggled and suffered. Life-force itself is blind. And this blind man knew nothing except how to suffer in accordance with the guidance it received.
>
> I learned too from Tolstoy the magnanimity of God. This was not because Tolstoy explained it to me; it was because of the fact that in whichever way a man may try to direct with his limited

awareness the life-force God has given him, in the end God will watch in silence. I kneel before the grandeur of God.

It may be that Christianity made Tolstoy unhappy. But the fault was not in Christianity.[190]

It will be evident from these extracts that Hirotsu's criticism was formulated on a higher plane than anything by Masamune Hakuchō. The language is at times unclear, though later essays were more lucidly stated, presumably because Hirotsu was attempting to convey ideas that were by nature more complex than the commonsensical observations typical of the criticism of Hakuchō. Whether or not Hirotsu's ideas successfully illuminate the art of Tolstoy, his courage in his convictions was noteworthy. He was sure that he had something new to say about Tolstoy and that he had every right to say it. Earlier Japanese critics who had discussed European literature, even Natsume Sōseki, had confessed they found it impossible to appreciate it in the same manner as someone who had been born within the culture that produced this literature, but Hirotsu made no such disclaimers. He had read Tolstoy attentively and discovered contradictions between the man and his philosophy, which he felt impelled to point out to Japanese readers. Hirotsu's essay marked the beginning of an independent Japanese attitude toward masterpieces of European literature, which hitherto had been accepted with unquestioning reverence.

Hirotsu nowhere stated what had led him to make his criticism of Tolstoy. Perhaps it was on emerging from a period of uncritical admiration, or after discovering "poisonous elements" within his idol. Hirotsu's next choice of an idol, however, remained one to the end: Shiga Naoya. Hirotsu's essay on Shiga is filled not only with testimony to Shiga's profound personal appeal, but may well be the finest analysis ever made of Shiga's special importance in the history of modern Japanese literature.

Hirotsu's essay opened with a description of why it was so much more difficult to analyze Shiga's writings than those of such contemporaries as Mushakōji Saneatsu, Arishima Takeo, or Iwano Hōmei, all of whom presented their views on life within their works. Shiga never offered his philosophy in an overt form; with a few exceptions, his works were devoted exclusively to what he had seen, heard, touched, or felt. In the literal sense of the words, he was always talking about himself. When Shiga described his experiences, he avoided explanations; his eyes were always fastened on the concrete rather than the abstract, the individual rather than the general. In this sense he was a consummate realist. Unlike the Naturalists, who often dropped into sentimentality despite their professions of objectivity, Shiga's vision was clear and absolutely unsentimental.

Shiga's style was so concise and simple that he could say as much in two or three lines as most authors in twenty or thirty. His materials were equally uncomplicated: for the most part he used materials that other writers had overlooked, often discovering something within the most trivial incident that permitted him to penetrate the surfaces of people and events. His skill at manipulating his materials was astonishing, but he was not an "artist" in the usual sense: his vision was too severe and uncompromising to permit him to search for beauty alone. He always observed both good and evil; indeed, he seemed incapable of shutting his eyes. Yet, though his gaze was invariably level-headed and acute, he never stooped to the mockery that was common among writers of his disposition. He manifested instead both melancholy and compassion, evidence that the compass needle of his mind never wavered.

Hirotsu was attracted above all by Shiga's character, as he discerned it through Shiga's writings. His almost morbid dislike of the inharmonious, unnatural, unjust, or ugly caused him to reiterate, so often that they became almost a mannerism, such words as *fukai* (disagreeable). Hirotsu admired the "oriental calm" of such an essay as "At Kinosaki." He concluded with his only expression of dissatisfaction:

> I can't keep hoping, most of all, that a man of Shiga Naoya's character will fight, as the times require. I believe that if ever Mr. Shiga, not fearful of the pain of his mind exploding, should press forward and confront life, more naked than ever before, he would display for the first time, in full force, what his keen intelligence, pure heart, and strong character can contribute to mankind.[191]

Shiga never fulfilled Hirotsu's hopes that he would "explode" and offer his intelligence and character to a cause. Instead, it was

Hirotsu himself who sacrificed everything else to righting the injustice of the Matsukawa trial between 1954 and 1961.[192]

Hirotsu participated in various ronsō. The best-known dealt with "the art of prose" and had Hirotsu and Satō Haruo on one side, Ikuta Chōkō on the other. Hirotsu opened the ronsō with the article "Sambun Geijutsu no Ichi" (The Place of the Art of Prose, 1924). He began by discussing "art for art's sake," as exemplified by the Phoenix Hall—Byōdō-in—in Uji, which has "wings" that stretch so close to the ground (for aesthetic effect) that an adult cannot pass underneath; the sole consideration of the architect was beauty, and the possible functions of the "wings" were not considered. But, Hirotsu insisted, modern prose literature cannot be justified in terms of pure art. He recalled Arishima Takeo's division of artists into three categories: (1) the pure artist, who is too completely immersed in his work to think of anything else; (2) the artist who cannot live without constant reference to his life and surroundings; and (3) the opportunistic, compromising artist who writes whatever suits the times or occasion. Arishima had dismissed the third category as being unworthy of the name of artist. He wished that he (like Izumi Kyōka) belonged to the first category, but had to confess that he was instead of the inferior second category. Hirotsu questioned Arishima's preference for the "pure" artist, finding it hard to imagine a writer so exclusively concerned with his art that he had no time to spare for the rest of the world. This led to the most celebrated remark of the ronsō: "Of all the many varieties of art, the art of prose is the one that neighbors most closely on human life. Its neighbors to the right include various other arts, including poetry, painting, and music, but to the left it abuts directly on human life." [193]

In November 1924 Satō Haruo published an article in support of Hirotsu's views. He noted the relative newness of prose as compared to poetry, reminding readers that although Aristotle had written a *Poetics*, nobody had written a *Prosaics*; indeed, the word "prosaic" had come to be a term of abuse. Satō thought that the art of prose could be traced back to Balzac, or at any rate to the time when writers first found it desirable in the course of a story to describe what the hero did to earn a living, or where he obtained the money he needed for his rendezvous with his girl friend.[194] Satō supposed that in ancient times prose was no more than a deformation of poetry, but modern poetry had tended to become increasingly like prose. Poetry typified mankind in the first bloom of youth, but prose represents mankind in its prime, when writers have come to know themselves and have received the baptism of reality.[195]

Ikuta Chōkō, replying to both Hirotsu and Satō, characterized recent Japanese literary critics as being afraid of scholarship; they were all too ready to deduce great truths from sudden flashes of illumination that lacked the benefit of scholarly backing. He disagreed with Arishima's descending order of writers, asking if men like Tolstoy, Dostoevski, and Strindberg, all of whom obviously belonged to the second category, should be considered inferior to Izumi Kyōka.[196] The essay continued in this manner, querying or mocking every statement by Hirotsu or Satō. Ikuta Chōkō was not a fool, but he often sounded like one or, at any rate, like a willfully uncomprehending man. His essay served no other purpose than to elicit from Hirotsu a more coherent statement of his views, including the admission that although he still revered Tolstoy, he could no longer read *War and Peace* with pleasure. He regretted this, but had to confess that he was now more attracted to new writers than to the nineteenth-century masters, the same discovery that Ikuta Chōkō had made years earlier.

The 1920s marked the apogee of Hirotsu's activities as a critic, though he published bungei jihyō, studies of Tokuda Shūsei and Shimazaki Tōson, and contributions to various ronsō even as late as 1951, when he and Nakamura Mitsuo debated the merits of Camus's novel *L'étranger*. The opinions expressed in this ronsō suggested that Hirotsu had fallen behind the times, at least in his capacity to appreciate new literature; [197] but Hirotsu had lost none of his humanistic concern.

SATŌ HARUO (1892–1964)

Satō's most important work as a critic was written during the Taishō era. A collection of the essays that had appeared between 1915 and 1926 was published under the intriguing title of *Taikutsu Tokuhon* (A Textbook of Boredom, 1926).[198] Despite the title, this is surely one of the most delightful examples of modern zuihitsu, and the critical insights are sometimes dazzling. The most striking feature of the book is the distinctive personality revealed on each page. Satō wrote with wit, a rare commodity in the Japanese literary criticism of this period, and with unerring discernment.

Although Satō was an unmistakable individualist, he was also conscious of belonging to the bundan, and sometimes discoursed on its functions:

> I get the impression that the bundan has become just another professional organization, no different from a fraternity of *geta* makers, a gang of rickshaw coolies, a bakers' guild, a gaggle of politicians, or the whole mass of officialdom. It is not my intention to slander the society composed of modern writers as being inferior to other societies; all I am saying is that it is no different from any other profession. That is the simple truth, but I wonder if members of the bundan do not think of the lives that they lead as being especially elevated? First of all, is it not true that our work, in relation to the amount of labor involved, is better paid than any other profession? Indeed, literature is now an economically viable occupation for anyone who has the talent to string together a few words; and if he has a modicum of practical wisdom, he can make a fortune as a writer; and, provided he has this practical wisdom, his literary ability is only of secondary importance. All one has to do is to spend ten years or so, like an apprentice serving out his term, close to the atmosphere of the bundan and one's manuscripts will somehow or other start to sell. . . . The poverty of members of the bundan is now a thing of the past. In this respect ours is a truly wonderful age. Does this mean, then, that literature is now so highly valued by society? And does literature itself enjoy such influence over society? No, that is naturally quite a different kettle of fish. In fact, it would be more accurate to say that the opposite is the case. I would even go so far as to say that literature, as a social phenomenon, has never had less authority than at present.[199]

Satō went on to explain this paradox in terms of the loss of the writer's autonomy: in exchange for being well paid, the writer is obliged to conform to the restraints that society has imposed on literature. Because literature is now a commodity for sale, writers have no choice but to obey the rules of the marketplace.

Satō's tone as he described the prosperous bundan created by Kikuchi Kan was not one of indignation but of amusement, and his opinions throughout *A Textbook of Boredom* make enjoyable reading. Only occasionally does he sound thoroughly in earnest, as when he discusses the vocation of the artist. Perhaps because of his readings in Oscar Wilde and George Moore, Satō early became convinced that he was a true artist, and he never had occasion to doubt it; his generalizations on the subject of what it means to be an artist therefore usually have autobiographical overtones. His confidence in his artistic judgments was absolute, as was his belief that whatever he chose to write would be of interest to everyone of taste.

In 1919 Kikuchi Kan published an article called "The Failure of Impressionistic Criticism" in which he deplored the irresponsibility of critics who merely relate their impressions, and urged them to draw up new criteria for judging literature that will be acceptable to all readers. Satō, in his reply, doubted that it would ever be possible to create such standards; but even if it were possible, they would be undesirable:

> I cannot believe that "creative criticism" has for its sole basis the silly aphorisms of Wilde, which Kikuchi quotes. I have been rather taken aback that Kikuchi should have reached such conclusions. Yes, I suppose it is true that impressionistic criticism does not contain a measuring rod applicable to all subjects. But in true impressionistic criticism the character of one man—the critic—itself becomes a measuring rod. . . . However, in our bundan at present the only kinds of criticism one finds are opportunistic criticism, timid criticism, and criticism that attempts to keep its lack of principles from being detected. Impressionistic criticism . . . has turned into a strange performance, which consists of the efforts of the critic to keep from showing himself honestly. . . .
>
> I am an impressionistic critic through and through. Everything I write is in terms of "I think." And it is my position that being true to myself is honesty. . . .[200]

Satō's confidence in the interest of whatever he wrote was substantiated by the essays in *A Textbook of Boredom*. Even when a book or an author he is discussing has been quite forgotten, his comments are absorbing in themselves. Perhaps the most striking essays are those in which he rated contemporary authors, often in a biting sentence or two. He was on the whole amiably disposed toward Mushakōji Saneatsu, but he could also write: "To read the

Complete Works of Mushakōji would be daunting, but his selected works will surely always be read. . . . An extremely small-format edition may suffice for the selected works." [201]

Satō had devastating observations to make on the lack of intellectual content in Tanizaki's work; [202] and he offered the caustic advice to Akutagawa Ryūnosuke that he should rid himself of his aversion to stripping himself naked and confessing, the only way for him to escape from the straitjacket of his reserve.[203] Other writers, like Kikuchi Kan or Kume Masao, fared even worse: Satō had nothing to say about the former, and about the latter he could praise only his ability to be up to the minute on what the public wanted to read.[204] He was more friendly about Hirotsu Kazuo, from whom major work might be expected in the future, but his conclusion was no less damning: "It may be that Hirotsu will exercise a greater influence on the next generation by his conversations than by anything he has written." [205]

The one contemporary whom Satō praised unreservedly was Shiga Naoya. The style of *Reconciliation* reminded him of classical Chinese in its bold lines, virility, and body, unexampled even in European literature. He continued:

> And it is not only a matter of style. He has portrayed with absolute realism, but at the same time with high density, a world that is extremely plain in its coloring. He has treated this poetryless world just as it is, and without in any way converting it into poetry, faithfully delineating the segment of reality he has chosen. Only if one first makes a clear mirror of one's mind can one reflect so much. Even I, who have the bad habit of always saying something slightly different from everybody else, have no way of opposing the accepted opinion that Shiga has discovered a new domain of literature, one filled with dignity and with a calm, underlying strength. I confess it: I find his dignity absolutely extraordinary.[206]

Satō's criticism is hard to distinguish from zuihitsu, but perhaps the difference was not of great significance. He knew instinctively what was good and bad in contemporary literature, and expressed his opinions with easy eloquence. Scholars who discuss the development of literary criticism in Japan sometimes dismiss everything before the arrival on the literary scene of the 1930s of Kobayashi Hideo as being unworthy of the name of criticism; but the novelist and critic Maruya Saiichi insisted that Kobayashi was preceded by Masamune Hakuchō and Satō Haruo. He observed that although the development of a new and more evolved form of criticism under Kobayashi's inspiration was a matter for congratulation, he could not help feeling a certain stiffness in Kobayashi's essays. He hoped that this was not merely a failure on his part to appreciate Kobayashi's subtleties; when he read the informal remarks made by Kobayashi in the course of a zadankai or in a dialogue with another writer he felt for the first time that Kobayashi was really addressing him, in an unconstrained, steady flow of ideas. This was precisely how Satō's essays always struck him.

Pre-Shōwa literary criticism was for the most part the work of amateurs, but these were exceptionally gifted amateurs; and on the whole it is more enjoyable to read them than the sometimes cryptic pronouncements of later critics, who often left their readers behind. The development of a more evolved kind of criticism, based on a knowledge of contemporary European criticism, was indeed a matter for congratulation, as Maruya stated, but it did not render obsolete the kind of criticism in which men like Masamune Hakuchō, Hirotsu Kazuo, and Satō Haruo had excelled.

THE SHŌWA PERIOD (FROM 1927)

AT THE BEGINNING of the Shōwa period two schools of literary criticism enjoyed special authority: one associated with the proletarian literature movement, and the other with the Modernists, especially the New Sensationalists.[207] The Modernists, notably Yokomitsu Riichi and Kawabata Yasunari, published some stimulating, if not always persuasive, essays, but the world of literary criticism of the late 1920s and early 1930s was dominated by Marxism; about 80 percent of the criticism published in literary or general (*sōgō*) magazines was by Marxists. There were not many peculiarly Japanese developments in Marxist literary theory, but (in part because of governmental pressure) factions had divided the movement. All factions accepted such basic principles as the class struggle, but differing weight was given to purely literary as opposed to social values. Some of the Marxist criticism is still worth reading, and the movement itself has proved to be of seemingly inexhaustible interest to scholars who have written about Japanese literature in the twentieth century. But the importance of the proletarian critics was vitiated by the scarcity of works of literary value written in accordance with the principles they advocated. All the same, the proletarian literature movement is more likely to be remembered for its criticism than for the novels, poetry, or plays it inspired.

Even the best works of proletarian criticism, however, rarely exhibit more than local variations on themes first conceived in Europe; there were no Japanese literary critics of the stature of, say, Georg Lukács or Christopher Caudwell. Proletarian criticism, along with the rest of the movement, was stamped out by governmental persecution in the early 1930s, and the critics were compelled either to renounce publicly their Marxist convictions or to write on exclusively nonpolitical subjects. It proved to be not impossible for the proletarian critics to find common ground with the militarists. Such slogans as "Asia for the Asians" could be subscribed to by both, though with different overtones, and the study of folk literature similarly could be made to serve as evidence of the glory of the Japanese race, in the right-wing manner, or to demonstrate that the common people had literary traditions even more important than those of the aristocrats. The persistence of Marxist convictions, however concealed during the decade of repression, was revealed by the astonishing rapidity with which the main figures of the proletarian literature movement regained their old authority after the war, and by the pervasive influence they exerted even on academic critics, who were anxious not to appear to be feudalistic remnants of the discredited "National Learning."

Marxist literary criticism of the postwar years was particularly concerned with the distinctions between "democratic" and "feudalistic" literature. This was true even of writing on the ancient Japanese classics. One professor dismissed *The Pillow-Book* of Sei Shōnagon as the work of a "spiritual cripple" because of her offensive remarks about the lower classes, and failed to mention the *Kokinshū* in his survey of Heian literature, presumably because the poetry was composed by members of the nobility.[208] *The Tale of Genji* was interpreted as the account of the struggle between the lower and upper echelons of the aristocracy, and the lives of the celebrated writers were intently studied in the hopes of proving that, contrary to common belief, they were members of the commoner class. Saikaku emerged as a powerful adversary of the Tokugawa regime; Chikamatsu's heroes and heroines died because of the contradictions in feudal society; and Bashō's poetry was filled with thinly veiled social comment. Such statements, not made with the intention of parody, acquired surprising authority.

Regardless of whether one admires or rejects this criticism, it was undeniably more systematic than the writings of Shimamura Hōgetsu or Masamune Hakuchō. It provided a framework of basic beliefs, which critics could apply to old or new works. Sometimes this ideological criticism provided fresh insights into hidden themes of which the authors themselves might not have been aware. Moreover, even the most committed Marxist critic was sometimes unable to overcome his love for literary works despite ideological differences: the martyred Communist writer Kobayashi Takiji addressed worshipful letters to Shiga Naoya, a writer who shared none of his enthusiasm for proletarian writings.

It is unnecessary here to describe the convictions of Marxist literary critics of the 1920s and 1930s; the principles involved will be familiar to anyone who has read Marxist criticism, regardless of the country where it was written. The extraordinary success of the Marxist critics in gaining control of so much of the literary world during the early Shōwa years was surely more a reflection of the political climate than of their intrinsic merits as critics.

It might be noted in passing that nonpolitical systems of criticism, whether the Modernism of the New Sensationalists or psychoanalytic criticism in the traditions of Freud and Jung, played a relatively inconspicuous role in Japan both before and after the war. Nonpolitical criticism tended to be individual, rather than the activity of a recognizable group. Only in the 1960s did the younger critics, especially those in the academic world, show real interest in such European systems of criticism as those of the Russian Formalists or Structuralism and attempt to apply them to Japanese literature.

It seems likely, however, that the first fifty or so years of Shōwa criticism will be remembered largely in terms of the work of one man, Kobayashi Hideo, who from the very outset of his career was strongly opposed to any kind of critical system, dismissing them all as mere "designs." It is hard to imagine what Shōwa criticism would have been like without Kobayashi, though we can be fairly sure that it would not have developed so greatly, nor would it have come to command the attention not only of persons professionally interested in literature but of the general public. Kobayashi's criticism was so skillfully and imaginatively written that his articles continued to be read even when the books or people he criticized had been forgotten. He was by no means the only critic of importance during the period, but he may be said to have created modern Japanese criticism.

KOBAYASHI HIDEO (1902–1983)

Kobayashi was born in Tokyo, the son of a professor at the Tokyo Higher Engineering School, and was educated at the most elite schools in the country: the First Middle School, the First High School, and Tokyo University. This education normally prepared young men for positions in the government, but Kobayashi, along with the friends he made at these schools, became passionately interested in literature, especially French literature. While still in high school he joined various *dōnin zasshi*, in which he published several short stories—his only works of fiction. He became friendly with Tominaga Tarō (1901–1925), a brilliant though short-lived poet, and it was through Tominaga that Kobayashi met in 1925 the more celebrated poet Nakahara Chūya (1907–1937).[209] Kobayashi fell in love with Nakahara's mistress, and eventually took her away, much to Nakahara's chagrin and anger. Kobayashi led a tempestuous life with the woman until after his graduation from Tokyo University in 1928; unable to endure the constant disputes any longer, he deserted her and went to Nara, to be near Shiga Naoya, the writer whom he most admired. He spent much of his time in Nara looking at old temples and sculptures with mingled pleasure and irritation that he did not know more about them.[210] He read the first two volumes of Proust, mainly because they were the only books he had with him, but Proust did not interest him much, and he never looked at his works again.[211] Kobayashi also spent some of that year in the Kansai wandering the streets of Osaka, as we know from a memorable passage in his *Mozart* (1946).

It was Tominaga who urged Kobayashi while he was still in high school to read Baudelaire, and before long Baudelaire and Poe (whom he read in Baudelaire's translation) became his favorite authors.[212] In 1929 he wrote an essay expressing indignation that the Japanese bundan considered Poe as a "writer of strange tales whose work is finished." He himself was sure that no serious literary criticism could be made that ignored Poe.[213] But the critical "meeting" for Kobayashi was with Rimbaud. Here is how he described this event twenty-two years later (in 1947):

> My first encounter with Rimbaud took place when I was twenty-three, in the spring. At the time, as I recall, I was strolling aimlessly through Kanda. An unknown man, coming from the opposite direction, suddenly knocked me to the ground. I was completely unprepared. I had never dreamed that such a tremendous charge of dynamite could be planted in the miserable little pocket-sized Mercure edition of *Une saison en enfer*, which I accidentally discovered in the stall outside a bookstore. The detonating device of this bomb was so sensitive that my shaky command of French was hardly even an issue. The little book exploded in great style, and for several years I was caught up in the whirlpool of the event called Rimbaud. It was definitely an event. Whatever literature may mean to other people, for me at least an idea, a conception, even a single word is an event, and it seems as if it was Rimbaud who taught me so.
>
> I allowed this "astonishing traveler," to use Mallarmé's phrase, to wander at will the length and breadth of my youthful spirit, but I have no way now of tracing the path left by his footsteps. Probably this is because I experienced to the extreme the reality of what is generally referred to vaguely as "influence." [214]

In 1963, during the course of a discussion with the critics Nakamura Mitsuo and Fukuda Tsuneari, Kobayashi suggested what had attracted him to Rimbaud even more than to Baudelaire:

> When I think back on it now, I realize that I had not found Rimbaud's images in Baudelaire. They're closer to a Japanese than Baudelaire's. That's what impressed me. . . . They're close to the images in a Japanese *uta* or haiku. . . . There's nature in them, nature. You won't find nature in Baudelaire. . . . Rimbaud's extremely real images accorded with something hidden deep in my consciousness, except that it was not my consciousness but what

might be called my racial consciousness as a Japanese, a question of analogy between the forms of the symbolic strength of things or of conception, call it what you please.[215]

This statement (which is somewhat less coherent in the original than in translation) was made informally, perhaps under the influence of liquor. It should not be accepted uncritically, but it suggests that Kobayashi in his sixties had come to recognize the Japanese core to his beliefs, though the major part of his career had been devoted to studies of European writers, painters, and musicians. The degree of the Japaneseness of his criticism is difficult to measure, if only because Kobayashi wrote so little about his literary interests before he fell under the spell of Baudelaire and the others. There can hardly be any doubt that his readings in French poetry and criticism had induced him to become a critic himself.

At Tokyo University Kobayashi's enthusiasm for Rimbaud, originally aroused in the manner described above, caused him to devote his first published essay (which appeared in 1926 in the journal of the French Department of the university), and his graduation thesis, presented in 1928, to Rimbaud; but he also read widely in other modern French writers, including Alain, Bergson, Valéry, and Mallarmé. Perhaps Bergson's influence proved in the end to be the most lasting: Kobayashi's distrust of general theories and universal systems, as well as his reliance on intuition, was probably confirmed by readings in Bergson.[216]

Kobayashi made his debut in the literary world with the partial translation of André Gide's *Paludes*, published in 1928. In the same year he began to publish anonymously in *Bungei Shunjū* a serialized biography of Baudelaire. His arrival in the literary world, however, came in 1929, when an essay submitted to the magazine *Kaizō* was awarded second prize in a competition for works of criticism by new writers. Kobayashi was astonished to receive only the second prize; even before writing his article he was self-confidently sure that he would take first prize. First prize was in fact awarded to Miyamoto Kenji for "Haiboku no Bungaku" (The Literature of Defeat), a criticism of the writings of Akutagawa Ryūnosuke by a man who would soon devote his full energies to the Japanese Communist party. Miyamoto's essay was his best piece of criticism and is now considered to be a classic, but he probably won first prize not because his essay was superior to Kobayashi's but because of the predominance of the left wing in the literary world of the time.[217]

Kobayashi's essay, "Samazama naru Ishō" (Designs of Various Kinds), opens with an epigraph by André Gide: "Doubt may mark the beginning of wisdom. But where wisdom begins, art ends." Kobayashi himself clearly doubted the validity of the "wisdom" provided by the different "designs," or theories of literature, he analyzed: "People say, 'It's easy enough to criticize somebody else on the basis of one's own tastes.' But it is equally easy to judge another person with a measuring rod. The hard thing is to possess tastes that remain constantly alive, and a measuring rod that is vibrant with vitality." [218]

Kobayashi obviously meant by the term "measuring rod" (*shakudo*) fixed standards; unlike critics who believed in the possibility of scientific, objective criticism based on unchanging standards, he insisted that criticism, if it is to be effective, must be personal and alive, susceptible of change as the critic's tastes mature. In this respect he resembled Satō Haruo, but he referred not only to his own personal tastes but to those of admired French critics.

> It is by no means clear to me what the literary historians mean by the term "impressionistic criticism," but one thing is absolutely clear: when I have models of impressionistic criticism before me— for example, the literary criticism of Baudelaire—I am swept away like a boat in the waves by his precise analyses and lively sensitivity. While under the spell of his sorcery, I am looking not at the form of his tastes or the form of a measuring rod, but at his dreams, which have assumed a form of incomparable passion. It is certainly criticism, but it is also a monologue.[219]

These beliefs, enunciated at the very outset of Kobayashi's career, would run through his entire work. He is always at once discussing himself and the object of his criticism, not using one for the sake of bringing out the other, but doubling the intensity of the light. His many admirers prize his writings, as he prized Baudelaire's, not for their persuasive exposition of a critical system but as testimonies to his passion. He claimed not to be interested in universality in criticism: "What artist, past or present, has aimed at that monster called universality? Without exception, they have aimed at the particular. . . . The supreme writer is always the most individual. Dogmatism and individuality are not the same thing." [220] But his writings, though individual, have appealed to such a wide variety of readers that they surely can be said to approach the universal.

The first system (or "design") discussed by Kobayashi in his essay was Marxist literary criticism, no doubt because it was the most prominent at the time. He wryly remarked that, just as Plato expelled poets from his *Republic*, so has Marx driven them from *Das Kapital*. He disliked the slogan "Art for the Proletariat!" It was easy enough to order artists to obey this rule, but hard for them to comply. If a work of art succeeds, it is not because of its ideology but because it has been "stained with the author's blood." [221] He next considered the "design" of "art for art's sake," of which he also disapproved, insisting that no work of art should "lose the smell of humankind." Toward the close of the essay he wrote disapprovingly of both New Sensationalism and "mass literature." In fact, he disapproved of all the "designs" he presented; there was no "design" that matched the one he had formed from his readings in French literature. In 1928, when he wrote this essay, critics were invariably identified as belonging to some "school," and for Kobayashi to reject them all made his position almost untenable. He persisted, perhaps in order to secure the "self-awareness" that he believed to be the basis of criticism.[222] Not until the mid-1930s would the influence of his criticism become apparent in the bundan, though from the start he attracted young writers, even those who could not fully understand him.

The difficulty of Kobayashi's writings was made an issue by writers who disliked him for whatever reason. In an essay (published in 1930) about Takii Kōsaku and Makino Shin'ichi, two novelists whom he "discovered," Kobayashi answered charges that Takii's writings were difficult: "So they are, but it is a contradiction in terms to speak of a masterly style that is easy to read. Difficulty is an adjunct of the best prose styles. . . . A masterly style defends itself from and resists being easily understood by inattentive readers." [223] Kobayashi declared that even works by such writers as Shiga Naoya or Tanizaki Jun'ichirō, which seem perfectly clear, have overtones or shadings that will escape the careless reader. His insistence on the crucial importance of style in literary expression was by no means unique, but he conveyed this concern by creating a distinctive style of his own. When no existing Japanese word expressed exactly the nuance he intended, he did not hesitate to coin new words or to use old words in unexpected senses. The syntax also departed from normal Japanese usage. Kobayashi saw no need to simplify or clarify his style; instead, he attacked from strength:

> I frequently hear the strange complaint that my criticism is difficult. I do not recall ever having advanced any difficult arguments. Nor do I recall having even mentioned any theories, except to state what absurd window-dressing difficult theories make. . . .
>
> I know. My criticism is a hundred times more difficult than your novels. But it is a thousand times easier than the novels of Balzac. It is a disgrace for anyone who pretends to be an author to find my simple arguments difficult. What is the easiest thing for you, anyway? You probably haven't the courage to answer, so I'll answer for you. Any kind of theory is difficult for your empty intelligences, and the only thing that is easy for you is real life.[224]

The tone of certitude is offensive, but perhaps not unnatural in a young critic. In 1936, replying to charges made about the obscurity of his expression, Kobayashi stated: "I have doubted and believed all sorts of things over the years, but if there is one thing I have always unwaveringly believed, it is the principle of the ordinariness of the critic." [225]

Kobayashi's use of the term "ordinariness" (*jinjō*) is puzzling. Surely he realized that his criticism was anything but ordinary. Probably he wished to distinguish himself from critics who resorted to high-flown, abstract arguments, instead of addressing themselves directly to the works of literature, art, or music they described. Kobayashi did not seek to persuade readers of any philosophy, nor to call attention to himself as a sensitive and superior being, but he described the work of criticism as "self-attestation" (*jiko shōmei*); his works of criticism were in fact discussed as segments of an autobiography, or even as "I novels" by Nakamura Mitsuo in his book on Kobayashi. The "I novels" of

Kobayashi were not revelations of personal secrets, in the usual manner, but form a spiritual autobiography, a record of his growth as he responded to the works before him.

Having established a reputation with "Designs of Various Kinds," Kobayashi was asked by *Bungei Shunjū* to contribute monthly literary chronicles (*bungei jihyō*). Obviously he did not much enjoy reading and discussing a typical month's production of Japanese literature. In a 1935 essay Kobayashi expressed his annoyance with authors who complained that he had not been sufficiently kind in his reviews, and asked sardonically what kindness contemporary authors have ever shown the critics. The only kindness a critic really wants from authors is that they will supply him with the basis for writing decent criticism; but present-day authors do precisely the opposite. Hirotsu Kazuo had expressed annoyance with the critics for having directed the full barrage of their erudition on a novel that had been written merely as a newspaper serial; but anyone who publishes such works should expect whatever criticism he receives. Referring to Hirotsu's novel, he added: "It would be easy to extract from *Fūu tsuyokarubeshi* (There Will Be Strong Wind and Rain) the dilemma of the intelligentsia. It would be equally easy to discover in this work the problem of the newspaper serial. The one difficult thing would be to be moved by this novel." [226]

Diving (1934), a novel by Funahashi Seiichi (1904–1976), had created quite a sensation in the bundan, largely because it dealt with Activism (*kōdō shugi*), the new literary philosophy introduced from Europe. Kobayashi thought that it would make better sense, rather than attempt to evaluate *Diving* as a work of literature, to look into the peculiarities of the bundan that makes a fuss over such novels. Kobayashi's irritation at having to read works of no intrinsic value made him doubt literary criticism that was focused on the bundan, and led to the sad conclusion: "If there were no such thing as bungei jihyō, critics today would have trouble eating." [227]

Kobayashi's article elicited sharp responses from critics who thought he was attempting to deprive them of a livelihood by attacking bungei jihyō, but he denied this, citing the instance of Sainte-Beuve's *Causeries de lundi* as an example of what might be achieved in this form, unlikely though it was in the Japanese literary world. He described the French critics who had impressed him most, adding: "It was they who taught me the art of literary criticism. No, I should say I learned everything from them. I was not taught one word, one syllable even, by the older Japanese critics. And it is only today, when I have come to make a living from bungei jihyō, that I have become aware of the jerry-built foundations on which we stand. Only by stretching myself on tiptoes am I able to get a glimpse of *their* bungei jihyō." [228]

Kobayashi felt unspeakably envious of the climate of criticism that had surrounded Sainte-Beuve, who had written, "True criticism is born of conversation." That was the case in Paris, but literary conversation in Tokyo could never give rise to anything resembling the criticism of the French writers. Sometimes, Kobayashi confessed, he tried imagining what it would be like if his own criticism was translated into French: "At the mere thought my hair stands on end." [229]

In 1934 Kobayashi had read the Japanese translation (by Kawakami Tetsutarō and Abe Rokurō) of Leo Schestow's *Philosophy of Tragedy*, a work that produced an immense impression on the Japanese intelligentsia.[230] Masamune Hakuchō declared that he had read the book three times. Kobayashi was impressed by this study of Dostoevski and Nietzsche, but he was by no means uncritical, and doubted that it would have any real influence on the Japanese.[231] But the relations between literature and philosophy, as traced by Schestow, disturbed Kobayashi. He contrasted the world of pre-1914 Russia, in which Schestow had lived, with modern Japan, where literature—at least until the introduction of Marxism—had been completely untouched by intellectual ideas. Marxist writers had cast doubt on the value of the literary works that Kobayashi most admired, notably the writings of Shiga Naoya, dismissing them as "individual fiction" as opposed to the "social fiction" that they advocated. This dispute over literary values was symptomatic of the confusion in Japanese society created by the introduction of ideas from abroad.

Schestow's philosophy of despair was of special relevance to both the proletarian critics, who had to stand by as their movement was crushed by the government, and to bourgeois critics like Kobayashi who feared that under the existing circumstances intellectual activity in Japan would surely be impeded if not brought to a halt. Kobayashi revealed at the conclusion of his second essay on bungei jihyō that he was planning a study of Dostoevski. His interest in the subject seems to have been aroused by reading Schestow, even though he did not agree with him.

The process of Kobayashi's alienation from modern Japanese literature was carried a step further in his next major essay, "Watakushi Shōsetsu Ron" (On the "I Novel"), published in May–August 1935. Kobayashi traced the history of the "I novel" back to Rousseau's *Confessions* and to such works of the same period as *Werther, Obermann,* and *Adolphe.* The creation of the "I novel" in Europe had coincided with the beginnings of the Romantic movement and with the increased recognition of the importance of the individual, but this did not hold true of its history in Japan, where the "I novel" had grown out of Naturalism. Kobayashi quoted Kume Masao's famous pronouncement (made in 1925) that, for all their unquestionable literary value, *War and Peace, Crime and Punishment,* and *Madame Bovary* were fictions, no more than popular reading matter, because their authors had not described the persons they knew best in the world, themselves. Kobayashi quoted Kume not because he agreed with him, but because his remarks typified what many Japanese writers of the period secretly felt. He traced the different developments of Naturalism and the "I novel" in France and in Japan; in France the "I novel," as represented by Barrès, Gide, and Proust, had represented an attempt to reassert the importance of human qualities in face of the determinism of Naturalism, but in Japan the modern urban society was too restricted to support the Naturalist thought imported from abroad, and the residual strength of the old literature was by no means spent. All that the Japanese Naturalists had learned from the French was techniques; in Tayama Katai's case, it was simply to look at the ground rather than at the heavens.

Kobayashi believed that the Japanese Naturalist fiction, unlike that written in France, lacked intellectual content, and tended to be directed toward producing increasingly refined techniques for describing as minutely as possible the real life of the author, his character, and so on; everything in a Naturalist novel served to promote the portrait of the "I." During the Taishō era the "I novel" had been criticized from many points of view, but no all-out negation was possible because those who attacked the "I novel" were dependent on the experiences of daily life for the materials of their creative work. Even if they treated these materials psychologically or through the sense perceptions, rather than realistically, their works were still "I novels." The only challenge to the "I novel" and similar writings derived directly from personal experience came from those who rejected "pure literature" and wrote for the pleasure and edification of the average reader. Kobayashi on several occasions devoted essays to the writings of Kikuchi Kan, whom he praised with a generosity unusual in so demanding a critic. He even wrote that Shiga Naoya and Kikuchi Kan were the only two literary men who had impressed him as being geniuses.[232] It is easy to imagine what impressed him in Shiga, but Kikuchi's chief contribution to literature was his success with the mass audiences of newspaper readers. Kobayashi had little specific praise for Kikuchi's works as literature; it was Kikuchi's attitude, so unlike that of the "I" novelists, who were indifferent to the average reader, which compelled his admiration. Kobayashi was willing to praise almost any kind of literature that resisted the mainstream of the "I novel." He even had some favorable words for proletarian literature; [233] he was apparently of the opinion that although the proletarian novels suffered from faults induced by the political tenets to which the authors were committed, these faults could be forgiven in the light of the authors' successes in dealing with intellectual preoccupations. He interpreted the successes of proletarian literature as victories over the "I novel," not over individualism. The essay on the "I novel" concludes with an expression of Kobayashi's uncertainties as to what the literary effects of tenkō, both in Japan and in such European instances as that of Gide, might produce: "The 'I novel' is dead, but I wonder if people have conquered the 'I.' The 'I novel' will doubtless appear again in a new form, as long as Flaubert's celebrated formula, 'Madame Bovary is myself,' continues to hold true." [234]

Kobayashi's essay was by no means restricted to a narrow consideration of the "I novel." For example, the last part of the essay is particularly concerned with the intellectual quality of literature. He contrasted an ineffectual though ambitious love story by Yokomitsu Riichi with Gide's *La porte étroite*; the translation of the latter had not only sold many more copies than Yokomitsu's book, but probably more than any work of popular fiction. The kind of truth about human beings found in Gide's novel or, to take another example, Maupassant's *Une vie*, attracted Japanese readers more than fiction that had been written with a mass audience in mind. Kobayashi's ideal was writing that was both engrossing and intellectually satisfying, and he seems to have believed that the ideals might be achieved by Japanese fiction in the near future.[235] This optimism does not at all suggest the gloom in the literary world of the mid-1930s, which is usually evoked by historians of the period who emphasize the traumatic nature of the experience of tenkō, but Kobayashi writes as if the chief obstacle to the creation of mature literature in Japan was the moribund "I novel." His optimism was not fulfilled by developments in the Japanese novel of the late 1930s; the best Japanese fiction of this period was in fact anti-intellectual.[236]

Kobayashi's disappointment with modern Japanese literature led him to the Japanese literature of the past, as well as to European literature, which had always been part of his daily sustenance. His love for the Japanese classics would be beautifully expressed in his essays of the war years, but during the period immediately after writing "The 'I Novel,' " Kobayashi was absorbed chiefly with European literature. Nakamura Mitsuo stated flatly that "no one since the Meiji era had been so powerfully affected by foreign literature" as Kobayashi.[237] He became the chief editor of the literary magazine *Bungakkai* (Literary World) in January 1935 and began the serialization of his *Dosutoefuskii no Seikatsu* (The Life of Dostoevski) in that issue. Publication went on until March 1937, but probably he did not realize how much of his life would be devoted to studies of Dostoevski, nor that Dostoevski would in fact serve as a kind of alter ego for him during the years after 1935. "The 'I Novel' " appeared a few months after Kobayashi published the first episodes of *The Life of Dostoevski*, but it has been claimed that this essay should be read as a preface to Kobayashi's studies of the great Russian author.[238] Kobayashi wrote, in an article on bungei jihyō to which reference has already been made:

> I have planned to make a long critical study of Dostoevski, not because I despise bungei jihyō, nor because writing them has become so unbearably tedious that I have taken to a study of the

classics, or anything that complicated. It is because I can no longer resist the desire to mold with my own hands, in the same manner that authors create human types, an image of this author. An image of my own and nobody else's.[239]

Kobayashi frankly admitted in *The Life of Dostoevski* his indebtedness to E. H. Carr's *Dostoyevsky* and to A. Yarmolinsky's *Dostoevski: His Life and Art*. Undoubtedly he also unconsciously absorbed ideas from other secondary works, but contrary to what he had earlier written about his bungei jihyō in French translation, he now felt such confidence in his Dostoevski that he would not have been ashamed to have it translated into any foreign language.[240] Japanese critics have not been as much concerned with the originality of Kobayashi's Dostoevski as with his success in identifying himself not only with Dostoevski but with the characters in the novels, notably Raskolnikov.[241] Regardless of the degree of originality, it was surely of great importance that a Japanese intellectual should have written with skill and assurance about a European author—neither disqualifying himself because of his nationality nor attempting to impart any specifically Japanese quality to his account. The most striking part of Kobayashi's writings about Dostoevski was probably the paradoxes. For example, he wrote: "In *Crime and Punishment* no crime is at any point committed, and nobody is punished." With respect to Stavrogin in *The Devils*, he asserted: "In the same way that Myshkin possessed nothing that could win the consent of the readers' ordinary conscience, there is absolutely nothing in the speech or behavior of Stavrogin that, in any sense, can satisfy the readers' cynicism. As the sagacity of *The Idiot* perplexed its readers, the innocence of *The Devils* surprises us." [242]

Such statements seem to reflect Kobayashi's fondness for paradox as a literary technique. In the essay "Gyakusetsu to iu mono ni tsuite" (Concerning Paradox, 1932) Kobayashi wrote disapprovingly of those authors—he mentioned Akutagawa by name—who relied heavily on paradox as a literary technique. He declared his preference for plain, straightforward expression, but, he added, sometimes a statement of great directness and simplicity contains a profound paradoxical meaning: "At the sources of a true paradox there must always be intense, direct observation; and there must be a keen intelligence intuitively aware of an inexplicable reality. A paradox is not something one plays with; it springs to life. It is the straightforward expression of an analyst who is sincerely tracing mutable reality in all its mutability." [243]

Kobayashi used paradox neither to startle nor to amuse, in the manner of Akutagawa portraying General Nogi or Lytton Strachey describing his eminent Victorians, but to convey the shifting nature of the phenomena he examined. In the case of his Dostoevski studies, some paradoxes were undoubtedly occasioned by Kobayashi's desire to prove that his book was not a mere rehashing of material in French or English books. One senses in his pages not only a challenge to Murry, Carr, Schestow, Gide, and the others, but a resolve to outdo them.[244]

During the late 1930s Kobayashi's major efforts were devoted to his study of Dostoevski, but he continued to write occasional articles about Japanese and foreign authors. He also found the time to participate in zadankai and even in ronsō. In 1936 he and Masamune Hakuchō carried on a ronsō about Tolstoy that has since been known as the "Thought and Real Life" debate. In the same year he also had a ronsō with Nakano Shigeharu on the language of criticism. In the ronsō with Hakuchō he challenged the authority of a senior who was the most respected critic of the past; in the ronsō with Nakano he confronted a respected member of his own generation. The difference of tone between the two is noteworthy.

The ronsō with Hakuchō began with an article by Hakuchō, which related his emotions on reading Tolstoy's last diary, which had been written in 1910 but had only recently been made available in Japanese translation. Hakuchō wrote:

Twenty-five years ago, when word reached Japan that Tolstoy had run away from home and died of illness at a remote country station, members of the Japanese bundan accepted as the truth the apparent fact that Tolstoy, no longer able to endure his abstract anguish with respect to human life, had set forth on a journey to seek salvation, and it stirred saccharine sentimentality. . . . But when one attentively reads this diary, which reveals that Tolstoy . . . was so afraid of his old lady and of the world that he slipped timidly from his house on a lonely journey, only to die miserably on the road, it is at once pathetic and comic, like seeing reflected in a mirror what life is really alike. Ah, our beloved and respected Tolstoy!" [245]

Hakuchō confessed that he had been moved more deeply by this diary than by any of Tolstoy's novels. Only when Tolstoy was eighty and his powers were declining had he first become aware of what an immense source of affliction a woman can be to a man. Such a reaction is what one might expect of Hakuchō, the famed nihilist, and the expression is in his usual direct, unpretentious manner.

In his essay "Sakka no Kao" (The Face of the Author) Kobayashi answered Hakuchō after first describing several other recently published works that had attracted his attention: a story by Hōjō Tamio (1914–1937), which described his life in a leper hospital; a letter from Flaubert to George Sand containing the revelation that man is nothing, artistic works all; and a letter by D. H. Lawrence in which he related the agonies it cost him to be a writer and his yearning to be delivered from this fate. Consideration of these three entirely dissimilar documents prepared the way for Kobayashi's rejoinder to Hakuchō:

Ah, our beloved and respected Tolstoy! Were you really afraid of your old lady? I don't believe it. . . . If Tolstoy's heart had not been burning with "abstract anguish with respect to human life" he probably would never have had to fear his old lady. If he had been Masamune Hakuchō, he might have knocked his old lady to the floor with one well-administered slap in the face.[246]

This sarcasm was followed by Kobayashi's own judgment on the relationship between art and life:

Intellectual ideas of whatever description arise from real life. But if a time did not come when ideas that had been given birth and raised to maturity finally parted from real life, what power would ideas have? That is the moment when the great writer, having died in his real, private life, is reborn in the "face" of an invented author. . . . It often happens that an impassioned intellect, which has left worldly wisdom behind, stumbles over the trivialities of actual life.[247]

Kobayashi went on:

> I do not understand the tastes of those who take pleasure in dis-
> covering our ordinary, human faces on great men and heroes. It is
> no more than sentimentality wearing the mask of realism.[248]

Hakuchō, replying, admitted that Tolstoy's running away
from home was probably occasioned by his "abstract suffering"
having assumed the shape of his wife, oppressing him to such a
degree that he could not remain in the same house with her. He
produced supporting evidence from another Tolstoy diary to the
same effect, and concluded: "Unless these two diaries are forg-
eries, there is absolutely no question but that Tolstoy detested his
wife and ran away from home because he was afraid of her. It is
as clear as if one saw it in a mirror." [249]

Hakuchō's article elicited a much longer reply from Kobayashi, entitled "Shisō to Jisseikatsu" (Thought and Real Life). He
described at some length Dostoevski's unspeakable behavior
toward even those who were closest to him; his works can be
interpreted as one long apologia for all his offenses. His biogra-
pher, though he was Dostoevski's closest friend, could hardly
overcome his distaste for the man. But, Kobayashi insisted, for
both Dostoevski and Flaubert, two geniuses possessed by the
creative daemon, real life was no doubt an "imaginary country."
The beliefs of such geniuses were obviously incomprehensible to
would-be literary masters who struggled to make real life seem
artistic.[250]

> The tragedy of Tolstoy's last years is not a symbol of life itself. To
> see in it a symbol of life itself is symbolic of the turn of mind of our
> Japanese modern men of letters who, like Mr. Masamune or Mr.
> Kanō,[251] are glued to real life and have kept struggling to refine
> their perceptions. What immense ideas Tolstoy had to bear up un-
> der before he could produce a living picture of life! It was not that
> he endured his wife's hysteria; he endured the cruel ideas that
> pressed him even to abandon the ideas of *Anna Karenina*.
>
> Thought does not exist apart from real life.[252] The social order
> is nothing but the sacrifices paid to thought. The strength of its

reality is in proportion to the sacrifices that have been made. . . .
Thought is brought to fruition by the constant sacrifice of real
life.[253]

Once again Hakuchō responded, this time questioning some
of Kobayashi's high-flown expressions and insisting on the importance of real life, as opposed to ideas, in the formation of an
author's work. Obviously, he and Kobayashi were talking at cross-
purposes, but Kobayashi dutifully replied with "Bungakusha no
Shisō to Jisseikatsu" (The Writer's Ideas and Real Life). Kobayashi recognized the impossibility of ever reaching a conclusion in
this ronsō, but this did not upset him: "Recent literary criticism
has acquired a strong tendency to find greater meaning in the
process of reaching a conclusion than in the conclusion that is
reached." [254]

Kobayashi's arguments were more complex and more difficult to follow than Hakuchō's. His dislike of realism as a standard
of literary worth, revealed in many essays, was brought to the fore
here because his antagonist was not only a prime exemplar of
realism in literature but a critic who prided himself on his level-
headed realism. Kobayashi found such realism inadequate to
cope with the mystery of Tolstoy's greatness. For Hakuchō and
others of the Naturalist school, Tolstoy's flight from home at the
age of eighty and death in an obscure railway station was the stuff
of literature; kinship was easily established between the Russian
novelist and the little Japanese portrayed in Hakuchō's stories,
whose lives end with a similar realization of the meaninglessness
of their accomplishments and even of their rare moments of joy.
For Kobayashi such considerations were immaterial.

The influences from abroad that had helped to form Masamune Hakuchō's outlook on literature came chiefly from English literary critics of the early twentieth century. Kobayashi
owed everything (he stated) to his readings in French criticism,
especially that of Baudelaire, Sainte-Beuve, and Valéry. An essay
by Kobayashi presents some of the problems found in Valéry; it
may take an average reader two or three perusals of a sentence
before he fully understands the meaning, but once he does he is
likely to be surprised and impressed by the economy of the argu-
mentation. The ronsō between Hakuchō and Kobayashi suggests

the differences between Taishō and Shōwa literary criticism. Hakuchō relied chiefly on his inborn literary preferences, backed by wide readings; Kobayashi was both deeper and more closely associated with the kind of criticism currently being practiced in the West.

That same year, 1936, the first of four exchanges of views between Kobayashi and Nakano Shigeharu appeared. It is usually treated as a ronsō though the articles were published over a period of three years. Nakano by this time had committed tenkō, and the proletarian literature movement was dead, but he still maintained—to the degree that it was possible—his left-wing convictions. Irritation with several of Kobayashi's essays, especially "The Face of the Author" and "Concerning Literary Chronicles," impelled him to write a slashing attack on Kobayashi in the article "Jun Nigatsu Nijūkunichi" (Leap Year, February 29th). The article opens with a description of gunfire and a heavy snowfall, followed by a brief report by an eyewitness of something that had taken place in the Akasaka section of Tokyo. Nakano did not explain why he had mentioned these seemingly unrelated occurrences, but any reader would have known immediately that he was alluding to the February 26, 1936, troop uprising at the Akasaka barracks after a snowstorm. With an indirectness that was presumably occasioned by fear of censorship, Nakano was calling attention to the urgency of the political situation in Japan, and upbraiding Kobayashi for his seeming indifference to all but literary matters. The attacks were leveled chiefly at Kobayashi, but Yokomitsu Riichi, the leader of the now defunct New Sensationalist group, was also subjected to harsh words:

> Yokomitsu Riichi and Kobayashi Hideo are doing their best, in the novel and in criticism, respectively, to run down everything that is logical. It is not that they have accidentally drifted into illogicality; they are antilogical, and they proclaim antilogicality to be the foundation of their work. They bandy about unfamiliar words with appropriate gestures, but their actions can be interpreted only as the last writhings of men who have lost all sense of logic.[255]

Nakano complained that the obscurities in the language of criticism by Yokomitsu and Kobayashi had fostered foolish epigones, citing a peculiar locution used by a college student, which could be traced back to Kobayashi. He also quoted the passage from "The Face of the Author" in which Kobayashi stated that ideas must eventually part company with real life, as an example of his unintelligibility.

Nakano quoted various excerpts from writings by Kobayashi to demonstrate that he had contributed nothing in the way of "basic criticism," whether the subject was contemporary Japanese fiction, Tolstoy's last diary, or Flaubert's letters to George Sand. He moved then to Kobayashi's politics:

> According to Hayashi Fusao, Yokomitsu and Kobayashi are both "progressive liberalist writers." I do not know in what sense Hayashi gave them this name, but I believe that their work, especially their recent work, is far from meriting any such appellation. I would not go so far as to say that their political stance is Fascist, but the progressive or reactionary nature of an author as an author is not determined by the political party to which he belongs or the system of political thought to which he subscribes. Regardless of their specific political opinions, the course that Yokomitsu and Kobayashi are following in their literary work, whether in contradiction to or in perfect harmony with their politics, is out-and-out reactionary.[256]

Nakano deplored the fact that there were people—"lazy university students with literary aspirations and some writers"—who bowed in worship before Kobayashi's antilogical, antirational pronouncements. As a matter of fact, however, the bumpkins straight from the country who had formed the Naturalist movement (he seems to be referring especially to Masamune Hakuchō) were more sophisticated than the city dandies typified by Kobayashi in that they were democratic, logical, and progressive: "These dandies who flaunt in rococo fashion vulgarly based or opinionated judgments and paradoxes have a penchant for citing foreign, especially French authors, but the modern French literary tradition was erected on the vanquished ruins of such attitudes. . . . Japanese literature, in order for it to grow, must use its straw sandals to kick away those dandies and their frippery." [257]

There could scarcely have been a less gracious evaluation of Kobayashi's worth as a critic. Nakano denied that Kobayashi had contributed anything to an understanding of the various works he had discussed, and implied that Kobayashi's recherché literary studies were a betrayal of the critic's responsibility. One might have expected that Kobayashi, so caustic in his debate with Hakuchō, would have been even more relentless with Nakano, an exact contemporary, but his reply, "Nakano Shigeharu-kun e" (To Nakano Shigeharu, 1936) is curiously mild. Perhaps he sympathized with Nakano who, like so many other Marxist writers, had been sent to prison and only recently released. Or perhaps he felt that there was justice in Nakano's criticisms. In any case, his response opened with a statement of his reluctance to publish a rejoinder to Nakano, despite the entreaties of magazines. When he finally wrote an answer, it was perhaps the closest he ever came to an apology for his life as a critic:

> According to you, I have done my utmost to create confusion in the language of criticism. Moreover, I have manufactured stupid epigones and blocked the progress of literature. . . .
>
> It so happens that I am not an illogical critic. You say that irrationalism is at the heart of my work as a critic. But I have no outlook on the world firm enough to characterize it as irrationalist or anything else. Besides, the turbulent cultural environment of our country today has not fostered in me any such view of the world. In the first place, never since modern criticism began in Japan have we once experienced anything that might be described as a serious confrontation between rationalism and irrationalism. . . .
>
> Ever since I published the reflective piece "Designs of Various Kinds" in *Kaizō*, I have been writing criticism from the position that critical methodologies, regardless of the kind, are no more than designs in which the critics clothe themselves, and that only if, after one has discarded all such designs, something remains to be said, can it be called true criticism. To this day there has been not the slightest change in this fundamental belief of mine. The miscellaneous pieces of criticism (I do not use the words "miscellaneous pieces" out of modesty; I think they definitely are miscellaneous pieces) I have written up to now, whatever the shapes they may have assumed on occasion, have in their basic principles been truly plain and simple. Perhaps they can't be called principles. But to call them irrationalism—that is ludicrous. And as for my stupid epigones, they can go to hell for all I care.
>
> My criticism has been labeled as subjective, arbitrary, psycho-

logical, irrational, and various other adjectives. As long as it doesn't go beyond adjectives, I suppose they are probably all applicable. But as far as I am concerned, one thing is definite: I have always come to a halt at the same place, and even if I go off somewhere, I always come back immediately to that same place. By the same place I mean the place where criticism becomes self-attestation, and where the opposite process is also true. Over the years I have doubted and believed all sorts of things, but if there is one thing I have always unwaveringly believed, it is the principle of the ordinariness of the critic. . . .[258]

You tax me with the ambiguity of my writings. You even go so far as to assert that I am incapable of speaking except ambiguously. Of course, much of the ambiguity comes from incompetence. I admit it. In addition, in the past there was a period when I tended toward ambiguity in language because I was strongly influenced by the French Symbolist poets. But, I assure you, I have never neglected to keep strict watch over the ambiguity of my words. I have tried always to relate my thoughts logically. In cases where I simply could not manage to speak logically, perhaps I have expressed myself hintingly or psychologically, but that is all. In such instances there can be only two reasons why my writings might appear to be ambiguous: it's either my lack of sufficient talent or insensitivity on the readers' part. . . .

You and I have been wounded by the confusion in a critical vocabulary that lacks both the universality of technical terminology and the reality of dialect. Surely you know that nobody has ever tried doing anything like manufacturing confusion. Confusion has been forced on us. In this respect you and I are the same. Now is the time for us to reflect on the wounds that we have been dealt by the particularism of modern Japanese culture. This is not, I think, a time for wounded men to be fighting each other.[259]

Nakano did not answer this article at once, but in March 1937 he published an essay expressing disgust with recent developments both in the literary world (including Kobayashi's bungei jihyō) and in the political world, as exemplified by the signing of the anti-Comintern pact between Japan and Germany in November 1936. He alluded to Kobayashi's article, but showed no signs of having been favorably impressed by its tone; on the contrary, he denounced Kobayashi, this time as an exemplar of the new bureaucratism of a Japan that now demanded conformity to nationalistic ideals.

Kobayashi undoubtedly had become involved in Japanese nationalism, whether or not he realized it. His essay on Kikuchi Kan, published in January 1937, expressed admiration for a writer who had deliberately shifted from "pure" to "popular" literature because he wanted to reach a public that had been untouched either by the proletarian literature movement or by Modernism. Kobayashi thought it was a mistake to stress the role of external pressure in the collapse of the proletarian literature movement; in point of fact, the proletarian writers had failed to capture even the readers to whom they should have most appealed. Kikuchi knew how to capture them. His writings intended for a mass audience have exactly the same literary qualities as the early works that established his reputation. He had the mysterious knack of writing what the public wanted without pandering to their tastes.

Kobayashi held up Kikuchi as the example of a writer who was not content with making an impression on his colleagues in the bundan. The collapse of the proletarian literature movement had ended pressure from the left on liberals, but it had increased the danger that the government might seek to crush elements in Japanese society that did not conform to its policies of militaristic expansion. Turning once more to France for inspiration, the Activists found a model to emulate in Antoine de St. Exupéry, a professional pilot whose poetic writings were filled with meditations on the dangers facing civilization. The Activists thought of themselves as humanists who had left their ivory towers and would use their works to express positively their concern over contemporary Japan. Kobayashi found the same dedication in Kikuchi. One critic, analyzing Kobayashi's writings on Kikuchi, decided that "It was not so much the personal bond with Kikuchi that moved him as the access Kikuchi seemed to provide to wider fellowship, plus, of course, Kikuchi's qualifications as a man of action." [260]

Kobayashi's career as a critic was not noticeably affected by the outbreak of the China Incident in July 1937, though chroniclers of the period often suggest that no writer could escape the oppressive weight of the atmosphere engendered by the war. In November he published "Sensō ni tsuite" (On War), an expression of his sentiments on what it meant to be a writer in wartime. He certainly did not oppose the war, not even when, in 1941, it expanded into the full-scale Pacific War. Kobayashi wanted his country to win, and he had no use for Japanese who continued their debates over peacetime issues instead of actively supporting the war effort.[261] He never wrote propaganda or the kind of patriotic journalism practiced by many other writers, but he cooperated as fully as he could without compromising his principle of self-attestation. In March 1938 he traveled to China as a special correspondent of *Bungei Shunjū*, entrusted with the pleasant task of presenting Corporal Hino Ashihei with the Akutagawa Prize for his novel *A Tale of Excrement*. Kobayashi was glad to carry out this assignment: not only was he eager to visit China for the first time, but he was deeply impressed by Hino's writings, especially the later *Wheat and Soldiers*. Kobayashi traveled to China, Manchukuo (as it was then called), and Korea six times between 1938 and 1944, for visits as long as six months. He wrote nothing that suggested dismay over what he observed. He also delivered addresses before such organizations as the Japanese Literature Patriotic Association and the Greater East Asia Writers Decisive Victory Assembly.[262] These activities would brand him after the war as a collaborator with the militarists. In June 1946 he was listed as one of those responsible for the war by the Communist-oriented periodical *Shin Nihon Bungaku*, but he was never formally accused of any offense.

Kobayashi's attitude of cooperation with the war effort remained constant, yet something seems to have changed within him. He continued until late in 1942 to publish serially his long study of *The Brothers Karamazov*, but during the remainder of the war years he wrote only rarely on the kinds of subjects that had engaged him previously; his other wartime writings were devoted to appreciations of medieval Japanese literature.

The series of essays beginning with "Taema" [263] (March 1942), Kobayashi's account of his impressions on witnessing a performance of the Nō play of that name, was collected in 1946 and published under the title *The Fact of Evanescence*. These essays, on such subjects as *The Tale of the Heike*, *Essays in Idleness*, the poets Saigyō and Sanetomo, and the concept of evanescence itself are written in a moving, elegiac style that is quiet unlike the almost aggressively masculine (though sometimes obscure) style of his ronsō articles and his comments on contemporary Japanese literature. These are not so much works of criticism as meditations on the Japanese past. Kobayashi during the war years was attempting to discover wherein lay the uniqueness of Japanese civilization. The pathos he found in the poetry of Saigyō or Sanetomo moved him especially. It was not that he never previously had shown any interest in classical Japanese literature, but his intelligence had been refined by studies of European literature, and he was profoundly under its influence. Even during the war years he by no means abandoned his love for French literature, but he now looked at his Japanese heritage with the double vision of the man born within the tradition, yet able to see it also from the outside.

The Fact of Evanescence contains none of the paradoxes and ambiguities that marked his early essays; the style is lucid, even crisp, as the following passage (from his study of *Essays in Idleness*) may suggest:

> Kenkō does not resemble anyone. Least of all does he resemble Chōmei, whose name is often linked with his. He did the same things that Montaigne did. Two hundred years before Montaigne was born. Far more sharply, concisely, and accurately. The writing is masterly. The often mentioned resemblances to *The Pillow-Book* are all on the surface; his precise, acute style is unique. The reason why it is not so striking on first acquaintance is that he was a master craftsman. "They say that a good carver uses a slightly dull knife. Myōkan's knife cut very poorly." [264] Here he is talking about himself and his keen awareness of his overly skillful style and the need for a dull knife. How is one to control eyes that see too well? That is the essence of the style of *Essays in Idleness*.[265]

The change in Kobayashi's style is apparent even in translation. The sentences are short, sometimes unfinished, and the meaning is transparent. It might be supposed that, in an essay published during the war, Kobayashi was allowing nationalistic sentiments to color his judgments, as when he opined that Kenkō was a better writer than Montaigne, though this is surely not the judgment of the world; but it would be a mistake to interpret him in that way. Kobayashi had read Kenkō and Montaigne carefully, and when he stated that Kenkō wrote "far more sharply, concisely, and accurately," that was undoubtedly what he believed.

Kobayashi interpreted Kenkō's statement about the master carver Myōkan as applying to Kenkō himself; the same might also be said of Kobayashi's remarks on Kenkō. He no doubt realized that he needed to dull his expression in order to make his meanings clear to readers. It may have come as a surprise to Kobayashi on rereading Kenkō, perhaps for the first time since he left high school, to find presented so appealingly ideas that he had admired in Montaigne and other French writers.

In other parts of *The Fact of Evanescence* the expression rises to poetic intensity. Nakamura Mitsuo referred to these passages as "prose-poems," rare examples of descriptions of poets and poetry that themselves become poetry.[266] This was probably not Kobayashi's conscious intent. but when he described the poets of the past their style presumably affected his. Perhaps, as Nakamura suggested,[267] he found in Sanetomo, as he had long before found in Rimbaud, "his own, solitary poetic soul." He had no need to remind himself of Rimbaud or Baudelaire when reading the Japanese medieval poets; their influence had entered his blood and taken permanent possession of his mind.

The title essay of *The Fact of Evanescence* is only three pages long, but it deserves its place at the heart of the collection. It opens with an episode quoted from *Ichigon Hōdan* (Brief Sayings of the Great Teachers), a collection of remarks attributed to priests of the Pure Land sect, which was probably compiled early in the fourteenth century.

> Someone related the story of a young woman at the Shintō shrine on Mount Hiei who falsely pretended to be a medium. Late one night, when the sounds of people had quieted down, she sat before the Jūzenshi Shrine and, beating on a drum, she cried out in a fervent voice, "It makes no difference any more. Please, oh please!" When someone insisted that she reveal what this meant, she replied, "When I think of the process of life and death and the evanescence of all things, nothing in the world makes any difference. So I say, 'Please save me in the life to come.' " [268]
>
> This is a section from *Brief Sayings of the Great Teachers*. When I first read it, it stuck in my mind as a fine piece of writing, but the other day I went to Mount Hiei, and while wandering aimlessly in the area of the Sannō Gongen, looking at the green leaves, the stone fences, and the rest, suddenly this short passage

flashed into my mind as if I were examining a fragment of a horizontal picture scroll of the period, and the different phrases of the text spread in my mind exactly as if I were following the course of the slender but strong lines of an old picture. This was the first time I had had such an experience, and I was extremely shaken. Even while I was eating *soba* at Sakamoto a while later, the strange feeling persisted. What was I feeling or thinking at the time, I wonder? It baffles me even now. Of course, one could say that I simply had a mild hallucination. That would be a convenient way of disposing of the matter, but somehow I do not feel I can trust such convenient evasions. I wonder why.[269]

After debating the meaning of this experience he passed on to a consideration of the nature of history:

The more one examines history the more it reflects back its immovable form. It is not susceptible to being perturbed by new interpretations or anything of the sort. It is not so fragile that it can be destroyed by such things. Once I came to realize this, I felt history was more beautiful than ever before. . . . The only beautiful things are those that are immovable and resist explanation. This was Norinaga's strongest conviction. Nowadays, when explanations positively abound, this is the most carefully guarded of all secrets.[270]

Kobayashi's distrust of methods of treating literature or history, stated in many essays, was here given in concentrated form: like Motoori Norinaga, who would be the subject of his longest study, Kobayashi believed in the uniqueness and ultimate inexplicability of historical events. No doubt it was for this reason that Nakano Shigeharu and other advocates of "scientific" methods of analyzing history accused him of being not only illogical but antilogical. But Kobayashi rejected the belief that it was possible to explain the present in terms of repeated patterns of historical evolution; for him every event was worth investigating—as Mori Ōgai's investigations into the lives of obscure figures of the past were worthwhile—because it was unique and irreplaceable. His conclusion concerning *mujō,* the evanescence of all things, was that it was not a specifically Buddhist conception but a term that describes the animalistic state of life in this world for man in the process of becoming a human being.[271] He concluded the essay:

"Modern man does not understand the fact of evanescence as well as that young woman who lived some time in the Kamakura period. This is because he has lost sight of the eternal." [272]

Kobayashi in this essay may seem to be executing the familiar phenomenon of "return to Japan" (*Nihon kaiki*). Perhaps there was an element of this phenomenon and it was not unrelated to the time of composition, the first year of a war with various countries of Europe and America. But it definitely was not a rejection of the West. It is true that Kobayashi broke off his study of Dostoevski in 1942 without completing it, but this was apparently not because of any ideological reason.[273] In any case, Kobayashi decided in the same year to write a book on Mozart. The actual writing of his *Mozart* was begun late in 1943, while he was in Nanking, planning the third meeting of the Greater East Asian Writers Decisive Victory Assembly. With the exception of an essay on the painter Umehara Ryūzaburō written in January 1945, Kobayashi devoted the last two years of the war entirely to his studies of Mozart.

Kobayashi's absorption with the music of Mozart was by no means recent. In his essay he described how, twenty years earlier, during his year of vagabondage, as he wandered through the Dōtombori amusement section of Osaka, suddenly the theme of the first movement of the Mozart Symphony No. 40 flashed into his head. He recalled:

> I have forgotten what I was thinking about at the time. Probably I was wandering around aimlessly as a dog, my head filled with useless words, the meaning of which I myself did not know—life, literature, despair, isolation, and the like. . . . As I walked through the crowded street, I could distinctly hear in the absolute silence of my head somebody playing the music. Trembling with excitement, I rushed into a department store to listen to the records, but the excitement did not return. I am not suggesting that there was any special meaning to this pathological sensation. It is simply that, as I start now to write about Mozart, my most vivid experience relating to him has flooded back into my mind.[274]

It has often been pointed out that, like others of Kobayashi's studies of artists of the past, his *Mozart* is a kind of self-portrait, or even an "I novel." Nakamura Mitsuo, in his praise of *Mozart*, said that Kobayashi had succeeded in identifying himself completely with Mozart: "If one wished to come even closer to Mozart, the only way would be to perform his music. Kobayashi approximated this by making music of his words." [275]

Before setting about the writing of *Mozart*, Kobayashi collected every book, record, and score he could find—not an easy task in wartime Japan. At no point did he explain whether or not he saw some connection between unhappiness over his increasing realization that Japan was losing the war and his turning to Mozart, but it is likely that, no less than the Japanese classics, the music of Mozart became his refuge. The particular importance of this essay to Kobayashi is suggested by the dedication to his mother, who died in 1946, the year that *Mozart* was published.[276] Nakamura believed that *Mozart* was a masterpiece that not only demonstrated the possibilities of criticism as a literary form but was itself a study of Kobayashi.[277]

The question may arise as to whether or not Kobayashi's perceptions of Mozart, however beautifully expressed, represent a genuine contribution to the world's understanding. Nakamura Mitsuo was sure that *Mozart* and the later *Kindai Kaiga* (Modern Painting) provided proof of Kobayashi's correct understanding of Western culture and not only Western literature.[278] Kobayashi derived all his information about Mozart and many of his perceptions from readings in European books, notably Henri Ghéon's *Promenades avec Mozart*, where he found the phrase *tristesse allante*, which seemed to characterize exactly his own feelings on hearing, say, the allegro movement of Mozart's G Minor Quintet, K. 516. For that matter, *tristesse allante* would not be an inappropriate description of Kobayashi's mood at the time of his writing *Mozart*.

Mozart was surely the right composer for Kobayashi to study during the dark years from 1944 to 1946, and his *Mozart* brought comfort to many readers. It might have been expected that, as life in postwar Japan returned to normal, Kobayashi would resume his career as a literary critic, but instead he turned his attention increasingly to art. He had become passionately fond of antiques, and perhaps even made a living as a dealer during the period when he stopped writing.[279] His essay on the painter Umehara Ryūzaburō, written in 1945 but not published until 1947, was the forerunner of a series of articles devoted to Japanese painters, including "Kōetsu and Sōtatsu" (1947) and "Tessai" (1948). Late in 1948 he began publication serially of *Gohho no Tegami* (The Letters of Van Gogh), and resumed his studies of Dostoevski with the first of several essays on *Crime and Punishment*. With the exception of eulogies for some friends who had recently died, he wrote little on modern Japanese literature.

At the end of 1952 Kobayashi traveled to Europe in order to study masterpieces of modern painting, and spent about six months abroad. In March 1953 he started to serialize *Modern Painting* in a magazine, but did not complete it until 1958. During this period he also wrote occasional essays, gave lectures, made broadcasts, took part in dialogues with writers, artists, and scientists, and wrote about golf. This long period of silence on literary matters might have induced readers to forget his importance as a critic, but his reputation only grew, and even people who were normally uninterested in criticism read Kobayashi's comments on whatever subjects happened to interest him. A collection of miscellaneous essays originally published monthly in *Bungei Shunjū* between 1959 and 1964 appeared under the title *Kangaeru Hinto* (Hints for Thinking) in 1964 and became a best-seller. Kobayashi was no longer writing for the limited audience interested in French poetry or medieval Japanese classics, nor for members of the bundan, but for the general public, serving as a philosopher, a guide to the appreciation of the remarkable things in the world. He was decorated by the Japanese government and invited to the Soviet Union. His *Complete Works* appeared in several different editions, and many books and essays were devoted to elucidating them. Lionized everywhere, he seemed no longer to have the time to make the concentrated efforts that had provided the basis for his major works. He surprised those who thought he was resting on his laurels by publishing, beginning in June 1965, his magnum opus, *Motoori Norinaga*, not completed until 1976. Writing this book was his principal occupation for eleven years, though he continued to publish occasional essays. In 1967 he was awarded the Medal of Culture (*Bunka Kunshō*).

The publication of *Motoori Norinaga* elicited new admiration. This work, over six hundred pages in length, attracted unusual interest from the reviewers, despite its forbidding contents. Rather in the way that Kobayashi's *Mozart* had reassured Japanese after the end of the war that they belonged to a worldwide community, *Motoori Norinaga* brought to Japanese, then enjoying unprecedented commercial prosperity, the reassurance that they possessed in their tradition a true thinker, a man who spoke with a voice that was worthy of being heard throughout the world. The book is masterfully written, but only Kobayashi's unique reputation can account for its popularity. His tastes, whether for the music of Mozart, the philosophy of Motoori, or for traditional orthography, were adopted by many critics. He had become, even during his lifetime, an almost mythical figure, the touchstone against whom other critics were judged and the pride of the world of Japanese letters. He had outspoken enemies too, but even they served as negative testimony to his commanding importance.

As Kobayashi himself insisted, he owed his literary formation to his readings in foreign literature. He was familiar also with many examples of European literature that he rarely discussed in his essays, including the drama of Ibsen and Nietzsche's philosophy, but his main interest was definitely French literature, and this preference may account for the unusually large number of young Japanese who have studied French literature at the universities. As for Japanese literature, his interest in contemporary writings was maintained for years by the necessity of writing bungei jihyō, but once he was freed of this burden he rarely discussed his contemporaries. He seems to have been uninterested in modern Japanese poetry—except for the works of a few friends—or in modern drama. His discovery of medieval Japanese literature during the war years was of great significance, but he seldom returned to it in later years. His attraction to Motoori Norinaga probably originated in the similarity in attitudes he detected between Motoori and himself: both men believed that the critic must go to the heart of the work he is considering and try to understand its meaning, rather than describe the historical background or attempt to force the work into an existing critical scheme.

OTHER MODERN CRITICS

It is grossly unfair to the many modern Japanese critics to lump them all together under one rubric, but Kobayashi's influence was so pervasive as to make many of them appear to be members of his school, or at least writers under his influence, regardless of how greatly their fields of interest might differ. The distinguished critic Nakamura Mitsuo (b. 1911) gladly admitted his indebtedness to Kobayashi, who had opened his eyes to literature and made him look directly at the works he discussed rather than across the structure of Marxist theory. Nakamura devoted himself mainly to modern Japanese literature, making his career in an area of criticism that Kobayashi had tended to disdain.

Kawakami Tetsutarō (1902–1980), though slightly older than Kobayashi and his senior at school, learned much from him. He knew more than Kobayashi about music and wrote well on the subject, but even his most penetrating essays never enjoyed the reputation of Kobayashi's *Mozart*. He was not only a devoted reader of Dostoevski but the translator of Schestow, and shared Kobayashi's interest in such writers as Gide and Baudelaire. His chief preoccupation, however, was modern Japanese literature, and he wrote impressively about such unorthodox figures as the poets Nakahara Chūya and Hagiwara Sakutarō, the novelist Iwano Hōmei, and writers like Ōsugi Sakae, the celebrated anarchist, and Okakura Kakuzō (Tenshin), the authority on Japanese art. *Nihon no Autosaidā* (Japanese Outsiders, 1960) was perhaps his best-known work of criticism. Kawakami's last major work, *Yoshida Shōin* (1968), in some ways paralleled Kobayashi's *Motoori Norinaga*: Kawakami, a member of a samurai family from the western end of Honshū, undoubtedly found it easy to associate himself with Yoshida Shōin, whose background was similar. Although Kobayashi and Kawakami remained close friends to the end of Kawakami's life, and there were many similarities in their interests, there were important differences too, some of which can be attributed to their dissimilar backgrounds.

Yoshida Ken'ichi (1912–1978), a close friend of both Nakamura and Kawakami, was above all a scholar of English literature. Much of his schooling was in England, and he spoke English perfectly; but he took the advice of his supervisor at Cambridge, G. Lowes Dickinson, who urged him to return to Japan if he wished to become a writer. He left Cambridge without graduating, but it was often in his thoughts. Soon after Yoshida's return to Japan he was introduced to Kawakami, who became a lifelong friend and fellow drinker. Yoshida's writings, whether on English poetry, popular Japanese fiction, or food and drink, were eminently civilized. He wrote with complete assurance and with obvious pride in an intricate, sometimes perilously involved literary style, which seems to have represented to him the way the Japanese language—as opposed to English—was most characteristically written.

Many other critics deserve mention, but it would not be easy to state in a few words the distinctive excellence of each. It is easier to suggest elements that most of them shared: a knowledge of European literature based on extensive readings, usually in Japanese translations; a familiarity with classical European literary criticism, though not much interest in twentieth-century developments; a love of the Japanese language and its expressive possibilities; a love of Western music, especially of the eighteenth century, but not of Japanese music; an admiration for popular writers like Hino Ashihei or Kikuchi Kan, who are usually not sympathetically treated in accounts of literature written by academics; a fondness for saké and a belief that only drinkers make amusing companions; and a nostalgia for the Japanese bunjin of old and their elegant pleasures.

Not all the critics shared every one of these tastes, and some are in fact contradictory, but the combination of seemingly disparate interests helps to account for the complexity of the modern Japanese literary intellectual. The discovery that a Japanese writer who has spent many years studying French poetry enjoys spending an evening in an old-fashioned restaurant where geishas keep his cup filled with saké and exchange improper remarks with him is likely to induce reflections—at least among some Western interpreters of Japan—on the superficiality of the Western veneer over the Japanese core. That a Japanese is a Japanese is a truism, and needs no comment, but the word "veneer" or any synonym that suggests that a Japanese who has spent his whole life studying European literature has probably never penetrated beneath the surface is not only insulting but untrue. If, for example, Kobayashi's studies of Dostoevski were translated into European languages and could be read by Western specialists, they might decide that he was unoriginal, insufficiently familiar with the background, handicapped by his ignorance of the Russian language, and so on, but they could not properly decide that Dostoevski was nothing more to Kobayashi than a superficial, rootless interest or an exotic diversion; the facts of his career prove otherwise. He stated that he owed nothing to Japanese predecessors when he became a critic. Perhaps if he had read Motoori Norinaga at an impressionable age he might have become a critic all the same, but it is hard to imagine a young twentieth-century Japanese becoming excited by Motoori. It was only after having devoted forty or more years of his life to European literature, music, and art that Kobayashi was ready for Motoori. He did not approach Motoori as a foreigner would, obviously; he had special insights into the Japanese language and into the intellectual climate of eighteenth-century Japan, which enriched his appreciation of a thinker who is nevertheless of world importance. But it was Kobayashi's familiarity with another tradition, and his absorption of that tradition along with the one that had come to him with the first words he spoke, that made possible an appreciation of Motoori that no Japanese who was exclusively grounded in his own traditions could have achieved.

Kobayashi typified not only the critics but all the best Japanese writers of the twentieth century. Few of them studied the Japanese classics after they passed their university entrance examinations, but as they matured they gradually, sometimes grudgingly, began to admit that Japanese literature had worthwhile elements, that a tanka, though so brief as to appear insignificant alongside a great European poem, conveys much through the music and the overtones of the Japanese language—in short, that they have reason to be proud of their own traditions. This is not the same as a rejection of the West; the West is still there, deeply ingrained, not an affectation; but the minds and hearts of these Japanese have also found place for their own literature.

The writings of Kobayashi, Nakamura, Kawakami, Yoshida, and other critics illumined the works of Europeans whom they treated; they studied these works and knew them well. If they sometimes emphasized unexpected aspects of the works they discussed, this does not necessarily prove they had failed to understand these foreign works. At their most successful they even turned to advantage their having been born within different traditions.

No one would have made such a claim for the Japanese criticism of the Meiji era. Through study of the West, in the light that had come from the West, the Japanese were able to understand as never before their own traditions and those of other countries, and to become citizens of the world of letters without surrendering the heritage of their birth.

NOTES

1. For a comprehensive treatment of early Meiji criticism, see Hisamatsu Sen'ichi, *Nihon Bungaku Hyōron Shi: Kinsei, Kindai Hen*, pp. 311–30.
2. See Kawazoe Kunimoto, "Kaisetsu," to *Kindai Hyōron Shū*, I, p. 11.
3. Quoted in Homma Hisao, *Meiji Bungaku Shi*, I, p. 209.
4. *Ibid.*, p. 211.
5. *Ibid.*, p. 213.
6. See *Dawn to the West: Fiction*.
7. This was the first series of *Waseda Bungaku*; the second series began, after the return of Shimamura Hōgetsu from Europe, in January 1906, and continued until December 1927. The magazine was revived once again in 1934 and publication continued irregularly through the war years until January 1949. The fourth series was inaugurated in January 1951.
8. Usui Yoshimi, *Kindai Bungaku Ronsō*, gives in two volumes an account of the principle ronsō from the one between Shōyō and Ōgai to the "People's Literature" ronsō of the mid-1950s. Postwar ronsō are extensively treated in the two volumes of the same author's *Sengo Bungaku Ronsō*.
9. See Tanizawa Eiichi, *Meijiki no Bungei Hyōron*, p. 25.
10. *Ibid.*, p. 24.
11. He referred specifically to the first four volumes of a projected twelve-volume series devoted to new authors, which the firm of Shun'yōdō was bringing out at the time. See Usui, *Kindai Bungaku Ronsō*, I, pp. 11–12.
12. *Ibid.*
13. *Ibid.*, p. 13.
14. Ōgai equated Shōyō's three "schools" with the *Gattungsidee, Individualidee*, and *Mikrokosimus* described by Hartmann in *Philosophie des Schönen*. Ōgai translated the German terms as *ruisō, kosō,* and *shōtenchisō*, which mean, roughly, "stereotype thought," "individual thought," and "microcosmic thought." See *Ōgai Zenshū*, XXXIII, p. 6.
15. Ōgai referred to p. 187 of Hartmann's work, where he expressed his contempt for the *Gattungsideal* and his respect for the individual. See *Ōgai Zenshū*, XXXIII, p. 7.
16. *Ibid.*, pp. 14–15.
17. Quoted by Usui, *Kindai Bungaku Ronsō*, I, p. 18.
18. *Ōgai Zenshū*, XXXIII, p. 21.
19. Tanizawa, *Meijiki no Bungei*, pp. 21–22. Tanizawa pointed out that not until 1921 was the ronsō described in a history of literature. Credit goes to Takasu Baikei for this discovery, which was followed by numerous other accounts of the

ronsō. It is now recognized as an important development in modern Japanese literary criticism.

20.   See Hisamatsu, *Nihon Bungaku Hyōron Shi*, pp. 363–64.

21.   Tanizawa, *Meijiki no Bungei*, p. 81. This is from the article "Byōga Roku-jun" (Sixty Days in a Sickbed) by Uchida Roan, published in 1926.

22.   See Tanizawa, p. 99.

23.   *Aibiki* was the name given to "The Rendezvous," a section of Turgenev's *Sportsman's Sketches*, which was translated by Futabatei and published in 1888.

24.   Uchida Roan, quoted in Tanizawa, *Meijiki no Bungei*, pp. 81–82. Tanizawa dismissed Roan's statement as the recollections of an old man who was set in his views and was writing with the object of entertaining readers, rather than of presenting empirical data. It is difficult, however, to imagine that (even if old age had made him mellow) Roan would have fundamentally changed his opinions about Ningetsu's worth.

25.   *Yamada Bimyō, Ishibashi Ningetsu, Takase Bun'en Shū*, p. 273.

26.   *Ibid.*

27.   *Ibid.*, p. 274. Ningetsu used the German word *Periode* throughout.

28.   Quoted by Usui, *Kindai Bungaku Ronsō*, p. 33.

29.   *Ōgai Zenshū*, XXII, p. 163.

30.   Quoted by Usui, *Kindai Bungaku Ronsō*, I, p. 34.

31.   Translation by Richard J. Bowring, in *Monumenta Nipponica*, XXIX (Autumn 1974).

32.   *Yamada Bimyō, et al.*, p. 276. Ningetsu developed his views on the absence of yūgen in "Ōgai no Yūgenron ni kotauru sho," written in December 1890 by way of response to Ōgai's rejoinder to his review of "Utakata no Ki."

33.   *Ibid.*, p. 275.

34.   See Hisamatsu, *Nihon Bungaku Hyōron Shi*, pp. 371–73, for examples.

35.   See Tosa Tōru, "Ryokuu to Edo," in Miyoshi Yukio and Takemori Ten'yū, *Kindai Bungaku*, II, p. 65. In the October 1907 issue of *Chūō Kōron*, an issue devoted to Ryokuu, Sasa Seisetsu called attention to the legacy of gesaku literature, which Ryokuu had inherited. See Inagaki Tatsurō, "Kaidai," in *Saitō Ryokuu Shū*, p. 457.

36.   He failed to describe the last two of his "sects."

37.   The effectiveness of this strange list of authors depends in part on the observance of the mid-Meiji practice of giving the names of foreigners in a transcription consisting of a kanji followed by katakana; the names of authors and such foreign dishes as "omelet" therefore look much alike.

38.   See *Ōgai Zenshū*, XXIII, pp. 467–522, for *Sannin Jōgon*, a series of comments on contemporary literature by three men, each using many aliases.

39.   See "The Founding of *Bungakkai*" by Michael C. Brownstein, in *Monumenta Nipponica*, Autumn 1980.

40.   Makibayashi Kōji, "Bungakkai no Romanchishizumu," p. 89, quotes two of the founders, Baba Kochō and Hirata Tokuboku, to this effect.

41.   *Ibid.*, p. 85.

42.   See *Dawn to the West: Fiction*.

43.   See the comments by Kinoshita Naoe in "Fukuzawa Yukichi to Kitamura Tōkoku," in *Kitamura Tōkoku Shū*, pp. 343–44.

44. Katsumoto Seiichirō (ed.), *Tōkoku Zenshū* (henceforth abbreviated as *TZ*), I, p. 299.

45. *Ibid.*, II, p. 26.

46. *Ibid.*, p. 28. Tōkoku's special interest in Bakin is further attested by his having read part of *Hakkenden* with the missionary George Braithwaite, whom he served as a translator and teacher of Japanese. However, the planned translation of one section into English apparently did not materialize. See *ibid.*, I, p. 284; and *ibid.*, II, pp. 422-23.

47. Yoshida Seiichi, *Kindai Bungei Hyōron Shi: Meiji Hen*, p. 498.

48. Presumably Tōkoku meant by this term the medieval poets and essayists who "fled the world" to live as recluses; but he also used the term "pessimist-poet" of people like himself.

49. *TZ*, II, pp. 25-26.

50. For these writers, see Donald Keene, *World Within Walls*. Tōkoku also mentioned the *kyōka* poet Utei Emba (1743-1822).

51. *TZ*, I, p. 353.

52. *Ibid.*, pp. 354-55. The appropriateness of Tōkoku's quotations from *Hamlet* is left for the reader to decide.

53. *Ibid.*, pp. 364-65.

54. *Ibid.*, p. 370.

55. *Ibid.*, pp. 370-71.

56. *Ibid.*, p. 370.

57. *Ibid.*, p. 277.

58. See the comment by Saitō Ryokuu, given in *Dawn to the West: Fiction*, chapter 9, note 27.

59. The revival of interest in Saikaku during the 1890s, which gave rise to the brilliant stories of Higuchi Ichiyō among others, was not considered by Tōkoku. In any case, the tone of these latter-day works on the licensed quarters is totally unlike that of Saikaku.

60. Quoted by Yoshida, *Kindai . . . Meiji Hen*, p. 516.

61. Sumiya Mikio (ed.), *Tokutomi Sohō, Yamaji Aizan*, p. 451.

62. *TZ*, II, p. 116. See also Satō Yasumasa and Satō Masaru (eds.), *Kitamura Tōkoku, Tokutomi Roka Shū*, p. 195.

63. Sumiya, *Tokutomi . . . Yamaji*, p. 467.

64. *TZ*, II, p. 148.

65. See Yoshida, I, p. 518.

66. *TZ*, II, p. 170.

67. *Ibid.*, p. 187.

68. See Katsumoto Seiichirō, "Kitamura Tōkoku no Shōgai, in *Tōkoku Zenshū*, I, pp. 12-14, for a detailed account of Tōkoku's pacifism. Tōkoku edited the journal *Heiwa* (Peace), published by the Japanese Pacifist Society from March 1892 to May 1893. His Quaker connections during this period undoubtedly contributed to his pacifism.

69. *Takiguchi Nyūdō* was in the Shinchō Bunko series as late as 1979.

70. Anesaki Masaharu (ed.), *Chogyū Zenshū* (henceforth abbreviated as *CZ*), II, p. 141.

71. *Ibid.*, p. 316.

72. Yoshida, *Kindai . . . Meiji Hen*, p. 586.

73. *Ibid.*, p. 587.

74. This periodization was made by Akagi Kōhei. Quoted by Yoshida, *Kindai . . . Meiji Hen*, p. 581.

75. For a discussion of the effects of the Sino-Japanese War on Japanese culture, see Donald Keene, *Landscapes and Portraits*, pp. 259–99.

76. Text in *Takayama Chogyū, Saitō Nonohito, Anesaki Chōfū, Tobari Chikufu*, pp. 23–26.

77. For a discussion of Chogyū's ronsō with Shōyō in 1898–1900 over historical plays and art, see Yoshida, *Kindai . . . Meiji Hen*, pp. 617–26. Chogyū believed it was more important to give freer rein to the imagination than to be faithful to historical facts; Shōyō insisted that the dramatist or artist must not alter facts to suit his convenience.

78. Yoshida, *Kindai . . . Meiji Hen*, pp. 616–17.

79. *Ibid.*, p. 631.

80. *Takayama Chogyū, Saitō Nonohito, et al.*, p. 63.

81. *Ibid.*

82. *Ibid.*

83. *Ibid.*, p. 64.

84. Yoshida, *Kindai . . . Meiji Hen*, p. 632. The quotation is from the essay "Sukorasuchikku to Bungakusha," published in June 1900.

85. *CZ*, II, pp. 302–08.

86. *Ibid.*, I, p. 426.

87. *Takayama Chogyū, Saitō Nonohito, et al.*, p. 68.

88. *Ibid.*, p. 81.

89. *Ibid.*

90. *Ibid.*

91. *Ibid.*

92. Quoted in Sadoya Shigenobu, *Hōgetsu Shimamura Takitarō Ron*, p. 59.

93. Translated by Burton Watson, in *Su Tung-p'o*, p. 89.

94. Sadoya, *Hōgetsu Shimamura*, p. 61.

95. *Hōgetsu Zenshū* (henceforth abbreviated as *HZ*), I, pp. 7–8.

96. Hōgetsu was generally negative, even about Saikaku's best works, but by no means so critical as W. G. Aston, who wrote of Saikaku in 1899: "He was a man of no learning. Bakin says that he had not a single Chinese character in his belly, and his books, most of which have very little story, are mainly descriptions of the manners and customs of the great lupanars, which then, as now, formed a prominent feature of the principal cities of Japan. The very titles of some of them are too gross for quotation." W. G. Aston, *A History of Japanese Literature*, pp. 268–69.

97. *HZ*, I, p. 33.

98. Sadoya, *Hōgetsu Shimamura*, p. 86.

99. *HZ*, VII, p. 153.

100. *Ibid.*, I, p. 201.

101. *Ibid.*, p. 209.

102. *Ibid.*

103. *Ibid.*, p. 210.

104. *Ibid.*, II, p. 15.
105. *Ibid.*, pp. 25–27.
106. Before Hōgetsu finally announced his out-and-out conversion to Naturalism, he published an unrelated but interesting essay in July 1907 on censorship. He deplored the actions of the authorities in banning a novel by Kosugi Tengai on the grounds of immorality: "this is not only an insult to the author but is persecution of literature and pressure directed against freedom of thought." On the whole, Hōgetsu remained aloof from politics and rarely took stands on public issues, but he had been impressed by British democracy, and perhaps he sensed the particular danger to Naturalism represented by censorship, which could ban books in the name of preserving the morality of the Japanese people. See *ibid.*, p. 36.
107. Kawazoe Kunimoto, *Kindai Hyōron Shū*, I, p. 261.
108. *Ibid.*, p. 262.
109. *HZ*, II, p. 49.
110. Yoshida, *Kindai . . . Meiji Hen*, p. 761.
111. Sadoya, *Hōgetsu Shimamura*, pp. 128–29, gives the results of a poll conducted in 1911 to determine favorite writers in various categories. Shimamura Hōgetsu was chosen as the favorite critic, with 13,692 votes.
112. *HZ*, II, pp. 107–8. See also Kawazoe, *Kindai Hyōron Shū*, I, pp. 292–93.
113. *HZ*, II, p. 112.
114. *Ibid.*, p. 117. The rebuttal by Gotō Chūgai, "Shizen Shugi no Mutokushoku," is given in Kawazoe, *Kindai Hyōron Shū*, I, pp. 420–29.
115. *HZ*, II, p. 125.
116. *Ibid.*, pp. 124–25.
117. Sadoya, *Hōgetsu Shimamura*, p. 310.
118. *Ibid.*, p. 248.
119. *HZ*, II, pp. 172–73.
120. Examples of the early Taishō ronsō are given in *Dawn to the West: Fiction*.
121. Masamune Hakuchō, "Bundan Gojūnen" (in *Bungakuteki Kaisō Shū*), p. 404.
122. *Ibid.*, p. 405.
123. *Ibid.* The authors are, of course, Kikuchi Kan, Akutagawa Ryūnosuke, Kume Masao, Satomi Ton, and Satō Haruo.
124. Translated by Geoffrey Sargent, in Ivan Morris, *Modern Japanese Stories*, pp. 101–37.
125. These are the concluding words of his essay "Bungei Sakuhin no Naiyōteki Kachi," where they meant that a true depiction of life was more important than ivory-tower artistry. However, the same words came to be used to mean that the writer's livelihood was more important than any display of artistry, and this is often cited as an explanation for Kikuchi's activities as leader of the bundan. See *Nihon Kindai Bungaku Daijiten*, IV, p. 476.
126. Quoted in Hisamatsu Sen'ichi, Kimata Osamu, Naruse Masahiko, Kawazoe Kunimoto, and Hasegawa Izumi, *Gendai Nihon Bungaku Daijiten*, p. 626.
127. Naoki's gō means literally "thirty-five." He started writing bungei jihyō at the age of thirty-one and called himself "Sanjūichi," adding one year to his

name with each birthday, until he reached Sanjūgo, where he stopped. The following quotation is from Hisamatsu et al., *Gendai Nihon*, p. 626.

128. Translated by John Bester as "The Realm Beyond," in *Japan Quarterly*, VII, No. 3.

129. Kagawa's novel was translated by I. Fukumoto and T. Satchell in 1922.

130. Tanizawa Eiichi, *Taishōki no Bungei Hyōron*, p. 89.

131. *Ibid.*, p. 90.

132. He may recall Coleridge's remark, "The writings of a contemporary, perhaps not many years older than himself, surrounded by the same circumstances, and disciplined by the same manner, possess a *reality* for him, and inspire an actual friendship as of a man for a man."

133. Chōkō later gained fame as a translator of English, French, German, and Italian works. He knew all these languages, but depended chiefly on his English. He read a fair amount of recent European literary criticism, but the uses to which he put this knowledge were not always impressive. Much of his essay on Fūyō, for example, can be traced directly to concepts absorbed from Johannes Volkelt, whose works had been introduced to the Japanese by Shimamura Hōgetsu. As an exercise in the application of European criteria to the writings of a recent Japanese author, the essay is of some interest, but Chōkō himself did not think highly enough of it to include it in collections of his criticism.

134. Inono Kenji, *Meiji no Sakka*, pp. 580–81.

135. Quoted by *ibid.*, p. 582.

136. For text, see Tanaka Yasutaka (ed.), *Kindai Hyōron Shū*, II, pp. 141–49. See also *Dawn to the West: Fiction*.

137. Hirano Ken, Odagiri Hideo, and Yamamoto Kenkichi (eds.), *Gendai Nihon Bungaku Ronsō Shi*, I, pp. 97–108.

138. Text given in *ibid.*, pp. 214–22; for a discussion, see Usui, *Kindai Bungaku Ronsō*, pp. 210–11.

139. The influence of Paul Morand on Japanese writers is discussed in *Dawn to the West: Fiction*.

140. Hirano, *Gendai Nihon Bungaku Ronsō*, I, p. 219.

141. *Ibid.*, p. 221.

142. Quoted by Inono, *Meiji no Sakka*, p. 588.

143. *Ibid.*

144. *Masamune Hakuchō Zenshū* (henceforth abbreviated as *MHZ*), VI, p. 10.

145. *Ibid.*, p. 66, from an essay written in May 1927.

146. *Ibid.*, p. 42, from an essay written in 1910.

147. He read Dante in the English translation by H. F. Cary, though he probably also consulted the partial Japanese translation by Ueda Bin and the complete translation by Ikuta Chōkō.

148. *MHZ*, VI, pp. 18–19, from an essay written in 1901.

149. Free translation of *amazake*, a sweet saké that even children can drink, and *ramune*, a bottled liquid of no alcoholic content. *Ibid.*, p. 20; written in 1905.

150. Yoshida Seiichi, *Kindai Bungei Hyōron Shi: Taishō Hen*, p. 45.

151. Quoted in *Nihon Kindai Bungaku Daijiten*, IV, p. 233.

152. *MHZ*, VI, pp. 22–23.

153. *Ibid.*, p. 87; written in 1927.

154. *Ibid.*, p. 90.

155. *Ibid.*

156. *Ibid.*, pp. 90–92.

157. *Ibid.*, pp. 36, 87.

158. *Ibid.*, p. 63.

159. *Ibid.*, p. 64.

160. See *Dawn to the West: Fiction.*

161. *MHZ*, VI, p. 22. Hakuchō went on to say of Ueda Bin: "For example, sensei will say, 'In order to appreciate Aston's discussion of Saikaku in his *History of Japanese Literature*, it is necessary to be able to read Dante in the original. The phrase *muyamuyamuya* at the end of his discussion of Saikaku is a quotation from *muyamuya* in Dante, an extremely famous passage.' " *Muyamuyamuya* is a meaningless combination of sounds, rather like "hocus-pocus."

162. *Ibid.*

163. See Yoshida, *Kindai Bungei Hyōron Shi: Taishō Hen*, pp. 45–46.

164. For the Ryūdokai, see *Nihon Kindai Bungaku Daijiten*, IV, p. 528. It is unclear when this group first met, but it was probably about 1900. Members brought their works to the various restaurants where sessions of the club were held and read them aloud, following which there were discussions. The name Ryūdokai was adopted in 1904 after it was decided to hold all future meetings at a French restaurant called the Ryūdo-ken. Members included Kunikida Doppo, Tayama Katai, Iwano Hōmei, Chikamatsu Shūkō, and Yanagita Kunio. It gradually turned into a social club, but in 1907, at the suggestion of Yanagita, eleven of the members founded the Ibsen Society, which assumed the literary functions of the Ryūdokai. The last important meeting was in 1913, the farewell party for Shimazaki Tōson before his departure for Europe.

165. Yoshida, *Kindai Bungei Hyōron Shi: Taishō Hen*, p. 48, states that it was against Hakuchō's wishes; but Yamamoto Kenkichi, in his article in *Nihon Kindai Bungaku Daijiten*, III, p. 234, makes no mention of unwillingness to resign.

166. The essays were on Natsume Sōseki, the Tokutomi brothers, Ozaki Kōyō, Iwano Hōmei, Mori Ōgai, Masaoka Shiki, Ichiyō and Chogyū, Tayama Katai, Futabatei Shimei, Kawatake Mokuami, Akutagawa Ryūnosuke, Osanai Kaoru, Tokuda Shūsei, Kōda Rohan, Shiga Naoya and Kasai Zenzō, Shimazaki Tōson, Tanizaki Jun'ichirō and Satō Haruo, Kikuchi Kan, and Nagai Kafū.

167. Hirano, et al., *Gendai Nihon Bungaku Ronsō*, I, pp. 163–64.

168. *Ibid.*, p. 154.

169. *Ibid.*, pp. 166–67.

170. *Ibid.*, p. 170.

171. *Ibid.*, pp. 172–74.

172. *Ibid.*, p. 186.

173. For criticism by members of the proletarian literature movement before Aono, see *Dawn to the West: Fiction.*

174. Hirano, et al., *Gendai Nihon Bungaku Ronsō*, I, p. 255.

175. *Ibid.* See also Tanaka, *Kindai Hyōron Shū*, II, pp. 318–19.

176. Hirano, et al., *Gendai Nihon Bungaku Ronsō*, I, p. 256.

177. *Ibid.*, p. 259.

178. *Ibid.*, p. 267.

179. *Ibid.*, p. 268.

180. Aono described it: "It is a reflection of the consciousness of belonging to the Japanese intelligentsia. Or, to put it in intellectual terms, it is a manifestation of the liberalistic thought of the intelligentsia. The keynote of liberalistic thought is the spirit of individualism; and if one pushes this spirit to its logical conclusion, it becomes democracy in the realm of politics, and the concept of the opposition between the individual and society in the realm of philosophy; it further becomes the concept of the individual as an independent entity. It can easily be seen how nihilism branches off at this point." Hirano, I, p. 272.

181. Hirano et al., *Gendai Nihon Bungaku Ronsō*, I, pp. 271–72.

182. Senuma Shigeki, in *Nihon Gendai Bungaku Shi*, II, p. 9, dates the beginning of the Taishō period in literary terms from 1910, the year of the Grand Treason case, and concludes it in 1930, the year before Japanese Fascism showed itself publicly by creating the Manchurian Incident.

183. Quoted by Yoshida, *Kindai Bungei Hyōron Shi: Taishō Hen*, pp. 48–49. Yoshida himself, after examining the evidence, came to the conclusion that, despite all that has been written about the enormous shock that the execution of Kōtoku exerted on Japanese of the time, most people, unfamiliar with the facts of the case, believed that Kōtoku's crime was a loathsome act of rebellion for which the death penalty was entirely justified. If this was true of the general public, it was even truer of the bundan, which prided itself on its lack of interest in matters that bothered the average Japanese. Ishikawa Takuboku was an evident exception.

184. Itō Sei, "Kaisetsu," in *Hirotsu Kazuo, Kikuchi Kan*, p. 504. "Nihilism," as used here, seems to have meant scepticism about all established values, especially those relating to literary activity.

185. *Ibid.*, p. 505.

186. Tanizawa, *Taishōki*, p. 164.

187. *Hirotsu Kazuo Zenshū* (henceforth abbreviated as *HKZ*), VIII, pp. 145–46.

188. *Ibid.*, p. 146.

189. *Ibid.*, pp. 159–60.

190. *Ibid.*, p. 162.

191. *Ibid.*, pp. 301–02.

192. The Matsukawa trial stemmed from the derailment of a train as the result of which three railway employees lost their lives. The event took place in August 1949. Arrests were made, mainly of railway union members. At the first trial in December 1950 the defendants were found guilty and five men were sentenced to death. Subsequent reviews of the decision led in 1959 to the Supreme Court's ordering a retrial, as the result of which the defendants were found innocent in 1961. Hirotsu Kazuo kept up a steady flow of articles on the subject and immensely aided the defense. There is a book in English on the subject, *Trial at Matsukawa*, by Chalmers Johnson.

193. *HKZ*, VIII, pp. 436–37.
194. Satō Haruo, *Taikutsu Tokuhon*, I, p. 140.
195. *Ibid.*, p. 144.
196. Hirano, I, p. 77. Ikuta's article was entitled "Ninshiki Fusoku no Biga-kusha Futari" (Two Aesthetes with Inadequate Knowledge).
197. Usui, II, pp. 211–34.
198. The title seems to have been Satō's modern equivalent of *Tsurezuregusa*. Maruya Saiichi's preface discusses the possible meanings of the title: (1) a text-book with which the reader is certain to be bored; (2) a textbook written when the author was bored; (3) a textbook that offers instruction in boredom. The last possibility is further divided into: (*a*) a book from which one learns how to be bored; and (*b*) a book from which one learns how to divert oneself when bored. Maruya Saiichi, "Kaidai," to Satō Haruo, *Taikutsu Tokuhon*.
199. Satō, *Taikutsu*, I, pp. 166–67.
200. *Ibid.*, II, pp. 233–34.
201. *Ibid.*, I, p. 182.
202. *Ibid.*, pp. 184–85.
203. *Ibid.*, p. 163.
204. *Ibid.*, p. 212.
205. *Ibid.*, p. 173.
206. *Ibid.*, pp. 175–76.
207. Criticism by members of these schools is found in the relevant chapters of *Dawn to the West: Fiction.* I have tried to avoid duplicating material.
208. See Saigō Nobutsuna, Nagatsumi Yasuaki, and Hirosue Tamotsu, *Nihon Bungaku no Koten*, published by Iwanami Shoten in 1953.
209. Nakamura Mitsuo, in *Ronkō Kobayashi Hideo*, pp. 35 and 64, called atten-tion to Kobayashi's particular interest in short-lived geniuses, including Sane-tomo, Rimbaud, and Mozart. Perhaps his early contacts with Tominaga and Nakahara influenced Kobayashi's interest in such figures, but he wrote sur-prisingly little of a critical nature about either of these friends. Kobayashi once stated: "There is no need for me to read works by my close friends. When I know everything that needs to be known about a work created by the hand of nature, works created by these works seem exceedingly boring." (From "Hi-hyōka Shikkaku, II" (1931), in *Kobayashi Hideo Zenshū* (henceforth abbreviated as *KHZ*), I, p. 179.
210. "Nenrei" (1950), *KHZ*, VIII, p. 228.
211. "Aki" (1950), in *ibid.*, pp. 190–91. He later described how difficult he had found it to read Proust's French at a pace appropriate to the precision of Proust's analyses of minute events.
212. *Ibid.*, XII, p. 287.
213. "Shiga Naoya" (1929), in *ibid.*, IV, p. 14.
214. *Ibid.*, II, p. 152.
215. Kobayashi Hideo, *Kyūyū Kōkan*, pp. 307–08.
216. Edward Seidensticker, "Kobayashi Hideo," pp. 448, 459.
217. Odagiri Hideo, *Gendai Bungaku Shi*, II, pp. 436–37. Odagiri is quoting Honda Shūgo, but clearly agrees with the opinion.
218. *Ibid.*, I, p. 12.

219. *Ibid.*, p. 13.

220. *Ibid.*, pp. 13–14.

221. Naturally, what Kobayashi meant by this unusual phrase was that the work is impregnated with the author's most deeply experienced feelings, not that he has been killed over his manuscript.

222. See Nakamura, *Ronkō Kobayashi*, p. 140.

223. "Ashiru to Kame no Ko, 3" (1930), in *KHZ*, I, p. 49.

224. "Ashiru to Kame no Ko, 4" (1930), in *ibid.*, p. 56. Kobayashi also remarked in the same passage:

> Just supposing that my criticism really is difficult. If so, it could only be for two possible reasons: the first is that my expression is technically clumsy; the second is that simple truths are far more difficult to relate than complicated theories. All the same, I can't help wondering what attitude the innocent young authors who complain that my criticism is too difficult for them to understand adopt when they amuse themselves by writing novels. Do they suppose that authors have the special privilege of being inept at criticism? Are we supposed to admire, as a fine old tradition of our people, the fact that young writers today have still not completely abandoned the attitudes of the gesaku writers of the old days?

225. *Ibid.*, IV, p. 170.

226. *Ibid.*, III, p. 107.

227. *Ibid.*, p. 108.

228. "Futatabi Bungei Jihyō ni tsuite" (1935), in *ibid.*, p. 111.

229. *Ibid.*, p. 113.

230. *The Philosophy of Tragedy* was the title given by the Japanese translators to Schestow's *Dostoejvski und Nietzsche* (1903).

231. Other critics expressed concern lest the translators had meant it when they said it was "sincere malice" that had induced them to present to Japanese readers so noxious a book. *KHZ*, III, p. 71.

232. *Ibid.*, IV, p. 87.

233. "It is quite true that perhaps not even one of their works is a masterpiece of the kind that will be read by future generations; and the characters who appeared in their novels may have been for the most part only a mass of imaginary beings. However, this was the result of their having been distorted by ideology that demanded exaggerations in accordance with literary theories; it was definitely not a failure or success that resulted from individual taste." *Ibid.*, III, p. 132.

234. *Ibid.*, p. 145.

235. Nakamura, *Ronkō Kobayashi*, p. 145.

236. *Ibid.*, p. 147.

237. *Ibid.*, p. 149.

238. *Ibid.*, p. 191.

239. *KHZ*, III, p. 117.

240. Nakamura, *Ronkō Kobayashi*, p. 181.

241. Kaga Otohiko wrote of Kobayashi's *Life of Dostoevski* that "it seems to have been heavily influenced by J. Middleton Murry's *Fyodor Dostoievski*, and

although I recognize its significance as a pioneering study in Japan, I have doubts as to its real originality." (In "Wa ga Kobayashi Hideo Zō," in *Kokubungaku Kaishaku to Kanshō*, August 1975, p. 79.) Nakamura Kennosuke, "Dosutoefusukii no Tegami are kore," in *Kobayashi Hideo*, p. 207, wrote: "Probably the only instances where Kobayashi Hideo began to approach Dostoevski himself, without depending on Gide or Carr, were in *Notes from the Underground* and *The Eternal Husband*." Nakamura referred specifically to correlations made by Kobayashi between these two works and a letter of Dostoevski's.

242. Quoted by Shimizu Takayoshi, *Kobayashi Hideo to Furansu Shōchō Shugi*, p. 107.

243. *KHZ*, I, p. 213.

244. Shimizu, *Kobayashi Hideo to Furansu*, p. 109.

245. Hirano Ken et al., *Gendai Nihon Bungaku Ronsō*, III, pp. 120–21.

246. *Ibid.*, p. 123; also, *KHZ*, IV, p. 152.

247. Hirano Ken, et al., *Gendai Nihon Bungaku Ronsō*, III, p. 123; also, *KHZ*, IV, pp. 152–53.

248. Hirano Ken, et al., *Gendai Nihon Bungaku Ronsō*, III, pp. 123–24; also, *KHZ*, IV, p. 153.

249. Hirano Ken, et al., *Gendai Nihon Bungaku Ronsō*, III, p. 125.

250. *KHZ*, IV, p. 165.

251. Kanō Sakujirō (1885–1941), an "I" novelist who enjoyed a considerable reputation in his day. Kobayashi earlier in this article had quoted Kanō's opinion that the tragic life led by Tolstoy in 1910 was symbolic of human life itself.

252. I have translated the Japanese word *shisō* as both "thought" and "ideas," depending on the context.

253. *KHZ*, IV, p. 166.

254. *Ibid.*, pp. 173–74.

255. Hirano Ken, et al., *Gendai Nihon Bungaku Ronsō*, III, p. 156.

256. *Ibid.*, pp. 158–59.

257. *Ibid.*, p. 159.

258. See above, p. 587.

259. *KHZ*, IV, pp. 168–71. Seidensticker, "Kobayashi Hideo," pp. 440–41, gives translations of some sections omitted here.

260. Seidensticker, "Kobayashi Hideo," p. 439.

261. *KHZ*, IV, p. 289.

262. See Kawakami Tetsutarō, *Bungakuteki Kaisōroku*, pp. 14–25; Iwaya Daishi, *Hijōji Nihon Bundan Shi*, pp. 5–61; and Keene, *Landscapes*, pp. 308–10.

263. Kobayashi preferred the pronunciation "Taima," but *Taema* is the correct name of the play.

264. From episode 229 of *Essays in Idleness*, translated by Donald Keene, p. 188.

265. *KHZ*, VIII, p. 25.

266. Nakamura, *Ronkō Kobayashi*, p. 159.

267. *Ibid.*, p. 161.

268. I have followed the interpretations given by Miyazaka Yūshō (ed.), *Ichigon Hōdan*, in *Kana Hōgo Shū*, p. 204, and Yanase Kazuo (ed.), *Ichigon Hōdan*, p. 108.

269. *KHZ*, VIII, p. 17.
270. *Ibid.*, pp. 18–19.
271. When he used the word "animalistic" he was referring to a remark made by Kawabata and quoted slightly earlier in the essay: "A living human being is a kind of animal in the process of becoming a human being."
272. *KHZ*, VIII, p. 19. For translations of other poetic passages from *Mujō to iu koto*, see Seidensticker, "Kobayashi Hideo," pp. 454–57.
273. It has been suggested that Kobayashi's inability to deal with Dostoevski's Christianity obliged him to break off his study. See *ibid.*, p. 458.
274. *KHZ*, VIII, pp. 75–76.
275. See also *Kawakami Tetsutarō Zenshū*, III, p. 305.
276. *Ibid.*, p. 303. The essay was published in the inaugural issue of the magazine *Sōgen*, in December 1946.
277. Nakamura, *Ronkō Kobayashi*, p. 171.
278. *Ibid.*, p. 48.
279. Etō Jun, "Kaisetsu," to *Mozart; Mujō to iu koto*, p. 190.

BIBLIOGRAPHY

Note: All Japanese books, except as otherwise noted, were published in Tokyo.

Akiyama Seikō. *Takayama Chogyū*. Sekibunkan, 1957.
Anesaki Masaharu (ed.). *Chogyū Zenshū*, 5 vols. Hakubunkan, 1904.
Asai Kiyoshi et al. *Hyōron, Ronsetsu Zuisō, I*, in Kenkyū Shiryō Gendai Nihon Bungaku series. Meiji Shoin, 1980.
Aston W. G. *A History of Japanese Literature*. London: William Heinemann, 1899.
Chiba Sen'ichi. *Gendai Bungaku no Hikaku Bungakuteki Kenkyū*. Yagi Shoten, 1978.
Etō Jun. "Kobayashi Hideo," in *Chosaku Shū, III*. Kōdansha, 1967.
———. "Kaisetsu," to Kobayashi Hideo, *Mootsuaruto; Mujō to iu koto*, in Shinchō Bunko series, 1961.
Hartmann, Eduard von. *Philosophie des Schönen*, in *Ausgewählte Werke, IV*. Leipzig: Wilhelm Friederich, n.d.
Hasegawa Izumi. *Kindai Nihon Bungaku Hyōron Shi*. Yūseidō, 1977.
——— (ed.). *Kōza Nihon Bungaku no Sōten, V*. Meiji Shoin, 1969.
Hasegawa Nyozekan et al. *Gendai Bungei Hyōron Shū*, 3 vols., in Gendai Nihon Bungaku Zenshū series. Chikuma Shobō, 1958.
Hashimoto Minoru. *Kobayashi Hideo Hihan*. Tōjusha, 1980.
Hijikata Teiichi. *Kindai Nihon Bungaku Hyōron Shi*. Hōsei Daigaku Shuppankyoku, 1973.
Hirano Ken. *Bungaku: Shōwa Jūnen Zengo*. Bungei Shunjū, 1972.
———. *Shōwa Bungaku no Kanōsei*. Iwanami Shoten, 1972.
———, Odagiri Hideo, and Yamamoto Kenkichi (eds.). *Gendai Nihon Bungaku Ronsō Shi*, 3 vols. Miraisha, 1956.

Hiraoka Toshio. *Zoku Kitamura Tōkoku Kenkyū*. Yūseidō, 1971.

Hirotsu Kazuo, Kikuchi Kan, in Nihon no Bungaku series. Chūō Kōron Sha, 1973.

Hirotsu Kazuo Zenshū, 13 vols. Chūō Kōron Sha, 1973–74.

Hisamatsu Sen'ichi. *Nihon Bungaku Hyōron Shi; Kinsei Kindai Hen*. Shibundō, 1952.

Hisamatsu Sen'ichi, Kimata Osamu, Naruse Masahiko, Kawazoe Kunimoto, and Hasegawa Izumi (eds.). *Gendai Nihon Bungaku Daijiten*. Meiji Shoin, 1965.

Hōgetsu Zenshū, 8 vols. Ten'yūsha, 1919–20.

Homma Hisao. *Meiji Bungaku Shi, I*. Tōkyōdō, 1935.

Inono Kenji. *Meiji no Sakka*. Iwanami Shoten, 1966.

Isoda Kōichi. *Sengo Hihyōka Ron*. Kawade Shobō Shinsha, 1969.

Iwaya Daishi. *Hijōji Nihon Bundan Shi*. Chūō Kōron Sha, 1958.

Katsumoto Seiichirō (ed.). *Tōkoku Zenshū*, 3 vols. Iwanami Shoten, 1950.

Kawakami Tetsutarō Zenshū, 8 vols. Keisōsha, 1969–72.

Kawakami Tetsutarō. *Bungakuteki Kaisōroku*. Asahi Shimbun Sha, 1965.

Kawazoe Kunimoto. *Shimamura Hōgetsu*. Waseda Daigaku Shuppanbu, 1953.

——— (ed.). *Bungaku 1910 Nendai*. Meiji Shoin, 1979.

———(ed.). *Kindai Hyōron Shu, I*, in Nihon Kindai Bungaku Taikei series. Kadokawa Shoten, 1972.

Keene, Donald (trans.). *Essays in Idleness*. New York: Columbia University Press, 1967.

———. *Landscapes and Portraits*. Tokyo: Kodansha International, 1971.

———. *World Within Walls*. New York: Holt, Rinehart and Winston, 1976.

Kinoshita Naoe, "Fukuzawa Yukichi to Kitamura Tōkoku," in *Kitamura Tōkoku Shū*, in Meiji Bungaku Zenshū series. Chikuma Shobō, 1976.

Kitamura Tōkoku, in Nihon Bungaku Kenkyū Shiryō Sōsho series. Yūseidō, 1972.

Kobayashi Hideo Zenshū, 12 vols. Shinchōsha, 1967–68.

Kobayashi Hideo in Nihon Bungaku Kenkyu Shiryō Sōsho series. Yūseidō, 1977.

Kobayashi Hideo. *Kyūyū Kōkan*. Kyūryūdō, 1980.

Makibayashi Kōji. "Bungakkai to Romanchishizumu," in Miyoshi and Takemori, II.

Masamune Hakuchō Zenshū, 13 vols. Shinchōsha, 1965.

Masamune Hakuchō. *Bundan Jimbutsu Hyōron*. Chūō Kōron Sha, 1932.

———. *Bungakuteki Kaisō Shū*, in Gendai Nihon Bungaku Zenshū series. Chikuma Shobō, 1967.

Matsumoto Ken'ichi. *Dosutoefusukii to Nihonjin*. Asahi Shimbun Sha, 1975.

Miyazaka Yūshō (ed.). *Kana Hōgo Shū*, in Nihon Koten Bungaku Taikei series. Iwanami Shoten, 1964.

Miyoshi Yukio and Takemori Ten'yū. *Kindai Bungaku*, 10 vols. Yūhikaku, 1977–78.

Mori Ōgai. *Ōgai Zenshū*, vols. XXII and XXIII. Iwanami Shoten, 1973.

Morikawa Tatsuya and Watanabe Hiroshi. *Atarashii Hihyō*. Shimbisha, 1971.

Morris, Ivan (ed.). *Modern Japanese Stories*. Tokyo: Tuttle, 1962.

Muramatsu Takeshi (ed.). *Shōwa Hihyō Taikei*, 4 vols. Banchō Shobō, 1972.

Nakajima Kenzō, Ōta Saburō, and Fukuda Rintarō (eds.). *Nihon Kindai Shōsetsu*, III. Shimizu Kōbundō, 1961.

Nakamura Mitsuo Zenshū, 16 vols. Chikuma Shobō, 1971.

Nakamura Mitsuo. *Meiji Bungaku Shi*. Chikuma Shobō, 1963.

———. *Ronkō Kobayashi Hideo*. Chikuma Shobō, 1977.

——— and Yoshida Seiichi (eds.). *Gendai Bungakuron Taikei*, II. Kawade Shobō, 1953.

Nakamura Shin'ichirō. *Meiji Sakka Ron*. Kōsōsha, 1978.

Nihon Kindai Bungaku Daijiten, 6 vols. Kōdansha, 1977–78.

Ochi Haruo. *Kindai Bungaku no Tanjō*. Kōdansha, 1975.

Odagiri Hideo. *Gendai Bungaku Shi*, II. Shūeisha, 1975.

Ōe Kenzaburō et al. *Kobayashi Hideo wo yomu*. Gendai Kikakushitsu, 1981.

Ōgai Zenshū, 38 vols. Iwanami Shoten, 1971–75.

Ōoka Shōhei. *Shōwa Bungaku e no Shōgen*. Bungei Shunjū, 1968.

Ōoka Shōhei et al. *Ronshū Kobayashi Hideo*, 2 vols. Mugi Shobō, 1966.

Sadoya Shigenobu. *Amerika Seishin to Kindai Nihon*. Kōbundō, 1974.

———. *Hōgetsu Shimamura Takitarō Ron*. Meiji Shoin, 1980.

Saitō Ryokuu Shū, in Meiji Bungaku Zenshū series. Chikuma Shobō, 1966.

Sasabuchi Tomoichi. *Kitamura Tōkoku*. Fukumura Shoten, 1950.

Satō Haruo. *Taikutsu Tokuhon*, 2 vols., in Fuzambō Hyakka Bunko series. Fuzambō, 1978.

Satō Yasumasa and Satō Masaru (eds.). *Kitamura Tōkoku, Tokutomi Roka Shū*, in Nihon Kindai Bungaku Taikei series. Kadokawa Shoten, 1972.

Seidensticker, Edward. "Kobayashi Hideo," in Donald H. Shively (ed.), *Tradition and Modernization in Japanese Culture*. Princeton, N.J.: Princeton University Press, 1971.

Senuma Shigeki et al. *Nihon Gendai Bungaku Shi*, I, in Nihon Gendai Bungaku Zenshū series. Kōdansha, 1979.

Shimada Kinji. *Nihon ni okeru Gaikoku Bungaku*, 2 vols. Asahi Shimbun Sha, 1976.

Shimizu Takayoshi. *Kobayashi Hideo to Furansu Shōchō Shugi*. Shimbisha, 1980.

Shinoda Hajime. *Yoshida Ken'ichi Ron*. Chikuma Shobō, 1981.

Sumiya Mikio (ed.). *Tokutomi Sohō, Yamaji Aizan*, in Nihon no Meicho series. Chūō Kōron Sha, 1971.

Takahashi Hideo. "Watakushi to wa nani ka," in *Yuriika*, VI, No. 12, 1974.

Takayama Chogyū, Saitō Nonohito, Anesaki Chōfū, Tobari Chikufu, in Meiji Bungaku Zenshū series. Chikuma Shobō, 1966.

Tanaka Hidemichi. *Bungaku no Tenshin*. Tairyūsha, 1976.

Tanaka Yasutaka (ed.). *Kindai Hyōron Shū*, II, in Nihon Kindai Bungaku Taikei series. Kadokawa Shoten, 1972.

Tanizawa Eiichi. *Kindai Nihon Bungakushi no Kōsō*. Shōbunsha, 1964.

———. *Meijiki no Bungei Hyōron*. Yagi Shoten, 1971.

———. *Taishōki no Bungei Hyōron*. Hanawa Shobō, 1962.

Ueda, Makoto. *Modern Japanese Writers*. Stanford, Calif.: Stanford University Press, 1976.

Usui Yoshimi. *Kindai Bungaku Ronsō*, 2 vols. Chikuma Shobo, 1975.

————. *Sengo Bungaku Ronsō*, 2 vols. Banchō Shobō, 1972.

Watanabe Hiroshi. *Kiki no Bungaku*. Chikuma Shobō, 1972.

Watson, Burton. *Su Tung-p'o*. New York: Grove Press, 1965.

Yamada Bimyō, Ishibashi Ningetsu, Takase Bun'en, in Meiji Bungaku Zenshū series. Kōdansha, 1979.

Yamanouchi Hisaaki. *The Search for Authenticity in Modern Japanese Literature*. Cambridge, England: Cambridge University Press, 1978.

Yanabu Akira. *Buntai no Ronri*. Hōsei Daigaku Shuppankyoku, 1976.

Yanase Kazuo (ed.). *Ichigon Hōdan*, in Kadokawa Bunko series, 1970.

Yoshida Ken'ichi Chosaku Shū, 32 vols. Shūeisha, 1979–81.

Yoshida Seiichi. *Kindai Bungei Hyōron Shi: Meiji Hen*. Shibundō, 1975.

————. *Kindai Bungei Hyōron Shi; Taishō Hen*. Shibundō, 1980.

————. *Nihon Kindai Bungaku no Hikaku Bungakuteki Kenkyū*. Shimizu Kōbundō, 1971.

————. *Rōman Shugi no Kenkyū*. Tōkyōdō, 1970.

————. *Shizen Shugi no Kenkyū*, 2 vols. Tōkyōdō, 1958.

————and Wada Kingo (eds.). *Kindai Bungaku Hyōron Taikei*, III. Kadokawa Shoten, 1972.

Yoshitake Yoshinori. *Meiji Taishō no Hon'yaku Shi*. Kenkyūsha, 1958.

GLOSSARY

Asahi Shimbun A newspaper, founded in 1879, that is nationally distributed. It enjoys special popularity among intellectuals.

Bakin Takizawa Bakin (1767–1848), an important writer of yomihon fiction, of which the best known example is *Hakkenden* (Eight Dogs).

Bashō Matsuo Bashō (1644–1694), the greatest of the haiku poets.

bundan The "literary world," which consists of influential writers and critics who judge the writings of others and award prizes that bring recognition to new authors.

Bungakkai A literary magazine, originally founded in 1893, which enjoyed great prestige in the Meiji period. A second series, issued in 1933, and a postwar series have maintained its reputation.

bungei jihyō Monthly (or weekly) literary criticism, carried in magazines or newspapers. Originated in the 1880s but first attained prominence in the 1920s with Masamune Hakuchō.

Bungei Shunjū A popular magazine of wide circulation, which publishes both literary and nonliterary works. Founded in 1923 by Kikuchi Kan.

bunjin A "man of letters" in the old-fashioned sense; the dilettante ideal of, writers who look back nostalgically to the past.

Danrin A school of haikai poetry, founded by Nishiyama Sōin (1605–1682), and known for its allusive and contemporary qualities.

dengaku A form of theatrical entertainment, originally related to agricultural ceremonies, but later taken up by the court in Kyoto; flourished especially in the early fourteenth century.

dōnin　A member of a group that publishes a magazine (as opposed to commercially published magazines).

dōnin zasshi　A magazine published by dōnin; a "little magazine."

engo　A related word; that is, a word connected to others in a poem by its overtones as well as its meaning.

fudoki　A gazeteer; refers specifically to the gazeteers compiled in response to an imperial order of 713 by provinces all over Japan.

Gekisaku　A magazine of the theater, founded in 1932 by Kishida Kunio and others, for publishing new plays and criticizing existing tendencies in the Shingeki theater. The first series contained 104 issues, published until 1940.

gembun itchi　The principle of unifying spoken and written languages, first achieved in the works of Futabatei Shimei and Yamada Bimyō.

gendaishi　"Contemporary poetry"; used in contrast to *kindaishi* (modern poetry), which came increasingly to refer to poetry composed before 1930.

Genroku　The name of an era (1688–1703), but used also to designate the culture of Japan from about 1685 to 1725.

gesaku　A general name for fiction composed from about 1770 to 1870, originally humorous.

gidayū　A form of sung and declaimed recitation to the accompaniment of the samisen; the name was derived from that of Takemoto Gidayū (1651–1714), the celebrated chanter of the Jōruri theater.

hagi　A plant (*lespedeza bicolor*) that bears lavender or white blossoms in early autumn. Often rendered as "bush clover."

haikai　A word originally used of the comic poetry in the *Kokinshū*, and later of the comic style of linked verse. It came to designate the poetry that grew out of comic linked verse, notably that of Bashō and his school.

haikai no renga　The comic style of linked verse.

haiku　A complete poem in seventeen syllables, divided into lines of five, seven and five syllables. The name was apparently invented by Masaoka Shiki.

heitan　"Plainness and blandness"—an ideal of Chinese poetry, especially of the early Sung Dynasty, which was adopted by Masaoka Shiki.

Hōgen Monogatari　A historical romance describing warfare that began in 1156. Probably written about 1220.

Hototogisu　A haiku magazine, founded in 1897 by disciples of Masaoka Shiki, and long associated with Takahama Kyoshi.

imayō　The "new style" of poetry, popular from the eleventh century. Each poem generally consisted of four lines of seven and five or eight and six syllables.

jidaimono　Historical plays, generally set in the distant past.

jōruri　The puppet theater, known today as Bunraku.

kaika　A term used in the early Meiji period for the "enlightenment," referring to the new culture imported from the West.

Kaizō　A leading intellectual magazine, founded in 1919. It carried many important works of fiction, especially in the 1920s and 1930s.

kakekotoba　A "pivot word," that is, a word with a double meaning, the first related to previous words, the second to the words that follow.

ka mo   Exclamatory particles, often used in poetry of the *Manyōshū* style to convey pity, compassion, etc.

kana   The Japanese syllabary, forty-eight phonetic symbols, each representing a syllable.

kanshi   Poetry composed in classical Chinese by Japanese.

katsureki   "Living history"—a term first used with derogatory intent of Kabuki plays that were faithful to historical facts, as opposed to the traditions of the Kabuki stage.

Kenkō   Yoshida Kenkō (*c.* 1283–*c.* 1350), a Buddhist priest, known especially for his collection of essays, *Tsurezuregusa* (Essays in Idleness).

-keri   A past, durative, or affirmative suffix, often found at the ends of lines of waka poetry. Sometimes used also for reported action or to indicate an emotional response to a new perception.

Kojiki   The oldest surviving Japanese book, presented to the court in 712.

Kokinshū   The first and best-known imperially commissioned anthology of *waka*, presented to the court in 905.

kokugaku   "National learning"—the study of Japanese (as opposed to Chinese) literature, history, and religion. The kokugaku movement flourished especially in the eighteenth century.

Kokumin no Tomo   Important periodical, founded by Tokutomi Sohō in 1887. Discontinued publication in 1899 after issuing 372 numbers. Mainly political in importance, but it published also original works of literature and literary criticism.

kokushi   "National poetry," a term favored by Yosano Tekkan, rather than the more usual *tanka*.

koto   A musical instrument with numerous strings (the exact number depending on the variety); the "classic" Japanese musical instrument.

Kwannon   A Buddhist divinity, also known as Kannon in Japanese and as Kwan-yin in Chinese.

kyōka   A comic variety of waka.

makurakotoba   A kind of epithet, used before the names of places, gods, etc. The meanings have often become obscure.

Manyōshū   The great collection of poetry compiled in the eighth century. Also written *Man'yōshū* and *Mannyōshū*.

masuraoburi   An ideal of manliness, associated with the literature of the warrior class.

Meiji   Reign name of Emperor Mutsuhito (1867–1912).

Mita Bungaku   A literary magazine, associated with Keiō University. Founded in 1910; advocated a "new romanticism," in opposition to the Naturalism of *Waseda Bungaku*.

mono no aware   "The pity of things" or "a sensitivity to things"; a quality conspicuous in the literature of the Heian period especially.

Motoori Norinaga   The scholar of National Learning; probably the finest premodern critic of Japanese literature (1730–1801).

Myōjō   "Morning Star"—a poetry journal founded in 1900 by Yosano Tekkan and associated with Romantic poetry. Discontinued publication in 1908.

Nihon-ha   The "Japan School"—the school of haiku associated with Masaoka

Shiki. After the newspaper *Nihon* (or *Nippon*) discontinued publication in 1906, the school shifted its forum to the magazine *Nihon oyobi Nihon-jin.* Led by Kawahigashi Hekigotō until Takahama Kyoshi returned to the world of haiku.

Nihon Rōman-ha Literary magazine, 1935–1938. The writers and critics for whom this was the organ were anti-Marxist, and devoted attention especially to the Japanese classics.

Nihon Shimbun (Nippon Shimbun) Newspaper, founded in 1889 as an organ of Japanism (*Nihon shugi*). The guiding spirit was Kuga Katsunan.

Nihon Shoki The first officially sponsored history of Japan, presented to the court in 720.

Nihon shugi "Japanism," a nationalistic variety of thought advocated at times by such men as Takayama Chogyū and Iwano Hōmei.

Pan no Kai "The Devotees of Pan," a group of writers and artists who met regularly at a French restaurant in Tokyo from 1908–1912, at first for discussions, later for social pleasure.

Po Chü-i The celebrated Chinese poet (772–846), whose works were extravagantly admired in Japan.

rabu "Love"–often used by Japanese of the Meiji period, with overtones of platonic love.

Rai San'yō An important kanshi poet and patriot (1730–1832).

Rekitei A poetry magazine, founded in 1935 by a group of poets including Kusano Shimpei, who remained associated with the magazine through its many vicissitudes.

renga "Linked verse," the composition of a poem, in one hundred or more "links," by two or more poets, supplying verses by turns. Effectively killed in the Meiji period by the unremitting attacks of Masaoka Shiki, who declared that renga was not "literature."

rensaku A series of tanka (or haiku) on related themes, typified by the rensaku of Saitō Mokichi.

risō An "ideal" in the Platonic sense, but also (as misunderstood by Tsubouchi Shōyō) an ideal that inspires a man when he is writing a work of literature.

rōnin A masterless samurai, who has been deprived of his normal work and source of income.

ronsō A literary dispute; one of the noteworthy features of Japanese criticism since the Meiji period.

saibara A variety of popular song that flourished in the Heian period; displaced in the thirteenth and fourteenth centuries by newer songs.

Saigyō The celebrated priest-poet (1118–1190).

Saikaku Ihara Saikaku (1642–1693), the most important writer of fiction during the Tokugawa period.

sakkaron "Discussions of authors"–a form of criticism that became popular during the Taishō period.

sakuhinron "Discussion of works," another form of criticism that became popular in the Taishō period.

Sanetomo Minamoto Sanetomo (1192–1219), the third shogun of the Kamakura shogunate, and a much admired poet.

sedōka A poem in six lines of five, seven, seven, five, seven, and seven syllables. Well represented in the *Manyōshū*, but increasingly rare thereafter.

seppuku Ritual disembowelment; known also as harakiri.

sewamono Domestic tragedies that described contemporary city life.

shasei "Portrayal of life"—an ideal of painting that was extended to poetry and prose.

shaseibun A composition in prose that embodies the ideal of shasei.

Shi, Genjitsu A poetry journal founded in 1930.

Shiki A major poetry journal, founded in 1934, at first as a quarterly. The editors included Miyoshi Tatsuji, Maruyama Kaoru, and Hori Tatsuo.

Shimpa A form of drama, created in the 1880s, that generally presented melodramatic events of contemporary life.

Shingeki "New Theater"—the mainstream of Japanese theater in the twentieth century, consisting of plays translated from Western languages and original Japanese plays in similar modes.

Shin Kokinshū The eighth imperially sponsored anthology of Japanese poetry. Completed in 1206.

shinkyō shōsetsu Mental attitude novels—a form of "I novel" that attempts to discover truths in small and often unimportant occurrences.

Shinsei Sha A group of poets of the early and mid-Meiji period headed by Mori Ōgai, who published the literary journal *Shigarami-sōshi* from 1889.

Shinshichō "New Thought Tides"—a literary magazine of Tokyo University, originally founded in 1907, and many times resuscitated.

Shinshi Sha The group of poets, headed by Yosano Tekkan and Akiko, who published the magazine *Myōjō*.

shintaishi "Poetry in the modern style"—the kind of poetry written from the early Meiji era under the influence of European poetry.

Shirakaba-ha The group associated with the literary magazine *Shirakaba*, founded in 1910 by Mushakōji Saneatsu, Shiga Naoya, and others.

Shi to Shiron An important journal of poetry and criticism of poetry, founded in 1928, that was widely respected for its advanced contents.

Shōwa The reign name of Emperor Hirohito, from 1926.

Sodō Yamaguchi Sodō (1642–1716), one of Bashō's important disciples.

SSS See Shinsei Sha.

Subaru A literary magazine, the successor to *Myōjō*, founded in 1909.

susuki A tall plant with a silvery plume that is typical of late autumn landscapes; sometimes translated as "pampas grass."

tabi "Bifurcated foot mittens," in the old phrase. A kind of sock worn with Japanese kimono, either white or black.

Taishō The reign name of Emperor Yoshihito (1912–1926).

taishū shōsetsu "Mass-market novels," not treated in this history.

Taiyō A magazine of general content, first published in 1895.

The Tale of the Heike English translation of the title *Heike Monogatari*, one of the major works of Japanese literature, written in the thirteenth century with later accretions. It treats the rise and fall of the Taira clan.

Tamenaga Shunsui A gesaku writer (1790–1843), the leading writer of *ninjōbon*, works that emphasized romantic attachments.

Tanabata The meeting of two stars on the seventh night of the seventh moon; a well-known Chinese legend that took root in Japan.

tanka The classic verse form, written in thirty-one syllables divided into five lines of five, seven, five, seven, and seven syllables. Earlier called *waka*.

tanshi A variant name for the tanka coined during the Meiji period.

tatami The floor covering, woven of a kind of grass, that is used in Japanese houses.

Teikoku Bungaku A literary magazine, closely associated with Tokyo Imperial University, founded in 1895 and discontinued in 1920.

tengu A long-nosed, winged goblin.

tsukinami Originally designated regular monthly meetings of tanka and haiku poets; later (especially under Masaoka Shiki's influence) came to have a pejorative meaning of uninspired compositions written to prescribed themes.

Tsurayuki Ki no Tsurayuki (884–946). A compiler of the *Kokinshū* (*c.* 905), and the writer of its celebrated preface. An important poet and also the author of the diary *Tosa Nikki*.

Uchimura Kanzō An important Christian leader (1861–1930) who influenced many writers of the Meiji period with his "churchless" Christianity.

uta Another name for the waka; also, a song.

utagokai Poetry gatherings in the imperial palace.

waka The classical verse form in thirty-one syllables arranged in five lines of five, seven, five, seven, and seven syllables. Also known as *uta, tanka*, and *tanshi*.

Waseda Bungaku The literary magazine of Waseda University, associated especially with Naturalism. Originally founded in 1891.

Yomiuri Shimbun A newspaper, founded in 1874, which was of great importance in the development of Meiji literature.

yūgen The ideal of "mystery and depth," found especially in poetry of the *Shin Kokinshū* and later, as well as in the Nō plays.

zadankai A group discussion, in which three or more persons participate, and which is later printed in a magazine or newspaper.

Zamboa A literary magazine, published between 1911 and 1913, in which a number of important works of poetry, especially by Kitahara Hakushū, appeared.

zangirimono "Cropped-hair plays"—refers to the Kabuki plays, especially those by Kawatake Mokuami, which depict the changes brought to Japan by the introduction of Western ways of life. The "cropped hair" of men who had formerly shaved their foreheads and allowed the rest of their hair to grow to full length epitomized these changes.

zatsuei "Miscellaneous compositions"—a section of a haiku magazine that is not restricted to verses on assigned topics.

zekku A quatrain in Chinese poetry (*chüeh-chü*), popular with Japanese writers of kanshi.

zuihitsu "Following the brush"—a kind of essay, popular with readers, who feel that it enables them to come close to favorite authors.

SELECTED LIST OF TRANSLATIONS INTO ENGLISH

Note: This list is not intended to be complete. A much fuller bibliography of translations, not only into English but into many other languages, is *Modern Japanese Literature in Translation: A Bibliography*, published in 1979 by the International House of Japan Library in Tokyo.

Anthologies That Include Poetry and Drama

Hibbett, Howard. *Contemporary Japanese Literature*. New York: Alfred A. Knopf, 1977.
Keene, Donald. *Modern Japanese Literature*. New York: Grove Press, 1956.
Mishima, Yukio, and Geoffrey Bownas. *New Writing in Japan*. Harmondsworth, England: Penguin Books, 1972.

Collections of Modern Japanese Poetry

Atsumi, Ikuko, and Graeme Wilson. *Three Contemporary Japanese Poets*. London: London Magazine, 1972.

Bownas, Geoffrey, and Anthony Thwaite. *The Penguin Book of Japanese Verse.* Baltimore: Penguin Books, 1964.

Fitzsimmons, Thomas. *Japanese Poetry Now.* New York: Schocken Books, 1972.

Guest, Harry and Lynn, and Kajima Shōzō. *Post-war Japanese Poetry.* Harmondsworth, England: Penguin Books, 1972.

Keene, Dennis. *The Modern Japanese Prose Poem.* Princeton, N.J.: Princeton University Press, 1980.

Kijima Hajime. *The Poetry of Postwar Japan.* Iowa City: University of Iowa Press, 1975.

Kirkup, James. *Modern Japanese Poetry.* St. Lucia, Queensland, Australia: University of Queensland Press, 1978.

Kōno, Ichirō, and Rikutarō Fukuda. *An Anthology of Modern Japanese Poetry.* Tokyo: Kenkyusha, 1957.

Ninomiya, Takamichi, and D. J. Enright. *The Poetry of Living Japan.* London: John Murray, 1957.

Ōoka Makoto (ed.) *Celebration in Darkness,* poems of Yoshioka Minoru and Iijima Kōichi. Rochester, Mich.: Katudid, 1985.

Rexroth, Kenneth, and Ikuko Atsumi. *The Burning Heart: Women Poets of Japan.* New York: Seabury Press, 1977.

Sato, Hiroaki. *Ten Japanese Poets.* Hanover, N.H.: Granite Publications, 1973.

———, and Burton Watson. *From the Country of Eight Islands.* Garden City, N.Y.: Doubleday, 1981.

Shiffert, Edith Marcombe, and Yuki Sawa. *Anthology of Modern Japanese Poetry.* Tokyo: Tuttle, 1972.

Ueda, Makoto. *Modern Japanese Haiku: An Anthology.* Tokyo: Tokyo University Press, 1976.

Poetry by Individual Modern Poets

Epp, Robert. *Treelike: The Poetry of Kinoshita Yūji.* Rochester, Mich.: Oakland University, 1982.

Furuta, Soichi. *Cape Jasmine and Pomegranates: The Free-Meter Haiku of Ippekiro.* New York: Grossman Publishers, 1974.

Hagiwara Sakutarō. *Howling at the Moon,* trans. Hiroaki Sato. Tokyo: University of Tokyo Press, 1978.

———. *Rats' Nests.* trans. Robert Epp. Stanwood, WA: Yakusha, 1993.

Heinrich, Amy Vladeck. *Fragments of Rainbows.* New York: Columbia University Press, 1983.

———. "My Mother Is Dying: Saitō Mokichi's Shinitamau Haha," in *Monumenta Nipponica,* XXXIII, No. 4, 1978.

Horiguchi Daigaku. *Rainbows.* trans. Robert Epp. Stanwood, WA: Yakusha, 1994.

Ishikawa Takuboku. *A Handful of Sand,* trans. Shio Sakanishi. Boston: Marshall Jones, 1934.

(Ishikawa) Takuboku. *Poems to Eat,* trans. Carl Sesar. Tokyo: Kodansha International, 1966.

Itō Sachio. *Songs of a Cowherd,* trans. Shio Sakanishi. Boston: Marshall Jones, 1936.

Kitasono Katsue (Katué). *Glass Beret.* trans. John Solt. Milwaukee: Morgan Press, 1995.

Kusano Shimpei. *Frogs & Others*, trans. Cid Corman and Susumu Kamaike. New York: Grossman Publishers, 1969.

Maruyama Kaoru. *That Far-Off Self.* trans. Robert Epp, 2nd ed. Stanwood, WA: Yakusha, 1994.

(Masaoka) Shiki. *Poenies Kana*, trans. Harold J. Isaacson. New York: Theatre Arts, 1972.

Masaoka Shiki. "The Verse Record of My Peonies," trans. Earl Miner, in *Japanese Poetic Diaries*. Berkeley: University of California Press, 1969.

Miyazawa Kenji. *Spring and the Asura*, trans. Hiroaki Sato. Chicago: Chicago Review Press, 1973.

Mushakōji Saneatsu. *Long Corridor.* trans. Robert Epp. Stanwood, WA: Yakusha, 1996.

Nakahara Chūya. *Depilautumn.* trans. Kenneth L. Richard and John L. Riley. Toronto: Joint Centre on Modern East Asia, University of Toronto, 1981.

Ōoka Makoto, *Beneath the Sleepless Tossing of the Planets.* trans. Janine Beichman. Santa Fe: Katydid Books, 1995.

———. *A String around Autumn*, trans. author and Thomas Fitzsimmons. Rochester, Mich.: Oakland University, 1982.

Sekine Hiroshi. *Cinderellas.* trans. Robert Epp. Stanwood, WA: Yakusha, 1995.

Shiraishi Kazuko. *Seasons of Sacred Lust*, ed. Kenneth Rexroth. New York: New Directions, 1978.

Takahashi Mutsuo. *Poems of a Penisist*, trans. Hiroaki Sato. Chicago: Chicago Review Press, 1975.

Takahashi Shinkichi. *Afterimages*, trans. Lucien Stryk and Takashi Ikemoto. Denver: Swallow Press, 1970.

Takamura Kōtarō. *Chieko and Other Poems*, trans. Hiroaki Sato. Honolulu: University of Hawaii Press, 1980.

———. *Chieko's Sky*, trans. Soichi Furuta. Tokyo: Kodansha International, 1978.

Tamura Ryūichi. *Dead Languages.* trans. Christopher Drake. Rochester, Michigan: Katydid, 1984.

Taneda Santōka. *Mountain Tasting: Zen Haiku by Santōka Taneda*, trans. John Stevens. Tokyo: Weatherhill, 1980.

Tanikawa Shuntarō. *At Midnight in the Kitchen*, trans. William I. Elliott and Kazuo Kawamura. Portland, Ore.: Prescott Street Press, 1980.

———. *Coca-Cola Lessons.* trans. William I. Elliott and Kazuo Kawamura. Portland, Oregon: Prescott Street Press, 1986.

———. *Map of Days.* trans. Harold Wright. Santa Fe: Katydid, 1996.

———. *Naked Poems.* trans. William I. Elliott and Kazuo Kawamura. Berkeley: Stone Bridge Press, 1996.

———. *With Silence My Companion*, trans. William I. Elliott and Kazuo Kawamura. Portland, Ore.: Prescott Street Press, 1975.

Tsuboi Shigeji. *Egg in My Palm.* trans. Robert Epp. Stanwood, WA: Yakusha, 1993.

Yosano Akiko. *Tangled Hair*, trans. Sanford Goldstein and Seishi Shinoda. Lafayette, Ind.: Purdue University Press, 1971.

Yoshioka Minoru. *Lilac Garden*, trans. Hiroaki Sato. Chicago: Chicago Review Press, 1976.

Modern Drama

Abe Kōbō. *Friends*, trans. Donald Keene. New York: Grove Press, 1969.
———. *The Man Who Turned into a Stick*, trans. Donald Keene. Tokyo: Tokyo University Press, 1975.
———. *Three Plays by Kōbō Abe*. trans. Donald Keene. New York: Columbia University Press, 1993.
Bell, Eric S., and Eiji Ukai. *Eminent Authors of Contemporary Japan*, 2 vols. Tokyo: Kaitakusha, 1930.
Hirano Umeyo. *Buddhist Plays from Japanese Literature*. Tokyo: CIIB Press, 1962.
Iwasaki, Yozan T., and Glenn Hughes. *New Plays from Japan*. London: Ernest Benn, 1930.
——— *Three Modern Japanese Plays*. Cincinnati: Steward Kidd Co., 1923.
Kikuchi Kan. *Tōjūrō's Love and Four Other Plays*, trans. Glenn W. Shaw. Tokyo: The Hokuseido Press, 1925.
Kinoshita Junji. *Between God and Man*, trans. Eric J. Gangloff. Tokyo: Tokyo University Press, 1979.
———. *Twilight Crane*, trans. A. C. Scott, in *Playbook*. New York: New Directions, 1956.
Kurata Hyakuzō. *The Priest and His Disciples*, trans. Glenn W. Shaw. Tokyo: The Hokuseido Press, 1922.
———. *Shinran*, trans. Umeyo Hirano. Tokyo: CIIB Press, 1964.
Mishima Yukio. *Dōjōji*, trans. Donald Keene, in Mishima, Yukio, *Death in Midsummer*. New York: New Directions, 1966.
———. *Five Modern Nō Plays*, trans. Donald Keene. New York: Alfred A. Knopf, 1957.
———. *Madame de Sade*, trans. Donald Keene. New York: Grove Press, 1967.
———. *My Friend Hitler*, trans. Hiroaki Sato in *St. Andrews Review*, IV, Nos. 3 & 4, 1977–1978.
———. *Tropical Tree*, trans. Kenneth Strong, in *Japan Quarterly*, XI, No. 2, 1964.
———. *Twilight Sunflower*, trans. Sigeho Sinozaki and Virgil A. Warren. Tokyo: The Hokuseido Press, 1958.
Nakamura Kichizō. *The Death of Ii Tairo*, trans. Mock Joya. Tokyo: The Japan Times, 1927.
Okamoto Kidō. *The American Envoy*, trans. Masanao Inoue. Kobe: J. L. Thompson, 1931.
———. *The Human Pillar*, trans. by Zoë Kincaid and Hanso Tarao. New York: Samuel French, 1928.
———. *The Mask Maker*, adapted Zoë Kincaid, trans. Hanso Tarao. New York: Samuel French, 1928.
Senda Akihiko. *The Voyage of Contemporary Japanese Theatre*. trans. J. Thomas Rimer. Honolulu: University of Hawaii Press, 1997.

Takaya, Ted T. *Modern Japanese Drama: An Anthology.* New York: Columbia University Press, 1979.

Tanizaki Jun'ichirō. *The Man with the Mandoline*, trans. Donald Keene, in *New Directions 24.* New York: New Directions, 1972.

Yamamoto Yūzō. *Three Plays of Yamamoto Yūzō*, trans. Glenn W. Shaw. Tokyo: The Hokuseido Press, 1935.

Yamazaki Masakazu. *Mask and Sword*, trans. J. Thomas Rimer. New York: Columbia University Press, 1980.

Modern Criticism

Anderer, Paul. *Literature of the Lost Home: Kobayashi Hideo—Literary Criticism.* Stanford: Stanford University Press, 1995.

INDEX